practical encyclopedia of crafts

THE WOMAN'S HOW-TO BOOK CLUB EDITION

Compiled by **Maria Di Valentin**
and others

Drawings by **Louis Di Valentin**
and others

STERLING PUBLISHING CO., INC. **NEW YORK**

ACKNOWLEDGMENTS

The following people, working under the editorship of David A. Boehm, have assisted in the editing of this book: Manly Banister, Rita Brown, Anne DePiano, Aileen Friedman, Burton Hobson, Anne Kallem, Barbara Klinger, Gordon B. Lander, Jane Lassner, Jennifer Mellen, Joan B. Priolo, and Maurice Siegel.

Some of the photographs in this book originally appeared in the following: Children of Czechoslovakia, © 1969, Sterling Publishing Co., Inc.; Chile in Pictures, © 1965, Sterling Publishing Co., Inc.; Ecuador in Pictures, © 1969, Sterling Publishing Co., Inc.; England in Pictures, © 1970, Sterling Publishing Co., Inc.; France in Pictures, © 1970, Sterling Publishing Co., Inc.; Greece in Pictures, © 1968, Sterling Publishing Co., Inc.; Iraq in Pictures, © 1970, Sterling Publishing Co., Inc.; Ireland in Pictures, © 1970, Sterling Publishing Co., Inc.; Japan in Pictures, © 1965, Sterling Publishing Co., Inc.; Korea in Pictures, © 1968, Sterling Publishing Co., Inc.; Malaysia in Pictures, © 1964, Sterling Publishing Co., Inc.; Mexico in Pictures, © 1968, Sterling Publishing Co., Inc.; Thailand in Pictures, © 1967, Sterling Publishing Co., Inc.

CONTENTS

WOOD

APPENDIX

INTRODUCTION

Many people believe that artistic talent is necessary to make craft objects. This is not true. Artistic ability helps, of course, but it is not essential. While an eye for color and design is certainly an advantage when planning original designs, the techniques of almost all crafts can be learned by anyone with just a small amount of manual dexterity. You will have to use your hands if you want to practice a craft, but this is really the only prerequisite.

If you can cut with a pair of scissors, draw a straight line with a ruler, and hammer a nail securely, you will not be limited in the things you can make. You already have many basic skills. Combining them with the step-by-step instructions and suggestions here will enable you to make many items which cannot be bought in this age of mass production. Crafts are the sanctuary from technological mediocrity.

The term "craft" too often scares potential creators away, and on the other hand, anything which involves using the hands can legitimately be called a craft. The editors therefore found themselves with two problems: to encourage readers to experiment and to prevent them from being inundated with hundreds of topics which could possibly be included in this ENCYCLOPEDIA. When we began to classify our list, we immediately eliminated certain fields. Electrical wiring was one area left for more technical books. Repairing items which are already completed was determined to be outside the intended realm. We left out crafts that are in fashion one day but out-of-date the next. We chose not to touch crafts which, in the beginning, require expensive or elaborate equipment. And we assumed that most readers are already familiar with the household crafts: sewing, for example.

Nevertheless, a considerable number and a wide range of crafts are included in this volume. Instructions for each craft are thorough, but since this is a general encyclopedia, instructions for very complex, detailed projects will not be found here. Occasionally we have added a brief section about the history of a craft when it was unusual enough to warrant attention, but on the whole we have stuck to the elementary techniques which give a basic understanding of what is involved in a craft. The most modern equipment and materials are suggested: epoxy cement, for example, is a new scientific advancement, as are self-hardening clays which do not need firing. In addition, the articles, in one way or another, list the materials needed to make an item (so they can be gathered before you start), give directions for specific easy beginning projects, and offer suggestions for making more involved objects. Read through an article before you begin, and preferably go over it several times to be sure you have the sequence firmly in mind.

We feel certain that other craftsmen have other ways of making things, and to these people we can only say that the process described is just one technique—but it works!

The editors' criteria for determining whether to include a certain craft were broad enough to leave room for a diverse assortment. New or unusual methods of working with ordinary equipment provided reason enough to admit an article. Paper, crayons, string, nails—these are everyday items, but they can still be used to make unusual objects. We also wanted to include crafts which can easily be completed in the average home. Your kitchen will usually provide adequate work space or, if you want to set up a permanent workshop, the basement or garage can be converted into a studio.

Occasionally we were unable to restrain ourselves from writing about an unusually fascinating craft, even though some fairly expensive material or equipment is necessary. If you are curious to try such a craft, we suggest that you first experiment with inexpensive materials in a professional studio or school before investing in elaborate tools.

Although the articles are intended to appeal to different levels of craftsmanship, there is one thing which all have in common. The editors instructed each writer to assume that the reader knew virtually nothing about the craft. This way, the instructions turned out to be complete, and no prior knowledge or experience is taken for granted. While the beginning stone sculptor probably has to be more dexterous than the beginning crayoncrafter, the instructions are just as carefully detailed for both crafts, although the articles are obviously not for the same audience. The writing style of each article has been geared to the level of craftsmanship expected.

Each writer was given the freedom to explain his craft the way he felt would be most helpful. For this reason, punctuation and other technicalities of style may differ among various articles; we were reluctant to tamper with the writers' words, or even spellings, for fear of distorting the meaning.

We have incorporated several aids to make the ENCYCLOPEDIA even more helpful. The bibliography in the appendix should be useful in furthering your knowledge of a craft. This list was compiled from suggestions by the authors of the articles. Still, we cannot guarantee that books other than the authors' own volumes approach the craft in the same way as here. In most cases, the books listed are more advanced and technical than our articles.

The ENCYCLOPEDIA is not meant to be read from cover to cover. It is meant to be used. After you learn the basic techniques by following the directions and making an object, you are to use your natural creativeness to make your own object to your own design, using the principles just learned. Many people who become interested and skilled in one craft soon become interested in others, and you may well become curious about additional crafts once you start with one. This ENCYCLOPEDIA is organized so that closely related articles follow each other. The major headings, which are arranged alphabetically, group together those crafts using the same materials and, frequently, the same equipment. All metal crafts are under that heading, for example.

Within these major headings, the articles are arranged alphabetically, except when it was more appropriate to begin a section with an article which generally discusses the materials to be used. Thus, Papercraft begins the *Paper* section, as a sort of introduction and preparation for the rest of the articles under that heading. Claywork (non-firing) is placed before Ceramics (kiln-fired), because the former builds up to the latter and contains basic information concerning clays, as well as coil and slab techniques.

To supplement the instructions in the text, drawings, diagrams and photographs appear on almost every page. Besides those drawn inimitably by Mr. Di Valentin, other artists, photographers, museums and agencies from all over the world have contributed illustrations. We hope they are helpful if not invalu-

able for the visual-minded. Illustrations in an article, if numbered, start from Illus. 1. Whenever possible, the picture and its description in the text are on the same page or the one directly opposite, so you will easily be able to follow what is being discussed. Finished projects of a variety of crafts are illustrated in vibrant color in the separate color section. The authors of the articles have examined the step-by-step illustrations for accuracy, and we have done our best to make sure they are correct.

Sometimes we refer to illustrations and pictures that appear in another section of the book. Many crafts use the same tools and equipment, and it would be redundant to show exactly the same tool twice. Also, sometimes detailed information found in one article seems relevant, but not vital, to another. With both pictures and text, we frequently refer the reader to the directions in the other article. Your ability in one craft will not be limited if you choose not to look up these references, but you will find the additional information and instruction helpful.

Other aids to help you in making craft items include a list of suppliers found in the appendix. To obtain equipment and materials, check this list. The names were compiled from many sources: authors' suggestions, craft catalogues, and advertisements. We have listed mainly American suppliers, and only a few from other countries, but many of these companies will ship overseas for a small charge.

Any index should be helpful, and we have tried to make ours as meaningful and worthwhile as possible. We have avoided listing pages where a term is only mentioned, not described, since a reference of this sort is only a bother to the reader looking for actual information. Listed in the index are projects, tools, methods, terms, and alternate names for the crafts included.

The editors hope, of course, that the entire book will be as useful and stimulating as we intended. Parents and teachers particularly will find this a clear, concise book packed with ideas for projects that children can make. Children too will enjoy browsing through the book for ideas. Adults will discover a myriad of crafts which will challenge their creative skills. By combining your skills with the directions and suggestions here, you are sure to improve your craftsmanship and produce spectacular creations.

THE EDITORS

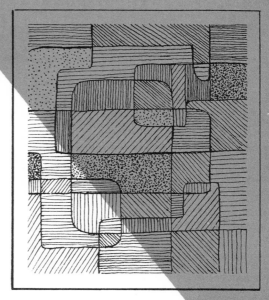

art materials

CRAYONCRAFT

The crayon, traditional tool of the nursery school, has grown up. The many new varieties of crayon now available can produce a number of effects interesting enough to satisfy the adult craftsman as well as the child. Oil painting and watercolor effects can be suggested with these new types. Various surfaces can be achieved—some dull, some transparent; others waxy, shiny, or enamel-like—depending on the type of crayon used. Among the new crayons are the chalk pastel, oil pastel, water crayons, and fluorescent crayons, in addition to the familiar wax crayon.

Crayons and Techniques

The *oil pastel crayon*, sold under different trade names, is a combination of materials that produces exceptionally brilliant colors. Its oil base makes it impervious to dust. It can be applied to many surfaces, such as brick, wood, cardboard, canvas, tagboard, cloth, cork and cement. It should always be applied smoothly, with parallel strokes. Turpentine can be lightly painted over a surface of oil pastels to produce interesting oil washes and to simulate an oil painting.

Water-soluble crayons, available in stick form, can be used to sketch directly on dry paper. If the sketch is then blended with a wet brush, a striking "watercolor" or "tempera" emerges. Dry water crayons applied to water-soaked paper result in brilliant and bold line drawings.

Fluorescent crayons are the brightest crayons made, and they are best used to produce exciting highlights in drawings that have been predominantly colored with oil pastels, water crayons, or wax crayons.

Chalk pastel crayons are an exciting medium because their colors are so intense. Broad, sweeping strokes of the chalk pastel create a soft, rich velvety texture that can be blended easily. Their color adheres well to all types of paper and also to cloth. They are especially useful for making posters and murals with bright and vivid designs.

While the point of the crayon is used for representational drawing, many interesting effects can be achieved by using the crayon's side and blunt end creatively. Cutting a notch in the side is a trick that enables you to get smoothly alternating bands of crayon and background color. Cross bows and circles are made by holding the crayon flat against the background surface and rotating it.

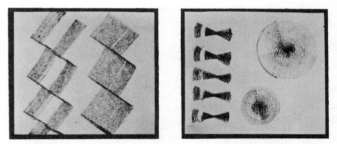

BY CUTTING THE SIDE of the crayon and rubbing it against the paper, you can make unique designs and swirls.

Background Materials

In experimenting with crayons, you will discover that there are many background materials that can be used to good advantage— and each has its own properties. Each type of paper, for example, has a unique surface character. Newsprint is thin and fairly smooth. Manila paper and white drawing paper have a

Condensed from the book, "The Complete Crayon Book" by Chester Jay Alkema / © 1969 by Sterling Publishing Co., Inc., New York

toothy surface that in itself becomes a textural element in your work. The various boards—cardboard and tagboard, for example—have surfaces that make them appropriate for certain designs. Experimenting will teach you best.

Cloth is another effective background material which is extremely popular today. You will find that cloth takes color best when the crayon stroke follows the weave of the cloth. Before crayoning, glue or tack to thick paper or cardboard the cloth you intend to use. Canvas, linen, tarlatan, and cotton are perhaps the most suitable fabrics. Colors can be set into these cloths by placing the material face down on clean paper and using a hot iron on the reverse side. Lift the iron as each section is pressed.

Sandpaper, which comes in a variety of grains and colors—ranging from coarse to fine and from black to tan—provides one of the most exciting surfaces that can be used for crayoning. Coarse sandpapers are best for rough, textural patterns, whereas fine sandpapers allow for a more subtle, detailed application. A transfer print can be easily made when sandpaper is used as background material. Execute the design with a wax crayon; then lay a sheet of plain newsprint paper down on a hard flat surface and place the original work face down on top of it. Apply a hot iron to the back of the sandpaper so that a little of the wax is transferred on to the newsprint. Pull the sheets apart and you will see the original design transferred and transformed—the original will have lost none of its beauty and the print will display a unique character of its own.

Stencils

Exciting designs, both non-representational and representational, can be executed with a crayon stencil. Use tagboard, a most durable material, to construct the stencil. For a non-representational design, cut from the tagboard an interesting shape—one with irregular edges

CRAYON ON CLOTH: The design here was heavily applied to cotton, but other cloths, such as canvas and linen, also provide excellent backgrounds.

USE A HOT IRON to set the crayon colors on cloth, as in this line design. With the areas of background cloth showing through, it could decorate clothing or be framed to hang on a wall.

CRAYON ON SANDPAPER: These four designs on sandpaper are similar yet different. Grouping them together like this makes an attractive composition on the wall.

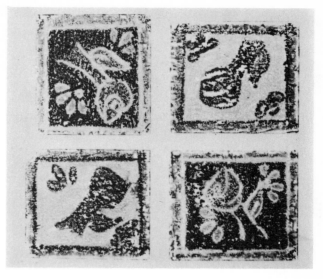

BY TRANSFERRING THE SAME DESIGN to white paper from sandpaper, you will create a completely different look.

and protrusions, perhaps something like a piece from a jigsaw puzzle. Lay this stencil piece on a waste sheet and apply crayon to the stencil's edges. Rub the crayon (oil pastels, chalk pastels, fluorescent or wax crayons) heavily along all the edges of the stencil. Then place the crayoned stencil on a large sheet of background paper, which will be the base for your final art. Rub or streak the crayon from the stencil's edges on to the background paper, using a tissue, a cotton wad, or your fingertip. After all crayoned edges of the stencil have been rubbed on to the background paper, return it to the waste sheet, re-crayon its edges and place it elsewhere on the background paper.

Make use of the stencil from which you cut the piece by rubbing crayon along the edges of the hole and then placing the stencil on the same background sheet. Now rub crayon inward from the edges of this stencil on to the background paper. Again, repeat the crayoning and place the stencil on different parts of the background sheet.

Consider the color scheme carefully. If your background is dark, use crayons that are light and preferably warm in color. If light-colored background paper is used, then select crayons that are darker.

An additional use can be made of this stencil technique by combining it with collage. Cut out bits of paper and paste them on a background. Then stencil over these, and around them, to create a diversity of color and shape not attainable with collage alone.

Crayon Encaustic

An age-old technique is painting with melted wax—the so-called encaustic technique. It is especially rewarding because of the variety of surfaces that accept melted wax. There are several ways to melt the wax crayons to be used. One way is to hold the crayon over a lighted candle. Then quickly apply the crayon to your selected surface before the wax hardens. Another method of melting is to place broken, peeled crayons in a muffin tin—one color to each compartment. Place the muffin tin atop any open-top metal box large enough to hold a 100-watt bulb. The heat from the lighted bulb will melt the crayons. A third and a simple melting method is to hold a lighted bulb close to crayon shavings, made by rubbing peeled crayons over a vegetable grater.

PAINTING WITH MELTED WAX: By dripping melted crayons on to burlap, a 3-dimensional composition was made. The textured surface combines with the varying rectangular shapes to make an interesting modern design.

Use a stiff bristle brush, a tongue depressor or a palette knife to apply the melted wax to your chosen surface. For thin layers of wax, paper is a very adequate background. For thick applications, matboard, cardboard, chipboard, wallboard, plywood, plasterboard or tiles can be used. Among fabrics, burlap holds wax very well, as does felt. Black velvet provides an exciting background for bright, rich colors.

Melted wax adheres to glass surprisingly well. Paint directly on the glass, leaving some of the glass transparent to complement the opaque wax portions of your design.

To get a variety of interesting surface textures for a melted wax crayon painting, vary the thickness of the wax that is applied. In some areas, build up the wax almost to a three-dimensional state, leaving surrounding areas thin and flat. To get a shiny surface, polish the finished painting with a soft cloth. To complete your work, spray it with a fixative.

THE CRAYON RESIST TECHNIQUE creates a textural pattern, as the paint leaves little wax bubbles on top of the wet crayon. The paper which was not drawn on with crayon absorbs all the paint.

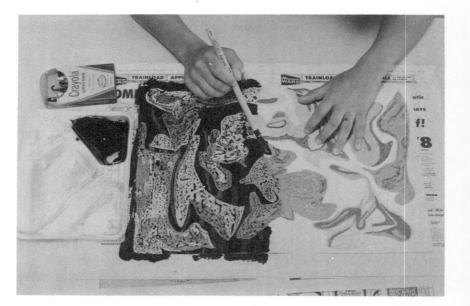

Crayon Resist

The crayon resist technique produces intense, brilliant colors that stand in great contrast to their background. First draw light colored lines, patterns and/or solid shapes upon light colored paper, using wax crayons or oil pastels. Then paint a dark colored wash over it—the wash may be of transparent watercolor, thinned tempera or dissolved water crayon. The wax lines resist the dark wash, but the paper absorbs it where its surface is not covered with wax crayon markings. Manila paper, tagboard, and colored construction paper are good background materials.

Another approach is to apply dark crayon colors to a sheet of dark colored paper and then wash over a paint, light in color, to achieve contrast.

Various techniques can be combined by craftsmen who wish to see the rather extraordinary effects that can be achieved by imaginative use of the crayon.

PAINTING ON WET PLASTER produces interesting and permanent effects. Because the plaster dries while the paint is already on it, the paint becomes virtually a part of the wall. Fresco paintings centuries old are still in good condition, since the paint lasts as long as the plaster to which it was applied.

FRESCO

Fresco is wall painting with water-mixed pigments on wet plaster. The paints permeate the wet plaster and are bound to it by the chemical action of the lime in the plaster. Fresco means "fresh," referring to the state of the plaster.

The painter-craftsman starts by transferring his prepared cartoon (or pattern) on to the wet plaster. The cartoon predetermines the design, the colors, and the chiaroscuro (lights and darks). The transfer may be done by either squaring or pouncing.

Squaring is dividing the cartoon and the wall surface into a series of numbered, corresponding squares. Each line within the cartoon squares is copied on to the wall squares.

Pouncing is done by making holes with a pin along the outlines of the design on the cartoon. The punctured cartoon is then placed over the wet wall surface, and a muslin bag filled with

Written especially for this volume by Maria and Louis DiValentin

powdered chalk is dabbed or "pounced" over the surface, leaving an outline of the design on the wall. A more primitive method is to indent the outlines of the design through the cartoon on the wet plaster surface with a pointed implement.

After the squares are filled or the cartoon paper is removed, the water-mixed pigments are applied to the wet plaster wall in sections which are freshly prepared, since, once begun, each part of the design must be completed without stopping before the plaster dries.

The craftsman must paint quickly in fresco, concentrating on the essentials. Perhaps only one small section can be done in a day. The fresco painter must know exactly how much color the wet plaster surface will absorb. As the plaster dries, the lime in it reacts chemically with the carbon dioxide in the air, forming calcium carbonate, which creates a film over the colors and binds them to the plaster, making them an integral part of the wall surface. Fresco colors are clear and pure, and the surface appears uniform and matte rather than glossy.

If too much paint is applied, loss of binding power will occur. Should this take place, part of the wall will have to be removed and replastered. To achieve dexterity and quick judgment, preparatory studies are absolute necessities.

An important point to remember is that colors applied to a wet wall may appear dark and strong, but become light and weak when dry. Therefore the craftsman must estimate beforehand just how the colors will appear when the mural is dry. Corrections are impossible in this technique, which is seldom employed today precisely because it is so difficult.

Usually bristle brushes of medium length are used. To clean, they should be washed repeatedly in lime water, then in soapy water, rinsed thoroughly in clear water, and then dried.

clay

CLAYWORK

Primitive people in every part of the world made pottery from clay which they found in river beds. They shaped it by beating and pounding, and then sun-baked it or fired it in open fires, making it hard and durable. Until the discovery of the potter's wheel and the kiln for baking clay (see Ceramics), these simple methods were the only ways early people knew of working with clay. With no more equipment than your two hands and some clay (different kinds can be bought in art supply or hobby shops) you can still make attractive and lasting clay objects, just as these primitive men did centuries ago.

CLAY GRAPES

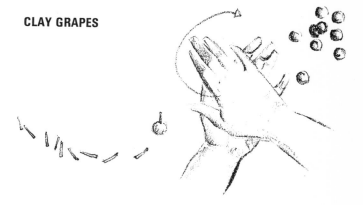

SHAPE AND DECORATION are the two most important qualities to consider when you design clay objects. By carefully etching around the rim with any blunt tool, you can turn a simple bowl into an elaborate serving dish or ornament for a shelf.

Besides natural clay, there are several new synthetic clays now being produced and sold. Some dry slowly, thus allowing you to take your time as you work without the clay becoming brittle. If the clay you are using does dry quickly, however, you can slow the process down and keep the clay soft by leaving a damp cloth over the clay when you stop working. When your object is completed, you will be grateful for the quick-drying clay, however, for the faster the clay dries, the sooner you will be able to use your creation. Some of these self-hardening clays do not need to be fired, as they really harden.

Some other new clays have substances added which hinder evaporation of their water content and thus allow you to work more slowly without danger of the clay drying before you are finished manipulating it. To achieve a dry, solid state, these clays may have to be fired in a kiln. You can obtain information about kilns from an art supply or hobby shop.

To get the feel of the clay, try making a bunch of grapes as your first project. Make each

Written especially for this volume by Jane Lassner

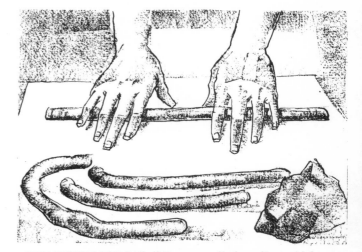

GRAPEVINE: Make stem, twigs and grapes and group them together to look like a natural bunch.

little sphere by taking a pinch of clay from your original clay block and rolling it between the palms of your hands until it is a fairly round ball. Make many of these, and when you have a sufficient quantity, make as many little clay stems as you have grapes. Attach a stem to each grape by simply pressing the end of the stem on to the ball.

Now make a long, thick vine, and attach the small stems to it. If you have a real bunch of grapes as a model, you will be able to notice all the differences in each grape and the manner in which they are clustered on the vine.

Coil Building

Coil building is one of the oldest methods of making pottery, primarily because it is very easy and requires no tools. This technique consists of rolling long coils or sausages of clay and placing them one on top of another to make vases, bowls, or any round or cylindrical object.

Form the coils by rolling the clay slowly— rapid motions may make the coils too thin before you realize it. Uniform thickness along the coils is the important thing to strive for when you roll.

When you begin to wrap the coils around, make sure that the bottom of the pile is made very carefully: it will bear the weight of the

ROLLING THE COILS: Roll "sausages" of a uniform thickness. Anyone can learn this primitive method of working with clay.

rest of the bowl or vase, and should therefore be coiled tightly and smoothed. Various tools may help you manipulate the coils into place and smooth the inside of the bottom, although your hands may do just as good a job alone.

After you have pressed and smoothed the base, build up the sides by adding more clay coils. Overlap the coils as you wind them, so that only half the thickness of the top coil extends above the one beneath it. Continue coiling until your bowl is as large as you want it.

Now you are ready to smooth the coil marks away. Keep your fingers damp as you work

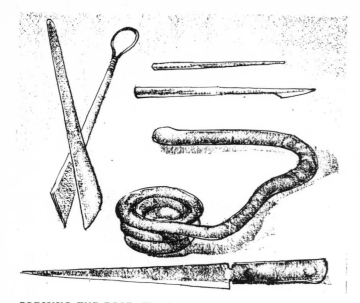

FORMING THE BASE: The base must be thick and sturdy. Use your hands or various tools (scrapers, putty knives, metal spatulas) to help smooth the coils.

with smaller coils, and place them inside one another so that the crock gets narrower and the spirals get smaller as you work. Smooth the inside walls as you progress, since you will not be able to reach inside the crock later.

SMOOTH THE CLAY by using your fingers. As you smooth, check to see that the bowl is not thicker in one place than another.

WRAP THE COILS around one another evenly and smoothly.

and press carefully, or the coils may separate from one another as they dry. Press the entire surface of the bowl until there are no uneven places, inside or out.

A crock, which is a shaped bowl, requires a bit more skill, but can be made in the same way as one that is not shaped. To make the crock curve in at the top, continue building

A CROCK MADE BY THE COIL TECHNIQUE is formed the same way as a bowl. This time, however, you must be sure to smooth the inside as you wrap the coils, since you will not be able to reach inside the crock once the neck is coiled.

Make the neck of the crock with rings laid on top of each other as before. The larger you intend to make the crock, the stronger you must make the original coils.

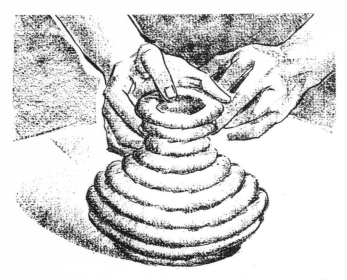

AT THE NECK of the crock, first narrow and then enlarge the opening.

Smooth the outside of the crock with your index finger so that all lines from the coils disappear. You can also use a wooden wedge or flat stick to make the surface even smoother.

To make your bowl or crock a permanent piece of craftsmanship, let the clay dry at room temperature for several days. Let it take its time: even placing the clay on a radiator would make the clay eventually crack.

If you have not used self-hardening clay, you should fire your object. Wedge the clay

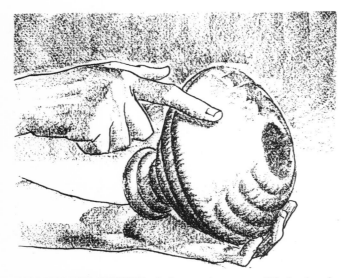

SMOOTH THE OUTSIDE of the crock as you did the bowl, with either damp fingers or a flat tool.

first to make sure there are no air bubbles in the clay which will explode in the kiln (see Ceramics). You can use a professional kiln to fire your bowl, or try the "home-fire" technique. Place the piece of claywork in a coal stove (gas does not give enough heat). To protect the bowl from smoky fuel, place a flower pot over the bowl. Fire up the stove in the usual way, and leave the bowl for about 6 hours.

If you want to fire your claywork in an already lighted furnace, warm the clay figure or bowl by placing it on top of an asbestos plate over a gas fire. Then put the clay into the furnace without a flower pot cover. Again, leave the object for 6 hours. If the color of the clay is uneven after this time, it has not been fired long enough.

COPY A BOWL by the slab technique. Press the clay slab in the basket, trim it, and let it dry naturally.

The Slab Technique

Besides making round pots with clay coils, you can also build objects from clay slabs. These slabs should be about $\frac{1}{4}$ inch thick. Pound them with your hands, or roll them with a rolling pin. You can cut round or square tiles from these slabs, and decorate them with patterns. Or, make another bowl following this simple method.

Press a rolled-out slab down with your thumbs into a suitable form. To make a bowl which is not too deep yet has an interesting relief pattern, use a woven basket as a mold.

After pressing the slab into the basket, smooth the inside with a sponge and cut clean edges with a knife. When the clay is dry, it will have shrunk and can easily be slipped from the basket. The result is a clay bowl with the woven design of the basket impressed upon it. The bowl may be fired, depending on the type of clay you used.

Hollowing-Out Technique

Bowls, pots or other hollow containers can be made from solid balls of clay. Teapots,

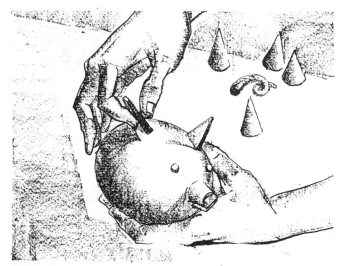

A PIGGY BANK is easy to make from a solid clay ball. Decorate its face and add legs, a tail and a nose at this stage.

MAKE A SLOT FOR COINS by forcing a wooden stick into the pig's body, at least one inch deep into the surface.

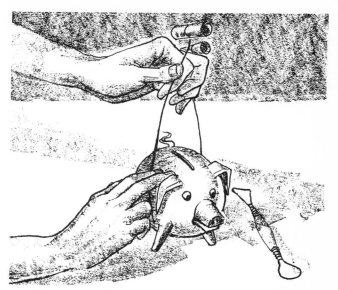

CUT THE PIG IN HALF with a wire. If the cut runs through the slot you made, you may have to reform the slot to keep it free of excess clay.

HOLLOW OUT THE PIG by removing the clay with a spoon or other tool. Although the inside does not have to be perfectly smooth, the pig will not be liable to break if the clay is evenly hollowed all around.

ash trays and even piggy banks can be formed in this way. Let's try the bank.

First, make a simple pig shape out of a solid ball of clay, and firmly attach ears, feet, a nose and tail. Next, use a wooden stick to make a slot for coins. Press the stick into the pig about $\frac{1}{2}$ inch, re-forming the clay around the slot to keep the surface round.

Take a wire, to which you have attached small wooden blocks on the ends for grasping, and cut the figure apart. Again, be sure that the area around the slice is kept clean. Hold the ends of the wire in one hand and keep the pig steady with the other. Slice firmly but slowly, and the cut will be even.

Carefully hollow out the inside of the pig. As the inside surface will not be visible, it does not have to be perfectly smooth.

To put the two halves of the pig back together again, apply slip to the edges of both halves. Slip is a mixture of clay powder, made from clay which has been dried and pulverized, and water. Smear the slip freely on both halves and press them together firmly. Any excess slip which oozes to the outside surface can be rubbed off.

Smooth the crack where the two halves were joined with your fingers, and then with a stick with a rounded end. Make sure that all parts of your pig are properly shaped, let it dry naturally, and then, if necessary, fire it to maintain its hardness.

PUTTING THE PIG TOGETHER again requires the use of clay slip as an adhesive.

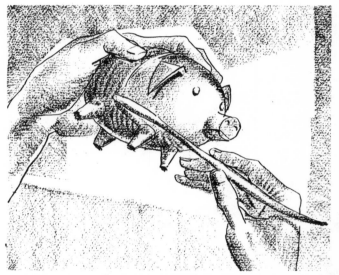

SMOOTH ALL SURFACES of the piggy bank carefully, to remove any finger marks and impressions.

CERAMICS

The word "ceramics" comes from the Greek *keramos*, which means potter's earth. Today, ceramics are defined broadly as *all* useful or ornamental objects made from clay or other earthy materials and hardened by fire. Such objects range from ceramics used in industry, such as nose cones in missiles, to pottery artifacts and sculpture.

History

Ceramics, dating back to the earliest earthenware pottery, is perhaps the world's most ancient art form. It antedates even the knowledge of metals and weaving. Interestingly, nearly all cultures the world over have independently discovered pottery.

While some pottery objects have been discovered that date back prior to 9000 B.C., the widespread use of fired clay vessels dates from 6000–3000 B.C. The early vessels of the Egyptian, Mesopotamian and Babylonian peoples were hand molded, either baked in the sun or fired in bonfires or in primitive open-pit fires such as are still in use

in parts of the world today. Glazed tiles have been found in Egypt which date back to 5000 B.C.

Various origins have been attributed to the discovery of the potter's wheel, and pottery with a turned foot, indicating use of a wheel, has been discovered in Northern Iran dating back to 4000 B.C. Pottery was usually the work of women the world over until the wheel came into use; thereafter potters were most often men.

Mediterranean ceramics reached their highest development with the black figure and red figure ware of the Greeks. But perhaps the most notable success in ceramics of any peoples was achieved by the Chinese who have an unbroken tradition of high accomplishment in earthenware, stoneware and porcelain which has lasted to this day. The earliest known Chinese pottery dates back to 4000 B.C. The Chinese claim to have discovered both the potter's wheel and porcelain. Certainly, they developed some of the world's richest glazes and most sophisticated firing techniques prior

ANTIQUE VASES from Crete show what handsome earthenware was made by ancient peoples (Illus. 1).

Written especially for this volume by Ruth Ullmann

EARTHENWARE has been called "the alphabet of archeology" because from studying pottery one can deduce the age of an object. This display is in the Iraq Museum in Baghdad (Illus. 2).

to modern times. It was from Marco Polo's trip to China that Europe and the West learned about porcelain in the 13th century A.D. Other achievements are recorded in the lustreware developed in the Middle East, the early pottery of Africa, and the pre-Columbian pottery of North, Central and South America.

The great revival of interest in ceramics in the 20th century—both in industry and as an art form—heralds what may be regarded as a ceramic renaissance.

The Process

The usual stages in making a ceramic object, after obtaining the clay and other necessary materials, are: (1) preparing the clay; (2) forming the object; (3) drying; (4) finishing the object; (5) bisque firing; (6) glazing or decorating; and (7) glaze firing.

Clay Bodies

Even for simple claywork an understanding of the different kinds of clay bodies is helpful. Clay bodies are blends of various clays or clays and other earthy mineral substances. These are blended to produce a clay body with the desired firing range and properties to achieve a specific ceramic purpose. For example, a desired clay may be very plastic to be suitable for throwing, less plastic for hand building, completely dense at a given firing temperature, or white and translucent when fired, or have the right properties for casting. There are three basic categories into which clay bodies used by the studio potter can be divided— earthenware, stoneware and porcelain.

Earthenware clay bodies: Used mainly for glazed household crockery and enamelware, as well as for unglazed baked clay such as bricks. Earthenware clay bodies can vary considerably in composition, but generally can be classified as a clay blend that has over 3 per cent absorption when fired. Earthenware clay bodies generally contain some iron and other mineral impurities, are blended of several clays, and often contain some quartz, feldspar and a little kaolin for body strength. Earthenware is "fired" or baked in an oven or kiln (see page 37) at a low temperature. The range is generally from cone 08 to cone 03,

1750° F. (950° C.) to 2040° F. (1115° C.). Although the clay matures at these temperatures, it remains porous and water will seep through until the ware is glazed.

Stoneware bodies: The clays used to make a stoneware body contain a high percentage of alumina (from kaolin) and silica (from flint), feldspars, and grog (crushed pottery), etc. to bring the body to a moderate to high firing range. Medium-fired stoneware matures at a range of cone 1 to cone 4, 2125° F. (1160° C.) to 2175° F. (1190° C.). Higher fired stoneware matures between cone 5 and cone 10, or 2200° F. (1205° C.) to 2380° F. (1305° C.). Properly compounded, a stoneware body will mature or vitrify at one of these temperatures; it will become impervious to water. However, stoneware is most frequently glazed and is increasingly popular with the studio potter because of the wide range of glazes that are possible.

Porcelain bodies: The clays used to make porcelain provide for a white, translucent body when fired to high temperatures, cone 11 to cone 16, or 2415° F. (1325° C.) to 2645° F. (1450° C.). Such bodies generally contain kaolin, feldspar, flint, and ball clay, and vitrify at a high temperature to produce the

STORING THE CLAY and keeping it moist requires a tightly sealed container like a rubber-covered drum (Illus. 4, above) or a "wet box" (Illus. 5, below).

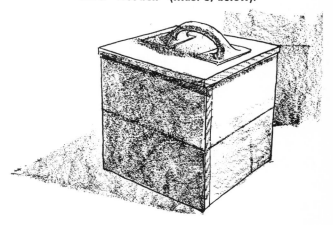

hard, semi-translucent, white characteristic of porcelain or chinaware.

Storing Clay

Natural clay is not only difficult to work with but difficult to find. The simplest solution is to purchase prepared clay from a ceramic dealer either in plastic, liquid or powder form. For simple claywork the plastic form is required. (Stoneware or porcelain require a high-temperature kiln.) It is important to keep modelling clay moist. Plastic bags or containers with tight-fitting covers can be used to store clay, or a tub covered with wet burlap. Pieces that are being worked on should be covered with damp cloths when stored away for the night. If they must be left for longer than

CHINESE PORCELAIN, in a green called celadon, from about 935-1392 A.D. is regarded as among the finest ever made (Illus. 3).

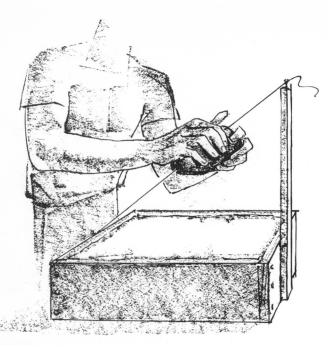

WEDGING: Clay must be kneaded to get the air bubbles out, or firing will cause your pot to explode. A good way to wedge is with a taut piano wire on a wedging box. Cut your lump in half over and over again (Illus. 6). If you want to add grog to your clay, do it at this time.

that, the cloths must be re-dampened periodically, or better still, construct your own "wet box" for storing the pieces. Otherwise, the clay will not remain in a workable condition.

Wedging

All clay must be wedged before it can be modelled properly. The kneading of clay into a mass of uniform consistency is called "wedging." Clay must be wedged prior to use for two reasons: (1) to distribute moisture evenly throughout the clay, and (2) to remove all air from the clay body. (If a piece is to be fired, air bubbles could cause an explosion in the kiln.) The best method of cutting large lumps of clay to be worked is with a length of strong but firm wire attached to two pieces of wood that serve as handles.

For small batches, hand wedging is satisfactory. The procedure is as follows:

1. Take a large ball (the size of a melon) and pass it over a taut, stretched wire to cut it in half.

2. Throw one half of the ball down hard on a wooden table or plaster slab.

3. Throw the second half, also cut-side up, down on the first, and knead the mass into one solid ball.

4. Now, bisect the new lump at right angles to the first cut and repeat the process 20 to 30 times, until there are no air bubbles showing on the cut surface. The texture should be smooth and fine.

There are other methods of wedging which can be used in combination with the process described above. The first and most widely used is the "jelly roll" technique which involves pressing the clay down with both hands, turning it, and pressing again, bisecting, slamming and rekneading the clay until it is air free and consistent in texture. The second method is called "Oriental wedging" and involves a rhythmic pressure from the right hand that makes the clay flow around. Generally, the potter will discover the method that best suits him. For large batches of clay, machines are commercially available for the wedging operation.

A wedging board is easy to make and is essential. Start by making a shallow box out of a few pieces of scrap wood. Then fasten an upright post to the front or back side of the

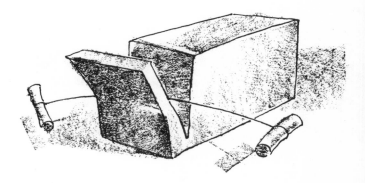

CUT A LARGE CLAY LUMP by slicing with a wire between two wooden handles. This device will come in handy again to lift a pot off of the wheel (Illus. 7).

box with nuts and bolts. Now pour plaster of Paris into the box to the very top, and with a straight stick evenly smooth off any excess of plaster at the top of the box. This will form the working surface. Plaster helps to absorb the excess water from the clay during the wedging process, thus eliminating bubbles of air. Most studio potters go one step further and anchor the wedging board, or the table it stands on, firmly to the floor.

Next, stretch a piece of nichrome, copper or rustproof piano wire, or any other strong (not less than 12 gauge), thin wire from the post to the front or back of the box. The wire must be absolutely taut to cut the clay cleanly and easily, and, for this reason, should be fastened down with a turnbuckle, available at any hardware store.

Preparing the Clay

There is one aspect of working in ceramics that should be taken into consideration from the start. Regardless of whether you choose to mix your clay body from dry materials, order it from a commercial manufacturer, or dig it from the ground, the clay body must be suited to the type of object desired and must be tested in the kiln to be used. In addition, the glazes must be tested on the clay body to be sure that both the body and the glaze will mature at the firing range of the kiln. Otherwise, the resultant clay objects may be defective.

Forming the Object

Ceramic forms in an endless variety of shapes and sizes can be created by a number of methods or combination of methods.

The Pinch Pot. Pinch forming is a simple natural method and a good starting point for the beginner. After wedging the clay, take a ball of clay the size of a peach. Make a hole in the middle and by pushing the clay outward, pinching it between your fingers and thumbs, form it into a cup or bowl-shaped piece. Continue the pressure around the piece until there is a uniform wall thickness of about $\frac{1}{8}$ inch.

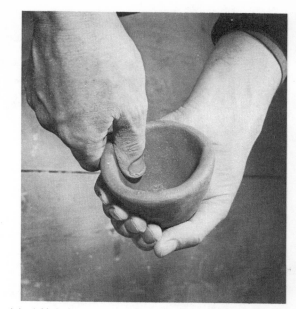

Photograph by J. M. Anderson. From "Ceramic Creations" by Robert Fournier

PINCH FORMING is the most elemental way of making a ceramic piece. Just use your thumb and fingers (Illus. 8).

Leave some of the clay at the bottom for a foot. Try to smooth both the foot and piece as much as possible. Then set aside for drying before further finishing.

Alternate Methods: The same cup or bowl could have been formed by the coil or (modified) slab methods described in the article on Claywork (see pages 22 and 24), or, as in Illus. 9, by molding the clay over a plaster

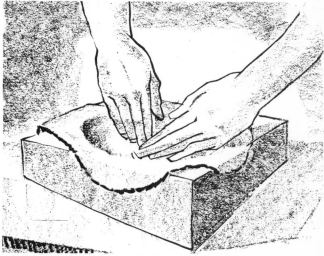

MOLDING a cup or bowl in clay over or into a plaster form is one method (Illus. 9). The others are by pinching, by coil, by slab, or by wheel.

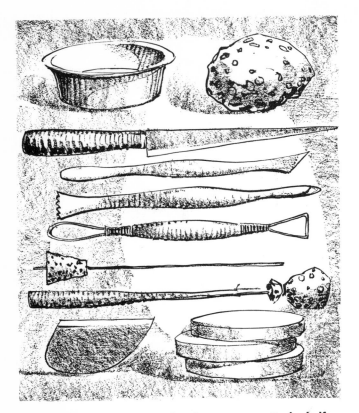

EQUIPMENT for ceramics: bowl, sponge, potter's knife, modelling tools, pricker, sponge stick, wooden rib and plaster bats (Illus. 10).

Throwing a Bowl

1. Fasten a plaster bat to the wheel head with three wads of clay. Try to center this accurately. (Illus. 12.)

2. Place or "throw" a wedged and rounded ball of clay on to the center of the bat while the wheel is spinning. (Illus. 13.)

3. Centering. Hold your left hand against the clay on the left side and press towards the center. With your right hand, push against the clay on the right side, with your right arm firmly braced against the frame of the wheel or anchored against the body with your elbow. Both your hands and clay must be kept wet. In centering, let the wheel turn at maximum speed (you might call this speed 4). Your left hand pushes inward while your right presses downward. Remove excess clay at the base. Allow the clay to run true by containing it rigidly in your hands and at the same time letting the clay rise up in the center. Repeatedly push down with your thumbs, and draw the clay up again in a wedging action until it has been pushed into a symmetrical disc right over the center of the wheel. It is absolutely essential that the symmetrical disc be running true before you proceed further.

4. Opening. The next step is to open and form the bottom of the bowl. While the wheel is spinning (at about speed 3), hold your thumbs together and push downwards into the center of the ball. The thickness of the

form, pressing and trimming as you mold. But perhaps the more usual methods of production for the studio potter are shaping at the wheel or using properly deflocculated or broken-up clay in slip form for casting.

Throwing at the Wheel

Throwing is an art that is best learned by working with an accomplished potter.

A few tools are necessary. There should be a *bowl for water*, a *natural sponge*, a *potter's knife*, a *wooden modelling tool* or two, and a *pricker*. A wooden or *rubber nib* is useful and a small sponge tied to the end of a stick is helpful for removing water from the inside of a tall piece. In addition, there should be a ready supply of *plaster bats* and, of course, a *wheel*. There are many different kinds of wheels, but the most commonly used are the kick wheel and the electric wheel.

KICK WHEEL: This is fine for the beginner. An electric-motor-powered wheel can come later (Illus. 11).

bottom is important, and must be decided at this point.

5. Pulling. Now draw the walls up into a cylinder at about the height of the finished

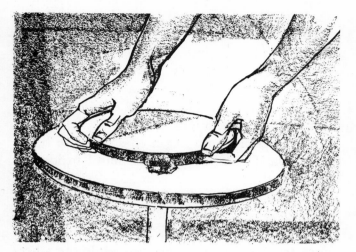

FASTEN A PLASTER BAT to the center of the wheel, using three lumps of clay to hold it in place (Illus. 12).

"THROW" A WEDGED BALL of clay on to the center of the bat while the wheel is turning slowly. This will become your pot (Illus. 13).

CENTERING: This is pushing the ball of clay towards the center so that it rises up between your hands (Illus. 14). To be sure you have centered the clay exactly, hold your finger or a blunt tool in a fixed position (almost touching the clay). If the space between the clay and your finger, or tool, is constant, the clay is centered.

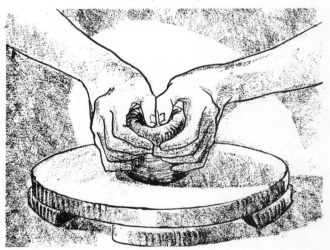

OPENING: Place your thumbs at the outer edge of the "centered" ball of clay and allow the centrifugal force of the moving wheel to pull your thumbs to the center. Now, apply pressure with your thumbs and "open up" the inner portion of your pot (Illus. 15).

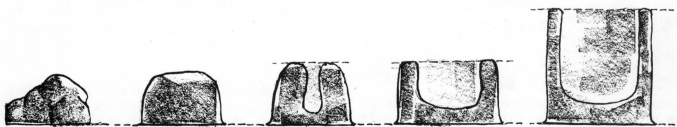

HOW A CYLINDER IS FORMED: The five steps from throwing a lump of clay at the wheel through opening and pulling (Illus. 16).

PULLING: Put one hand inside the opening with the flat part of your fingers braced against the inside wall. (Thumb is outside.) With the other hand outside, apply pressure and pull upwards slowly. The walls will rise gradually (Illus. 17).

bowl. There are many ways to position the hands, but generally this step is carried out by using both hands—the left inside the form and the right outside—and squeezing the lower wall between thumb and fingers and pulling slowly upward, with both hands raised together. This step may have to be repeated several times until the walls are the right thickness for shaping. The wheel should now be spinning at what might be speed 2.

6. Shaping. Next begin to shape the bowl. Place the fingers of your left hand inside the piece and a finger or knuckle of your right hand on the outside. Raise both hands together, with gentle pressure between them, so that the wall thins out and moves upwards and outwards. Then shape the rim while the wheel is turning slowly, and smooth the inside with a rubber rib. Trim the top with a pricker if it is uneven and finish with the hands.

FINISHING: Use the wire modelling tool to shape and smooth the base (Illus. 19).

SHAPING: Raising and thinning all the time, shape the upper part of your pot into a graceful neck. Speed of the wheel is reduced for shaping (Illus. 18). To widen the base of the pot exert slightly more pressure from the inside.

7. Finishing. Use a wooden tool to finish the base and a sponge to fine-finish the rim.

8. Lifting. The bowl is now ready to be lifted off the wheel. Let it remain on the bat

thickness, shapes, and turning speeds he desires. To check this, cut practice pieces in half to note the thickness and evenness of the walls until each piece has walls $\frac{1}{4}$-inch to $\frac{1}{8}$-inch thick, with a thicker wall at the base to allow for trimming of the foot.

NOTE: Throwing movements, after the initial throwing of the clay on the bat or wheel, vary with the shape of the object desired. The bowl is the easiest shape to make on the wheel and the student is encouraged to start throwing cylinders as soon as possible.

LIFTING: If you threw the pot directly on the wheel head, instead of a plaster bat, you would have to lift it after drying slightly. This is done with the type of wire and handles you used to slice the clay lump. Be sure you hold the pot loosely as the wire cuts close to the base (Illus. 20).

for the initial drying. Pieces also can be thrown directly on the wheel head and then cut with a wire and lifted off the wheel, but this requires care and skill and is not recommended for the beginner. (See Illus. 20 if you want to try.)

Only practice will help the potter gain the control necessary to achieve just the right wall

CYLINDERS: If you can throw cylinders, you can throw any shape vase. Practice pulling until you have mastered this (Illus. 22).

Drying

Regardless of the forming method used, a clay object must be allowed to dry to a leather-hard state before finishing. This is to prevent its being deformed in the finishing or trimming process. Ordinarily, drying is a long or two-stage process.

Often a piece can be dried by leaving it at room temperature for a few hours. Large pieces and pieces that must be joined or cannot be finished right away have to be covered with plastic or placed in a damp closet to prevent too rapid drying which causes breaks, or undue strains.

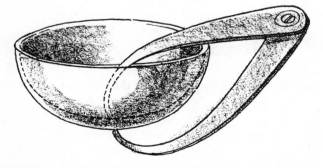

CHECKING bottom thickness is necessary before inverting a pot on the wheel head (Illus. 21).

Finishing or Trimming the Piece

The Pinch Pot: The leather-hard pinch pot piece. can now be turned over, the bottom scraped flat and the foot trimmed with a wire trimming tool. The rest of the surface may be finished by smoothing lightly with a damp sponge and light fingering movements.

The Wheel-Thrown Bowl: Trimming wheel-thrown objects is called "tooling," because in this process the potter uses trimming tools, which are applied only to objects in the leather-hard state.

1. Measure the bowl outside and inside to determine bottom thickness before inverting it on the wheel head. (Illus. 21.)

2. Then invert the bowl on the wheel head and center it, by bringing a pointer towards the bowl on a slow-moving wheel until the pointer just evenly touches all sides of the bowl at the lowest point where tooling is desired. Stop the wheel and firmly press coils or small lumps of clay against the bowl to secure it to the wheel head.

3. Begin tooling with the wheel operating at slow speed. Using a round-ended tool, carefully and firmly bring it down on the bottom of the bowl just slightly away from the middle. Leave a knob of clay in the center. The tool will bite into the clay, taking off some of the excess until the base is even. Remove the knob only when the bottom surface is level. It is a guide as to how much clay you have removed.

4. Decide on the foot rim diameter and cut away excess clay from the bottom wall.

5. Establish the visible foot rim on the bowl's contour after support clay has been cut away.

6. Tool the foot rim on the middle of the bottom surface. This is only one style for foot-rimming a bowl. You must decide which shape will best suit your ware.

Decorating

If handles are desired on a bowl, pitcher or mug, these must be fashioned and applied to the leather-hard ware and then allowed to dry

THE FOOT: Any bowl in leather-hard state, whether thrown at the wheel or made by coils, can have its foot trimmed in this fashion. Use the banding wheel, turning slowly, for bowls made by coils. Trim the foot of a "thrown" bowl on the potter's wheel (Illus. 23).

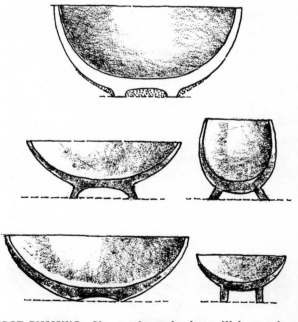

FOOT RIMMING: Choose the style that will best suit your bowl (Illus. 24).

together before firing. If the ware is to be incised or otherwise decorated with clay additions, this too should be done at this stage. Handles are most frequently pulled from a

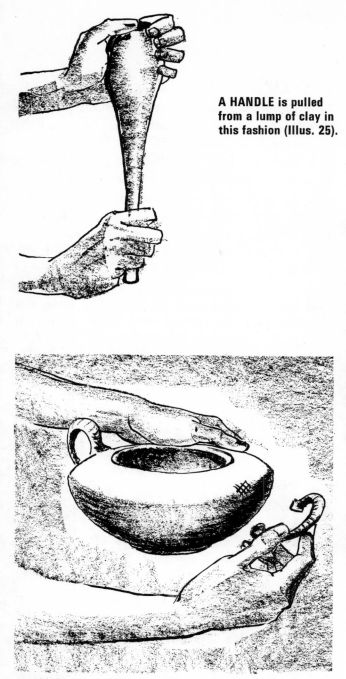

A HANDLE is pulled from a lump of clay in this fashion (Illus. 25).

AFFIXING HANDLES is done by scoring the spot of attachment and using slip as the adhesive (Illus. 26).

Bisque Firing

Clay objects must be dried slowly to prevent warpage and the development of cracks or strains. Even after the ware has been well dried at room temperatures, some moisture remains to be driven off in the kiln. In addition to free water, chemically combined water is present in the clay, and this must be eliminated before the ware can be considered matured. At the

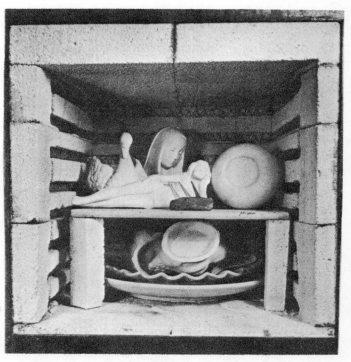

LOADING the kiln for bisque (or biscuit) firing is done by stacking in almost any manner (Illus. 27).

same time, clay minerals are crystallized in the firing, thus adding strength to the ware so that it can be more easily handled for glazing.

Most studio potters fire their ware twice. The first firing is called a "bisque" or "biscuit" firing because the kiln is fired at a lower range than would be suitable for the complete maturation of the clay body. Loading a bisque kiln is called "stacking," for the pieces may be stacked one in another, smaller pieces placed inside larger ones, or just may touch. Care must be taken, however, to avoid uneven

lump of clay and affixed by means of scoring the pot and using slip or slurry and a coil of clay to secure them to the pot.

In some cases, colored clay slip decoration also is applied to greenware (unfired pottery) at this stage and fired in the bisque.

strains which could damage the ware. It is wise to plan the loading so that kiln space is used most economically.

Ware can be placed on the floor and shelves of the kiln—thicker and heavier pieces at the bottom, which is cooler, and thinner or lighter ware, which can better withstand the rapid temperature changes inside the kiln, on a supported shelf or shelves in the upper areas. The shelves (top side) and the floor must have been previously coated with kiln wash. A visual cone pat or pyrometer is used to help determine the firing range desired. (See Firing section for full details.) This is placed near a peephole so that the potter can see inside the kiln while it is firing.

The firing range of bisque kilns varies widely depending on whether the potter wants soft or hard bisque wares. But in every case, the range is lower than for the maturation of the clay body and glazes to be used. For example, a potter firing his glazed ware to cone 5, stoneware, might choose to fire his stoneware bisque to cone 07, which is a range for earthenware.

Glazing

Glaze is a coating of glass formed on a clay object while it is being fired to maturity. It is glaze that gives ceramic ware its brilliant tones, fills the pores of bisque ware to make it waterproof and washable, and enables ceramic sculpture to endure harsh weather.

Glazes are made by mixing together a number of finely ground minerals and earth materials, combining these with water and Epsom salts (to prevent settling) and possibly a gum to help bind the glaze to the ware.

There are many different glazes and the potter must experiment with compounding them. The important thing to remember is that the glazes to be used must mature at the same temperature as the clay body to which they are applied, so that glaze and clay fuse properly.

Every glaze has three main ingredients: (1) a glass-forming substance (silica which comes from flint, clay and feldspar); (2) alumina (supplied by clay) to give the glaze body and

GLAZING: To make a ceramic object waterproof you must glaze the inside (Illus. 28).

POURING OFF EXCESS GLAZE: After the glaze has been poured into the pot, turn it around several times to make sure the entire inside surface has been covered. (Usually only one application of glaze is necessary for the inside of a pot.) After it is dry, you can begin to glaze the outside (Illus. 29).

DECORATING AN INCISED PLATE WITH GLAZE: The lines have been incised before the bisque firing. Now you brush glaze on the areas to be colored (Illus. 30).

and fuse together. In addition, oxides of various metals are added to provide color, i.e., iron = brown, copper = green, cobalt = blue, etc., and other ingredients are added for special effects. Glazes are usually classified by the flux they contain and are referred to as lead glazes, alkaline glazes and feldspathic glazes.

Glazes may be applied to freshly sponged bisque ware by several means: brushing, sponging, dipping, pouring, or spraying in a spray booth. The inside of the ware is glazed first, allowed to dry, and then the outside is glazed. Sometimes colored clay slips are used under a transparent glaze. Often one glaze is applied over another which has dried on the ware; this creates special effects. Oxides mixed with water are also sometimes brushed on, and for lustreware, metallic oxides, which melt at a lower point than the glazes, are applied after the glaze firing, and the ware is fired again at a lower temperature.

Generally, it is safer to glaze ware that has been bisque-fired than to glaze greenware

to make it stay on the ware; and (3) a flux or melting agent (lead, borox, sodium, potassium, calcium, etc.) to make all the ingredients melt

SPRAY GLAZING should be done only in a spray booth. Don't let the glaze stay in the tubing overnight, but wash it out thoroughly after each using (Illus. 31).

BRUSH GLAZING: The first coat may be applied horizontally, the second coat vertically after the first is dry, and perhaps a third coat diagonally will be necessary (Illus. 32).

(unfired ware). However, glaze can be put on unfired clay ware and fired to maturity in a single glaze firing.

Firing

There are many different kinds of kilns in which ware can be fired and in which heat is supplied by wood, coal, gas, oil or electricity. Most studio potters use electric or gas kilns. Electric kilns produce an oxidizing atmosphere throughout the firing cycle. Gas kilns can be used to provide a reduction atmosphere at various times in the firing, producing different chemical effects on the glazes and clay body.

Before glazed ware can be placed in a kiln it must be dry-footed—that is, all glaze must be scraped and washed away from the rim on which the ware is to stand in the kiln. A glazed object should not be placed in the kiln unless the glaze has been previously tested. This is to avoid trouble in the firing.

Loading: Kiln shelves, floor, stilts and lid must be given a coating of kiln wash—a mixture of equal parts of kaolin and flint mixed with water. This is to prevent damage to the kiln and kiln furniture, and to prevent the glazed piece from sticking to any surface. Only one side of the kiln shelves should be coated with wash; the underside is not coated to avoid having any kiln wash drop on to the ware below and ruin the glaze.

Glazed pieces that cannot be dry-footed are placed in the kiln on stilts. In loading a glaze kiln, you must take great care to leave space around each piece, and be sure that no glazed piece touches any other. Glaze kilns are not loaded by stacking pieces one in another. The kiln should be loaded with an efficient and economical use of the space, and most potters plan their shelf arrangements before loading so that pieces need not be shifted about.

Temperature: Kiln temperatures are measured by pyrometric cones or pyrometers. Pyrometers are devices for measuring kiln temperatures by means of a thermocouple and are useful when used in combination with an

A TOP-LOADING KILN is least expensive and most suitable for a beginner (Illus. 33).

A SIDE-LOADING KILN has the advantage of shelves and less need for stilts (Illus. 34).

automatic cut-off on electric kilns. Pyrometric cones are made of clay to which fluxes have been added so that the cones become soft at known temperatures.

Cones are shaped like pyramids and each bears a number. The peephole in a kiln serves really as an observation post through which a cone may be watched. Usually cones come in a wad of dried clay, which holds them up.

Place the wad where it can be seen through the peephole. When the heat reaches the predetermined temperature, the cone begins to bend and the kiln needs to be shut off.

For each glaze firing (also for bisque) a cone pat is made. For example, if you want to fire your kiln to cone 5, at 2201° F. (1205° C.), you set three cones—cone, 4, 5, and 6—in a pat of clay in a row slanting in the direction they will bend, cone 5 in the middle. Place the cone pat so that it can be seen through the peephole in the kiln. When cone 4 bends, it is a signal to keep careful watch for the bending of cone 5. When this cone bends, the desired temperature has been reached and you can turn off the kiln.

Cones numbered with a zero before the first digit (01, 02, etc.) have melting points which decrease as the numbers increase (cone 01 melts at 2030° F., and cone 09 melts at 1706° F., for instance).

The Firing Cycle: This varies with the type of kiln used, the firing range desired, the density with which the kiln is loaded, the climates and whether it is a bisque or glaze firing. In all cases, however, the firing cycle must begin slowly and only gradually is the kiln brought up to the required temperature. The cooling process is also as slow as possible and it should take as long for a kiln to cool down as it does for it to heat up.

In an electric kiln, a glaze firing, for example, begins slowly with the kiln set on low and with the lid slightly propped open to allow

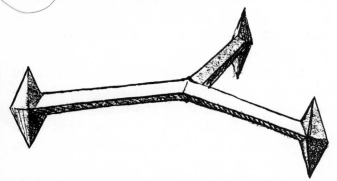

STILTS: Double pointed stilts are available in different sizes and must be coated with kiln wash so that no glaze can stick to them (Illus. 35).

water and other vapors to escape. Next, turn the kiln to medium heat, with the lid propped open slightly. Finally, close the lid and set the kiln to high. Shut-off comes only when the proper temperature has been reached, as checked by the automatic cut-off and the visual checking of the cone pat. Then the cooling process begins.

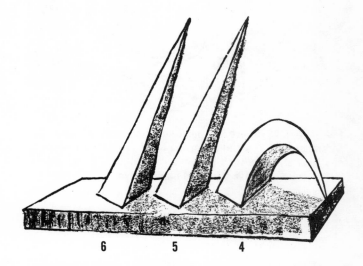

CONES: These are usually placed three in a row. The cone bearing the number corresponding to the temperature at which your ware will mature is placed in the middle (cone 5 here). Cone 4 has already melted (2129°F.). Now you must watch the cones carefully (through the peephole) and when cone 5 has melted (2201°F.), turn the kiln off. If you wait until the heat of the kiln causes cone 6 to melt (2246°F.), your ware will be damaged (Illus. 36).

The procedures are slightly different with a gas kiln, where measures are taken to "reduce" the ware several times during the firing, and the damper is left open at the end for a few minutes to permit the escape of gases.

Unloading: Once the firing and cooling cycles are completed, the kiln may be slowly opened. It may be "cracked" by opening peepholes and lifting the lid or door slightly.

After an hour or two, the kiln should be sufficiently cooled down to permit full opening. The ware is then unloaded, using gloves and tongs which have been heated at the gripper end.

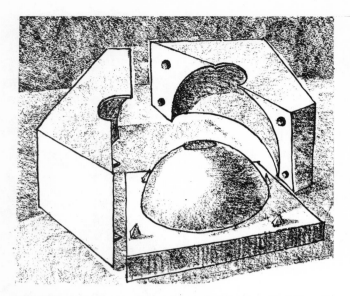

PLASTER CASTS are for making duplicates of your best ceramic ware. You can make the mold (usually a tri-partite) and pour slip into it to form the cast (Illus. 37). Or you can have the mold made for you.

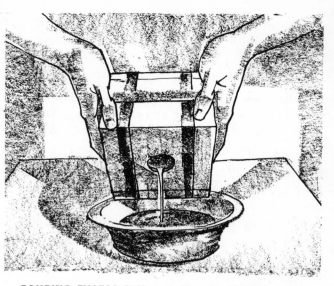

POURING EXCESS SLIP out of the mold (Illus. 39).

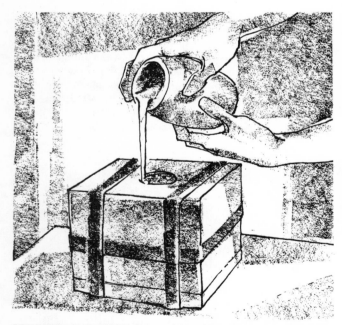

POURING SLIP INTO the mold, which has been securely banded (Illus. 38).

Casting

Casting by pouring a clay slip into a plaster cast is often used when shapes must be reproduced in large quantities. A clay slip (clay to which enough water has been added to make it a liquid and to which electrolytes, such as soda ash or sodium silicate, etc., have been added to deflocculate the mixture, i.e., to prevent its becoming a sticky mass) is prepared. The studio potter is better off purchasing this commercially. Casting slip should weigh 30 ounces per pint.

The Mold: Casting is always carried out in plaster molds so that the water is readily absorbed. Solid casting is made by filling the mold with slip, allowing it to set and then pouring off the reservoir of slip, if any. The *mold itself determines the thickness of the walls.* In hollow or drain casting, however, the slip is poured into the mold and left there until it has cast solid to the right wall thickness; the excess is then poured off and the mold allowed to harden. All cast pieces require some trimming and great care must be taken in removing them from the mold.

MOSAICS

ROMAN MOSAIC: This rabbit, composed of glass tesserae, sitting among mushrooms was made by the Romans in the 1st century B.C.

The word "mosaic" derives from the Greek *mouseios*, which means "belonging to the muses." A mosaic is composed of small pieces of differently colored materials, called *tesserae*, arranged to form a design from their different colors and textures. Mosaic is considered an outgrowth of the ancient decorative art of inlaying, and was practiced in Mesopotamia at least as early as 4000 B.C.

Because of the infinite color possibilities and

Condensed from the book, "Making Mosaics" by Edmond Arvois / © 1964 by Sterling Publishing Co., Inc., New York

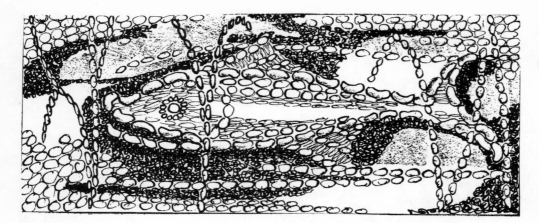

DRIED PEAS, beans and even coffee beans can be used to make colorful mosaics.

the durability of most tesserae materials, mosaics have never been equalled as architectural adornment. In the early Christian period and through the greater part of the Middle Ages in the Byzantine Empire and Italy, they were used as the chief method of wall decoration.

The basic requirements for making a mosaic are: (1) a design, (2) tesserae of almost any material, (3) a base, and (4) an adhesive or a cement.

Mosaic Stones

The tesserae which form your mosaic can be either natural stone, glass, tile, or small pieces of various materials—beans, seeds, gravel, or bits of paper. Marble, agate, and onyx are the most common of the natural mosaic stones. Most mosaics are now made with materials created specifically for the purpose. These are classified as follows:

Glass tile, about ¾ by ¾ inches (20 mm. by 20 mm.) is often called *Venetian glass tile*

because it was first made in Venice. It comes pasted on sheets of paper about a foot square or in bulk form by the pound, in single or assorted milky colors.

Byzantine tile, another glass tile measuring about ⅜ by ½ inches (10 mm. by 10 mm.), is also called "smalti tipo antico." Made in large sheets and then split by machine, the surfaces are often slightly irregular, which increases the reflective qualities of the tile. It is sold in bulk only, and is available in a wide range of milky colors. These little tiles are suitable for decorating small objects.

Ceramic tile, measuring about ¾ by ¾ inches (20 mm. by 20 mm.), is made of clay with a colored glaze. It comes pasted face down on sheets of paper or face up on sheets of open-weave fabric. It is also sold in bulk form by the pound in single or assorted colors. The color range is moderate. Colored unglazed ceramic tile is also available.

Glazed ceramic tiles are also available in shapes known as "brick tile" which are sold in

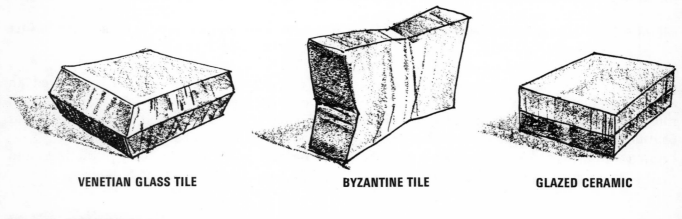

VENETIAN GLASS TILE   BYZANTINE TILE   GLAZED CERAMIC

foot-square sheets containing assorted sizes: $\frac{3}{8}$ by $\frac{3}{8}$ inches; $\frac{3}{8}$ by $\frac{5}{8}$ inches; and $\frac{5}{8}$ by $\frac{5}{8}$ inches. Other varieties include foot-square sheets of glazed ceramic tiles shaped like leaves of various sizes (leaf tile) and random shapes and sizes (pebble tile), sold in foot-square sheets and in bulk bags.

Porcelain tile, measuring about $\frac{3}{8}$ by $\frac{3}{8}$ inches (10 mm. by 10 mm.), comes in a limited range of colors. It is particularly suitable for decorating small objects.

Other tiles or materials include small pieces of stained glass and colored ceramic bathroom tile which can be broken up into small pieces, as well as various decorative plastic tiles.

Adhesives

A variety of adhesives are used to form the bond between the pieces of the mosaic and the base. Temporary adhesives include wallpaper paste (an excellent paste can be made by mixing flour and water thoroughly), library paste, and rubber cement. Rubber cement has two advantages: the excess can be removed when dry by rubbing, and when it is applied to only a single surface, the bond is not permanent. However, when rubber cement is applied to both surfaces and allowed to dry before joining, an almost permanent bond is achieved.

More permanent adhesives include mucilage, model aircraft cement, contact cement, hoof or hide glue (such as that used by furniture makers), mastic (used in mounting plastic or cork floor tile), polyvinyl resins, and—the most permanent of all—epoxy cement. Epoxy comes in two tubes or jars, one the cement and the other the hardener. Epoxy cement should be mixed immediately before use in small quantities. NOTE: When handling epoxy, always wear gloves and avoid contact with the eyes.

Cements and Grouts

In addition to general purpose adhesives, there are mosaic cements and grouts. Cements can serve as a bed for mosaic pieces, while grouts are used to fill the spaces between the pieces of a mosaic after they have been set in a bed or cemented directly to the base.

Cement should be mixed to the consistency of modelling clay, while grout should have the consistency of heavy cream—that is, heavy enough to be worked by hand, but thin enough to fully penetrate the spaces between tesserae.

Portland cement can be bought in bags and comes in two shades, grey and white. The grey is stronger, but the white can be dyed more easily by the addition of ground pigments. Portland cements can be stretched by mixing, using the proportion of one part cement to three parts clean medium-grain sand. The sand-cement mixture should be used for large mosaics, particularly those which will be left out-of-doors. The mixture can be colored with water-soluble dyes. Cement should be cured slowly to prevent cracking. Cover the finished mosaic with wet cloths or wet newspapers for several days until the cement has hardened.

Magnesite, a non-waterproof cement used in flooring work, forms a close bond with wood or composition hardboard mosaic bases, in contrast to the poor adhesive qualities of concrete. Its setting time can be controlled. For small mosaics, fine-grain patching plaster ("spackle") is excellent as a cement or a grout.

Plaster of Paris has a very short setting time which necessitates working quickly. A commercial "plaster retarder" can be used, or white vinegar can be added in place of water to lengthen the setting time. However, both tend to weaken the resultant plaster.

Baseboards and Edging

The choice of a baseboard must be determined primarily by the dimensions of the mosaic and its purpose. Almost any stiff, strong surface can support a mosaic—heavy cardboard, a metal plate, a sheet of plywood, masonite, wallboard—even plain wood can serve. All wood baseboards require water-

BOWLS, DISHES AND VASES become more attractive and colorful when decorated with mosaic tiles.

proofing with sealer, shellac or varnish to prevent warping. Various pieces of furniture can be used as a base for inset mosaic. Tables and benches are natural objects for mosaic decoration, but consider also the possibilities of book ends, lamp bases, bowls, serving trays, jewel boxes, and wooden chests.

A border or edging is essential not only to contain the mosaic on the baseboard, but also to conceal the rough edges of the tile and the bed. You may wish to use a temporary border while making your mosaic so that the permanent border will not be marred or damaged.

Either wood or metal edgings can be used for most projects. The most usual width of edging is one inch—but this width depends somewhat on the size of the mosaic and the part you want the edging "frame" to play in your completed design.

The thickness of wood edging is generally $\frac{1}{8}$ inch and metal edgings vary from $\frac{1}{20}$ to $\frac{1}{8}$ inch. The more supple or malleable metals are advised for rounded or curved baseboards.

When cutting borders, frames, or edging materials, a mitre box is useful. It holds both the work to be cut and the saw at the correct angle. For perfect joints, a mitre box is essential.

Tools

While many kitchen utensils such as knives and spatulas are very useful, you will need the following special tools for making mosaics:

1. Heavy cellulose sponge for wiping away excess grout from the face of the mosaic.

2. Tweezers for holding tesserae while applying adhesive and for placing small tesserae on the base.

3. Flexible-bladed scraper or putty knife for forcing grout into the open spaces between tesserae.

4. Plasterer's trowel for applying and smoothing large areas of cement.

5. Plastic scraper for removing excess grout or mosaic cement from the face of the mosaic (a metal scraper would scratch).

6. Small round-tipped paint brush for applying watercolors or touching up, etc.

7. Cutting nippers—the best nippers have carbide cutting edges and long handles.

Cutting

The technique of cutting tesserae is easily learned. Never place the entire tesserae in the mouth of the nippers. Rather, use the side of the nippers to "bite" the stone. The edge of the cutters must lie in the same line as the cut you wish to make.

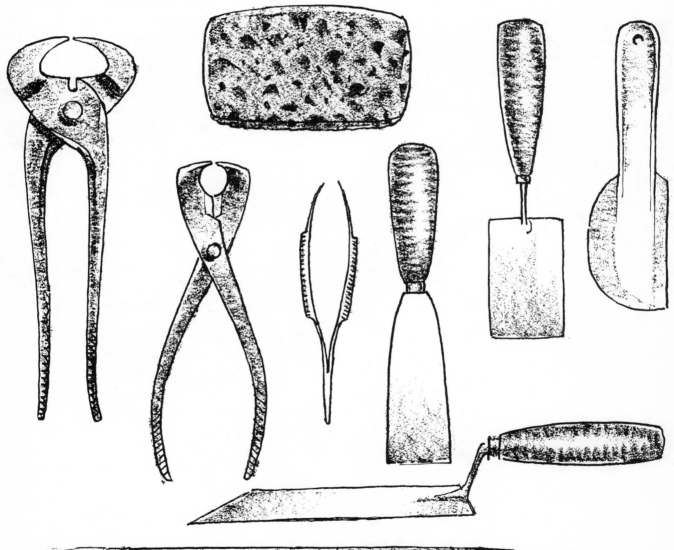

TOOLS FOR MOSAICS include a sponge, various knives, scrapers and brushes for applying cement, and cutting nippers and tweezers to cut and place the tiles.

Whole tesserae can also be cut with a hammer with a sharp cutting edge. The traditional method of cutting tesserae is with a chisel and mallet. However, diamond or carborundum cutting wheels or a steel-wheel glass cutter can also be used. Tesserae can even be placed in layers of newspaper or cloth and struck with a hammer to produce random shapes and sizes.

Finishing and Waxing

Although portland cement is relatively impervious to liquids, other cements, such as plaster of Paris, quickly absorb moisture. To avoid staining, first clean the face of the mosaic using a commercial mosaic cleaner, and then coat the tesserae and the grout-filled spaces between the tesserae with a silicone preparation called a "sealer."

If the grouting cement is plaster of Paris, two *thin* coats of white shellac or a synthetic varnish should be applied, instead of the sealer. A final coat of clear paste wax, highly buffed,

will make the mosaic finish tougher and more durable.

Indirect Method

To attach tiles to a vertical surface, the only practical way is by the reverse or indirect method. This method also assures accuracy and uniformity in horizontal designs. First draw the design full scale in reverse on a sheet of brown wrapping paper. Place the tesserae face down on the paper and keep them in place with a temporary adhesive. Smooth a bed of relatively soft cement over both the vertical surface and the backs of the tesserae. Then press the paper holding the tesserae against the cement bed and allow it to set. It is important that the cement is forced into the spaces between the tesserae. When the bed has begun to set, moisten the paper with a sponge and carefully peel it off. As long as the bed has not hardened too much, the tesserae can be shifted and adjusted.

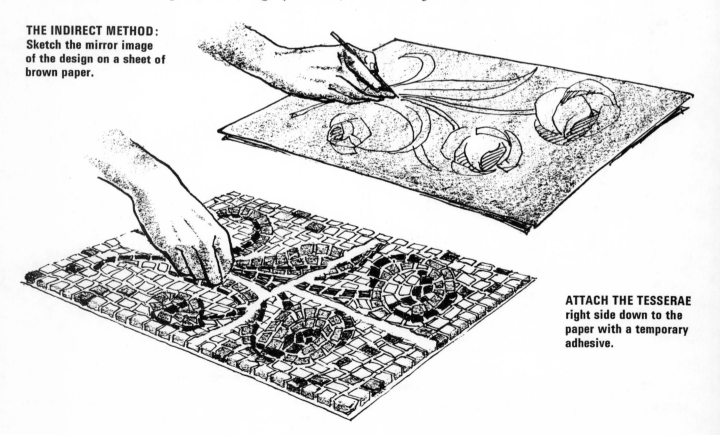

THE INDIRECT METHOD:
Sketch the mirror image of the design on a sheet of brown paper.

ATTACH THE TESSERAE right side down to the paper with a temporary adhesive.

THE PAINT BRUSH should be used to apply adhesive to the small tiles.

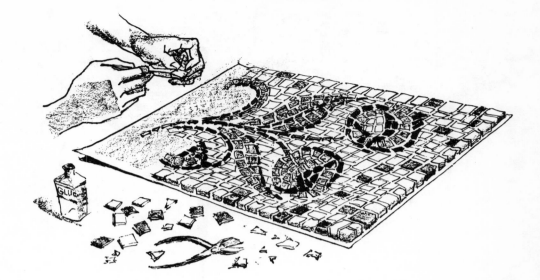

THE CARTOON: Cut the brown wrapping paper into four pieces and lay each piece into the bed of mosaic cement.

REMOVE the paper after the mosaic cement has dried sufficiently.

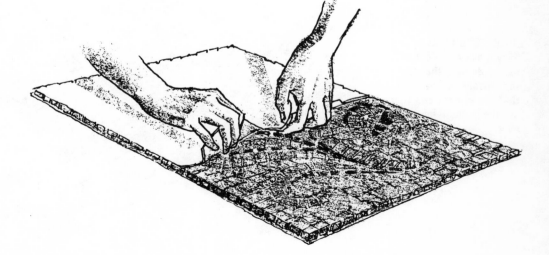

THE FINISHED TABLE with mosaic top. Dark plastic edging was fastened to the baseboard.

A Mosaic Cheeseboard

An attractive and practical project to make is a mosaic-topped cheeseboard. Fix the tile tesserae you have chosen with a permanent adhesive to a breadboard base, and grout them with a thin mixture of mosaic cement and water. The grout in the spaces between the tesserae can be smoothed with a table knife or a nut pick. Copper scouring pads will remove any mosaic cement left on the surface. Be sure to wipe the surface clean with a sponge before applying sealer and finish.

The edge of the breadboard can either be stained or covered with a row of tesserae. A piece of felt glued to the underside of the board with rubber cement will prevent scratches on furniture.

Inlay for a Table Top

Decorating an entire table top with mosaic stones takes patience and care, but requires no techniques other than those used for making the cheeseboard. If you wish to mosaic only a small portion of a table top, a few preliminary steps are necessary.

Cut a hole in the top of the table, in the size and shape you desire your inlay to be. With wood screws, attach a piece of plywood larger

A CHEESEBOARD is an easy mosaic project to make. Be sure that the top surface is level and that the cement and tiles are the same height all over.

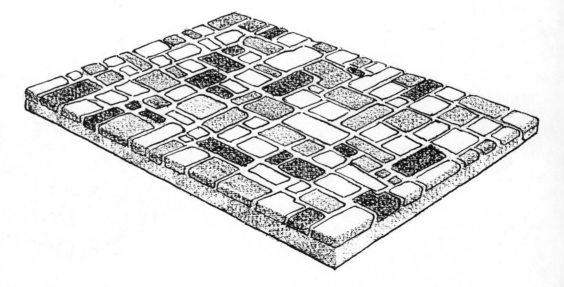

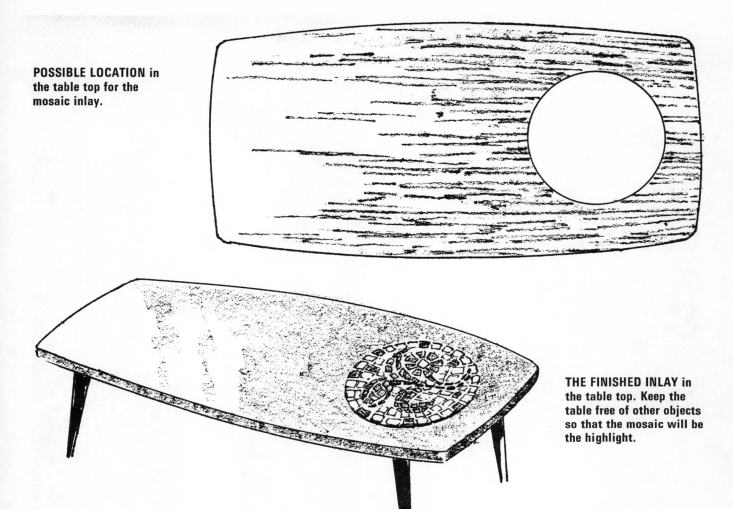

THE FINISHED INLAY in the table top. Keep the table free of other objects so that the mosaic will be the highlight.

than the hole to the underside of the table: this piece will be the base for your mosaic panel, and the sides of the hole will serve as the edging. Apply two coats of shellac to the plywood and the raw edges of the hole, but be careful not to get shellac on the surface of the table.

Using one of the permanent adhesives, fix the individual tesserae to the plywood. When this has dried, fill in the areas between tiles with grout and top with a sealer. If the table top is thicker than the tesserae, it may be necessary to build up a bed of cement on the plywood to bring your completed mosaic up level with the surface of the table.

"MEDITATION," clay sculpture by Louis Di Valentin, cast in bronze.

SCULPTURE

Sculpture may be broadly defined as the art and craft of representing observed or imagined objects in solid materials and in three dimensions. There are two basic types of sculpture: (1) *statuary* in which figures or shapes are shown in the round, and (2) *relief* in which figures or shapes are projected from a background or solid surface, either in low (*bas*) or high (*haut*) relief.

Sculpture is one of the oldest and most widespread of the visual arts and one of the more difficult to master, since it requires not only skill but patience and much physical labor and craftsmanship to complete a work. Often sculpture involves working out a piece from more or less resistant materials over a long period of time. Casting or other methods of forming the sculptured work requires many procedural steps.

A sculptural work can be produced either by direct carving or by modelling. Modelling is a method of producing a work in clay, wax, or plaster and then reproducing it in plaster, bronze or other materials.

Modelling can also be used to fashion a piece of terra cotta (clay that is to be fired in a kiln) and then fired to the appropriate temperature in a kiln to mature the clay. The terra cotta piece is then sanded and finished with suitable patinas.

There also are many other techniques employed by contemporary "new material" sculptors. These are artists and craftsmen who prefer to work in the newer materials made possible by modern technology. For example,

MODELLING a figure in clay over an armature for plaster or bronze casting later is the customary procedure for beginners in sculpture.

metal sculptures employing wire, sheet steel, tin, aluminum, chrome or other modern metals can be fashioned by welding, soldering, cutting, etc. Here the major tool is often the soldering iron or torch, while refinishing is done with files, hammers, chisels and jigs. (See Metalcrafting on page 149.) Other sculp-

Condensed from the book, "Sculpture for Beginners" by Maria and Louis DiValentin | © *1969, 1965 by Sterling Publishing Co., Inc., New York*

tors prefer to work with glass or use light to represent three-dimensional form.

Still other contemporary sculptors choose to make their works from the various types of plastics that are now available and use such items as plexiglas, polyester resins, plastic foam, and vinyl, to mention only a few. In the case of plastic sculpture and collage, entirely new methods for forming are used, depending upon the materials employed and the method of forming. (See Sculpture and Collage in Plastics.) Often, too, contemporary sculpture combines various "new materials" such as plastics, acetates, paper, acrylic paints (see Acrylic) and other synthetic and natural materials.

History

The earliest known works of sculpture date back to times when man worked on bone and ivory with stone tools, carving his works. Early sculpture included carved spears, axe handles, and fertility statues.

While various cultures have produced sculpture reflecting their civilizations, in the Western World there seems to have been an unbroken line of descent from the early Stone Age works of Africa to the sculpture of Egypt and the similar developments in the parallel civilizations of the Middle East and Mediterranean. The further development of sculpture by the Greeks to the highly humanistic realism and idealism of classical Greek sculpture led to the creation of some of the most magnificent sculpture in the West. The style of the Greeks was subsequently adopted by the Romans, and later came into its full fruition in the High Renaissance work of Leonardo da Vinci and Michelangelo. Most early work was carved, but a number of civilizations also developed high techniques in bronze casting.

During the Middle Ages, sculpture in the West became a miniaturist art. Larger works were again fashioned by the Gothic and Byzantine artisans, and in the 19th century following the High Renaissance work of the master sculptors, the humanistic, idealistic

CLASSIC SCULPTURE may be seen in museums all over the world. This is Nike or the Winged Victory of Samothrace, which holds a featured place in The Louvre, Paris.

tradition was again revived. Sculpture of the 19th century in this tradition is perhaps best exemplified by the work of Rodin—generally bronze casting.

In the 20th century, Western sculpture has kept pace and has paralleled the developments in painting styles. Sculpture in the 20th century has been cubistic, futuristic, constructivist, suprematist, abstract and minimal in style, and since World War II contemporary sculptors have turned increasingly to the use of newer materials—metals, glass, rubber, plastics, celluloid, paper, etc.—to fashion their works. Today, "new material" sculpture is taken for granted and many works since 1940 are made from the newly developed synthetics.

Nearly all other civilizations the world over also independently produced fine 3-dimensional works. The wood carvings of Africa, ivory, jade and cast bronzes of the Far East, stone and gem carving of Central and Latin American civilizations, and the wood, straw, and woven work of the Oceanic peoples are only a few examples of the diverse cultural achievements in sculpture.

Terra Cotta

Terra cotta is a common clay of open, coarse-grain structure which permits drying with a minimum of warping. It has been used for forming sculptural and architectural pieces for thousands of years and generally requires firing to maturity in a kiln to an average temperature of 2070 to 2320 degrees F.

"Terra cotta" is a term borrowed from Italian and means "cooked earth." Although the term has been used more broadly in the past to refer to all kinds of fired clay objects, today it is used in a more restrictive sense to apply only to sculpture and architectural uses of the material. Terra cotta sculpture may be fired unglazed or glazed with monochrome or polychrome ceramic glazes. Fired terra cotta pieces (unglazed) may also be decorated subsequently with lacquers and glazes.

What really differentiates modelling in terra cotta from modelling in oil-based clay is that a terra cotta piece cannot be fired in a kiln if it contains an armature.

Only very small statuary can be successfully fired when solid. Medium-sized and larger works *must* be hollow in form with evenly built up sides or walls to survive the firing process.

Direct Modelling in Terra Cotta

To make a small unglazed terra cotta sculpture, all that is required are:

several pounds of terra cotta
a table or modelling stand
water, sponge and modelling tools (the same as listed below for modelling in oil-based clay)
firing and glazing facilities

Rather than invest in expensive kilns, have an experienced potter or sculptor fire your work for you at the start or use the firing facilities at an art school, unless you need a kiln also for ceramics and/or enamelling.

TERRA COTTA: This statuette can be fired in a kiln since it was not made on an armature.

The first step is to wedge the clay properly (see page 30) so that it is smooth and consistent. Now make sketches of the subject and determine the final size and form of the piece. Remember that clay shrinks in the drying and firing process.

Assuming that the subject is a small head or bust, there are several ways of proceeding. First, take a ball of clay the approximate size of the head and begin with fingers and clay-work tools to work this into a shape that roughly resembles a head. Add to the clay by using small pellets of clay, fasten these on by scoring the surfaces and adding slip (clay suspended in water) to the spot where the addition is to be made. Then work the pellet into the other surface with your fingers and tools to combine the clay pieces. The roughly shaped head can then be hollowed out with a knife and wire

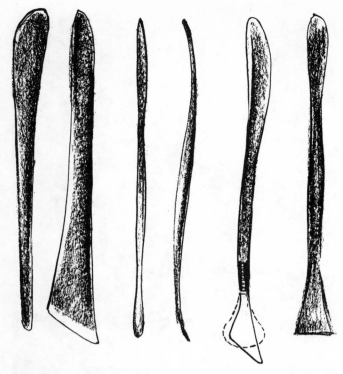
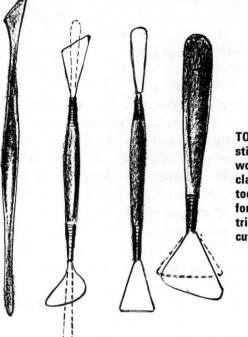

tools, and finished with the same modelling instructions given below for modelling the head in oil-based clay. Subtractions are made by cutting away the unwanted surfaces with wire modelling tools.

An alternate method for obtaining the basic hollow shape on which to base the modelling is to build it up by using the coil or modified slab method of pottery formation (see page 24). This may take some time for a large piece, but has the advantage of initially being hollow and of the correct basic shape. Additions are then made by adding small pellets of clay wherever needed; subtractions are made by cutting away excesses with wire modelling tools. The coil or slab methods may also be used to make free-form sculpture.

Always be sure to wrap a terra cotta sculpture in damp paper towels under a plastic cover to ensure keeping the piece moist between work sessions. Similar care must be taken also with the terra cotta supply which can be wrapped in plastic sheets and stored in a metal or wooden container.

The modelled piece can be smoothed or finished by sponging with a soft elephant ear sponge or, if desired, the surface can be texturized while the piece is still damp. Once bone dry, it is difficult if not impossible to make further refinements. When the finished sculpture is complete, allow it to dry slowly. Too rapid drying will result in cracks and strains developing either before or during the firing process. When the piece is completely dry (bone dry to the touch) it may be fired in a kiln. It is wise to test the clay prior to firing the modelled piece if the maturity temperature is not known; usually, however, the clay supplier can provide this information.

If the sculpture does not require glazing, it can be fired slowly and directly to maturity in a suitable electric or gas kiln. If the sculpture is to be glazed, it is wise to fire it twice—first to the bisque state (lower than to maturity) and then—after glazing the piece with suitable glazes that mature at the same point the clay does (see page 38 for glazing methods)—firing the glazed terra cotta sculpture to maturity. All the techniques used for glazing pottery and loading a glazed kiln apply to this stage of decorating and firing glazed terra cotta.

Unglazed but matured terra cotta can also be decorated with patinas and lacquers applied after the piece has been fired and sanded to smoothness.

Alternate Methods of Forming in Terra Cotta

All sizes of terra cotta sculpture also can be produced in hollow form by making a plaster mold and pouring in deflocculated clay slip. Large terra cotta sculptures can also be made by first building a model over a suitable armature and casting a waste mold (or piece of mold) of the work and then pressing clay into the plaster mold or molds. When leather-hard, join these terra cotta sections at the seams with slip and clay pellets. It is wise on a large hollow piece to permit the air to escape from the interior by puncturing the piece with several small holes in places where they will not be conspicuous. These air holes will help to prevent any explosions in the kiln.

Modelling with Oil-Based Clay

Cast sculptural pieces are generally modelled first in moist oil-based clay, plasticine, or wax.

Modelling in clay is a good way to begin exploring the various methods of creating sculpture. Only a few supplies are needed:

several pounds of an oil-based clay or plasticine

a table top, revolving modelling stand, or a turntable which can be placed on the table or stationary modelling stand

a bowl of water

a sponge and some clay modelling tools

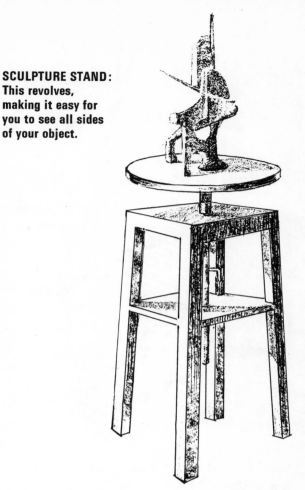

SCULPTURE STAND: This revolves, making it easy for you to see all sides of your object.

An oil-based clay is preferable since it remains moist and soft during the work process.

Tools for modelling less than life-size clay pieces include: looped wire tools to cut away clay, make hollows and concave areas; wooden stick tools used to add clay to the model, flatten a piece, or to "draw up" the clay; callipers and proportional dividers for measuring and enlarging a work proportionally. Similar tools, but larger in size, are used on

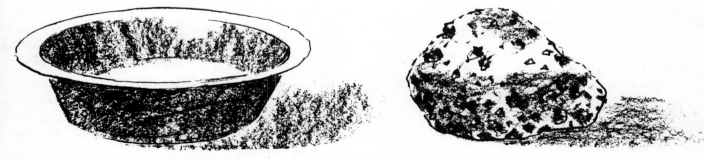

SPONGE AND BOWL: You must keep your clay damp while working on it.

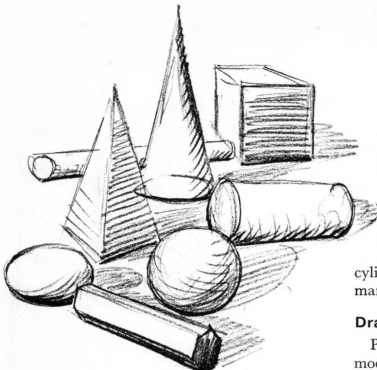

THE BASIC SHAPES: Surprising as it may seem, these are the only shapes you need to know how to make in order to form a good many objects in clay: cylinder, oval, sphere, cube, cone, and pyramid.

life-size and large pieces, and sculptors also use a wooden mallet to pound clay into shape. The best tool of all is an "educated thumb," and all sculptors develop dextrous fingers to work their pieces into shape.

The Basic Shapes

The first task for the student sculptor is to get acquainted with the clay material. Wedge the clay so that it is smooth and consistent in texture (see page 30 for complete instructions). Now take a large pinch of clay and feel it between your fingers. Roll the clay into a sausage shape. Now take a larger lump of clay and roll this into a ball. Keep adding to this until you can paddle it and shape it into a perfect square. Then with a knife, cut the square diagonally across and down into two wedge-shaped pieces. Soften the angles of the wedges, round them off and bring the long sides up to a point until you have shaped two cones. Take one cone and build up the pointed end until enough clay has been added to make a cylinder. The ball, cube, cone and

cylinder are the basic shapes from which many objects can be modelled in solid form.

Drawing and Sketching

Perhaps the most important prelude to modelling is to draw and sketch forms you want to create as sculpture. Only by studying nature or a live model will fine sketches result. The first step in creating a model is to have an absolutely accurate sketch, at least one-fourth the size of the proposed figure, with the movement and proportions absolutely exact. This can then be enlarged by pointing, by using the callipers and proportional dividers. Actually, sketches should be made of the proposed figure from all views—front, back, sides, and top.

Modelling a Bear

Small animals or forms can be modelled from solid clay without use of an armature as a support. Start by taking some clay and working it into small sausage-like shapes. These will form the legs. Next take some clay and form a ball for the head, a larger oval or egg-shaped form for the body, and two triangular clay parts for the ears. Also form a rectangular base, slightly larger than the final dimensions of the bear on which to mount the animal.

Now join the head and body. Use a wooden tool to join the edges of the two pieces, working one form into the other. Seal by brushing slip

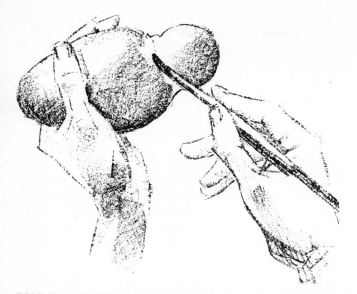

BEAR (Step 1): After rolling the body as an oval and the head as a ball, clap them together, and fill the joint with slip (a liquid form of clay).

BEAR (Step 2): After attaching the nose (a cone flattened out), the legs (cylinders shaped narrower at the lower ends), and the feet (flattened eggs), put the bear on its rectangular base.

BEAR (Step 3): Use wire tools to trim away excess clay and shape the features.

BEAR (Step 4): After the eyes are tooled out, and the ears made to stand up, sponge off the bear. These simple steps prove how easy it is to become a sculptor. Your finished bear may not be artistic, but you are on your way.

on. Cut away any excess with a wire tool and use the fingers to indent or build up the form with additional clay pellets. Now attach the nose and legs.

When satisfied with the general outlines of the piece, attach it to the base at the legs and then complete the ears and facial features with wire tools. Use wooden tools to give softness to the form. A light sponging is also helpful in finishing the piece.

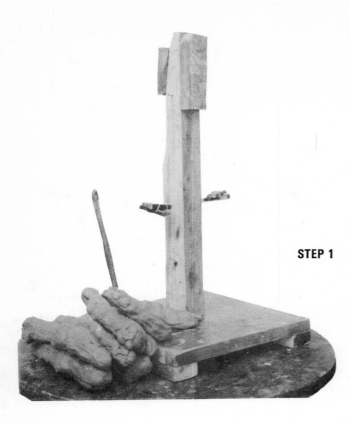

STEP 1

Making an Armature

Larger sculptural works require an armature for support, prior to beginning the modelling in clay. An armature is simply an understructure which acts as a support for the proposed piece. An armature is usually constructed from pipe, rods, wiring, burlap, or wood. It is secured to a base and is constructed to resemble in a crude way the form being modelled. The purpose of the armature is to support the clay and hold it in place so that the piece will not collapse before it is finished.

Building an Armature for a Life-Size Bust. The first step is to take a very strong, flat baseboard and join a wooden 2 × 2 or a lead pipe to it right in the middle. Next, fasten a crossbar to the upright at about the point below the neck where the shoulders of the bust will be. Secure the crossbar to the upright with copper tubing, or by wooden dowels in bored holes. A few loops of the copper tubing can first be formed above the crossbar to supply the support necessary for the head.

Simple armatures can be purchased at any art store, but most professional sculptors construct armatures to meet the particular requirements of their proposed sculptures.

Lead or galvanized pipe is frequently used in building armatures, since this will not erode, and chicken wire, burlap, plaster, bricks, and iron rods are used as well. The important thing to remember when building an armature is that the understructure must always be smaller than the finished work and must resemble crudely the piece so that support will be adequate. Needless to say, each armature will vary according to the pose, size, movement and shape of the modelled sculpture.

Modelling a Head and Bust

You are ready to begin modelling once you have selected your subject, made careful preliminary sketches to scale, and translated the proportions of the sketches to work out the proportions of the model.

STEP 1. Prepare the armature and work the clay into manageable lengths.

STEP 2. Mass clay on the armature, thumping it on with your hands. Put on as much clay as needed to approximate eventual size. Remember clay will shrink in drying. Keep the clay moistened and cover the bust with damp cloths between work sessions.

STEP 3. With a wire tool dig out the eye sockets under the brow. Establish the central line from the sternum through the neck, chin, mouth, nose, forehead, over the top of the head and down the back and neck.

STEP 4. With wire tools establish the large planes and high points, measuring distances for proportions and relating the parts to each other.

STEP 5. Establish the high point of the zygomatic bone—the bone which extends along

STEP 2

STEP 3

STEP 2: Use your hands to thump the clay on to the armature. Put on enough clay to approximate the eventual size of the head and bust. Mass the clay on, one small wad after another.

STEP 3: After you have enough clay on the armature and have smoothed it out into the general shape of a head, nose, neck, shoulders and chest, start taking away clay. Use a wire tool. First, dig out the eye sockets, after putting a horizontal guide line across the brows. Put another guide line through the whole center of the head, front and back, down through the chest.

STEP 4: Look at your model or photograph and notice the high planes and points—the top of the head, the tip of the nose, the jutting chin, the ears. Measure distances on your model and on your sculpture. Since this is a life-size bust, you should have no trouble getting the dimensions and proportions right.

STEP 4

the front or side of the skull beneath the eye socket. Add the ears, placing them properly in relation to the jaw, brow, and nose.

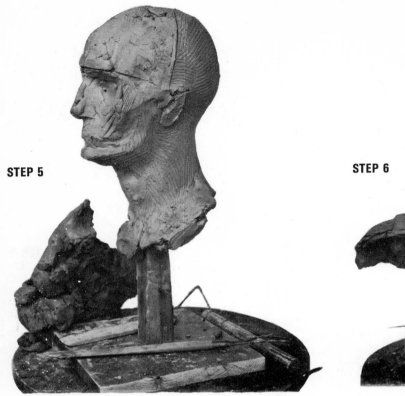

STEP 5

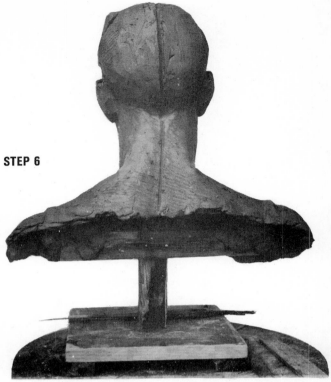

STEP 6

STEP 5: The bone beneath the eye socket is more or less prominent in each person. Work on this until you form it properly. Then place the ears in relation to the brows and jaws especially.

STEP 6: Revolve your stand and model the back of your sculpture.

STEP 7: Hair on top of the head is created from an added wad of clay.

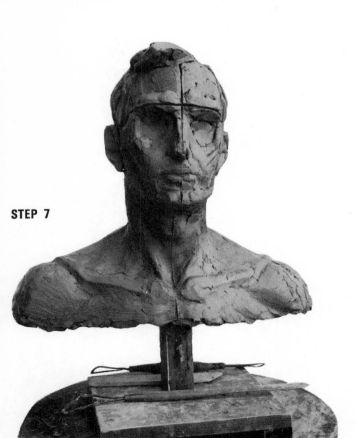

STEP 7

STEP 6. Remember to work on the back of the bust as well as on the front. Check all sides of the work by spinning it slowly on the revolving stand. Make clay pellets and add these where necessary. Be sure the base of the skull overhangs the base of the neck.

STEP 7. With a wooden tool, add clay and press it in to create the hair mass. Treat hair as a mass form which grows out of the skull.

STEP 8. Check to see that the bone and muscle structures are accurate and that the

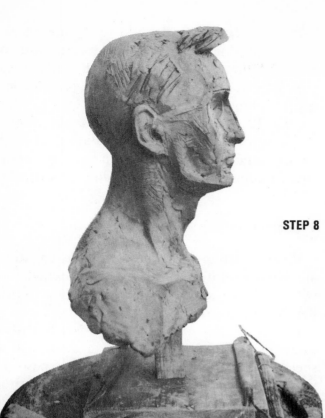

STEP 8

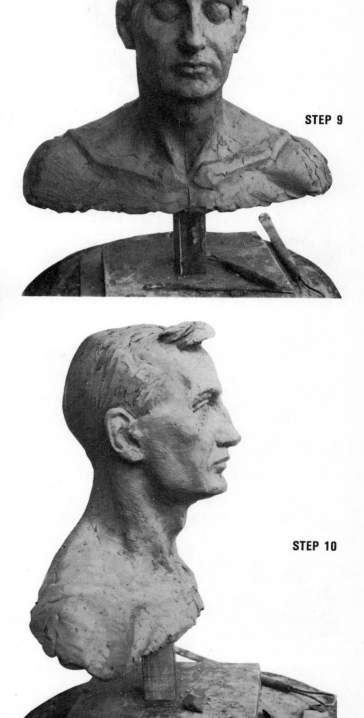

STEP 9

STEP 8: As you can see in this side view, the long vertical muscle (the sterno-mastoid) in the neck has been built up. Also the jaw line has been emphasized by building and tooling away.

STEP 9: With the shoulder muscles and bones (deltoids and clavicle) fully developed, you can switch your modelling to the eye sockets which need to be rounded out and eyeballs developed. Eyelids come last. Finish the mouth and lips.

STEP 10: After you are satisfied with all of the features (ears, nose, eyes), soften the rough lines with your wooden tools. Flatten some areas, round others. Blend the clay over apertures. Put lines in the hair. Observe your model always as you work.

STEP 10

sterno-mastoid muscle in the neck and the shoulder girdle are firmly indicated.

STEP 9. Using tools, model the deltoids and the clavicle, relating muscles to bone structure. Place eyeballs in the sockets. Model the eyelids and other outer areas.

STEP 10. Flatten or curve areas with wooden tools; soften areas and blend together.

STEP 11. Indent and build up where necessary, using fingers to model and wire tools to create hollows. Keep turning the model to view it from all angles. Also, check proportions while looking down on the model.

STEP 12. With small wooden tools, model the nose, mouth, ears and lids, adding all final details and keeping the underlying bone structure in mind. A knowledge of anatomy will help.

Plaster Casting

Plaster casting—that is, making a negative and then a positive plaster cast of the model—will preserve your clay sculpture in a more permanent form.

Casting is not only a difficult job but also quite messy. Unless you have a studio or a special room you can use for this purpose, it is best to have a plaster caster do the casting for you. If you do attempt it yourself, try a very small piece or a head at most. Prepare the area by covering the floor and everything else in the room with newspapers. Wear a smock or other protective clothing.

Powdered plaster has the peculiar property of whisking itself through the air and settling as a thick white dust everywhere, even in adjoining rooms.

If all of this has not discouraged you, then prepare the following items for the making of a mold:

25 pounds of casting plaster
2 mixing bowls, a large one and a small one
1 large spoon
bottle of liquid blueing
cooking oil
liquid soap
2 chisels
some brushes
piece of burlap
1 scraper
1 hammer
some plaster tools
1 tin snips
metal strips

PLASTER CASTING: The first thing to do is to place metal shims as shown to divide the bust into two sections (Illus. 24).

Into the water in the large mixing bowl put two tablespoons of liquid laundry blueing which can be obtained in liquid form or made from powder. Now, into this blue water, very carefully sift some plaster, enough of it until it comes to the surface. Use no more than that; otherwise your plaster will be too thick. Use your spoon to stir, but don't lift it out. Stir under until it looks like thick blue cream. Now dip the smaller bowl into the mixture and get some of the plaster out. From your smaller bowl, scoop some plaster in your hand and fling it gently but firmly on to the front half of your clay model (Illus. 25). The plaster may run off; catch it as it does and throw it back on. Continue until you have a thin coat all over the front. This colored film of plaster will guide you later on.

Blow gently through your mouth so that the plaster runs definitely into the nostrils and

Have all these items on a separate covered table beside your casting stand. Dip your spoon and bowls in cooking or olive oil. If you are going to cast a head or other three-dimensional piece it cannot be done in one piece but must be cast in two sections. The back of the head has to be sectioned off. This sectioning is done by using shims, which are small metal strips about 1½ by 3 inches. Use snippers to cut these metal shims to the size and shape you need.

These small metal shims are inserted into the clay head all around, starting from the top of the head, down the sides, through the temples, behind the ears and vertically down the sides of the neck (Illus. 24). Cover the back of the head with tissue paper so it won't get splattered while you are plastering the front part of the mold.

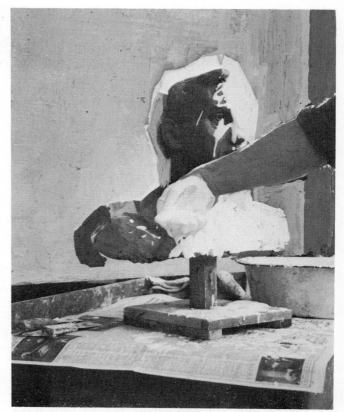

FLING liquid plaster by the handful on to the clay sculpture until the front is covered to a thickness of ¾ inch, thicker at the seams. (Illus. 25).

HOW THE FRONT LOOKS when it has been completely covered with its first thin layer of plaster (Illus. 26).

SECOND PLASTERING: This is a thicker mixture, the consistency of whipped cream. Be sure it covers (Illus. 27).

THE BACK: Make V-shaped "keys" where the shims were before you begin to fling plaster on the back of the head (Illus. 28).

eyes and other deep places. Make sure every single part of the surface is covered (under the chin too). Put extra plaster all around the edge in front of the shims. Make a thick wall edging. This must be strengthened. It is very important to build up this thick seam. Scrape the plaster off the edges of the shims with your scraper. They must be clear so they can be pulled out later.

The plaster will now have begun to set. If you have any left over in your bowl, scrape it out and discard it. There will always be some wastage, but this is to be preferred over not having mixed enough plaster. Scrape your bowl clean. If some plaster still adheres, bend the rim of your bowl inward towards the middle and this will loosen it.

After your plaster has set enough and is beyond the smeary stage, you can brush it all over lightly with oil.

Now mix a second batch of plaster, this time without the blueing and thicker in consistency than the first coat. Add this as an outer shell, which should be about 1 inch thick (Illus. 27). Dip some burlap strips in the plaster and bind them around the shell. (This is not really necessary on a small piece of sculpture.)

Once again clean and grease your bowl. Remove the tissue paper from the back of the clay head. If you view your model from in back you will note the 1-inch edge of plaster

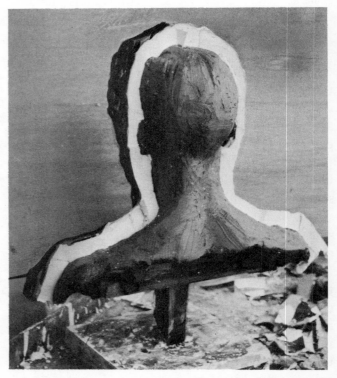

AFTER SETTING for an hour, the plaster has dried and the back mold has been removed at the key line (Illus. 29).

all around the top of the head and vertically down the sides. In this plaster rim edge (from which you must remove the shims with pincers), cut some small notches with a little knife or spatula. These notches are called keys. Make them V-shaped. They will serve to fit the two sections of the mold together later when you have the second section of the mold cast.

Grease the 1½-inch edge carefully. Now begin again as you did for the front (Illus. 28). Put blueing in the water and mix plaster and complete all of the steps as you did before.

Allow 30 minutes to about 1 hour for the plaster to set. Next, pry the two sections apart. Ease a thin chisel into the seam (but not near a key). Use gentle pressure back and forth. When the mold starts to open put a knife blade on each side and gently and gradually pull the back section away from the front. By this time you should be able to lift it away without difficulty. Do not worry about having "destroyed" your clay figure. You have preserved it in plaster.

When you have separated the two sections, begin to dig out the clay from inside your mold. Be sure to use a blunt tool. Try to keep the clay as clean and free from plaster bits as possible because you will be re-using the clay for your next piece of sculpture. Also have a receptacle or box ready in which to store it.

Before you have gotten all the clay out you will reach the armature, which you must remove from the mold very carefully so as to not cause any damage to the plaster. Remove gently any clay that remains. If you have used plasticine (oil-based clay), water will not dissolve it from the deep or tiny crevices. Nevertheless, you must remove every trace of clay from your mold without damaging or scratching it.

After the two sections have been cleaned, they must be soft-soaped or shampooed. With a soft brush, work the soap (boil 1 part soap and 3 parts water) over every single part of your mold. You must do this for about 10

THE PLASTER MOLD with its innermost layer of blue is now the object you will work with, and your original clay bust will probably be destroyed. Soap the mold and pick out bits of clay. Clean out the soap, oil the inside of the mold, and you are ready for the next step, which is pouring new white plaster into the mold for your actual cast (Illus. 30).

minutes. The entire surface must be covered. (Don't forget the ears.) Let the mold soak for about 15 minutes; then remove the soap. With your brush, pick up the soap. Each time you do, squeeze it from your brush with your fingers. Repeat this over and over until you have picked up all the soap. Now you can very lightly brush on a few drops of oil, but only on the high points.

When you have the two sections of the mold cleaned, soaped, and oiled you can use either of two methods for making a cast. You can pour each section separately or you can bind both together as one shell and pour the plaster into the entire unit.

If you are going to do each section separately, mix enough plaster to line the molds about

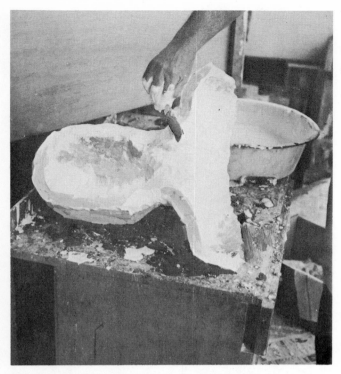

MAKING THE TWO HALVES FIT: Before the new plaster has set completely, clean the edges of your cast, so that when the halves are bound together they will fit tightly (Illus. 31).

1 inch thick. Don't stir the plaster too long or it will set too fast. If you want to fill both sections immediately, you will have to work rapidly without interruptions. Pour in only a little at first (Illus. 30), then tilt and twirl the mold so the plaster gets in and around everywhere. Blow the plaster into every crevice. Keep the seam clean, but cover the mold thoroughly.

After both sections are filled with 1 inch of plaster, clap the two sections together firmly, fitting the two sections into the notched keys. Now dip burlap (2″ × 3″ pieces) into thick plaster and place these patches (soaped) along the seam for reinforcement—at the top of the head, several others on each side, others on the neck. You can also tie the two sections together with cord, but the burlap patches should be enough to hold them firmly together.

There is another method of plaster casting.

After you have cleaned and soaped the mold, fit the two sections together and put strips of burlap dipped in plaster along the seam. This is an open-bottom hollow shell. Stand it upside down on the table. Put a support under it so it won't tip over or move. (You can wind a thick old towel and encircle your upturned mold to keep it steady.) Mix the plaster, dip some out with the smaller bowl and pour it into the shell, tilting and turning around and around gently but firmly so the plaster covers the entire inside surface. Make sure there is a goodly layer over all. Don't fill the head. You can drip out some of the loose, running plaster as you go along.

Repeat pouring, more slowly, allowing the consecutive layers of plaster to set. Tip out the excess. When you think you have a 1-inch-thick cast you can stop pouring and twirling. Wait about an hour or so. In the meantime you can be clearing away the trash and splattered newspapers to get ready for the chipping.

Once again spread clean newspapers around and on the stand and on the floor. Get set to chip away the outside shell. With a mallet and a dull chisel tap away the burlap strips you have placed around the seam. Don't chip too deep and don't force your tools. Begin at the seam and slowly remove the outer shell. Hold the chisel in place at right angles resting your hand against it and tap it with the mallet. Pull your chisel back as soon as it cracks the plaster. The white outer shell will gradually chip, crack and come off in pieces (Illus. 32). Sometimes large pieces will come off with one stroke. Sometimes the blue layer may be still left attached to the cast. Remove this gently with a light tap on your chisel. If some small blue patches remain in the ears or nostrils, you can use a plaster tool to get them out. Always proceed with caution. Always be ready to pull your chisel away. The back of the head is usually easy to chip and uncover, coming off in one or two big pieces.

Take extra care around the ears. You can easily snap them off and ruin your work.

CHIP AWAY the outer plaster mold from the plaster cast carefully, using a dull chisel, tapping gently with a mallet. Here the head is beginning to appear (Illus. 32). Use a small chisel gently around the ears.

Don't be discouraged if you dig or nick your cast. This happens sometimes to the most experienced casters. Minor repairs or patching should be done as soon as possible while the cast is still fresh and moist.

To patch, mix a small amount of casting plaster in a halved hollow rubber ball. This makes a very useful and very easily cleaned receptacle. Sift the plaster into the water; don't stir. Allow it to stand. Run a knife through the mixture. If the cut does not disappear but remains visible, the plaster is ready to be used for filling in or patching. Before you apply the plaster go over the damaged spot, applying water with a wet brush. Make sure your patching plaster is properly prepared as described above; otherwise, your patched areas will dry out darker and harder than the rest of the cast.

There are, of course, other kinds and methods of casting. For example, there is casting by means of a glue mold or a piece mold. These are best left to expert casters. They are complex, smelly, and messy and seldom attempted even by professional sculptors.

Of course, bronze casting must be done at a foundry. If your piece of sculpture is going to be cast in bronze, then you will deliver the plaster cast (positive replica) to the foundry, where experts in molten metal will pour and cast it for you. The bronze cast is made hollow, about $\frac{1}{4}$ inch thick. It is a difficult, intricate and expensive process. If you arrange to visit a foundry, you will find it a very interesting place, and you will also realize just how complicated the bronze casting process is.

Finishes for Plaster Casts

If you want to display a plaster cast, there are a number of interesting ways to finish it.

Ivory finish. To achieve an ivory finish, paint the cast with two coats of shellac. Mix 2 parts of white shellac to $1\frac{1}{2}$ parts of alcohol. Apply from the top downwards. After drying, apply a second coat.

Darker color. To obtain a darker color, add sepia or yellow ochre in powdered form to the second coat of shellac. Go over the cast with melted beeswax thinned with turpentine to get a soft, glowing effect.

Bronze finish. For a simulated bronze finish, apply two coats of alcohol wood stain; one in dark oak, the other in redwood. On the second coat, brush some bronze powder very lightly on the high points. When dry, add a coat of wax and polish with a soft cloth.

Bas-Relief

Bas-relief is sometimes defined as sculptured drawing, or raised drawing. It has the dimensions of length and breadth, but its third dimension, that of depth, varies. Bas (low)-relief generally has a flat background, is not in the round, but only elevated in part. Where a sculptured form is designed only to project a small degree from the background, it is bas-relief. When the design is raised enough to appear detached from the background and

BAS-RELIEF from ancient times: Portrait of Hesire c. 2750 B.C., now in the Egyptian Museum, Cairo, as rendered by Louis Di Valentin.

projects at least half the natural circumference, it is said to be high-relief.

A good bas-relief requires the knowledge and execution of good drawing. The sculptor must be adept in draftsmanship, in the use of charcoal and pencil, to draw at least the outline of his subject, whether it be a profile of a head or of the entire body. Here you will learn how to do a bas-relief portrait. However, you can apply the same basic procedures to any bas-relief.

To begin your portrait, outline on paper, with pencil or charcoal, the profile of the sitter's head. You will use your drawing as a guide for your work in clay.

On an easel, place an appropriate-sized shellacked wooden board upon which to pack and level the clay. With charcoal, mark out the area of the board which will contain the clay. On both the left and right sides of the marked-off area, nail a strip of wood to the board to set the thickness or depth of the clay background, which will be about ½ inch. Pack on your clay between the wooden strips to the level determined by them. Add the clay on the board little by little and bit by bit until the board is covered with an even distribution of clay.

Now take a straight-edge and, holding both ends, press down to draw it across the clay, diagonally from top to bottom, horizontally, and from left to right. Scrape down firmly. Draw the straight-edge over the surface of the clay until you obtain an even and level plane. Fill in any hollow places or spots with more clay where needed, and smooth out again.

With a wooden sculpture tool, copy the outlines of your drawn profile in the smooth-surfaced clay. Place the portrait outline in the clay, so that you leave more space in front of the face than in back. This is best for compositional purposes, so the profile will not look as if it were walking out of the designated area. Reliefs using figures must also be composed so they are well framed.

Cut away the background around the profile

STEP 1: Set up your shellacked board on an easel and mark off the area for bas-relief.

STEP 2: Nail wooden strips as side boundaries and pack ½-inch-thick bits of clay between them.

STEP 3: Firmly level the clay by drawing a straight-edge across it in different directions.

STEP 4: Incise the outlines of the drawing into the smooth, clay surface with a wooden tool.

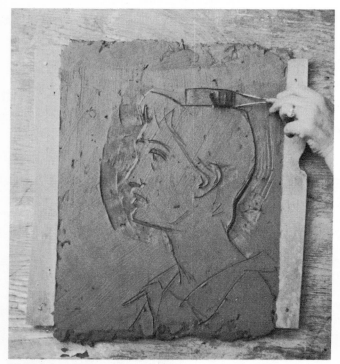

STEP 5: Lightly scrape away a layer of clay around the outline of your subject with a wire tool. The profile will now be in relief against the background, which you will eventually scrape to an even thickness all over.

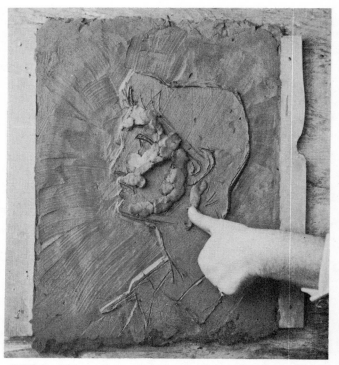

STEP 6: Add small masses of soft clay to the high points—cheekbone, jaw, temple. Don't press so hard that you disturb the underlayer.

STEP 7: Form the medium structural points, such as the nostril and upper jawbone. Then fill in all the areas between high and medium points. Add shoulder, hair and ear.

STEP 8: Using a flat wooden tool, define the various planes of the face. Note that the outer edge of the eye is closer to you than the inner edge, for instance. Observe and render.

with a wire sculpture tool. This cutting away of the background must be performed very lightly and cautiously. It is done to give rise to your outlined profile. Eventually the entire background will be cut away to an even depth.

The next step is to add clay to build up the form. Use bits of clay that are well-worked and soft. Use the thumb to establish these structural high points. Press the softened bits of clay on firmly, but do not press hard enough to dislodge the underlayer of clay. Use no tools, just your thumb.

Fill in all the middle planes. Add protruding points. The closest point to you will be the highest. The shoulder, in profile, is the highest point because it is closest to you.

After placing the clay masses, define the

planes more exactly, separating the areas closest to you from those furthermost from you. Use a flat wooden tool to do this.

The next to the last step is to model and blend the clay. Keep the planes distinct, but work one into the other smoothly. Refine and designate the planes and variations, but always keep the anatomical structure. Scrape away the background so it is level.

Last to be dealt with are the details, the many small planes and curves.

In order to do a good bas-relief you must have the sort of training which is required for sculpture in the round, even if bas-relief does not present as many problems. The knowledge of handling clay as material is essential. You may also put to use your knowledge of casting

STEP 9: Blend the clay so that the planes are distinct but flow smoothly into one another. Treat the hair as a mass. Begin adding details—eye in its socket, eyebrow, etc.

STEP 10: This is what your bas-relief will look like when complete. All the many planes are defined, blended and softened, and the background is leveled off.

plaster to make a permanent model of your clay relief.

Incised Bas-Relief

(*See illustrations on next page.*)

Bas-relief may be produced by incising or carving away the clay surface rather than by adding to it. You begin in the same way with a drawing made on paper to be used as a guide while working in clay. Prepare a board as before with wooden side strips to contain the clay area. Level a smooth, clay surface about $\frac{3}{4}$-inch thick by drawing a straight-edge over the packed clay. With a wooden tool, outline the subject in the soft clay, drawing as you would with charcoal or pencil. Next, use a wire tool to cut down into the clay below the surface.

The deepest cut is the outline; the shallowest cuts are those for the closest planes.

After you have made all your necessary cuts, model and blend the planes with a wire tool. All modelling and cutting is done below the original $\frac{3}{4}$-inch deep clay surface. Hair is suggested with indented strokes.

With a wooden tool, refine and designate the planes and areas. Lastly attend to details. Soften and blend the planes lightly.

INCISED BAS-RELIEF: With your wooden tool, outline the subject on smoothly-packed clay, ¾-inch thick.

CARVE DEEPER into the clay than before with your wire tool. Cut deepest at the farthest receding points of the outline—top of head, farther cheek, etc. Do not cut high points on near side; leave the clay. Make shallow cuts for planes in between.

INCISED BAS-RELIEF: With wire tool, model below the surface.

REFINE AND BLEND modelled planes with your wooden tool. Add details last. Indicate hair with incised strokes.

fabric

BATIK

Batik (ba-*teek*) employs what is known as a "resist" technique; wax is used to resist dye. Parts of a cloth that are covered with wax will not dye, and a contrasting design is created. Beautifully decorated fabrics can be made by painting or drawing a design with wax on cloth, dyeing the cloth, and then removing the wax. The cloth may be rewaxed and dyed several times in order to make intricate designs with many colors.

Traditionally, smooth fabrics have been used for batik because the close weave takes fine detail and the wax penetrates completely through the cloth. By using different types of fabrics, however, you can create unique and interesting effects. You can also use your imagination to experiment with different ways of applying wax. Part of the enjoyment of batik comes from the surprisingly good results you often get by experimenting.

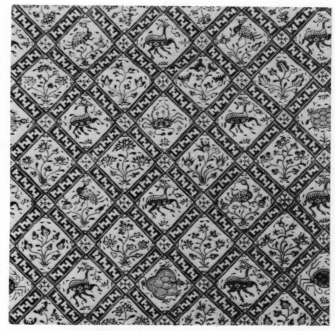

THE TJEPLOK PATTERN, one of the four basic Javanese designs, uses animals and flowers within squares.

The Traditions of Batik

The origin of the craft of batik is unknown, but it has been used as a method of decorating cloth for many centuries in the Orient. The first batiks were probably made in Egypt or China. From there, the craft spread to Persia, India, and other countries. One of the earliest preserved examples of batik, Indian screens dating from A.D. 710 to 794, show a perfection of design and technique that would indicate a highly developed art.

The Javanese people of Indonesia have been creating batiks for hundreds of years, to be used in making clothing. Among these people, the art of batik developed and became an important part of their lives. The earliest travellers to Java in the 16th century described single pieces of beautiful batik work with intricate designs which the people had worked for months to produce. There were four basic patterns of these designs in classical Javanese batik. Towards the end of the last century, however, batik artists began to experiment with a greater variety of designs and were influenced by the tastes of outsiders, particularly the Chinese. American batik has been greatly modified from the traditional painstaking designs of the Javanese.

Materials

Following are the basic materials you will use in all batiking projects. Additional materials for the projects in this article will be listed at the beginning of each project.

Condensed from the book, "Batik as a Hobby" by Vivian Stein | © 1969 by Sterling Publishing Co., Inc., New York

JAVANESE BATIKS made in the 19th century had strong outside influences. The batik here is very Chinese in both subject and design.

Wax: Many types of wax mixtures can be used; paraffin and beeswax are the most common. The batik wax that art dealers supply is usually a mixture of the two. They can be mixed in equal parts or three parts beeswax to two parts paraffin.

A dye bath up to 90 degrees F. can be used with paraffin, which is more brittle than beeswax. Paraffin can be obtained in grocery stores. Beeswax, the more flexible wax, can take a higher temperature dye bath, up to 110 degrees F. Beeswax is sold as dressmaker's beeswax.

Heat Source and Container for Wax: Wax may be melted in the top of a double boiler, in an electric frying pan, or in a pot. Be careful not to overheat the wax; either a hot plate or a stove burner covered with an asbestos pad is a good heat source.

The wax should be heated to at least 170 degrees F. It should be stirred occasionally, and the liquid should be allowed to cool a little before waxing the batik. You can test it by waxing extra scraps of cloth.

While working, turn the heat off under the pot and reheat when necessary. Be careful when handling the pot of wax, and avoid getting any water near the wax container.

Dye Bath Containers: A small glass or china bowl is needed to mix the powdered dye with very hot water. The concentrated liquid dye is then added to clear, lukewarm water in the dye bath container and mixed thoroughly before the batik is placed in it. This container should be large enough so that the batik may be fully immersed in the dye.

Dyeing may be done in a plastic or enamelled pan, or in the sink or bathtub if the piece is large. Dye stains may be removed from enamel with bleaching cleanser, or by letting a solution of bleach and water stand. You should not use metal pans.

Rubber Gloves for handling the batik when wet with dye.

Tongs to pick up the batik from dye or from hot wax.

Iron and Papers for Removing Wax: Since wax and dye tend to clog the vents of a steam iron, it is better to have a plain electric iron for use in removing the wax from a batik. You will need newspapers to absorb the wax and some unprinted absorbent paper, such as paper towels and plain newsprint, to place next to the batik.

You should have a work table and space for your tools near the hot plate or stove. If not, set the pot of wax on a pot holder or asbestos pad near where you are working. Protect the floor with newspapers.

Fabrics and Dyes: The project directions tell the type of fabric to use and give instructions on how to use the dyes. Batiks may be made on white, colored, or print fabrics. Synthetics do not dye well with most dyes, and should be avoided. Household dye (good for cottons and linens), special dyes (needed for silk or synthetics), and commercial batik dyes can be used.

To prepare the fabric, wash it with detergent and water, removing all fillers and finishing materials. Rinse in water without using fabric softener, and let dry. Iron the cloth smooth, and then begin the project.

Can-Decorated Place Mats

Materials:

    white cotton cloth, 14″ × 19″, unhemmed, for each mat
    empty cans of different sizes
    one package household dye, which dyes about 3 yards of material
    pot holder
    household waxed paper
    dry-cleaning fluid (optional)
    white vinegar (optional)

For this project, empty cans of various sizes are used as stamps to decorate a place mat. You may use an all-cotton broadcloth, percale, or even an old sheet. Wait until you are finished batiking before you hem the mats. You may wish to practice first on an extra piece of cloth.

Lay the prepared cloth flat on newspapers, or cardboard, which you have covered with waxed paper. The newspapers or cardboard act as insulation for the work surface.

Completely remove the top of each can and punch a hole in the closed end or remove it.

SAFETY PRECAUTION: Use a pot holder to hold the can. It will get too hot to hold while it is in hot wax.

Pick up a can with a pot holder and dip the open end into the wax. Hold it so that just the rim of the can is covered with wax. Count 30 seconds to allow the metal to heat, then lift the can and tip it to shake off excess wax drops into the pot. Quickly move the can over the cloth and press it until liquid wax appears all around the rim.

Make a design of rings, using several different sizes of cans for variety. If you make drips, you may either start over or incorporate dots into the design by using a brush to drip wax. When you have finished making your design, turn the batik over and peel the waxed paper from the cloth. (Do not peel the cloth from the paper, as this will crack the wax on the batik.)

APPLYING THE WAX: After shaking off the excess wax, press the can on the cloth until liquid wax appears all around the rim of the can.

TO MAKE AN INTERESTING DESIGN, vary the size of the cans. Overlapping the circles will create new geometric areas.

WET THE CLOTH TO BE DYED with lukewarm water before you immerse it in the dye bath. Move it gently with rubber gloves or tongs until the color is as deep as you want it.

Check the dye package for special directions. Household dyes are usually mixed with only hot water, but we will use lukewarm water. Heat two cups of water until bubbles begin to form; then add the dye to it. The solution will be about 190 degrees F. Stir to mix thoroughly. Strain the concentrated dye through a wet cloth into the dye bath container. Fill the container with enough lukewarm water (80–90 degrees F.) to cover the material. Unless the

package directions of the dye advise differently, add 1 tablespoon uniodized salt to each gallon of liquid, or 1 teaspoon to the quart, to act as a dye fixative.

Wet the place mat with lukewarm water before immersing it in the dye bath. Move it gently every few minutes, checking the color frequently. (When wet, the batik looks twice as dark as when dry.) Remove it from the bath with tongs or rubber gloves, and rinse it in lukewarm water until the water runs clear. Do not squeeze or wring the cloth. Save the dye until the batik is dry; you can rewet the cloth and dye it again until the color is right.

Let the place mat dry thoroughly, hanging smooth and flat. Do not dry in the direct sun.

To remove the wax, place a heavy layer of newspapers on an ironing board, with a layer of plain absorbent paper on top. Lay the batik on the absorbent paper, cover it with another layer of absorbent paper, then a final layer of newspapers. Run an iron, set one setting lower than the type of fabric used, over the papers covering the place mat. As the wax melts, it soaks into the papers, which you discard and replace with fresh papers, both on top and on the bottom, until no more wax is absorbed from the cloth.

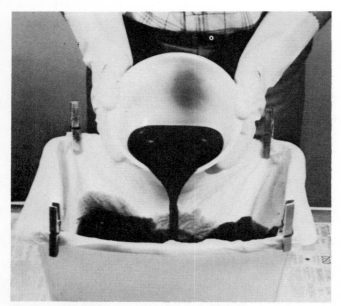

MIXING THE DYE: Concentrated dye should be poured into a container of lukewarm water by being strained through a wet cloth. Secure the cloth to the container with clothespins so your hands are free to pour the dye.

IRONING THE WAX OUT: After the batik is dry, iron the wax out on to layers of absorbent paper. The top layer of newspaper was left off here to show you how the wax is absorbed by the paper.

Some wax will be absorbed by the cloth around the previously waxed areas. To get rid of the remaining wax rings, the batik must be cleaned in a solvent. Take the mats to a professional dry-cleaner, or clean them yourself with a non-flammable solvent, available at department stores or through distributors of supplies to the dry-cleaning trade. Pour the solvent into a bowl, and immerse the batik.

Squeeze gently until the stiffness is gone, and hang the mat up to dry.

If you wish, when the mat is dry and the solvent smell is gone, lay a cloth soaked in white vinegar over the batik, and steam iron it to set the dye. Hem the mat, and press with an iron to finish it. When the mats become dirty, dry-clean or wash with a mild detergent.

REMOVING THE WAX: The cloth around the wax circle will absorb some wax as you iron it on to paper. To remove the wax completely, the cloth must be cleaned in solvent or by a dry-cleaner.

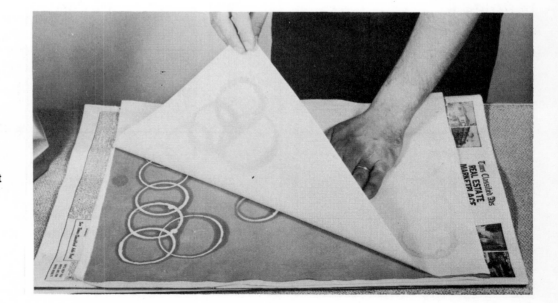

Mixing Colors in Dyeing

In the next project, and in most batiks you will make, more than one dye color is used. Dyeing one color over another causes the colors to mix on the cloth and become a third color. The following chart will give you an idea of the resulting color when one color is dyed over another.

Mixing colors also depends partly on the length of time the batik is in the dye bath. Tints of a color are formed by adding more water to the dye, or by immersing the fabric in the dye bath for a very short time.

Use the chart as a guide to help plan dyeing sequences, dyeing from the lightest color to the darkest. When using a large number of colors, painting the dye on the cloth is often better.

	over yellow produces	over red produces	over blue produces	over orange produces	over green produces	over purple produces	over brown produces
yellow	deep yellow	orange	green	light orange	light green	reddish brown	yellowish brown
red	orange	deep red	purple	dark red-orange	brown	wine red	dark reddish brown
blue	green	purple	deep blue	brown	blue-green	bluish purple	very dark brown
orange	light orange	dark red-orange	brown	deep orange	light greenish brown	reddish brown	golden brown
green	light green	brown	blue-green	light greenish brown	dark green	dull purplish grey	olive green
purple	reddish brown	wine red	bluish purple	reddish brown	dull purplish grey	deep purple	dark reddish brown
brown	yellowish brown	dark reddish brown	dark grey	golden brown	dull greenish brown	dark reddish brown	dark brown

A Brush Design Pillow

Materials:

two 15″ × 15″ squares of cotton cloth
two packages household dye
stiff, synthetic bristle brushes of good quality,
    such as oil or house painting brushes
cleaning fluid (optional)
pillow stuffing

Use a finely woven cotton cloth such as percale, muslin, or broadcloth. Wash the fabric; then cut it into squares—two pieces of cloth for each pillow. You may wax both cloths to make a design on both sides of the pillow, or wax only one for the front of the pillow. The back can be dyed in the last dye bath to match the color of the front.

Two colors of dye are needed. Some suggested color combinations are turquoise and green, yellow and brown, or pink and red.

Brushes about 1 to 2 inches wide are useful for filling in large areas. Smaller lines may be made by using the narrow side of a flat brush, or by trimming the bristles to a point with scissors or a razor.

To wax, lay the washed and ironed cloth on newspapers covered with waxed paper. Dip the brush into the hot wax, then press it against the side of the pot to squeeze out the excess wax. You can make an abstract design by painting a few swirling strokes on different parts of the cloth. The wax should be hot enough to penetrate the cloth with each brush stroke, making the area look wet. Work quickly, allowing the brush to miss a few spots, as this will add texture to the finished batik. Let the wax drip or splash in spots to add to the design. Everything covered with wax now will stay white. Leave enough cloth unwaxed to allow for the next two colors.

When you are through using the brush, press the excess wax out against the side of the pot, and lay the brush on waxed paper to cool with the wax still in it. Be careful not to bend the bristles after they cool.

After the batik has cooled, turn it over and peel the waxed paper from the cloth. Check the back to see that wax has gone through. If an area seems too thin, lay the cloth on waxed paper and rewax the back. The batik is now ready for the first dye bath, which will be the lighter of the two colors you have chosen—turquoise, for example, if you have chosen the turquoise and green combination.

MAKING AN ABSTRACT DESIGN: Place the cloth on newspaper and waxed paper and, using a ½″ wide brush, paint the hot wax with abstract swirls.

THE AREAS WAXED FIRST will remain white. The cloth is now ready for its first dye bath. Turquoise was the first color used here.

Dissolve the dye in hot water, and mix it with the lukewarm dye bath as you did when making the place mat. Wet the batik and immerse it in the dye. Remove the batik, rinse it until the water runs clear, then hang it up to dry. Do not use a dryer or iron to hasten drying.

When the batik is dry, you are ready for the second waxing. After the wax is hot, set

TO KEEP THE FIRST DYE COLOR on the cloth, splash on more wax. These newly waxed areas will remain turquoise.

the brush in the pot until the solidified wax in the brush melts again. Proceed as before, brushing wax on the colored areas you want to save. You should rewax any white areas where the wax is cracked, thin, or peeling. Let the batik cool, and peel off the waxed paper.

Prepare the second dye bath as before. If the dye pan is stained from the first bath, clean it with bleaching cleanser. Dye as you did the first time.

USE A CONTRASTING COLOR for the second dye bath. Dark green was used here to make the white and turquoise areas stand out.

After the batik is dry, you may remove the wax completely as with the place mat. If you do not want to use cleaning solvents, dip the entire batik in wax and then merely iron the wax out. The batik will be slightly stiff, but the colors will be about as bright and dark as they were when the dye was wet. There will be no wax rings around the brush strokes, because the background will have had a wax coating also.

To finish the pillow, place the two squares together inside out; sew three sides together and part of the fourth, leaving a hole for stuffing. Pull the material right side out, stuff, and hand-sew the opening shut.

Selecting, Enlarging, and Transferring a Design

Ideas for batik designs such as the one in your next project may be adapted from many sources. Look at embroidery patterns, posters, illustrations, or simple abstract designs, remembering that flat, two-dimensional designs are generally easier to do. Rather than copying designs exactly, take advantage of the nature of the wax. By applying wax of different temperatures, and thick or thin layers of wax, you can obtain variations in texture and color.

A design can be drawn freehand on the fabric with pencil, charcoal, or blackboard chalk. Or, if you prefer, you can make a small sketch, then enlarge the design on paper, and transfer it to the fabric.

To enlarge a design, first sketch it on graph paper. If you do not have graph paper, draw a grid of uniform squares across your sketch, using a ruler and a pencil. Then draw the same number of squares on your pattern paper as you have on the sketch. You can enlarge the sketch to any size. After drawing the squares, in each large square on the pattern paper, copy the portion of the design exactly as it appears in the same square on the smaller sketch.

You may transfer the design on to the cloth by placing the pattern under the cloth, taping both to a window and tracing the lines of the pattern. You may also cut out the design elements, lay them on the cloth, and trace around them with pencil or charcoal. Or transfer the design with a tracing wheel. Lay the pattern on a soft surface and run a dressmaker's tracing wheel around the outlines of the pattern. Then lay the punched pattern on the cloth. Powdered charcoal can be rubbed through the holes to transfer the design.

It is also helpful to have a color sketch and a list or diagram of the steps in waxing and dyeing.

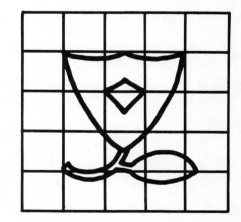

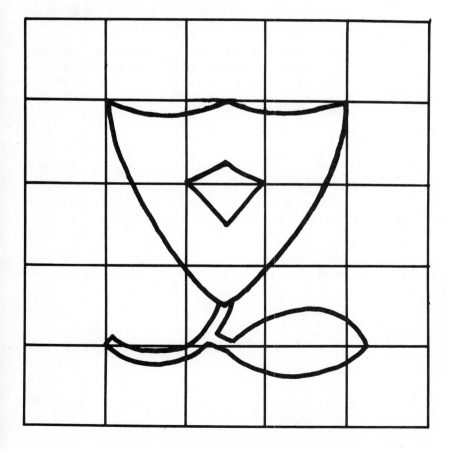

THE SQUARING-OFF METHOD: The smaller diagram represents your original design which you mark off by squares. To enlarge the pattern, draw a bigger grid with the same number of squares. It will not be difficult to copy the design square by square, and the original proportions will be maintained.

"Partridge in a Pear Tree" Wall Hanging

Materials:

white cotton corduroy, 18″ × 24″
dyes—red, yellow, green, brown
No. 10 flat oil painting brush for waxing
flat ½-inch wide brush for painting dyes
four one-quart jars
small glass or china bowls
waxed paper
newspapers
paper towels

Materials for framing:

four pieces moulding or half rounds, 20
   inches long for top and bottom frames
two pieces black twill tape, each 3 inches long
two pot holder or drapery rings
small finishing nails
carpet tacks or stapler
paint

To make the interesting batik for this project, you fill in the background with wax and leave a stencil-like design which you paint with dyes. The corduroy used for the illustrated batik had six wales or ribs to the inch. You can also use the standard, finer corduroy. Make sure the pile runs towards the top of the design. The cloth feels smooth when your hand brushes in the direction of the pile.

USE A BRUSH TO PAINT the bird, tree and pear with dyes. Only their silhouettes will show; details will be added in a dye bath. This hanging can be seen in color on page B.

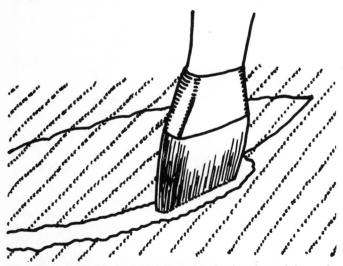

TO WAX THE BACKGROUND, hold the brush upright and parallel to the outline. Wax the background up to the lines of the design.

Lay the corduroy on newspapers covered with several sheets of waxed paper. Keep the wax hot the entire time you are waxing, in order for it to go through the thick cloth. Dip the No. 10 brush in the hot wax; then press out the excess against the side of the pot. Hold the brush so the flat side is parallel to the outline of the design and the handle is upright. Touch the bottom of the brush on the cloth close to the outline, until wax flows up to the line. Daub the wax around all the outlines first, then fill in the background solidly with wax. Outline the silhouette of the bird, but do not paint wax on the wing, leg, bill, or eye. Leave each entire leaf as well as the tree and pears unwaxed.

ENLARGE THIS PATTERN to make the partridge in a pear tree.

To wax the border, hold the brush upright, and paint a line of wax on the top and bottom of the border. Allow an extra margin of cloth on the outer edges of the borders. Divide the border into squares. Paint all the diagonals in one direction, and let the wax cool completely before waxing diagonals in the other direction. Turn the batik over and rewax any areas on the back where the wax failed to penetrate.

You may use household dyes, or the commercial batik dyes which tend to be more colorfast. Mixing according to the manufacturer's directions, add 1 tablespoon uniodized salt to each gallon of liquid batik dye, or 1 teaspoon to the quart. Mix a quart of each color in the jars. Since you will paint the dyes on, they need to be stronger and look darker than if you were going to dip the cloth in the dye. To test the strength of the colors try the dyes on a piece of scrap cloth that has been dampened and wrung dry.

The entire cloth may be wet before dyeing, or you may wet a section at a time with the small brush. Blot excess water out of the unwaxed areas until they are just damp. Dip a spoonful of each color of dye into a small dish. The red and yellow should be bright, full-strength colors. The basic brown and green should be fairly dark. Mix light green and light brown by adding water to the dark dyes in separate dishes.

Being careful not to paint any of the waxed area, use the small brush and paint the upper and lower triangles in each border yellow. Paint each pear yellow. To make the shading on the pears, blot the pear dry with paper towels; then paint light brown along the left edge of each pear, extending the shading across the bottom of the pear. Paint the leaves light green. The tree trunk is light brown, shaded along each edge with dark brown. The brown dye will run into the bird if the area is wet. The central triangles of the border are red. Let the batik dry completely and wax the branch before painting the bird red. Shade the edges of the bird with brown.

After the first dyeing is complete, let the batik dry thoroughly to set the dye; then rinse out the excess dye. If any areas need retouching, blot dry, redye, then rinse. Let the batik dry again.

Wax the areas that are finished—the border, tree trunk, and pears. Cover half of each leaf with wax. Let the wax flow to the line, to form a straight line down the middle of the leaf. Fill in the remainder of the half leaf with wax. Similarly, hold the brush upright and wax the bird's head and body, leaving unwaxed areas for a bill, eye and wing. Leave the leg unwaxed.

ADDING DETAILS TO THE HANGING: Wax the bird's head and body after they are painted with dye, but leave unwaxed areas for a bill, eye and wing. Wax half of each painted leaf. The shaded areas represent wax.

Paint the unwaxed half of the leaves dark green; paint the wing, eye, bill and leg of the bird dark brown. Let the batik dry; then rinse the excess dye out of the leaves and bird.

Let the batik dry thoroughly before the final waxing. Then wax the leaves and bird, and go over the pears and tree trunk again to make sure they are completely covered with wax.

Crackle lines, interesting in themselves, will help to integrate the background with the rest of the design. Run cold water over the batik to chill the wax. Crack the wax by bending the batik backwards diagonally and across, so there are a number of cracked places when you look at the back. Wipe off water drops from the front and back of the batik with towels; then reseal both the front and back of the bird, pear, and tree design with wax. Do not rewax the background.

Make a clear, lukewarm dye bath sufficiently large to cover the entire batik. Add the yellow and green dyes, warmed, that you have left in the jars. Wet the batik, then immerse it in the dye. After the color looks deep enough, rinse the batik, saving the dye. Most of the dye will rinse away from the surface, leaving only a tint. Redye and rinse until you are satisfied with the color.

After a final rinse, let the batik dry thoroughly before ironing the wax out. Iron with many changes of paper; the batik will be stiff. Since this is a wall hanging, it is not necessary to remove every trace of wax.

Trim any ravelled edges from the batik. With tacks or staples, attach the top to the flat side of a piece of stained or painted moulding. Put a piece of twill tape through each pot holder ring and tack the ends to the moulding as in the illustration. Fasten a second piece of wood over the first with

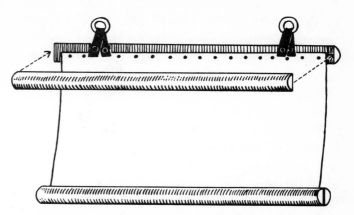

HANGING THE CLOTH: Tack the batik to one strip of moulding. Attach rings for hanging and cover with a second strip of moulding, so that both sides of the cloth are protected.

finishing nails and spot the nails with paint. Use the same method, without the tape and rings, to finish the bottom.

Other Methods for Batik

Making Crackle Lines: Crackle lines often enhance a batik design by giving an interesting texture to plain areas. Cloth should be starched to get the best crackle. Iron the washed and starched cloth and wax as you normally would. For crackle, the wax should be pure, or at least 75 per cent, hard paraffin, which is more brittle than beeswax.

You can apply wax to the cloth for crackling either by painting it on or by dipping the

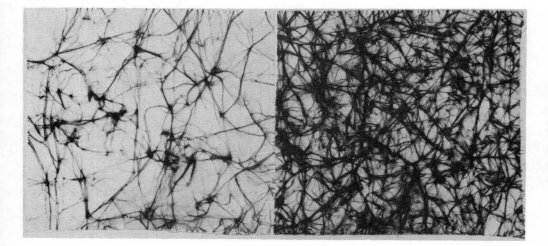

THE CRACKLE TECHNIQUE is done by crushing cloth which has been completely covered with wax. Light crushing produced a few lines in the crackle on the left, while heavy crushing made many more lines in the cloth on the right.

cloth into the wax. If you dip the cloth into the wax, paraffin should be no more than 131 to 140 degrees F. (5 to 10 degrees above its melting point). Check the temperature with a thermometer, such as a laboratory immersion thermometer, that is made for use in liquids.

When you dip the cloth, make sure it is completely covered with wax. Pull the cloth out with tongs and let it drain, turning the cloth to keep the wax coating even. Hold the cloth in the air until the surface is dry.

It is very difficult to control the temperature of the wax if you are painting it on. It must be at least 170 degrees F. in order to penetrate the cloth. The coating must be thick and smooth. Wax both sides of the cloth *two* times.

After the wax coating has cooled, chill the cloth with cold, running water up to 60 degrees F., or dip it briefly in ice water. Crush the cloth, bending it back and forth with your hands. After crushing lightly and straightening out the cloth, hold it to the light to get an idea of the number of lines. If you want more, crush it again. If you want only certain areas to have crackle, reseal the wax where no crackle is desired by repainting the area with wax, or by touching it with the tip of a warm iron to melt the wax.

After straightening, soak the waxed cloth several hours or overnight in the dye. The dye bath should cover the cloth completely. You may need to weight the cloth with some heavy, glass object. After the dyeing is finished, rinse the batik until the surface is free of all dye spots. Let it dry thoroughly before you iron the wax out.

The Tjanting and How to Use It: The word "batik" comes from a word that means to draw and write, and batiks are "written" with a tool called the tjanting (pronounced *chahn-ting*). This tool, which is used to apply wax in fine lines or dots, has been used for centuries in the Orient to make extremely complex designs for clothing. It consists of a handle, a reservoir to hold the wax, and a spout through which the wax flows. Commercially made tjantings are often available through art supply dealers. These are made from brass tubing and hold a small amount of wax. You can make a tjanting yourself which holds a larger amount of wax.

Whether you use a commercial tjanting or make your own, some practice is needed before you will be able to make smooth lines without blotches. To begin, fill the tjanting by pouring wax into it, or by dipping it into the wax. The larger tjanting should be no more than one-third full, the commercial tjanting no more than one-half full. Do not hold the tjanting over your batik until you are ready to wax.

To warm the wax to the correct temperature and to melt wax clogging the spout, place the bowl of the tjanting over the flame of an alcohol lamp. (Lamps are available through laboratory or art supply dealers; they burn denatured alcohol, which you can buy at a drugstore.) As you hold the tjanting over the flame, you will see the wax moving in waves or lines across the bottom of the can. Pass the spout briefly through the flame until the wax starts to drip out. If the temperature is about right, the wax will drip slowly and steadily. If

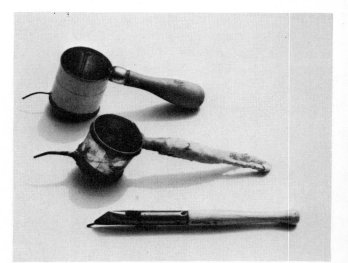

DIFFERENT KINDS OF TJANTINGS: A home-made tjanting is at the top of the photo. It was made from a can, a fine brass tubing spout, and a wooden handle. In the middle is a tjanting made with an oil can spout; the handle is of wire wrapped with rags. At the bottom is a commercial brass tjanting.

the wax spreads, it is too hot. If the wax builds up, it is too cold.

Hold a small rag under the spout to keep the wax from running out, and move the tjanting to the batik. Remove the rag when you are ready to draw, and quickly move the tjanting along the lines of the design, with the spout barely touching the cloth. After the line is completed, place the rag under the spout to prevent drips on the cloth.

Keep the wax at the correct temperature by periodically reheating the tjanting over the alcohol lamp. When you are finished using the tjanting, pour the wax remaining in the reservoir back into the pot of wax.

Making Dark Outlines: The natural way to draw with the tjanting is to use it like a pencil, outlining the design with wax. After the cloth is dyed, the wax line is lighter than the background. However, there are times when you might prefer a dark outline around an object.

The illustration shows a bird made with a dark outline and a bird with a light outline. The light line was drawn directly with the tjanting, then dyed. The tjanting was also used to form an outline for the second bird. The background and interior of the bird were filled in with wax, leaving an unwaxed channel which became a dark outline after the cloth was dyed. The entire cloth must be covered with wax to make a dark outline, and the outline has to be the last step if you are going to use more than one color. Leave an unwaxed channel around each object as you cover succeeding colors with wax.

Making a Repeat Design: Repeat designs are most effectively made on thin materials such as nylon, chiffon, voile, or organdy. These designs can cover the entire batik or can be confined to the border of the cloth.

An over-all repeat design is created by folding the cloth into four layers, then waxing

MAKING A LIGHT OR DARK OUTLINE: The bird at the top left was outlined in wax with a tjanting. Dyeing the cloth resulted in a light line on a dark background (top right). In the cloth on the bottom left, everything except the bird's outline was waxed, so that after dyeing, the outline showed up dark on a light background (bottom right).

while the cloth is still folded. The cloth may be folded into fourths diagonally, lengthwise, or once in half, then in half again to make a smaller square. Do not fold the material into more than four layers (or organdy into more than two) because the wax will not penetrate any further layers. Press the fold and pin the edges together if necessary to keep the cloth from slipping as you press. After the cloth is dyed and the wax is ironed out, open the folds. After the cloth is opened, each of the four sections of the design is a mirror image of the other. This type of design is most effective when part of the design touches the fold.

Repeat borders are made in a similar way. For a picture with a repeat border around it, wax the central picture first with the cloth laid flat and paint the dyes on. Then crease the cloth in half and pin it to a board. Wax the border design along the three unfolded edges, and paint the dye on. After the batik is dry, carefully iron the wax out of the border only. Unfold the cloth and iron the wax out of the entire batik. The result is a central design surrounded by a symmetrical border.

BURLAP CRAFTING

Even a coarse fabric such as burlap can be made into any number of unusual art objects to use in your own home or give as gifts. If you use burlap from a potato sack, you will have to wash the fabric before you work with it. Burlap (in some places called jute or sackcloth) can also be purchased by the yard in a variety of colors, and because of its loose weave is ideal for stitching with thread and yarn.

If you are planning to use a potato sack, use a mild detergent to wash the burlap. Dry it in the shade, as burlap will fade. To brighten the color, add a few drops of vinegar in the final rinse. Washing the burlap will ensure full shrinkage before you stitch it.

A Lamp Shade

To get the "feel" of the burlap and learn how it reacts to handling and cutting, cover a faded lamp shade with this durable fabric. Do not choose too dark a color, as the light must shine through.

Cut a rectangle from the burlap (after having preshrunk and washed it, of course). The length of the rectangle should be equal to the circumference of the shade you are decorating, plus 1½ inches. The width should be equal to the height of the shade, plus 3 inches. On each long side of the burlap, fold over 1½ inches and pin with straight pins. Insert a very fine wire in this hem and stitch the hem tightly by machine. Then sew the top and bottom so that the burlap is shirred and fits over the shade. Twist the wires together to secure them and snip off any loose ends.

A LAMP SHADE can be covered with burlap to liven up a corner in any room. Be sure to shrink the fabric before you cut and stitch it.

Painting on Burlap

Before you paint on burlap, make sure your fabric is absolutely clean of any soil or grease. Dirt will prevent the paint from adhering properly to the burlap surface.

Condensed from the book, "Creating with Burlap" by M. J. Fressard | © 1970 by Sterling Publishing Co., Inc., New York

PAINTING ON BURLAP is simple enough for a child to do with success. The neutral color makes a good background for bright paint.

Acrylic polymer paints are very satisfactory for applying to fabric. First, however, put a base of acrylic emulsion gesso on the burlap. This provides a smooth white surface on which you can sketch your design and then paint. If you are unsure of a design, it would be wise to plan on paper, cut out the paper patterns, and trace them with chalk on to the burlap.

Use a rather wide brush, from ½ to 1 inch, as any picture on this rustic fabric should be bold, not detailed and fussy. The cloth is coarse and you should choose an appropriate design.

THIS BURLAP PAINTING tells the story of Little Red Riding Hood through a series of pictures.

A Burlap Wall Hanging

Burlap makes an excellent background for non-painted items. Scraps of fabric can be sewn or glued, as can string, leaves and twigs, or any combination of these. The harlequin on the right was made exclusively from cloth remnants which had been saved for a project such as this. His costume is composed of random colors, but there is still a plan to the picture because of the forethought which the designer used.

To make a cheerful picture like this, draw your design on paper in the size you want the finished collage to be. Lay the paper figure on the burlap and trace it in chalk. Next, lay the paper pattern on another piece of material, such as cotton, of a color which will be suitable for the main features of the figure. (Yellow cotton was used for the harlequin.) Cut this cotton figure out, place it directly over the chalk outline on the burlap, and glue the two fabrics together with a glue recommended for textiles.

Make paper patterns for other parts of the picture also—here, for example, the bird, hat, and flowers required separate patterns. After all the general outlines are in place, use more paper patterns to plan the details of the picture—for example, the harlequin's costume and his face.

THIS BRIGHTLY COLORED HARLEQUIN is made of scraps of fabric sewn as appliqués on a burlap background.

Decorating Burlap with Wool or Thread

Because burlap is loosely woven, one individual thread can easily be removed and replaced with another of a different color. Interesting patterns can be made by alternating

A BUSY SCENE made of fabric sewn on burlap. The pleasant appeal of this wall hanging comes from the random shapes and sizes of the various pieces.

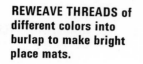

REWEAVE THREADS of different colors into burlap to make bright place mats.

colors and weaving above and below different numbers of threads, thus changing the length of the stitches.

Two important rules must be remembered when reweaving burlap: remove and replace only one thread at a time, and always go over and under an odd number of threads. If you do not follow the odd-number rule, the remaining burlap threads will be too loose.

In addition to yarns, laces and trims can also be rewoven into burlap by removing several threads together. Trims can be purchased at variety stores in different widths and patterns. Abide by the rule of odd-numbered threading as before, although now the number of threads you skip will have to be quite large (5 or 7) to show the trim off to its best advantage. Decorate several rectangular pieces of burlap with lace or trim, hem the edges securely, and you have made a set of place mats.

An Embroidered Pillow

Besides being a background for reweaving with wool and laces, burlap is an excellent fabric to embroider on: its loose weave and thick threads aid stitching evenly, since one can easily count the number of threads to be included in a stitch. Planning a design on graph paper before you pick up the needle will ensure a symmetrical design, and because burlap is so evenly woven, transferring the design to the fabric will be simple.

LACES AND WIDE TRIMS can be rewoven into burlap. Several threads must be removed together to allow for the additional thickness of the decorating trim.

HOMEMADE PILLOWS: Decorate a burlap square with stitching and sew it to another square on three sides. Loose foam rubber or feathers are common stuffing materials.

Use a variety of embroidery stitches to decorate a piece of burlap 1 inch larger on each side than you would like your finished pillow to be. Cut another piece of burlap the same size as the first, and either decorate it also or leave it plain. Stitch the edges of both pieces to prevent unravelling.

Place the two pieces with their right sides against each other, and stitch them together by machine, leaving an opening for turning and stuffing. Turn the pillow cover right-side out and insert a pencil through the opening in to the four corners to make them stick out.

Stuff with a suitable material, making sure that the corners are tightly packed and that there are no lumps in the pillow. Stitch the opening closed by hand.

FELT CRAFTING

Even very small children, if they are able to cut out and glue paper together, can likewise make amazingly attractive and imaginative creations from colored felt. The soft, easy-to-handle material is ideal for cutting and does not unravel like most fabrics. Felt comes in a large selection of colors, with or without adhesive backing and requires only scissors, glue, a strong needle and heavy cotton thread.

The Material

Felt is a collection of woollen fibres rather than a pattern of woven threads, thus giving it several advantages over other materials:

1. You can cut it up without worrying about the direction of the weave.

2. There is no risk of unravelling.

3. The smooth surface has an especially soft and attractive appearance.

4. You can glue and sew pieces without bordering or hemming them.

5. You need only a strong needle and heavy cotton thread for all stitching.

6. Because it is so flexible, you can manipulate and stuff it easily.

In addition, as you will see, you will find good use for leftover pieces. It is a wise idea to keep, from the beginning, a drawer or box for any odds and ends. You will soon discover that this "scrap basket" has become a valuable treasure chest!

Felt comes in a wide selection of colors, but only a few basic colors are needed for the projects described here. Buy red, yellow, sky blue, dark blue, orange, pink, brown, white, grey, black and green, if you want a large assortment.

Enlarging and Reducing

To reproduce a design the same size as the pattern, place a sheet of transparent paper on top of it, and trace carefully. Unless your design is extremely simple, it is often better to cut out the different parts, such as the head, feet, wings, and so on, rather than cutting out a whole outline.

If you want your design in a larger size, trace the outline in the same way. Then divide the entire area surrounding the pattern into equal squares. Now take another sheet of paper and carefully draw the same number of squares on it, but, say, twice as large. Then, following the original tracing, fill in freehand each large square with the corresponding part of the outline. You will have a figure twice as large as the original.

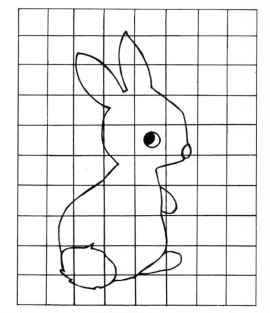

THE SQUARING-OFF METHOD: To enlarge or reduce a picture, draw a grid over the original. Copy the design freehand, square by square, on to another grid, either larger or smaller.

Condensed from the book, "Felt Crafting" by Jacqueline Janvier | © 1970 by Sterling Publishing Co., Inc., New York

Glueing

Unless there is an adhesive backing to your felt designs, you can simply apply any number of glues known to be used with textiles. Be sure not to use too much glue in one area. Small amounts will do a good job. The salesman can give you the best information.

Background

You do not necessarily have to use another piece of felt as a background for your designs. Beautiful effects can be produced with backgrounds of cloth, cardboard, canvas, construction paper and burlap. For best results, test the different effects by placing the pattern down on its background without glueing it. If it is appealing, apply the glue.

A child's greatest thrill is making something with his hands, especially if it is a toy which he can later play with. This satisfaction can be greatly increased if he can make his toys simply and effectively from cut-out pieces of colorful felt.

Stuffed Dolls

To make stuffed dolls, you must cut the pattern in a double thickness. Since patterns do not generally include hems for stitching, allow at least $\frac{1}{8}$ inch extra before cutting.

For stuffing, you can use different materials. Old rags serve well for this. Cotton is probably the best for stuffing because it leaves the least number of creases and gives the doll a very soft feeling. Foam rubber is very light and easy to handle.

Before stuffing, sew the doll either by machine, or by hand, using firm, overcast stitches and leaving an opening at the most convenient spot. For leg support, bend a piece of wire and make a framework in the form of a small arch. Then stuff the doll carefully and neatly sew up the slit.

The stuffing process is really very simple. Use a pencil or the flat top of a nail to push the stuffing into difficult corners. Be careful not to puncture the felt.

Instead of using felt for the parts of the face, you can embroider the features on with solid color thread. To make the nose stand out, pull the threads together very tightly. Use black thread for the eyebrows and very small pieces of white felt, fastened to the head with black thread, for the eyes.

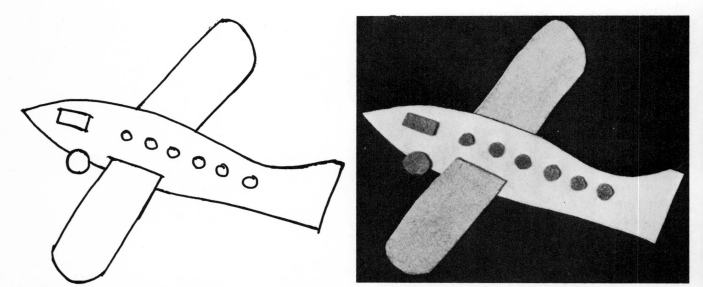

AIRPLANE: Begin a flat felt composition by making a sketch of the object's outline. Draw in the details, to be added after the basic shape is cut. Then cut out the felt according to the shape and size you designed.

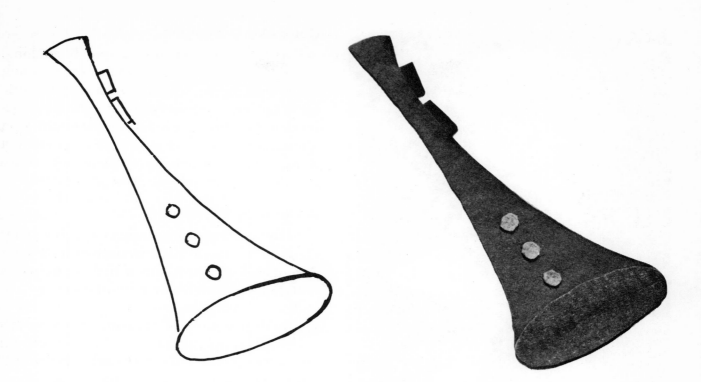

MUSICAL HORN: To enlarge the horn from the original drawing (above) to the actual size of the fabric pieces (right), use the squaring-off method.

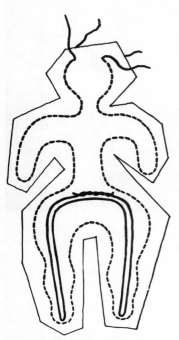

FEATURES OF THE DOLL may be stitched on the doll's face with heavy thread or yarn. If you want to use different items to decorate the doll, add buttons and trims.

A WIRE SUPPORT makes the legs stiff. If the wire is sturdy enough, the doll should be able to stand up by itself.

STUFFING THE DOLL: Leave an opening in the head to insert the stuffing through. Pack it tightly with a pencil or knitting needle.

A FELT PICTURE is well suited to framing and hanging on the wall. Lively colors help brighten up any corner.

Contrasting Designs

For framing purposes, a one-dimensional doll on a contrasting background can be hung in a child's room. A little girl's face and a little boy's face are expressive and animated. Experiment with different expressions before making a final selection. All details, such as position of arms, posture, hairstyle, clothing and colors can be varied in any way that pleases you.

A Game of Ninepins

What can you do on a rainy day? Take your child to a carnival right in his own bedroom! A game of ninepins with a little music is an entertaining pastime for rainy days.

To make the pins, follow the patterns shown. Cut each pin (three of each animal) out of felt in double thickness. Use as many different colors as are available. Sew each one together with very tight overcast stitches of strong

NINEPINS: Make three each of these colorful felt pins. To make them stand up by themselves, put a heavy weight near the bottom and place stuffing over it.

thread, approximately $\frac{1}{8}$ inch from the edges, but leave the bottom open for stuffing.

Now stuff the pins with cotton or rags. To get as perfect a stuffing as possible, smooth the felt down constantly as you stuff so it will not be lumpy. Place a piece of lead or other heavy object into the middle of the pin or as close to the base as possible. This is for balancing the pin. Cover the base of the pin with a round piece of felt and sew it up.

The last step is to make the parts of the head, using the patterns. Sew these pieces on; do not glue them. In addition, make a ball out of rag-stuffed felt to throw at the pins.

Now, remove the pillow from a bed and set the pins up on the bed as if they were on a shelf at the carnival. Let your child knock down the pins with a soft ball. For variation, set the pins up as they would be in a bowling alley, on the floor.

Rolled Felt

Let's go on a safari into deepest Africa! A whole jungle scene can be created with pieces of rolled felt.

ROLLED FELT: Make a 3-dimensional scene out of felt by rolling felt into animals and trees.

To make a palm tree, cut a long band of green felt. (See next page.) Roll it around a thin rod which will represent the trunk of the palm tree. Fluff the strips out so they hang gracefully. Insert a large needle in the base of the tree and use this to stick into a cardboard surface to hold the tree up.

The Crocodile. To make the head, cut out one piece of felt and fold it in two, following the

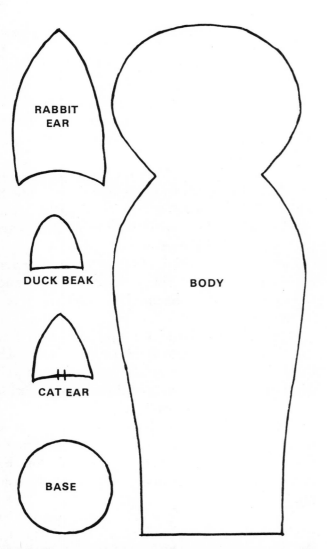

PATTERNS FOR THE NINEPINS: Enlarge these to the size you want, using the squaring-off method.

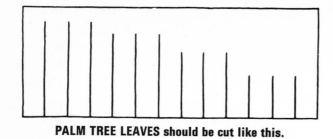

PALM TREE LEAVES should be cut like this.

dotted line shown in pattern "A." For the tongue, cut a piece of red felt as in "B," and four pieces of black felt for the feet as in "C."

Make the body by cutting out five green felt rectangles measuring $1\frac{1}{2}$ inches $\times$ 21 inches; $1\frac{1}{2}$ inches $\times$ 18 inches; $1\frac{1}{2}$ inches $\times$ 16 inches; $1\frac{1}{2}$ inches $\times$ 14 inches; and $1\frac{1}{2}$ inches $\times$ 12 inches, corresponding to the five segments of the animal's body. Roll each of these rectangles (each $1\frac{1}{2}$ inches long) and stitch them closed. Sew the tongue to the lower jaw of the head along the folded line. Sew on plastic pearls for the eyes. Attach the head to the largest of the five rolls; then join these rolls (starting with the largest and ending with the smallest) together by threading a strong cord through the middle of the rolls.

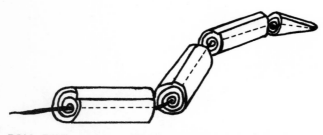

ROLL FELT around itself and stitch it securely. Insert a piece of wire through the middle and bend the felt roll any way you want.

Finally, sew a tail made from a 3-inch-long triangular piece of felt to the end of the body and attach the four feet by sewing two on the first section of the body, and the other two on the third section.

The Giraffe. The 10-piece orange giraffe includes a felt rectangle 2 inches $\times$ 9 inches for the body; four 1 inch $\times$ 2 inch pieces for the legs; one $1\frac{1}{4}$-inch $\times$ 3-inches for the neck; one 1 inch $\times$ 2 inches for the head; two $\frac{1}{4}$ inch $\times$

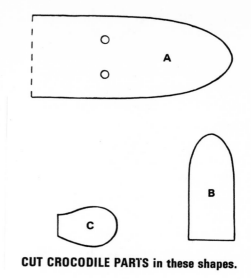

CUT CROCODILE PARTS in these shapes.

$\frac{1}{2}$ inch for the horns; and one $\frac{1}{8}$ inch $\times$ $\frac{1}{2}$ inch for the tail.

Roll and sew each piece—head, body, and legs. Roll the neck the long way, and fringe it on the open end to make a mane. Then insert a piece of wire through it and attach the head. Sew the horns on to the head and the legs on to the body.

The Elephant. Following the patterns, cut out the different parts of the elephant: two ears of white felt—pattern "A"; two tusks—"B"; the head—pattern "C" with a slit to pull the ears through. "D" is the yellow tail pattern.

For the main portion of the body, cut a black rectangle about 2 inches $\times$ 21 inches, and four smaller white rectangles $1\frac{1}{2}$ inches $\times$ $4\frac{1}{4}$ inches for the legs.

Next, roll the band for the body and sew together. Do the same with the legs. Insert the ears through the slit in the head. Attach the head and tail to the body and glue on the tusks. Add two white buttons for the eyes.

The Monkey. Using brown felt, cut out a band $1\frac{1}{4}$ inches $\times$ 8 inches for the monkey's body, four pieces $\frac{1}{2}$ inch $\times$ 6 inches for the head, and a band $\frac{1}{4}$ inch $\times$ $2\frac{1}{2}$ inches for the tail.

Roll the band for the body tightly and then stitch it together at the closing seam. Do the same for the head. Then roll lengthwise, less tightly, the pieces for the arms and legs, and

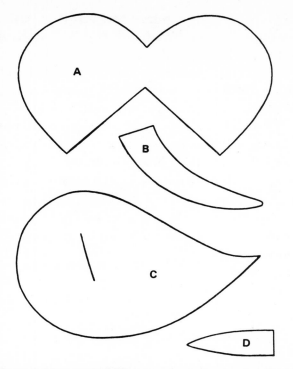

TO MAKE A FELT ELEPHANT, cut ears, tusks, head and tail like these.

Next, place all the pieces of the flowers down on the felt background, making sure they are in the desired positions. Put down the stem and leaves first, the petals and center next and position the flower planter over the stem ends. Move the flowers around until you have found the most appealing arrangement, and then apply glue to the back surface to hold the patterns in place. Allow the glue to dry completely.

Border the felt background with strips of felt or make a regular frame with wood. Your colorful flower arrangement will then be ready to be given as a gift or hung in your bedroom or den.

hold them in place with a few stitches at each end, about $\frac{1}{4}$ inch in from the rolled edge. Lock the thread well at each end. After preparing these four pieces, put them together in pairs, and sew them to the monkey's body. Last, attach the tail and a double piece of elastic or a rubber band to the neck. Hang the elastic from the top of the palm tree so the monkey can climb up and down the tree when you pull him by the tail.

Felt Flowers

Make and frame an attractive flower pattern using contrasting colors of felt and glueing the cut-out pieces to a background. Follow the simple drawing, and cut out the individual petals, the center, stem and the surrounding leaves of the flowers.

Make two or three flowers from each of the patterns. Create your own patterns as well. Retrieve a dark piece of felt from the scrap basket and cut out a planter. The planter can be rectangular, square, or any other shape you create.

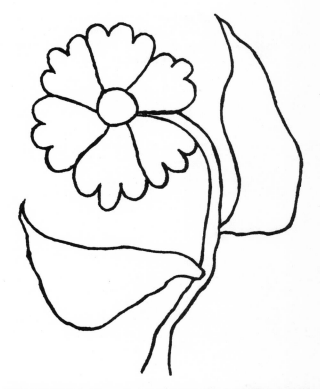

FELT SCRAPS make colorful flowers. Don't limit your color combinations to those you have seen in nature: the flowers that are admired most are the more unusual designs.

Leftovers

After completing several projects, it is time to turn your attention to the treasure chest filled with remnants. You can now make use of these bits and pieces.

THIS COAT OF ARMS is from the old French province of Foix. If your family has a coat of arms, copy it in felt. Or, create your own design with your hobbies illustrated in bright colors.

Cut several circles and add a colorful scalloped or embroidered edge—you have a practical and useful set of coasters. With other scraps and remnants, piece letters together using different colors. Make name tags; label books; and monogram shirts and jackets.

Coats of arms are always simple in design. Whenever possible, contrast the background with the design. A large shield would make an exciting decoration for a classroom or child's room. Make several as identification for a group or club. Designs can be found in many books and encyclopedias and can provide an opportunity for you to experiment with different shields.

MACRAMÉ

Many amateur craftsmen look for a hobby which allows them to create whimsically as they work. With macramé, an old European handicraft using cord, twine or yarn, you can create many different articles by using a variety of knots from these materials. The word "macramé" is from the Arabic *magramah*, meaning "fringe," as pieces of macramé were originally used to fringe such large objects as rugs and wall hangings. With the renewed popularity of macramé today, examples are found in innumerable places: replacing jewelry as a headband or necklace; in a waistband or belt; lined, for a handbag; or even forming an entire garment.

Many artists enjoy making an ambitious project with little or no plan in mind: with macramé, you can create as you work, changing designs and colors at will. And because materials are inexpensive and available at any grocery, hardware or variety store, even a large project can be made cheaply.

Materials

A *Working Base* (Abbr.: WB) is important, for it will hold your work secure. A polyurethane foam pillow, found in most variety stores, is ideal, for it is firm enough to hold the pins tightly. The upholstered arm of a chair or even nails on a wood board will work just as well, however.

Plastic- or *glass-head pins* are needed to attach the cords to the WB.

You should also have a *ruler* and *scissors* with which to measure and cut the strands.

The *cord* or *twine* is, of course, the material which makes the finished object. Any thickness will do, from a thin cotton cord to the thickest

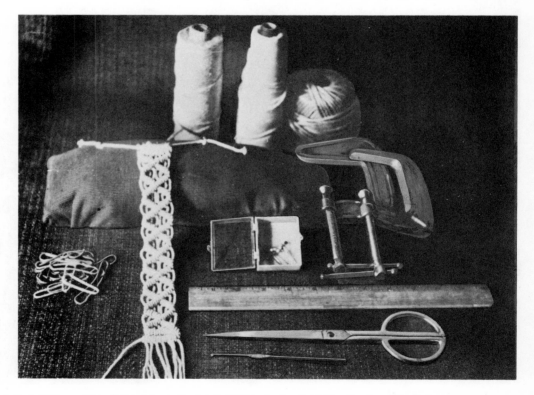

TOOLS AND AIDS for macramé include a Working Base (a small polyurethane pillow), cords and yarns, pins with heads, a ruler, scissors, rubber bands, and a clamp for holding the work.

Condensed from the book, "Macramé" by Imelda Manalo Pesch | © *1970 by Sterling Publishing Co., Inc., New York*

rug yarn. The yarn should be firmly and evenly twisted, of a uniform thickness for its entire length, and strong enough to handle the tension of knotting. Elastic or soft yarns are not suitable. The type of cord you choose naturally determines the delicacy or durability of the finished project.

Basic Knots

Before you begin knotting, you must mount the cords on a Foundation Knot Bearer (Fnd. KB), the cord to which all the others are attached. Cut a strand about 10 inches long; this will be the Fnd. KB. Make a *Bead Knot* (BK) on both ends.

Bead Knot: Bring one strand of cord around itself, and draw the end through the space made. (See below.) Fasten the Fnd. KB to the WB with pins through the BK's, to keep the piece secure.

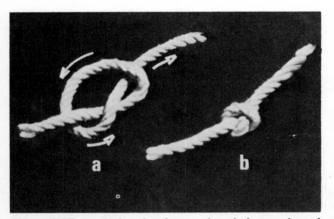

BEAD KNOT: a—end twisted around and drawn through. b—completed bead knot.

Mounting the strands is done by taking a long strand and folding it in half to form a loop at one end. Place the loop behind the Fnd. KB; then take the two cord ends and place them through the loop. Pull tightly and let the ends hang down. You have just mounted two cords. (See next column.) At each mounting, attach with a pin to the WB. When you are finished mounting, the cords are numbered from left to right (#1, 2, 3, 4, etc.).

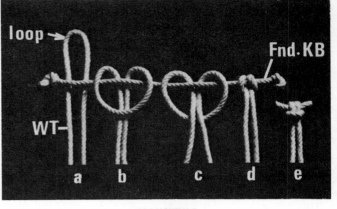

MOUNTING

Double Knot (DK): Take the first cord on the left (#1) and lay it horizontally to the right over all the cords. This cord is the *Knot Bearer* (KB), the cord which carries the knots or around which the knots are made. The other cords are called Working Threads (WT), those cords which are twisted around the KB to make the knot.

Pass the WT under the KB and around towards the left; then repeat, so that the KB is caught between the two twists. Pull tightly downward, being sure to *hold the KB taut while twisting the WT*. A DK may be made going either left or right. By making DK's across several successive WT's, you will make what is called a Horizontal DK bar (Hor.DK bar).

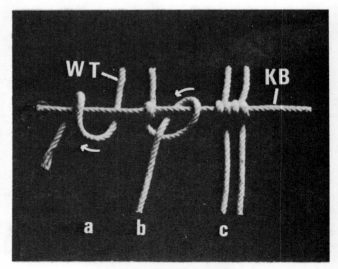

TYING A DOUBLE KNOT

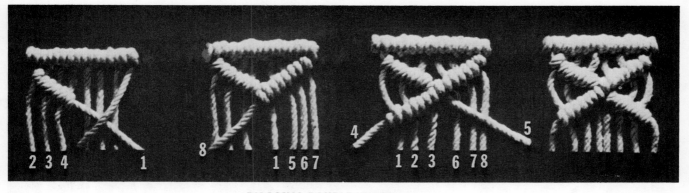

DIAGONAL DOUBLE KNOT BARS

To make a Diagonal DK bar (Diag DK bar), going either to the left or the right (L Diag DK bar or R Diag DK bar), lay the KB diagonally across the WT, rather than horizontally. To make two Diag DK bars crossing each other to form an "X," as shown above, do the following: if you have eight cords, #1 and #8 are KB's, and the middle six cords are WT's. Make three Diag DK's in each direction. Then, using KB #8, make a DK with KB #1, and continue the DK's as before, using #8 as the KB for #4, 3, and 2, and #1 as the KB for #5, 6, and 7.

Collecting Knots (CK)

Using a long cord as the WT, tie a group of

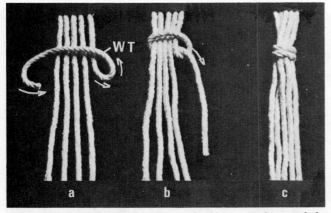

COLLECTING KNOT: In a, WT is twisted over and around. In b, WT is drawn through space. In c, 2 CK's make a secure knot.

cords together by twisting the long cord over itself and the group, behind the group, and through the space made. Pull it tightly and repeat, to make the knot more secure. Cut the cord ends evenly to the desired length. A tassel made like this may be either sewn or pasted on to the edge of an article.

Simple or Square Knot (SK)

Using two cords, bend the left cord to the right and place it behind the right cord (*a*). Then bring the (original) right cord under the left, and pull the end through (*b-c*). Now, reverse this: place the right cord behind the left this time (*d*), and draw the left cord over and through the space (*e*). Pull both ends tightly. (See illustration on next page.)

Flat Knot (FK)

A Flat Knot is easy now that you know how to do a Square Knot, as a FK is a SK with two middle cords caught between the outer cords. Bend #1 over #2 and #3, and bring #4 under #1 and through the space made between #1 and #2 (*a* and *b*). Pull the ends to position the cross properly, and then reverse the steps: bend cord #1 over #3 and #2, and bring #4 under and behind #1. Draw #4 through the space between #3 and #1 (*c* and *d*). Then pull the ends tightly.

A row of SK's or FK's form a "sinnet"; it

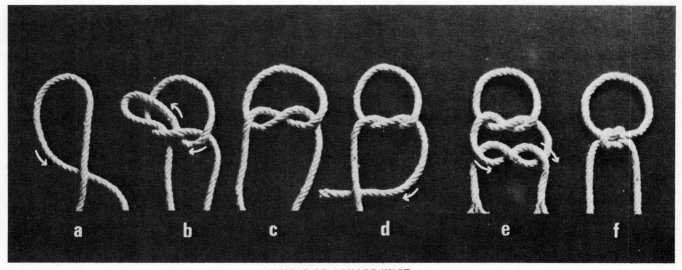

SIMPLE OR SQUARE KNOT

is also possible to have a sinnet of Half SK's or FK's, using only the first half of the knot.

A *Collecting Flat Knot* (CFK) is a FK with more than two filler cords in the middle. A CFK makes very attractive tassels for decoration.

Projects to Make

As you have probably realized from learning these few knots, macramé is not complicated, yet it can be used to make a wide variety of objects. The projects described here are only suggestions: use your imagination to make other things, and create your own original designs.

Decorative Band

This decorative piece could be a wall hanging, as it is in the illustration, or, made longer, a belt or headband. The design is very simple: it uses Diagonal DK bars. Any packaging cord you might have around the house is suitable here. Measure and cut four strands, each 80 inches long, and another piece 10 inches long for the Fnd.KB. Make a BK on each end of the shorter cord and mount the four longer strands on the Fnd.KB. Fasten each cord to the WB with a pin, and number the cords #1 to #8 from left to right.

Using #1 as the KB, make a Horizontal DK bar across the WT's (that is, make seven DK's,

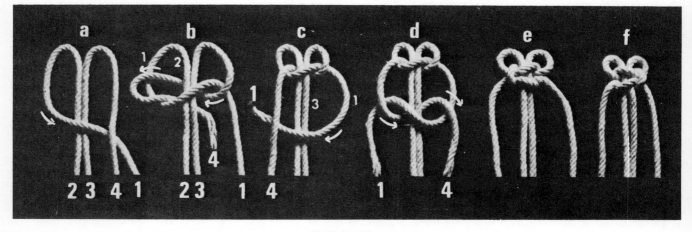

FLAT KNOT

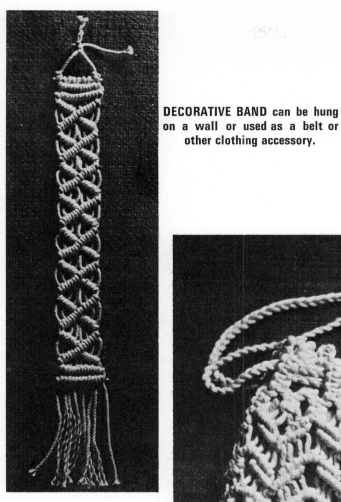

DECORATIVE BAND can be hung on a wall or used as a belt or other clothing accessory.

each using WT in succession). Then reverse the direction and make a Left Horizontal DK bar, with #1 again as the KB.

Now divide the cords into two groups of 4. Lay #1 diagonally to the right across the next three cords, and make the Diagonal DK bars, as explained before.

To finish, use #1 as KB and make two Hor. DK bars as you did at the start. Cut the cord ends evenly, leaving about 1 inch for fringe.

The 80-inch cord will make eight sets of bars, so if you want a longer band with more

HANDBAG is made in one piece. Instructions begin on the next page.

crosses, cut longer cords. Should you decide to lengthen the piece after already cutting the cord, you may attach a new piece by firmly knotting by SK or BK to the old piece. Tack the ends on the underside of the article.

Off-White and Gold Handbag

This bag is made in one continuous circular piece. Other bags may be made in separate pieces, later attached either by sewing with a needle and thread, or by knotting on the inside with SK's. The front and back of a 2-piece bag might even be different designs.

Here, the design is the same around the bag. You can adjust the size of the bag by adding multiples of eight cords. Cut strands four times the desired length of the bag and, instead of mounting the way you did before, mount this way: make two separate 2FK's (a 2FK is one FK on top of another) and fasten each to the WB, side by side. Then take a cord from each group and tie 4FK's, to make the second row. Make a third row of 2FK's, joining the sinnets of FK's in the same manner as you just did.

The main design is made using 8 cords (#1 to #8).

Series I: Starting with #4 as KB, make a Closed Double L Diag DK bar. Double bars, one diagonal bar after another in the same

direction, may be "open" or "closed," depending on the way in which their ends are finished. For an open bar, first use #2 as KB, over #3 to #6. Then in the second bar, use #1 as KB, and #3 to #6 as WT's. For a closed bar, first use #1 as KB over #2 to #6. Then in the second bar, use #2 as KB over #3 to #6 *and* #1. Thus, the end of the first bar is closed. Reverse the Closed Double Diag DK bar, now going right. Repeat across the row, joining KB's by SK.

Start ½ inch away from preceding bars:
Series II: SK(#4 and #5). Repeat Series I.
Repeat Series II once more, making three rows of Double DK bars.

Series III: Introduce the second color: fasten a loop (140 inches, doubled) at the left side of #1 and, using these new cords as WT's, make Open R Diag DK bars with #1 to #4 as KB's. SK two colored cords and then reverse on the right half. SK again two colored cords and then reverse on the right half. SK again two colored cords. Repeat across row.

Series IV: Same as Series II. Then CFK (#2 and #7 as WT's) at center. Reverse Series II.

Series V: Repeat Series III.

Series VI: Reverse Series II twice.

To finish, take a new strand for KB, about 22 inches long, and make a Hor.DK bar, using each of the cords as WT's. Take two strands from the front and two opposite strands from the back and tie them into an SK, then form a tassel with two CK's. Repeat along the edge of the handbag. Insert a drawstring braid through the second row at the top, and line with fabric if you wish.

Place Mat (12 inches by 16 inches)

A set of macramé place mats will add a special interest to your table, and because you are the creator, you can make them in any color, or even in contrasting colors, if you wish. The best cord to use for a place mat is either cotton or sisal, only $\frac{1}{10}$ of an inch thick for easy handling of the cords. Begin by cutting 30 strands 4½ times (doubled) the length of the

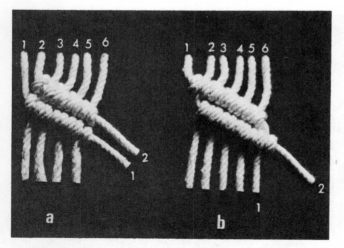

"OPEN" BARS (a) are not finished off as "closed" bars (b) are, by using the KB as a WT in the next bar.

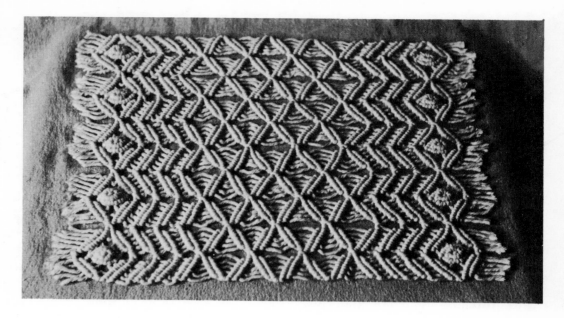

finished mat. Then mount 30 loops by the method first described here; you will have 60 strands with which to work. The design is based on multiples of 12, and is repeated five times across the row. Begin the knotting about 1 inch away from the mounting line.

In Row I, make diamond motifs with a "bud" in the center in the following way:

Series I: SK #6 and #7). Closed Double L Diag DK bars, starting with #6 as KB and #5 to #1 as WT's. Reverse on the right half and join the KB's between groups by SK.

Then make a "bud" at the center, about $\frac{1}{4}$ inch from the bars:

Sub-Ser. #1: R Diag DK bar (#3 as KB with #4, #5 and #6).

Sub-Ser. #2: L Diag DK bar (#3 as KB with #2 and #1).

Sub-Ser. #3: R Diag DK bar (#3 as KB with #4 and #5).

Sub-Ser. #4: L Diag DK (#3 as KB with #2).

Now reverse: Sub-Ser. #5: L Diag DK (#5 as KB with #3 crossed over #4).

Sub-Ser. #6: R Diag DK bar (#2 as KB with #3 and #4).

Sub-Ser. #7: L Diag DK bar (#6 as KB with #5 and #4).

Sub-Ser. #8: R Diag DK bar (#1 as KB with #2 and #3).

Push up the DK's on each KB so that the inner petal pops up.

Sub-Ser. #9: R Diag DK (#3 as KB with #4). You have made an outer petal now, and the "bud" is completed.

Series II: Reverse Series I.

Row II to Row IV: Same as Row I Series II, omitting "bud."

Row V: Same as Row I Series I.

Row VI: Same as Row I Series II.

Row VII: Same as Row I Series I.

Half the place mat is finished. To complete the entire piece, reverse the above directions, from Row VII to Row I. At the end, trim the cord ends to about 1 inch. Pull out the Fnd.KB at the mounting line, and trim those cord ends the same as the others.

NEEDLECRAFT

Stitching with a needle and thread is one of the oldest crafts known to man or woman: even early man had to devise some method of attaching pieces of animal fur together to make clothes, and using needles made of bone with threads made of hair was the most practical way. Today, of course, needles are of durable steel and thread comes in many natural and synthetic fibers, a multitude of thicknesses, and an infinite number of colors. Needlecraft has progressed from its original function, that of keeping seams together, to the elaborate and decorative art it is today. The designs you can create on cloth with a needle and thread are unlimited.

Embroidery

In the Middle Ages, Bible stories were visually depicted by embroidering on cloth. Since most people could not read at this time, pictures, particularly cloth pictures, were the easiest way to teach the populace stories from the Bible. Sometimes an expert embroidress worked for many years on one piece, or several women worked together on a large design. Embroidery during the Middle Ages was a very skilled craft and was valued highly: it appeared on clothing, cushions and bed linens.

In our modern age, when fabric comes in different textures and colors, embroidery is not so common as it used to be. When it does appear on a manufactured article, the price of that article is often more than we would like to pay. The best solution, if you admire this art and look towards its revival, is to embroider your own designs. This is a hobby which has delighted many for centuries because it offers hours of quiet pleasure with extremely beautiful and lasting results.

The equipment you need can be found in most sewing and department stores, although you probably have several items already. A selection of needles with both large and small eyes is necessary; a packaged assortment can be purchased. While you are buying the needles, also pick up a small pair of scissors for clipping threads. If you are accustomed to using one, a thimble may be helpful; some sewers would not dream of stitching without one, while for others they are merely a hindrance. An embroidery hoop is one piece of equipment you may believe is optional: it holds the fabric taut, however, and helps you make neat, even stitches with no puckering. These hoops are inexpensive and come in several shapes and sizes. The fabric and thread you use depends of course on what type of article you are embroidering: if you are making a monogram on silk, for example, fine thread—either silk or one of the new synthetic threads—should be used. On burlap or other coarse cloth, use thicker thread.

While you learn and practice your stitches, use a piece of cotton fabric with no design on it. Save your practice pieces: some valuable items in museums are "samplers," those squares upon which girls once practiced. Perhaps a sampler of your own will be colorful and decorative enough to be hung.

Written especially for this volume by Jane Lassner

PRACTICE STITCHES often form interesting designs without any pre-planning. Samplers, as these practice pieces are called, can be framed and hung as pictures. The mistakes which a beginner might make only add to the charm of the sampler and, as the stitching improves, can tell an interesting story about the progress of the embroiderer.

Running stitch: The running stitch is the simplest stitch of all to learn, and is the basis for many decorative stitches. As you will do for all stitching, thread the needle and tie a knot near one end of the thread. Insert the needle into the fabric from the underside to the top, and then from the top to the underside about $\frac{1}{4}$ inch away. Repeat, letting the needle come through the fabric $\frac{1}{4}$ inch from where the last stitch ends. Running stitches can be any length, but both stitch and space should be equal.

INTERLACED RUNNING STITCH

Variations and elaborations of the running stitch can be made: the *interlaced running stitch* or the *whipped running stitch*, for example, are only two possibilities. Lace two rows together

RUNNING STITCH

WHIPPED RUNNING STITCH

with a new color, or with the same color simply to vary the texture.

Double-running or *Holbein stitch:* Make a row of regular running stitches on the fabric. Then turn the piece and go back over the same area, filling in the spaces with stitches to make a continuous row of stitches on both sides of the fabric.

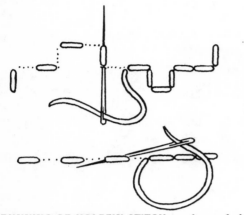

DOUBLE-RUNNING OR HOLBEIN STITCH can be made in any direction.

Cross stitch: A cross stitch forms an "X" on the right side of the fabric. It is one of the easiest decorative stitches to make, since you can ensure even stitches by always skipping the same number of threads with each stitch. Entire pieces of embroidery have been worked using only the cross stitch and its variations. If you

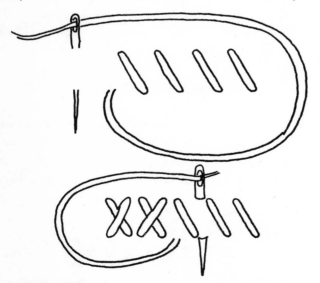

CROSS STITCH: To ensure even crosses, first stitch a row of half crosses. Then reverse direction and complete the crosses.

are making several cross stitches in a row, work all diagonals in one direction down the row first, then complete the crosses by reversing direction. This will result in the top stitches of all the crosses going in the same direction.

Herringbone stitch: Make your stitches in the direction opposite your over-all sewing: if you are going right, take right-to-left stitches. This stitch resembles the cross stitch, but the stitches are longer. It makes a secure hem stitch, particularly for stretch fabrics, as the cross stitching allows the stitches to move with the fabric's elasticity.

HERRINGBONE STITCH

Chain stitch: This stitch can be used either to outline areas or fill in designs. Because of its versatility, it should be carefully practiced and perfected. Bring your needle through to the right side of the fabric and make a loop with the thread, holding it down with your finger. Begin your next stitch from inside the loop through which the needle last emerged, making a small stitch within the loop and drawing the needle out over the thread. The stitches should be precise and round like links in a chain.

Straight stitch: The straight stitch can be made heading in different directions to create different effects. On the right side of the fabric the stitches will look like vertical sticks, either

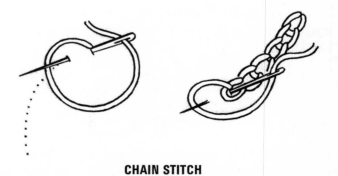

CHAIN STITCH

parallel in a row, or radiating from a central point. You can make an attractive flower-like pattern by sewing straight stitches in a circle, with one end of each stitch meeting at one point.

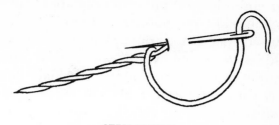

STEM STITCH

STRAIGHT STITCH: Stitches can be made like sticks in a row, or radiating from a central point.

Satin stitch: Made of straight stitches sewn very close together, the satin stitch will add a smooth, luxurious look to your work. When you want to cover a large area completely with the satin stitch, break it up into smaller sections. From one side of the area to be stitched, take a stitch straight across the area to the other side, bringing the needle up on the original side close to where the first stitch began. Make the edges neat and even. The satin stitch will produce a raised pattern which contrasts nicely with the surrounding flat

stitches. To raise the satin stitch even more, first make a base of small running stitches, and then go over the area with satin stitches.

Stem (Outline, Crewel) stitch: This stitch is very good for both outlining and filling entire areas. To stitch from left to right, you will take right-to-left stitches. Make a simple running stitch from left to right, but instead of bringing the needle through on the right, come up alongside the stitch you just completed, about midway down its length. Make all stitches exactly the same length, particularly if you are making a linear design where the stitches will be very noticeable. Once you have established a rhythm, regularity and precision will come automatically.

Back stitch: To make the back stitch, begin at the right, take a stitch to the left, and come to the surface of the material in front of the starting point, leaving a space the length of the stitch just made. Then insert the needle in the end of the stitch on the right side of the fabric and carry it through one complete stitch-space further to the left.

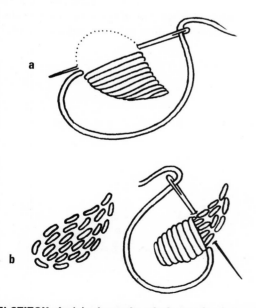

SATIN STITCH: In (a), the satin stitch stands alone, while in (b) it covers running stitches, which raises the pattern.

BACK STITCH resembles the Holbein stitch on the front side, but the reverse sides are different.

Practice these basic stitches until they become second nature to you and are neat and even. Now you are ready to use your embroidering talent by planning and executing a design.

An embroidered gift is always appreciated, especially in our modern times of mass-produced goods. A set of napkins or place mats would be welcomed by any woman and can be as simple or as complicated as you like. Since this is your first project, do not make a very elaborate design: first build your confidence by making an easy pattern and then progress to more difficult things.

Designs which have already been planned and sketched on fabric can be purchased at most needlecraft and department stores. These are good to work on if you want to practice your stitches before attempting an original piece, and the resulting tablecloths, napkins, bibs and pot holders you can make from these kits are usually quite attractive. If you want to make an entirely personal article, however, draw your own pattern on paper and transfer it to the fabric.

A simple design for a beginner would be a plain geometric pattern in straight lines. Following the threads of the fabric will help you keep the pattern straight. Plan a pattern on graph paper—each line on the paper can represent one thread of the fabric—and decide which stitch you will use for each part of your design. The color scheme should also be determined at this point in your planning.

An alternate method of making an original design is to fold a piece of paper of a basic shape—circle, square or diamond—into quarters, and make random snips with a scissors. It does not matter what shapes you cut, for whatever you cut out will be repeated symmetrically when you unfold the paper. You should be able to produce many interesting and attractive patterns this way.

There are several methods you can use to transfer your design to the fabric. Special types of carbon paper specifically meant for use on fabric can be purchased, along with a

SIMPLE GEOMETRIC PATTERNS, planned first on graph paper, can be embroidered with the basic stitches. Fill in some areas with color and leave others open for varied designs.

Illustrations from the book, "Creative Embroidery" / © 1960 by Sterling Publishing Co., Inc., New York

BY FOLDING AND CUTTING PAPER, you can design either symmetrical abstract compositions or more representational scenes.

tracing wheel. Place the colored carbon paper face down on the fabric, with the design you created on top of the carbon paper, and roll the tracing wheel firmly over the lines of the design. The color from the carbon paper will be transferred to the fabric along the lines you outlined, and the color will wash out later.

For fabrics which cannot be washed, such as velvet, or for fine fabrics which might tear if the sharp tracing wheel went over them, tack marking is recommended. Trace the design on to smooth tissue paper and pin this into the exact position you want it to be on the fabric. Using a thread which contrasts with the fabric, stitch along the appropriate lines of the design through both the tissue paper and the material. The tissue paper can then be torn away and the design will be clearly marked by the stitches.

Crewel

Once you have mastered the basic embroidery stitches, you will have no trouble progressing to crewel. The only difference between the two crafts is that crewel uses wool worsted yarns exclusively (that is, wool yarns that are combed smooth with long combs). The wool worsted fibers can be stitched on to any fabric. Crewel yarn is two-ply, available in small hanks, and comes in a variety of colors. The needles come in different lengths and eye sizes, the higher numbers representing finer needles. The finest is #8, and heavy work is done by a #3 or 4. Needles can be purchased in a packaged assortment. It is wise to use a needle slightly larger than the yarn, so that the yarn will not be worn down by continual rubbing with the fabric.

As in embroidery, an embroidery hoop which you hold in your lap or an embroidery frame which is self-supporting is very helpful. Since crewel yarn is thicker than embroidery thread, the background upon which you stitch may also be larger and bulkier. There are frames which stand on the floor and adjust to any height or angle: you may want to invest in one of these if your work is particularly cumbersome. A frame which clamps to the table or can stand in your lap may prove just as useful for you, however; or the simple embroidery hoop which you hold yourself may be sufficient. Naturally, you are the best judge of what kind of support you need for your project.

Beginners, with the good intention of keeping their work neat and even, often stitch too tightly. This stretches the crewel yarn and makes it thin. Be careful when you stitch that you do not make this mistake. Your stitches should be as tight as the background upon which you are stitching.

Some materials on which crewel yarns look very beautiful and where the yarn and fabric blend are: linens, twill weave wool and antique satin. Save delicate fabrics and synthetics to use for embroidering with thin threads which can be washed with the background.

Complicated stitches are usually avoided in crewel; the wool yarns are too thick to allow many intricate patterns. The simple stitches—Holbein, stem, satin, cross and straight, for example—are as attractive as the more complicated ones with their parallel rows and intertwining cords.

The *split stitch* is one stitch used in crewel which is not usually used in embroidery. Here the thickness of the crewel yarn is an advantage. Take a small forward stitch along the line to be worked, and instead of bringing the needle up ahead of where it entered the fabric, bring it up midway along the first stitch. Instead of coming up next to the first stitch as you did in the stem stitch (see page 117), however, split the yarn itself exactly in the middle.

SPLIT STITCH

Appliqué

The word appliqué comes from the French *appliquer* meaning "to put on," and the Latin *applicare* meaning "to join or attach." As it is now used in needlecraft, appliqué indicates the placing of one piece of material over another, attached with decorative stitches (embroidery stitches are usually used). Interesting effects can be achieved by varying the fabrics appliquéd on to one another: contrasting or different colors and textures, or plain and patterned fabrics, or transparent and opaque materials. These create pieces which, besides being beautiful to look at, seem to invite being touched as well.

Remembering that the aim of appliqué is thus to emphasize contrasting colors and textures, keep the design simple and fairly large. Intricate designs are difficult to stitch and are not necessary to make an attractive piece. While many contrasts are desirable, the different fabrics being joined should have the same laundering qualities. It is wise to wash both the appliqué and the base before stitching, since their amount of shrinkage may differ. Also, do not appliqué pieces on the bias: keep the threads of both the appliqué and the base running parallel to each other. You will thus avoid uneven pulling.

Once you have planned an outline on paper, transfer it to the fabric (transferring is explained on page 119) and add about $\frac{1}{4}$ inch around the outline for a hem, which you will turn under and stitch. Cut the appliqué out and, if the design has straight edges, simply fold the hem under and stitch with any hem stitch, being careful not to let the stitches show on the right side. If the edges are curved, however, use the template method of hemming:

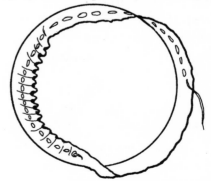

TURNING AN EVEN HEM ON A CIRCULAR APPLIQUÉ

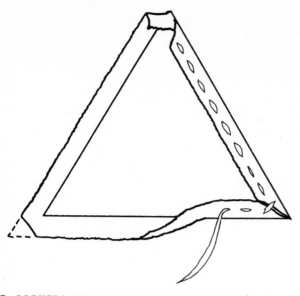

THE CORNERS OF A TRIANGULAR APPLIQUÉ must be mitered, or trimmed, so they lie flat.

cut templates of stiff paper in the proper size and shape that the finished appliqué is to be. Take a loose running stitch around the edge of the hem, and gather the hem evenly so that it lies flat against the template. Iron the hem. Then release the stitches, remove the template, and stitch down the hem allowance along the ironed folds. This method can also be used for sharp corners where folding the fabric under another hem is necessary. Of course, if the material being appliquéd is not woven, such as felt, plastic or leather, it will not ravel or fray along its edge, and thus does not have to be hemmed. It can be stitched to the base material with its raw edges exposed, or decorative stitching may be added. Some

common decorative edging stitches are the following:

Buttonhole stitch: The stitches should be taken very close together. When the needle emerges from the fabric it goes over the loop of thread formed at the end of the stitch before. To make the buttonhole stitch stand out and be raised more, stitch over a groundwork of a basic stitch, such as the running stitch.

Blanket stitch: The only difference between this and the buttonhole stitch is that blanket stitches are more widely spaced.

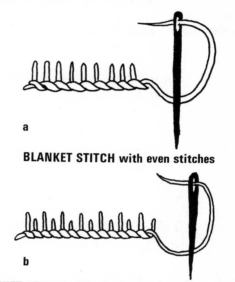

a

BLANKET STITCH with even stitches

b

BLANKET STITCH with alternating long and short stitches

By making these stitches very close together, you can eliminate the need for a hem: they will suffice to prevent unravelling. Before you cut away the hem allowance, and before the appliqué is stitched on to the background, make either buttonhole or blanket stitches with a heavy embroidery thread all around the design. The loops should lie on the design line and the spokes point inward. When you have completed the stitching, cut away the excess material close to the loops. The appliqué can then be applied in the same way as it was when it had a hemmed edge.

Pins can hold the appliquéd pieces temporarily in place before they are stitched. The pins should be placed at right angles to the lines of the design; this helps prevent

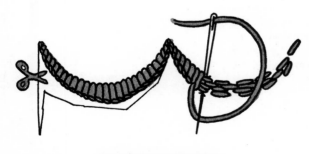

BUTTONHOLE STITCH

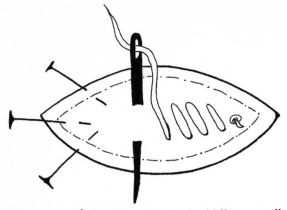

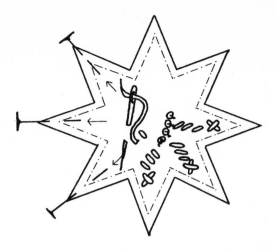

PINNING APPLIQUÉ TO FABRIC: Pins should lie perpendicular to the stitches around the outside edge. This keeps the appliqué flat, and allows stitching while the pins are still inserted.

DECORATIVE TOP STITCHING is also practical: it attaches the appliqué to the underlying fabric even more securely.

puckering. The beauty of appliqué comes from the decorative stitching which is used to hold the piece in place on its background. The stitching must be sufficient to hold the pieces flat. With simple shapes, you can begin stitching at one side and work across to the other; with more complicated pieces, begin in the middle and work outward. Never attach a piece by putting a line of stitches around the edge or the piece will not lie flat.

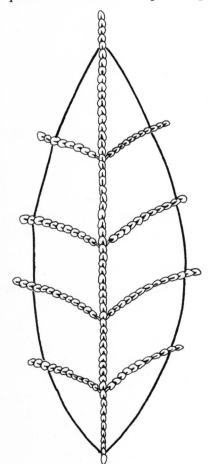

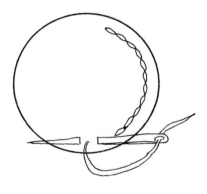

SOME ATTRACTIVE STITCHING PATTERNS. Appliqués which are already hemmed, or those cut from fabrics which do not require hemming (felt or plastic, for example), can be top-stitched with a number of good-looking stitches. Fasten the appliqué first with small even running stitches, and then top-stitch with any thread or yarn which is suitable to the fabrics.

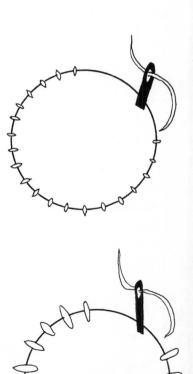

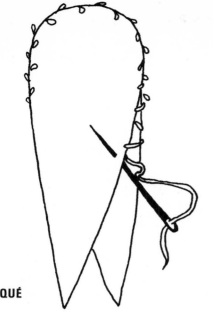

INLAID APPLIQUÉ

The advice so far has dealt with *onlaid* appliqué, where there are two thicknesses of fabric where the appliqué lies. *Inlaid* appliqué, where there is only one layer throughout, requires further instructions, however, since there is no background on which to stitch the appliquéd pieces. Instead, the pieces are joined together by various decorative pieces. The resulting article looks somewhat like a mosaic or collage, and is actually a mosaic made of cloth.

Inlaid appliqué has traditionally used materials that are closely woven, such as flannel, or that do not fray, such as felt or leather. The pieces must be accurately cut out for the design to be successful. Trace the design of a single piece on to both the background fabric and the fabric from which the appliqué will be cut. Using very sharp scissors, cut out the shape from the appliqué fabric, and then cut the same shape away from the background material. The appliqué should fit exactly into the area cut away. Take a stitch in the background material, then in the appliquéd piece, and then in the ground material again. The union can be hidden by thin cording, or by a line of close stitching. The herringbone, buttonhole and blanket stitches are frequently used.

Quilting

Sitting by the fireside with your legs covered by a warm quilt and a dog by your side is a scene that many people think belongs to a former age—that it is not geared to today's fast-moving world. While your home may not have a fireplace, and while you may not own a dog, you can certainly make yourself a quilt to warm you on cold days. Mass-produced quilts can be purchased, but making your own will give you great satisfaction and pride.

Technically, quilting is a method of fastening together two or, more often, three layers of fabric with a diamond or square pattern of stitches. The three layers are a base, usually a solid piece of fabric; a filling, which may be a thin layer of cotton or a synthetic material; and the covering material. This upper layer is generally finer than the base, as it is this side of the quilt which is meant to show. The pattern of stitches which holds the layers together is worked with this layer intended as the right side.

One often hears the term "patchwork quilt," which means that the upper layer is composed of small triangles, squares or other shaped

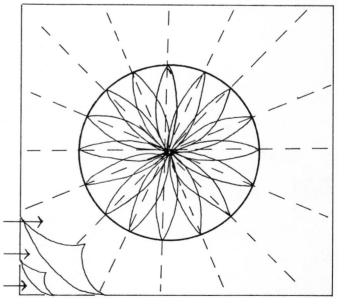

THREE LAYERS OF A QUILT. The dotted lines represent loose running stitches which temporarily hold the layers together. After the layers are securely attached by the permanent stitches, remove the running stitches.

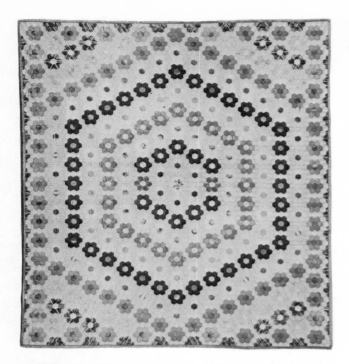

PATCHWORK QUILT: Made of small pieces of fabric sewn together, a patchwork quilt involves much work. The patches here are all the same shape; they were cut from the same template, or pattern.

quilted, as can many other articles where the extra thickness that the middle layer gives is desired.

Make a small article for your first project, so that you can get the feel of the craft and decide whether you enjoy it, without committing yourself to a large project. A pillow is a good item to start with; one side of the pillow will have a quilted pattern and the other side will be plain.

Almost any type of smooth fabric can be quilted. A solid color is often preferable to a pattern, since the beauty of quilting lies in the stitching you add yourself. Linen, silk, wool, flannel and cotton are all good fabrics to use; materials which split easily, such as taffeta and satin, are not practical. Small stitches strain these fabrics, and the shiny surface causes eyestrain when working closely. The backing material can either be similar to that used for the upper layer, or a less expensive fabric.

The padding must be chosen carefully, however. There are several varieties of cotton batting that are made especially for quilting which can be purchased in fabric stores. Batting made from synthetic fibers is often fluffy and therefore desirable, but because of its bulk cannot be worked with fine stitches. Ready-made bias binding can be bought to

pieces of varied fabrics, pieced together to cover. The small shapes are usually sewn together with a running stitch. A quilt need not be patchwork, however, nor is the art of quilting even limited to making quilts. Cushions, seat covers and pot holders can be

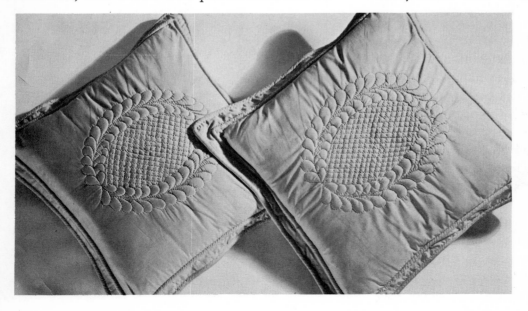

QUILTED PILLOW COVERS make good beginning projects, since they are small enough to finish quickly. This quilted pattern, an oval wreath with a feathery effect, is not too complicated for a beginner. Sketch the pattern on paper first, and then transfer it to the fabric.

Photographs from the book,
"Quilting as a Hobby"
Sterling Publishing Co., Inc.

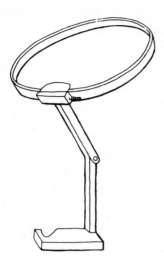

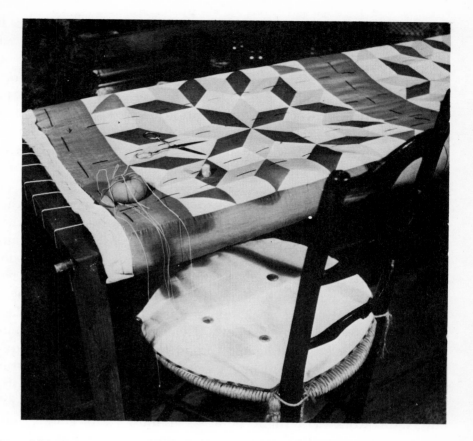

A QUILTING HOOP (above) is easy to handle and can be moved around. A quilting frame (right) consists of two poles set on a frame. The ends of the quilt are wrapped around the poles until the quilt is stretched taut.

put around the edges of your piece if it is to be a quilt, or you may cut your own bias strips from fabric. If the quilted article is a pillow or a seat cover, binding will not be necessary.

Designing the lines along which you will stitch is the most important step in making an attractive quilted piece. Since the purpose of the stitching is to hold the three layers of material together, the lines of stitching should be uniformly spaced. There should be very few areas with no stitching at all.

Cut the material to be quilted (all three layers) larger than the desired finished size, as the material will shrink when it is stitched. Next, transfer the quilting pattern on to the top layer. Use a ruler as a guide to make straight lines, using a pencil or chalk to draw geometric patterns. Or, to transfer curved lines on to fabric, put the pattern on tracing paper and puncture holes no more than $\frac{1}{8}$ inch apart along the pattern lines with a pin. The holes will allow chalk to go through to the fabric along the pattern lines.

After you have transferred the design to the top layer of material, lay the backing layer down flat, right side down, and then place the middle padding layer on top of it. Then lay the top material down, right side up, and pin the layers together, taking great care that the layers do not slip out of position. To keep the layers together without pins while you are stitching, you should tack them together with running stitches. From a point about in the middle of the piece, stitch toward the edge. Work a few lines of tacking at the same time by having several needles threaded and working each needle forward a few stitches at a time. Never tack toward the middle, only from the middle. Many lines of tacking will ensure smooth quilting: tacking keeps the layers firmly together while you stitch. After you have completed your stitched design, remove the tacking threads.

After having been tacked, the layers should be put in a quilting frame or hoop. Thread your needle and make a firm knot at one end of the thread. Generally, threads which are the same colors as the background are used, since the beauty of quilting usually lies in the raised pattern obtained by stitching rather than from color. Sewing silk is a good thread to use, since it is stronger yet finer than cotton and has an attractive sheen. It works well on linen, cotton, silk, and wool material.

The length and type of stitches you use depends on the thickness of your work: a piece with a heavy layer of batting cannot easily be worked in fine detailed stitches. The customary range is between 8 to 16 stitches per inch. The most popular stitches for quilting are the back stitch, chain stitch and running stitch. The needle should pierce the work at right angles only, and each stitch must be made in two separate movements. If you pick up the stitch before pulling the thread to the wrong side as in other forms of sewing, you may not take in enough of the bottom layer to bind all the layers firmly together. If the needle enters the work at a slight slant, as it must when you make a stitch using only one motion, the stitch may pull the layers out of position.

To avoid unsightly puckering of the top layer, always work from the middle towards the edges. This will make the top layer lie

smooth and flat. To ensure a neat bottom layer, you can either line the piece after stitching so that no threads show on the underside, or else neatly end each line of stitching. A new thread will thus be used for every line of stitching.

Color can be added to a quilted pattern in several different ways. Patchwork, where the top layer is composed of small pieces stitched together, is popular for quilting: the stitches which join the top layer to the padding usually lie along the lines where the shapes were joined. Onlaid appliqué is another way to add color. The onlays can be attached to the top layer before quilting, so that the stitches go through the colored pieces as well as the background, or after quilting, so that the appliqués hide part of the stitching. With an appliquéd quilt, there will be two aspects of the design to be considered: that of color, and that of stitching. If you make a crazy quilt, one with a random assortment and placement of colors, you will probably want to stitch in a regular pattern. Besides being necessary to hold the layers together, the regularity of the stitching creates order in a beautiful but nevertheless haphazard arrangement of colors.

Needlepoint

In needlepoint, a background made of woven canvas threads is entirely covered with stitching. The finished result often resembles tapestry, and the two crafts are sometimes confused. Tapestry itself, however, is a woven fabric, while needlepoint is the application of different colored threads on a woven canvas background. Because canvas is so sturdy, needlepoint can be used in places that get a lot of wear: chair seats and backs are common uses, as well as handbags and pin cushions. After being stretched and mounted, a colorful needlepoint article can also make an attractive wall hanging.

The beauty of needlepoint designs comes not only from changes in the color of the threads, but also from a variety of decorative

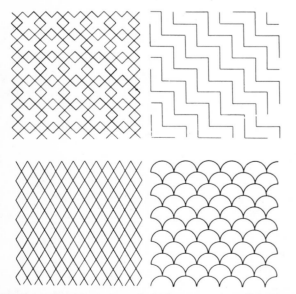

QUILTING DESIGNS to be stitched as an over-all pattern.

stitches. A canvas background with a pattern already stamped on it and the colors already indicated can be purchased in needlework stores. Practice on these and perfect your stitches before planning an original needle-point design.

When you do feel ready to create and execute your own pattern, plot it on graph paper and transfer it to the canvas background. Either keep your original paper pattern to refer to for color and types of stitches, or paint the design in different colors on the canvas itself. Geometric shapes, such as those suggested on page 126, are not difficult to stitch; the straight lines of the design are easily converted into straight lines of stitching.

Before you begin any needlepoint, however, treat the edges of the canvas to avoid fraying. Bind the edges with masking tape, or else work diagonal stitches over the edges. If you stop working on your needlepoint for a while, the canvas should be rolled, not folded, when you put it away. The creases made by folding the canvas are difficult to remove.

There are two types of canvas, Congress (woven in single threads) and Penelope (woven in pairs of threads). Both types come in different gauges, with different numbers of threads per inch. The gauge you choose will determine the size of your stitches and, therefore, the appearance of the finished article, either delicate or rugged. Coarser canvas, with fewer threads per inch, is used for needlepoint rugs, while finer canvas is stitched with thinner wool, to be used as a handbag or other finely designed article. The choice of canvas, Congress or Penelope, and the gauge of the threads thus depend upon the intended use of the needle-point article.

Before you begin stitching, consider the types of threads available. Crewel wool is a fine 2-ply wool, and several strands may be used in the needle at once to cover the canvas threads completely. Tapestry wool, being 4-ply, is thicker, and thus only a single strand at a time is used on loosely woven canvas. Use

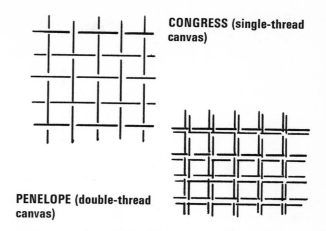

CONGRESS (single-thread canvas)

PENELOPE (double-thread canvas)

DETERMINE WHICH CANVAS to use before you design the stitching pattern and colors.

cotton and silk threads only on a very fine canvas. They are good for fine details and highlights when used with wool in a design. For carpets and rugs, use rug wool, which comes in various thicknesses and colors.

Choose your thread carefully: a thread which is too thick for the canvas background will cause puckering, while one which is too fine will not cover the canvas threads completely. Since drawing the thread through the canvas wears the thread down, use short lengths of thread (18 inches is the standard length) so that each inch of thread will not go through the canvas too many times.

To estimate the amount of yarn you will use on a particular needlepoint article, work a 1-inch square sampler on the same background and with the same thread you will use on the article itself. Note the amount of yarn used, and figure the number of square inches to be covered on your canvas. (To figure square inches, multiply the length of the canvas times the width, both measured in inches.) Now multiply the number of square inches times the length of thread used to stitch one square inch, and you will have an estimate of the amount of yarn necessary to cover the entire canvas.

Starting a thread in most types of stitchery is done by making a knot in one end of the

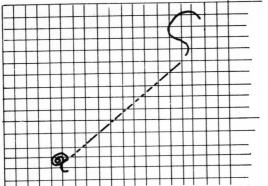

STARTING A NEW THREAD: Starting on the right side, make a stitch which emerges again on the same side at the exact spot where the first stitch should begin. The thread will be secured later on the wrong side by other stitches, and the knot on the right side can be cut off.

thread. In needlepoint, however, knots only cause lumps on the underside of the piece and are therefore avoided whenever possible. Instead, start a new thread in the following way: make a knot at one end of the thread, which you will cut off later. Bring the needle from the right side to the wrong side near the space where the first stitch is to be, and then up again to the right side in the position of the first stitch. The thread will be covered by stitching and thus secured in that way; when that is done, clip the knot off. If there is already enough stitching done, a new thread can be started by running the thread through the stitches on the wrong side. This method is also the way to fasten off a thread.

Now that the preparation for needlepoint stitching has been explained, you are ready to learn a few common needlepoint stitches. Learn and practice these before you plan a design, since you will be better prepared to plan one which is suited to needlepoint if you are familiar with the stitches you will be using.

Cross stitch: The cross stitch in needlepoint can be worked on either Congress or Penelope canvas and over any number of threads. The top stitch of every cross stitch on a piece of needlepoint must always be in the same direction—usually from the bottom left to the top right. You can either make each complete stitch individually, or make a row of half stitches, then reverse and complete the crosses. Making them by rows will ensure even stitches.

Half cross stitch: The half cross stitch does not cover canvas as completely as other stitches do. It uses little yarn and is practical for things which will receive little wear. To make a row of half cross stitches, start at the upper left corner of the canvas, at a point that will be the bottom of the first stitch. Make a row of half cross stitches as you would make the first half of a row of cross stitches. To make a row directly under the first, turn the canvas around and stitch as you did the first row.

Continental stitch (also called the petit point or tent stitch): The continental stitch resembles the half cross stitch, except that here the canvas is

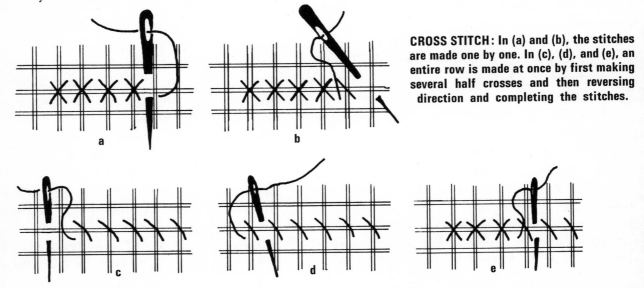

CROSS STITCH: In (a) and (b), the stitches are made one by one. In (c), (d), and (e), an entire row is made at once by first making several half crosses and then reversing direction and completing the stitches.

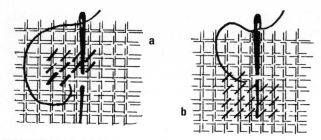

HALF CROSS STITCH: To make several consecutive rows, stitch from left to right, as in (a). For the next row (b), turn the canvas: the stitches will still be made from left to right.

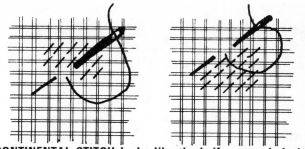

CONTINENTAL STITCH looks like the half cross stitch, but both front and back are covered with yarn.

covered on both the front and the back, and more thread is used. The finished piece wears well due to the extra wool. The layer of wool on the back makes this stitch very practical for upholstery and pillows. Begin stitching at the upper right hand corner of your canvas and work as shown in the diagrams. Always work from right to left; turn the canvas when making a return row so you are still heading left.

While some stitches are common and are named, you may in your stitching invent one that you have never seen before. Its absence in a needlepoint book does not mean that you should not use it, however: new stitches are always being discovered, and they can be just as beautiful and practical as the standard stitches. Some variations of the common stitches are shown here, to make you aware of other possibilities.

Once your needlepoint piece is stitched, it needs very little care to keep it looking as fresh as it does at the beginning. If it should need cleaning, brush the surface with a clean rag dipped in carbon tetrachloride or other cleaning fluid. The colors will return to their original brightness.

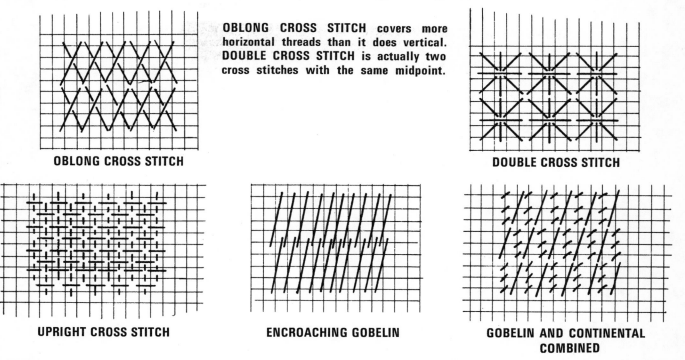

OBLONG CROSS STITCH covers more horizontal threads than it does vertical. **DOUBLE CROSS STITCH** is actually two cross stitches with the same midpoint.

OBLONG CROSS STITCH

DOUBLE CROSS STITCH

UPRIGHT CROSS STITCH

ENCROACHING GOBELIN

GOBELIN AND CONTINENTAL COMBINED

UPRIGHT CROSS STITCH, which looks like a cross stitch turned 90°, is made by stitching several rows of running stitches and crossing them with perpendicular rows. **ENCROACHING GOBELIN,** so named because one row encroaches upon the next, is sewn the same way the simple overcast stitch is. **GOBELIN AND CONTINENTAL COMBINED** is made by first sewing all the continental stitches, and then going over the area to make the Gobelin stitches.

After having been worked in diagonal stitches, the canvas is sometimes diamond-shaped rather than square. To block the canvas back to its original square shape, fasten the needlepoint piece right side down with thumbtacks to a piece of soft wood, the top of which you have marked with the proper size and shape of the canvas. Place the four corners of the piece on top of the four corners of the wood, and fasten all around the edges. If the yarn is not colorfast (that is, if the color runs when wet), sprinkle the needlepoint liberally with salt. Wet it thoroughly with cold water and let it dry. When you remove the thumbtacks, it should retain the square shape.

To mount needlepoint pictures, block the piece to a square shape. Stretch it over heavy cardboard or plywood of the same size as the stitched area of the canvas. Push pins (for cardboard) or tacks (for $\frac{1}{4}$-inch plywood) through the canvas on the *edge* of the cardboard or plywood. Using heavy thread, make big but tight stitches in the loose canvas on the back of the board to hold the canvas taut. Frame this as you desire.

To make a needlepoint pillow, trim the canvas of the blocked needlepoint piece to 1 inch and stitch the edges of the canvas to the back of the needlepoint by overcasting. Cut a piece of fabric for the back of the pillow the same size as the needlepoint, plus a $\frac{1}{2}$ inch seam allowance. Turn this seam allowance to the inside and stitch it in place. With an overcast stitch, attach the needlepoint top to the fabric back on three sides. Insert a pillow form (if foam rubber, it should be exactly the same size as the finished needlepoint) and stitch the fourth side closed.

TIE-AND-DYE

Give your fabrics a "mod" look without giving in to the high cost of living. Decorate drapes, shirts, pants, and even umbrellas with colorful "cloudy" effects by using this rapidly growing craft, that consists simply of knotting and dyeing. Use only colorfast dyes for your projects. Fine fabrics, such as silk and nylon, require more and tighter knots than cotton.

The secret to tie-and-dye is protecting certain areas of the fabric while the remainder of the cloth is soaking in a dye bath. These protected areas will become patterned sections once the cloth is dry. The tying process determines the degree of protection your selected areas receive when placed in the bath.

METHOD 1: Tying the cloth.

Tie Techniques

You can use a long or a square piece of cloth. Start by tying a knot in the middle, and work your way out to the ends. Make the knots more or less uniform. Tie with string, thread, cord, yarn, or raffia, as tightly as possible, knotting the ends. You might wind some cellophane tape around the knot for additional protection. Or you might tie the string in a latticed pattern for a different effect. How much dye penetrates the cloth depends upon how tightly or loosely it has been bound and the dyeing time. When untying, look for the two ends that were knotted together. Pull these away from the bound cloth and insert the point of a scissors into the space and cut the string.

METHOD 1. Pinch a small section of cloth between your thumb and index fingers. Tie

EQUIPMENT FOR TIE-AND-DYE: Raffia, string and cord are used for tying the cloth. By wrapping the cloth around various household objects—marbles, wooden balls, buttons, screws—only part of the cloth will be dyed. Hang the cloth with clothespins to dry.

Photographs from the book, "Batik som hobby" by Gunnel Edenholm and Gudrun Ahlberg | © 1965 by ICA Forlaget

this section. Repeat this procedure several times in different sections of the same cloth.

METHOD 2. Lay the material out on a flat surface. Next, lift the cloth from the middle, allowing it to hang freely. Tie the portion between your fingers as tightly as possible. In addition, make several more ties around the remaining area of the cloth, leaving spaces between each tie.

METHOD 2.

METHOD 3. Place solid household objects within the cloth, then tie around these objects. The purpose of placing an article within the material is to allow the dye to penetrate only partially the area around the tie.

METHOD 4. Fold the cloth into a double triangle, using an oblong-shaped piece of cloth and tie the knots in the corners.

METHOD 5. Stripes can be produced by folding the cloth and binding it in a bundle of accordion pleats at right angles to the first fold. Make a solid band of binding around the bundle.

The Dyeing Process

Attach a string long enough to pull the fabric out of the dye bath and to use later for hanging up to dry. You are now ready to bathe the material. To protect the working surface, spread out several sheets of newspaper. Use a pan deep enough to hold the entire piece of material. Follow the directions on the dye package and prepare the water-and-dye mixture in the pan. Be sure that the mixture is colorfast.

Dip the knotted material into the prepared bath. Press it down to make sure that the entire piece is covered by the water. After a few minutes, remove the material from the dye bath, squeeze it out, and hang it on the piece of string with one or two spring-type clothespins. Allow the dye to dry completely before untying the knots. Unknot very carefully so as not to damage the cloth in any way. The areas which had been knotted should now show circular designs. If the dye has not been distributed evenly, retie and redye in the same color.

If you decide to dye the material with more than one color, replace all or most of the

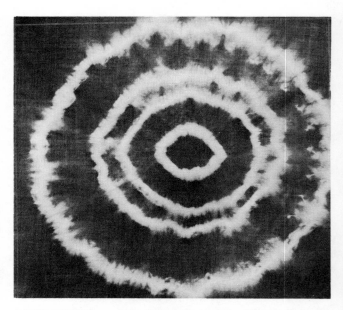

AFTER DYEING, a cloth tied by Method 2 will look like this.

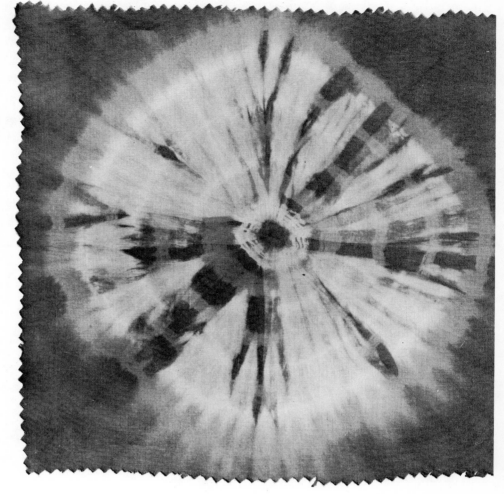

SEPARATE DYE BATHS produced the different degrees of color in this cloth.

original knots after the fabric's first bath. Or, you might tie a few more knots. For each additional color, you have to place the material into a new dye bath. When redyeing with new colors, arrange the cloth so that the part not already dyed will be near the surface and the areas which have been dyed will be bundled into the middle of the tied-up cloth, if you don't want them to mix.

Avoid using an excess of colors as the designs will begin to overlap and possibly ruin the intended effect.

Tie-Dyeing Clothes

After you have dyed one or two pieces of material, select an article of clothing to be tie-dyed. The procedure for curtains, a shirt, or a pair of pants will be the same in each case. Tie several knots and dip the article in a dye bath. Remove material from the bath, allow it to dry completely, and then untie the knots.

Tie-Dyeing Umbrellas

Remove the rib tips from an old umbrella, allowing the umbrella cover to fall free of the metal rib arms. Should there be small pieces of thread holding the cover from falling free, slice the threads with a safety-edged razor.

Proceed from here as you would in other tie-and-dye projects. Make several ties with string and place the material into a dye bath. If more than one color is to be used, tie extra knots after the first color has dried. Repeat the process, leaving the original knots tied.

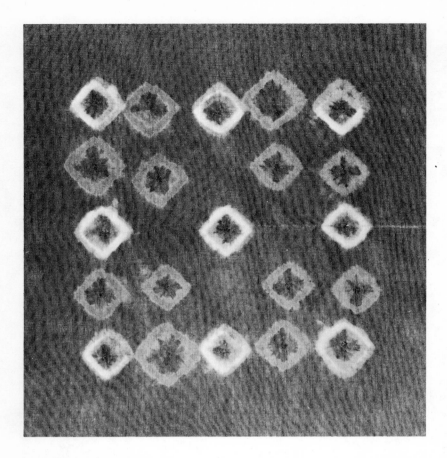

When all desired colors have been applied and the material dried, remove the string and tug on the material lightly. Replace the tips on the ends of the metal ribs. Open and close the umbrella a few times to stretch the material back into its proper position. Your tie-and-dye umbrella is now complete. Because the dyes are colorfast, you need not worry about the colors running in the rain.

WEAVING

Weaving, reduced to fundamentals, is a process of interlacing threads to form cloth. After forming a foundation of taut threads called the *warp*, the weaver goes over and under the warp threads at right angles with threads known as the *weft*. Designs are formed by varying the patterns of interlacing warp and weft threads, and by using different colors and materials.

This basic principle applies to all looms, no matter how complicated they might seem to you at first. Before long you will realize how simple the process of weaving actually is, even though it is one of the world's most intriguing crafts.

The best loom for a beginner is the versatile square weaver, which is easy to make and use. On it you will be able to make any number of things such as scarves, baby blankets, and even handbags, while you learn to produce patterns comparable to ones woven on a 4-harness loom.

Making a Square Weaver

This loom is designed for weaving 4-inch squares which you can sew together later on to form almost any yarn article. Although you can make larger square looms, this size is preferable, since with it you will be able to use a 5-inch or 6-inch needle which will pick up the warp threads all the way across the loom in one simple operation.

To make the loom, cut four pieces of soft wood such as pine or bass $\frac{1}{2}'' \times \frac{1}{2}'' \times 5''$ long, and mitre (dovetail) the corners. Glue the

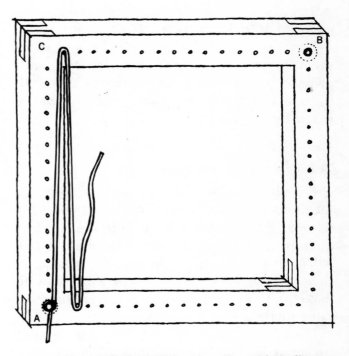

Illus. 1. THE SQUARE WEAVER, shown here with the first row of warp, is easy to use. You can turn out any number of articles on it, from blankets to berets.

pieces together, and reinforce each corner with a small nail if the loom does not seem sturdy enough. To form the top of the loom upon which you will wind the warp (Illus. 1), you will need 16 $\frac{3}{4}$-inch headless or casing nails for each side of the loom. If headless nails are not available, buy 1-inch nails and cut off the heads with a wire clipper.

The first step is to mark dots along each of the four 5-inch sides of the loom, starting $\frac{1}{4}$-inch from the inner edge of the lower left-hand corner (A). To ensure that your woven squares

Adapted from the book, "Weaving as a Hobby" by Marguerite Ickis | © *1968 by Sterling Publishing Co., Inc., New York*

will be straight, before you drive the nails in, draw a guideline in the middle of each side of the loom. Measure your dots against this guideline to be sure they line up in a straight row in all directions.

Illus. 1 shows how the nails are set. First, drive in one nail in each of two corners A and B which are diagonally across from each other. Then add 15 nails $\frac{1}{4}$ inch apart along the four sides. The two corner nails will give you a count of 16 nails in each row.

Now set your nails on each dot and drive them in at least $\frac{1}{4}$ inch deep, so they will provide a firm frame for weaving. When all the nails are in place your square weaver is ready for the warp.

The Warp and the Weft

For this you will need a ball of 4-ply or medium-thick wool yarn in the color you have selected for your square. If this is your first attempt at weaving, a solid color dark square will give better results, since it will appear to stay cleaner. Later on you will learn how to make patterns on the square weaver, using this same method.

Place your loom in front of you so that corner A is near your left hand. Tie the yarn 1 inch from the end on to the nail in corner A, and begin to string the warp by carrying the yarn inside the line of nails to your left, up around the first nail near the upper left-hand corner of the loom (C), back down to the nail next to where you began, back up again, and so on until you reach the upper right-hand corner (B) of the loom. This completes the warp. While you are stringing, *try to maintain an even tension*, since the warp is the foundation of the final woven square.

To measure the amount of yarn you will need for the weft, wind it around the outside of the nails on your loom eight times, and cut it off. This will leave you with plenty of yarn to spare. If the square is to be woven in two colors and you have the loom strung with the

background color, tie on the weft or pattern thread at this point and measure the length in the same way. Thread your 5-inch needle with the yarn. Now, starting at corner B, weave from right to left by passing the needle over the first warp thread, under the next warp thread, and so on, across all 31 threads. You will bring the needle out over the warp thread just above corner A. Pull the yarn through gently, and loop it around the nail above A before you begin the next row.

The second row must be woven opposite to the first. To do this, you must go *under* all the threads you went *over* in the first row, and *over* those you went *under*. Since you went over the last thread in row 1, start row 2 by going under the first thread, over the second, and so on, across the row from left to right. The third row should be woven just like the first row, the fourth row like row 2, etc. Thus every *other* row will be alike. Continue weaving back and forth across the loom until there is a loop round each nail in the loom. Your square will be complete when you bring the thread out beside the nail in corner A.

While you are weaving the weft, be very careful not to pull the yarn too tight or your square will be uneven. By passing the needle over the warp at a sharp angle (Illus. 2) each time you weave a row, and then easing the yarn into place gently with your needle, you will be able to control the tension at all times, and avoid unevenness.

After cutting off some of the excess weft thread, carefully push the square off the nails, and weave the two left-over ends into the edge of the square. At corner B you will find an extra loop of yarn left. Draw this in along the two woven edges and you will have a perfect square with 15 loops on all four sides. These loops at the edges of the woven square will be matched with those of the next squares you make.

Sew your squares together with a darning needle and yarn to form scarves, a baby blanket, or anything you like. Block the finished

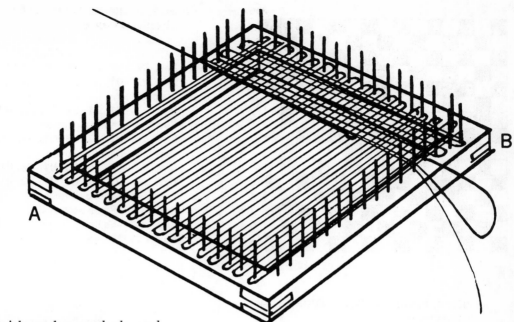

Illus. 2. WEAVING THE WEFT will complete your square. Always maintain an even tension throughout the threading of both the warp and weft so that your squares will be smooth and even.

article by covering it with a damp cloth and pressing lightly with a warm, not hot, iron.

As soon as you have mastered the one-color square, you are ready to go on to the next step: designing and weaving your own patterns.

Pattern Weaving

In most pattern weaving, the loom is first strung with warp threads, and then the pattern is woven in with weft threads carried on a needle.

There are many interesting weaving materials on the market, but for small looms such as the square weaver, it is important to use only those materials which have elasticity. If you do not string your loom with a thread that will "give," the warp threads may become too taut before you finish weaving. Four-ply wool yarn gives the most satisfactory results on a square weaver, but you may want to experiment with other materials when you have more experience.

If you weave the weft over and under, as you did in the first project, in a color which contrasts with the color of the warp threads, the result will be a plain or *tabby* weave. This produces a tweedlike effect.

By varying the over-one under-one weave, however, you can achieve a multitude of

patterns with the same two contrasting colors. To do this, you skip over or under two or more warp threads with the weft occasionally. Although this can be done at random, it is so simple to block out your own weaving designs in advance that random weaving is not recommended.

To plan a design, take a piece of graph paper and block off as many squares as you have warp ends on each side of your loom. For example, your square weaver has 16 nails on each side, so make a graph 31 squares wide and 31 squares long. Each square represents what will show when the woven cloth is right side up. If the weft is passed under the warp, the warp will show, and vice versa. Where the warp will show, color the graph square solid. Where the weft thread will show, leave the graph square blank.

Weaving graphs are usually read from right to left, and since weaving always starts at the upper right-hand corner of the loom, instructions are planned to read back and forth—first to the right and then to left. Study the graphs and weaving directions in Illus. 3-8 carefully, and compare them with one another. This will

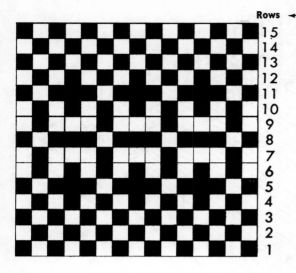

Rows ←——— Illus. 3. A SIMPLE PLAIN WEAVE PATTERN.

15
14
13
12
11
10
9
8
7
6
5
4
3
2
1

Directions:

O = Over
U = Under

Row #1—U1, O1, U1, O1, U1, O1, etc. (plain weave).
Row #2—O1, U1, O1, U1, etc. (plain weave) (left to right).
Row #3—U1, O1, U1, O1, etc. (plain weave).
Row #4—Same as row 2.
Row #5—U1, O1, U3, O1, U3, O1, U3, O1, U1.
Row #6—Same as row 2.
Row #7—O1, U1, O3, U1, O3, U1, O3, U1, O1.
Row #8—U1, O1, U3, O1, U3, O1, U3, O1, U1.
Row #9—Same as row 7.
Row #10—Same as row 2.
Row #11—Same as row 5.
Row #12-15—Same as rows 1-3.

Illus. 4. PLANNING SMALL SQUARES. ——→

Directions:

Row #1—Plain weave from right to left—O, U, O, U, etc.
Row #2—From left to right—U, O, U3, O, U, O, U, O, U3, O, U.
Row #3—O, U2, O, U2, O, U, O, U2, O, U2, O.
Row #4—U2, O, U, O, U2, O, U2, O, U, O, U2.
Row #5—U, O, U, O, U, O, U3, O, U, O, U, O, U.
Row #6—Same as row 4.
Row #7—Same as row 3.
Row #8—Same as row 2.
Repeat rows 3 to 8 inclusive.
Last row #15—Plain weave, U, O, U, O, etc.

15
14
13
12
11
10
9
8
7
6
5
4
3
2
1

Weft thread
Warp thread

Illus. 5. PLANNING SMALL SQUARES. ——→

Directions:

Row #1—Plain weave—U, O, U, O, from right to left.
Row #2—From left to right—O, U, O, U3, O, U, O, U3, O, U, O.
Row #3—U, O, U2, O, U2, O, U2, O, U2, O, U.
Row #4—U3, O, U, O, U3, O, U, O, U3.
Row #5—Same as row 3.
Row #6—Same as row 2.
Repeat rows, 3, 4, 3, 2, 3, 4, 3.
End with a row of plain weave.

15
14
13
12
11
10
9
8
7
6
5
4
3
2
1

Weft thread
Warp thread

Illus. 6. DIAGONAL WEAVE. ——————➤

Directions:
Row #1—Plain weave—U, O, U, etc.
Row #2—U2, O2, etc., end O1.
Row #3—O1, U2, O2, U2, O2, etc.
Row #4—O2, U2, O2, U2, O2, etc., end U1.
Row #5—U1, O2, U2, O2, U2, O2, U2, O2.
Row #6—Same as row 2.
Repeat 3, 4, 5 and 2.
Last row weave plain.

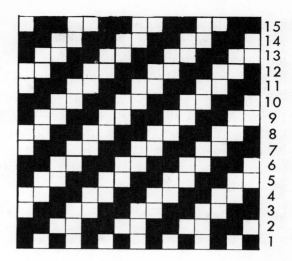

15
14
13
12
11
10
9
8
7
6
5
4
3
2
1

25   3
24   4
23   5
22   6
21   3
20   4
19   5
18   6
17   3
16   4
15   3
14   6
13   5
12   4
11   3
10   6
9   5
8   4
7   3
6
5
4
3
2
1

◄—————— **Illus. 7. HERRINGBONE WEAVE.**

Directions:
Row #1—U, O, U, etc.
Row #2—O2, U2, etc., end U1.
Row #3—U1, O2, U2, O2, U2, O2, U2, O2.
Row #4—O1, U1, O2, U2, O2, U2, O2, U2, O1.
Row #5—O1, U2, O2, U2, O2, U2, O2, U2.
Row #6—U1, O1, U2, O2, U2, O2, U2, O2, U1.
Row #7—Same as row 3.
Repeat 4, 5, 6.
Repeat 3, 4, 5, 6.
Repeat 3, 4, 3.
Repeat 6, 5, 4, 3.
Repeat 6, 5, 4, 3.

Illus. 8. IRISH CHAIN. ——————➤

Directions:
Row #1—Plain weave, O, U, O, U, etc.
Row #2—U3, O, U3, O, U3, O, U3.
Row #3—O3, U, O3, U, O3, U, O3.
Row #4—U, O, U3, O, U3, O, U3, O, U.
Row #5—U3, O, U3, O, U3, O, U3.
Row #6—Same as row 4.
Row #7—Same as row 3.
Repeat 2, 3, 4, 5, 6, 3, 2.
Row #15—Plain weave, O, U, etc.

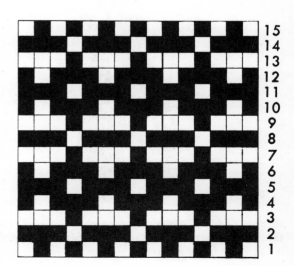

15
14
13
12
11
10
9
8
7
6
5
4
3
2
1

WEAVING ■ **139**

give you practice in working with graphs and eventually planning your own. All of these patterns are designed for weaving back and forth on the square weaver, and as in all weaving graphs, it is wise to make a few practice rows before attempting a project. Later on you may wish to weave these patterns on a 4-harness loom, but they will give you surprisingly good-looking results on your square weaver.

What to Make

The projects you can make on your square weaver are almost innumerable. Those that follow are only a few possibilities. Weaving is economical, too, for the amount of yarn required is less than half the amount commonly used in crocheting and knitting. You will also find your square weaver ideal for using up odds and ends of yarn, for you only need about 4 yards of yarn to make a 4-inch square. Although you can use as many colors as you like in a square, the yarn should always be of the same weight and quality, or your square will be uneven.

An Attractive Scarf. Decide first how large you want the scarf to be. For children, 8 inches (2

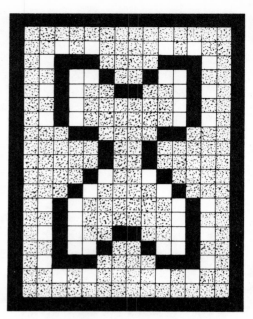

Illus. 10. GRAPH DESIGN for afghan or baby blanket.

squares) in width and 32 inches in length (8 squares) is a good size, while an adult's scarf should be at least four squares longer. The width of an adult's scarf is optional.

Now plan your design. You might make an equal number of squares in tabby weave or two solid colors, which you would sew together alternately, fringing the ends of the finished scarf.

If you do not wish to use any of the designs you have learned from Illus. 3-8, this would be a good time to try an original design of your own. You could plan a design which would incorporate half solid color squares and half patterned ones, or weave all patterned squares.

An Afghan or Baby Blanket. An afghan is an excellent project for using scrap yarn, and after you have completed a scarf or two you should have little difficulty in making even a rather large blanket, since this consists of nothing more than a number of the squares you have already learned how to make sewn together.

Before you begin to weave, draw a graph containing as many squares as you plan to

Illus. 9. SCARF. Tie the strands with a slip knot, and make the knot as near the end of the scarf as possible. Trim the ends of the fringe so that all threads are of even length.

weave for the afghan. A good size is 16 4-inch squares wide and 21 4-inch squares long, but you may vary this according to your needs. A better size for a baby blanket is nine squares one way and eleven squares the other.

Plan on the graph (Illus. 10) the number of finished squares you will want in each color, and fill in each square with a crayon of the appropriate color, as shown in the illustration.

When your design is satisfactory to you, weave the squares, counting carefully to make sure you weave the right number of each color or pattern. If you do not have enough yarn for a solid color border, which requires 70 squares for the afghan and 38 for the baby blanket, buy three 4-ounce skeins of 4-ply wool for this purpose.

Sew all the finished squares together with matching colored yarn, and reinforce the outside edge by crocheting one row of single crochet stitches all around the edge.

Illus. 12. CHILD'S BERET made of small squares.

Illus. 11. HANDBAG made of small squares.

Handbag or Knitting Bag. Make a paper pattern the size of the bag you want, making sure that it is at least two squares wider than the base of the handle you have chosen (Illus. 11). Divide the pattern into 4-inch squares to determine the number of squares needed for the bag. Weave the squares into any design and sew them together with matching yarn.

Block the squares into shape, and add a lining of soft material. With matching yarn,

fasten the lined squares to the holes which most wooden or plastic handles have at $\frac{1}{4}$-inch intervals for this purpose. A wide variety of handles is available at most department stores.

Berets for Children. An attractive beret (Illus. 12) is easy to make and a perfect gift for a child. It requires 13 4-inch squares, and enough extra wool for a pompon on top.

Sew 9 woven squares together to form a large square (3 squares each way). Add a single square to the middle of each of the 4 sides of the large square (Illus. 13). Fold these

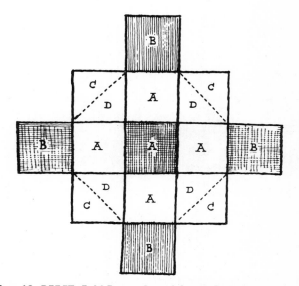

Illus. 13. BERET. Fold B over A, and C over D. Stitch along the dashed lines.

back to form the underside of the beret. Next, fold the corner squares of the original large square diagonally across, turning them back so that their edges meet those of the undersquares (Illus. 14). Sew the matching loops together, starting at the beret's outer edge and working towards the middle, which will form the opening for the head. Sew each seam only half the length of the square, and fit the beret on to the head.

Determine now if the seam should be shorter or longer in order to make the opening fit the head, and make any necessary adjustments. Reinforce the beret's edges by overcasting them with yarn in a matching color.

To make the pompon, cut matching yarn into 4-inch lengths. Tie a string of the same yarn around the middle of a group of 4-inch threads, folding the ends together so the strands are all the same length. Wrap a piece of yarn several times around the top of the pompon, approximately $\frac{1}{4}$ inch from the looped ends. Knot securely, and cut off any excess thread. Spread the strands to form a half ball, and trim the ends evenly. Using yarn and a large needle, attach the finished pompon to the top of the beret.

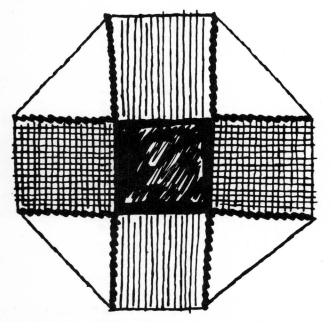

Illus. 14. FINAL SHAPE of the beret (from below).

Looms

All looms are basically like the square weaver, a framework across which the warp threads of a fabric are held taut while the weft is being interlaced at right angles. The loom was first developed many thousands of years ago because almost any woven article contains so many threads that going over and under each one would be an impossible task without a substantial frame to hold the foundation firm, and some sort of device to lift alternate threads so that the filling could be passed through, instead of being tediously interlaced according to the desired pattern. No matter how complicated a loom may seem, its purpose is to simplify the process of weaving, a fact that the beginner should be encouraged to remember.

The principal parts of a loom (Illus. 15) are the *harnesses*, which lift the warp threads to form openings (known as *sheds*) through which the filling can be passed; the *heddles*, which are metal needle-like devices with an opening through which the warp ends are threaded (these are attached to the harnesses); the *reed*, a comb-like rod which keeps the warp ends evenly separated and is also used to *beat* the weft shots into place after they have been passed through the sheds; the *warp beam*, a roller at the back of the loom on which the warp is wound before it is drawn up over the loom for weaving; the *cloth beam*, a roller at the front of the loom on which the material is wound as it is woven; and the *apron bars*, to which the ends of the warp are attached.

Looms are generally identified by the number of harnesses they have: the 2-harness loom, the 4-harness loom, and so on up to large commercial looms which have 26 harnesses. The best loom for you after the square weaver is not necessarily the smallest; since the 2-harness loom will only produce variations of the plain weave because it can only lift alternate threads forming only two sheds, and the 4-harness loom will produce any weaving pattern, the latter is definitely recommended.

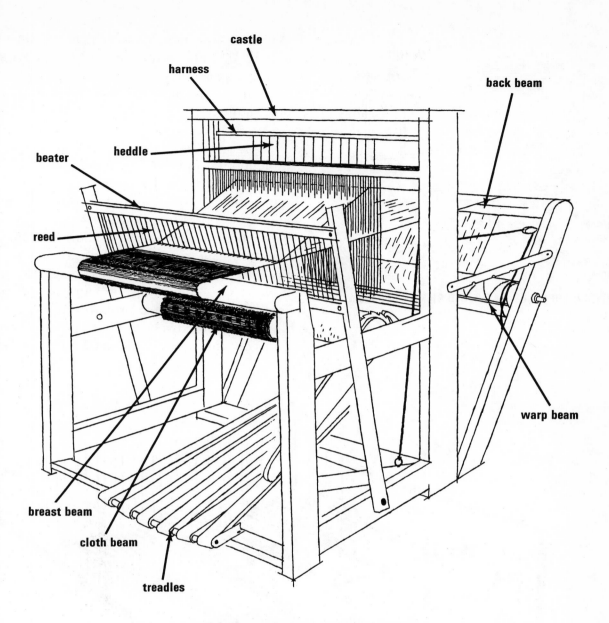

Illus. 15. FLOOR LOOM, with 4 harnesses.

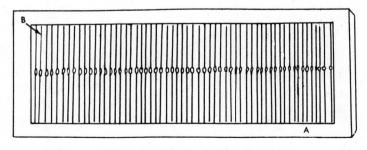

Illus. 16. HARNESS (A) showing the heddles (B).

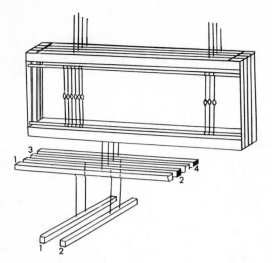

Illus. 17. TREADLES, LAMS AND SHAFTS of a loom.

With the 4-harness loom, which will lift every fourth thread, you can form twills, satin weaves, overshot patterns and lace variations as well as the plain weaves—and the cost is not significantly greater than the 2-harness loom.

Looms are available in various styles. The table loom is operated by hand levers, while in the floor loom the harnesses are raised (Jack-type looms) or lowered (counterbalanced looms) by pressing down *treadles*, or pedals, with the feet, obviously a more comfortable way to weave since the hands are free to pass the weft through the various sheds. However, table looms have the advantage of being small in size, and are probably preferable for the apartment dweller. There is no difference between the counterbalanced and Jack-type

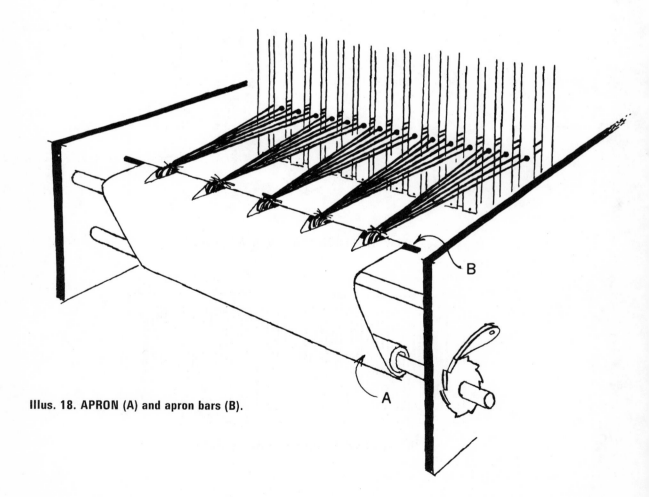

Illus. 18. APRON (A) and apron bars (B).

Illus. 19. TABLE LOOM with 4 harnesses. If your space is limited, you might consider a table loom, which is operated by hand levers.

Illus. 20. FOLDING LOOM. This is another very convenient loom when space is at a minimum.

looms as far as the weaver is concerned; they simply function on different mechanical principles.

The width of the loom is another thing to consider. While a width of 20 inches is a possibility, the recommended width is 36 inches, which will be sufficient to weave everything from place mats to suiting.

All looms come disassembled, but include detailed instructions both for assemblage and *dressing*, or threading the warp on to the loom. In addition, all weaving texts give complete directions for this process.

Reading Pattern Drafts

The basic principle of weaving over and under taut warp threads with weft threads, carried on a shuttle, applies to all weaving patterns and all looms. You will find pattern drafts that are different from those used here. The symbols inside the graph squares can be letters, numbers or shadings. But it doesn't really make any difference what the symbols are, since all you need to know is the sequence of warp-over-weft crossings. The pattern block is repeated as many times as desired across the warp and until the desired length of the material is reached. The sample drafts here

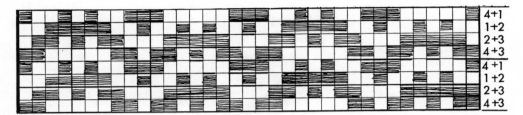

Illus. 21. THREADING DRAFT. Honeysuckle design.

Illus. 22. TREADLING. Honeysuckle design.

Illus. 23. VARIATION of the treadling draft, with tabby. Honeysuckle design.

(Illus. 21, 22, 23) show three different ways of drafting the very same pattern. As you can see, the end result will be the same no matter how the draft is filled in. You will find hundreds of weaving patterns, and suggested applications for them, in weaving books and magazines, together with instructions on the kinds of yarn to use, appropriate colors, and so on.

As explained, the best loom—and the most versatile—for the home weaver is the 4-harness loom. By pressing down the first and third harnesses, you will lift every other end, thus forming an opening, or *shed*, through which the weft thread can be thrown, or *shot*, to form a plain tabby weave (over one and under one). By instead pressing down every harness in turn, lifting only each fourth thread, and moving each time to the left, you will be forming a simple left-hand twill weave. To make a right-hand twill, you would simply reverse the *treadling*, or pressing down of the harnesses, starting from the opposite side of the loom. Hundreds of different patterns, including all the overshot variations, can be formed by changing the treadling or threading different numbers of threads in the harnesses or putting in more than one shot in each shed. It is impossible to discuss these possibilities here, but a bit of experimentation at your loom will give you enough practice to weave any patterns to be found today.

metal & glass

METALCRAFTING

Metalcrafting, the art of fashioning beautiful and useful objects, is based upon a knowledge of the metals themselves and metalworking techniques. The better a craftsman knows his materials, methods, and use of tools, the better he can use his imagination towards superior craftsmanship. In this section you will learn the characteristics of metals, the most commonly used techniques, and the hand tools that the craftsman uses in his craft.

Metals were used for ornaments, utensils, plates and jewelry as long ago as 3000 B.C. The first metals to be found in a metallic state in nature were gold, silver, copper and tin, and they were the first to be used. When men found methods for combining metals to form alloys, bronze (copper and tin) and pewter (tin and an alloy) were added to the list. Iron and a form of steel came into use about 1000 B.C. These metals comprised the metalworkers' raw materials until the 18th century when the discovery of zinc added brass (copper and zinc) and nickel silver (copper, zinc and nickel) to the list. The final, very important metal to become available to the metal craftsman, in the 19th century, was aluminum.

Metals Used in Metalcrafting

The ten metals, namely gold, silver, copper, pewter, brass, bronze, nickel silver, aluminum, and wrought and cast iron, used since ancient times, are still used today. Gold and silver, due to their cost, are principally used for jewelry work and for fashioning small objects. Illus. 1, 2, and 3 show some jewelry work using precious metals and incorporating several metalworking techniques. Bowls, plates, cups, trays, and an infinite variety of shaped articles are made from the less precious metals.

Your choice of metal depends upon the object you want to make, the color and finish you like, and your personal taste in form.

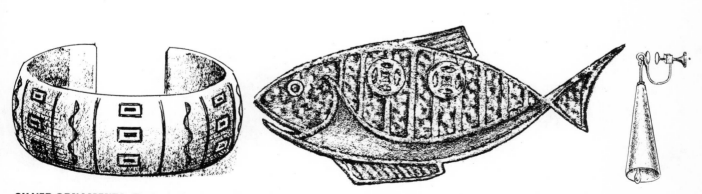

SILVER ORNAMENTS: Typical of what you can make as an amateur metalcrafter are these: a chased bracelet (Illus. 1), an etched pendant (Illus. 2) and a teardrop earring (Illus. 3).

Written especially for this volume by Henry H. Simons

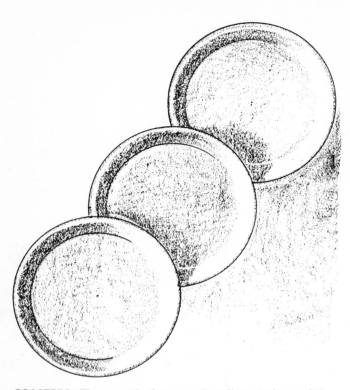

TRAY OF COPPER: Complete directions are given on page 156 to enable you to make this tray (Illus. 6).

COASTERS: These can be hammered easily out of any of the ten metals except iron (Illus. 4).

Illus. 4 shows hammered coasters which can be made with aluminum, copper, brass, or any of the ten metals other than iron. Illus. 5 is a dish made with copper with an engraved design. Illus. 6 is a tray made of copper. This is the project you will work on to familiarize yourself with some common metalworking techniques. Illus. 7 shows household items made of pewter, a metal which lends itself beautifully to metalcrafting.

Metals for craft work can be obtained from various supply companies. (See Appendix.) Mill supply houses are a source for brass, bronze, aluminum and steel. Since, sometimes, a mill supply requires a minimum order which may be far more material than you require, your local hardware merchant may be able to obtain a small quantity for you.

DISH OF COPPER: Engraved with a design, this handsome deep dish is simple to make (Illus. 5).

PEWTER: Don't overlook this metal for household items (Illus. 7).

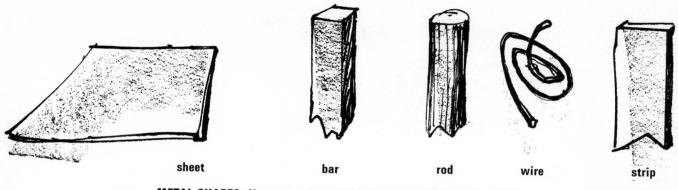

sheet   bar   rod   wire   strip

METAL SHAPES: You can order metal in any of these forms (Illus. 8).

Metals are available in the shapes shown in Illus. 8. When ordering specify the kind of metal, the shape, the dimensions, and the quantity. Thickness of sheet stock is usually stated in metal gauge sizes. Table I shows the gauge size that corresponds to a given metal thickness for some of the more common thicknesses.

TABLE I

Metal Thickness	Gauge Size
.075 inches	14
.067 "	15
.060 "	16
.054 "	17
.048 "	18
.042 "	19
.036 "	20
.033 "	21
.030 "	22

Metal Characteristics

Malleability and Ductility. When a metal is malleable it can be hammered without cracking. When a metal is ductile it can be deformed without tearing. These two characteristics are required for making formed objects, such as cups, bowls, and dishes.

Annealing. This is the process of heating a metal to a high temperature, but below the melting point, in order to soften it for further work. Most metals "work harden" after being hammered, formed, or shaped. They become hard, lose their malleability and ductility, and become difficult to shape or form further. Annealing puts the metal back into a workable condition. You would need a torch or kiln to anneal.

Density. This is the relationship of weight to size. Copper is about eight times as dense as wood. Our comparisons of the metals will be made with reference to copper.

Nobility. A metal that resists attack from air and chemicals is called noble. Of the metals you will be working with, gold is the only completely noble metal. It does not tarnish or discolor.

Solderability. The ability of a metal to be joined to another metal or to itself, by means of a soft solder or brazing alloy, is known as its "solderability." (Soldering and brazing are explained on page 161.)

Metal Descriptions

Gold is an extremely dense metal, bright yellow in color with a high degree of malleability and ductility. It can be worked to very thin sections without annealing; 100%, or 24 carat, gold is too soft to use for jewelry; 22 carat (92%), 18 carat (75%) and 14 carat (60%) gold are alloys of gold, silver and copper which are used in jewelry. These alloys give longer-wearing properties without appreciably affecting nobility or ductility. Gold is $2\frac{1}{2}$ times as heavy as copper. To preserve the nobility of gold, use only silver brazing or gold solder alloys for joining.

Silver in the 100% pure state is seldom used. Instead, an alloy of 92% silver and 8% copper, known as sterling silver, is the metal used for silver work. Sterling is a bright metal, with good malleability and ductility, about $1\frac{1}{4}$ times as heavy as copper. Annealing is required when heavy work is done. Silver tarnishes due to the sulphur gases in air, making its surface appear grey and lacklustre. Silver brazing alloys should be used for joining.

Copper is a beautiful reddish metal. When freshly polished, it has a bright lustre, but it will tarnish in air to a black-red color. In metalcrafting it is used in the pure state, since, after working, it is tough enough to resist abrasion. When ordering, request cold rolled and annealed copper. This will give you a smooth, soft material ready for working. If worked extensively, however, copper requires annealing. It is readily solderable with soft solders or brazing alloys.

Pewter is very soft, white-silvery when new. It will tarnish with time to a grey brownish metal, losing some of its lustre. The softest of the craft metals, about $1\frac{1}{4}$ times as dense as copper, it does not need to be annealed unless severely worked. Soldering requires a special low melting solder with glycerin as a flux.

Brass and bronze, alloys of copper, have a yellow-red color. Brass is slightly less malleable than copper, and is used like copper. Bronze, less ductile than brass, is used mostly for casting. Both alloys require annealing, and both tarnish to a dull golden color. Their density is the same as copper.

Nickel Silver, also known as German silver, is a white metal resembling silver in appearance, but is an alloy of copper and zinc. It has a malleability similar to brass. Often used in place of silver in jewelry work, as well as for hammered products, it does not tarnish as badly as brass. It requires annealing when worked, and solders readily with soft solders.

Aluminum is a malleable and ductile metal. Whitish and slightly less bright and silvery than silver, aluminum does not tarnish in the same way that other metals do. When attacked by air, aluminum allows a coating to be formed, which is transparent and adheres to the aluminum very tenaciously. As a result, the coating forms a protection against further attack by air and allows aluminum to retain its color. Aluminum requires annealing. Lightest of all craft metals, about one-third the density of copper, aluminum can only be soldered with difficulty and with special fluxes. You would be wise to plan to use riveting methods for joining.

Wrought Iron (or mild steel) is a grey-appearing metal with a dull lustre. It has a low malleability and a fair amount of ductility, and is used mainly in wire and strip work. Frequent anneals are required. Iron corrodes easily, producing a reddish scale. As a result, objects made of iron must be painted, varnished or plated to protect the surface. Iron can be soldered or brazed, if care is used. The density of iron is slightly less than that of copper.

Cast Iron has no ductility or malleability, and is therefore used to make cast or machined objects only. It must be protected with a protective coating after completion.

Tools

Illus. 9 through 15 show the basic tools used for most of the metalworking operations you will encounter. There is no need to go out and buy all the tools immediately. Pick them up as each project is planned. In time you will have an impressive kit.

Hammers. Illus. 9 (*a*) shows a planishing hammer, (*b*) a chasing hammer, (*c*) a ball-peen hammer. These are used for forming metals through raising. The light tack hammer (*d*) is used for delicate hammering of metal. The rawhide mallet (*e*) is used for flattening and straightening a sheet without marring it. The wooden mallet (*f*) is used for raising metal when a smooth finish surface is desired.

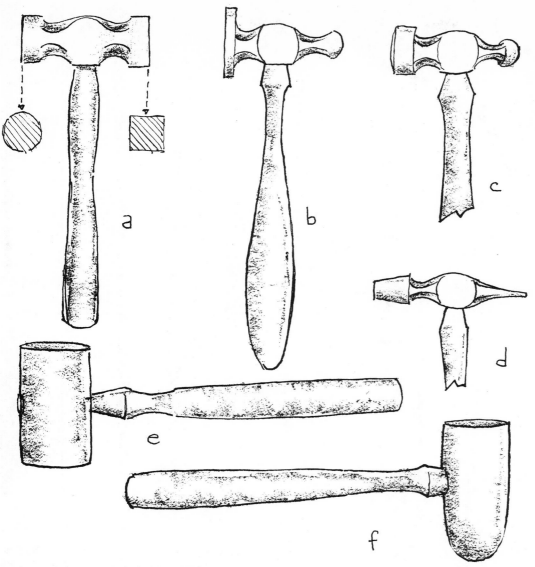

HAMMERS FOR METAL
(Illus. 9): (a) planishing,
(b) chasing, (c) ball-peen,
(d) tack hammer,
(e) rawhide mallet,
(f) wooden mallet.

Pliers. Illus. 10. A side-cutting pliers with serrated jaws (*a*), a flat-nosed pliers 4 inches long (*b*), and a thin-nosed pliers for work in close places (*c*) will serve adequately as a starting set.

Drill. If you are not lucky enough to have an electric drill, the hand drill shown in Illus. 11 will work well. Obtain twist drills up to $\frac{1}{4}$ inch in size.

PLIERS (Illus. 10): (a) side cutter with serrated jaws, (b) flat-nosed, and (c) thin-nosed pliers will all be needed for bending, holding, and snipping.

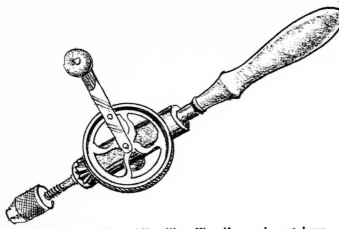

A HAND DRILL (Illus. 11) will suffice if you do not have access to an electric drill.

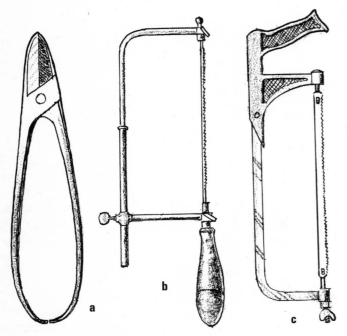

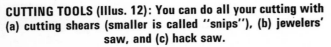

CUTTING TOOLS (Illus. 12): You can do all your cutting with (a) cutting shears (smaller is called "snips"), (b) jewelers' saw, and (c) hack saw.

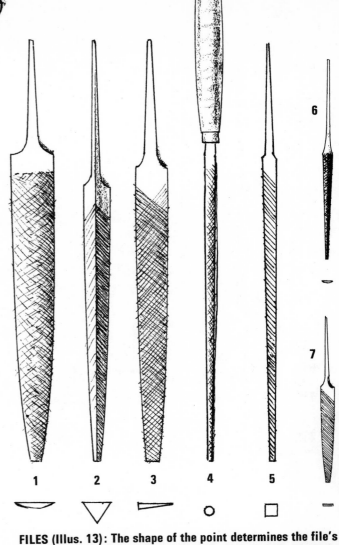

FILES (Illus. 13): The shape of the point determines the file's use. Use a universal handle (shown on #4) for all but the little needle files.

Cutting Tools. Illus. 12. A 10-inch cutting shears (*a*), a 5-inch jewelers' saw with *#2* blade (*b*), and a hack saw (*c*) will enable you to do all the cutting you need.

Files. Illus. 13 shows the various shaped files you should have. A smooth cut file 6 inches long is a good size. Using the five shapes on the left, and the two small "needle" files at the right, you will be able to handle all your filing work. You will need in addition a file brush and a universal handle to place on the file you are using.

Miscellaneous Tools. Illus. 14 shows two types of punches (*a*), a set square (*b*), a 6-inch steel rule (*c*), a scriber (*d*), a 6-inch compass and dividers (*e*) and (*f*), and an awl (*g*) for accessory operations.

Worktable. A sturdy bench with a hardwood top fitted with a vise, Illus. 15, mounted about 12 inches from the left-hand side of the bench is all you will need to start.

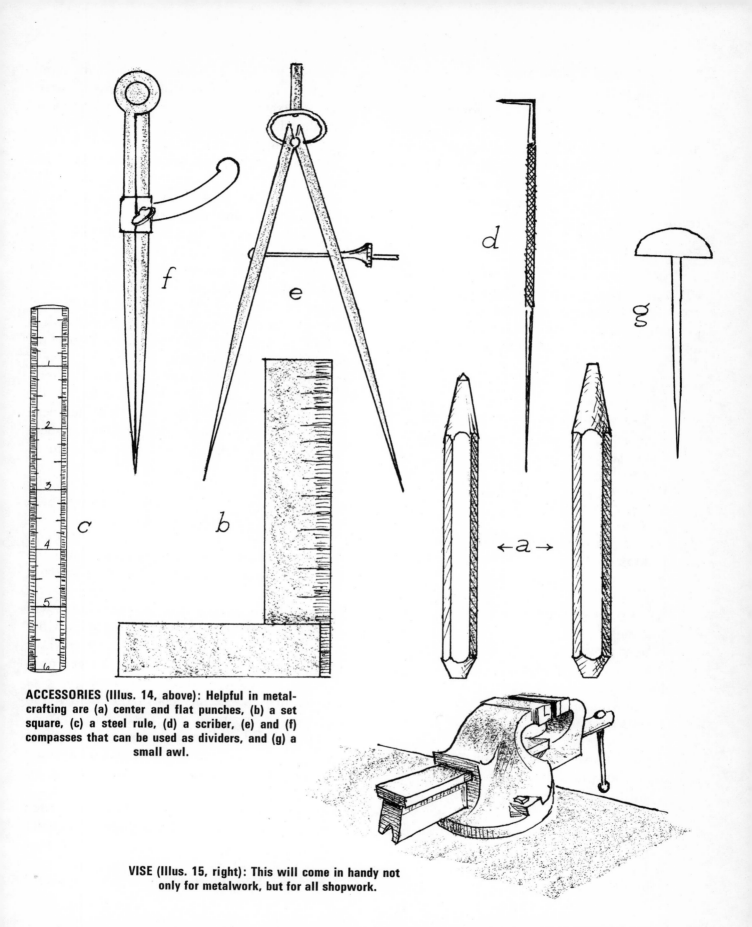

ACCESSORIES (Illus. 14, above): Helpful in metal-crafting are (a) center and flat punches, (b) a set square, (c) a steel rule, (d) a scriber, (e) and (f) compasses that can be used as dividers, and (g) a small awl.

VISE (Illus. 15, right): This will come in handy not only for metalwork, but for all shopwork.

Metalworking Techniques

The operations of metalworking fall into four broad classes: forming or shaping, decorating, finishing, and joining. We will make the decorated tray with handles shown in Illus. 6. When you have finished this project you will have become familiar with a number of the most commonly practiced and most popular techniques of the craft.

Etching

This process consists essentially in transferring a design on to the metal, painting the areas not to be etched with a coating impervious to acid, and etching the exposed areas with an acid to produce a design.

Materials (in order)

  6-inch compass
  tracing paper
  a 12-inch diameter sheet copper disc, 18 gauge
  cleaning fluid
  fine steel wool
  6-inch file
  center punch
  dividers
  a small jar of white tempera paint
  cellophane tape
  #2 pencil and carbon paper
  scriber
  scrap piece of copper
  soft rags
  rubber gloves
  2 wooden clothespins
  bicarbonate of soda
  old newspaper
  newsprint pad at least 14 by 14 inches
  2 artist's brushes, #2 and #5
  1 pint of asphaltum varnish
  a glass or plastic dish or tray, 1 inch deep by 13 inches wide for etching
  1 pint nitric acid
  a 13-inch dish for cleaning varnish from copper
  a $\frac{1}{2}$ gallon plastic container
  1 quart turpentine

STEP 1. Draw a 5-inch circle with your compass, in the middle of a 12-inch square piece of tracing paper. If you do not wish to use the design shown here, pick any design that will fit into the 5-inch circle and leave $\frac{3}{4}$-inch to 1-inch space on each side of it inside the circle.

Now trace the design in the middle of this circle on the tracing paper.

STEP 2. Clean the copper with cleaning fluid and remove tarnish with the steel wool. File the edges of the copper smooth. Now find the middle of the copper disc by laying the tracing paper on the disc so that they fit exactly and tapping the middle point of the circle with a center punch. This point will be important for this and all later work.

Using the center point, scratch a 5-inch circle on the copper with your dividers. Paint the inside of this circle with white tempera paint. When the tempera is dry, place a sheet of carbon paper face down, over the painted circle. Place the tracing paper, with the design face up, on top of the carbon paper on the copper disc, so that the outside edges match exactly, and tape the paper to the disc.

Now transfer the design to the painted copper by drawing, with a #2 pencil, over the design on the tracing paper. Use firm pressure but do not gouge. Remove the tracing and carbon papers. A clear copy of your design will show on the painted copper. Using the scriber shown in Illus. 14, you will scratch the whole design into the copper. It is wise at this point to practice with the scriber on a scrap piece of copper first to get the feel of the scriber and discover what pressure is needed to make a sharp cut and still be able to round a curve easily. (In fact, whenever an operation appears difficult or strange to you, it is always good practice to go through the operation with a scrap test.) After you have scribed the design into the copper, wash the copper with water and wipe dry with a soft rag. You are now ready to start the etching process.

STEP 3. You must follow some important

safety precautions for working with acids. Wear rubber gloves. Use wooden flat-edged clothespins for stirring the solution and lifting the copper. Always pour *acid into* water, never water into acid. Have some bicarbonate of soda (baking soda) handy, to sprinkle on spills for neutralization.

Clean both sides of the disc with fine steel wool. Then clean both sides with the cleaning fluid. Now handle the copper disc at the edges to prevent any dirtying of the metal. Dirty or oily metal will not take a protective coating well. Cover your workbench with several thicknesses of newspaper to keep your bench from being dirtied. Place a clean sheet of blank newsprint on the newspaper on your workbench. Place the copper, with the design facing down, on newsprint. With the #5 brush, paint the entire back side of the disc with asphaltum varnish. Touch up void spots (they will show up as red spots) with more varnish. Place two sheets of newsprint paper over the fresh varnish. These will stick to the copper.

Wait 5 to 10 minutes until the varnish has partly set and turn the disc over so that the design is now on top. Proceed to paint the top surface and the design. Remember, all the parts of the copper that are covered with the

varnish will be protected from the etch. After etching, the exposed parts (the unpainted lines) will appear and feel like a depression, and the protected portions will seem to be raised. Illus. 16 shows the appearance of the asphaltum painted copper. Note that the portions of the design that appear dark will be unetched. Also note that the outer edge of the disc has about $\frac{1}{4}$ inch asphaltum running over on to the newsprint. This helps protect the edges from the etching solution. Use the #2 brush for fine work and the #5 brush for the remainder. Allow the asphaltum to dry overnight. Trim away any excess newsprint when dry.

The next operation should be performed in a kitchen or basement sink. Place the etching tray on the drainboard of the sink, and use the sink for rinsing.

Prepare an etching solution as follows: Measure the number of cups of water it takes to fill the etching tray $\frac{1}{2}$ inch deep with water. Wearing gloves, and being very careful, add $\frac{1}{3}$ cup of nitric acid to the water in the tray for every cup of water used. Mix thoroughly with a wooden clothespin. Place the cover back on the nitric acid bottle and store it in a safe place.

Then, slide the plate carefully into the etching tray that contains the nitric acid solution. Cover the tray with a piece of cardboard or an inverted cardboard box. Etching will be complete within $1\frac{1}{2}$ to 5 hours. After $1\frac{1}{2}$ hours, remove the plate from the solution, by lifting it to the edge of the tray with clothespins and then picking it up in your fingers. Rinse it in the sink very thoroughly. Remove one glove and check the depth of etch with

RAISING: How to use a wooden mold with a recess to hammer dents into a piece of metal. As a start, make four impressions $\frac{3}{4}''$ from the edge of the plate (Illus. 17).

your fingernail. Be careful not to disturb the protective varnish during this test. A good etch will be $\frac{1}{3}$ to $\frac{1}{2}$ the thickness of the copper. Put back and continue to etch until the depth you want is reached.

When you have the depth of etch you want, rinse the plate thoroughly again and dry it. Pour the acid solution into a half gallon plastic container, and store it for future use. Remove the asphaltum varnish by placing the dried plate in a tray containing turpentine. Allow it to remain in the turpentine until the varnish and the newsprint on the bottom come off easily. Work with rubber gloves to protect your hands, and use soft rags. If turpentine does not remove all the varnish, use steel wool to clean the last bits away. The plate is now ready for shaping.

Raising

One of the most commonly practiced techniques in metalcrafting is shaping a metal by hammering it against a mold or block in order to raise part of it in relation to the starting material. The additional tools you will need are:

a 12-inch mold with a 10-inch hollow
a wooden mallet (Illus. 9f)
a rawhide (buckskin) mallet (Illus. 9e)

STEP 1. Turn the plate to the position you would like the design to be when you mount handles on the right and left. Draw a pencil line through the middle of the disc horizontally. This will be your reference point later for mounting the handle properly. Place the disc over the mold so that the edge of the disc and the edge of the mold correspond exactly. Hit the copper with the round end of the wooden mallet at the four points of the compass and at the outer edge of the mold. This aligns the disc in the mold. Illus. 17 shows the plate in the mold with the lines for centering the handles and with the four impressions in the copper. Note also the angle at which the mallet strikes the metal.

STEP 2. Continue to hammer the copper with light blows, but now move it continuously in one direction. Each blow should slightly overlap the previous blow. Go round a number of times with light blows rather than trying to raise the edge in one go-round. The middle of the plate does not require hammering. Working the edge will give you the depth you want.

In working, the plate may tend to buckle. If it does, turn it upside down, place it on a flat surface and straighten the edges with the rawhide mallet. The proper way to strike with this tool is to hit so that the mallet comes down *flat* at the bottom of the stroke.

After the completion of the hollowing, pits and scratches can also be smoothed out with the rawhide mallet, by placing the spot over a hardwood block held in a vise and hammering.

The plate is now ready for handles.

Making and Mounting Handles

This part of the project will demonstrate the method of joining known as riveting. Additional tools and materials required are:

> 2 pieces of copper strip, ¾ inch wide by 14 inches long, 16 gauge
> round dowel rod ⅝-inch in diameter by 4 inches long
> a drill with a ⅛-inch twist drill
> 4 rivets of copper ⅛-inch in diameter and ⅜ inch long
> a ball-peen hammer for riveting (a riveting set is optional)
> a side-cutting pliers

STEP 1. Straighten and flatten the copper strips with the rawhide mallet. Place a strip under the dowel with 3 inches extended and bend the strip around the dowel. Work at a slight angle, making four turns spaced ⅛ inch between turns. When the turning is finished, cut the ends off, to be equal in length. Form the handles to the shape of the plate bottom by placing the handle in the mold you used for the plate and hammering to shape. Make two handles in this manner.

STEP 2. Place the plate and one handle in the mold, with the handle underneath the edge of the plate. Extend the inner portion of the turned part of the handle ½ inch from the edge of the plate. Center the handle in relation to the pencil line through the center that you made in the raising operation. See Illus. 19.

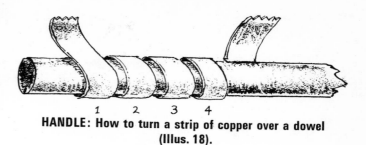

HANDLE: How to turn a strip of copper over a dowel (Illus. 18).

Now scribe a mark ½ inch from the inner edge of the plate and in line with the center of one of the strips of the handle. With your center punch, dent both the plate and handle at this spot. Drill a ⅛-inch hole in the plate and handle at these dent marks. File the burr caused by drilling. Place the handle under the plate with the holes matching and insert a rivet with the round head up.

STEP 3. Prepare a rivet set by holding the round end of a rivet against a hardwood block and striking the rivet to make an indentation in the block (Illus. 20). Then take the plate and handle with the rivet inserted, turn it upside down and place the head of the rivet in the block you have just prepared. Press the plate and handle as close together as you can. Cut the rivet so that ⅛ inch protrudes. Use your

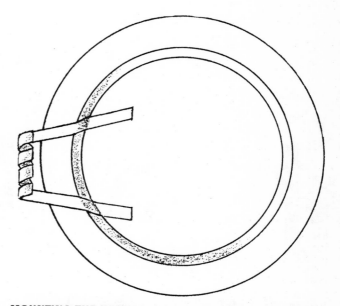

MOUNTING THE HANDLE: Diagram of how the handle looks underneath the plate. Drill holes before mounting (Illus. 19).

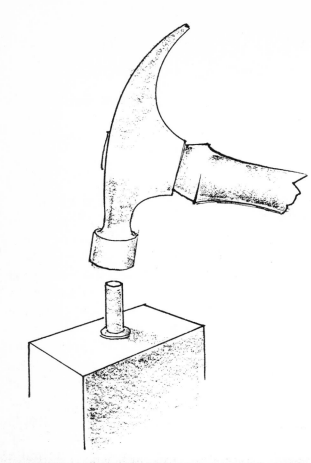

PREPARING A RIVET SET: With a hammer and rivet make an indentation in a wood block. This will become the rivet set (Illus. 20).

side-cutting pliers for this. Now spread the rivet by striking it with the flat side of the ball-peen hammer. Illus. 21 shows the steps taken in riveting when a rivet set is used. If you do not have a set you will not be able to round the rivet finally, but this may not matter to you. Care with the ball end of the hammer should give you a neat finish anyway.

Place the tray with one side of the handle riveted, back into the mold, line up the handle so that it is parallel to the side. The second side should be equal in distance from the guide line to the first. Scribe and punch as for the first side. Remove from the mold, and drill a hole through both plate and handle at the same time. Rivet as before. Repeat the whole operation for the second handle.

Finishing the Plate

The finishing operation is required to bring out the best in the piece you have made. It always starts with polishing.

Additional Materials:
   coarse steel wool
   jeweler's rouge
   fine pumice
   liver of sulphur
   clear lacquer

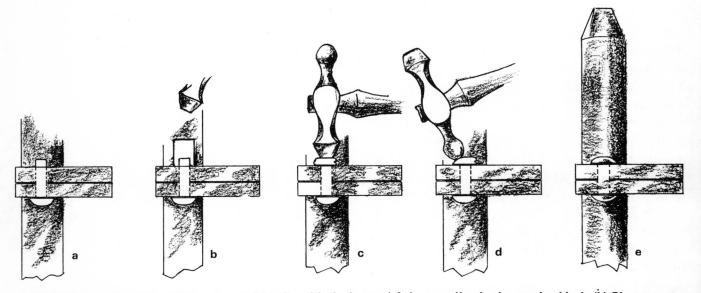

RIVET STEPS: (a) Rivet through the plate and handle with the bottom of rivet nestling in the wooden block. (b) Rivet set compressing the two parts together. (c) "Upsetting" the rivet by hammering. (d) Rounding rivet with ball-peen hammer. (e) Shaping rivet with the rivet snap (Illus. 21).

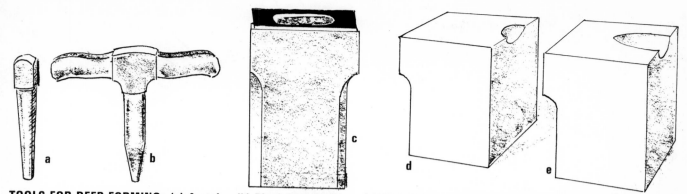

TOOLS FOR DEEP FORMING: (a) A stake. (b) Planishing hammer. (c)(d)(e) Different molds for raising and shaping (Illus. 22).

STEP 1. Take out the deep scratches and marks with coarse steel wool. Follow this with the fine steel wool. To obtain a high lustre, rub with jeweler's rouge or fine pumice on a soft rag. To protect the metal from tarnishing and to maintain its brightness, it must be coated with a clear lacquer or constantly waxed.

STEP 2. A long time ago some craftsman found that he could help nature along in the tarnishing process, and he produced results that outdid in beauty the natural ageing process. This so-called antiquing is a process in which the metal is treated with a solution of liver of sulphur (potassium sulphide). Because of the irregularities of surface produced in etching, the copper is affected unequally by the solution. When subsequent polishing is done, the effect is that of a beautifully aged piece of metalware.

The process is simple. Dissolve a pea-size lump of liver of sulphur (obtained from your craft dealer or drugstore) in $\frac{1}{2}$ cup of hot water. Rub this on to the copper surface with a soft rag. Allow it to dry. Polish with fine steel wool, pumice or rouge. Experiment for effects. The process can be repeated as often as desired until you obtain the effect you want.

Now that you have seen how gratifying metalcrafting can be you will want to be able to tackle other, and perhaps more intricate projects. A brief description of other techniques and tools, and the bibliography in the back of the book should help you.

Deep Forming

The tools shown in Illus. 22, are those used for forming bowls, cups and other deep objects. The hammering principle is the same as you used in making the plate. The pewter ware of Illus. 7 was made with tools such as these.

Chasing

Designs can be placed on metal by two other popular methods, namely chasing and engraving. Chasing is a process in which a tool pattern is repeated by tapping a shaped tool with light strokes of a chasing hammer. The tool is moved along the work and the result is a design made by the repeated pattern. Illus. 23 shows some of the tools and a schematic of the chasing stroke. The bracelet in Illus. 1 was decorated by chasing.

Joining by Soldering and Brazing

Soldering and brazing are used to join parts together in jewelry and in metalcraft work. Soft soldering uses lead-tin solder, melting in the range of 400° F. Heating of the part is accomplished with a soldering iron for smaller parts, or a torch for larger parts.

Brazing is a process similar to soldering. It uses an alloy of silver and copper for joining, and a torch for heating. Brazing finds its greatest use in jewelry and precious metalwork. Illus. 25 shows soldering irons and a very handy propane gas torch. (Also see Nail Sculpture or Stained Glass Crafting.)

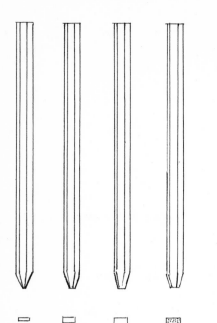

TOOLS FOR CHASING (above) illustrate some of the shapes and designs available (Illus. 23a).

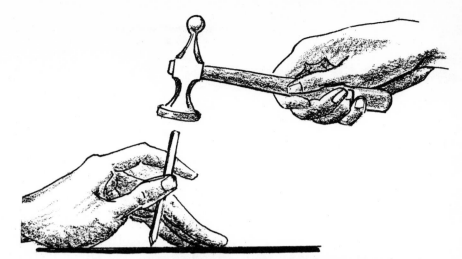

CHASING: How to hold the chasing tool at the correct angle of stroke. Repeated strokes make the design (Illus. 23b).

ENGRAVING: A variety of tools are available for incising lines. The stroke is a push with the hand in the position shown (Illus. 24).

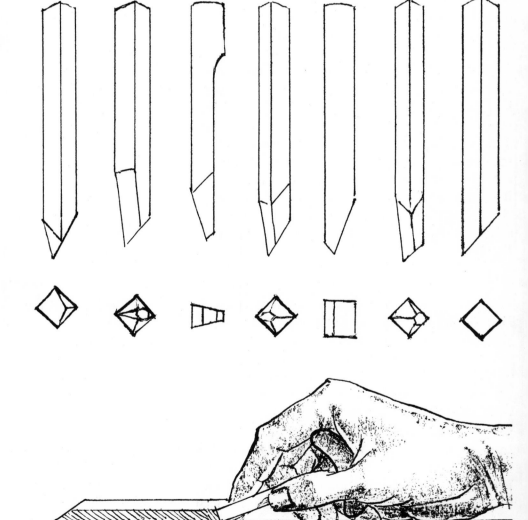

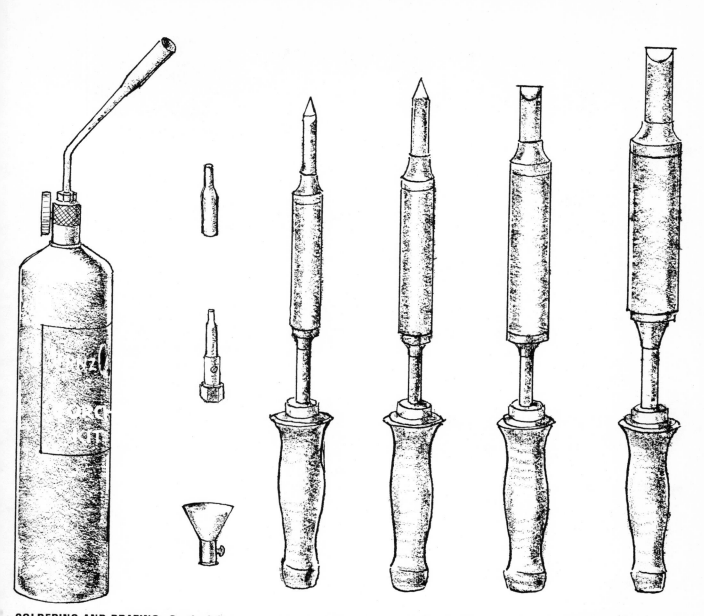

SOLDERING AND BRAZING: On the left are a propane torch and several shaped tips. This torch is used for both soldering and brazing. On the right are several shapes and sizes of tools used exclusively for soft soldering (Illus. 25).

Engraving

Decorations made by the engraving method allow you to give vent to your artistic inclinations. The design is carved into the metal with tools such as are shown in Illus. 24. Illus. 5 shows a bowl with engraved decoration.

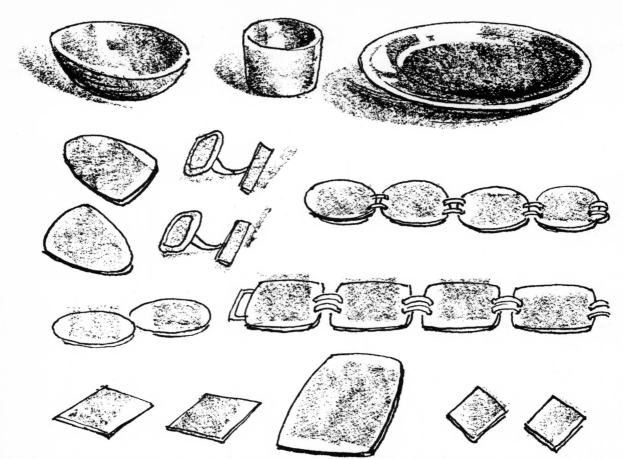

PRE-FORMED COPPER SHAPES: As a beginner, you can start enamelling faster if you purchase the shapes you want to decorate—bowls, cups, plates, cuff links, bracelets, earrings or pendants.

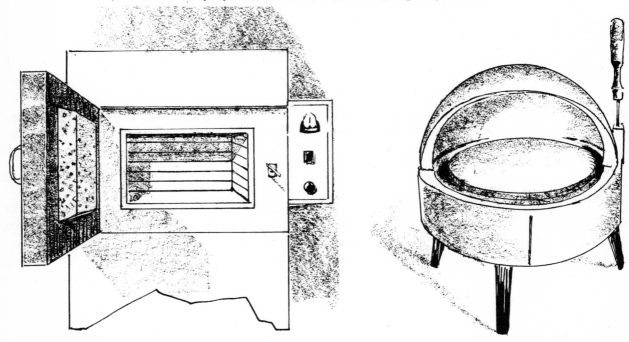

KILNS: (Left) An electric kiln that is ample for enamelling and (right) a typical domed kiln.

ENAMELLING

Enamelling is the technique by which glass colored with metallic oxides is fused on to a metal surface. While many craftsmen make their own metal shapes, *pre-formed copper shapes* are available in such a wide variety of forms (cuff links, earrings, pendants, bowls, ash trays, boxes, trays and so on) that these are recommended for all but the most experienced enamellist.

Metals suitable for enamelling are copper (the least expensive and most widely employed), silver, gold, aluminum, pinchbeck, brass and stainless steel. Until you are very experienced, it is best to confine your efforts to pre-formed copper shapes.

The cardinal rule of enamelling is cleanliness. *Enamel powder* will not adhere to any surface that is not absolutely clean and grease-free, so the first step is to clean meticulously the surface to be enamelled. A new, inexpensive and *safe acid compound* is now available as a substitute for the traditional nitric acid cleaning solution. It is a dry acid compound for pickling, sold under various trade names. Add one tablespoon of it to each cup of water in a large glass container (always, always add acid to water).

Heat the copper shape for 10 seconds or so in a *kiln*. (You will need a large one for ceramics work or you can get a small domed kiln as illustrated here.) This will loosen scale and burn away grease. Let it cool (never add a hot metal object to the acid solution or you may be seriously burned and the metal will surely warp). Immerse the metal in the pickling solution, and leave it there until the surface is pink, clean and shiny. Remove it with *tongs* (you must not touch the clean surface with

Tongs

your fingers, which will deposit grease on the surface) and rinse it under cold running water.

If the metal surface is not completely clean, or if you want it to show through transparent enamels, you may polish it further by rubbing with *fine steel wool* or emery paper. Wipe again with a soft cloth, and then with vinegar or household ammonia to make the surface alkaline.

If you are working with children, a solution of 1 cup of vinegar mixed with $1\frac{1}{2}$ tablespoons of salt is an effective substitute for the acid solution, though acid will do a more thorough job of cleaning.

In case the new dry acid compound is unavailable, here is the traditional acid mixture: Add 1 part of *nitric acid* to 5 parts of water in a large, heat-resistant glass container. Heat and cool the metal as before, and immerse it in the solution. Swish it around with your tongs until it is clean. Rinse and polish as before. You may store the acid solution, tightly covered, until it turns brown with dissolved metal.

Characteristics of Enamels

There are three different kinds of enamel: the opaque, the transparent, and the opalescent. Most often used are the opaque enamels. Because they completely cover the color of the metal over which they are fired, they are

Written especially for this volume by Jennifer Mellen

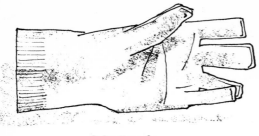

Asbestos glove

especially suitable for enamelling on copper. Since transparent enamels allow the surface underneath to show through, they are used over more precious metals, such as gold and silver, as well as over opaque enamels. Opalescent enamels are seldom used because they are quite scarce. They have an iridescent glow rather than the clear, glassy quality of the transparent enamels.

Ready-to-use enamels are available in various forms, but the best way to buy them is in powder ground to 80-mesh (the powder will pass through a strainer with 80 square openings to the square inch). Enamel powder ground to 80-mesh is used for nearly every enamelling technique, with the exception of the "painting," or Limoges technique, which requires enamel ground to 200- or 250-mesh. Although unwashed powders are less expensive, no saving really results in the end as up to 50% of the powder is lost in the washing process.

Enamels also have three firing characteristics: soft-firing enamels mature at 1400 degrees F., medium-firing enamels at 1450–1500 degrees F., and hard-firing enamels mature at 1600 degrees F. You will need *kiln cones* to tell you how hot your kiln is. Although some colors (black, white and beige especially) are available in all three categories, most colors are *either* soft-, medium- or hard-firing. Soft-firing enamels burn away sooner than do the more durable hard-firing enamels (which are generally used for counter-enamelling), while the medium-firing enamels are suitable for most purposes. The only way to determine the firing characteristics of each color you buy is to fire a small test sample on a scrap of clean copper and note the results on the label of the jar in which the enamel is to be stored.

The test sample is also an invaluable guide to the exact color of the enamel powder. This is very important because one of enamelling's cardinal rules is that you cannot mix colors as you can oil or watercolors. Yellow and blue enamel will *not* make green, but will remain separate and distinct from one another after firing. Hundreds of color gradations are available, however, so you will not find this a disadvantage if you have made a test sample which you can use to pick out an exact shade at a glance from your stock. For each enamel color, you should also add the manufacturer's number to the label giving the firing characteristics so that when you re-order you will be sure to get the same color. Manufacturers frequently change the descriptive name of the colors, but they always retain the original number for each one.

Cleanliness cannot be overemphasized. Keep your enamel powders tightly capped at all times, for the tiniest speck of dust or grease will loom large on the surface of a finished project. Should transparent colors appear muddy after firing, you will have to clean the powder: Place it in a glass jar. Fill this with ordinary tap water, and siphon off or carefully pour out the water into another jar. Repeat the process until all the impurities have been removed and the water runs clear. Dry the powder on blotting paper thoroughly before rebottling. You can save yourself this tedious chore by keeping each color separate and away from breezes and stray dust at all times.

A Sample Project

Before commencing a complicated project, make a small sample first. This will save you hours of indecision later on, and the grief of spoiling a project because this simple precaution was not taken. These samples need not be discarded, for with the addition of a jump ring and a chain they make handsome pendants or key chain fobs for gifts.

Adhering and Firing

After cleaning the metal to be enamelled, coat the surface with an adhesive solution so that the enamel powder will adhere evenly. A *gum tragacanth* solution is usually employed. To prepare this, soak the lumps or flakes of gum tragacanth overnight in water.

On the following day, cook the solution (be sure there is enough water so it will not burn) over low heat until it becomes more fluid and the gum dissolves completely. When cool, dilute the mixture with tap water until it is quite thin and strain it through a 200-mesh sieve (a strainer with 200 square openings to the square inch).

When you apply the adhesive solution to the metal surface it should be as clear and fluid as water. Ready-to-use adhesive is available commercially, and you may find that the higher cost is balanced by its time-saving qualities.

Using a soft, clean brush, paint the adhesive over the surface to be enamelled. Sift the enamel powder over the tacky surface through an *80-mesh strainer*, covering the surface evenly but not too thickly. Two thin coats are always better than one thick coat in enamelling, and even the simplest one-color objects must be sprinkled and fired several times. Build up the layer of enamel powder slightly at the edges, however, as this is where it tends to burn away more.

Before you can fire this base coat, you must let the object dry completely, until every trace of water has evaporated, or it will bubble and crack the enamel coating while it is in the kiln. Either hold the object on your *enamelling fork* just in front of the open door of the hot kiln (always wear *asbestos gloves* when using the kiln) or dry the piece in a low oven for 25 to 30 minutes. When working with children always use the latter method.

If you dry it just outside the kiln, almost immediately you will see a little cloud of steam rising round the object. This is the water evaporating. Pull the object away instantly or it will overheat.

To fire, put the object inside the kiln on a *firing stand* on *stilts*, using an enamelling fork and gloves. If your kiln has a glass door, you will see the powdery surface begin to change color and liquefy.

When it becomes smooth and brilliant, and the metal is heated to a light red (this should take no less than 2 and never more than 4 minutes, depending on whether you have used a soft-, medium-, or hard-firing enamel), the firing process is complete.

Enamelling fork

Remove the object with your fork, and leave it on an *asbestos slab or stone* to cool in a draught-free area. The surface will continue to change colors until it is cool enough to be touched with bare hands. Then it will show the color it will always retain. This is one of the most interesting aspects of enamelling, for the gradual color changes are quite beautiful.

If the surface has dents or holes, you can assume that you sprinkled too little powder on the surface the first time. If the surface appears granular, you under-fired.

It is always better to under-fire than to over-fire, for the under-firing is easily corrected, but there is no solution for over-firing. Continue to sprinkle and fire until the surface is smooth and even, and you are satisfied with its appearance. Do not build up so many layers, however, that the enamel is overly thick and puts an unbearable strain on the metal. File the oxidized edges of the metal with a *metal file* and polish the enamel surface with a *carborundum rubbing stone* under running water to complete the project.

Since metal expands and contracts at a different rate than the enamel coating, it is always wise and often essential to coat both sides of the metal with enamel, to seal and reinforce it. This is called counter-enamelling. When in doubt as to whether or not to counter-enamel, do so. Always choose a hard-firing enamel for the underside coating, since it will have to withstand as many firings as will be necessary for the top coat.

To counter-enamel, after you have finished sprinkling the top of the object, turn it over on a firing stand very carefully, touching the clean surface as little as possible. (Be sure your stand has little metal stilts or points on which to balance the very edges of the object.) Remove any finger marks with vinegar or ammonia before painting the surface with adhesive solution and applying the enamel, and do not forget to allow the enamel to dry completely before firing. Place the object upside down on its stand into the kiln and fire

as usual. If you should hear a cracking sound while an object is being fired, simply leave it in the kiln until the surface heals. The cracking is a result of the metal contracting.

There are many decorative techniques in enamelling. Try them when you have become familiar with the medium, and have some experience with simple techniques such as applying colors through stencils, using sgraffito (scratching a design through unfired enamel on top of a contrasting fired enamel surface), and using commercial chunks and threads of enamel barely fused to the surface. Never attempt to be precise, except in cloisonné (see below) for the colors are simply not easy to control. The 200-mesh powders mixed with adhesive solution can be painted or pushed into shapes and delicate patterns on the surface (as in the Limoges technique), but this is a demanding and difficult process suitable only for experts. Explore the many relatively simple possibilities first.

Cloisonné

Derived from the French *cloison* (cell), cloisonné is the only technique in enamelling

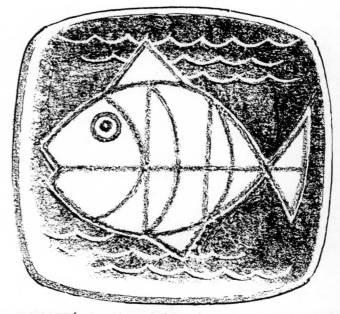

CLOISONNÉ: In this technique you separate the enamel colors with wire barriers, instead of allowing them to flow together.

CHAMPLEVÉ: Less exact than cloisonné, the champlevé process starts with the etching out of little depressions in the metal. These are filled with enamel and fired until colors are fused to the metal.

that permits precise separation of enamel colors, which if not "restricted" tend to flow together during the firing process. Wire barriers fused to the metal-and-enamel surface in the cloisonné technique prevent this. Cloisonné was used for thousands of years by the Chinese, particularly during the Ming Dynasty.

While intricate cloisonné designs are very beautiful, your first attempts should be restricted to simple designs and few colors until you become skilled. After counter-enamelling a base coat of enamel on to the object (a brooch, for example), glue on fine silver wire in the shape of your design. Tweezers or a jig (see Wirecrafting, page 206) are useful to bend the wire.

Fire briefly so that the wires sink into the first coat of enamel as it melts slightly. When the object is again cool, the wires will be firmly affixed and ready to receive enamel powder mixed with a thin solution of gum tragacanth thinned with water. Add as little binder to the enamel powder as possible to avoid lengthy drying periods.

When each "cell" has been filled to the brim with enamel pap, set the object aside until it is thoroughly dry, at which time you will fire it at 1500 degrees F. for approximately 3 minutes. Usually the enamel will shrink below the surface of the wires during the first firing process, so repeat the procedure if necessary. You may slightly overfill the cells

the second time, as excess enamel can be filed away after the object is cool.

A final polishing with a carborundum rubbing stone is necessary; a glass brush will polish the wire and enamel surface to a higher gloss.

Many variations are possible in cloisonné: the areas around the cells may be filled in as well, or the cells may be left completely empty, the wires forming the only design.

Champlevé

In order to create a less precise separation of colors than that achieved with cloisonné, depressions are etched out of a metal surface with acid and then filled with enamel. This is called champlevé.

After the design has been painted on to the metal surface with asphalt paint, immerse the object in a glass container filled with a 50/50 solution of water and nitric acid. (Always add acid to water.) It will take approximately 10 hours to etch away the necessary $\frac{1}{16}$ inch of metal.

After rinsing the etched object in cold running water, apply enamel powder moistened with gum tragacanth mixed with water to the excavations. After the pap has dried, fire the object at 1500 degrees F. for 2 to 4 minutes, or until the enamel "fuses." If the colors do not completely fill the excavations, repeat the application of pap and fire again.

NAIL SCULPTURE

Nail sculpture, a unique yet simple hobby, is sure to provide you with many hours of fun and satisfaction as you make interesting compositions from the humble nail. How to bend nails in almost any shape and fasten them to each other by soldering with an iron is explained in the easy-to-follow directions here.

Nails can be used in ways that release them from their customary role and convert them into attractive articles for home or office decorations. Any type nail can be used, providing it is free of rust, grease, and other dirt. We will only use iron nails for the sculptures described here, however. The equipment you need for sculpturing with nails is available in most hardware and department stores, plus many arts and crafts shops.

Tools for Soldering the Nails

To connect the iron nails so they stay together permanently, you will need soft, acid-core solder. Other types of solder are good only on metals other than iron, such as copper and brass. You can form a stronger bond by applying rosin flux to the nail surface: it removes any oxides (the substances that form naturally when iron is exposed to air) which may be on the nail. Solder without rosin flux is not potent enough to do a good job, and a strong bond cannot be formed unless the oxide is removed.

To solder nails together, there are three different tools to choose from: a soldering iron, soldering torch, or for best results, a large butane burner. Although one source of heat will do the job adequately, for very large projects two sources may make the job easier. You should have at least two pairs of pliers and a small vise for holding to aid in bending and twisting the nails. Certain projects may even require the assistance of another person: he can hold the nails while you use two hands for twisting and soldering.

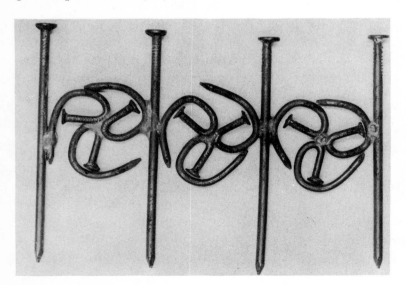

BENT NAILS AND STRAIGHT NAILS are soldered together with a soldering iron to make sculptures you never dreamed of before.

Condensed from the book, "Nail Sculpture" by Elmar Gruber | © 1968 by Sterling Publishing Co., Inc., New York

A nonflammable surface is necessary to use under all the projects you do involving soldering. In many cases, a firebrick or ordinary brick will be sufficient. For higher intensity heating, however, use an asbestos mat $\frac{3}{8}$ inch thick placed on top of several bricks to protect the work area. The mat can also serve as a surface to lay out and design your sculptures.

A hammer and file to smooth off rough edges completes the list of required tools, except for the nails, of course. Keep your work area well lighted, and keep your tools in a special storage place close to the work area. After a tool is used, return it to its proper place before using another tool. These precautions may seem a bother, but they may also prevent a serious burn that could result from carelessly handling the hot tools.

The Soldering Process

The actual process of soldering is relatively easy. First, clean the areas you intend to join to remove any oxide which would prevent a good union. Heat these areas with whichever tool you are using—the soldering iron, torch

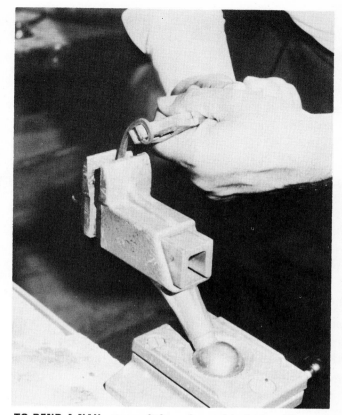

TO BEND A NAIL, secure it in a vise and twist it with a pair of pliers.

THE TOOLS YOU WILL NEED are assembled here. Shown are a butane burner, an electric soldering torch, nails, solder, rosin flux, pliers and a vise, laid out on an asbestos mat.

or burner—and dab the heated portion in rosin flux. Heat it again slowly, increasing the heat little by little and melting the solder over the joint. If the tips of the soldering iron itself become coated with solder, file the excess off and then dip it in the flux.

When the project has been soldered and sculptured to your satisfaction, it must be cleaned of excess greasy solder in a hot detergent, using a soft brush. This will prevent the acid in the rosin flux from rusting the nails. Colorless varnish can then be brushed on for added lustre.

Paper Weight

Before you begin any project, be sure to look at the soldering iron's cord and plug to see that they are not frayed or cut. Plug the iron in and test its heating capacity, making sure that all parts of the iron work properly. Make a general check of your other tools: be sure the mat and bricks are correctly placed.

An easy piece to put together for your first project is a paper weight, made to look like

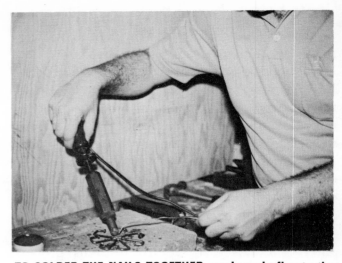

TO SOLDER THE NAILS TOGETHER, apply rosin flux to the areas to be joined. Then heat the solder with the iron and let it flow over the joint.

the rays of the sun. The procedure will allow you to learn the proper soldering methods at the same time you are making a useful object.

Take 19 nails and lay them out in a circular sun-ray fashion, but do not allow the tips to touch. Hold the butane torch over the nail

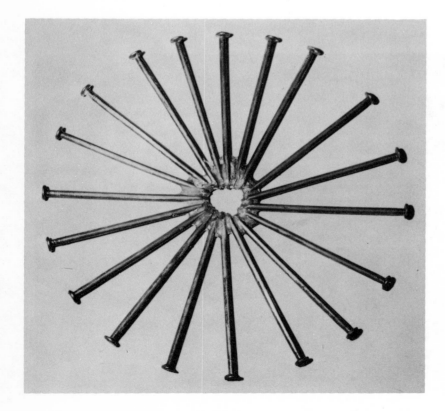

THIS PAPER WEIGHT is a simple design. It would make a good project for a beginner, as it offers much practice in soldering.

points and heat them for a brief moment. Next, with the pliers, pick up a nail, dip it in rosin flux, and return the nail to its place in the circle. Repeat this process systematically until all 19 nails have been treated with rosin flux. Then, using the torch again, slowly increase the heat, and melt the solder over the tips of the nails. Make sure that the solder falls between each of the nails for a good bond.

Allow the solder to cool for several minutes and then use your file to smooth away any prominent lumps. Dab some rosin flux over the area which was heated and wipe it down with a cloth. Using fine steel wool or sandpaper, rub the nails to a smooth and shiny finish. Finally, place one or two coats of clear varnish over the nails, to keep them looking as polished as they do now. The finished product is heavy enough to make an excellent paper weight for your home or office.

Lettering

Wherever we go, we are surrounded by the written word—in directions, signs, names and numbers. The lettering of the messages we read makes a big difference in the way they impress us. It is therefore extremely important to make a sign as attractive as possible, without distorting the message.

Letters which are both attractive and readable can be sculptured with nails and solder. Naturally, the easiest way is to form the letters with straight nails. After you gain some experience, you may want to try to make

NAILS CAN BE BENT to almost any degree, to form letters that are more curved than the ones below.

letters by bending the nails into the necessary curves, using a pair of pliers and the vise.

Use a very small amount of solder when connecting nails to make letters. If you use too much, it will detract from the neat appearance you want for the letter, and require additional work when you file away the excess.

Decorative Holders for Candles

While colorful or oddly shaped candles may have become popular lately, an unusual holder can enhance the appearance of even an ordinary candle, as well as providing a safe, nonflammable container. If your candle is round, you will want to make a round holder for it. The nails must therefore be curved: use a wood dowel to bend the nails around. Before

LETTERS MADE WITH NAILS create unique effects, as the pointed letters here show. They could be used to announce the name of a family over a door or mailbox, or even as the name of the house itself.

THE CANDLESTICK ON THE RIGHT is made of bent nails which were soldered together.

you solder the nails together, bend them all uniformly, according to the design you have chosen, by putting one end in the vise and bending the other end over the dowel with a pair of pliers. When all the nails have been bent, solder them together.

The candle itself can easily be attached to the holder by another nail. Bend the nail to a 90° angle, and solder its head to the holder so that the tip points upward in the center of the holder. Warm the tip of the nail before pushing the candle down on it.

The holder below is a different type: here the candle rests directly on the nails, rather than being encircled by them. Bend a number of nails to an identical shape with the vise and a pair of pliers. Place them in a circle on your nonflammable mat so that their heads touch. Then heat the heads and solder them

NAILS MUST BE CURVED VERY CAREFULLY to ensure that they are all uniform. If the candlestick is level and does not rock, then the nails have been bent the same amount.

together. The most important step when constructing this holder is the bending of the nails: if their curves are not uniform, the holder will wobble—not only an unsightly but also an unsafe characteristic for a candle holder to have.

Dripless candles that burn down the center are best for these two holders which are open at the bottom.

Abstract Designs

Providing instructions for abstract designs is superfluous, as one's imagination is the best guide to an interesting object. Abstract nail sculptures are an inexpensive source of unique gifts for others, as well as decorative objects for your own home. Using nails that have been uniformly bent, design a pattern of geometric

THIS FLAT ABSTRACT NAIL SCULPTURE could be hung on a wall, or used in a practical manner, as a trivet for a hot plate at the table.

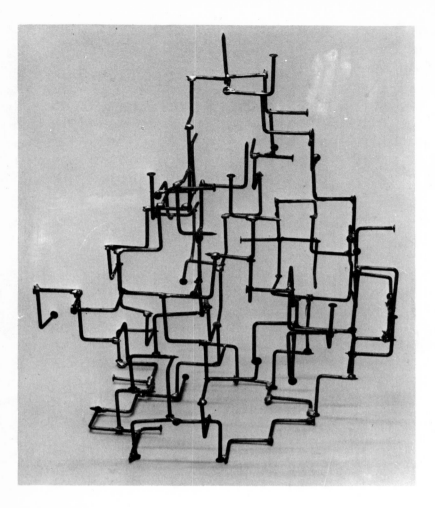

forms. Solder these together and look at the composition. You may decide that it looks fine as it is, or you may want to add more nails to build a more complicated structure. Take care to avoid an excessive use of solder over each joint.

The taller your structure becomes, the more planning you should do to make sure that it is properly balanced if you want it to stand by itself. The base must be wide enough to maintain the weight of the design without the sculpture falling over.

REPOUSSAGE

The French word "repoussage" may scare some people away from this craft—since the name is foreign, some may imagine that all sorts of complicated instructions are involved. Actually, repoussage is the easy craft of embossing on soft metal, using special tools. It is not messy, can be done almost anywhere, and requires only a minimum of equipment. You can make many different objects with an infinite number of designs—no two ever have to be at all alike. Wall plaques, coverings for boxes, name tags for bottles, and even jewelry—all can be made in your own home with just a little practice.

Metal, of course, is the most necessary material. The kind of metal you buy—aluminum, copper, pewter, bronze and brass are the most common—determines the qualities of the finished object. In general, sheet metal not thicker than 0.4 mm. (20 gauge) and preferably 0.1 or 0.2 mm. is best to work with. It is malleable, yet at the same time sturdy enough to withstand the pressure you apply to shape it to your design.

You will need a pair of shears to cut the metal to the size you want. While jewelers' shears make the best cuts because they are made to work with metal, even simple kitchen scissors will do.

A hard rubber mat is necessary. It provides both the resistance and the suppleness necessary for an embossing support.

A basic set of three boxwood modelling tools and various metal styluses will be useful. Practice with some metal scraps to see what kind of lines each tool makes.

A grease pencil will mark a pattern on the metal. It is wise to plan your design with the pencil before embossing, since the lines are easily rubbed out.

A hammer and chisel, while not necessary for your first projects, will be helpful later on when you want to punch holes in the metal, perhaps for a nail or screw. A flat-nosed pliers to bend the metal is another piece of equipment you may want later, when your talent for embossing has progressed.

Before you begin a project, experiment with

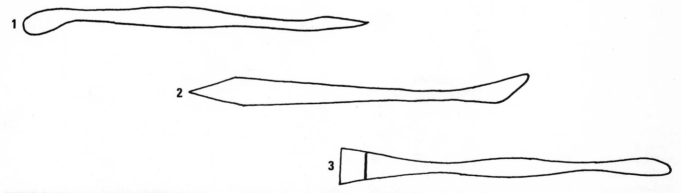

THESE BOXWOOD MODELLING TOOLS are available in art supply and craft shops. Notice that each tool has two different ends which can be used to define a design (Illus. 1).

Condensed from the book, "Repoussage: The Embossing of Metal" by Yves Meriel-Bussy | © 1970 by Sterling Publishing Co., Inc., New York

the metal you plan to use. A sheet of aluminum about 0.1 mm. thick is a wise choice for a beginner, as its thinness makes it easy to work with. Take each of your tools and make lines, circles, loops—all sorts of designs. It is important to get the feel of the metal before you begin any project. Press firmly enough so that your lines show, but not so hard that you break through the metal with your tool. After you have made several lines, turn the sheet over and define the outlines with the pointed end of the No. 2 tool.

A Sunburst

Do you feel confident enough now to make a real design? Practice until you can make pleasing lines, and then make a fancy sunburst to hang in your living room or den. Draw a simple pattern at first, and then later make a more elaborate design, with fancier rays and more decoration on the face.

From a sheet of aluminum approximately 0.1 mm. thick, cut out a 4-inch square. Place this square on a flat hard surface in order to avoid making an impression on the metal,

FROM THE BACK, after turning your practice sheet over, define the outlines more clearly with a pointed tool (Illus. 3).

THIS SUNBURST DESIGN is only one of many designs you can make (Illus. 4).

and trace with a grease pencil the diagonals of the square. Their point of intersection is the middle of the sheet. Measure about 1 inch from this point on each diagonal and use these four points as a guide to mark a circle. Then measure 1 inch from the circle on each diagonal—these will be the sun's rays. Draw in a number of rays to use as a guide for the embossing. Do not worry if you make a mistake because you can erase the pencil easily by rubbing with your finger or a cloth.

Now place the square on your rubber mat. Using the rounded edge of the No. 1 tool, move it in a circular fashion within the outline of the sun, exerting a constant and consistent pressure all the time (Illus. 5). As soon as you have formed a hollowed-out depression, turn the sheet over and define the edges of the repoussage with the sharp end of the No. 2 modelling tool (Illus. 6). Turn the sheet back over again and continue hollowing it out even deeper with the No. 1 tool. Repeat this operation as many times as necessary until you obtain the desired amount of embossing, taking care not to overdo it, thereby weakening the metal.

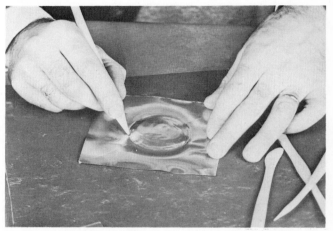

TURN THE SHEET OVER after you have hollowed out the circle. Define the edge of the outline with the pointed end of the modelling tool (Illus. 6).

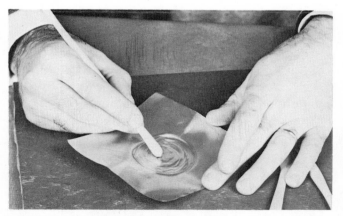

TO BEGIN THE SUNBURST, outline a circle on the metal with a grease pencil. Then, using the rounded end of the No. 1 tool, make circular movements from the middle to the edges of the circle. Keep an even pressure on the tool (Illus. 5).

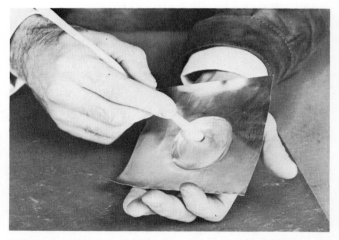

TURN THE METAL right side up again and increase the depth of the hollow. Repeat this procedure until the circle is as deep as you want it (Illus. 7).

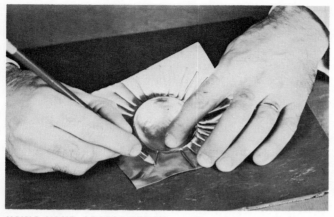

USING YOUR GREASE PENCIL, outline the rays of the sun (Illus. 8).

DEFINE THE OUTLINES of both the circle and the rays. Then, as shown here, flatten the metal between the rays with the flat edge of the No. 3 tool (Illus. 9).

Draw in the rays of the sun with your grease pencil and then work them in the same way as you did the circle. Turn the sheet over and sharpen the edges of the rays with the pointed end of either the No. 1 or No. 2 tool. Flatten the areas around the rays with the wide end of the No. 3 modelling tool. When you are satisfied with the effect, make an interesting sunburst design in the circle. The sunburst shown in color on page A is an elaborate example of what you can make.

Decorative Boxes

Of all the materials which you might choose to cover simple wooden boxes or chests, embossed metal is certainly one of the richest-looking and most attractive. It transforms the

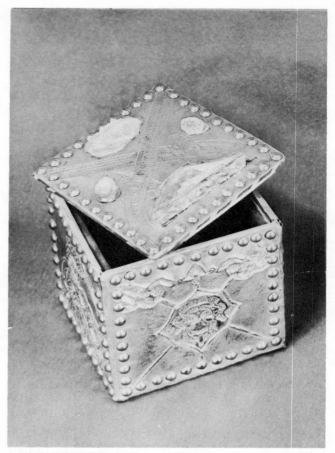

A SIMPLE WOODEN BOX was transformed into this beautiful chest by a covering of embossed metal (Illus. 10).

most commonplace cigar box into a receptacle fit for a king's rings!

The first step in covering any box with metal is to measure all the dimensions of the box and outline this area on a piece of paper. Begin with the lid, adding $\frac{1}{2}$-inch to each end of the two long sides so that you will have an overlap to turn under later. Make the pattern for the sides of the box in the same way, adding $\frac{1}{2}$-inch on each side, top, and bottom. Draw the bottom exactly to fit the dimensions of the box.

On your paper outline, design the pattern you will want to appear on the metal. It can be decorative, with crosses and circles, or picturesque—a nautical scene, perhaps. When the drawing suits you, place the paper pattern on the metal. Using a modelling tool, hard pencil or ballpoint pen, go over your design just hard

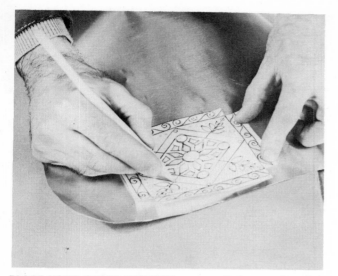

PLACE YOUR PAPER PATTERN on top of the metal and go over the design hard enough to transfer the lines to the metal (Illus. 11).

enough to make the lines appear on the metal. Be sure you have the rubber mat underneath your work. Now cut the metal to the required size, and carefully work with your tools to emboss the metal. After all the pieces have been worked—four sides and the top, plus a flat piece of metal for the bottom—you are ready to cover the box.

Before glueing the metal on the box, test each piece against the box to make sure they will fit exactly. Fold under the $\frac{1}{2}$-inch margins you allowed—or more, if you find your piece too big and if doing so will not spoil the design—and place glue on the wood surfaces to be covered. Epoxy glue is best suited for holding two surfaces such as wood and metal together. While the glue is drying, you may want to staple the metal pieces to the wood with an ordinary stapler, or, for a greater bond and more decoration, use carpet tacks with rounded tops on your box. (See Illus. 10.) Be sure to trim off any sharp tips that protrude into the inside of your box.

Your chest will be even more elegant if you provide it with four little wooden or cork legs which you can varnish. For a really finished look, line the interior with felt or any fabric that will hide the roughness of the folded-over metal.

A Copper Bracelet

By now you are probably amazed at the results of your efforts—you have learned the basic techniques of repoussage, how to make

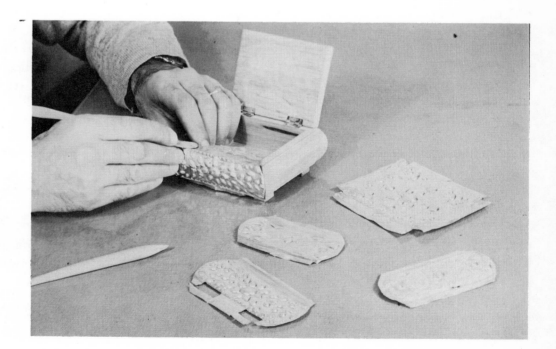

HOLD EACH PIECE OF METAL up to the box to make sure it is the proper size. Then glue it securely to the wood and add carpet tacks if you wish (Illus. 12).

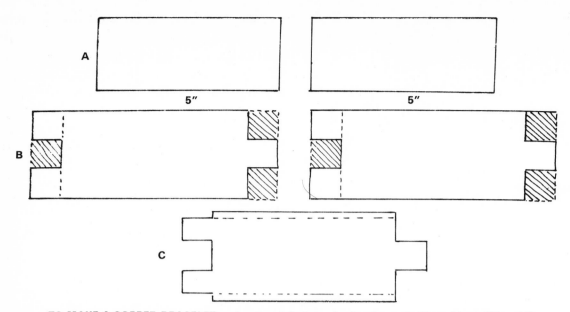

TO MAKE A COPPER BRACELET, cut out metal pieces in the shapes indicated here (Illus. 13).

handsome wall plaques, and you have even covered boxes with embossed metal of your own creation. But you have only begun to explore the decorative possibilities of repoussage, and you are now ready to create three-dimensional objects whose form, as well as design, will be executed by you.

Jewelry is an exciting thing to make, for it calls upon your imagination, taste, and manual skill. A bracelet can be made from two rectangular pieces of thin copper set on two thicker pieces, and attached together by a hinge on one side and a hinge clasp on the other.

Using 0.2 mm. thick copper, cut out two rectangles 5 by 2 inches each. Divide the 2-inch width into three equal parts $\frac{2}{3}$ of an inch wide, and measure in from each end $\frac{2}{3}$ of an inch.

Mark these areas with your grease pencil, as in Illus. 13 B. Cut out the shaded areas. With the point of a metal stylus, trace a light continuous line $\frac{1}{10}$ inch in, using a ruler as a guide. Heat these edges *slightly* to make them more malleable, and then use your pliers to fold the $\frac{1}{10}$-inch strips over almost completely. These edges will serve as grooves to hold the embossed copper sheets you will now make.

From a sheet of copper not more than 0.1 mm. thick, cut out two rectangles 4 by $1\frac{3}{4}$ inches. To give them a patina, heat them red hot and wipe off the coat of oxidation. Cool. Decorate these sheets of thin copper with repoussage, according to your taste. The four designs in Illus. 14 are suggestions for embossing.

DESIGNS to emboss on a copper bracelet (Illus. 14).

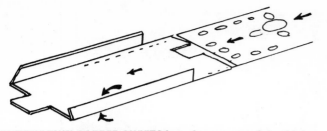

PUT THE THIN COPPER SHEETS into the grooves of the thicker sheets and close the grooves completely with a pliers (Illus. 15).

Once you have completed the repoussage, slide these pieces into the grooves that you made on the 0.2 mm.-thick pieces (Illus. 15) and close the grooves over completely with the pliers. These decorated pieces should be shorter than the base sheets by approximately the length of the notches.

Now you must join the two sections of the bracelet together. First, fit the two pieces together in the notches you cut out earlier. Begin by heating the ends of these sections to make the copper more malleable; then, using a pliers, carefully roll the ends round a nail as shown in Illus. 16. You will thus be able to form hinge rings without taking the risk of flattening the metal. Once the operation is finished, remove the nail.

To form the sections into an arc, shape them round a bottle or tin-can. Join them to each other by putting a copper rod through the hinge rings on one of the ends. This copper rod should be bent into tiny rings at each of its ends (Illus. 17).

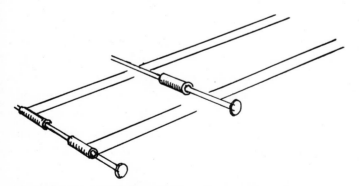

ROLL THE CUT-OUT ENDS of the copper base around a nail, to form rings for the hinge of the bracelet. After rolling the ends, remove the nail (Illus. 16).

Make the clasp on the hinge on the other end by inserting a sliding rod (Illus. 18), this time forming a tiny ring on only *one* of the ends of the rod. With a chisel and hammer, punch a small hole near the edge of one of the sections of the bracelet as shown on the bracelet in Illus. 18. A little chain fastened in this hole and in the ring of the sliding rod will secure the clasp.

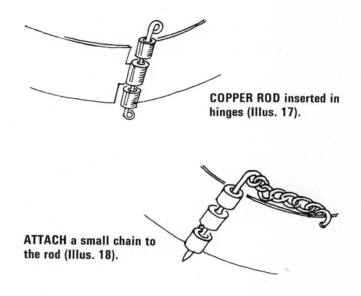

COPPER ROD inserted in hinges (Illus. 17).

ATTACH a small chain to the rod (Illus. 18).

Coloring the Metal

Beautiful colors can be created in the metals you use by a variety of techniques. Heating copper, for example, not only makes it more malleable, but also, depending upon the intensity of the heat and the duration of the exposure, the copper undergoes a color change. It passes progressively from a fiery red to deeper hues, with a whole succession of intermediate tints.

A Bunsen gas burner is ideal for this type of heating, where you are passing the metal in and out of the flame. Be sure to use a heat-resistant base such as an asbestos mat during your heating. Wipe the copper with a clean rag after it cools.

COLORED METAL: This was heated in a Bunsen burner to color it before it was embossed (Illus. 19).

COLORING THE METAL: Hold with a pliers and pass it through the flame. Experiment to determine how long you should heat the metal to achieve various colors (Illus. 20).

THE UNUSUAL EFFECT seen here was obtained by quickly moving the metal in and out of the flame (Illus. 21).

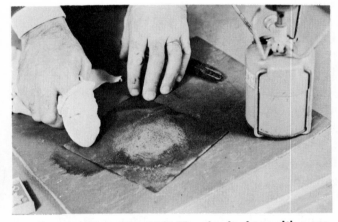

AFTER THE METAL HAS COOLED, wipe it clean with a rag. You are now ready to emboss (Illus. 22).

To achieve color changes on aluminum, you could let it oxidize naturally. However, this takes a very long time, and you are probably eager to begin your project. To make an artificial "patina" (the name for the layer of oxidation) on aluminum, you have two possibilities: you can brush a black varnish on the metal, and wipe it off lightly with a rag while the varnish is still damp; or you can apply a mixture of India ink and fixative with an atomizer. For another effect, spray or brush oil paints on selected areas. The paint covers completely, so be selective in choosing the areas you paint. Whatever method you choose to color the metal, or even if you leave it in its natural shiny state, your creations will make lovely gifts—and metal is one substance that will last for many years to come.

STAINED GLASS CRAFTING

Working with stained glass is an exciting and challenging activity. You can create practical objects, such as a stained glass table top or a shimmering stained glass panel for a room divider, or you can make mobiles, murals, door panels and lamps.

A small area in your home is all you need for a suitable work area. A few specialized tools are needed, but the rest of the equipment can be found around the house.

The technical demands of stained glass crafting are not difficult. After you learn the basic skills, you can soon work on such projects as hanging pendants and bonded glass designs. The larger projects such as stained glass home windows require planning, patience and precision. The results are stunning creations in stained glass that can be admired and enjoyed by all.

The projects described here are only a beginning and merely show the various techniques to follow.

Kinds of Stained Glass

Stained glass varies in texture, color, thickness, degree of transparency, etc. Each type produces its own artistic effect. In selecting glass for different projects, use the type that is most appropriate for the particular use. Where it is desirable to see through the glass, choose "antique" glass (modern glass made by the old hand-blown method) for its clarity and transparency. For windows you do not want anyone to see through, use a denser, more translucent glass such as seedy antique, marine or cathedral glass. For areas that receive a lot of sun, a glass with deep dense color is recommended. For windows that receive a minimum of light, use light-colored textured glass. The texture helps it hold the light.

These are the names of the more common types of glass:

1. Antique hand-blown glass, usually English or European.
2. English Streaky (a beautiful textured glass with color variations).
3. Blenko glass, an American hand-blown glass.
4. Cathedral glass—a rolled glass with heavy regular texture.
5. Opalescent glass—used a great deal about 50 years ago, a vari-colored translucent glass.
6. Rondels—round pieces of glass with a swirl in the middle.
7. Flashed glass—refers to glass with one color over another color, used for acid etching. One side is very smooth; the opposite side is the one to score when cutting.
8. Marine Antique—an American rolled glass in light colors.
9. Seedy Antique—blown glass with little bubbles trapped inside.

Cutting the Glass

Straight line cuts are the easiest to make, so use rectangular shapes for your first projects. If you do use curved shapes, be sure they are outside curves (convex) and make them as gently sloped as possible. Also try to avoid having to cut pieces less than 1 inch wide.

To cut stained glass, you first score it with a cutter and then break it along the scored line.

Condensed from the book, "Stained Glass Crafting" by Paul W. Wood | © 1969 by Sterling Publishing Co., Inc., New York

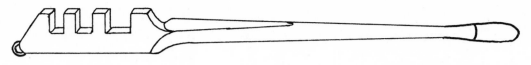

GLASS CUTTERS have wheels that do the scoring. Use kerosene or turpentine on the wheel in order to keep it working smoothly. Notice that the notches are of different sizes—these are used to break off pieces of glass.

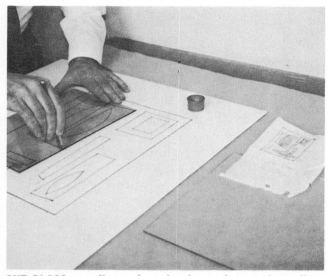

CUT GLASS on a flat surface that is sturdy enough to allow bearing down. When the glass cutter is scoring properly, it will make an even, biting sound. The small container on the right holds the kerosene.

To score the glass, hold the cutter with the wheel pressed downward against the glass, the notched edge of the cutter towards you. The ball end of the cutter goes between your first two fingers: your thumb and index finger

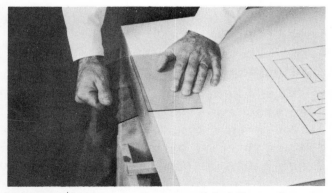

BREAKING GLASS is easily accomplished if you place the scored line slightly beyond and parallel to the edge of the work table. It should snap off evenly if you have scored it properly.

should be in position to bear down on the shoulders of the cutter. Dipping the wheel in kerosene or turpentine occasionally will lubricate it and make your job easier.

Be sure you have the glass on a flat, sturdy surface. Bear down firmly with the cutter wheel beginning at the edge away from you. Draw the cutter towards you steadily, maintaining the downward pressure all the way to the other edge. Bear down hard enough so that the scoring shows clearly on the glass, but remember you are only scoring the glass, not trying to cut all the way through it!

After the glass has been scored, you are ready to break it. If you are breaking the glass along a straight line and if you have enough glass to hold it firmly on both sides of the line, hold the pattern piece flat against the table with one hand with the scored line along or slightly beyond the edge. Grasp the excess glass firmly with your other hand and snap downward. The glass will break off along the scored line.

To cut off pieces less than 1 inch wide, score the glass as above, but break it off by tapping from below with the cutter along the length of the scored line. Keep tapping from edge to edge until the glass breaks off along the scored line. Curved cuts are scored in the same manner and also broken by tapping. Cut very thin pieces by first scoring the glass, then breaking off the piece using one of the notches on the side of the glass cutter. Uneven protrusions of glass along the cut edge can be smoothed off by working away at them with the notched teeth of the cutter. (This is called grozing.)

Stained glass is also available in 1-inch-thick cast blocks called "dalles." The pieces are

NARROW PIECES of glass should be broken off by tapping along under the scored line holding the glass near the surface of the table so that when the glass piece breaks off it will not shatter. When breaking a very thin piece, use the notch on the side of the cutter nearest in size to the thickness of the glass you are cutting.

EACH CURVE is tapped out until a final deep curve is reached. A curve sharper than the one shown here would require two pieces of glass joined by a lead at the sharpest part of the curve.

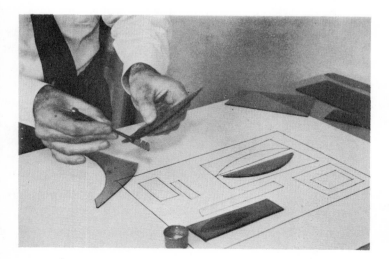

UNEVEN PROTRUSIONS of glass are broken off with very small bites of the teeth of the glass cutter. Check the colors of the overlapping pieces of glass as you go along to be sure the effect is what you want.

THICK GLASS requires a piece of wood as heavy as a butcher's block for a base. Always score and cut first through the middle of the glass to relieve the inner stress, which will make the other cuts easier. The glass is broken along the scored line by a sharp crack on a cold chisel inserted into the block.

chipped or "faceted" on the edges and cast in a form using concrete instead of lead to bind the pieces of glass together.

For cutting thick glass you need a heavy piece of wood, ideally a butcher's block, but a 4″ × 6″ piece of wood about 30 inches high will do. If you can find an old tree stump, this will make a sturdy support. Insert a 2-inch cold chisel sharp edge up in the top of your block. *Always wear gloves and goggles for cutting.* The first cut should be down the middle of the dalle. Score the 1-inch-thick glass exactly as you score thin stained glass sheets. After scoring, place your hands on the ends of the dalle with the score line in the middle and bring the dalle down to the cold chisel, lining up the cold chisel edge directly underneath the scored line. A good sharp crack should break it cleanly.

For cuts that are not rectangular, you must use a chopping hammer. A sheet metal hammer or mason's hammer of fine tempered steel

is best. Keep the hammer sharp for cutting. Place a paper pattern over the glass piece. Using the wood block as a base hold the glass at a 45° angle with one edge on the block. Chip away a little bit at a time from the edge of the glass until you reach the paper pattern. Turn the glass piece over and put the paper pattern on the back. Now chip away again until both sides of the glass piece match the pattern.

Faceting gives added sparkle to the glass. If a piece looks too dark, a facet can effectively lighten it. A color that is too flat can be enriched by a facet. Faceting is done by striking the edge on the face side of the glass. Hold the piece in your left hand with the edge to be faceted facing up. Strike the edge with your cutting hammer about $\frac{1}{4}$ inch down from the face and a semi-circular chip will fly off of the piece leaving a light-refracting facet, shaped like a fish scale.

NON-RECTANGULAR CUTS on thick glass are made with a chopping hammer. To avoid undercutting of the glass piece, hold the piece at a 45° angle to the wood block. Chip small pieces at a time, first on one side of the glass, then on the other, until the final shape is reached.

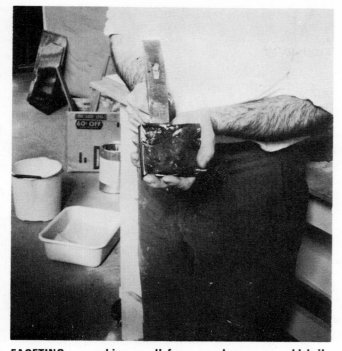

FACETING, or making small faces or planes, can add brilliance to a dull or dark piece of glass. With the cutting hammer in one hand and the glass in the other, strike the edge of the glass. A semi-circular piece will fly off. When you facet thick pieces of glass, save these "fish-scale" chips for use later on in your bonded or fused glass panels.

Bonding Glass

Glass can be permanently bonded to glass by using epoxy glues. These come in two tubes or jars, one the cement or "base" and the other the hardener or "reactor." Follow the manufacturer's instructions for mixing and hardening time and you will have a clear, strong, permanent bond. When using epoxy, work in a ventilated area. A few people have skin which is sensitive to epoxy materials but you can wear gloves if this applies to you.

A Simple Project—Bonded Glass Panel

Select a piece of clear window glass the size of a window pane. Choose the stained glass for your panel by holding pieces of various colors up to the window to see the appearance with light coming through. The color effect is often quite different than when seen against a solid surface.

Now sketch a design out full size on a sheet of white paper. Use charcoal, crayon or a dark pencil, because the outline must be dark enough to show through when you later cut colored glass directly over this pattern. The outside dimensions of your design must, of course, be limited to the size of the pane of clear glass you have selected.

With the epoxy bond technique you can use two or more layers of stained glass, but the pieces of the upper layer must fit within the shape immediately below so that they can be glued down properly.

In making your design and choosing your glass for the upper layer, remember that using two different-color pieces of glass, one on top of the other, gives the same effect as mixing paints—blue and yellow appear as green, red and blue as purple, and yellow and red as orange. Study a color wheel if you are not familiar with primary, complementary and mixed colors.

When all of the pieces for your panel have been cut, put the pane of clear glass down on top of the pattern and brush on clear epoxy glue over the area where the stained glass is to go, and only that area. Following the pattern,

A BONDED PANEL: When making a bonded panel, the clear epoxy glue must be brushed on in a thin, even film. The working time of epoxy glue is short, so be sure all of your glass pieces are properly cut and ready before you begin spreading the glue on the pane of clear glass, which is laid over the paper pattern.

lay the pieces of stained glass in place. Repeat the same procedure with your second layer if you have one. For each bonding (glueing), lay the glass on a flat surface to keep the pieces from slipping out of place before the cement hardens.

The finished bonded glass panel may be installed directly against an existing window pane. A thin bead of putty around the edge of the glass panel will hold it securely in place.

Leading Glass

Traditional stained glass crafting involves the use of lead came (grooved rods) to join the pieces of glass together. The technique itself has varied little since medieval craftsmen created the inspired windows in the great cathedrals. We now use extruded lead cames instead of casting them ourselves, an electric soldering iron rather than one heated in a fire and a steel wheeled glass cutter instead of a hot rod of iron—but other than this the essentials of the craft remain the same.

A More Difficult Project—
A Leaded Glass Panel

In planning a large project, you will want to follow the professional practice of making several preliminary designs to scale—1 inch or ½ inch to 1 foot is customary. Stained glass designers use pen and India ink to indicate lead lines and watercolor for the glass areas, as this closely approximates the final effect of the panel. Using a pencil, sketch your design lightly to the above scale. Block in the lead lines and border with India ink and apply transparent washes of watercolor (the India ink will not be dissolved by the watercolor).

When you have decided on the final design, you must then enlarge the selected sketch to full size. (This is called a "cartoon"—the traditional name used for full-size detailed drawings.) Charcoal is an excellent medium for this full-size drawing. Lines can be easily changed and shifted when necessary—it is black enough for indication of lead lines—

and when you are satisfied with the look of it, it can be sprayed with fixative to prevent smudging.

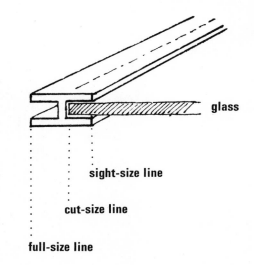

There are three vital measurements that go on your full-size cartoon (see illustration).

1. Full-size line—This represents the outer edge or perimeter of your leaded panel.

2. Sight-size line—This line indicates the inside line of the lead came.

3. To determine the cut-size line—Take a piece of lead came and place it with the outside edge on the full-size line. Where the glass itself will end when inserted in the came is the cut-size line.

Once your full-size cartoon is completed, you still need two additional full-size sheets —one for your paper pattern for cutting glass and one as a working drawing, to serve as a leading guide. Put two blank sheets on your table with the full-size cartoon on top and pieces of carbon paper in between. Trace the three perimeter lines—full-size, cut-size, sight-size—first. Use a straight edge for this and for any other straight lines that you will trace. Now trace down the *middle* of each lead line, pressing down firmly so that the lines will show on the two lower pieces of paper.

While your sheets are still tacked down, number each individual segment that will be a cut piece of glass. Start at the lower left

A LEADED GLASS PANEL: You need three full-size sheets of paper and two pieces of carbon paper. Label the top sheet, "cartoon"; the middle sheet, "paper pattern"; and the bottom sheet "working drawing."

and end with the upper right segments. Later on when the pattern is cut apart, you will keep the numbered pattern with the piece of cut glass so you will always know its relative position in the panel.

Now separate the sheets and you are ready to cut your paper patterns from one of the copies. A professional double-bladed pattern shears is very useful here but perhaps not readily available. Two single-edge razor blades taped together with a $\frac{1}{16}$ inch wood or cardboard spacer in between make a good substitute (see drawing).

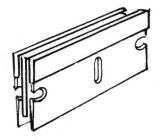

The two razor blades or shears cut the paper patterns and allow for the width of the lead heart which, of course, comes between each piece of glass. However, cut the outer perimeter cut-size line with a single blade.

Using the paper patterns, cut the pieces of selected glass. Glass must be cut very accurately to the paper pattern or leading will be difficult. As each pattern of glass is cut, lay it in place on top of the working drawing.

When all pieces are cut you are ready to begin leading. Take the glass segments off your working drawing and place *in proper order* next to your work bench or table. Staple or tape your working drawing to the top of your work bench.

Before lead came is used, it must be stretched to straighten it and take up any slack. A vise and pliers are the only tools you need. Place one end of the lead in the vise. Hold the other firmly with the pliers. Pull

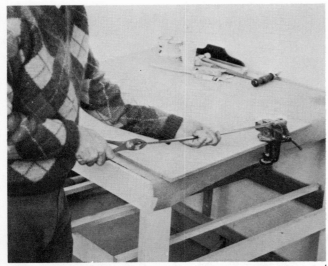

LEAD CAME must be stretched in a vise with a pliers in order to straighten it before using. When stretching short pieces, pull with just enough force to straighten them.

with enough pressure so that the 6 foot length of lead stretches 2 inches or 3 inches. Leads must also be opened by running a sharpened pencil down each groove to force the lead apart.

The principal kinds of lead came are:

1. Standard lead cames, as large as 1 inch and 1½ inches in width—used mostly for long, thick, straight lines.

2. "U"-shaped came used in edging panels and in lamp shade edges.

3. Came with an open heart—used for insertion of reinforcing rods when it is desirable to hide them.

4. Thick cames for use with unusually thick glass or when glazing two thicknesses of glass together.

5. Came with off-center heart. Used for edges to allow more trimming area in installations.

To begin the actual leading of your panel, nail two ¼-inch-thick wooden strips at right angles to the panel on the lower left line marked full size. Start leading from lower left corner of panel. Place the first piece of came against the wood strip covering the lower edge of the panel. Place the second piece of lead at right angles to the first, against the other wood strip. Open up the edge of one came, so that the other one may slip under it slightly as they meet.

A handy and inexpensive tool for cutting lead can be the sharpened reverse (bottom) side of a linoleum cutting knife. A firm, slightly rocking motion directly down on the lead is the best way to cut. Keep your knife sharp.

Now insert the first piece of glass into the lead grooves at the lower left. Tap it in slightly with the wooden handle of your knife. Next place a piece of lead along the top of the glass, fitting the glass into the groove. Now add the second piece of glass and so forth with each piece. Where leads meet at the joint, the end of one can be fitted into the side of the other, or butted. All the pieces of glass and lead are put down in this manner, until the other two edges are reached. Then the two remaining perimeter leads are put down. Any leads meeting the outside leads should fit into the groove. Place

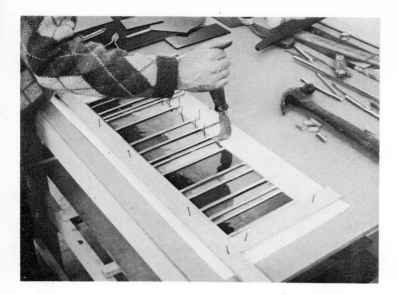

A LINOLEUM CUTTING KNIFE is a good implement for lead cutting. Trim the ends of the lead strips as close to the glass as possible without actually touching the edges.

CURVED PIECES of glass are leaded by bending a length of came directly to the curve of the glass, trimming the ends, and then fitting the piece into the panel.

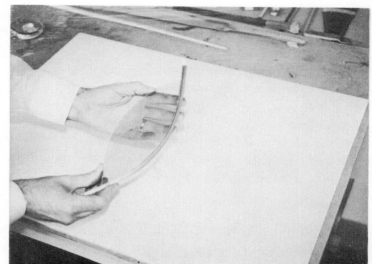

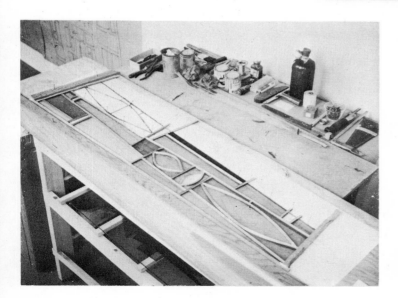

TO HOLD THE PANEL together before soldering, place a ¼-inch wood strip against the last piece of lead at each end. Tap them until each piece of the panel is firmly against the adjoining pieces. Then tack the wood strips down so nothing will slip.

$\frac{1}{4}$ inch wood strips against the last two outside leads and tap against them with a hammer until everything is firmly held. Tack these last two wood strips down and this will hold your panel for soldering.

Soldering

If you have a new soldering iron, the copper tip must be "tinned" before you can use it. If this is the case, plug in the iron and bring it up to "hot" (6–8 minutes). Sprinkle rosin on the flat piece of copper and rub the tip of the iron into the rosin, at the same time holding the solder next to the tip. The solder will flow on making the tip shiny.

The first step in actually soldering the joints is to use your brush to put a drop or two of flux at the point where two pieces come together. Now touch the hot iron tip to the joint and simultaneously touch the solder to the tip. The solder will run across the joint, bonding it together. The solder should flow evenly over the joint, although this may require a little practice. Fortunately, even joints that are not soldered too smoothly have that interesting "handmade" look.

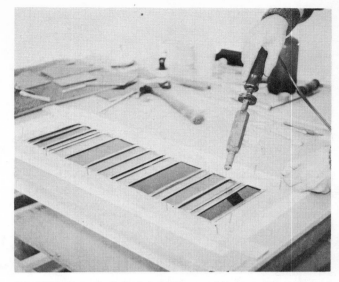

BE SURE that all of the joints on one side are soldered before turning the panel over to solder the joints on the other side. Before the second side is soldered is the time to make any changes that are necessary, so check the panel carefully for cracks in the glass or an arrangement that does not satisfy you.

After soldering all joints on one side, remove the wood strips and carefully hold the panel up to the light. At this point you can, if necessary, change a color or replace a piece of glass that has cracked. Put the panel down unsoldered side up and pry up the lead rim around the piece to be changed. Cut a fresh piece of glass slightly smaller than the first one and place it in the lead. Press the lead down and solder at the joints. When you are satisfied with the appearance of the panel, solder all joints on this side.

Installing a Panel

The final process before installing your window is to putty the panel. Lay the panel flat on your work table and, with your thumb and fingers, press white lead putty into all the lead grooves on one side of the panel, to seal them. Carefully press down on all the leads with a putty knife and cut off any excess putty with a sharp pointed piece of wood. Repeat this operation on the other

A NEW SOLDERING IRON requires "tinning." The hot iron tip is rubbed into rosin and solder is then applied. When the tip is shiny, it is ready to be used. Be sure to use plenty of solder while tinning the tip.

PUTTY is the last step before installing your panel. Use a stiff-bladed putty knife for pressing down the face of the lead strips. All excess putty must be scraped and cleaned off and then polished with a soft cloth. The finished gleaming panel is shown on the right.

side of the panel. Sprinkle whiting on the panel and scrub the glass and lead with a stiff brush to clean off the remaining putty and dirt. Polish with a soft cloth.

To install the panel in a door, cut an opening allowing $\frac{1}{8}$ inch clearance all around. Fasten $\frac{1}{2}$ inch wood molding around the inside of the opening. Run a band of putty against this molding and press the panel into place. Now nail inside molding into place against glass panel.

Glass in Concrete

This method produces a jewel-like panel of 3-dimensional richness. In effect, a wall of concrete with openings of glass is created, the cement acting as a bonding agent for the glass and a structural wall as well. The technique has been further refined, using epoxy cement as the binding agent. Because of its great strength, the epoxy cement allows great width variation in the cement areas from fine lines to wide areas. However, for this project, use ordinary cement.

Since facet glass castings are heavy, it is wise to keep your panels to approximately 10″ × 20″. To store the casting while it is curing, you will need a working base of $\frac{1}{2}$ inch wallboard about 24″ × 30″.

First cover the wallboard base with wax paper. This prevents any concrete from sticking to it. Now nail wood strips so that they form a rectangle of the correct size. Within the rectangle arrange the pieces of glass according to your pattern. Keep the pieces of glass at least $\frac{1}{2}$ inch from each other and at least 1 inch away from the wood form.

When you are satisfied with the arrangement of the pieces, sprinkle an even layer of screened sand into the form and around the glass pieces to a depth of $\frac{3}{8}$ inch. Now place lengths of thin wire on the sand between the glass, criss-crossing your panel. Sprinkle water on the sand until it is uniformly damp. This will prevent the concrete from drying too rapidly and cracking.

A WALLBOARD BASE provides a working form for a panel in concrete. Wax paper covers the wood so the cement will not adhere to it. The paper pattern is laid under the wax paper and the pieces of glass positioned over it, at least 1 inch away from the wood.

SPRINKLE an even layer of screened sand all around the glass pieces, filling the entire form. Then dampen with water to prevent the concrete from drying too fast. This is an important step.

POUR THE CONCRETE, making certain you follow the manufacturer's instructions to the letter. Pour carefully and evenly to a depth of about $\frac{1}{8}$ inch from the top of the glass. Remove drips from the glass immediately with a wet cloth.

Follow the manufacturer's directions for mixing the concrete. It should have a flowable consistency. Using a jar or a tin can, pour the wet concrete carefully into the sand. Fill up the form with concrete to within approximately $\frac{1}{8}$ inch of the top edge of the stained glass pieces. Do this evenly over the entire casting area. Use a small trowel to even it off. Any cement which falls on the surface of the glass should be removed with a damp rag before it has a chance to harden.

The surface of the wet concrete can be sprinkled with sand, gravel, or marble chips. Parakeet or bird gravel which is readily available works very well and imparts a nice sand-toned finish to the surface of a panel. Sprinkle gravel evenly over the entire panel and set it aside to cure in a cool damp place for three days.

After curing, remove the wood strip form and turn the entire casting over into whatever sand remains on the wax paper. Now you are ready to pour the other side. There will be approximately $\frac{1}{4}$ inch depth to receive your second pouring. Replace the wood strips around your panel and repeat the pouring process on this side. Again sprinkle the surface with gravel and allow to cure two or three days longer.

Glass in Epoxy Cement

The casting procedure itself is similar to that used in casting in concrete. There are, however, a few important changes.

1. All facets must be filled in with putty or plastilene before casting or the cement filler will run in and cover them up. Trim the putty so that it is even with the cut edge.

2. Place 1-inch strips of cardboard completely around the inside of the wood form. This will adhere to the epoxy and provide the proper depth for the second casting.

3. Follow the manufacturer's mixing directions for casting epoxy. Wear gloves while handling epoxy and use a rag dipped in alcohol for cleaning any spilled epoxy off the glass surfaces.

4. After pouring the reverse side of the panel, remove plastilene from the filled-in facets and clean them with alcohol.

CASTING WITH EPOXY CEMENT: Although the process is basically the same as with ordinary cement there are important rules to follow. Fill the facets with plastilene. Clean the edges of all glass pieces with denatured alcohol, as epoxy cement will not adhere to a dirty or greasy surface.

A KILN is necessary if you intend to fuse, or inlay, glass. A peephole is provided for looking in at the glass panel during the firing. This kiln has a peephole on the left side, shown here with the plug removed.

Fusing Glass

Fused glass, sometimes called inlaid glass, is a relatively simple technique that can be successfully performed even in a small kiln. (You will need a kiln for ceramics and enamelling, in any event.) There should be at least a 1-inch space between the panel and the sides of the kiln. Warpage will occur if the glass is too close to the heating element. When designing for fused glass, allow a ⅛-inch space between the individual pieces of glass. When fired in the kiln the glass needs this much space for expansion. All of the glass including the base panel and the cut segments should be of the same type of glass so that the amount of expansion will be the same all round. This means less likelihood of glass cracking during firing.

First cut the base panel by placing a sheet of clear or very pale glass over your pattern and cutting out the shape. Groze off any sharp edges—sharp points of glass may curl up during firing. Now cut the design segments from pieces of colored glass placed over the paper pattern.

When all of the glass pieces are cut, position the base panel over the paper pattern and glue each design segment to the glass base, using casein glue or rubber cement. Only a tiny amount of glue should be used, applied with a toothpick to two or more strategic points on each piece.

After the glue is dry, turn the panel upside down on the kiln shelf or tray so that the design segments are underneath the base panel, not on the top surface. The kiln shelf or stainless steel tray must be covered with a coat of kiln wash or separator to prevent the glass panel from fusing to the shelf itself during firing.

Although glass generally fuses at about 1400 degrees F., it is difficult to predict the precise temperature for any one type as different kinds of glass fuse or melt at varying degrees of heat. Glass also reacts differently in different size kilns, so it is necessary to run some trial tests to determine the correct temperature for fusing in any one kiln. If the edges of the test glass are still angular and sharp after firing, this indicates that higher heat is needed. If there are tiny, needly points of glass around the edges, the piece is overfired and less heat is indicated.

History

The existence of colored glass can be traced back to the Near East where, about 7000 B.C., because of its variety and beauty, it had much the same value as gem stones and was indeed worn as jewels for personal adornment. The earliest known glass workshops were in Alexandria, Egypt, where the craft grew and flourished following the invention of the blowpipe. The blowpipe enabled the craftsmen to control the size, shape and thickness of the glass products.

Under Roman rule, Egyptian glass and glass makers were brought to Rome where early records indicate the first use of glass in window openings, primarily simple pieces of translucent glass set into masonry openings to form decorative patterns.

The advent of Christianity changed the status of stained glass from a minor craft to a major art, and with the decline of the Roman Empire, the hub of glass manufacturing shifted to Byzantium. Here, under Emperor Constantine, the use of glass in window openings for decorative and symbolic meaning reached a high degree of development in the "Great Church of Divine Wisdom" (Haggia Sophia), unfortunately destroyed by fire in A.D. 532.

From Byzantium the craft and the craftsmen spread to Europe, appearing almost simultaneously in France, Germany, and Italy in

This 13th century stained glass at Chartres cathedral in France is an excellent example of medieval windows. The earliest known school of stained glass in France flourished in the 12th century.

the 6th century and reaching England in the year 680. The oldest surviving stained glass windows are those of the "Prophets" in Augsburg Cathedral, Germany. They show such a high standard of artistry and craftsmanship that many earlier windows must have been completed in order to perfect the technique.

The existence of skilled craftsmen set the stage for the great glories of medieval stained glass. The intense religious feeling of the times, the architectural developments which allowed glass to be used in great expanses, and the creative genius of the medieval artist-craftsman all combined in the 12th and 13th centuries to produce the inspired windows of the Gothic cathedrals in France, Germany, and England. Strong vibrant colors, bold use of lead to delineate form, and harmony between the window design and the architecture characterized Gothic stained glass.

After medieval glories, church art, particularly stained glass, began a slow decline. Windows became lighter in color. Forms and figures were modelled more and more as in easel painting with a consequent loss of emotional impact. This decline was due to the Black Plague which greatly reduced the ranks of first-rate craftsmen and to the Reformation with its opposition to over-decoration in the church. This led eventually to the actual destruction of many fine windows.

The 20th century has brought a revival in the art of stained glass. Distinguished modern artists such as Matisse, Braque, Leger, and Chagall have designed and executed works of great originality and beauty to equal the best of medieval glass. Coventry Cathedral in Warwickshire, England, is an outstanding example of the superb art and craftsmanship provided by contemporary artists and designers in stained glass. The great baptistry window designed by John Piper contains 198 separate panels of leaded glass between its deep mullions and rivals in size and grandeur the great cathedral windows of the past.

Today in almost any contemporary building you are likely to find stained glass playing an important decorative role. Area dividers, murals, walls and windows of shimmering beauty, delicate mobiles, colorful mosaics of stained glass—all show that this most ancient of materials can also be one of the most modern.

Stained glass windows can be found today in new churches and synagogues everywhere, as well as in other contemporary buildings of every kind. This modern window group is in the First Presbyterian Church in Stamford, Connecticut.

TIN-CAN CRAFTING

Tin cans are used to hold almost any food, from sardines to peaches to soup. A common problem, however, is what to do with the can after its original function, that of holding food, is no longer necessary. With some imagination and a few tools, you can make attractive objects from these otherwise useless containers.

"Tin" cans are not made entirely of tin— they are actually rolled iron which has been coated with a thin layer of tin and then lacquered to combat the acids of their contents. Historically, the tin can developed as a result of a reward offered by Napoleon for a process that would preserve food for his field armies. A Frenchman, Nicholas Appert, is credited with the discovery in 1795 of hermetically sealed tins, which led to the development of the tin-plated can in 1823.

Used tin cans acquire a brilliant patina the more they are handled, and their malleability makes them ideal for cutting, curling, twisting, puncturing and stamping in many shapes and designs.

Tools and Equipment

The essential tools in tin-can crafting are relatively few—shears, pliers, work gloves, an ice pick, a ruler, and a grease pencil. Three different kinds of shears are necessary: 1—a light metal pair with a strong spring; 2—an ordinary pair of kitchen quality; and 3—a pair of tin shears, or tin snips, which have a compound leverage. For large heavy cans, a fourth pair—electrician's tin shears or sheet-metal worker's tin shears—is useful. In addition, for very fine work, a Wiss 3M heavy-duty compound leverage snips with double serrations is helpful. A pair of engineer's pliers and a pair of needle-nose pliers complete the essential tools.

Other equipment you will want includes templates and gauges of heavy cardboard. With templates you can divide can lids into equal segments simply by putting marks in the desired notches with a grease pencil or crayon and then connecting the opposite marks with ruled lines. A gauge for measuring even strips can be made out of a ¾-inch wide strip of cardboard.

Manipulating the Tin

Cutting: The light spring shears are used for short cuts and thin strips, the kitchen shears

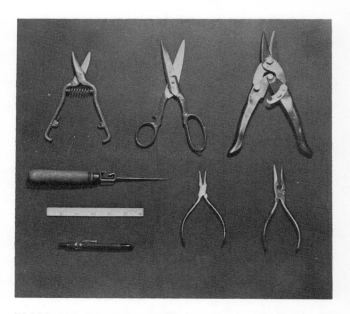

TOOLS FOR TIN-CAN CRAFTING: When purchasing tools, take a piece of tin with you to see how the tools will work. All of the tools shown here are inexpensive.

Condensed from the book, "Tin-Can Crafting" by Sylvia W. Howard / © 1964 by Sterling Publishing Co., Inc., New York

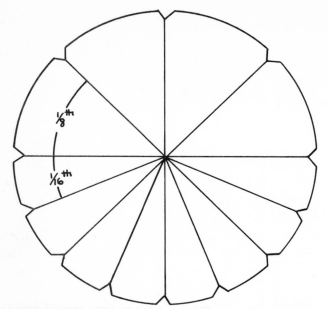

A METAL TEMPLATE which is divided into equal segments is useful for accurately marking a sheet of tin and for making several pieces of tin the same size.

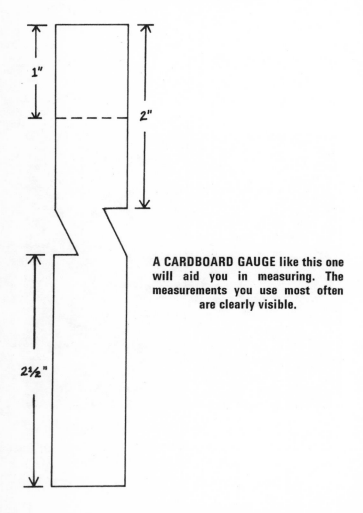

A CARDBOARD GAUGE like this one will aid you in measuring. The measurements you use most often are clearly visible.

for long cuts with serrated edges, and the tin shears for difficult cuts, such as heavy can rims and the first cut on heavy seams. The lids of cans should be cut off very cleanly with a can opener.

Curling: The engineer's pliers are used for ordinary curling of narrow strips of light- or medium-weight cans, and the needle-nose pliers for heavy-weight cans, or for wide curls. Strips that are cut from the top rim to the base can be curled with both pliers. With the needle-nose pliers grasp a strip at the base and turn it at right angles to the others, while using the engineer's pliers at the same time to hold the open end of the strip and twist it gently into a large coil. Correct any sharp angles that might occur by removing the pliers and pressing the strip firmly between your fingers until a smooth arc returns. (Wear work gloves for safety when handling sharp metal.)

CURL TIN STRIPS by holding one end in your gloved hand and twisting the other end with a pliers.

Arching and bending: Strips can be bent by holding a wooden block ($\frac{1}{2}$ by $\frac{1}{2}$ by 5 inches) tightly against the bottom of the can and bending the strips over it. They can then be arched by running them slowly between the right thumb and forefinger in the desired direction. Heavy gloves are necessary for this procedure since the cut edges are often very sharp.

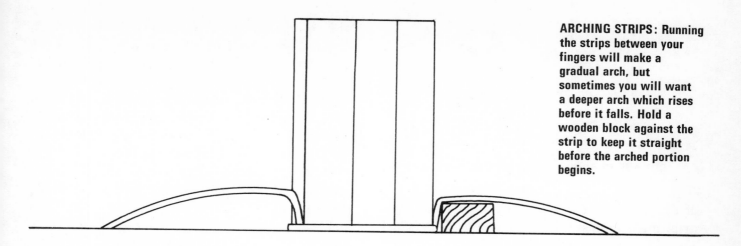

ARCHING STRIPS: Running the strips between your fingers will make a gradual arch, but sometimes you will want a deeper arch which rises before it falls. Hold a wooden block against the strip to keep it straight before the arched portion begins.

Spokes

If the circumference of the tin can is evenly divisible by 8, you can divide it into 8 equal spokes by wrapping a tape measure around it and marking with a grease pencil where you will make the 8 cuts. If the circumference is not easily divisible by 8, however, wrap a strip of paper around the can and cut it to the exact circumference. Then fold the strip in half three times so that there are 8 equal sections and wrap the paper around the tin can edge. The crease lines of the paper should be transferred to the tin with a grease pencil, and the lines can then be cut along the marks.

Patterns

Patterns generally are transferred to the can bodies or lids by taping them on the tin and cutting the paper and tin all at once. If the pattern needs enlargement or reduction, however, the squaring-off method is used, by ruling a grid of equal-sized squares over the design. Then, to enlarge the design, a larger grid of the same number of squares is made and the design is transferred freehand, square by square. For reduction, the transfer is made to a smaller grid.

Centerpiece

Medallions, plaques and other symmetrical decorations require a central design around which you can add flourishes. With a No. 2

tin can, or any can lined with shiny gold, divide and mark the lid with a template into eight sections. Place a small coin or other round object in the middle and mark a circle around it. Cut the eight lines with the spring

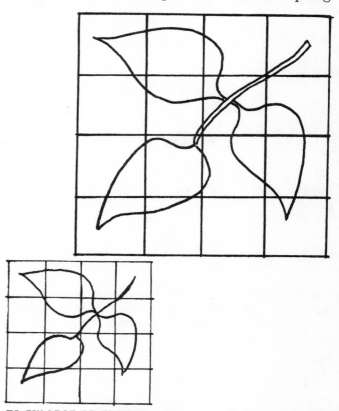

TO ENLARGE OR REDUCE a design, use the "squaring off" method. Mark off the background of the pattern you wish to use in squares. On another piece of paper, draw squares, either larger or smaller, and draw that part of the pattern which appears in each square of the original into the corresponding square of the new size pattern.

CUT AND CURL strips along the lines shown here.

shears as far as the circle, then cut a narrow strip down each side of the eight sections. Curl with the engineer's pliers towards the gold side. Make three more cuts in each section within the narrow strips, along the lines indicated above. Turn one at a time with the pliers towards the middle and curl outward, as shown above. Continue until the entire lid has this pattern. This basic piece can be mounted on a larger lid and embellished by adding a button, earring or pin in the middle.

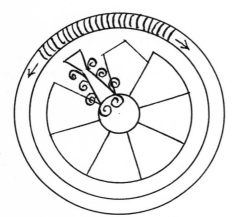

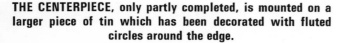

THE CENTERPIECE, only partly completed, is mounted on a larger piece of tin which has been decorated with fluted circles around the edge.

Sea Horse

The sea horse plaques (next page) have been "tooled" to give a textural effect to the tin. After enlarging the pattern (right) to the desired size and tracing the decorative motif, attach the paper firmly to the *reverse side* of the tin with cellophane tape. With an ice pick, make a hole through the eye and through

the tip of the tail, where you will later attach the sea horse to a wood background. Tool the raised portions of the sea horse *before* cutting him out, as the surrounding metal will help to support the area you are working on. Using a short-handled, blunt screwdriver with about a $\frac{1}{4}$-inch point, tap very carefully with a hammer on the *reverse side* to raise the design.

Care must be taken that the tin is merely raised and not punctured. For best results, experiment to find the proper "touch" on another piece of tin first. The tooling will give the sea horse an attractive convex effect, as well as forming the details of the design. This tooling method can be used in any number of ways to highlight special decorative features such as bird feathers or fish scales.

Plaque from a Coffee Can

For this plaque, you will need a 1-pound tin coffee can, the metal lid from a cottage cheese carton (approximately $3\frac{1}{2}$ inches in diameter)

SEA HORSE PATTERN: Enlarge this picture according to the "squaring-off" method described on the previous page.

A COFFEE CAN LID forms the base of this wall plaque. The center portion is raised by being placed on a washer of wood or leather.

MOUNT the sea horse plaques on finished wood panels and hang them where they will receive lots of attention.

or a centerpiece made from tin, and a string of imitation pearls, beads, or a metallic chain. The colors of this plaque will depend upon the brand of coffee the can contained, so consider this before you begin. The upper ring or collar of the coffee can is not soldered on and can be removed with the engineer's pliers. The kitchen shears should be used to cut both sides of the side seam. Bend this piece containing the side seam back in a loop, to be used later as a hanger.

Divide the can body into 16 spokes approximately 1 inch wide. (Surround the circumference of the can with a piece of paper and fold the paper in half four times to get 16 equal sections.) Next, bend the base of each spoke over a wooden block to make them uniform. Each spoke is then divided into five equal parts and the ends cut in gradations of $\frac{1}{2}$ inch to 1 inch (see below). Each of these strips can be curled with pliers. The middle of the centerpiece can be filled with all kinds of decorations—odds and ends of metallic threads, beads, chains or imitation pearls.

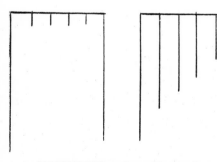

MEASURING and marking strips.

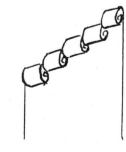

CURLED strips.

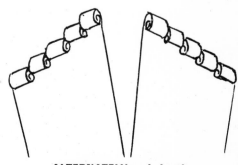

ALTERNATELY curled strips.

WIRECRAFTING

For wirecrafting, you can use almost any kind of wire, from iron coat hanger wire (which is often painted and usually too springy) to aluminum wire (which is very light but not very rigid) to silver and platinum wire (which is very expensive). The best wires for substantial craft projects are brass, copper and mild steel. The tools you use for wirecrafting are essentially the same as those for other metalcrafting (see pages 149, 161). You must add some equipment, most of which is easily made. Known as jigs or fixtures, the equipment is designed to bend wires and bars, and act like the molds and stakes used for shaping flat stock.

Three types of finished objects result from wire work: jewelry, household furniture, and art objects. Illus. 1 shows necklaces made by combining round and flat wire. The bracelet of Illus. 2 was made by twisting and partially flattening wire and then curving it to form a bracelet. Illus. 3 shows the combination of

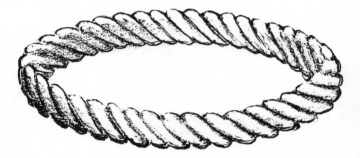

BRACELET combining several techniques in wirecrafting (Illus. 2).

WIRE PATTERNS on this bracelet are first formed and can then be soldered or brazed on to the sheet metal (Illus. 3).

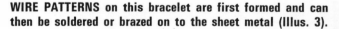

NECKLACES: These attractive shapes can be formed out of silver or any type of metal wire (Illus. 1).

LOOPED WIRE BRACELET: These loops are formed over a dowel and twisted together (Illus. 4).

Written especially for this volume by Henry H. Simons

ORNAMENTS: These imaginative creatures are made of looped thin wires and wire mesh (Illus. 5).

sheet work with wire work. It has a design of flat wire soldered on to a formed sheet. Illus. 4 is a bracelet made from copper coils mechanically joined.

A growing craft, with practically no limits, is using wire or wire combined with other shapes to make pleasing and exciting objects of art. The insects shown in Illus. 5 were made with wire and wire gauze. Illus. 6 shows the very interesting spatial designs that can be made

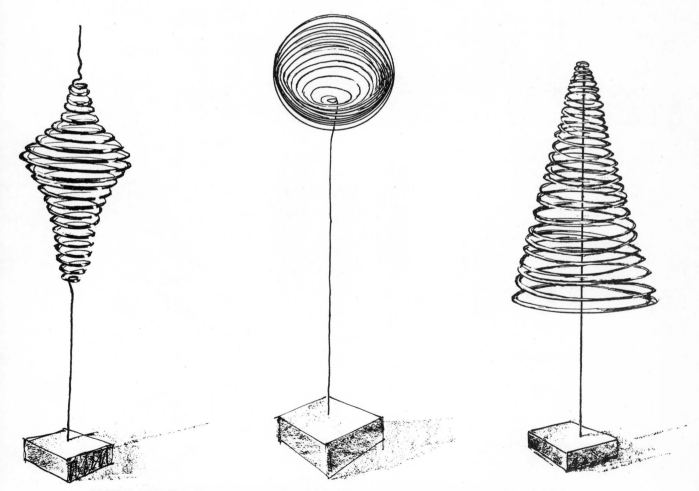

SPATIAL DESIGNS: These can be made with hanger wire or any wire of about 16 gauge (Illus. 6).

HAMMERED LEAF JOINED TO WIRE: This attractive decoration is brazed, but could be soldered (Illus. 7).

CONE-SHAPED BOWL: The wire stand is brazed to this silver container (Illus. 8).

Photographs from the book, *"Metal and Wire Sculpture"*

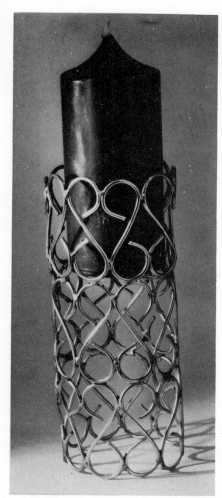

CANDLE HOLDER: This is one of the projects described in the text (Illus. 9).

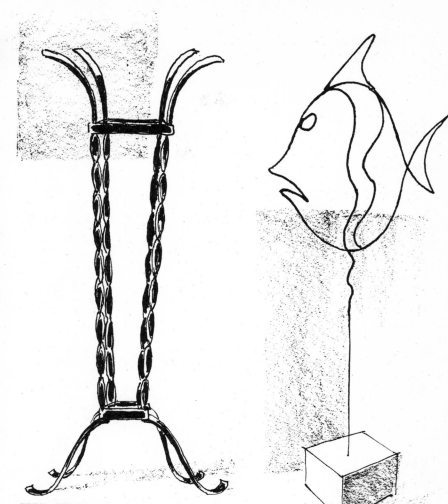

FERN STAND: Wrought iron is a soft iron which can be twisted like this (Illus. 10).

THIS FISH WAS FORMED in the jig shown below (Illus. 12b).

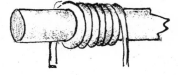

COPPER COIL being formed over a wooden dowel (Illus. 11).

JIG used to form wire is made by placing two nails in a small wood block and clipping off nail heads (Illus. 12a).

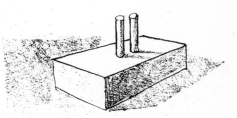

from wire. In Illus. 7, sheet and wire were combined to give a beautiful leaf and stem design.

The candle holder made from bent wire (Illus. 9), the candy bowl (Illus. 8), and the fern stand (Illus. 10) made with twisted and shaped bar stock, are a few examples of useful and ornamental household pieces that can be made with wire.

You will make three projects using tools that are typical for wire work. The major new tool (not in Metalcrafting) is a jig needed for bending and forming wire. The fixture around which wire is coiled is known as a mandrel (or core). The size and shape of the coil is determined by the size and shape of the mandrel.

Illus. 11 shows a dowel used as a mandrel for making a light copper wire coil. Illus. 12*a* shows a jig for making simple bends. The wire fish (Illus. 12*b*) was bent on this jig. Illus. 13 is

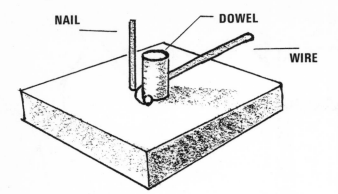

LARGE JIG: The dowel is screwed to the block from the bottom. The wire gets bent and then pushed forward (Illus. 13).

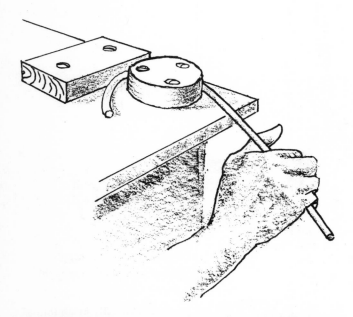

HEAVY-DUTY JIG: Two blocks of wood screwed down act as a forming guide. A similar jig will be used in a project in the text (Illus. 14).

a simple jig made with a dowel rod and nail in a block of wood. When the wire is inserted between nail and dowel and gradually wound around, each successive bend forms a curve or loop. For making bends with heavy wire and with bar stock, you need a jig similar to Illus. 14. The scroll work for one of our projects will be made on a modified version of this jig. To make right-angle bends, a vise (Illus. 15) or an anvil and hammer are used.

Planning is an important part of every project. To aid you in determining the amount of material you will need for any given project, Table I gives the weights and lengths of brass, copper, and silver wire for the most used gauge sizes. Very often material needed can only be purchased at industrial supply warehouses. There is usually a minimum charge. With careful planning you can obtain enough material for a number of projects for this minimum charge. For example, one local supplier stated that for the minimum a 1-pound spool each of 14 gauge brass, 18 gauge brass, 14 and 18 gauge copper, and 1-foot squares of 18 gauge sheet copper and brass could be obtained. This will be enough material to make the first two projects and still leave an appreciable amount for future use.

Table I
Length and weight of several gauges of wire

Gauge #	Diameter in inches	Approx. ft/lb copper & brass	Approx. ft./Troy oz, silver
14	.064	80	7
16	.051	125	10
18	.040	205	17
20	.032	320	27
22	.025	515	43
24	.020	810	70

The lower the gauge number the thicker the wire.

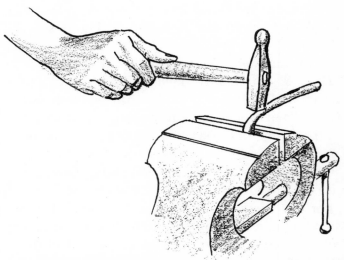

RIGHT-ANGLE BEND has to be made in a vise like this or on an anvil (Illus. 15).

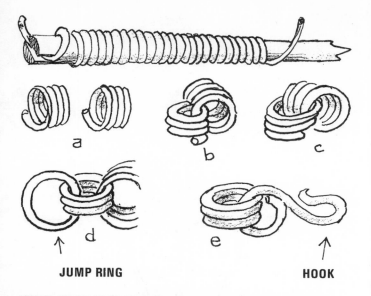

JUMP RING   HOOK

STEPS IN MAKING THE COILED BRACELET over a notched pencil (Illus. 16). Make the loops first, then cut them (a), join them (b) and (c), add jump ring (d) at one end and hook (e) at the other.

PROJECT: **Coiled Copper Bracelet**
Materials and Equipment:

    soft copper wire, 18 gauge, 50 feet
    soft copper wire, 14 gauge, 1 foot
    wire-cutting pliers
    small can clear lacquer (spray can if available)
    soft rags
    pumice
    steel wool

Wind a continuous coil of 18 gauge copper wire on a notched pencil, as shown in Illus. 16. Guide the coils with your fingers while bending, to keep the coils close together. Remove the coil from the pencil and cut it with your pliers into sections with four coils in each section (Illus. 16a). Approximately 20 sections will make the bracelet. Join the links together by inserting the end of one link over the four coils of a second as shown in Illus. 16b and turn one section over the other. This will give you a pair of links as shown in Illus. 16c. Add more links in a similar manner until the chain is complete. To make the bracelet, add a jump ring at one end and hook at the other. Make the jump ring by turning one coil of 14 gauge

copper around a pencil and cutting (Illus. 16d). Make the hook by coiling two rings from 14 gauge copper, unwinding one coil, bending it into a hook with your fingers, and twisting it 90 degrees (Illus. 16e).

Complete the bracelet by polishing the wire with steel wool and wet pumice on a rag, until a high lustre is obtained. Coat the bracelet with clear lacquer in order to maintain the shine. (See Illus. 4.)

This same bracelet can be made of silver wire when you feel you have mastered the technique. You can even insert a semi-precious stone in the center coil by modifying that coil to hold the stone or hang charms from the coils.

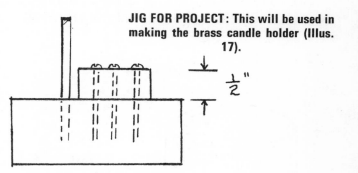

JIG FOR PROJECT: This will be used in making the brass candle holder (Illus. 17).

PROJECT: **Brass Candle Holder**

For this candle holder you need to solder together a number of curved brass wire pieces to form a lacy tube. Two jigs will be needed, a bending jig to bend the brass wire to shape, and a soldering fixture to hold the pieces while soldering.

STEP 1. *Making a bending jig.*
Materials and tools:

    1 wooden dowel, $\frac{3}{8}$-inch diameter, $\frac{1}{2}$-inch long
    1 finishing nail, 6-penny size, $1\frac{1}{2}$ inches long
    2 small wire nails, 17 gauge, $1\frac{1}{2}$ inches long
    hammer and saw
    1 wooden block (2 × 4 cut 4 inches long)

Nail the $\frac{3}{8}$-inch dowel on to the block with the two 17 gauge nails. Hammer the larger nail into the block in the position shown in Illus. 17. To determine the spacing between the nail and the dowel, place a short length of 14 gauge wire next to the dowel. Position the nail so that there is a small clearance for the wire between the nail and dowel.

STEP 2. *Making a soldering fixture.*
Materials and tools:

1 wooden dowel rod, 6 inches long by 1½ inches diameter

several sheets of asbestos 6 inches square by .050-inch thick

1 package brads, 17 gauge, ⅜-inch long

Wrap the asbestos around the dowel so that it makes a smooth, tight fit. Start the asbestos by nailing one edge to the dowel. Wrap and nail the second edge flush to the first. Do not overlap.

Cut a circle of asbestos 1½ inches in diameter. Nail this to the top of the dowel rod (Illus. 18).

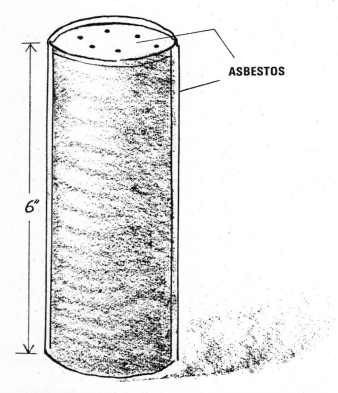

SOLDERING FIXTURE: This asbestos-covered wood dowel, 6" high, is used as an aid in soldering and assembling the candle holder (Illus. 18).

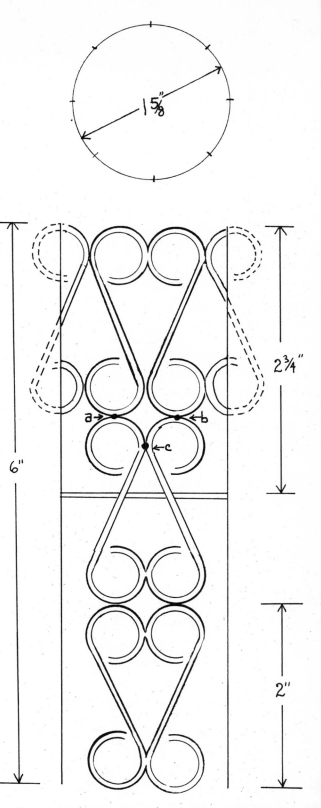

CANDLE HOLDER LAYOUT: The curved pieces form the body of the piece. Top view (above) shows the size of the brass plate which will fit across the middle (Illus. 19).

STEP 3. *Planning and layout.*
Materials and equipment (in addition to above):
  brass wire, 14 gauge, 15 feet
  soft copper wire, 22 to 28 gauge, 2 feet
  brass sheet, 18 gauge, 2″ × 2″ square
  1 small smooth file
  1 propane gas torch
  1 medium soldering iron with wedge tip
  1 1-lb. spool of 50/50 solder (50% tin–50% lead) of the solid type, .032 (20 gauge)
  1 small can of petrolatum type soldering flux

Illus. 19 shows the way the individual curved brass pieces are to be laid out and joined. Note that the pattern is one of alternately upright and inverted swan shapes.

The layout will enable you to determine the number of pieces in each row, the number of rows, and the size of the brass circle. To determine the length of straight wire you will need to make one curved piece, curve a piece of solder to the shape of the piece. Straighten the solder and measure its length. This will turn out to be $4\frac{1}{4}$ inches if you follow this size layout.

STEP 4. *Bending the brass curves.* (Illus. 20.)
Using the bending jig made in Step 1 (Illus. 17), place a $4\frac{1}{4}$-inch length of 14 gauge wire between the dowel and nail so that $\frac{1}{4}$ inch sticks out beyond the nail. Holding the wire in the middle, bend it around the dowel. The motion is a slight pulling action while at the same time hugging the dowel. Bend till there is $\frac{1}{8}$ inch between the straight portion of the wire and the start of the bend.

Reverse the wire and repeat at the opposite end. Make 24 such pieces.

STEP 5. *Soldering.*
Make a disc by drawing a $1\frac{5}{8}$-inch circle on the 2-inch square brass sheet. Cut the circle with a tin snips and file the burrs. Be sure to file in one direction, forward only, not back and forth.

Arrange eight curves around your soldering fixture (Illus. 18) in the following manner.

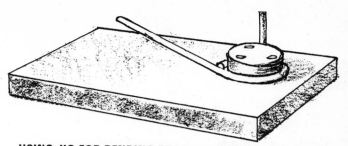

USING JIG FOR BENDING BRASS CURVES: Here you have to pull in order to hug the dowel and form an almost closed loop (Illus. 20).

Encircle the fixture with one strand of fine copper wire, leaving a clearance of slightly more than $\frac{1}{16}$ inch between the wire and the fixture. Twist the copper wire to maintain the circle. Insert eight of the curved pieces of brass you have made between the wire and the asbestos, by sliding them in. Lay the fixture down on its length. Tighten the wire, by twisting, so that the pieces can be moved, but will not fall down when the fixture is held upright. Adjust the pieces now so that the tips extend $\frac{3}{4}$ inch above the end of the fixture. Tighten the copper wire to hold them firmly in place. Place the fixture in a vise, so that the bottom of the curves clear the vise.

Trim the brass disc with a file so that it fits inside the circle of pieces. When a good fit has been obtained, mark with a pencil the points at which the disc and curves touch. Remove the disc and notch these points to a depth of about $\frac{1}{32}$ inch. Place the disc back, adjust the curves to fit into the notches, tighten the copper wire, and proceed to solder.

With a pencil, place a small dab of petrolatum flux at the junction of the disc and each curved wire with a pencil. Cut eight pieces of solder each $\frac{1}{16}$-inch long. Place a piece of solder on each of the fluxed meeting points of the disc and the brass curves. Make sure that the solder touches the wire curves. Light the torch (page 163) with a 2-inch flame. "Play" the flame over the disc with a circular motion, starting from about 2 inches from the disc and moving closer. Continue this circular motion while moving closer to the disc until the solder

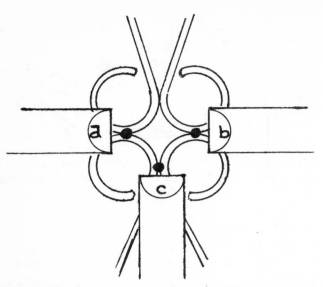

SOLDERING IRON POSITIONS: Where to place the tip and spot of solder for the three points (Illus. 21).

melts and flows. Remove the flame. When the solder has frozen, the disc will be soldered to the eight curves. Allow the part to cool thoroughly, and remove the copper wire used as a clamp. Prepare for the soldering of more brass curves to make the complete holder.

Build up a second row of eight curves on top of the first row of curves, using the copper wire as a clamp. Tighten the clamp and lay the fixture so that you are looking directly at two curves. Place a small dab of flux at the meeting points of the curves, marked a, b and c, in Illus. 19. Make sure that the curves touch each other. Illus. 21 shows the positioning of the soldering iron when soldering a, b and c. Hold the iron in one hand and a short length of solder in the other. Touch the spot to be soldered with the solder every few seconds. When it becomes hot enough, the solder will melt and flow to make a good joint. When the solder flows, remove the iron IMMEDIATELY. Allow the solder to freeze before going to a new joint. Be careful to supply heat to each joint as quickly and for as short a time as possible, so as to prevent softening of the previous joint.

Turn the fixture 1/8th turn so that a new curve faces you. Adjust the pieces so that they touch, and solder as before. Continue until the

row is completed. Allow the parts to cool thoroughly.

Turn the fixture upside down and proceed to add the last row. Use the same soldering procedures as before.

STEP 5. *Cleaning and finishing.*

Remove the flux residue by wiping with a rag dipped in cleaning fluid. Polish as explained in the procedure for the bracelet. Coat the holder with clear lacquer.

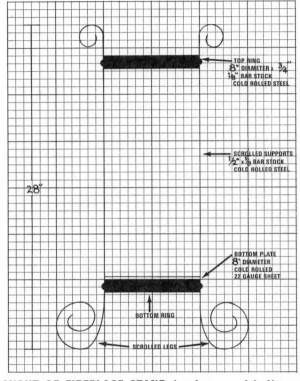

LAYOUT OF FIREPLACE STAND (made to scale). You will follow this in making the detailed patterns shown next (Illus. 22).

PROJECT: **Fireplace Tool Stand**

This stand is made by means of riveting together scrollwork legs made from cold rolled steel.

STEP 1. *Layout.*

The layout (Illus. 22) is made to scale. You will have to make the full-size patterns, shown in Illus. 23, 24 and 25 so that you can follow the pattern as you bend the iron.

Use $\frac{1}{4}$-inch graph paper for ease in scaling up.

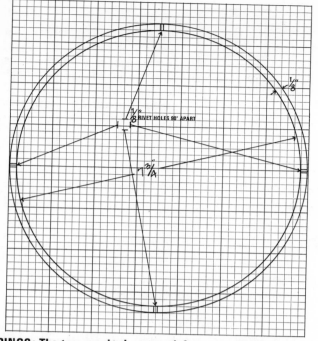

RINGS: The two required, one each for top and bottom of the fireplace stand, are made from bar stock, 25″ long. The material is cold rolled steel, $\frac{1}{8}$″ thick by $\frac{3}{4}$″ wide. Drill holes as indicated (Illus. 23).

STEP 2. *Making the bending jig.*
Materials and equipment:

    1 piece of 2 × 4 lumber, 6 inches long
    2 dowels $1\frac{1}{2}$ inches diameter, 1 inch long
    4 wood screws, 2 inches long

Mount the dowel rods on the 2 × 4 by means of the wood screws as shown in Illus. 26.

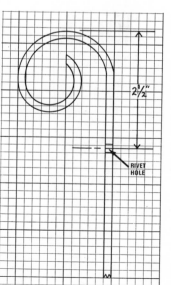

PATTERN FOR TOP PART of the stand leg. You will form this from the other end of the 42″ length (Illus. 25).

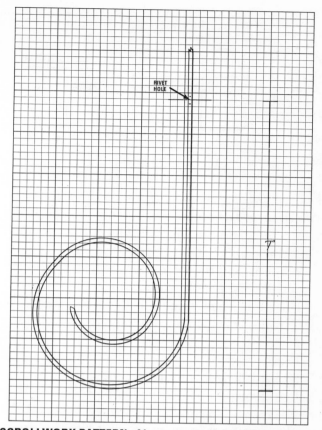

SCROLLWORK PATTERN of bottom part of stand leg, showing rivet hole placement. Start with 42″ length of cold rolled steel, $\frac{1}{8}$″ thick by $\frac{1}{2}$″ wide, and make this four times (Illus. 24).

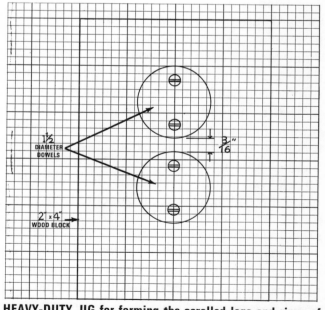

HEAVY-DUTY JIG for forming the scrolled legs and rings of the fireplace stand (Illus. 26).

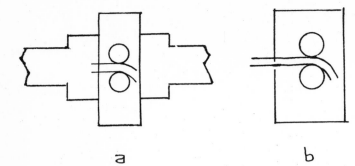 

STEPS in bending circles and scrolls: (a) shows the bar just after the first bend; (b) shows the curve being continued through pushing the bar forward; (c) shows the curve 1/4 completed (Illus. 27).

a   b   c

STEP 3. *Bending iron into circles and scrolls.*
Materials and additional equipment:

- 6 5-foot lengths of cold rolled steel, $\frac{1}{8}$ inch thick by $1\frac{1}{2}$ inches wide
- 2 3-foot lengths of cold rolled steel, $\frac{1}{8}$ inch thick by $\frac{3}{4}$ inch wide
- 1 9" × 9" sheet of cold rolled steel, 22 gauge
- 8 iron rivets $\frac{1}{8}$ inch diameter by $\frac{1}{2}$ inch long
- 2 rivet sets
- 1 hack saw
- 1 pint black stove enamel
- 1 tube or jar of bonding cement

Place the bending jig in a vise. To bend the circle, use the $\frac{3}{4}$-inch bar stock. Although only 25 inches of material are needed to make the ring, the metal is ordered longer so that there is work space at the end of the bend. Illus. 27 shows the several stages of bending the bar. The bend is accomplished by moving the bar forward after each bend. The further the movement the larger the circle. Compare the shape of your curve after each movement. Cut the excess of unbent metal when the circle is completed. Bend the two ends to meet.

The technique for bending the scroll is similar to that for the circle. Start the movement of material with small distances and increase gradually. Practice with some scrap. Check your pattern constantly. Bend four legs using the $\frac{1}{2}$-inch bar cut to 42 inches long.

STEP 4. *Drilling holes for rivets.*

Measure the distance indicated in your pattern for the placement of the rivet holes. One hole will be 7 inches up from the bottom scroll, the other will be $2\frac{1}{2}$ inches down from the top scroll. These are the points at which the ring will be riveted. Punch a center mark in the center of the bar at these points and drill holes. Each leg will have two holes. Clean drilling burrs with a file.

Drill holes in the two rings in the position indicated on the pattern.

Each ring will have four holes.

STEP 5. *Assembling the stand.*

The rivet set is shown in Illus. 28. The larger hole is known as the snap and is used to hold the round head of the rivet during the riveting operation. It is also used to round out the "upset" (flat) part of the rivet after the hammering is completed. The smaller hole,

RIVET SET: The larger hole of the two at the top is the snap, and the smaller is the set hole (Illus. 28).

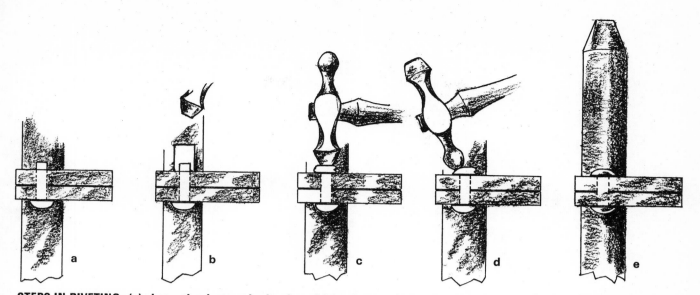

STEPS IN RIVETING: (a) shows the rivet set in the vise with head of the rivet through the two pieces to be riveted and sitting in the snap hole; (b) shows the two parts being snugged by using the set hole of a second rivet set; (c) shows the upsetting (flattening) of the rivet; (d) shows the forming of a rivet; (e) shows the shaping of the rivet using the snap hole of a second rivet set (Illus. 29).

also called the set, is used to bring the two surfaces to be riveted snugly together.

Illus. 29 shows the riveting steps. Place the rivet set in the vise. Join one leg to one of the rings by placing a rivet through the two. Have the head of the rivet facing inwards, and have the leg outside the ring. Place the rivet head into the snap of the rivet set (Illus. 29). Close down the two parts with the rivet set (Illus. 29b). Cut the rivet so that slightly more than $\frac{1}{8}$ inch sticks out. Spread the rivet with the hammer (Illus. 29c). Work the edges of the rivet with a ball-peen hammer (Illus. 29d). Round the rivet using the rivet snap (Illus. 29e).

Add the other legs to the ring in the same manner as the first leg. Now add the bottom ring to the four legs.

STEP 6. *Making and assembling the bottom plate.*

After the legs have been riveted to the top and bottom rings, measure the distance inside the stand. Draw a circle of this diameter on the 22 gauge sheet steel. Cut with a tin snips. File the edges smooth.

To secure the plate to the bottom ring of the stand, a bonding cement, sometimes called "cold solder" is ideal. Paint the cement at the junction points of the ring and the legs. Place the circle on top of the bottom ring and hold it down with a weight. Allow it to harden overnight.

STEP 7. *Finishing.*

Clean the stand with cleaning fluid. Steel wool all surfaces. Wipe clean. Paint with black stove enamel. This will give you a distinctive and lasting finish.

Now that you have become familiar with some of the basic techniques, tools and materials, of wire working, you can go on to create your own objects. Plan and design, lay out on paper, and invent your own jigs when you need something special.

natural
materials

BASKETRY

Basketry is one of man's earliest manual arts. Primitive men used grasses, straws, willow branches, reeds and twigs—in fact, any coarse, moderately flexible material at hand—to weave strands together, in and out, under and over, to form baskets. Modern basketry follows much the same procedure, but it uses a wider variety of materials and weaves.

In general, there are four kinds of materials to choose from:

straw (made from dried rushes or grasses, such as wheat, oats and barley)

hollow reeds (which may be round or flat)

cane (which may be round, split to half round, or flat)

and raffia (which is made from a palm plant and can be threaded through a needle).

The straws and raffia are often made into braided or plaited strands before the basket weaving is begun, or braided over stationary rods in the basket-making. Straws and braids are sometimes sewn round the nucleus (strands that form the base and structure for the sides) instead of, or in addition to, being woven.

You will need some tools: scissors, thimble, awl, pliers or pincers, tape measure, and blunt large-eyed tapestry needles. Your materials can be obtained at a craft supply shop or a wholesale millinery supplier.

For your first basket, choose a style to copy. No matter whether you have selected straw braids, reed, cane or raffia, you will start by making a nucleus (or by using a round, rectangular or elliptical wood base). The

EXAMPLES OF WEAVING: Check pattern (left) is a simple weaving method. Each strip goes over one perpendicular strip, and then under the next one. In twilled two's (right), strips go over and under two consecutive strips at a time, rather than one. In twining (below), two strips are woven between sturdy support strips and are twisted over and under each other.

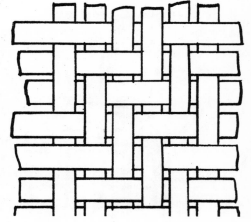

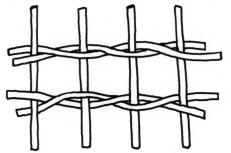

Written especially for this volume by Maria and Louis DiValentin

receptacle will be built up by rows of strands woven round this nucleus in a way that resembles building up rows of clay in coil pottery (see Claywork). To form the nucleus (or base), cut strips to a size that equals the width of your proposed base *plus* the height of two sides of the planned basket. Weave the middle parts of these strips over and under or in a wheel spoke arrangement. The base part of the nucleus should be tight enough to hold weight and loose enough to be flexible. The whole advantage of a basket over another type of container is that it is not rigid.

Since you have woven only the middle parts of your strips, you should end up by having equal lengths on each side of the woven base. These are the spokes that will be used for the building of your basket's sides.

If you are working with cane or semi-pliable reed, you will now need to soak the spoke ends in water to make them bend upward to form the network for the basket's sides. Squeeze the strands while wet with a pincers at the point where they turn upward, and they will stay set.

Now take strands or braids of slightly smaller diameter or width, making sure they are

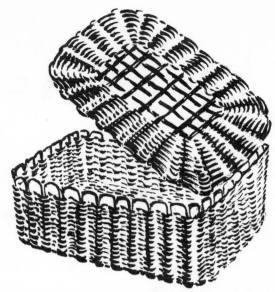

A FINISHED BASKET WITH A LID. Even if the nucleus of the basket is round, you can make a rectangular basket, depending on how you bend the strips to form the sides. The lid should correspond to the measurements of the basket.

flexible (if not, soak them) and weave them in and out, over and under the side spokes that you have just bent. Build up the sides, row on row.

When you have built up the sides as high as you want to go, you must finish off the top. This is done by turning down and twisting the side spokes in and out of each other, all around, to form a finished edge.

If you want to make a wooden or cork base for the basket (instead of a loose bottom), you must bore holes $\frac{1}{4}$ inch from the outer edge for the spokes to go through. You must have an even number of holes. Take each side spoke, bend it in half and thrust one end through each adjoining hole. Leave the spokes standing upright. Continue around the base using each strand to make two adjoining spokes. The loop on the underpart of the base gives the basket strength.

Basket lids may be flat, curved or peaked. Begin with a nucleus, and "coil out" until you have reached the exact size of the basket. The lid can be woven or sewn on to the basket along one side with raffia. A knob and loop will hold the lid closed. To make the knob, start with a ring of straw or raffia about the size of a wedding ring. Completely cover this

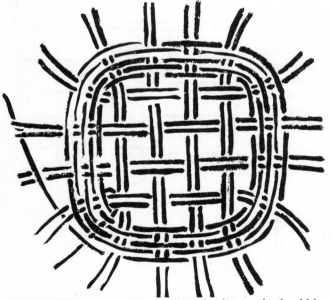

THE NUCLEUS forms the base of the basket, so it should be firmly woven. Bend the strips up, soaking them if necessary, to form the supports for the sides.

ring by winding the circumference with more straw or raffia. Weave strands of your material until it curves over the top of the ring into the size of a marble. It will be hollow unless you insert a wooden bead or button before you make the central ring. The loop is easy to braid and attach.

A basket handle can be made of braided straw, cane or reed. Attach it through the sides of the basket, not the top edge.

The shape of any basket is determined by the weaving. The nucleus can be round, and you can still make a rectangular basket, if you set your stakes or spokes rectangularly as they leave the base. As you weave you must keep shaping, bending, and pulling the strands into the shape you want. Commercially, baskets are shaped over wooden blocks or molds. As a craftsman, you will not want to use a block.

The term *randing* in basketry means weaving in front of one stake and behind the next, working with one cane. *Pairing* means working with two canes. *Upsetting* or *waling* means working with three canes, weaving each cane in front of two uprights and in back of the third.

Raffia

Making objects of raffia is similar to weaving baskets. The raffia itself is a strong string-like fiber made from the leaves of the raffia palm of Madagascar. It can be used more easily than cane (which needs soaking to become flexible) but raffia objects tend to lose their shape.

Start by making a table mat. In using raffia strands, you will need a large-eyed needle made especially for the purpose. To start a raffia nucleus, you need to make a loop of a few strands, and sew a few rings of raffia thread around it. Now continue looping raffia with firm stitches through the loop until you have a strong enough nucleus for your mat. The central hole should be kept as small as possible. The nucleus can be changed from a circle by sewing strands across it and by pulling

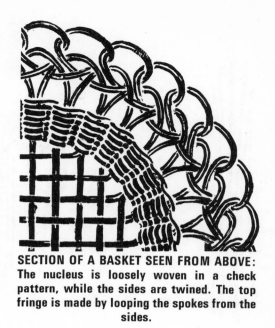

SECTION OF A BASKET SEEN FROM ABOVE: The nucleus is loosely woven in a check pattern, while the sides are twined. The top fringe is made by looping the spokes from the sides.

out the corners. When you have your nucleus set, bind any loose ends in.

With a tail (as the loose end of a strand is called) of raffia, stitch around the nucleus until you have a complete circle. When you come to the end of a strand and have to thread a new strand, pass the needle through the tail of the previous strand, and fasten all together with a long stitch into the row before. Each new row of stitches will go into the row you have just sewed, not into the nucleus. Sew on, with each coil being sewed into the preceding coil. If you want a non-circular mat, manipulate the work as you go, pulling it into the desired shape. The nucleus to a large extent determines the shape of this piece.

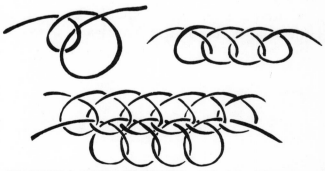

TO MAKE A DECORATIVE EDGE, curl the spokes around each other and insert them back into the body of the basket. A new strip forms the second row.

STRAW, which grows wild in many fields, can be dried and woven with no elaborate advance preparation. The stems are evenly shaped and make good bases. Attach the portion containing the seeds for decoration.

When you have finished your table mat, press it with a hot iron over a moistened cloth over the right side of the work.

A coaster or a tumbler holder is made the same way as a table mat—the coaster is merely smaller. For the tumbler holder start with a mat slightly larger than the base of the glass. Turn up and sew the sides. Keep fitting the tumbler into the little basket as you work, to get a perfect fit. Sew high enough up the tumbler side to protect the hand when the tumbler is held.

Raffia can be braided or woven with a basket weave, or woven on a small loom like yarn. Raffia is especially suitable for making bottle holders, decorative leaves and flowers, hats, bags, dolls, lamps, stars—even shoes. The strand ends of raffia can be turned back and stitched, or can be knotted to form a fringe.

Raffia can be dyed almost any color.

Straws

Almost all objects made by weaving or braiding raffia can also be made of straw or grass. Straw naturally varies in color from white to gold, has a hard, shiny surface (where raffia is soft) and comes in textures and thicknesses that vary widely. Wheat, oat and barley straws differ in hardness. Wheat is best for hat making, oat for making toys and animals. Reeds and flax are like raffia too but less pliable.

SCULPTURE IN THE HOME: A revival in interest in the decorative value of sculpture is taking place, so make sculptures with your own home in mind. This living room has a dramatic effect because of the varied pieces of bronze and white plaster in a setting of redwood and white walls and rug.

REPOUSSAGE, AN EASY CRAFT: This striking ornamental sunburst plaque can be made by a child using a wooden modelling tool on a piece of aluminum. Embossing, stamping, hammering, intaglio, patinas, are all easily accomplished with simple tools and paints on inexpensive sheets of metal.

From the book, "Batik as a Hobby," by Vivian Stein. Sterling Publishing Co., Inc.

BATIK is a technique of decorating fabric by a method known as "wax resist," that is, wax is used to resist dye. This batiked corduroy wall hanging depicting the "Partridge in a Pear Tree" is described on page 88.

BATIK PLACE MATS, made with cookie-cutter and tin-can patterns, are easy to make and would be a good project to start with. Instructions are on page 81.

From the book, "Batik as a Hobby," by Vivian Stein. Sterling Publishing Co., Inc.

BASKETRY: A turkey made of real feathers and a braided raffia head. Braiding is an essential process in producing any form of basketry whether you use straw, reeds, cane or raffia.

From the book, "Batik as a Hobby," by Vivian Stein. Sterling Publishing Co., Inc.

BATIK REPEAT DESIGNS are best done on thin materials. The border of this organdy wall hanging has a repeat design made by folding the cloth in half, then waxing while the cloth is folded.

From the book, "Creative Enamelling and Jewelry-Making," by Katharina Zechlin. Sterling Publishing Co., Inc.

ENAMELLING is an exciting craft that can be accomplished easily, economically, and without special artistic ability. The child's red plate with its effective train design employs the cloisonné technique (which uses thin wire as a color barrier), as does the green brooch. The link bracelet was decorated with red and blue flowers on an opaque white enamel background using the Limoges (fine brush-work enamel background) technique.

BURLAP: One of the easiest of fabrics to work with, burlap can be used as a background material for cloth pictures, string pictures, montages; it can be rewoven with other materials; embroidered (as shown here); or used as a base for tapestry. Burlap now comes in a wide range of colors and weights.

From the book, "Creating with Burlap," by M. J. Fressard. Sterling Publishing Co., Inc.

PAINTING ON BURLAP is easily done using the new acrylic polymer paints which are applied over a base of acrylic emulsion gesso.

From the book, "Creating with Burlap," by M. J. Fressard. Sterling Publishing Co., Inc.

Photographs on this page from the book, "Creative Paper Crafts," by Chester Jay Alkema. Sterling Publishing Co., Inc.

CARDBOARD AND CRAYON combine to make a unique wastebasket. A gallon-sized cardboard milk carton was covered with tagboard. Crayons and ink wash were applied to a long sheet of tagboard which was then wrapped around and glued to the carton, and the design was then etched with a fine pencil point. To protect the etching, a coat of shellac or light varnish should be applied.

COLLAGE: A VARIETY of paper patterns have been united by pen and ink lines to form this collage. However, you need not be restricted to paper—any number of natural or man-made materials can be added to a collage to provide texture.

From the book, "Acrylic and Other Water-Based Paints," by Judith Torche. Sterling Publishing Co., Inc.

ACRYLIC, A VERSATILE PLASTIC: Acrylic polymer paints have revolutionized the arts and crafts world. Used by the fine artist for painting, they are also employed by craftsmen as adhesive, sculpting materials, or glazes. This collage is bound to the surface with acrylic base medium, and acrylic modelling paste is used to achieve thick impastos.

From the book, "Ikebana Simplified," by Olive Scofield Bowes. Sterling Publishing Co., Inc.

IKEBANA, or Japanese flower arranging, combines a love for flowers with an interest in beautiful design. This arrangement is in the Rikka tradition, one of the four great Ikebana styles. (Arranged by Sofu Teshigahara.)

THE SEIKA STYLE of Ikebana in the informal manner is shown in this graceful orchid arrangement. The silver moon container is of a traditional Japanese design. Notice that the foliage is from another variety of flower.

From the book, "Ikebana Simplified," by Olive Scofield Bowes. Sterling Publishing Co., Inc.

MOBILES: LIGHTNESS OF MATERIAL is the essential ingredient in constructing a successful mobile. This fish mobile is made of crepe paper strips and tissue paper stretched on wire frames. However, any lightweight material such as papier mâché, plastic foam, glass or thin metal can be used in constructing mobiles.

From the book, "Creative Paper Crafts," by Chester Jay Alkema. Sterling Publishing Co., Inc.

From the book, "Potato Printing," by Susanne Strose. Sterling Publishing Co., Inc.

POTATO PRINTING offers all of the advantages of block printing—but all you have to have on hand is a sack of potatoes. Peel, clean, and cut them into various shapes, color with poster paints or watercolors, and stamp on to paper or fabric.

POTATO circles and wedges form this brilliant floral bouquet which would be a suitable design for an apron or stationery. While your potato stamp will give many impressions, you should cut fresh stencils every day.

From the book, "Potato Printing," by Susanne Strose. Sterling Publishing Co., Inc.

Page J ■ **POTATO PRINTING**

From the book, "Potato Printing," by Susanne Strose. Sterling Publishing Co., Inc.

GEOMETRIC SHAPES: Squares and triangles are combined to form an abstract design, appropriate for a man's necktie, perhaps. When printing on fabric, remember to use fine material such as silk, linen or cotton. Fabrics of coarse texture do not print well. Be sure to make a separate stencil for each color that you use.

COLORING PAPERS: Watercolors applied to wet watercolor paper causes an interflow of color. Watercolor paper is quite sturdy and your colored paper can be used in making gift boxes, envelopes, greeting cards or book covers.

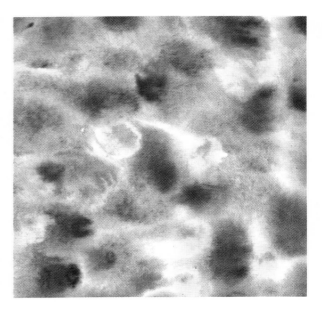

From the book, "Coloring Papers," by Susanne Strose. Sterling Publishing Co., Inc.

COLORING PASTE-COATED PAPER results in this unusual design. The paper is coated with cellulose paste upon which highly diluted watercolor is applied at the top of the paper. This is allowed to drip down the sheet. Then the paper is coated again with paste, colors brushed across it, and the brush is then manipulated to produce the effect shown here.

From the book, "Coloring Papers," by Susanne Strose. Sterling Publishing Co., Inc.

THE SEIKA STYLE of Ikebana in the informal manner is shown in this graceful orchid arrangement. The silver moon container is of a traditional Japanese design. Notice that the foliage is from another variety of flower.

From the book, "Ikebana Simplified," by Olive Scofield Bowes. Sterling Publishing Co., Inc.

MOBILES: LIGHTNESS OF MATERIAL is the essential ingredient in constructing a successful mobile. This fish mobile is made of crepe paper strips and tissue paper stretched on wire frames. However, any lightweight material such as papier mâché, plastic foam, glass or thin metal can be used in constructing mobiles.

From the book, "Creative Paper Crafts," by Chester Jay Alkema. Sterling Publishing Co., Inc.

From the book, "Potato Printing," by Susanne Strose. Sterling Publishing Co., Inc.

POTATO PRINTING offers all of the advantages of block printing—but all you have to have on hand is a sack of potatoes. Peel, clean, and cut them into various shapes, color with poster paints or watercolors, and stamp on to paper or fabric.

POTATO circles and wedges form this brilliant floral bouquet which would be a suitable design for an apron or stationery. While your potato stamp will give many impressions, you should cut fresh stencils every day.

From the book, "Potato Printing," by Susanne Strose. Sterling Publishing Co., Inc.

Page J ■ POTATO PRINTING

PAPER WINDOW TRANSPARENCY: One of the most spectacular possibilities in working with paper is in simulating stained glass windows. Black construction paper provides the leading that holds pieces of colored cellophane and tissue "glass." Notice here that although the shapes on each half correspond exactly, the colors do not, giving this simple window an interest it might have lacked.

Photographs on this page from the book, "Creative Paper Crafts," by Chester Jay Alkema. Sterling Publishing Co., Inc.

THREE-DIMENSIONAL PAPER FIGURES: This free-standing bird is made of strips of construction paper which can be glued, stapled, or taped together. Pipe cleaners are attached to the inside of the body and legs for additional support.

PAPER STRIP SCULPTURE need not be limited to the birds shown here—you can use this simple method to make relief pictures, hats, mobiles, or whatever else your imagination dictates.

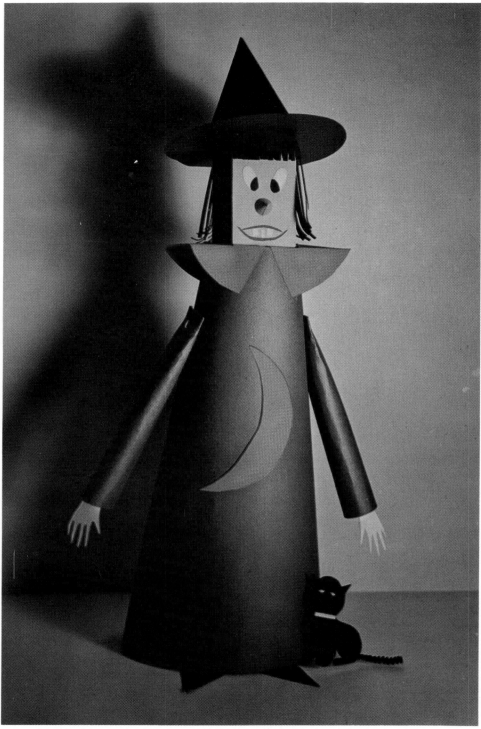

From the book, "Creative Paper Crafts," by Chester Jay Alkema. Sterling Publishing Co., Inc.

PAPERCRAFT: CYLINDERS, CUBES, CONES AND CIRCLES—basic geometric shapes—are all used to advantage in this Halloween witch who is entirely composed of construction paper.

DIORAMA: A scene viewed through an opening is known as a diorama. A cardboard box provides an excellent background for settings such as this. However, other kinds of material, such as metal, paper, or fabric, might be suitable. This diorama is composed of a paper background washed with watercolor. Gravel, stones, shells, and paper fish suggest the ocean floor. An assortment of scrap articles can be used in composing dioramas.

Photographs on this page from the book, "Creative Paper Crafts," by Chester Jay Alkema. Sterling Publishing Co., Inc.

PAPER WEAVING: Many decorative and functional objects can be made or covered with woven paper. Here, diagonal and curved slits were cut into a folded red paper loom giving a radiating design when yellow and blue strips were woven across. There are many everyday weavable materials that could be added—shoelaces, bias binding, hair ribbons, even grass!

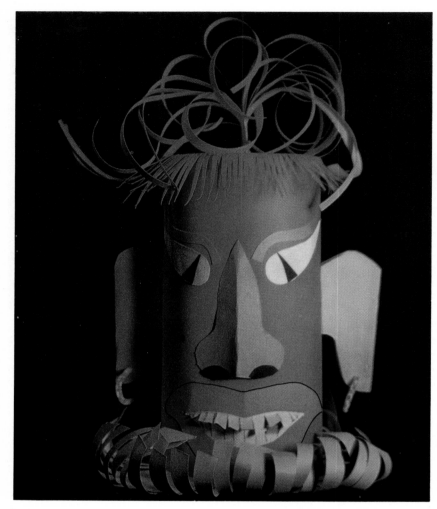

MASKS: An exotic mask made of nothing more than construction paper. Paper bags, papier mâché, tinfoil, or wood, all are possible materials for masks.

From the book, "Creative Paper Crafts," by Chester Jay Alkema. Sterling Publishing Co., Inc.

STAINED GLASS EMBEDDED IN EPOXY CEMENT: Thick facet glass cast in concrete makes a rich, colorful panel. Although ordinary concrete can be used, the new epoxy cement makes an excellent binding agent because of its great strength.

From the book, "Stained Glass Crafting," by Paul W. Wood. Sterling Publishing Co., Inc.

Page P ■ MASKS–STAINED GLASS CRAFTING

STAINED GLASS, once the domain of professional artisans and found only in church windows, has today entered the home. Now, the home craftsman can produce windows, panels, lanterns, and other ornamental objects to enhance a modern or traditional decor.

From the book, "Stained Glass Crafting," by Paul W. Wood. Sterling Publishing Co., Inc.

From the book, "Making Mosaics," by Edmond Arvois. Sterling Publishing Co., Inc.

MOSAICS: A plain bottle and a clay pot are transformed into decorative vessels by the application of tile tesserae. The mosaic technique can be applied to almost any surface, using any number of materials for tesserae—from pebbles to glass—and simple tools. You can ornament window sills, fireplaces, kitchen walls, or floors to suit your own taste.

From the book, "Stained Glass Crafting," by Paul W. Wood. Sterling Publishing Co., Inc.

GLASS MOSAICS can rejuvenate old tables or add a bright touch to a new plain one such as this, which has a frosted glass base to allow light to shine through the glass tesserae.

From the book, "Designs and How to Use Them," by Joan B. Priolo. Sterling Publishing Co., Inc.

WOODWORKING is a satisfying craft which enables you to create practical as well as decorative objects. A plain, easy-to-make wooden plate can be turned into a unique server with the application of an enamel or lacquer design.

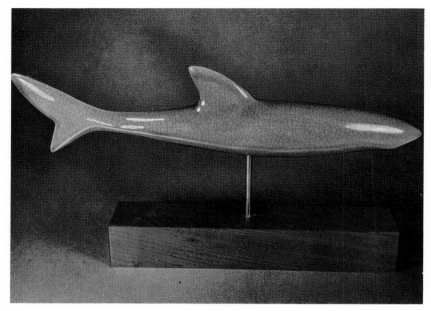

From the book, "Ceramics—and How to Decorate Them," by Joan B. Priolo. Sterling Publishing Co., Inc.

CERAMICS: A shark, simple in form, has a crackle glaze. Many special glazing effects can be achieved by sponging, dipping, pouring or spraying.

GLAZING A DEEP BOWL: A background of grey-green and brown underglaze sponging was used and a line design of black underglaze applied over the sponging. Several sgraffito accents have been added. This view is looking directly down into the bowl.

From the book, "Ceramics—and How to Decorate Them," by Joan B. Priolo. Sterling Publishing Co., Inc.

WEAVING is an age-old handicraft, but modern fibers and fabrics have opened up a new dimension to the beginner. With a simple handloom, the craftsman can turn out impressive woven articles.

From the book, "Small Webs," by courtesy of the copyright owner, ICA-Forlaget Aktiebolag, Vasteras, Sweden.

From the book, "Macramé," by Imelda Manalo Pesch. Sterling Publishing Co., Inc.

MACRAMÉ, an ancient craft practiced by southern Europeans in the 14th to 16th centuries, has recently become popular again. Colorful wall hangings such as this one can be made with almost any thread, yarn, cord or string. By alternating the basic knots used, the lines of color can move across the piece in varying directions.

From the book, "Papier Mâché and How to Use It," by Mildred Anderson. Sterling Publishing Co., Inc.

PAPIER MÂCHÉ is one of the most versatile processes imaginable. Essentially, it is actually turning paper back into the wood it originally came from, either by using paste-coated paper or the pulpy mass called "mash," made in an electric blender. A revolution in papier mâché has taken place with the use of the new epoxy resins as a surface finish, which provide a strength and hardness never known before. Now, even papier mâché furniture is possible!

From the book, "Making Paper Flowers," by Susanne Strose. Sterling Publishing Co., Inc.

PAPER FLOWER MAKING: Crepe paper offers many advantages for making paper flowers—the range of colors is wide, the paper can be crimped, pinched, stretched, curled or rolled. For frilly flowers like these chrysanthemums, it is ideal. However, all kinds of paper can be used depending upon the kind of flower you wish to make.

A CRAYON MOSAIC is composed of melted wax crayons poured on to tin foil to harden. When solidified, broken layers are glued to paper and India ink and pen used for the defining lines. There are many such new crayon techniques today.

Photographs on this page from the book, "The Complete Crayon Book," by Chester Jay Alkema. Sterling Publishing Co., Inc.

CRAYON ETCHING: An unusual negative-positive etching can be executed with the use of chalk and crayon. Here, stylized poinsettia blossoms are positioned amidst a tightly woven pattern of geometrically etched shapes.

From the book, "Creating with Beads," by Grethe La Croix. Sterling Publishing Co., Inc.

BEADCRAFT: The colorful wooden bead necklace was made using the "matting technique," which can be applied to such objects as table mats, tumbler holders, or picture frames. From a few basic threading methods, you can create a wide range of objects. Bead embroidery decorates the two round cloth-covered boxes. Leather, felt or any material that can be sewn on directly can be embroidered.

CERAMIC CREATIONS: This simple hollowing-out technique can produce any number of fine articles, such as the piggy bank, the owl or the vase.

From the book, "Ceramic Creations," by Robert L. Fournier. Sterling Publishing Co., Inc. Photograph by John Anderson for Diana Wyllie filmstrip "The Potter's Craft."

IKEBANA

The origins of Ikebana, Japanese flower arranging, go back forty-five centuries when the art was developed in order to create flower offerings fit for Buddha. Priests were the artists and schools were formed to ensure that the traditions, scrupulously developed, were correctly handed down. But through the ages, the delicacy and beauty of Ikebana have attracted many people. Many wished to imitate the fineness of its line, its harmony and intrinsic grace. Priests long since have stopped acting as custodians of the art and the art has grown away from its strictly religious beginnings. Today, anyone can participate who wishes.

If you practice, give attention to the prerequisites of various Ikebana styles, have a love for flowers and a capacity for deriving special pleasure from the simplicity of Ikebana—you will create flower arrangements that will bring important personal rewards, not the least being the satisfaction of introducing something quite beautiful into your own home.

The four important traditional styles of Ikebana are Rikka, Nageire, Seika and Moribana, each with its own variations. The most practical way of differentiating one style from another is to observe the manner in which the stems emerge from their containers.

In Rikka all stems emerge together in a vertical shaft for a few inches above the rim of the container. In the Nageire style, all stems emerge individually, in slanting lines, generally forming a triangle. In Seika all stems are grouped closely together to appear as one. In

MAIN STEM VERTICAL: This is the identifying characteristic of a Moribana arrangement.

Moribana, plant material duplicates the natural growth pattern and the base of stems is usually concealed by such material as leaves, small flowers or moss.

Small cluster flowers are best suited for Ikebana designs because they maintain an Oriental feeling. The small refined size of cluster narcissi are more appropriate than the flamboyant size of large trumpet daffodils. Small carnations and chrysanthemums are most suitable. When selecting flowers according to color, remember that a monochromatic harmony is composed of tints and shades of one color; an analogous harmony is composed of a small group of touching colors on a color wheel, such as orange, yellow and green or green, blue and violet. Complementary colors are those opposite each other on a color wheel, such as red and green, blue and orange, or violet and yellow.

The ideal branches for Ikebana are those with graceful natural curves. The leaves on branches or the needles on evergreens should be reasonably small or short. The leaf size has to be in good proportion to additional

Condensed from the book, "Ikebana (Japanese Flower Arranging) Simplified" by Olive Scofield Bowes / © 1969 by Sterling Publishing Co., Inc., New York

CUT UNDER WATER: The stem end should not lose its moisture (Illus. 1).

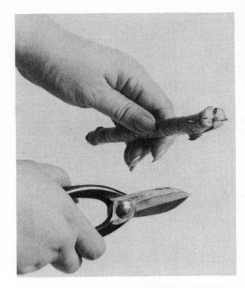

SPLIT WOODY BRANCH STEMS
to allow absorption of more water
(Illus. 2).

materials and to the container. Branches that have the twigs arranged in an alternating pattern along the branch are more pleasing than those that have the twigs arranged opposite each other.

Most flowers and foliage are perishable. Their freshness and durability can be extended by proper care and conditioning. Flowers picked when young will obviously keep longer than flowers that have been in full bloom on the plant for a number of days. Beware of flowers that remain open for one day only, such as the morning glory, daylily, and hibiscus. Cool temperatures, about 60 to 65 degrees F., are best for maintaining freshness in flowers. An arrangement will last longer if it is put in a cool place overnight out of air currents. It should also be kept out of direct sunshine as excess heat will dehydrate petals and leaves. A light, misty spray of water, twice daily, will help to maintain moderate humidity. Cut material should be placed in a deep container of water and kept in a dark, cool, draft-free place for an hour or two before you begin your arrangements. Tepid water will cool to correct temperature in this time.

There are various hints helpful to know in preparing stems:

1. Cut the stem end while it is under water (Illus. 1).

2. Split or crush an inch or two of stem ends on all woody branches (Illus. 2 and 3). This allows the material to absorb more water. Woody stems should be split or crushed as

CRUSH STEM ENDS that are difficult to split (Illus. 3).

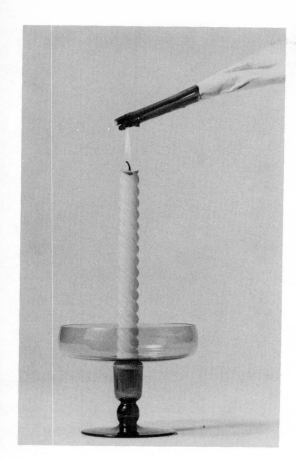

MILKY SAP MATERIAL must be burned to make the stem into charcoal that absorbs water easily (Illus. 4).

RUB DRY SALT on cut ends that are difficult to condition (Illus. 5).

soon as they are removed from the tree or shrub and they should then be plunged immediately into deep, tepid water. This procedure applies to evergreen branches, flowering branches, foliage branches and all other material that has a hard-textured stem.

3. Dip stem ends in 2 inches of boiling water if the plant material has a hard exterior and a spongy interior. Protect the rest of the stem, flowers or leaves from the steam. Boil the stem ends for 5 minutes. This forces air into the stem, expanding it. The secret of this procedure is to plunge the stems into cold water immediately after boiling. Now the stems contract and draw up fresh water. Stems may be recut when ready to arrange. This method applies to many garden flowers such as amaranth, gerbera, peony, hydrangea and snapdragon.

4. Burn stem ends on all material that has a milky sap, a juicy stem or branches noted for wilting. Place 1 inch of the stem end over a hot flame until it glows red (Illus. 4). Protect the rest of the material from the heat. Burning the stem changes it to charcoal, which is porous and absorbs water easily. While the stem is still glowing plunge it into cold water. Some materials which will need this treatment are aster, bellflower, Christmas rose, dahlia, Oriental poppy, oleander and poinsettia.

5. The salt method is used two ways. If material is difficult to condition, use the boiling water method and add 1 teaspoon of salt to the water. Otherwise, dry salt may be rubbed on the cut ends (Illus. 5). The salt helps to preserve the moisture within the stem. Try salt for amaranth, anemone, calla lily, cosmos, Nandina and lilac.

6. Sugar may be added to the water for tulips and verbena. The flowers will last much longer, as the sugar supplies carbohydrates to the plant tissues. Add 1 teaspoon of sugar to the container.

7. Alcohol or Japanese sake may be used to keep flowering wisteria or anemones fresh. Place freshly cut stem ends in either one for a half-hour (Illus. 6).

Fortunately, most material needs no special treatment. The above suggestions are given to solve special problems and should only be used where necessary.

Essential to the art of Ikebana is the careful positioning of the natural elements in con-

AN ALCOHOL DIP for a half-hour is needed for flowering anemones and wisteria to keep them fresh (Illus. 6).

Illus. 7

CUTTING A STEM requires a sharp tool (Illus. 7), a clean cut (Illus. 8), and firm pressure (Illus. 9).

Illus. 8

Illus. 9

tainers. To do this, you will need a pinholder, which can be purchased in a florist's shop. It is sometimes referred to as a needle-holder, or a frog or a kenzan. A holder which has fine, sharp pins closely spaced is far superior to coarse, dull pins more widely spaced. Anchor the pinholder to a dry container by placing a small piece of floral clay under it, and, with firm pressure, twisting the pinholder at its desired position until it becomes well adhered.

The following basic instructions and illustrations explain how to cut, trim, and secure stems and branches most effectively.

To cut branches or stems, use sharp scissors, shears, or clippers (Illus. 7). Squeeze the cutters with firm pressure (Illus. 8), and make a clean cut at the desired point (Illus. 9).

To place a small branch on a pinholder, cut the end on a slant (Illus. 10). Place the branch straight up in the holder (Illus. 11). Then slant

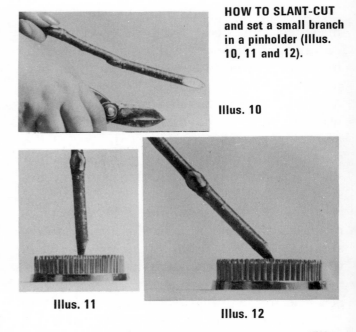

HOW TO SLANT-CUT and set a small branch in a pinholder (Illus. 10, 11 and 12).

Illus. 10

Illus. 11

Illus. 12

the branch, with the cut end facing up (Illus. 12). If reversed, the branch will not stay in

Illus. 13

Illus. 14

Illus. 15

LARGE BRANCH HANDLING: Slant both sides of the stem (Illus. 13), counterbalance the holder with a weight (Illus. 14) and insert stem (Illus. 15).

Illus. 16

Illus. 17

Illus. 18

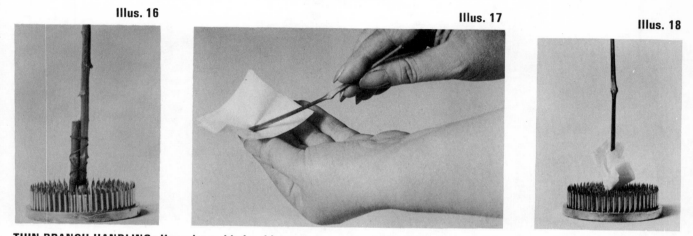

THIN BRANCH HANDLING: Use wire to bind a thin stem to a support (Illus. 16). For very thin stems, wrap them in paper (Illus. 17) and stick paper and stem into the holder (Illus. 18).

place. The bark is softer than the inner wood, and will press into the pins more easily.

To handle big branches, cut the end so that it is slanted on both sides. This produces a flat triangle (Illus. 13). Place an extra pinholder upside down on the first holder to counterbalance the weight of the branch (Illus. 14). Place the branch in the holder as shown in Illus. 15.

To handle thin branches, add an extra piece of stem to the base of the first one, and bind them together with wire or thread (Illus. 16).

To hold very thin stems, such as sweet peas, wrap a small square of paper around the end of the stem (Illus. 17). Place the wrapped stem in the pinholder (Illus. 18).

Illus. 19

BENDING: Grip with both thumbs and slowly bend regular size branches (Illus. 19).

To bend regular branches, use both hands, grip with the thumbs, and exert pressure on the branch, bending it slowly (Illus. 19). Use the same technique to bend grass, but twist the

Illus. 20

Illus. 21

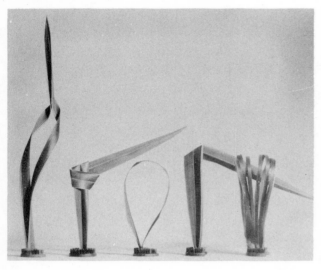

Illus. 22

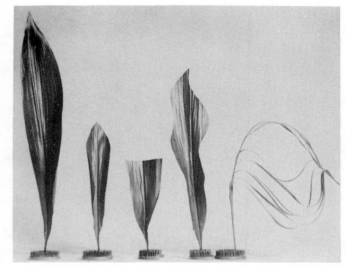

Illus. 23

HANDLING LEAVES: You can twist the stems of grass or leaves (Illus. 20) or make loops in them (Illus. 21 and 22). Leaves may also be cut to shape or shredded (Illus. 23).

BENDING LARGE BRANCHES: You may either cut a triangular slash out of one side of the branch (Illus. 24), or cut a wedge off completely (Illus. 25) and wire the slanted edges together to form a bend (Illus. 26). Use the wedge in this or another slash.

Illus. 24

Illus. 26

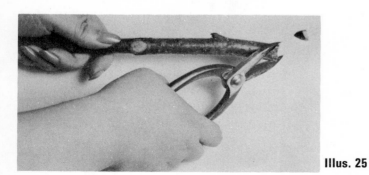

Illus. 25

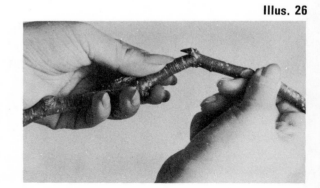

Illus. 27

Illus. 28

Illus. 29

Illus. 30

TRIMMING A FLOWER SPRAY: When a branch is heavy with leaves (Illus. 27), trim out some of the smaller leaves and branches (Illus. 28). Do the same with a full fruit tree branch (Illus. 29 and 30), and with a berried vine (Illus. 31 and 32).

stem a bit (Illus. 20). To bend leaves, hold the end of the stem. With the other hand gently twist the leaf (Illus. 21). Besides twisting the leaf, you can knot it or shred it as shown in Illus. 22. Leaves may also be cut and re-shaped as in Illus. 23.

To bend large branches, cut a slash at the point where the branch is to be bent (Illus. 24). Clip a small triangular wood wedge (Illus. 25) and insert it into the slash (Illus. 26). Several cuts and wedges may be needed, depending upon the degree of the desired curve.

Trimming methods: By eliminating excess material the beauty of a stem, vine, or branch is revealed. Simplicity of line is important in Ikebana. Illus. 27 shows a flower spray before trimming. Illus. 28 shows the same stem after several small leaves and small side branches have been removed. Illus. 29 shows a fruit branch before trimming; and Illus. 30 shows the same branch after many leaves have been

Illus. 31

Illus. 32

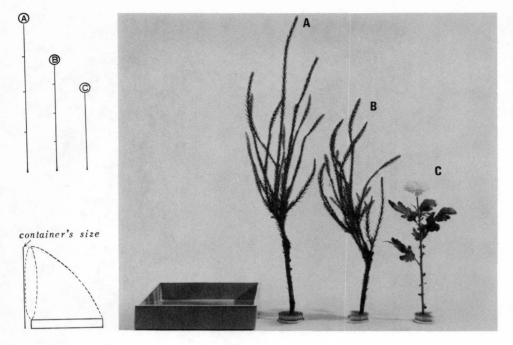

container's size

MORIBANA uses a shallow container and three main stems: A, tallest, B, next, and C, smallest (Illus. 33).

removed. A berried vine before trimming is seen in Illus. 31. Illus. 32 shows the same vine after many leaves have been removed.

Moribana Designs

Arrangements in the category of Ikebana called Moribana are composed of three main stems which will be referred to as A, B and C. Any additional materials used will be called fillers, numbered 1, 2, 3, etc. The A stem is always the main stem—choose the best shaped and strongest looking branch or stem. The length of the A stem will vary, according to the sturdiness or delicacy of the branch, and also according to the nature of the container. Since the plant material and the container are always together, they should be well related in scale, texture, color and pictorial quality.

The size of the A stem should be equal to the width plus the height of the container, or it may measure two or more times the width of the container.

The character of the plant material and the nature of the container influence the measurement. The larger the plant, the larger the container. Delicate stems may be cut longer,

sturdy ones shorter. A thick-walled container may take a taller design than a thin-walled one.

It is always safer to start with stems a bit too long, as they may be shortened to improve the design. Once cut, of course, it is impossible to replace the piece of stem.

The B stem measurement should be three-fourths the length of A.

The C stem measurement should be three-fourths the length of B.

The Moribana Upright Manner

To create a Moribana arrangement in the upright manner, anchor the pinholder to the left front of the dish. Place the A stem in a vertical position at the left side of the holder, leaning it slightly left and forward. Place the B stem at a sharper angle to the left and front. Place the C stem (a flower) at a sharp angle to the right and front. (See Illus. 34, 35, 36.)

To better understand the position of the stems, observe the two accompanying diagrams which show the degree of the angles, as seen from the front and above the arrangement. The two fillers, numbered 1 and 2, are added near the middle to complete the design. (See Illus. 37.)

A

Illus. 34

B

Illus. 35

C

Illus. 36

Illus. 38

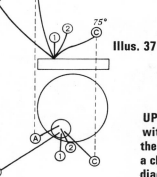

Ⓐ *10°*

45°
Ⓑ

① ②

75°
Ⓒ

Illus. 37

Ⓐ

① ②
Ⓑ   Ⓒ

UPRIGHT: Moribana in this manner accents the vertical, with the tallest material (A) placed first (Illus. 34) in the holder. Next, B is swung outwards (Illus. 35) and C, a chrysanthemum, to the right and front (Illus. 36). The diagrams (Illus. 37) show the angles and overhead view. The finished arrangement (Illus. 38) is simple and balanced with two more chrysanthemums as fillers.

Additional flower leaves (chrysanthemum in this arrangement) are used to cover the pinholder and conceal the bareness at the lowest part of the design. Do *not* make an even ring of foliage around the base. This creates an unnatural effect. Any added foliage should appear to be attached to the flower stems. A small amount of moss or pebbles may be added close to the pinholder to give the design a finished look and a natural appearance.

All plant material needs a constant supply of fresh, cool water to remain in a fresh condition. You must therefore add water to your arrangement. (After being conditioned in tepid water, flowers and foliage should be kept in deep, cool water until they are placed in an arrangement.) You may fill your container with fresh water after anchoring supports and before you begin to arrange flowers, or the water may be added as soon as the design is completed. This applies to all containers, the dish you used in this arrangement and the vases or pin cups you will be using in later arrangements.

Every Ikebana arrangement can be made in reverse. Naturally, the best side of flowers and branches should face the observer. If your plant material looks best facing the opposite way, it would be advantageous to place the pinholder in the *right* front of the dish and reverse (left to right) the entire procedure for placing the stems.

A Variation of Moribana Upright

This design differs from the usual Moribana Upright Manner in as much as the plant material is divided between two pinholders instead of being contained in one.

In Illus. 42 the A and B lines are in the front left pinholder and the C line is in the rear right pinholder. The fillers are arranged in the pinholders according to the diagrams. Filler number 6, a small cluster of flowers, is in the left holder, adding variety of size to that group. This is a very pleasing variation and may be created with two or three different kinds of flowers. An attractive combination could be forced springtime branches, such as flowering quince or peach, in combination with small garden flowers. Notice that the stem measurement of this design adheres to the basic one in which A is equal to the width of the dish plus its height.

The unoccupied expanse of water in most Moribana arrangements is an important part of a design, adding a tranquil effect and helping to balance the arrangement.

The Moribana Slanting Manner

In this style the pinholder is secured at the rear right side (Illus. 44). (An alternate position could be the left front as in the first design.) The A stem inclines forward, while the

| Illus. 39 | Illus. 40 | Illus. 41 |

TWO PINHOLDERS are used in this variation of Moribana Upright. Stems A (Illus. 39) and B (Illus. 40) go into the left holder, and C, the lowest (Illus. 41), into the right holder.

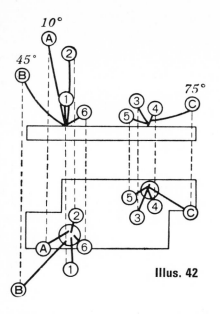

Illus. 43

MORIBANA UPRIGHT

FILLERS add variety of size to this Moribana Upright. The water expanse is an important part of the arrangement, shown finished in Illus. 43.

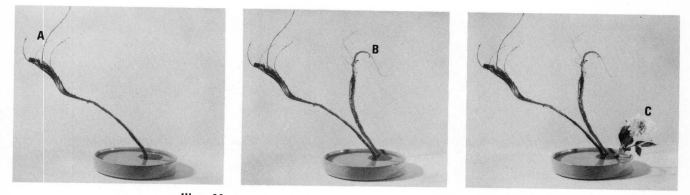

Illus. 44

Illus. 45

Illus. 46

B stem is at the rear. The C stem (a flower) to the lower right completes the imaginary triangle formed by the ends of the three main lines. This triangular pattern is characteristic of Ikebana. Emphasis is on the lovely slanting line of A, making this a suitable design when you use naturally curving line material.

Place the A stem at the left front of the pinholder, extending it left and at the same time slanting it forward. Place B stem at the back of A, slanting it slightly to the left. Place C at an angle to the right, also tilting it forward. The two extra flowers, one lower than the other,

MORIBANA SLANTING:
Typical of this manner is the triangular pattern (Illus. 44, 45, 46, 47) with A, B and C all slanting. With curving line material, this is a good design.

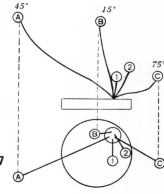

Illus. 47

Illus. 48

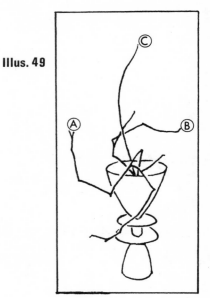

Illus. 49

are simply to add to the design. An additional leaf or two will disguise the pinholder. The diagrams (Illus. 47, previous page) illustrate the degree of the angles as seen from the front and above.

Occasionally basic measurements are disregarded in the Slanting Manner. The individual characteristics of the material are allowed to determine the most attractive positions, demonstrating that there is some freedom of expression within Ikebana.

The Moribana Cascade Manner

This style of Ikebana is ideal for vines, for materials which twine or suspend, or have great natural flexibility. The individuality and the significance of the Cascade Manner lie in the emphasis on line and movement. To bring out these characteristics to best advantage only a few materials are arranged together. Because

Illus. 50

MORIBANA IN THE CASCADE MANNER: For vines with a low container on a tall stand this is ideal (Illus. 50).

the A stem curves downward, choose a container, as in Illus. 51, with a tall stand.

Let A stem curve sharply to front and downward, swinging to the left. Place B stem behind it, to curve in the opposite direction, for balance. Place C stem almost upright behind these two lines, since one is cascading forward and the other is horizontal. No filler is used in this arrangement as the C stem has sufficient leaves attached to it. If a shallow container is used for this design, the arrangement should be placed on a shelf or near the edge of a table to allow room for the A line to cascade.

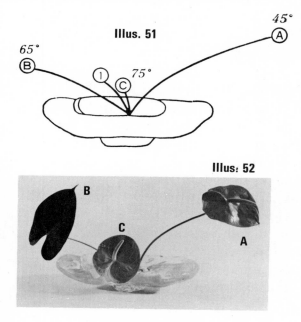

Illus. 51

65°

45°

75°

Illus: 52

The Moribana Horizontal Manner

Plant materials often dictate the manner in which they are best displayed. The beauty of some is brought out by an erect line; some will appear more graceful when placed in a slanting position. Use the Horizontal Manner for material that will be best shown in a low widespread arrangement. This is appropriate for a dinner or coffee table. (See Illus. 51, 52.)

Using flowers that bloom one to a stem, such as anthurium, place the A stem in the holder extending to the right at a sharp angle. Place B to extend to the left in a slightly lower position than A, and toward the front. Place C at the middle of the front, very short-stemmed

and slanted downward. The one filler is a leaf placed behind C.

Nageire Designs

The effect of the Nageire style of Ikebana is casual, uncluttered and informal. A tall container is used and much of the art lies in positioning the natural materials in these containers with a minimum support. The Japanese technique consists of using pieces of light branch material to support the lines of the design. This requires much patience and dexterity and similar results can be achieved by using pinholders positioned within the container; chunks of Oasis (a water-absorbent foam block) cut to fit into the container; or some such substance as chicken wire, crumpled lightly and wedged down inside. Your finished Nageire arrangement will not reveal whether you used a traditional Japanese method of support or one of these "Western" shortcuts.

As in Moribana, there are three main stems which again we will refer to as A, B and C. Any additional material will be called fillers, numbered 1 and 2. Rarely are there many fillers in a Nageire design. Again, the A stem is always the best shaped and strongest looking branch or stem.

The A stem measures twice the height of the vase plus the diameter of the opening. The B stem is three-quarters of A, and the C stem is three-quarters of B or one-half of A. These measurements include only the visible portion of the material, and the length of stem resting inside the container must be in addition to the prescribed lengths. If a stem curves sharply, it may appear short in the finished arrangement, but if you have begun with the correct lengths you will be working correctly.

The Nageire Upright Manner

This is a basic upright style for a tall vase arrangement. The principal consideration is to achieve a tall, slender design. Only a part of the opening in the vase is to be used for the

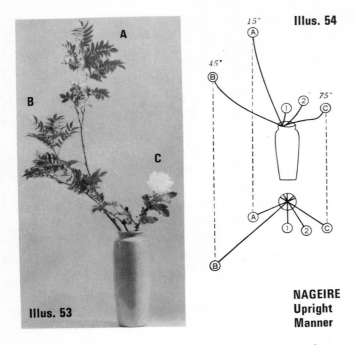

Illus. 54

Illus. 53

The Nageire Cascade Manner

Select graceful branches for the A and B lines, as they must suspend in natural curves, clearly defined and uncluttered.

Place the A line to the far left of the opening. Use a branch which has a natural curve near the container rather than one which would need force to bend it into a sharp cascading position. Place B, which is an angular line, towards the back of the container, slanting it to the right to counterbalance the A line. Place C (a spray of flowers) on an angle to the left but close to B, and tilted slightly to the back. Standard measurements are not adhered to for a cascade design due to the irregular characteristics of the line material.

The Nageire Slanting Manner

This is an ideal style for displaying natural, gracefully curving lines of plant material. (See Illus. 55 and 56.)

Place the A stem so that it slants forward and to the left, at a moderate angle. Place B in back of the A stem, in a nearly vertical line. Place C (a flower bud) in a relatively horizontal position and to the right. The two open flowers, which are the two fillers, unify the design and add an accent at the middle of the triangle formed by the main lines.

placement of the stems. The lines rest against the front of the rim.

Place the A stem at the left front, slanting it slightly forward. Place the B stem at approximately the same spot, but at a sharper angle both to the left and to the front. Place the C stem (a flower) to the right, at a sharp forward slant. Fillers 1 and 2 are added near the middle to complete the basic triangle formed by the three main lines. As a guide follow the step-by-step indications in Illus. 53 and 54.

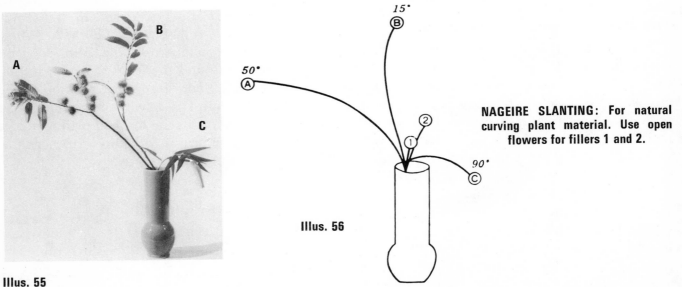

Illus. 56

Illus. 55

NAGEIRE SLANTING: For natural curving plant material. Use open flowers for fillers 1 and 2.

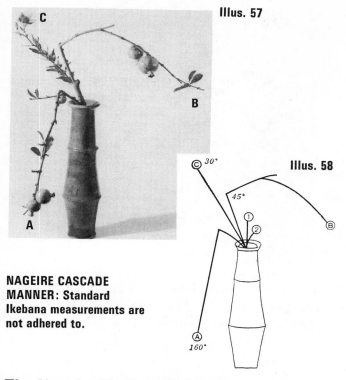

Illus. 57

Illus. 58

NAGEIRE CASCADE MANNER: Standard Ikebana measurements are not adhered to.

The Nageire Horizontal Manner

Main line branches of simple, clean lines are appropriate for this type of Nageire.

Place the A and B lines so they will cross at the vase opening and extend in opposite directions. Firmly fixed main lines provide a good foundation for the rest of the material. Both A and B must slant a bit forward. Place the C line (a flower) so that it is in a central position, slanting sharply forward. The one filler, another flower, arches up and to the left. (See Illus. 59 and 60.)

As in Moribana designs, all of these Nageire designs may be constructed in the reverse position if the beauty of the plant material would be displayed to better advantage. In all cases water must be added as soon as the design is completed.

Seika Designs

Seika is the classical style of Ikebana. Chronologically, Seika styles followed the Nageire. Again, the Japanese changed their concept of arrangements from the casual effect of Nageire to the strict formality of Seika designs. This type became so highly popular that a wide range of Seika styles were formulated.

Seika arrangements are governed by exacting rules for placement of line and stem arrangement. The designs presented are based on three main lines, which are easily duplicated by a beginner.

However, Seika designs are commonly constructed using three, five, seven, nine, etc., lines (always uneven numbers), although three of these lines are still considered the main ones. When a large number of lines are used in a design, it is usually one composed of foliage leaves of one variety, such as aspidistra leaves.

Seika designs are fascinating. There is an infinite variety of containers that have been used for these arrangements. Imaginative pieces range from antique bronze containers of elaborate design to hanging crescents (see

Illus. 59

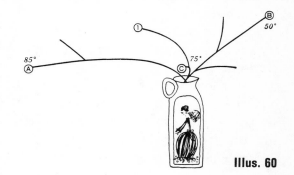

Illus. 60

NAGEIRE HORIZONTAL MANNER calls for simple, clean lines.

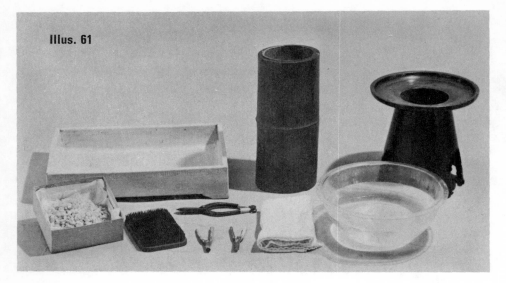

Illus. 61

SEIKA EQUIPMENT: Forked sticks and pebbles, along with vases and pinholders (Illus. 61).

color page I), boats and ceramic dishes. Many bamboo cylinders are fashioned with two or more openings, one above the other, as are some of the newer ceramics. If you should browse through old library books on classical Japanese arrangements, you will be impressed by the distinctive containers used for Seika designs.

You have a choice of four methods for supporting stems in Seika arrangements.

1. Use a forked stick (a crutch) inside medium and tall containers. This is the traditional Japanese equipment.

2. If heavy stems will not balance properly, use a Western prop, and fasten a pinholder beneath the forked stick. Conceal the pinholder with a layer of white sand. The forked stick maintains the appearance of traditional Japanese technique.

3. If you cannot master the use of the forked stick, rely on a pinholder or pin cup inside the container.

4. All low-dish arrangements require a pinholder. The Japanese have accepted its use as standard equipment to anchor stems in a shallow container.

Three Seika designs made with a combination of flowers and foliage are presented here. The three main lines are referred to as A, B and C. The types of containers used in these designs are correct for the particular styles.

Measure the A stem to extend one and one-half times the height of the container. To emphasize the stature of tall material such as gladioli, the A stem may be three times taller than the container.

The B stem is two-thirds of A.

The C stem is one-third of A.

The Seika Formal Manner (Shin-style)

This style is always slender, barely wider than the width of the container. Reverse the usual procedure by placing the C stem first. Place it at the middle front. Follow this with the A stem filler behind C. Next put the combination A-B stem at the rear. Illus. 62, 63, 64 will guide you. After the material is properly grouped, put in a side-stick over the forked stick to hold stems in place.

One basic rule must be observed in all Seika designs. All stems must be grouped to appear as one, and stems must be bare or plain for a few inches above the rim of the container.

FORKED STICK: This is how to use one with a Seika formal arrangement (Illus. 62).

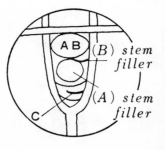

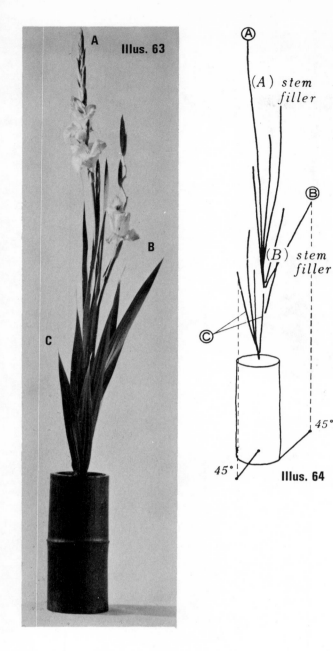

Illus. 63

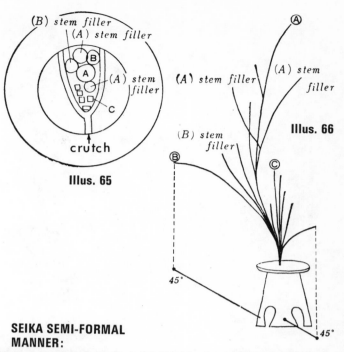

Ⓐ (A) stem filler

Ⓑ (B) stem filler

Ⓒ

45°

45°

Illus. 64

Ⓑ (B) stem filler

Ⓐ (A) stem filler

Ⓐ (A) stem filler

Ⓒ

crutch

Illus. 65

Illus. 66

45°

45°

SEIKA SEMI-FORMAL MANNER:
The crutch or forked stick holds the three stems (A, B, C) and 10 fillers in place (Illus. 65, 66, 67).

The Seika Semi-Formal Manner

(Gyo-style)

There is more freedom in the semi-formal type of design. Lines curve away from the center. Branches may extend beyond the width of the container. There is depth and rhythm in the design.

As in the previous arrangement, follow the illustrations (65, 66, and 67) for line placement. Insert numbered fillers.

Illus. 67

Illus. 68

Illus. 69

SEIKA INFORMAL: Assembled like a Moribana arrangement, this has the holder in the middle. The pinholder is hidden by pebbles in the finished design shown in Illus. 69 (Illus. 68, 69, 70).

SEIKA VARIATIONS include use of a double-opening container, or even a 3-level container, each opening filled with a different material. However, the identifying characteristic of Seika is having stems closely grouped to appear as one stem.

The Seika Informal Manner (So-style)

A pinholder is used in this shallow-dish design. Anchor it in the middle. This differs from Moribana where the holder is to one side. However, the design is assembled like a Moribana arrangement.

Place the A stem in the pinholder at a slight angle. Next, place the B stem to the left, leaning away from A. The C stem is a group of short flowers with their own foliage. Place C to the right front, slanting it a bit to the right. The fillers are pieces of the main line materials. In such a Seika arrangement, where the stems must be bare as they arise from the dish, the pinholder is concealed by placing a group of pebbles around it. As in other Ikebana designs, water must be added.

Illus. 70

Stem C added to stem A

Rikka Designs

Historically, a Rikka design is the oldest stylized form of Ikebana. Rikka is a tree-shaped pattern of 7 or 9 main lines. One is a central branch. The others are upper, middle and lower branches which are arranged around the central branch. The placement is never crowded; instead there should be a feeling of airiness throughout the design. All stems are grouped together at the base, in a bundled effect, and arise vertically from the container.

The Rikka Formal Manner

The traditional container for this type of design is a bronze vase or urn. Use a forest tree branch for the central line (usually an evergreen). Place this line in a vertical position. It may be quite tall in proportion to the height of the container. Each successive branch should be a different variety of tree, shrub or flower.

**RIKKA
FORMAL**

Illus. 71

**RIKKA
SEMI-FORMAL**

Illus. 72

Some fillers may be used but the design should not be packed. Maintain open areas between each branch so that the beauty of each will be apparent. Skillful selection of materials and strategic pruning enhance the design. All stems are bundled and tied at the base, or all stems are inserted into a bundle of slender pieces of hollow bamboo fastened together with straw. The bamboo holds the water. You may also use pinholders or pin cups and camouflage them with a ring of bamboo tied together.

The Rikka Semi-Formal Manner

A bronze container or bamboo cylinder is suitable for a semi-formal design. The same main lines are used. In this variation the tall central branch should curve slightly. In a similar manner the side branches have more fluid lines. The central branch may consist of any type of material, whether tree, shrub or

Illus. 73

flower. The branch pattern and stem arrangement are the same for all Rikka designs.

The Rikka Informal Manner

A shallow metal container is appropriate for an informal arrangement. All lines, including the central one, are quite horizontal, and often of a sinuous nature. The informal Rikka style may have been the inspiration, centuries later, for Moribana designs or per-haps for Bonsai trees, growing in shallow dishes, as there is a similarity of feeling.

At the present time smaller versions of Rikka arrangements are being made for the home. In the newest Ikebana schools modern adaptations of Rikka designs are a challenge to the artist. Some are constructed around massive pieces of weathered wood combined with a variety of plant material, and are placed on a tray or board.

LAPIDARY
(Gem Cutting)

Gem material minerals are found everywhere—the gravel beds of mountain streams, rock quarries, big city excavations, and newly blasted road cuts. Probably the easiest place to find attractive stones is on the gravel bars of beaches, and beachcombing for agates is popular in many parts of the world.

What if you are a casual browser and decide that you would like to polish one of your finds? There are thousands of amateur lapidaries to consult, there are a few magazines, gem and mineral societies in many places, and a few schools for the lapidary. Do not go out and buy equipment before you have a chance to try out the craft with tools belonging to someone else. A dealer, an amateur lapidary, or a mineral collector can put you on the right course. While it is possible (and has been done) to teach yourself to grind and polish gem material, instruction is surer and easier. It is *not* a difficult craft to learn; and the creation of enduring beauty is reward enough, even if the polished gem stones are not valuable.

What makes a stone a gem stone? It must be beautiful; it must be rare; it must be fashionable; and it must be comparatively hard and durable. Opals rate low on durability but so high on beauty and fashion that opal gem rough is sold by the ounce and retailed by the carat. Malachite, the beautiful green opaque gem stone from the Russian Urals and the old Belgian Congo, rates high in beauty and

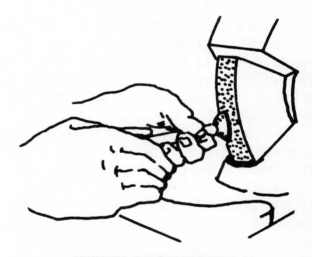

GRINDING A CABOCHON (Illus. 1).

low in rarity and hardness. You buy malachite rough by the pound and because of the quantity available and its ease of working you see it in cigarette boxes and ash trays.

To cut stones from their rough natural state until polished and ready for setting in a piece of jewelry requires a number of stages: (1) sawing into rough slabs or slices; (2) trimming; (3) rough grinding or lapping; (4) finish grinding; (5) dopping; (6) sanding or smoothing; (7) pre-polishing; and (8) polishing.

In any case, let us suppose that you have found some agate which you want to cut and to work in a shop. The trail starts with a diamond saw.

Written especially for this volume by Joe Rothstein

Slabbing

Sawing a stone is not like sawing wood or metal, since many minerals are harder than the strongest steels. A circular whirling metal blade is used, but it does not do the cutting itself. The actual cutting is done by an abrasive with which the rim of the saw is "charged," meaning that it is bathed or its notches filled with the abrasive. The best abrasive is diamond powder or grit, since the diamond is the hardest material known. Even the softest gem rough is "rock" hard, and must be slabbed by such a saw. This is the initial step.

Gem material comes in chunks; slabbing saws range from 10 to 20 inches in diameter; a chunk about 5 to 6 inches in diameter is all that can be handled by the ordinary saw. So you need a slabbing saw, which in principle is no more than the cheese slicer in the grocery.

Hold the gem material to be slabbed firmly in a clamp and run the saw to eat its way slowly through the hard stone. Heat, of course, is generated and, to dissipate this heat of friction, the bottom of the saw has to be immersed in a light oil coolant. When you take the oil-soaked gem slab out, put it into a box of sawdust or wrap it in newspaper or paper toweling—anything to take out as much of the oil as possible. The next day it will be ready for trimming.

Slabbing saws are expensive, bulky, and messy, and most lapidaries who work at home prefer to buy their slabs from dealers. It does save time, and also you can select a design that appeals to you rather than gamble on finding a good design hidden inside the chunk of gem rough. A craft school will charge a student a small fee to slab his rough material. Some affluent, large lapidary clubs have set up schools and charge their members a nominal fee, too. Dealers will charge about three times the price of a school or club in order to realize a profit. The price will vary according to the size and hardness of the material and also the quantity.

Cabochons

Gem material which depends on its translucency for beauty should be slabbed to $\frac{1}{8}$ of an inch, but the usual thickness for an opaque stone is $\frac{1}{4}$ inch. From this you can get a cabochon which is just about the right height. Cabochons (from the French meaning "bald head") are all you will be concerned with at the start—faceting will come after some 100 hours of practice in "cabbing." The easiest stone for a beginner is an oval, and the most rewarding gem material for a beginner is agate. After some half dozen ovals, your second style will be a "round" which is simply a complete

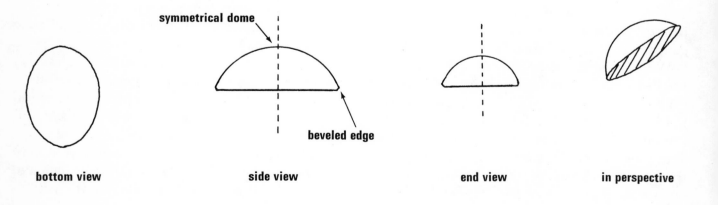

bottom view   side view   end view   in perspective

FIRST STEP is simple cabochon oval (Illus. 2).

circle. Then come squares, rectangles, even hearts and crosses—all "cabs," as cabochon shapes are called. You will branch out with amethyst, moonstone, and the two types of jade minerals, nephrite and jadeite, and other gem stones soon enough.

Scribing

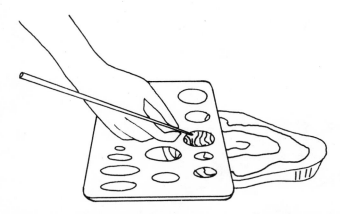

SCRIBING: Using a template to mark outline of stone (Illus. 3).

Look at your slab and notice the way the design is arranged. Think out where you want a large gem, where a small one, where an oval is best, etc. Then, take a template. A template contains the popular cut-out shapes of gem stones, and is best purchased. Templates are made to standard millimeter sizes so that after you have cut and finished the stone you can have it mounted. Not all types and sizes of mounts (called "findings" in the jewelry trade) are readily available, so unless you work in silver and make your own jewelry, you have to select a size that is available. An 18 × 13 mm. stone, which is a popular ring size, is good for a beginner.

With your template, you will mark or "scribe" your slab with outlines of the shapes you want to cut, using an aluminum rod about $\frac{1}{8}$ inch in diameter. Scribing with a pencil is not good enough. The graphite of the pencil washes off in the handling, whereas the mark left by an aluminum rod stands up fairly well.

If it does lighten up in handling, it is no great chore to scribe it again.

What you scribe will become the base of the stone so it is important to pick the side of the slab with the prettiest design for the top of your cab. For some psychological reason, novices frequently seem to think they are scribing the top of the stone. The next step is the trim saw.

Trim Sawing

A law in the machine shop which applies equally well to crafts is to use a machine only for the purpose the manufacturer intended. A trim saw does only that, it trims! If you have a slab of material 8 inches in diameter, it must be sawed down to a workable 4 inches on the slabbing saw before the trim saw can handle it.

Remember, a slab of a stone high up in the hardness scale should be no more than $\frac{1}{4}$ inch thick for the trim saw. Stones low in the hardness scale can be a mite thicker although "getting by" situations are not recommended in lapidary work. Hardness for minerals is measured on the Mohs scale, which consists of ten typical minerals arranged in decreasing order of hardness, as follows:

10. Diamond
9. Corundum (ruby and sapphire)
8. Topaz
7. Quartz
6. Orthoclase (feldspar)
5. Apatite
4. Fluorite
3. Calcite
2. Gypsum
1. Talc

The scale is not a calibrated one—it is only a measure of the ability of one mineral to scratch a softer one. The range of hardness between diamond and ruby is greater than that between ruby and talc.

The trim saw is also a metal saw with its rim embedded with diamond dust (Illus. 4). It has a flat bed and make use of it! Do not attempt to lift your slab off the flat bed or try to slab a large round beach pebble on a trim saw be-

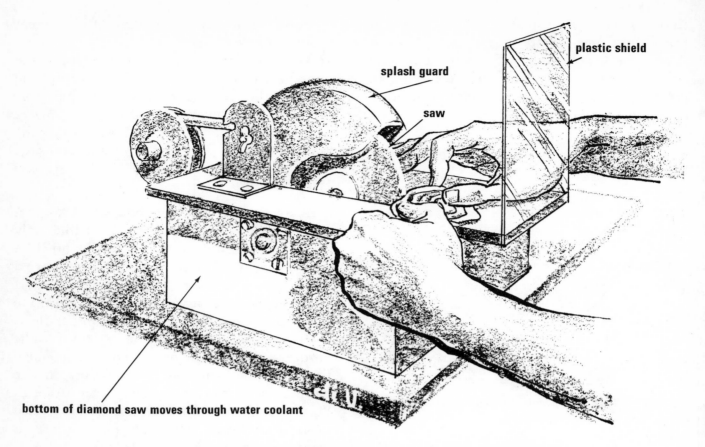

TRIM SAW: Always feed at right angles. The cuts must be very straight (Illus. 4).

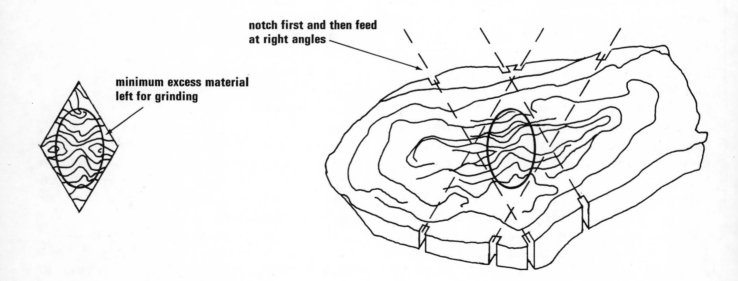

SAWING ANGLES: Allow for width of saw blade when feeding into trim saw (Illus. 5).

cause you do not have access to a slabbing saw. The diamond blade will bind and bend and will be ruined. Even if it does not bend the blade, using the trim saw for other than flat slabs tends to strip the diamond from the saw and shorten its life.

The proper way to use a trim saw is to hold the slab firmly down on the flat bed and feed it slowly and gently through the blade. Apply finger pressure as close to 90° to the blade as possible to ensure a straight cut. There are NO CURVED cuts possible on the trim saw. The coolant used in the trim saw is usually water, and plenty of water must be dripping off the splash guard before you send the gem material through. Illus. 5 shows the sawing angles you should use.

Grinding

Everyone has seen the sparks fly as a knife is sharpened against a wheel. The wheels used in lapidary are made of this same silicon carbide, but are cemented together with a bonding agent which is designed especially for the lapidary. The grains of silicon carbide are referred to as grits; and the lower in number the grit size is, the coarser the grains, and the faster the excess gem material can be removed. Unfortunately, the coarser the grit size, the deeper the scratches left on your gem stone. The objective, as you know, is the removal of even the tiniest scratches, eventually, from your gem material. When you have achieved that, you have polished the stone.

So, begin with a 100 grit wheel with your agate. Agate is a variety of quartz and has a hardness of 7. The silicon carbide of the wheel has a hardness of slightly over 9, and will grind stones over a hardness of 7, but slowly. Practice on agates first. With more experience you can try topaz (hardness 8), emerald and aquamarine (hardness $7\frac{1}{2}$–8), and tourmaline (up to $7\frac{1}{2}$), in fact, everything but ruby and sapphire (hardness 9).

Hold the rough stone gently against the 100

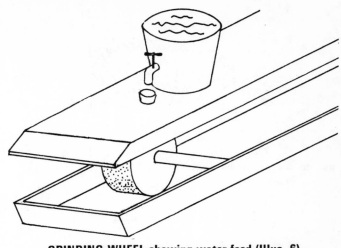

GRINDING WHEEL showing water feed (Illus. 6).

grit wheel, making sure water is dripping slowly on the wheel. The wheels are mounted in a manner to keep the silicon carbide dust away from the bearings. Again, these are made especially for the lapidary. If you are fortunate enough to connect your water supply to the house plumbing, fine; but if not, a bucket and a funnel or connecting hose will do. The wheel does not use so much water that refilling the pail becomes a tiresome chore. Illus. 6 shows a grinding wheel with a homemade water supply that will save a plumbing bill.

Do not grind dry. It will become obvious to you that you will get better visibility by dry grinding, but you could also wind up with silicosis of the lungs. The wheel works more efficiently when wet, you need to keep the gem stone cool or it will crack, and the silicon carbide dust mixed with agate dust does not hang in the air for you to breathe.

Keep the stone moving across the entire left-to-right surface of the wheel. Holding it in one spot will wear a groove in the wheel and ruin it for good work. The wheel should remain flat. If it becomes grooved, then it should be trimmed with a hard steel dresser, or better yet a diamond-tipped dresser.

The wider and larger the diameter of the wheel the better. Settle for a wheel 6 to 8 inches in diameter and 1 to $1\frac{1}{2}$ inches wide—most lapidary equipment for the craftsman

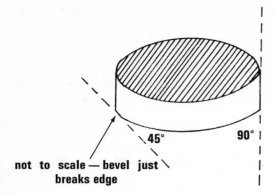

SHAPE BEFORE DOPPING (Illus. 7).

not to scale — bevel just breaks edge

45°   90°

bevel around the base of the stone on the 220 wheel. Now wash the stone and get ready for the next step—dopping.

Dopping

Dop sticks can be cut from any convenient doweling. They will vary in size from $\frac{1}{8}$ inch to $\frac{1}{4}$ inch, depending on the size of the stone. You need an alcohol lamp, a pair of tweezers, and a special dopping mixture of wax and shellac made especially for the lapidary. Hold the dopping cement over the alcohol lamp's flame (not in it, as that will make the cement brittle) and pull the softened wax on to the end of the dop.

A flat piece of steel can be used to roll the wax into a neat shape. The steel is cold and will dissipate the heat of the wax. You need just enough wax to cover $\frac{3}{4}$ of the base of the stone. After you have the dop stick end coated, pick up the agate with a tweezers. Gently heat the agate and the wax on the dop stick simultaneously, to the point where the wax adheres to the gem stone. At this juncture, remove both from the heat, and form the wax around the base of the agate and stick as shown in Illus. 8.

calls for this size. The wheel does the work. Do not push. Don't overload the capacity of your wheel. A wheel $1\frac{1}{2}$ inches wide is not made to grind out the base of a 5-inch ash tray. It will unbalance your wheel and the "chattering" it causes is anathema to a sensitive lapidary.

As you grind your agate, notice that material is being removed quite slowly and you can control the shape easily. Grind down to the marks made by your aluminum pencil, as you want to achieve the shape in Illus. 7. The final step of this stage is to put a small 45°

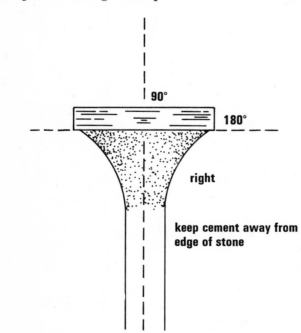

90°   180°

right

keep cement away from edge of stone

wrong

DOPPING (Illus. 8).

It cannot be stressed too strongly about not letting the wax flow over the boundaries established by the base of the stone; keep at least $\frac{1}{16}$ inch away from the bottom edge. You can grind away excess wax on a grinding wheel, but if you get wax on a sanding cloth (which is the next step) you ruin the quality of the abrasive.

At first use the flat edge of your tweezers to shape the hot wax around the dop stick and the stone. As the wax cools, you can use your fingers. Dipping your fingers into some cold water prior to molding the wax is a good trick for a beginner, but after you get the feel of it, that will not be necessary. When your fingernail cannot penetrate the wax, you can put it aside to cool. By this time the wax is set, and there is no danger that the stone will slide off the 180° (horizontal) position. A piece of discarded plastic foam packing about 2 to 3 inches thick is a convenient inexpensive stick holder.

The stone will cool gradually until it is at room temperature. Do not cool it under the water tap—the stone may break.

Shaping on the Grinding Wheel

Wash the stone and then go back to the 100 wheel. Hold the dop stick so that you can see the bottom of the stone. This is important. If you go through the scribed mark, you will lose the shape of the stone. Using a rotating motion and working over the entire surface of the wheel, bring your stone to the desired shape.

No one can help you with this—no one can see through your eyes—and here is where the artistry lies. Shaping the gem stone in a pleasing, symmetrical form to best utilize the color, design, and texture of the gem material is an art. A sculptor can look at a block of marble or granite and visualize a flow of line from which will emerge a finished piece. A lapidary must be able to visualize the same thing with a piece of gem rough. For the first few stones and maybe more, stick to striving

for symmetry. Free form and experimentation can come much later.

In striving for symmetry you must keep in mind that the shape of the stone is controlled from the top as shown in the following sequence:

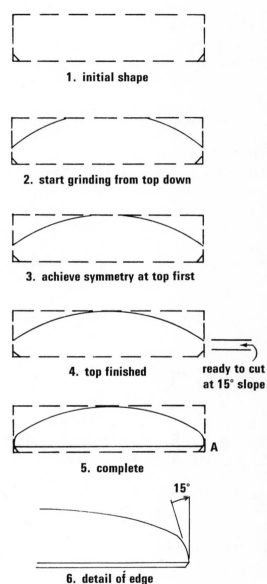

1. initial shape

2. start grinding from top down

3. achieve symmetry at top first

4. top finished

ready to cut at 15° slope

5. complete

15°

6. detail of edge

SHAPING A STONE: At point 5A bevel will remain—this just barely breaks the sharp edge of the stone to prevent chipping, for ease of handling, and for mounting in jewelry (Illus. 9).

In spite of being confronted with this type of illustration and actual models of the shape desired, beginners work from the bottom much too often. If this does not actually spoil the shape of the cab, in most cases it lessens the height of the stone. Check the shape of your stone often. Don't grind too long in one place or you will get a flat space. Keep rotating the stone. Somewhere along the line, the dop stick, your fingers, and the wheel become one instrument for beauty.

No matter what the curve of the dome may be, the bottom edge must be about 15° to accommodate a bezel or prong setting (Illus. 10).

When your stone is just about finished—say $\frac{1}{16}$ of an inch to go—switch over to the 220 grinding wheel after washing your stone thoroughly. From now on this is the rule: wash and scrub your stone between each step. Your final shaping is done here. The abrasive is actually gouging out the stone. So, on the 220 wheel, remember to let the wheel do the work. Let it hit the high spots gently so that you get as smooth a finish as possible.

Get a jeweler's loupe, a magnifying glass with the lens set just about the right distance from your eye in the plastic holder. You will need one ranging from 3 to 5 power. The higher the power, the greater the magnification. High magnification, such as the diamond merchant's expensive 10-power corrected loupe, is not needed or advised as the field is too small. After a final check with the loupe to be sure that your shape is symmetrical, that there are *no flats* (all surfaces must be rounded) and that there are no really deep scratches or lopsided areas, you are ready for the sanding operation. Now scrub the stone for the next step.

Sanding

The easiest sander to work with is a metal drum which has a rubber coating about $\frac{1}{4}$ inch thick, in which a series of air holes have been left. Over this, a standard circular belt of sanding cloth fits. This abrasive cloth, made to be used wet, comes in 320 and 500 grit. Notice the grit is getting finer as you progress. As the drum spins, centrifugal force tightens

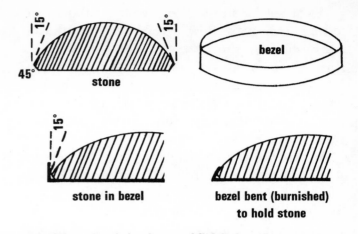

STONES are beveled at base and finished at 15° at edge to fit bezel mountings (Illus. 10).

the cloth on the drum (because of the air holes) so that it does not fall off. Keep the cloth wet by using a wet sponge in any convenient dish.

All you do in sanding is remove scratches. Your agate will begin to take on some character and may even begin to look polished.

Rotate a small section of the stone against the wet sander, applying firm pressure. Look at the stone under the loupe and you will observe the marked contrast between the scratches left by the 220 grinder and the results of 30 seconds of sanding. Keep at it until all the scratches have been removed. On small stones, work with a circular motion over the entire stone. On large stones in the 40 × 50 millimeter range you may have to work on a small, localized area. Work wet—it increases the efficiency of the operation. Dry off the stone with paper toweling to look at it under the loupe. If an area is not sanding, it is possible that you have a flat spot so large that the sander will not remove it. Regretfully, you will have to go back to the 220 grinding wheel and start over again.

There comes a point in your work with the 320 sanding cloth when the gem stone is shaping up and you can see reflections which give you a happy feeling. Scrub up at this point and switch to the 500 sanding cloth.

Now you really tackle the job in earnest. When you finish here there will be absolutely no scratches observable under the loupe. Agate will look polished after this operation. Other stones may not have the gloss of an agate, yet if there are no scratches left, they are ready for the next step. Wash and scrub the stone with soap and water as usual using a good nail brush.

Pre-Polishing

Pre-polishing is done on a hard leather-coated wooden disc, using a fine grained silica powder, called "tripoli." Mix up a slurry of tripoli and water in a small sterile jar (baby food size) using a heaping teaspoonful of tripoli and fill the balance of the jar with water. Use a small paint brush about $\frac{1}{2}$ inch to $\frac{3}{4}$ inch wide and reserve it exclusively for tripoli use.

Apply the slurry to your flat wheel with the brush. This wooden wheel has had a coat of rubberized sponge of thick texture glued on to it. After this a coating of leather has been applied and folded over the edge of the wood and tacked down into a permanent arrangement. Then a flexible piece of shoe-maker's leather has been glued on. This last piece of leather will wear out, but it can be renewed.

After the wheel is charged with the tripoli slurry, apply the gem stone with a firm, rotating pressure. As you become experienced you will learn how to use greater pressure. There is practically no cutting action here. If scratches show up, it means that your homework has not been done and again you must retreat a step, to the sander, and perhaps even further back, to the grinder. Do not get discouraged.

If the stone is sanded properly, a few minutes on the tripoli wheel is sufficient. Now your agate is taking on a gloss. Other gem materials may not take the high mirror gloss of agate on tripoli, but all should appear "almost polished." If you do come up with a small scratch, it is sometimes possible to "bear down" on that isolated area and take it out on tripoli, but this is better left to advanced lapidaries. Now scrub up well again—the last step is coming up and this really is the grand finale.

Polishing

Again you can use the same type of wooden disc as for tripoli, although a good many lapidaries prefer a hard felt wheel about 1 to 3 inches wide and 6 to 8 inches in diameter. The slurry this time is made with either tin or cerium oxide in the same proportions as for the tripoli. A clean brush has to be used exclusively for tin or cerium oxide (they are interchangeable). Charge the wheel, work wet, apply strong pressure and rotate the stone against the polishing disc. The pressure in this instance is strong enough to get the agate hot, but not enough heat should be generated for the wax to melt or the stone to fall off. There is a theory that as you get the stone hot, the surface flows and the polish is better. In any case you should now have achieved a mirror finish. Once you see the results of your handiwork, you will be a lapidary for life.

The stone can be removed from the dop by heating the wax in the alcohol lamp flame until soft. Inserting a knife blade between the stone and the dop stick will do the rest. No need to pry. Any wax adhering to the stone comes off in alcohol. A few minutes spent soaking the base of the stone in a shallow dish of alcohol will allow you to scrape the stone clean in seconds. If you are in mass production, put the stones into the freezing compartment of the refrigerator overnight. The cement contracts faster than the agate and by morning the stone just falls off. If necessary, clean with alcohol.

Notice that no mention has been made of motor speeds, or revolutions per minute (RPM) of the various wheels. All this information is readily available from the people who make the abrasives and lapidary equipment. In general, grind on fast speeds, and sand and polish on slow speeds. If you have both sanding drums and grinding wheels working off of the same motor, be sure you are working with the proper pulley.

Faceting

This process is merely putting flat faces (facets) on transparent gem material to make it sparkle. Making a flat surface is easy. Matching one side of a flat surface with another is not so hard either. To make a *multitude of matching surfaces* of different shapes and slopes at different angles—to produce a sparkling gem stone—is an art.

Start with a cylinder. For a quick example, take a fresh round crayon or a fresh round piece of chalk and rub the blunt end on a piece of fine sandpaper at an angle of 45° until you feel you have come ¼ of the way to the middle. Turn it 180° (one-half of the 360° circle) and repeat the process. Turn the crayon 90°, then 180°, going through the complete circle and you will wind up with four side facets on your crayon or chalk, like this:

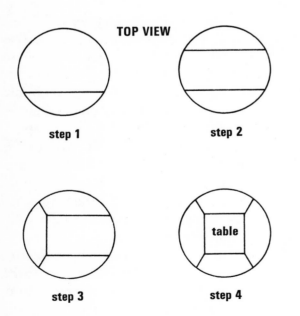

TOP VIEW

step 1

step 2

table

step 3

step 4

FACETING: Making facets on piece of chalk or crayon (Illus. 11).

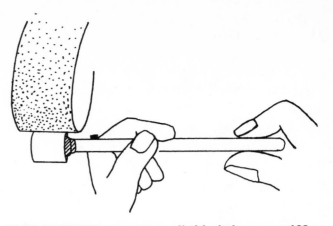

HAND GRINDING quartz to a cylindrical shape on a 100 or 220 grinding wheel before faceting (Illus. 12).

Obviously, the facets are not faces of precisionlike beauty. In the late 19th century and well into the 20th, to put some precision into faceting, an apparatus called the "jamb peg" was developed. This was used in combination with a flat disc called a "lap" which revolved and acted as a grinder. The sharpened end of a dop stick (opposite to the gem end) would be placed in a hole in the jamb peg at the angle desired against the lap. Then, when you turned your dop stick 180° or 90° to make your second facet, you would have a precision-cut object. This would work with crayons, or with a clear, unflawed, transparent piece of quartz which is going to be the first stone you will work with. You have now gained the skill to rough grind on a 100 or 220 wheel a cylinder of quartz about 15 mm. long which roughly approximates your snipping off the blunt end of a piece of chalk 15 mm. from the end.

With the jamb peg method (Illus. 13), you could proceed to cut facets in this quartz cylinder with some skill and confidence. However, let's set aside your cylinder of quartz until you have looked at modern faceting equipment.

Sometime about the second quarter of the 20th century, the idea was developed of replacing the jamb peg with a fixed arm that could be set by a protractor, tightened at the correct angle, and locked in place on a notch

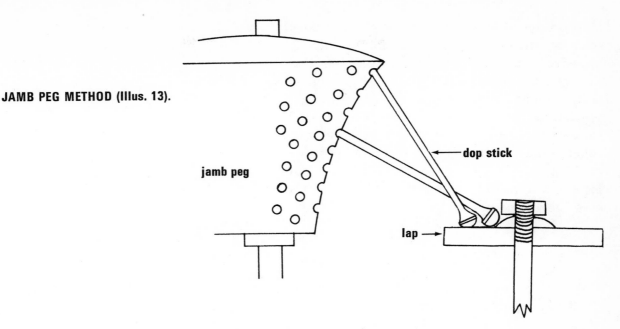

JAMB PEG METHOD (Illus. 13).

jamb peg

dop stick

lap

in a 360° rotating gear. After you set this device on 45° and make your first cut, you can raise the arm from the lap, turn your stone through a 90° arc and lock it back into place at a 45° angle. Then you can bring your arm back to the lap and confidently cut your crayon to an exactly matching 45° angle. (See Illus. 14 which shows this faceting head.)

There are many devices like this on the market that come complete with instructions,

run quietly, require little water for coolant, and can be set up in the corner of your living room. A basement workshop is recommended, but the living room does promote togetherness. Incidentally, many women are lapidaries who cut cabochons and go on to faceting. They not only become experts but prize-winners.

The removable lap in Illus. 14 is made of copper or brass for quartz. For a beginner, laps already scored and impregnated with diamond dust are recommended. Laps must

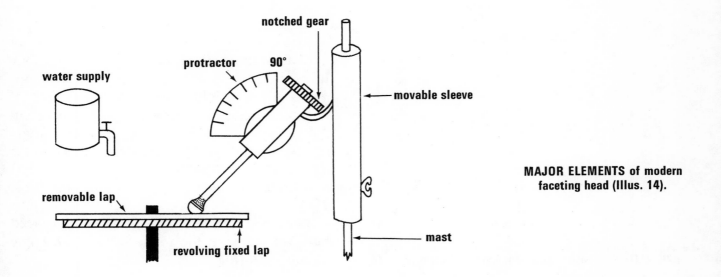

water supply

notched gear

protractor

90°

movable sleeve

removable lap

revolving fixed lap

mast

MAJOR ELEMENTS of modern faceting head (Illus. 14).

be scored first with a knife—that is, grooves must be cut into the lap in order to hold the abrasive. After the lap is scored, it is then impregnated with a diamond powder mixed with a light oil for handling. The diamond powder is ground into the lap by a smooth rocker made of a polished piece of agate, or a roller especially designed for this purpose. Now, as in the case of cabs, before you cut, look at the objective or end product—in this case a brilliant cut stone:

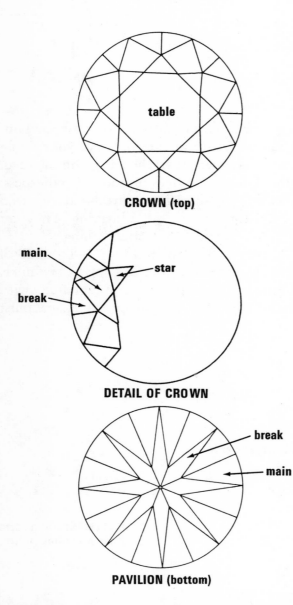

BRILLIANT CUT with names of individual facets (Illus. 15).

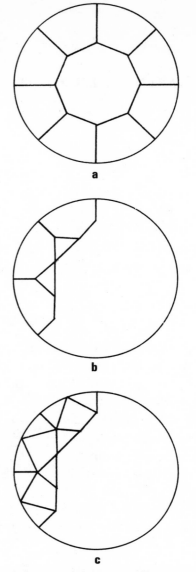

CUTTING THE CROWN FACETS (Illus. 16).

Remember the experiment with the crayon and its four facets at 45° as you moved four times through a 360° circle? Now you are going to cut eight facets on a cylinder of quartz, moving the rotating gear through a 45° arc instead of 90° and an elevation angle of 40° instead of 45°. After you finish these eight facets, the table (or top of the stone) will be in the shape of an octagon (see Illus. 16a).

Then you cut eight triangular stars, spaced half way between the main facets at an angle of 20°. (See Illus. 16b.)

And finally you cut the sixteen breaks at an angle of 46°. (See Illus. 16c.)

Sounds simple, doesn't it? Some authorities like the star facets cut at an angle of 25° rather than 20°, and even as high as 30°. The breaks can be cut at 43° rather than 46°. Put two lapidaries together and you get three answers sometimes.

The table, on which there is never a fight about the angle, is a flat 180°. Some people like to cut the table first, and others after they have cut the crown facets. The table should be approximately a little more than half the stone's diameter at the girdle. You must keep a record of the angles you use.

Polishing Facets

Wash the stone thoroughly. Take off your removable lap and put on a lucite lap scored in the same way, but this time scored to hold cerium oxide powder. Polish the facets at the same angles you used for cutting. The main girdle facets are a matter of judgment as to angle of cut after you have cut the first experimental one. You adjust to the correct angle—where it will fit in with the main and star facets.

Transferring

In order to cut the pavilion (bottom) you must invert the stone. The pavilion must be centered in exactly the same manner as the crown. Transfer dops that come with the faceting head are provided by the manufacturer. With a little deftness the transfer can be accomplished expeditiously and neatly. Faceting is an art.

Cutting the Pavilion

Note again what the pavilion looks like. You are going to cut eight main facets, and then proceed to cut eight breaks (Illus. 17). The eight main facets are cut at 42° and the breaks at 44°. Both could be cut at 43°. Polish as for the crown.

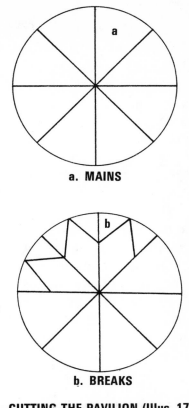

a. MAINS

b. BREAKS

CUTTING THE PAVILION (Illus. 17).

The width of the girdle is a matter of choice. If too thick, it loses its beauty; if too thin, it is liable to chip. In any case, the girdle is going to be cut and polished at an angle of 90°.

Matching

In the crown, the star facets touch each other around the table. The girdle facets of the crown are cut so as to reach the bottom of the star facets, and at the same time touch in the middle of the main facets. When you transfer, be sure that the main facets of the pavilion are aligned with the crown mains, so you can cut the pavilion facets in corresponding positions.

Optics

Because of dealing with the mineral kingdom, lapidaries must know a little science. Some pick it up by trial and error. Sometimes this is fine. The brilliant cut for a diamond was discovered by trial and error before it was mathematically proven by the science of optics to be the ideal one.

Light hitting the surface of a gem stone is reflected. Therefore, the more flat surfaces you put on a stone the more reflection and the more sparkle. However, some stones break up or disperse the light into more rainbows than others, giving still more sparkle.

The angle at which light hits the stone is the same angle at which it will bounce off the stone. When light goes from a less dense to a denser medium, it bends on entering the denser medium. This is refraction. Light entering a stone obliquely from the air bends upon entering the stone. That is to say, the ray of light is refracted. The angle of refraction will vary with the density of the stone. Now you can see why angles for different varieties of gem stones are established, and why the beauty of a particular gem stone may demand its own cut—such as a step cut for an emerald.

If you are going into faceting seriously you must read books. Even with expert instruction you will have to compile your little booklet of technique as you go along. You will find that your instructor has read all the books, and there are many.

The gem world is divided into two parts, the world of diamonds and the world of colored stones. Diamonds are an industry. The machinery and equipment are made for manufacturing processes and production line techniques. The training needed falls into trade union apprenticeships. No one does the whole stone. The divisions of labor can be likened to a production line. One man knows only the technique for a particular bench or workplace. A diamond man who wants to facet colored stones must begin exactly where a novice does —cutting an agate cabochon!

You have learned to cab and facet. The whole world of colored stones is open to you. You can go out and dig for gem minerals, some of which make beautiful or unusual cabs, stones different from any to be seen in Cartier's or Tiffany's or any jeweler's. You might join one of the clubs that hunt for treasure. The life is exciting, both in finding the gem material and in exposing its beauty in the shop. Incidentally, the fraternity of cutters and collectors is a friendly one. Do not wait for an invitation. All clubs are open to guests. All lapidaries love to show off their equipment and their cut gems.

If you are sedentary and would like to buy the gem material, there is no loss of status because you use the "silver pick." Besides visiting dealers individually, there are concentrations of dealers at various gem shows. You can drift from booth to booth, examining the slabs ready for the trim saw, or holding the expensive, transparent, gem aquamarine under the strong light to check for flaws. There is competition for prizes. You might enjoy the non-competitive displays of museums and advanced collectors. Above all there is a sense of being a part of a world of enduring beauty created by a fraternity of creative people to which you now belong.

SCRIMSHAW

Scrimshaw is the art of carving on shells, ivory teeth and other hard natural surfaces. Often ink or pigment is rubbed into the incised lines to make them even more striking. Whalebone and whales' teeth are the most commonly used substances which are carved. At one time sailors carved elaborate boxes from whalebone and ivory (there is one in Whitby, England, dating from 1665), and walking canes and kitchen utensils have also been carved. Nowadays, however, the machinery of modern whaling factories grinds down the whalebone, and only the whales' teeth are available for carving.

A large tooth weighs about a pound, but as whales are usually killed before they reach maturity, this size tooth is difficult to find. The average whale's tooth weighs about 7 ounces. Some teeth are pointed and some are rounded, depending upon the position of the tooth in the whale's mouth. The outside of the tooth is enamel and is harder than the inside ivory core.

Whales' teeth can be obtained from certain suppliers, while other pieces of ivory are more difficult and expensive to find. The instructions given here deal specifically with scrimshaw on whales' teeth.

As you will probably want to stand the finished tooth on a shelf, the bottom edge, where the tooth entered the animal's jaw, will need to be smoothed and leveled. Clamp the tooth in a vise and saw across the base of the tooth with a hacksaw. Start your cut by using a triangular file, and pour plenty of water on to the surface to lubricate the cutting process. As much of the base is hollow, leveling the base is not difficult. Stand the tooth upright to make sure it is level and will not tip when on display. Keep smoothing until the tooth can stand by itself.

Next, smooth the sides of the tooth. There are ribs and depressions on the sides, necessary for the whale when biting, but a nuisance to the carver. Use either a file or a power drill fitted with an abrasive disc or a small grindstone. Work slowly and carefully. You do not need to grind away too much of the tooth: just grind enough to make a flat plane for drawing and carving. Fasten the tooth to your workbench with a clamp and proceed to smooth it. The outside layer of enamel is very tough and resistant to damage, but once you get through to the ivory layer, the heat from the rapidly revolving grindstone may scorch. Lubricate the surface with water to prevent the heat from building up, and stop often to see how the smoothing is progressing.

Unlike every other kind of sculpture, the tooth in scrimshaw is always polished *before* it is carved. Rub the tooth with the finest sandpaper, and then abrade it with a wet cotton cloth dipped in powdered pumice. Finish polishing the tooth with whiting, putty powder (oxide of tin) or precipitated chalk, and wipe the tooth with a dry cotton cloth. Traditionally, whales' teeth were polished with sailmaker's wax or whale oil, but these polishes darken the teeth to the color of honey. The scrimshaw will be very attractive if the background is left natural, although you may prefer the darker color.

What you draw is up to you, of course. While marine subjects are traditionally carved

Written especially for this volume by Dr. Carson I. A. Ritchie

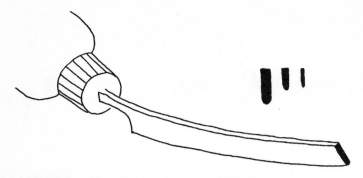

A ROUND SCORPER produces the markings shown above the tool here. Scorpers come with various tips to make different sized and shaped grooves—round, square or angled. See page 402 for pictures of other scorpers.

in whales' teeth, other designs may appeal to you more. Flags, birds, and castles were commonly carved by 19th century sailors, but any scene, as long as it is not too elaborate, can be carved.

The safest and most practical tool for you to use for engraving is a *scorper*, the tool of the professional ivory carver. It is a chisel with a fine tapered triangular point and a mushroom handle. Sharpen it often while you work. Put the tooth in the vise with the side to be engraved towards you. Cradle the handle of the scorper in the palm of your right hand and push against the tooth, away from you. To prevent you from cutting too deeply into the line, or from going off the line, put a brake on your progress by pressing the ball of your left thumb against your right as you carve.

Another carving tool which you may use is an *eskimo style*. With this tool, you can hold your work in one hand and the style in the other. The eskimo style is made from a wood dowel $\frac{3}{8}$ inch by $\frac{1}{2}$ inch by 3 inches. Round one end of the dowel and cut a notch about $\frac{3}{4}$ inch from the end. This notch is for your fingers, so you can maintain a firm hold on the tool. Drill a hole through the rounded end of the dowel. Saw a nail in half and sharpen both ends of it. Cement the nail into the hole.

By using the eskimo style as a pencil, you can easily carve the most complicated scrimshaw.

While you are cutting the lines, the ivory shavings will fall into the recesses. Either blow or brush them out with a stiff brush.

The final process in scrimshaw is inking the lines. Take a pen with a fine elongated point and, using India ink, draw along the *inside* of the lines. India ink is black, but diluted poster paints will provide other colors if you want them. Finish by rubbing the tooth with a piece of fine sandpaper to remove any ink which has gone outside the lines.

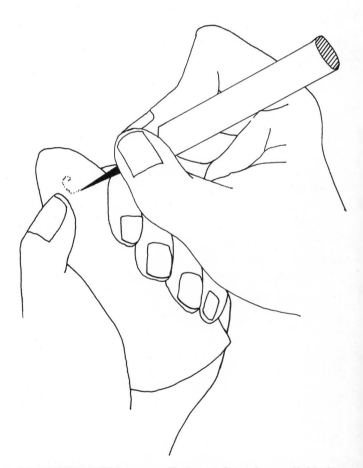

AN ESKIMO STYLE can easily be made at home. Hold the tooth you are working on in one hand and the style in the other, as if you were writing.

STONE CARVING

In stone carving, the sculptor achieves the shape, form, texture and mass of his work by removing pieces of the stone with tools until the form emerges from the stone. Carving requires strength, discipline, and perseverance, for the character of the stone itself demands overcoming difficult obstacles and develops steadiness of hand and mind.

The Nature of Stone

Stone is not as easy a material to carve as soap and wax are, but it should not be awe-

FAMOUS MONOLITH: Found on Easter Island, off the coast of Chile, this probably dates from the 11th or 12th century.

some. Stone varies greatly from soft soapstones to hard granites. The beginning carver should select a soft stone such as unfigured marble or limestone.

Stone is classified in three major categories: igneous, sedimentary and metamorphic.

Igneous: Igneous stone is formed by the action of fire and is extremely hard. It includes the granites and basalts.

Sedimentary: Sedimentary stones are formed by the action of water or from deposits of sediment in the beds of lakes and the sea. These are stratified stones and include limestone and sandstone.

Metamorphic: Metamorphic stones are igneous and sedimentary stones which have been physically transformed by the natural action of pressure, heat and chemistry. This category includes marble, soapstone, slate, alabaster, onyx, and all the gem stones.

Stone can be obtained from quarries, sculpture suppliers, tombstone companies and wrecked buildings. Gemstones can be found in areas frequented by "rockhounds," and pebbles can be picked up free of charge at nearly every beach.

Testing the Stone

It is wise for the beginner to learn first how to test a stone. Flaws may make a stone unsatisfactory for carving. For example, cracks, soft streaks, veins and stratification might cause deterioration of the stone. Watch out also for pebbles, fossils and air pockets in metamorphic rock which could cause difficulties in carving.

A simple test is to tap the stone lightly with

Written especially for this volume by Maria and Louis DiValentin

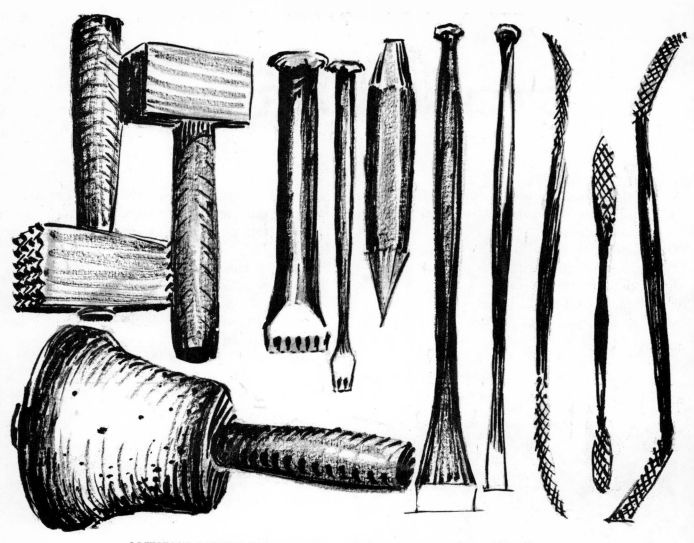

SOFTSTONE CARVING TOOLS consist mostly of light chisels, picks and mallets.

a steel hammer. If the sound rings clearly, the piece should be all right; if the sound is more like a dull thud, however, the stone is considered "dead" and unsuitable for carving.

Another test is to wet the entire stone with water. A deep-grained dark streak through the piece may be a sign of a crack or layer that will cause difficulties.

Tools and Supplies

The supplies and tools needed for stone carving vary with the type of stone to be carved. In general, however, the beginner will need: (1) stone suitable for the desired sculpture; (2) a sculpture stand which permits carving on all sides of the stone; (3) tools; (4) a forge and grindstone for sharpening the tools; (5) abrasives for finishing and polishing; and (6) goggles to wear while chipping stone. Dust masks also are helpful when filing and sanding.

Hand tools for soft stones: Hand tools include a variety of chisels with flat blades and points, bush hammers, picks and iron mallets in varying weights, toothed chisels (also called frosting tools) in varying widths and numbers of points, pointed and angled chisels, and curved rasps and rifflers. A long hand drill is used for boring holes.

Hand tools for hard stones: Tools for working

granite and other hard stones are essentially the same as those for softer stones, but they have carbide tips for greater durability and are generally heavier. These tools can be used on the softer stones but the softer stone tools may *not* be used on granite since the stone will dull them too quickly.

Power tools: Some power tools can be used on stone and are helpful in speeding up the carving process. These include pneumatic roto-hammers with points shaped like those on the hand tools; pneumatic drills with masonry bits, which are helpful for removing large chunks or opening up a concave area; and circular saws, drills, sanders and grinders, also used in certain phases of carving, finishing and polishing.

Finishing tools: The tools used depend on whether the sculptor wishes a smooth or rough surface, but generally, files, rasps, sanders and grinders, pumice or other rubbing stones, wet-dry sandpaper, carborundum papers and polishing powders are used.

Sharpening tools: Stone carving tools must be kept sharp, usually by working their edges on a grindstone. Tempered steel blades used in stone carving tools require occasional re-tempering. The best way is to place the tools in a forge of coal and charcoal until they reach a cherry-red color. Use tongs to remove them from the fire and hammer and shape them on an anvil. Return the tool to the fire after it cools, and when it is cherry-red again, dip the tip into cold water for three seconds; then rub it on a sand board.

In cooling, the colors will go from white, to gold, to bronze, to purple, and finally to blue.

Blue-tempered tools are used to carve marble, and bronze- or gold-tempered tools are used to carve harder stones. When the right color has been reached, dip the tool in cold water to hold the temper at that point. Chisels used for final details should be hard-tempered, since they are used for light surface carving, but remember that hard-tempered tools will break

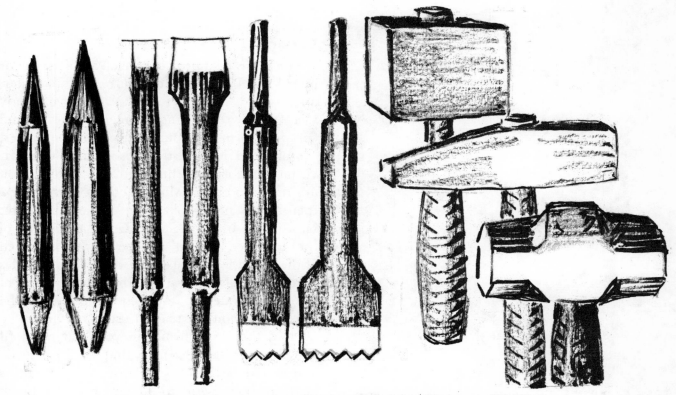

GRANITE CARVING TOOLS are much heavier and the drills have carbide tips.

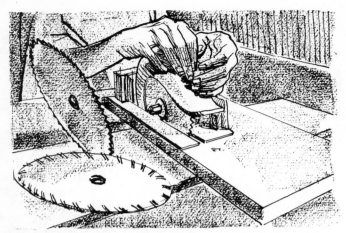

REVOLVING SAW BLADES may be used for cutting and smoothing marble.

if they are used against granite or other hard stones.

Do not use oil stones for sharpening stone-carving tools, as oil will stain the stone. While carving, keep a piece of wet soft stone or a grindstone handy on which to rub and sharpen the tools.

HOLD THE CHISEL midway down the shank, loosely.

DRAW AN OUTLINE of your work, as you envision it, when you have the stone set up at a convenient height.

Carving

For your first project, select a soft stone or marble such as sandstone, Caen or alabaster, all of which are easy to cut and carve. Study your stone carefully and then select a simple and compact form for your first piece—perhaps a cat or head in a restful pose. Once you can visualize a form nestling within the stone, you are ready to carve. Make sketches of the work, then a clay model of it, and place this within view of the block or stone. Draw an outline of the intended design on the surface of each of the five sides of the stone (that is, on all sides except the base). Transfer the central point of the clay model to the central point in the stone. Now you are ready to start carving.

Hold the chisel firmly in your left hand (if you are right-handed), so that the end to be hammered will not break off. The point is held at about a 45° to 90° angle to the block about midway down the shank. Swing the hammer with the right hand. Move around the stone to see if it can be worked better from one angle or another. Work at a height that is comfortable so you can take advantage of the size and shape of the block, carving it on all sides so that no material is wasted or unnecessary sculpting required.

Remove only small pieces of stone at a cut. If you discover a vein within the stone, work carefully around the area bordering the vein. This area will be soft and crumbly and requires care. Frosting tools may be lightly tapped along the stone to create a lined effect or add texture. Flat chisels are generally used for smoothing or to create lines. A long point is used for rough blocking and texturing. Curved rasps and files finish and smooth a work. Some sculptors prefer to leave stone rough or textured; others prefer a smooth surface or a combination of smooth and textured surfaces.

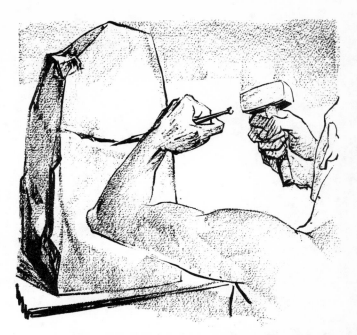

THE LONG-POINTED CHISEL is used for rough blocking-out.

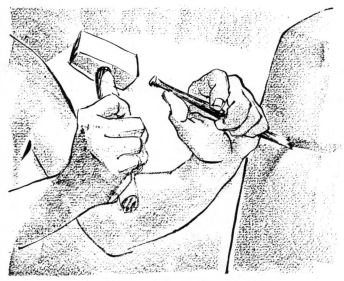

THE FLAT CHISEL is used to create wide lines.

Soft stones can be finished with rasps and files and then rubbed with pumice or other rubbing stones, wet-dry sandpaper, carborundum papers and polishing powders, and finally coated with wax, terrazzo sealer or silicone and buffed to a high shine.

Actually, no general instructions can be given regarding the methods used to carve stone. For one thing, each individual stone will vary and the sculptor may find, after doing several pieces, that he prefers to work with some tools rather than others.

But some general observations may prove helpful to the beginning sculptor. Study your stone carefully before beginning and then make sketches. Corrections in stone carving are more difficult to make once the piece has been started. Deep carving and sudden changes in direction of the planes and masses help produce strong contrasts and create dramatic elements, while smooth-flowing surface planes suggest poise and soft movements. Always keep the five surfaces of the free-standing sculpture in mind. Work around the stone and try to make the sculpture interesting for both the eyes and the hands. Remember that a free-standing sculpture not only exists in terms of the physical material from which it is made, but also includes the space around it and the light reflected on its surface planes.

When selecting the stone to be carved, consider whether the sculpture is to be placed outdoors or inside. Only the finer grained marbles and other hard stones are used for outdoor sculptures.

Out of the rough shape, model the head first.

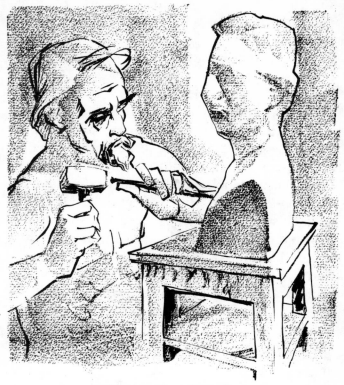

Next, work on the neck.

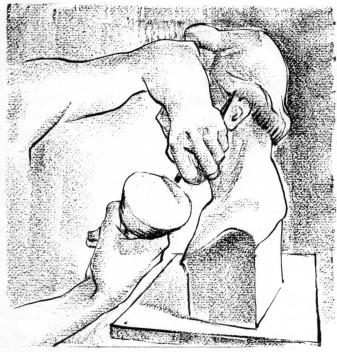

Go back and finish off the ears, nose and facial features with the bell-shaped mallet.

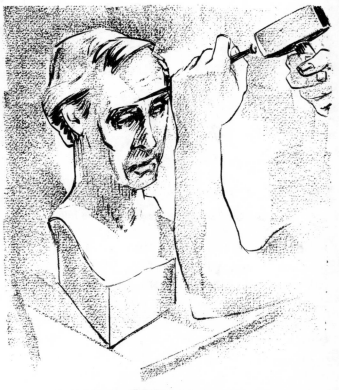

Finish the eyes.

Smooth down the planes around the mouth and nose.

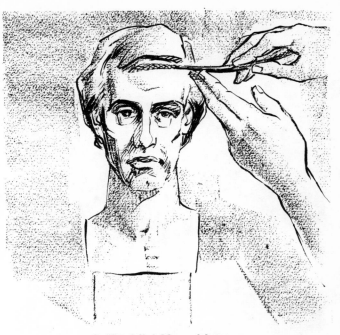

Do final finishing with a rasp.

More Advanced Carving

After having carved several pieces from soft stones, try working something harder, such as Indiana limestone. This stone is excellent for outdoor pieces, since it hardens with the weather.

You may want to work in marble or another metamorphic stone. These are among the most popular stones used by contemporary sculptors. Marble varies greatly in color and texture: some are translucent, opaque, figured, mottled, veined and striped, and the colors can be white, blue, green, pink, gray or black.

All marbles are good stones for the creative talents of the student and professional artist. Generally, sculptors working in marble polish it to a smooth surface. For example, Belgian marble while being worked is a gray, but with much polishing with an emery stone, coarse sandstone, fine sandstone, pumice stone, English bone, putty powder and oxalic acid, it finally takes on the shine of a black mirror.

Granite is quite a rugged material and is not recommended for the beginner. However, granite makes excellent outdoor sculptures since it is so durable. When granite is carved, the stone is first blocked out with a pneumatic drill to remove the large portions of excess stone. Compressed air is forced through a rubber tube in a metal holder by means of a hammer, made to vibrate at high speed against the stone. The stone is then carved with heavy chisels and hammers to the desired form.

There are other good kinds of metamorphic stone which are not as expensive or popular as marble, but which still should be considered by the sculptor. These include: soapstone (talc or steatite), African wonderstone, lava or feather rock, pebbles and gem stones. Pebbles can be as soft as soapstone or as hard as granite; test a pebble with a nail, and if it can be scratched it can be carved with stone-carving tools.

History

People carved stone even before they painted or built dwellings. The earliest remaining examples of carved sculpture are approxi-

ANCIENT GREEK carvings of lions in marble are on the island of Delos.

mately 15,000 to 17,000 years old, from the Old Stone Age. These early works were fashioned with chipped stone tools and were symbolic rather than representational. Many of the early sculptures were used for ritualistic purposes.

Though carving in stone dates back to prehistory, 20th-century artists have rediscovered stone as a medium for artistic expression. In the 19th century, stone statues and architectural works were the work of stonemasons copying the artist's model from plaster, clay or sketches. In the early 20th century, however, when Jean Arp, Constantin Brancusi, Barbara Hepworth, Henry Moore and others began working directly in stone, there was a tremendous change in style.

When the artist again returned to working directly in stone, a great deal of experimentation and innovation took place. This resulted in a variety of new approaches, with the artist expressing his feeling for volume, interlocking masses, textures, surface planes, linear movements and spatial patterns in his work. This variety can be seen today in the open or perforated smooth sculptures of Henry

Moore, which define shape and space in terms of negative forms as well as the positive forms; in the elongated forms of Lehmbruck; the heavy, massive works of Maillol, and the rugged natural simplicity of Modigliani's works.

HENRY MOORE, son of a Yorkshire coal miner, is considered one of the world's greatest sculptors in the modern manner. This is one of his works set out on the grounds of his Hertfordshire studio.

paper

PAPERCRAFT

Paper is probably the most versatile material you can work with: it can be cut, curled, colored, curved, used as a background, or even form the main parts of a paper arrangement. The type of project you want to make will determine the materials you need: paper of any kind—construction paper, tissue, cellophane, crepe paper, wallpaper or even cardboard—is suitable for something, and having only one kind on hand is no reason to postpone experimenting with this craft. A pair of scissors will be necessary — a small safety pair meant specifically for children's paper cutting is sufficient. Tape, glue and coloring materials, such as crayons, paints and pencils, are additional supplies you will probably want. To decorate certain animals or human figures even more elaborately, you might want to attach spare buttons, yarn, fabric or pipe cleaners to the paper.

Weaving with Paper

Flat 2-dimensional objects made from paper may be flat to the touch, but they are not necessarily dull in appearance. Some exciting things can be done with just paper and scissors by weaving strips in and out of a paper background. Insert one point of your scissors into the middle of the paper as shown in the illustration on this page. Cut a long slit, ending your cut about 1 inch from the edges of the paper. Do not limit yourself to straight, parallel lines, however; curves which come close together and then spread apart again create interesting optical illusions when contrasting papers are woven into the background.

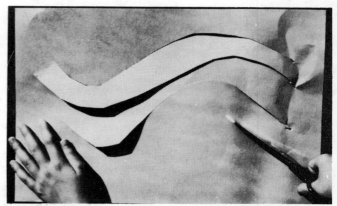

A PAPER LOOM: You can weave an attractive pattern on a large flat piece of colored paper by first cutting a series of lines—straight, wavy, or jagged. For your first attempt, keep the slits wide apart. Then try making cuts of varied spacing and design. Later on, you can make a folded paper loom, beginning your slits from the folded edge. This will give you a symmetrical pattern.

To weave the strips—whether they are ones you have cut from paper, or bits of yarn, lace, ribbon or any other trim—hold them in your right hand, the background paper in your left, and insert the strips one at a time over and under the bars. While an asymmetrical, or uneven, pattern is certainly desirable for some projects, you might want to try another design. To vary the symmetry, you can change the space between the slits when you cut them, or skip some slits when you weave, or use several colors for strips. The shapes which result will be varied—some small, some large, some rectangular and some square.

Slits can also be cut diagonally or in a combination of diagonal and straight lines. Unusual and exciting optical illusions can be made by using vibrant colors woven into diagonal or V-shaped slits. Another variation

Condensed from the book, "Creative Paper Crafts" by Chester Jay Alkema | © 1967 by Sterling Publishing Co., Inc., New York

(Left) A RHYTHMIC FLOW of lines is the result of weaving colored strips of paper into a non-folded paper loom. Here a striking effect is achieved by weaving black and white strips into a grey loom.

(Below) THREE-DIMENSIONAL WEAVING: A unique basket can be made by weaving directly on to a gallon-sized milk carton. The vertical strips (warp) are cut and pasted on first and then the horizontal strips (weft) are woven in and out. Any size or shape of container or box can be decorated in the same way.

of the weaving technique is to weave on to a background which has been cut and shaped, instead of a whole piece of paper. Perhaps an animal needs only his tail woven to make him realistic, or a farmhand can wear a checkerboard shirt.

The patterns you weave can be framed as they are, or they can surround a metal, plastic or cardboard container to make an exciting wastebasket. You can use these woven designs any place you want a decorative touch.

STAINED GLASS WINDOWS can be reproduced brilliantly using black construction paper, colored tissue paper, cellophane and a little imagination. Notice that the large simple shapes are just as effective as the more complex shapes in the middle panel.

Paper Window Transparencies

Stained glass is a beautiful medium, particularly when the colors are lit with sunlight (see Stained Glass Crafting). You can, however, simulate the effect of stained glass with paper. The translucency of both tissue paper and cellophane lets light shine through just as stained glass does. Mount different shapes on sturdy black construction paper, to imitate the lead in stained glass windows, hold the paper composition up to the light or a window, and the effect will be dazzling. While religious subjects are common designs of stained glass windows, you are certainly not limited to these. Any design, either abstract or representational, will be attractive in simulated stained glass, as long as it is colorful.

To make the construction paper frame, fold black construction paper in half lengthwise, resulting in a design which will be identical on the right and left sides. Trace the areas in the design you have chosen on to the black paper. Keeping the paper folded, cut out the shapes, but leave narrow strips between the cut-out areas. These are the mock lead strips, which also act as a backing upon which you will glue the cellophane or tissue. Open the construction paper now and make any corrections or further cuts if they are necessary.

Now cut the tissue or cellophane shapes. Take the paper you have chosen for a certain area and place the construction paper frame over it. Trace the shapes on the translucent paper, but cut it slightly larger than the shape itself to allow a margin for glueing. If your

BLACK CONSTRUCTION PAPER forms the base of a window transparency. After folding the paper in half the long way, lay out the design in chalk on one half, keeping the paper folded. In this way, each side will be identical.

CUT OUT THE SHAPES, again keeping the paper folded. The remaining black strips serve as "leading." Now open the paper up and clean up any ragged or wobbly edges.

TRACE around the construction paper frame by placing each section over a piece of your chosen colored tissue or cellophane and outlining the shapes. When you start to cut, remember to leave a small margin to allow for glueing.

MOUNT your transparencies on a window that receives strong sunlight. Here an abstract paper window transparency is flanked by two Christmas ornaments made in the same way but hung by strings from the top of the window.

Paper Mosaics

Paper imitates not only stained glass, but also a number of other durable objects: for example, stone, tile and metal. Mosaics made from these objects have existed for centuries (see Mosaics), and among the chief reasons for their enduring popularity are the colorful designs which result when bright tesserae (the bits of material that form the mosaic) are combined in an interesting pattern. While stone tesserae are cemented on to a backing and then filled in with grout, paper tesserae can easily be glued on to construction paper. While a bright background might detract from the design, a

window is symmetrical, you might choose to balance your colors evenly also. Elmer's glue or library paste are both good glues to use here.

Holiday ornaments are another use for translucent papers which allow the light to shine through them. The black construction paper not only outlines the colored tissue, but extends beyond to form designs of its own. By leaving enough space in the construction paper at the top to punch a hole, you can hang the ornament by a thread which will be almost invisible, or by gold or silver cord. These translucent ornaments should be placed near a window or other strong light source to achieve the most beautiful effects.

PAPER MOSAICS: A mosaic made up of varicolored paper tesserae can depict almost anything you wish—from landscapes or abstract designs to fanciful or representational figures, such as this joyous clown who would make a fine wall decoration in a small boy's room.

Monofold Animals

The instructions about paper have so far dealt only with 2-dimensional designs. But you can fold, curl or score paper to make it stand up by itself. By folding paper and cutting out some animals, you can make a whole menagerie.

Because animals are symmetrical on both sides of their body, they can easily be made from one piece of paper which has been folded in the middle. This fold will form the top of the animal—either his back or his head—and the edges of the paper will become his feet. Draw the outline of the animal before you cut, and then cut through both thicknesses of paper. Leave the two sides of the animal attached along the fold. The body of the giraffe (long neck) or llama (shorter neck) shown here was cut in this way, and his head—a single thick-

basic color—black, beige or white—will make the tesserae stand out, and thus add to the attractiveness of the mosaic.

When you plan a paper mosaic, first outline the areas you are going to fill in with different colors. Keep the design and the areas of color fairly large and simple: the paper tesserae will make the mosaic appear busy enough. The scenes might look flat, but this is an inevitable result of the mosaic technique: shadows and subtle changes of color are difficult to make, so very little 3-dimensional effect will be achieved. The beauty of a mosaic lies not in its realism, however, but rather in its colors. Try to place strongly contrasting areas next to one another to emphasize this.

SUPPORT can be given to slender-legged animals and people by glueing pipe cleaners to the inner sides.

ness of paper decorated on both sides—was attached with glue in a slit made in the fold.

This animal was painted with a dry sponge lightly dipped in tempera paint and stamped on the paper. His ear and eye were cut from construction paper, and the eyelashes were made from a curled piece of construction paper cut into a fringe.

Use a variety of materials to decorate your figures. Cotton for a kitten's or a rabbit's fur adds realism and a real "touch" appeal. Button eyes, a ribbon collar, and pipe cleaner whiskers would make your animals even more decorative. You may find as you glue scraps to the basic paper form that the additional weight puts a strain on the figure's legs and hinders his standing alone. To remedy this, attach pipe cleaners on the inside of his legs for additional support.

Creations from Basic Shapes

Three-dimensional geometric forms can be transformed into startling creatures by adding decorations of paper and other scrap items. The cylindrical form is ideal for parts of the human body: the trunk, arms, legs and head can all be made from paper cylinders and attached to form a whole body. Animals can be constructed in basically the same manner, only the cylinder will probably be turned on its side to suggest the long and low shape of a horse, dog or cow. Decorating the animal will hide the line where the end of the paper is attached by staples, tape or glue.

Cones provide even more possibilities for decorating than cylinders. They are a perfect shape for 3-dimensional people, and the wide base makes the figures steady and able to stand

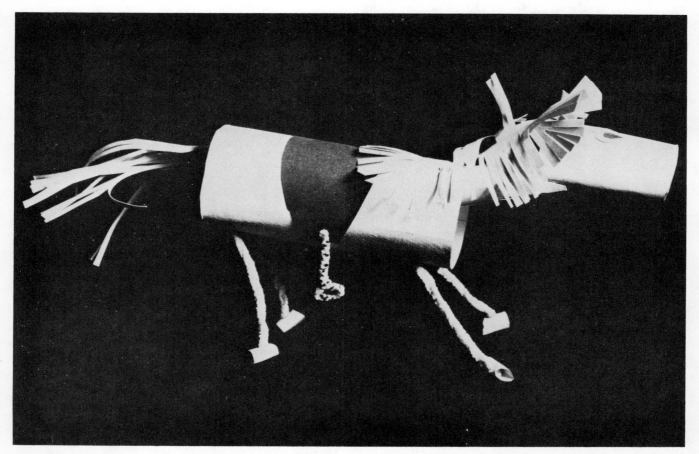

Cylindrical shapes are used to good advantage when making animals. The head and body, as well as the little hoofs, are constructed from paper cylinders. Pipe-cleaner legs and stirrups and slitted-paper mane and tail complete this horse.

PEOPLE are easily constructed from cylindrical paper shapes. These figures are almost entirely composed of cylinders of various sizes, lengths and widths.

by themselves. The little doll is made from a cone, on top of which curled fringe has been layered. To make the ruffles of her skirt, cut paper strips and curl them by running the strip tightly along a scissors blade. Then cut slits in the curled strips and attach them to the cone.

The doll's arms are made of "cat-stairs," two paper strips held perpendicular and folded alternately one over the other. Cat-stairs are not rigid, but bounce and move to imitate real-life actions. The construction paper shawl and hat, placed upon a table tennis ball head which has been decorated with twine hair, complete the costume of this paper doll.

Cones are also suitable for wild insects and weird creatures from other planets. Use pipe cleaners for arms and legs, sponges for hands and feet, and strips of thin foam rubber to make a head.

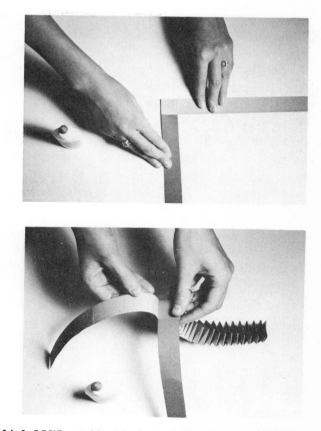

(Left) A CONE provides the basic body shape for this doll, while (above) CAT-STAIRS are used for her arms. Cat-stairs are also excellent for making long necks, tails and legs.

Paper Strip Sculpture

Another way of making 3-dimensional paper designs is to use paper strips of varying lengths. Free-standing sculptures of all sorts can be made, using glue, tape or staples to hold the strips together.

Relief pictures can also be made from paper strips attached to a flat background. Naturally, only the outlines of shapes will show and no interior details will be possible. Large curves representing hollow areas are therefore best and are quite graceful. There are several methods you can use to attach the strips to a paper background. The simplest is transparent tape. Small paper tabs, the same color as the background, might be bent and glued on to the background and the inside of the paper strips. If you do not want the paper strips to show at all, cut small slits in the background with a razor, slip the tabs through, and glue them to the back of the picture.

The Diorama

When you feel you are an expert in the field of papercraft, you can combine all the techniques you have learned so far and make a diorama. A diorama is a scene viewed through an opening, perhaps in a cardboard box with the front side cut away, so that it seems to be upon a stage. While the background and figures in the scene will probably be of paper, you can add very realistic details by using articles from real life. Scraps of cloth can dress your figures, leaves and twigs can form a forest, and a small piece of carpet could transform a simple cardboard box into a living room fit for your most elegant dolls.

By assembling several figures and decorating the box in the appropriate manner, you can make the stage design from a scene in a book, if you wish. Curtains over the opening will add a dramatic flourish to your diorama. Experiment and use any items you want to decorate the basic paper figures. A colorful example of the kind of diorama you might make is shown in the color section.

BOOKBINDING

In ancient times, before bookbinding began, manuscripts were kept in rolls. In order to do away with this tedious job of rolling, and to keep the many sections flat and uninjured, the manuscripts were placed between thin wooden boards for protection. These first wooden covers were decorated with metal mounts. Then came leather-covered boards with jewels, enamel, filigree, ivory carvings, etc., all beautifully tooled.

Before printing with movable type became widespread (c. 1500) monks prepared books with the artistic help of the town jeweler and goldsmith. During the Renaissance, Italian craftsmen decorated the covers and spines of books with gold geometrics; the English used small dies; and the French used their talents and ingenuity for fine decoration. Today, fine book cover designs are popular and many outstanding artists are employed to create covers and jackets.

The hand binding of books is one of the less familiar of modern-day crafts, but offers much pleasure for those who like creating and designing their own uniquely bound books. Limited editions and special printings of a particular book are often bound by hand.

Cover paper can be used on the outside of as well as inside the bound cover. Be sure the grain of the paper you select runs parallel to the spine of the book. Many types of covering are available: rice paper, silk, Japanese papers, and colored papers, as well as bond and laid papers.

There are also special book cloths, such as vellum and buckram, which may be bought in small quantities from commercial bookbinding firms and supply companies. Linen, denim, sailcloth and many thin cloths that have both strength and beauty can also be used. All cloths may be combined with paper.

Natural leather for a cover may be left simply with its own texture, or it may be stained, dyed, gilded or painted. Leather can later be tooled after covers are made, in real or imitation gold, yellow, black or any other color. For designs, symbols may be used, such as coats of arms, figures, or any design created with the imagination of the craftsman.

Leather is often used for spine and corners of the book, sometimes in combination with paper, metal, wood, enamel, ivory, and precious stones. Onlay, inlay and mosaic are used principally to make more sumptuous, elegant and splendid designs. Stiff seasoned cardboard (known as binders' board) is usually used as a cover board.

Bookbinding at Home

You can gather your favorite issues or articles of a particular magazine, theatre programs, catalogues or photographs and keep them in a neatly bound book with evenly cut pages. You can even add a hard cover to your favorite paperback. Binding your own books can be done right in your home.

Although various materials are needed for binding, many are probably already present in your house and have been used for other craft projects:

Written especially for this volume by David A. Boehm and Theodore Tuck

flexible glue and brush
hammer and nails
awl or ice pick
book press
punch guide
drill and bits
file, rough edge, or sandpaper
paper cutter (or access to one)
needle and thread
starched cheesecloth, called "crash"
cover material and cardboard
plastic cover for a working surface.
bone folder

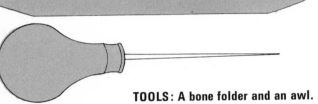

TOOLS: A bone folder and an awl.

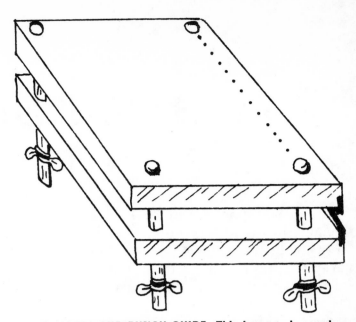

BOOK PRESS AND PUNCH GUIDE: This homemade wooden apparatus will serve several major purposes, and will be your main piece of equipment.

Prepare a proper work area. It must be large enough to allow several sizable devices and tools to be out at once. It would also be wise to spread a large plastic cover over the area to protect the surface from glue which may spill.

Binding requires the use of a specific instrument which you can make at home. This is a combination punch guide and book press. The guide part is used to line up the signatures (as the folded sections are called) so that you can punch holes in them with an awl or ice pick. The book press is also used to hold the signatures together for glueing, sanding and sewing.

Making a Book Press

To build the press part, you need two boards (same measurements): $\frac{3}{4}$ inch thick, 14 inches long, and $7\frac{3}{4}$ inches wide. These two boards are to be connected by four $\frac{3}{8}$-inch × 6-inch carriage bolts with wide wing nuts.

In each corner of the two boards, with a bit drill holes wide enough to accommodate the carriage bolts. Be sure the holes line up. Place the bolts through the holes with a washer and

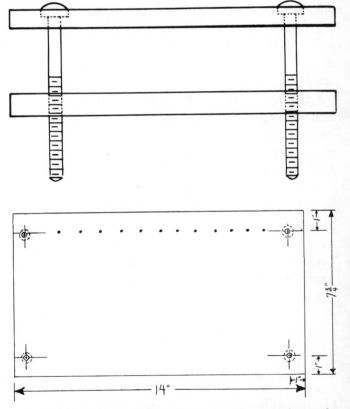

HOW THE PRESS IS MADE: The upper diagram shows the bolt position and the lower drawing shows the small drilled holes.

wing nut on each of the bolts. When the nuts are tightened, the boards will be drawn close enough together to press the signatures so that sewing, sanding, glueing and other operations can take place.

Making the Punch Guide

Take the top board of your press and drill holes along one length $\frac{1}{2}$ inch apart and only big enough for an awl or ice pick to go through. Now when you want to punch holes in the signatures for needle and thread to go through, all you need do is set this top board on the press and squeeze the folded signatures between them. The holes will guide your awl through the signatures, making all the holes uniform.

As an additional guide, cut a piece of cardboard or wood to go on the bottom layer of the press. Keep it loose so you can slide it into position and anchor it with masking tape. This will help assure that all the signatures will punch in the same place.

Preparing the Signature

The signatures you will handle at the start should contain no more than 16 pages. These

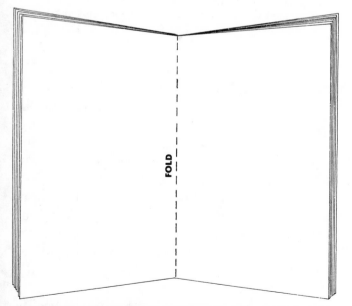

FOLD WITH THE GRAIN down the spine. If you follow this rule you will avoid wrinkles.

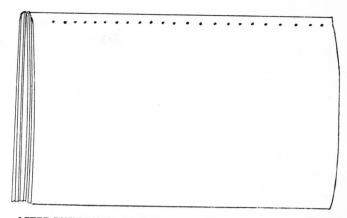

AFTER PUNCHING, this is how the folded signature will look.

16 pages are the result of folding four larger sheets. Each sheet folded once makes 4 pages (a folio). When you do the inserting (also called collating or gathering) of the four folios into each other at the fold, you get a 16-page signature.

Fold your signatures so that the fold along the spine (whether first fold or not) is with the grain of the paper. Place corner on corner before folding. Use a bone folder, especially prepared for paper, to crease the folio. Always run the bone folder over the folded part of the sheet to get the air out.

If your signature consists of a double fold, place corner to corner again, and press the air out as you fold. Improve the crease wherever you can to prepare it to be punched.

Signature Punch

Place the gathered signature into the press, placing it so that the first and last holes will be $\frac{1}{2}$ inch in from the top and bottom edges, and $\frac{1}{4}$ inch in from the spine. Affix the cardboard block to assist you in lining up. Jog the signature towards the guide block by tapping it gently with the side of your hand. Clamp down the press once you have the signature in position, take the awl or ice pick with the other and place it in the first hole at either end. Push and turn it until it penetrates the folded end of each sheet of the signature and passes through the bottom leaf. An awl is all

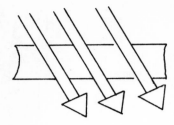

DIRECTION for filing the edges of the piled signatures before sewing.

right for punching holes in ½-inch thick signatures, but you will need to drill with a bit through the holes in thicknesses of more than ½ inch.

When the hole is complete, move the awl to the next hole and repeat the process until you have placed evenly spaced holes along the folded edge. Upon completion of all the holes on the guide, remove the signature from the press and it will be ready to be sewn.

If your signatures have already been stapled (such as theatre programs), remove the staples *after* punching.

Sewing the Signatures

Place all of the signatures (in order) neatly lined up with spine overhanging into the book press and tighten the screws. Using a file or sandpaper, lightly rub from top left to bottom right across the spine of the folded edges. Filing or rubbing the edges will open up the fibers of the paper and let the glue seep in better later on. Also it increases the bond between the crash to come later and the folded edges.

Remove the signatures from the press and place them on the table. One at a time and in order, begin sewing them, using an overcast stitch. Linen and nylon threads provide the most strength and wear. Number 16-3 (thickness) thread and a 1/0 (hardness) needle are recommended.

Start the stitching by tying a knot at the first hole and carry the thread up through it. Then push the needle down through each subsequent hole. Stitch until you reach the next-to-last punched hole. Come around the spine of the signature as usual, but this time come up and start on the second signature.

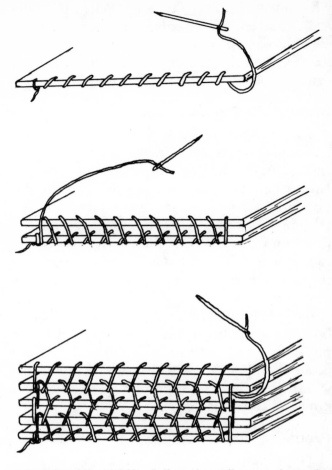

THE OVERCAST STITCH: Follow these diagrams in sewing one, two and more signatures, but be sure to pull the stitches tight (shown loose here for clarity). The spine of the book must be tight, and the knotted ends hidden.

Place it on top of the first signature, as in the illustrations. Now, as you stitch, the needle will pass through both signatures. The drawings show the signatures with space between them, but in actuality, there should be no space. The spine should be tight.

Continue adding signatures in the same fashion until each has been sewed by itself and to the adjoining signature. Make sure the stitching is tight, but not tearing the folded edges. End the stitching by making a knot at the end across from the starting knot. Hide the loose end, knotted into the backbone sewing. Hide the first knot in the same way.

End Papers

Take two sheets of paper no smaller than the size of the original paper sheets used to make signatures. Fold these the same way, producing two separately folded end papers about the same size as your regular pages. They can be blank, white or colored, or printed. Grain must be in the same direction as the spine.

The end papers are to be attached to the inside edge of the first and last leaves of the book and later pasted down on the inside of the front and back covers. Next, take these two end papers (one at a time) and put a strip of glue on a folded edge of each. Now, glue each end paper down at the folded edge of the first and last leaf.

Attaching the Crash

Crash is a mesh material, usually starched cheesecloth. If you cannot get crash easily, use gauze for bandaging. Cut a strip 3 inches wide (for a 1-inch thick book) just short of the full length of the spine. You will attach this to the signatures with its central 1 inch on the spine, on the outside of the end papers. This strip will later be glued to the cover. It serves as the link between the two (cover and signatures).

Press the crash strip now against the spine after you have given the spine a generous coating of glue. Even it out so that an equal amount (about 1 inch) hangs loosely on each side of the spine. Glue again on the outside of the crash, while wet. Allow the glue to dry while in the press.

Preparing the Cover

While the inside pages are drying, make your covers. Book covers are sections of cardboard covered with any of a number of materials: buckram, binder's cover paper, and even leather. (See illustration.) The kind of cover for this project has a square card in the spine. This card should be equal in width to the signatures of the book, plus the thickness of the side boards.

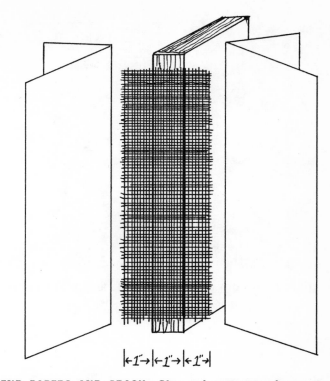

|←1″→|←1″→|←1″→|

END PAPERS AND CRASH: Glue end papers to the sewn signatures, then glue the crash strip to the spine, as shown here.

CUTTING THE COVER BOARDS: Step 1. Even the thickest cardboard can be cut through by repeated strokes of a knife along a metal straightedge. First cut the boards to a size equal to the size your book pages will be after final trimming, allowing ⅛-inch overhang on top, bottom and outside. You will need a front cover and a back cover exactly alike.

SOFTEN THE EDGES of the cut boards in this fashion with your bone folding tool. Step 2.

COVER MAKING: Step 3. Cut the cover material to size, and lay it down perfectly flat on your worktable. Step 4. Glue the cover material completely. Now lay the cover boards down in position, allowing a ½-inch margin for the cover material to overlap equally on all outsides of the board. The cardboard in the spine must be the height of your cover boards, and equal in width to the thickness of the sewn signatures plus the thickness of the cover boards.

After the cover boards have been mounted in the cover material, you are ready to do your cornering.

Making a square corner over the cardboard is simple. If you have used a soft material, such as binder's cover paper, there are only four steps to make for each cover. Each time you fold and glue, be sure you press the cover material tightly against the sides of the boards. Fold and glue as separate operations.

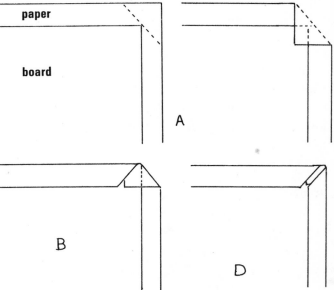

SQUARE CORNER with paper over board. Step C is the bottom edge folding.

A: Fold and glue the paper at an angle over the corner of the cardboard.

B: From the top, fold down the flap and glue it.

C: From the bottom, fold up the flap and glue it.

D: From the side, fold over the flap and glue it.

In every case, make the folds one at a time first, and apply the glue to one flap at a time. Apply pressure while the glue is drying to assure a tight bond. After finishing the corners and flaps of the front cover, do the same with the back cover. The spine top and bottom get folded and glued at the same time as the cover top and bottom.

If heavier material is used, such as buckram or leather, a scissors cut is needed first to prevent excessive build-up in the corners and allow the end papers later to adhere perfectly.

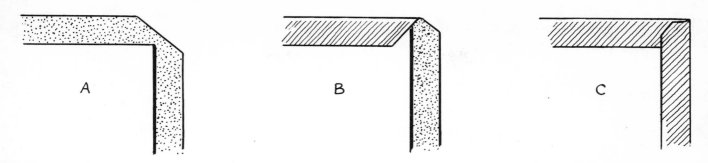

WITH HEAVY COVER MATERIAL, cut an oblique corner first (A). Fold down the top flap, covering the corner of the board (B). When you fold down the side flap (C), you will make a tight corner without too much build-up.

Following the illustration, cut at an angle across the material slightly above the corner of the cardboard.

Fold down and glue the top flap, making sure that the tip of the board is covered. Next, fold over and glue the bottom flap, then the side flap.

To make joints in the cover, you will need to put a score line halfway between the edge of the spine cardboard and the cover cardboard on each side of the spine. Scoring is simply making a line so that the cover will open easier at the most desirable point. Take a straightedge (such as a ruler) and with the edge of your bone folder draw a line in the exact spot where you want the joint.

Then when the cover is on the book it will lift up readily and not tear away from the spine.

Paper Cutting

A paper cutter may be needed to straight-cut the sheets of paper which make up your signatures. Without it, the pages might come out lop-sided, rough and uneven.

A desk-top paper cutter, normally found in an office or school, may be sufficient for a start. With this, you can cut a single folio at a time. If you are going on to bigger things, get a paper cutter with a clamp in an appropriate size depending on the number of folios you expect to cut at one time. Each cutter comes with specific instructions describing the number

GLUEING is a craft in itself. Always glue from the middle outwards and glue the corners last. Better to spread two thin coats than one thick one, and spread each evenly to avoid blobs and bumps that will prevent the cover material from lying flat. Try glueing on a waste sheet before you experiment on cover material.

of pages or approximate thickness it is capable of cutting.

At the beginning, cut the folios one by one before inserting and sewing. Cut the end papers to the same exact dimensions.

If your book consists of signatures that have been doublefolded, you will have to trim off the heads, and you will need a paper cutter with a clamp for this. If you want to cut a book consisting of five signatures of 16 pages each after sewing, you will need a sizable cutter with a clamp.

Binding Check

Before you "case in" your book, check to see that the following steps are complete:

Signatures sewn and edges of end papers tightly glued down.

Crash securely attached to spine and loose from end papers.

Cover material and cardboard neatly attached to each other.

All glued areas dry and secure.

Casing-In

When you are ready to attach the signatures and crash to the covered cardboard (or "case") —in other words, ready to case-in—double-check to see that all the edges of the signatures and end papers are smooth and even. If not, you have not made your cuts right or else the signatures have not been lined up right. If the spine is not much out of position, then go ahead.

Spread a generous amount of glue over the spine and one of the pasted end papers. Place this, glue side down, on to one of the cardboard covers, with the backbone touching the spine. (Be sure it is right side up and forward.) Glue the other end paper (now facing up) and pull the spine up straight. Push the second cover down flat on the glued end paper. Press firmly with your palm and fingers from the center outward towards the edges. Take the bone folder and use its edge to crease the scored joints.

Place the book carefully in the press so that the wood boards of the press are flat against the side boards and not touching the spine. Tighten the screws and leave the book overnight.

Open the press after approximately 10 hours. The end papers should be freed, and any excess glue scraped away. Your book is now ready

REBINDING A PAPERBACK: Once you know a little bookbinding, you can put all your favorite paperbacks in board covers.

for a permanent position among other books of value.

Rebinding a Paperback

Old paperbacks which bring back fond reading memories but look worn and ugly can be bound with a new cover in the same fashion. The new cover will not only be hard but it will protect the valued pages far longer than the original soft binding.

Grab the inside of the book (first page to last) with one hand as close to the spine as possible. With your other hand, peel off the cover slowly. If necessary, precut the area around the spine with a single-edged safety razor. Separate the entire cover, front and back, from the text. Be very careful not to destroy the paper on the glued spine which has held the signatures together.

Place the text in the press and tighten the bolts. With your file or sandpaper, make several passes over the folded edges of the spine. This will remove any lumps left from the first cover and smooth the surface in preparation for the new. It will also make the paper porous so that the new glue will be absorbed and hold.

Sew the signatures together as one, after punching the pages in your punch guide. Glue your end papers on. Freely spread glue over the surface of the spine. Take a 3-inch strip of crash just as you did before and continue on with the casing-in as before. When you get finished, you will have a hardcover paperback. Before returning the newly covered book to its place on the shelf, check the spine area and the inside of the cover for any pages or sections that may have become loose.

What has been described in this section is only the beginning of the bookbinding craft. You can make many innovations as you bind your own old magazines or any books or piles of greeting cards or any treasured items which you would like to preserve from deterioration by the air. Information is available in a good many books (see Bibliography in the Appendix) which describe other stages in bookbinding for the studio craftsman.

CARDBOARD CRAFTING

If you are a paper specialist, you will recognize cardboard as a particular form of paperboard, carefully made of wood and vegetable fibers. If you are a layman, cardboard is the roll around which paper towelling is wrapped, or a gift box, or the stiffener that keeps a laundered shirt from wrinkling. Cardboard is the paperboard on which an artist sketches, or the paperboard from which a bookbinder forms the hard covers for books. In short, cardboard is that material which one finds everywhere and which, for the cardboard craftsman, becomes the base material for any number of practical and decorative pieces.

Materials

In addition to cardboard, whose weight you will choose depending on its future function, you will also need materials to cover it: paper, cloth, leather or leatherette, plastic, braid and other various trims, as well as the adhesives required to join the covering material to the cardboard. In general, a bookbinder's flexible glue should be used to join fabrics to cardboard, and a paste, which is a semi-solid substance, should be used to join paper to cardboard. Wallpaper paste is good to use when paste is required. Rubber cement is an all-purpose adhesive that can be used when either glue or paste would suffice. The so-called quick drying glues which come in tubes, specifically those with an acetone base, should be avoided.

Tools

Only a few tools are needed: a sharp knife, a ruler, a bone folding tool, and a pair of scissors. However, those who intend to do more than the very simplest projects in cardboard crafting should acquire other tools: a compass, flat file, edging tool, and emery paper. You might want some very specialized tools, such as a steel hand punch and a nail set. The hand punch is used to make holes in the cardboard, always punching through from the outer (exposed) surface of the work to the inner (hidden) surface so that all rough edges will be concealed. The nail set is for sealing the grommets (the circles of metal) that will be put around the holes to reinforce them.

The cardboard craftsman should remember that cardboard can do many things: lie flat, stand on a base, support sides to fold, pleat like an accordion, or hold a pad of paper or the pages of a book. Its versatility is apparent, and only a few techniques are needed to put that versatility to use.

Techniques

There are three basic steps in cardboard crafting: (1) cutting the materials to be used; (2) glueing or pasting the covering material to the cardboard base; and (3) pressing and drying the finished product.

Before cutting the cardboard, it is imperative to measure carefully, using a T square for accuracy. The square can then be used as a cutting edge. Several shallow cuts are preferable to one deep cut. Covering materials can be cut with either a knife or a shears.

When the materials have been cut and are ready to be joined, decide whether to use paste or glue. Whichever adhesive you select should be spread on the work by beginning at the

Condensed from the book, "Cardboard Crafting" by Inga Granit | © 1964 by Sterling Publishing Co., Inc., New York

middle and working towards the edges. It is better to apply two thin coats, rather than one thick one. Spread the thin layers of adhesive *evenly*. Applying the adhesive to the cardboard or to the covering material is best decided with each project. If the surface to be covered is an interior surface or is in some other way difficult to get at, it is usually easier to coat the covering with the adhesive and then join it to the cardboard.

Pressing and drying are important parts of the glueing and pasting work. The purpose of pressing is to hold the work firmly and in the proper shape and position until all expansion and shrinking have stopped. Weights—dictionaries, encyclopedias or blocks—should be used that completely cover the work being pressed. Remember that too much weight is as undesirable as too little.

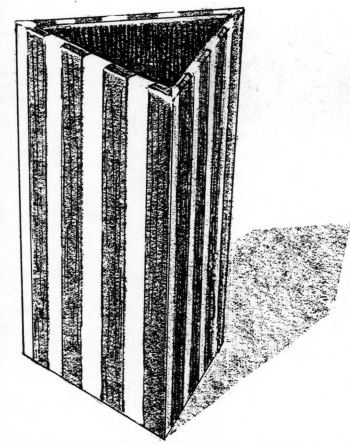

A WASTEPAPER BASKET is easy to make from cardboard. Attach the pieces together and cover with fancy paper, and you can add a decorator's touch to any room (Illus. 1).

Triangular Wastepaper Basket

For the base, cut a piece of heavy cardboard into a triangle $5\frac{1}{2}$ inches on each side. For the sides, cut three pieces $5\frac{11}{16}$ by $13\frac{13}{16}$ inches. Cut covering paper—either with an adhesive back or fancy giftwrap—to a rectangle measuring $14\frac{9}{16}$ inches by $17\frac{1}{4}$ inches. (This allows for an additional $\frac{3}{8}$ of an inch on the top and bottom of each side for folding over the edges, and $\frac{3}{16}$ of an inch at each end for overlap at the seam.)

Join the sides of the basket together using 14-inch strips of 1-inch wide brown wrapping paper (kraft paper). Glue this wrapping paper on the seams inside and outside of the basket.

The inside of the basket should be covered with a sturdy fabric such as canvas. This piece is cut $13\frac{3}{16}$ by $16\frac{11}{16}$ inches. Use glue liberally and spread it over the fabric evenly before laying the canvas on the inside of the basket. Glue a matching triangular piece on the bottom inside from edge to edge.

The final step is to wrap the basket in an outside covering paper. Glue this paper around the sides so there is a margin to turn over the bottom edges of the basket. Then cover the underside of the bottom of the basket, edge to edge, with a matching piece of covering paper or with plain brown wrapping paper.

Trinket Tray

Here is a small tray that you can use either to hold trinkets or as a desk caddy. You will need medium-weight cardboard, textured paper, kraft paper, and paste and glue.

Using the cardboard, cut out the tray and compartment dividers to the dimensions shown in Illus. 3. Score the tray halfway through the thickness of the cardboard along the score lines shown in the diagram, and fold the sides up.

Tie the sides in place with cord. From kraft paper, cut out four strips measuring $\frac{3}{4}$ by $3\frac{1}{8}$ inches; fold these in half lengthwise and paste them along the outside of the four corner joints. Split the part of the kraft paper hanging

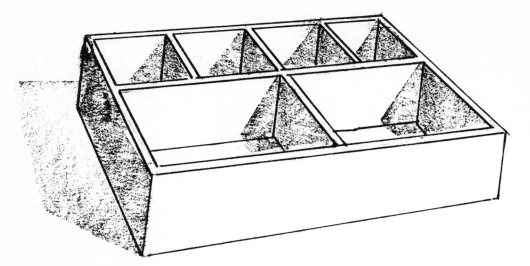

A TRAY WITH DIVIDERS is a practical place to keep those small items which often get lost. By being in separate compartments, safety pins, thumbtacks, earrings and rings will not be misplaced any more (Illus. 2).

over at the bottom and fold each piece under the base of the tray.

Cut the textured paper for the covering of the sides in a long strip measuring $28\frac{3}{8}$ by 2 inches. (This can be in two pieces, each measuring $14\frac{3}{8}$ by 2 inches; these two pieces must be bigger in total than the single sheet because the two diagonally opposite corners require an overlap.) The covering for the bottom of the tray—of the same material—measures $7\frac{7}{8}$ by $5\frac{5}{8}$ inches.

Use paste to mount the textured paper covering. Coat the paper with paste and then apply it to the sides of the box. The ends of this textured paper strip (or strips) should join at

a corner of the box, where a slight overlap of one end over the other can be made. Fold over the edges, top and bottom. A small triangular gore should be cut out at each corner to make the edges neat at the corners. Now mount the bottom covering.

Fit the compartment dividers into place. Use glue to fix them and also reinforce them using strips of kraft paper $\frac{5}{8}$ of an inch wide.

Cut out the covering for the inner sides of the tray and the compartment dividers from a matching unpatterned end paper. Cover the bottom of each compartment last. Use a bone folding tool to flatten all surfaces and to make the corners sharp.

USE THESE DIMENSIONS to make the trinket tray. To enlarge the tray, multiply each measurement by the same number. This will keep the sides in the proper proportions to each other (Illus. 3).

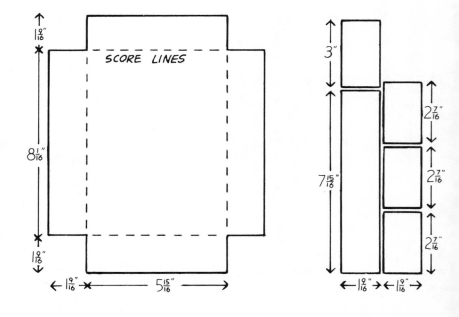

A DECORATIVE BACKING for a pad of paper makes a more interesting telephone pad than a plain tablet, and also supplies a hard surface to write on (Illus. 4).

Telephone Pad

Keep this pad handy near the telephone. It is meant for taking messages in the office or at home. You will need the following:

heavy cardboard
medium-weight cardboard
light canvas or buckram covering material
end paper
filler pad
glue and paste

Cut a piece 7 by $4\frac{3}{4}$ inches from heavy cardboard and a piece $6\frac{1}{2}$ by $4\frac{1}{4}$ inches from medium-weight cardboard. These will form the two-piece base.

Cut the covering from light canvas or buckram in two pieces, $7\frac{3}{4}$ by $5\frac{1}{2}$ inches, and $6\frac{7}{8}$ by $4\frac{5}{8}$ inches. Also cut out the mounting strip for the pad from the same material; make this $2\frac{3}{4}$ inches by the width of the pad you intend to use. Preferably get a pad with tear perforations as shown in Illus. 4. The filler pad can be replaced when it is used up, so be sure to select a pad for which you can obtain identical replacements.

Cut a piece of end paper $6\frac{1}{2}$ by $4\frac{1}{4}$ inches. This will cover the underside.

Round off the corners of both pieces of cardboard and bevel the edges slightly, using the bone folding tool.

Spread glue on one side of each piece of cardboard. Glue the larger piece of covering material on the larger piece of cardboard and the smaller covering on the smaller cardboard. Press each covered piece of cardboard.

Now glue the smaller piece of cardboard on the covered surface of the larger piece. Press again.

Spread glue on the top edge of the pad and fasten the mounting strip to the pad, folding it over the top of the pad as shown in the illustration. Fold the mounting strip under the pad and apply glue to the outside of the mounting strip. (If the rubber cement is used to attach the pad to the base, removal and replacement of the pad will be made easier.)

Paste the end paper on the underside of the base. Press again to seal the end paper to the base and to make sure the pad is solidly glued.

CARDBOARD OF THE DIMENSIONS SHOWN will provide a big enough backing for the average-sized pad of paper (Illus. 5).

$7\frac{3}{4}$ 7" $4\frac{3}{4}$" $5\frac{1}{2}$"

$6\frac{7}{8}$ $6\frac{1}{2}$ $4\frac{1}{2}$" $4\frac{5}{8}$"

$6\frac{1}{2}$" $4\frac{1}{2}$" $2\frac{3}{4}$

COLORING PAPERS

Anyone can buy manufactured colored papers, but you can make your own! Your friends will appreciate your sending them letters on beautifully colored stationery and presents wrapped in hand-colored gift papers with ornamental decorations of your own creation.

The few really beautiful papers that can be purchased are comparatively costly. Making your own is inexpensive. The enjoyment alone from experimenting should induce you to prepare your own colored papers for writing and wrapping papers, posters and even imaginative lamp shade creations.

Children will find coloring papers an exciting adventure. Adult supervision is recommended because of the ease in which stains occur and the use of toxic fluids in certain projects.

Before You Begin

Before starting any of your projects, lay several sheets of old newspaper over your work area and on the floor, to protect against spills. Have your paper, cups, brushes and other material close enough to reach without getting up. When working with wood stains and paint, all material should be handy so as not to give liquids a chance to dry before using them.

Wood Stain Coloring

The following materials are needed for coloring paper with alcohol-soluble wood stain:

wood stain in various colors
spirit or alcohol (for mixing colors and cleaning)
absorbent white paper
broad brushes
plastic cover or newspaper to protect work area
rubber gloves

Dissolve several wood stains according to instructions on the can and then apply each color with even brush strokes to your paper. Continue this process until the entire paper is covered with your selection of colors. Overlap the stains for additional effect.

Geometrical figures play an important part in modern design. Using circles and triangles,

WOOD STAIN comes in various colors. When it is applied to paper, it creates interesting grades of color, from the lightest shade to the darkest.

Condensed from the book, "Coloring Papers" by Susanne Strose | © 1968 by Sterling Publishing Co., Inc., New York

try some freehand patterns in different color stains. Once again, overlap the designs. Experiment and you will find that you get interesting color combinations without half trying.

The finished product can be framed or used as a book jacket cover.

Watercoloring

Watercolors have long been popular with children, and coloring with watercolors to produce a useful item is even more exciting. Choose projects that are not difficult, thus allowing the younger child a sense of freedom. Watercolor paper and tempera paints are all the materials needed from a store. A sponge, and adhesive tape are probably already in the house and have been used for other crafts.

To begin, tape the paper to the work area. Cover all the edges. This will allow curl-free work. Prepare a color in a paper cup. Dilute this mixture, and apply it with a sponge using even strokes. Allow this to dry and use the newly shaded paper as stationery or add a design with a brush point using a contrasting color. The dark design on a lightly shaded

PAINTING OVER PASTE: Twisting the brush while applying paste to paper creates a relief effect. The paste absorbs different amounts of paint, producing variations in the depth of color that appears.

background can be used as a book cover or for wrapping paper.

Coloring with a Base of Paste

Using a cellulose paste, such as the type used for wallpaper, you can give your drawings a colorful 3-dimensional appearance. The paste will make the different colors stand out, and, if the paper is moistened properly, the paint will take on a vein-like appearance as it does in the felt-tip pen project.

First moisten the paper (avoid soaking) with a sponge and then apply the cellulose paste. Twist the brush as you go. The twisting produces high and low areas in the paste. Additional paste can be applied to raise selected areas of the design.

Immediately after applying the paste, dip your paint brush in diluted watercolors, and carefully brush over the whole surface. Be sure that no pattern is left uncovered. If you are careful to allow only a small time lapse between sponging the paper and applying the diluted watercolors, the paints will spread into each of the areas producing a satisfying finish. After the paper has dried, it can be polished with floor wax.

WATERCOLOR applied to folded paper makes either a symmetrical or a repeating design.

MARBLED PAPERS: To create unusual swirls, add diluted oil paints to thinned paste and mix them gently. Place the paper on top of the paste. The design will transfer to the paper.

Marbled Papers

Swirl color and marble effects can be obtained with oil colors and diluted paste. The marbled finish is sometimes used for wrapping papers and posters, and for the end papers of books. The texture is rich in appearance, but in actuality, costs very little to produce.

Pour some diluted paste into a tray which is larger than the paper you wish to dye. The consistency of the paste should be loose enough so that it is lump-free, yet thick enough so that it adheres to the paper surface. Next, in several paper cups, prepare your oil colors diluted with turpentine.

Let some of the diluted oil paints drip off a brush into the paste. The paint will remain in globs on the gluey surface and will not mix. Take the tip of your brush and swirl the little globs around in the paste mixture. This will produce a fascinating variety of marble-like patterns.

Carefully place a sheet of paper on the surface of the paste-and-paint mixture. Lightly pat the top of the paper with a dry brush so that no air bubbles are permitted between

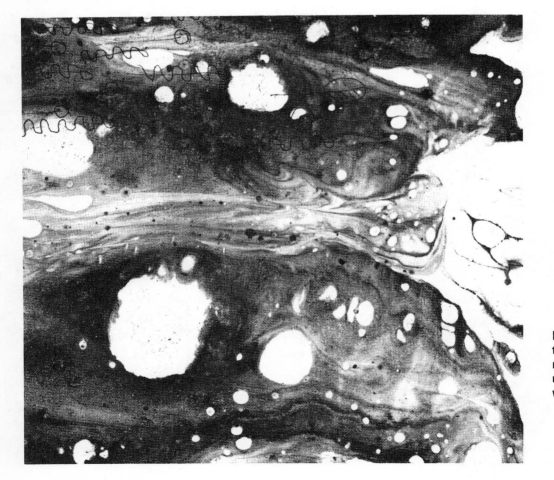

BY ADDING OX GALL to the paste-and-paint mixture, more unusual and unique circles and swirls will appear.

paper and paste. The colors will stick to the paper.

Because it is unavoidable that the paper will pick up some of the gluey paste solution, it is advisable to have a second tray with just water ready to remove any sticky mass. Fill this second tray the same way as the first—just covering the bottom surface. Place the paper in the tray and move it from side to side. This will remove the excess glue from the paper's surface.

Ox gall (obtainable in art supply shops) added to the diluted oil colors will produce new life in the design. It sets the marbling in motion, propels outward, mingles drops with adjacent drops and forms blister-like shapes. The transfer procedure from tray to paper is the same as before.

Felt-Tip Pens on a Wet Surface

An even less messy way of getting a water-color effect is by using several colored water-

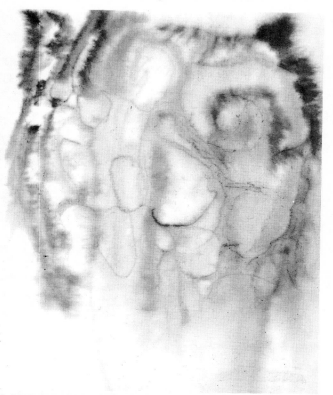

A FELT-TIP PEN applied to wet paper makes lines which run into the paper and seem to disappear as they get lighter. No mixing of paints is necessary to create these unique patterns.

soluble felt-tip pens on a wet surface. Water-color paper and a corner table are all you need to fill many hours of coloring fun. Diluting paints and dripping sponges are unnecessary here.

Attach a piece of paper to your drawing area by taping all around the edges. This will prevent the edges from curling when the paper is wet. Using tissue paper or a paper towel, dip it into water and then dab the drawing surface until the entire area is wet.

With the felt-tip pen, make circular designs on the moistened surface. Include in your design freehand motions and geometric figures. Watch how the ink spreads away from the main line in a vein-like fashion.

If the water dries while you are still drawing, dab some more water on the paper without touching the design. Do not soak the paper. Soaking will cause the first part of the design to run more than desired.

Children, as well as parents, will enjoy working with felt-tip pens because it does not involve mixing. You can get right down to actual drawing projects simply by removing the top of the pen.

Ink Spraying

One very amusing pastime for children is blowing bubbles. Now, employing the same technique, a child can color paper or fabric by spraying a permanent design using an ink diffuser. Trees, stars and geometric forms are easy to cut and can be combined to make a colorful design.

On a free section of wall in the kitchen or basement, hang several sheets of newspaper to protect against spills. On this, hang a piece of blank paper or fabric. Next, using construction paper or light cardboard, cut a stencil design and pin it to the blank piece of paper.

Open a small bottle of ink and insert the diffuser. Inhale and then place your mouth on the diffuser and blow lightly until little dots of ink begin to spray on to the stencil. When the

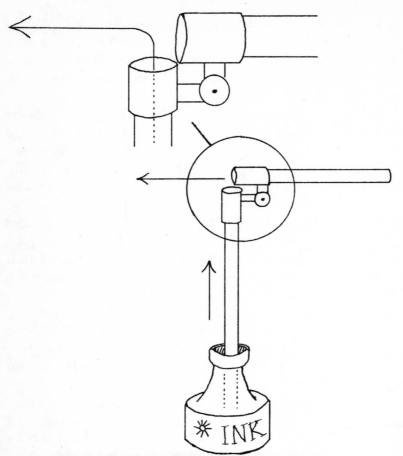

USING THE INK DIFFUSER to spray ink on paper.

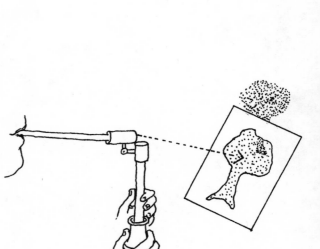

A STENCIL is a piece of paper with a design cut out from the center. Place the stencil on another sheet of paper and blow ink over it.

stencil area is filled with dots, remove the stencil and let the design dry.

Once the first design is dry, replace the stencil. Only this time, place it at an angle and overlap the original ink design. You can reproduce the same design again and again or change the stencil continuously. Each time a stencil is placed, spray it with a different color.

THE STENCIL can be moved and sprayed again, creating interesting overlapping patterns.

ORIGAMI

Origami is the art of folding objects from a single sheet of paper without cutting or pasting. The word comes from a combination of two Japanese words: "ori," fold; and "kami," paper. Originally, origami was used for ceremonial purposes in Japan, as well as for pleasure.

Today, origami experts still insist that no cuts be made or any paste used; others, however, permit limited incisions and some paste. This article *only* refers to the traditional use of paper folding. Origami can be both simple enough for children to enjoy and complex enough to stimulate the creative adult.

TRADITIONAL ORIGAMI FIGURES

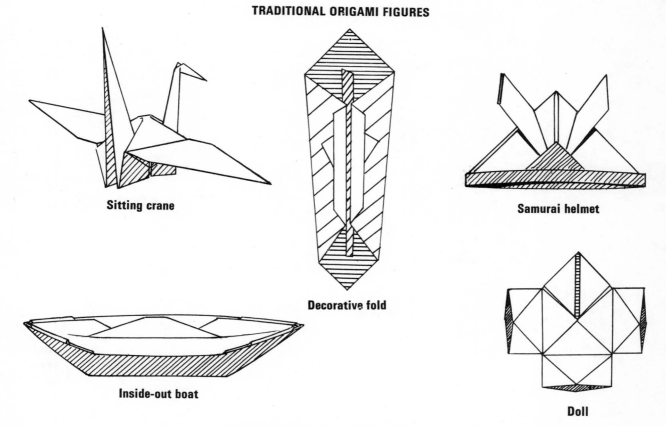

Sitting crane

Decorative fold

Samurai helmet

Inside-out boat

Doll

Written especially for this volume by Nancy Hom

SYMBOLS

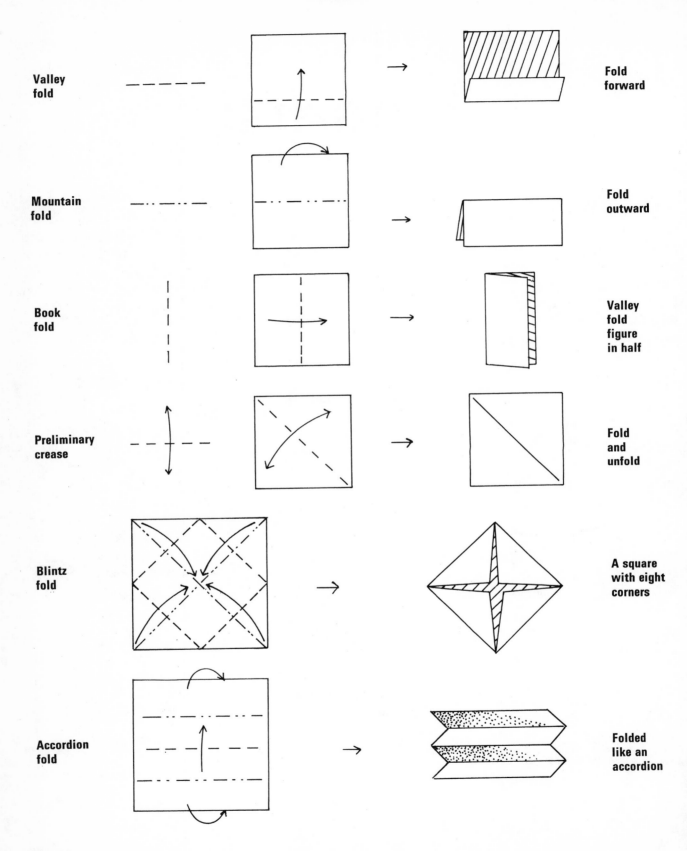

Valley fold

Fold forward

Mountain fold

Fold outward

Book fold

Valley fold figure in half

Preliminary crease

Fold and unfold

Blintz fold

A square with eight corners

Accordion fold

Folded like an accordion

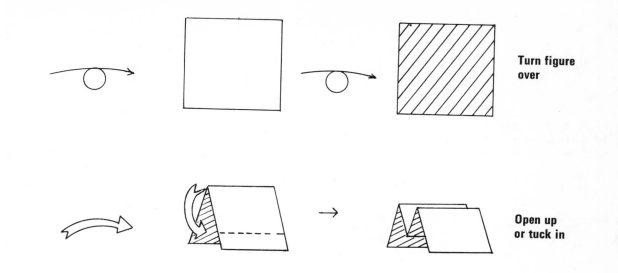

Turn figure over

Open up or tuck in

All you need besides airmail-type paper are square pieces of colored paper, aluminum foil, or aluminum foil backed with kraft paper.

For larger objects requiring greater strength a new material called Forbon is recommended. By wetting one side, you can obtain the necessary flexibility needed for making sharp creases and folds, while the dry side helps retain the rigidity needed to hold the crease.

The diagrams here give explicit instructions on how to fold various objects and you should practice these at the start until you can invent your own original origami designs.

Basic Folds and Symbols

All origami folds should be made with neat, sharp creases to obtain good straight lines. Use a finger or fingernail to make creases sharp. Sometimes it is wise also to make preliminary creases to ensure that the folds are made along the lines indicated. If the paper becomes crumpled, take a new sheet and start over.

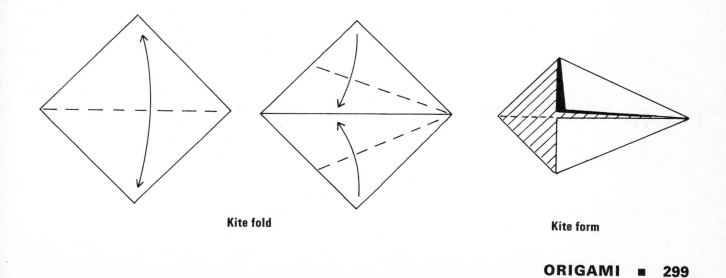

Kite fold   **Kite form**

HOW TO FOLD A BOX

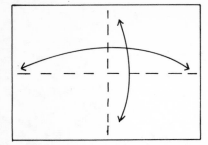

1. Begin with a sheet of paper 8½" x 11" and make creases for vertical and horizontal center lines.

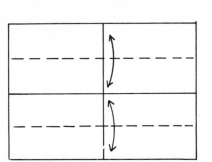

2. Fold the narrow sides up to the center line. Then unfold.

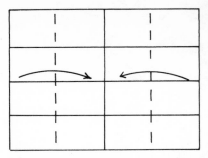

3. Now fold the wide sides to the vertical center line and unfold again. (Fold the first sides narrower than the second if you are using a square sheet.)

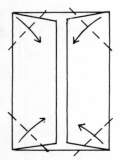

4. Using the valley fold, diagonal-fold corners from the folded edges to crease lines.

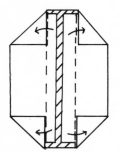

5. Now the raw edges may be folded over the folded corners.

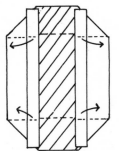

6. Open up the sides and, as shown, reverse the folds.

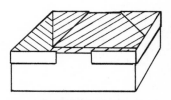

7. The finished box.

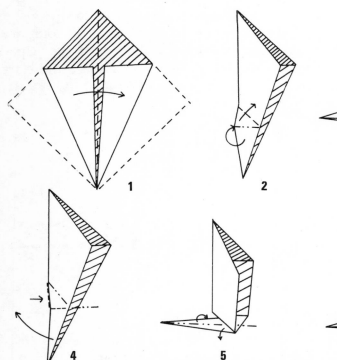

THE FOOT FOLD

1. Begin with a kite form and book-fold the paper.
2. First, valley-fold up and then mountain-fold down. Point fold to the left.
3. Then unfold.
4. Open up "foot" and valley-fold, pointing to the left.
5. From the bottom of the figure, push up the center line and mountain-fold the point.
6. The completed foot fold.

THE INSIDE REVERSE FOLD

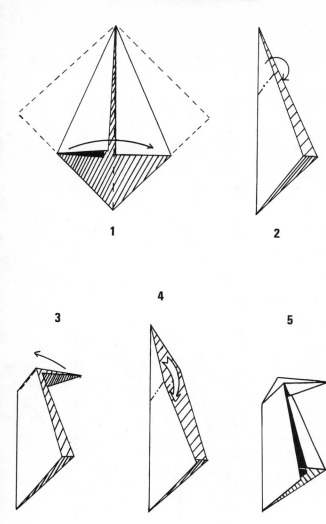

1
2
3
4
5

THE OUTSIDE REVERSE FOLD

1
2
3
4
5

1. Begin with the kite fold and book-fold the sheet in half.
2. Mountain-fold the top at any angle you wish toward the open edges.
3. Unfold.
4. Open the figure slightly and use the old creases to bend the point down into the flaps. Then valley-fold the vertical fold.
5. The inside reverse fold, completed.

1. Begin with the kite fold again and book-fold the sheet in half.
2. Valley-fold the top towards the folded edge.
3. Unfold.
4. Open the figure and bend the point, along the creases, down outside the flaps. Then valley-fold the vertical fold.
5. The outside reverse fold.

How to Fold a Box

Folding a box is a good first project for the paper folder. Start with a sheet of paper $8\frac{1}{2}$ inches × 11 inches in size. If you want to make a box with a cover, take another sheet of paper slightly larger and follow the box directions. It will fit over the smaller box as a lid.

More Advanced Folds

To produce some of the more sophisticated origami objects such as the traditional Japanese sitting crane, knowledge of some of the more advanced origami folds is needed. Follow the diagrams to make the inside reverse fold, the outside reverse fold, the crimp fold, the foot fold, and the square preliminary fold.

THE SQUARE PRELIMINARY FOLD

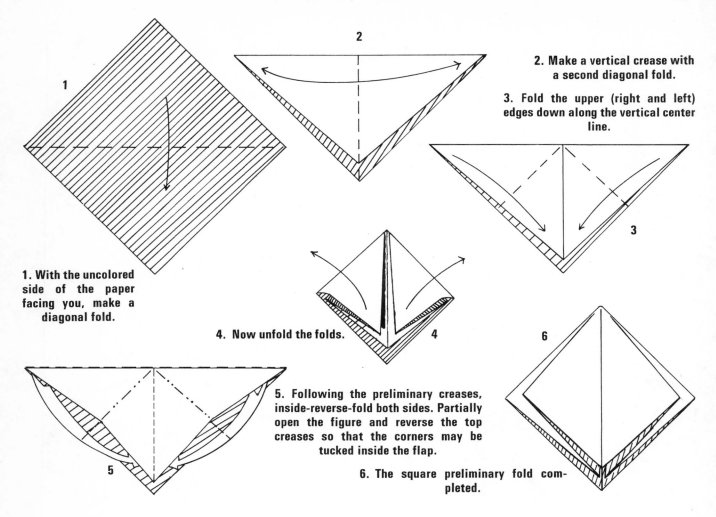

1. With the uncolored side of the paper facing you, make a diagonal fold.

2. Make a vertical crease with a second diagonal fold.

3. Fold the upper (right and left) edges down along the vertical center line.

4. Now unfold the folds.

5. Following the preliminary creases, inside-reverse-fold both sides. Partially open the figure and reverse the top creases so that the corners may be tucked inside the flap.

6. The square preliminary fold completed.

THE CRIMP FOLD

1. Beginning with the kite fold, book-fold the sheet.
2. Accordion-fold the top of the figure by valley-folding down and mountain-folding up.
3. Unfold.
4. Open the top flap and accordion-fold the sides towards the bottom.
5. The completed crimp fold.

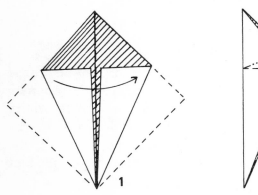
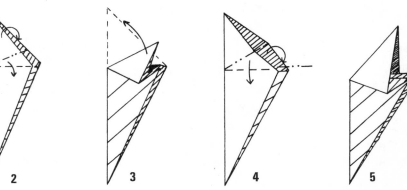

Now try the bird base:

THE BIRD BASE

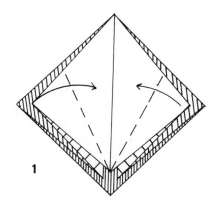

1

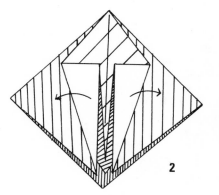

2

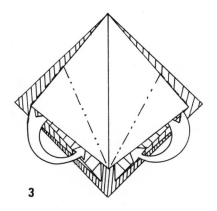

3

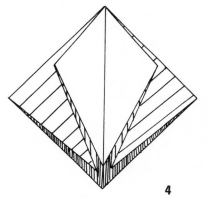

4

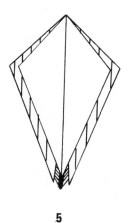

5

1. Beginning with the square preliminary fold, fold the bottom portions of the uppermost flaps to the center line.
2. Unfold the flaps.
3. Using an inside reverse fold, tuck the corners of both flaps inside.
4. Now repeat Steps 1-3 on the other side.
5. The completed bird base.

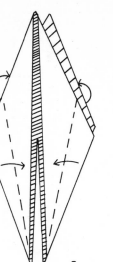
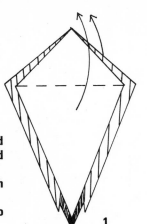

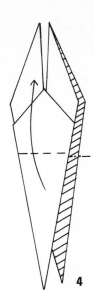

Start with bird base.

1. Fold bottom points upward on each side to form diamond shape.
2. Fold lower side of each diamond to middle line.
3. Book-fold side corners to middle.

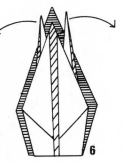
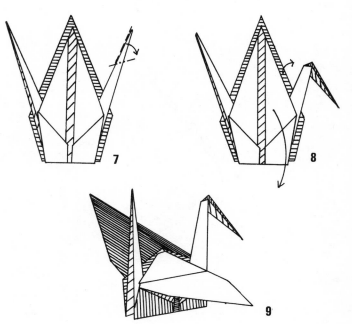

4. Fold in valley-fold each bottom point to top points.
5. Book-fold each side again.
6. Ease out the two narrow points to form head and tail.
7. Make inside reverse fold for beak.
8. Fold wing flaps down.
9. The sitting crane.

The Sitting Crane

Anyone who has developed enough skill in origami to fold the traditional Japanese sitting crane is no longer a beginner. In fact, once this degree of accomplishment has been reached, you are well on your way to having mastered the initial stages of origami.

PAPER FLOWER MAKING

Paper flowers are at their best when they are made to imitate but not copy a natural flower. Use the structure of the natural bloom as the basis for the structure of the paper flower, but then allow the paper flower its own uniqueness. Imaginatively crafted, paper flowers have a lightness and gaiety entirely of their own.

The craftsman can use tissue paper and crepe paper as well as stronger, stiffer materials like thin cardboard, metal foil, and drawing paper to construct his flowers. Each blossom made will have stamens or a pistil or both. Stamens are rather like long slender threads with a knob-like form at their upper ends; they surround the pistil—often a tubular structure but also having varied shapes—which is located in the center of the flower. Each flower will have petals and a base to which the flower parts are fixed; it will be supported by a stem with leaves.

There are several methods for making pistils and stamens:

(A) Draw a fine flower wire through a cotton ball or a bead; then twist the projecting ends of the wire together, leaving the longer end for the stem.

(B) Pierce two holes in a small disc of light cardboard, pass the wire through the holes and twist the ends of the wire together; the long end will be the stem.

(C) Paste tissue paper or crepe paper over a small cardboard disc and wind wire around its base, leaving enough for the stem.

(D) Crumple small bits of paper together, put them in a square piece of tissue paper or crepe paper and then fasten the paper together—with wire—into a pouch shape.

(E) For stamens, cut a strip of crepe paper or tissue paper. (If you use tissue paper, which is very thin, always cut at least four sheets together at a time.) Cut fine fringes along one edge of the strip, then gather it along the other edge, and wrap wire around it, leaving one end of the wire for a stem.

pistils   **stamens**

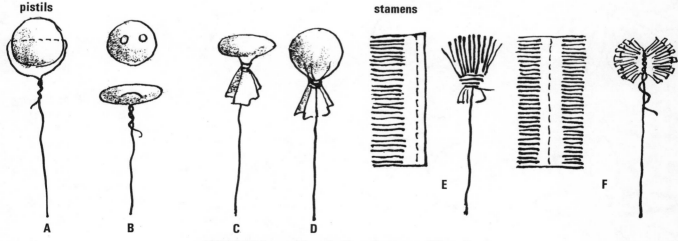

A   B   C   D   E   F

METHODS for making pistils and stamens (Illus. 1).

Condensed from the book, "Making Paper Flowers" by Susanne Strose | © 1970 by Sterling Publishing Co., Inc., New York

(F) Fold a strip of paper lengthwise, cut fringes along the doubled edge, open the strip, and wrap wire around the center line formed by the fold.

To combine a pistil with stamens, gather the fringed strip you have made around the stem already formed by the pistil and fasten the paper by firmly encircling it with wire below the fringed edge.

Although petals can be made by folding paper into various geometric shapes and cutting, they can also be made by a free-hand cutting of a disc of tissue paper or by cutting them from strips of crepe paper. Because crepe paper has a grain, it must be handled differently from tissue paper. Unfold the roll of crepe paper to a thickness of layers that your scissors can easily cut. Then cut the strip with scissors going across the grain. Never make disc petals from crepe paper.

Using tissue paper, cut your discs from a thickness of several pieces of paper and pierce the center of the discs. Cut petals into various shapes, as shown in the diagram. To prevent the layers from slipping while you are cutting, keep a firm grip on the middle and cut around the middle. Paper clips can also be used to hold the paper together.

To complete the blossom draw the wire stem of a bundle of stamens through several pierced petals. Press a small amount of modelling wax against the underside of the petals to form a receptacle. If you use both stamens and pistil, put the pistil in the middle of the stamens. A blossom so made will be very much like apple or cherry blossoms, poppies, cornflowers or daisies.

In order to complete the wire stems, use ribbon of silk or crepe paper, $\frac{1}{4}$ to $\frac{5}{8}$ of an inch wide, and glue it at an oblique angle to the stem under the blossom and roll the ribbon spirally around the wire.

For leaves, use double layers of tissue paper or crepe paper cut into whatever shape leaf you wish; insert a piece of wire between the two layers of the same shape and glue the layers together. The wire forms the main vein of the leaf and the leaf's stem.

Another method of making leaves is to cut a strip of crepe paper and considering one edge of it the bottom, cut triangular shapes almost to that bottom edge. Gather the strip at the bottom and wind a piece of wire around it.

petals

G

CIRCULAR PETALS: Using a compass for accuracy, make a circle and cut petals from it. Insert a bundle of stamens through a hole in the middle of the petals, and crease the petals so they stand up (Illus. 2).

FOR A LEAF cut two layers of green paper and insert a wire between the layers to form the main vein (Illus. 3).

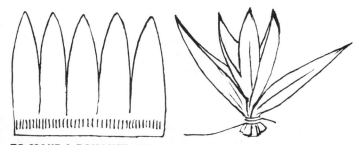

TO MAKE A BOUQUET of leaves, cut a row from green crepe paper or tissue paper, and gather the bottom together. Secure it with wire and separate the leaves (Illus. 4).

Spread the points on top. This method is especially useful for making bouquets and wreaths.

Crepe Zinnias

A lovely flower to construct is a zinnia—a blossom which has stamens dominating. For

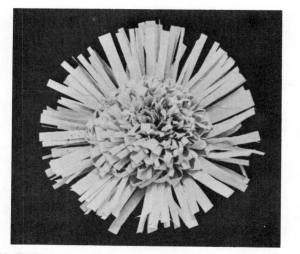

THIS ZINNIA is made by tying several stamens together. Zinnias are noted for their warm colors (Illus. 5).

the stamens, take a strip of crepe paper approximately 4 inches wide. Fold the paper (with the grain running vertically) about one-third of its width, along its entire length. Fringe the folded edge with scissors and roll the strip into a bundle. Secure it with flower wire. Make the petals by gathering a strip of crepe paper, fringed on a single edge, around the stamens. Cover the wire stems as indicated before.

WHEN MAKING A PEONY, remember that the inside petals are small and close together, while the outside petals are large and wide open. Peonies are usually a shade of red (Illus. 6).

Peonies

For a large brilliant blossom such as a peony, use a small wooden rod about $\frac{3}{16}$ to $\frac{1}{4}$ of an inch in diameter and with the aid of glue and flower wire assemble the blossom to this stem petal by petal.

First cut the petals. For the central portion, use smaller petals, and gradually increase the size of the petals as they reach the outer rows. (For example, you can combine petals that are 4, 5, and 7 inches in length.) Stretch the petals slightly, and partially glue and partially wire them to the stem. Cover the receptacle that is formed by glueing on it a piece of green crepe paper. Cover the stem as described previously.

One of the tremendous advantages of paper flowers is the remarkable color combinations that can be achieved. You can follow nature or depart completely from it. Bright orange blossoms can be combined with pinks; turquoise with darker blues and purples. Any color combination that pleases the craftsman—and suits his decorating needs—can be used.

Imaginary Flowers Made of Metallic Foil

These blossoms are all cut out of a circle. You can use either metallic foil or white drawing paper. In this kind of work, precision is of the utmost importance; therefore, you should use a compass for drawing. Make a large circle to mark the outer diameter. Use a smaller, inner circle to mark the point from which the petals start. The uncut middle of the circle forms the fused part of the corolla (Illus. 7).

The sector that is cut out of the circle has a tab for glueing one cut side to the other. The surface of the inner circle is thus formed into a cone, representing the tube of the corolla

FOR BRIGHT EFFECTS, cut petals out of metallic paper. Cut away a part of the circle and join the circle to form a cone (Illus. 7).

where the petals come together. Depending on the size of the cut-out sector (one-fifth, one-quarter, one-third, two-fifths, one-half, three-quarters of the circle), a blunt or a pointed cone results (see Illus. 8).

The petals may be cut in different ways, depending on the length and shape you desire. It is important that the petals are always arranged radially.

WHEN CUTTING THE CIRCLE, cut a large section to make petals which are close together, forming an unopened flower. A small piece cut from the circle makes an open flower. In the bottom row are suggested petal shapes for you to cut (Illus. 8).

THESE PAPER PETAL SHAPES were cut from drawing paper. They can be curled and folded to make three-dimensional flowers, or glued on paper in a scattered arrangement for a flat design (Illus. 9).

Naturally, the blossoms also need stems. A pistil or stamens are attached to a wire as described previously.

One or two flower rosettes made from the cut-out circle are attached with glue, and a pre-shaped receptacle, made of modelling wax, is pressed against the point of the tube. White blossoms have white stems; the leaves may also be white. You can cover white drawing paper with narrow strips of silk, crepe paper, or glazed paper.

Blossoms made of metallic paper, on the other hand, require stems and leaves made out of matching metallic paper. The effect may also be heightened if you use gold beads for making the pistil, and cut tinsel for the stamens.

Because a full-bloom effect is desired for this kind of flower, use at least two, and even three or four petal rosettes; they may be of different sizes, shapes, and colors.

Finally, the petals are drawn over the blade of a scissors to curl them either upward or downward, and to make them lose some of their stiffness.

You can use metallic flowers to adorn a nicely wrapped Christmas present, embellished with a few twigs. You will double the receiver's pleasure, and you will also feel rewarded because of the satisfaction you have derived from your work.

ROSETTES OF METAL FOIL assembled in layers make cheerful decorations (Illus. 10).

SCISSORSCRAFT

Scissorscraft involves more than cutting paper dolls and doilies, yet many people ignore this interesting craft because it seems too childish. True, children can and should experiment with scissors and paper. Remember when you yourself cut valentines and snowflakes? But now, with a mature imagination and an agile, adult pair of hands, you can cut fine and complex lines in paper to produce intricate and sophisticated designs. As with most arts, practice is necessary before you can create pieces worthy of a museum spot—but in the meantime, you will cut many interesting figures to decorate your own home and amuse your family and friends.

One advantage to the art of scissorscraft is the many things you can do with your cuttings once they have been perfected to your satisfaction: mount one on cardboard and frame it to hang in your home; spray or spatter paint around it, and when you remove the cutting, the shape will remain, outlined by the color surrounding it; or take your cutting to a professional printer and have him make several hundred greeting cards or sheets of stationery for you. Because you are the artist, the design will be your very own.

Materials

Equipment for scissorscraft is remarkably easy to obtain; in fact, you probably already have everything you need.

Scissors, of course, are the prime tool you will use. Have at least two sizes, one large and one small. The large ones are for cutting the outlines of figures and other large areas; with them, you can even make curving lines if you wish. The small pair of scissors should have pointed, not rounded, blades, for with this pair you will be cutting very small bits of paper away from your design.

Paper is also necessary. As you experiment, you will discover which thickness you prefer to work with. Different weights are suitable for different figures: thin tissue paper is more suitable for cutting a scene with much detail, as small areas can be cut away easily. Construction paper, which is heavier and sturdier, is best for scenes with large solid areas and wide curves as outlines. Cut the same pattern—a flower, perhaps—in several different colors. Group them together on a contrasting background and you will have a colorful garden that never has to be watered.

To keep your cuttings on their background, glue them carefully. Rubber cement has several advantages which make it ideal for most projects. By applying the cement to the back of the design only, and by placing the design on the background while the cement is still wet, it is easy to position your cutting. Excess glue—or smears of glue on the background caused by sliding the design into the correct position—can be easily removed by dabbing or gently rubbing them with a ball of dried rubber cement.

For permanent bonding with rubber cement, both the back of the design and the background paper must be given a thin coat of cement which must be thoroughly dry before the pieces are joined. Be sure you have positioned your cutting carefully before joining the surfaces.

For small or delicate designs, the easiest method of glueing is to place a small amount of

Condensed from the book, "Scissorscraft" by Lini Grol | © 1970 by Sterling Publishing Co., Inc., New York

glue on a piece of scrap cardboard. Then dip the end of a small strip of paper in the glue, making sure both sides of the strip get a thin coat of glue. Slide the strip between the cutting and the backing upon which it has been positioned. Remove the strip and press the cutting firmly on the cardboard to make sure that the two stick together. Begin this process in the middle of the piece and then spread to the corners. This way, there is less danger of wrinkling or moving the cutting out of position.

A Pine Tree

For your first project, begin by cutting out a simple pine tree. Using your large scissors, cut several trees out at once by cutting through three or four layers of paper. You can make each tree just a little bit different when you put your forest together.

The illustrated pine tree is one possible outline. If this is your first project, you might wish to copy the design. When you gain more experience and have confidence in your dexterity you will want to make your own designs.

Still using the large scissors that you used to cut the outline, cut branches, as shown in Illus. 2. Leave an area at the bottom to represent the ground so that your tree will not be left standing in mid-air.

Because this is a tree in the wintertime, holes were cut in the tree to show the snow which has settled on its branches. The method shown in Illus. 3 is called "hollow cutting," and results in an area cut out of the paper, without cutting through an edge to get to the inside. To make these cut-out areas, pierce the paper with a pin to make a small hole. Then insert one point of the small scissors into that hole and cut away the desired area.

You can add more details, if you wish, by making feathery pine needles on the ends of the branches. Use your small scissors again, and snip carefully to achieve this delicate result.

Leaves

You can cut as many different kinds of leaves as there are different kinds of leaves to cut. The one illustrated here is only one example of the possibilities. To get other ideas, just look at some real leaves. Notice whether the edges are smooth or scalloped. Turn the leaf over to examine the tiny veins. Look at the stem: is it short and stubby or long and graceful?

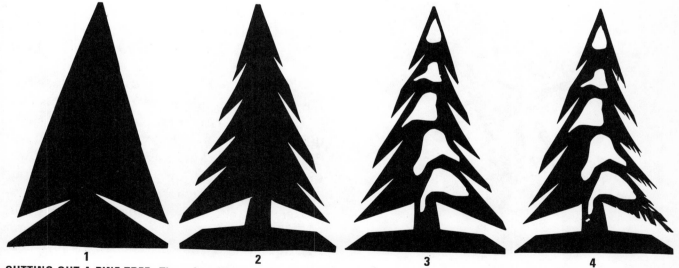

CUTTING OUT A PINE TREE: These four illustrations show different steps. The first is the basic outline of the tree. In the next step, cut the branches. Next, hollow cut the areas to represent snow. In the final picture, use fine pointed scissors to cut small snips for pine needles (Illus. 1 to 4).

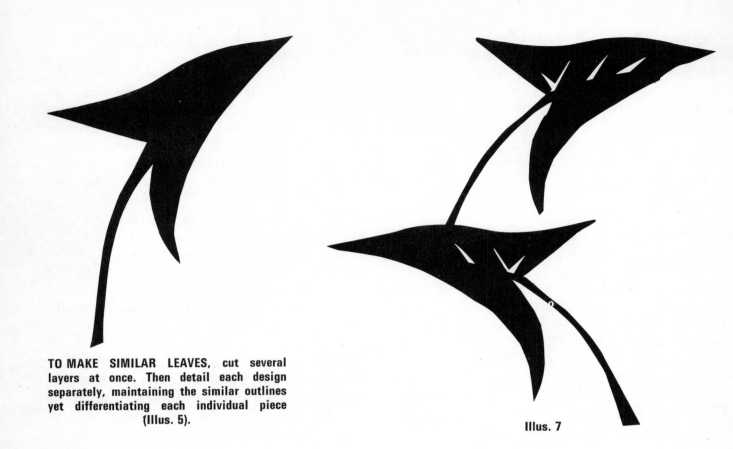

TO MAKE SIMILAR LEAVES, cut several layers at once. Then detail each design separately, maintaining the similar outlines yet differentiating each individual piece (Illus. 5).

The leaf in Illus. 5 is very simple to cut out with large scissors, for the lines are sweeping

Illus. 6

and there is no detail. In the next illustration, the veins were added by using the smaller scissors. Because hollow cutting would be too difficult to do in these tiny areas, another method was used to get inside the leaf: cutting in from an edge. You can see the small cut where the stem and the leaf meet. Once that snip is made, you are inside the leaf and can cut as you like.

While it makes little difference whether the cut to the inside shows or not on this leaf, in some projects it may make a great deal of difference—in a face, for example. But you will discover, after experimenting on your own, that if you make only one cut with your scissors and later glue the two sides close together, the cut will not show. You can cut into your picture as often as necessary without making unsightly holes. Make an arrangement of leaves and frame your composition (Illus. 7). Try different color combinations to show the four seasons.

THIS FLORAL ARRANGEMENT is an example of a folded scissors cutting. The right and left sides are symmetrical (Illus. 8).

THE RIGHT SIDE of the design was refined by more cutting (Illus. 9).

Folded Scissorscraft

You may frequently find that you want to make a picture that is symmetrical on both sides, but when you try to cut each side freehand, there is always some slight difference and the two sides are never quite identical. If this happens to you—if, for example, you are trying to make a scene and its reflection in a lake, or a human figure viewing himself in a mirror—then try folding the paper and cutting both sides together, almost as you did when you cut two layers to get two leaves. Here, however, there is an important difference; when you are finished cutting and detailing your picture and it is opened, you will want the two sides to be attached to each other.

Therefore, be careful not to cut completely through the fold. You can make small cuts on the fold, but at least one small area must be left untouched if the two sides are to remain together.

The flowers in Illus. 8 were cut this way. While you might want to create slight differences in either side when you hollow cut and add other details (see Illus. 9), at least your picture as a whole will be balanced, since you will have begun with two identical sides.

The exquisite Halloween scene in Illus. 10 is an example of what can be done by folded cutting. The group of trees on the right was cut together and then separated, and some detail was added to the "real life" trees. Their reflections would not show this detail, of course. Notice this too in the jack-o'-lantern's face: in the scene above ground, he has a toothy grin, but his reflection lacks those teeth. The witch and bat were cut separately and then glued on to the same backing as the rest of the scene.

Uses for Your Designs

You can use your cuttings in any place that you would use an ordinary picture, and even in designs where a painting or sketch would not be particularly interesting. This unique craft adds a special touch wherever it is used.

Mount the cuttings on cardboard and frame them to hang in your home, for example. Cut animals or flowers for your children's rooms, or make a likeness in profile—or *silhouette*—of a member of your family.

Take the mounted cuttings to a professional printer. He will photograph your cutting, make a printing plate from the photograph,

Illus. 10

and duplicate the design as many times as you like. You can design note paper or greeting cards with a personal design on the front. This is one way to make sure that your neighbor doesn't choose the same Christmas card you do! The delicate and detailed designs in Illus. 11, 12 and 13 were all duplicated by a printer for note paper.

If you want to try reproducing the design yourself, you should make the cutting out of sturdy construction paper. Spray paint or ink directly on the cutting, and then press it on another piece of paper. In planning this project, remember that the design will be reproduced in reverse. While a printer can reproduce an infinite number of copies by his

INDIANS are particularly suited for cutting out of paper: the fringe on their jackets and their feathers is represented by quick sharp cuts with a small pair of scissors (Illus. 11).

EVEN DELICATE FLOWERS can be cut from paper. Use tissue paper and the smallest scissors you own. Handle the cutting very carefully until it is securely mounted on cardboard (Illus. 12).

THE BACKGROUND of this is the solid area, and the flowers are white. If you have this printed, you will be able to make the background any color you want it (Illus. 13).

method, you will be limited depending on how sturdy your paper is. Usually only a few copies can be made this way.

To make your cutting permanent and useful at the same time, try this idea: place the cutting between two sheets of plastic. Ironing with a warm (not hot) iron should melt the plastic enough so that the sheets stick to each other with your cutting neatly sealed inside. Use these as place mats for your dinner table, or make smaller pieces for bookmarks. The number of possibilities you create depends only on your imagination. Practice until you can cut anything your imagination suggests!

plastic & leather

ACRYLIC

During the past decade, water-soluble plastic type paints have become a new medium not only for the fine artist but also for the commercial artist and craftsman. The popular use of these acrylic polymer paints is due to the ease and speed with which they can be used; their versatility, convenience and low cost are among the reasons for their widespread and successful use. Acrylic paints can be used not only as paint, for which they are well suited, but also as an adhesive, a sculpting material, a glaze, and a dye for fabrics.

In making a collage, acrylic medium is very useful as an adhesive for sticking sand, cloth, paper and other materials on to the designated surface. The medium is also very useful to weatherproof papier mâché. When saturated with polymer medium instead of flour and water, the paper pulp dries faster and becomes quite durable. You must be sure the base has

ACRYLIC MEDIUM is used in this collage as an adhesive for a wide variety of materials. Some areas are painted as well. The high relief lends this collage a sculptural quality. "Assemblage and Construction," by Judith Torche. Taken from *Acrylics and Other Water-Based Paints.*

Written especially for this volume by Jane Lassner

ACRYLIC MODELLING PASTE is combined with acrylic medium and matte medium in this collage. The surface is painted with acrylic colors. "Collage in Brown," by Judith Torche. Taken from *Acrylics and Other Water-Based Paints.*

hardened, or it will tend to bend. When decorated with acrylic colors, objects made of papier mâché can be displayed outdoors.

Acrylic modelling paste and gel mixed together can be used as bas-relief sculptural material. The acrylic paste can be modelled with the fingers, and when thoroughly dry can be carved and sanded just like stone or clay. Such things as beads, jewelry, decorated frames and inexpensive sculpture can all be made with acrylic modelling paste.

Several layers of acrylic paste can be built up on a wood or masonite block, then sanded down smoothly and given a coat of acrylic medium. The block can then be finely tooled and inked for block printing. Ink, wipe and print in the usual way. (See Wood Block article.)

Acrylic colors and medium can also serve to glaze ceramic objects simply by painting the object (see Ceramics). Glazes of acrylic do not need to be fired.

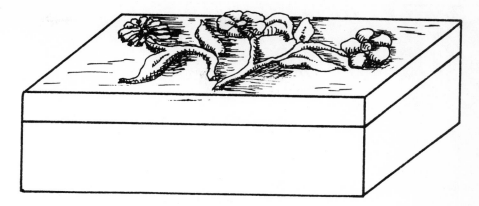

It is also possible to decorate fabrics with acrylic jar colors, either by directly applying the paint or by silk screening. (See Screen Process Printing.) In silk screening, prepare a glue-type stencil, mix the jar acrylic color with acrylic medium and squeegee it on to the fabric.

When using acrylics as a paint, use a palette of glass, porcelain or formica. Acrylics can be easily removed from such surfaces with water. Never mix acrylics with oils or oil solvents, nor with vinyl. Wash brushes thoroughly with soap and water. Clean acrylic paintings with mild soap and water only. Transparent acrylic watercolors can be washed if given a spray of acrylic matte varnish as added protection.

Water-based acrylic paints are made by grinding pigments in a binding medium

FABRIC DECORATING with acrylic paint is easily accomplished with the use of stencils. The paint is brushed directly on to the fabric. (For silk screening, see Screen Process Printing.)

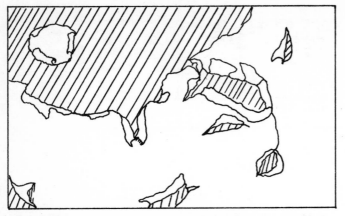

PEELING will occur on glass (shaded area) or metal if the acrylic paint is handled.

together with modifying ingredients. The base medium for polymer paints is made of fine particles of acrylic plastic resin suspended in water. When the water evaporates, it leaves a clear, strong, adhesive, waterproof binder which makes the pigments both brilliant and durable.

Some of the many advantages of acrylics are: they thin with water and are therefore non-yellowing and non-cracking, they are non-toxic and they can be used on canvas, cloth, paper, wood, clay, board, masonry—on any surface that is not slick or glossy. They can be used on metal or glass, but should not be handled or strips may peel off, as the two surfaces do not adhere firmly to each other. The paint dries very quickly, so overpainting can be done almost immediately, in contrast to the lengthy wait necessary when using oil paints.

To prepare a canvas or board that is not already "sized," cover the surface with acrylic gesso (acrylic base medium with titanium white pigment). This gesso serves the same purpose as traditional gesso, which is a coating of plaster or chalk applied to a support to produce a smooth, level surface.

Use a nylon brush (not bristle or hair) for painting with acrylics. The brush should be kept wet with water or base medium while you are working. Should the paint dry, water will wash the brush clean quickly and easily.

Watercolor effects can be achieved with acrylics if a small amount of paint is mixed with water to get the characteristic transparent quality. Regular watercolor techniques can all be used. When dry, an acrylic painting does not need glass framing.

Acrylics can also be adapted to the tempera and casein technique. Used as it comes, directly from the jar, the consistency will be that of casein. Overpainting can be done almost immediately and it will not disturb the underlayer. It has a definite advantage over the casein and tempera paints because it will not yellow or chip. If an egg yolk is mixed with the acrylic colors, the sheen and surface of regular egg tempera will be achieved, with the added assurance that on a flexible support the surface will not crack.

The oil technique may also be employed with acrylics, which come in tube colors as well as the more liquid jar form. Palette knife marks, brush marks and thick impastos can all be achieved just as with regular oil colors. A small amount of acrylic color mixed with polymer medium or acrylic gel, or with a mixture of both, will result in brilliant glazes which dry in minutes and allow any number of overlays in a short period of time. Acrylic gel lengthens the drying time and allows slower manipulation of the paint, if that is what you desire. Corrections can be made immediately and there is no need to scrape or wash out mistakes. Besides being quick drying, acrylics are less expensive to work with than ordinary oil paint.

BEADCRAFTING

The craftsman who works with beads to create jewelry, to adorn simple objects, or to fashion something as functional as a room divider enjoys the awareness that he is participating in a tradition as old as man. Cultures quite primitive left behind examples of their own efforts to create with beads. Very early did it occur to man that to bore a hole through a round, or long, or square object and then to string one with another resulted in an object pleasant to look at and pleasurable to wear. That the first crude necklaces quickly developed into an amazing skill can be clearly seen in the displays of finely designed and finely wrought examples of ancient beadcraft found in great museums throughout the world.

Thus, the satisfaction to be derived by the bead craftsman is two-fold—that which comes from the creating of something of beauty and also that which comes from participating in a craft with a great tradition of skill and imagination.

Beadcraft can of course be highly complex. But it need not be. Quite lovely objects can be produced with only very simple techniques.

Materials

A good work surface is one covered with a piece of felt or velvet in a neutral color so that the beads will not roll about unnecessarily. The beads should be collected and all of one kind kept in a glass jar or small saucer so that they can be reached easily. And since the greater part of beadcraft involves stringing, the stringing material should also be near at hand. Stringing material can be ordinary string, thread, wire filaments, plastic cord, or nylon fishing line (which is especially good because of its durability). Occasionally a threading needle or two is required and this also should be readily available.

One of the most delightful aspects of beadcraft is the opportunity to choose from among the enormous variety of beads available. Although we most often think of beads as round, they may also be oval, or cylindrical, or tubular. Rectangular bars, with a hollow through which thread can be passed, can also be put to good effect in beadcraft. And the materials of which beads of all shapes are made are almost without limit—there are wooden beads, and glass, crystal, silver and gold and other metals and minerals, ceramic beads, and beads of jet. Let your imagination guide you in your choice.

A Necklace with Looped Thread

A simple but rewarding project for the bead craftsman is the single-strand necklace. Decide on the desired length and then select the threading material, preferably nylon fishing line, and the beads. Tie a knot at one end of the thread—40 inches makes a good length—establish your pattern, and begin to thread until the necklace is completed. Tie the two ends of the thread together. (A suggested pattern—string one small glass bar, then five small round beads of one color followed by three small beads of another color, five beads the same as the first five and one glass bar. Repeat until you reach the end of your thread.)

Condensed from the book, "Creating with Beads" by Grethe LaCroix | © 1969 by Sterling Publishing Co., Inc., New York

A Two-Thread Necklace

Illus. 1 shows a bead positioned midway on a long thread. The bead is then fastened to a piece of cardboard or a pin cushion and one

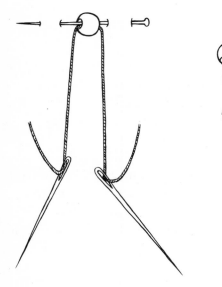

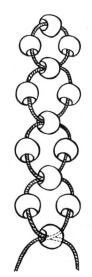

THE BASIC THREADING TECHNIQUE is shown in the diagrams on the left. You can vary this technique by using different beads for the left and right positions than you use for the top and bottom ones, or use bars instead of beads, as in the project on the next page. (Illus. 1 to 4.)

bead is threaded at the left side of this first bead and two at the right of it; the threads are then crossed through the last of the first four beads, thus connecting them (Illus. 2); the two threads are then pulled downwards, pulling the beads together (Illus. 3) and the process is continued (Illus. 4) until the desired length is achieved.

The apparently complex necklace of bars and beads shown in Illus. 6 is made entirely by the two-thread technique, as you can see by the pattern in Illus. 5. To make this necklace for yourself, all you need to determine is the number of bar and bead "frames" you will need to fill out the necklace to the desired length.

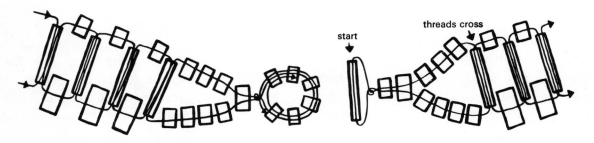

DIAGRAM OF A TWO-THREAD NECKLACE: At the right is the start of the necklace. Threads cross in the second bar, and the necklace continues in the basic technique. At the left is the end of the necklace, attached to a circular closing. (Illus. 5.)

A TWO-THREAD NECKLACE: This necklace made of bars and beads is diagrammed on the preceding page. The clasp is made of a bar which fits inside a circle of beads. (Illus. 6.)

A Necklace with Pendant and Fringe

With the two-thread technique and the macramé knot shown in Illus. 7, you can make an interesting necklace with pendant and fringe. The threading diagram is shown in Illus. 9.

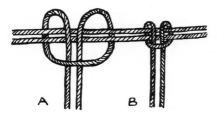

THE MACRAMÉ KNOT is easy to do and results in two threads hanging down. (Illus. 7.)

Begin your necklace with pendant by selecting two threads (preferably nylon) of the same length (25 inches, approximately) and thread eight beads so that they fall in the middle of the two threads (the shaded beads in the diagram). Secure these two threads to something stationary so that the eight beads will not move. Using the macramé knot, fasten one long thread in front of the first of the eight beads. Do the same after each of the other beads. By using the macramé knots, you have two threads of the same length hanging after each of the eight beads (nine double threads in all, which hang from the original two threads).

Thread one bead to each of these nine double threads, and then using all but the first and last of the hanging threads (see diagram), work in the basic threading pattern shown in Illus. 1–4 to make nine horizontal rows. (Note from the diagram that the first horizontal row has nine beads, the second eight, and so on, until row 10 is reached, which will contain eight beads.)

Row 11 is made by simply threading nine beads; row 12 by threading somewhat larger beads. As you follow the diagram, you will see that the threads cross for row 13 and that eight beads are used. Remember that the two threads on either end of the pendant are still hanging free. Row 13 ends the pendant and leaves the threads ready for the fringe to be added.

Now string a vertical row of beads to each of the two threads that have been hanging free, starting with row 2 of the pendant. When you reach row 12, pass each of the two outside threads through the large beads. You will now continue to use these threads for the fringe. Note that the fringe is ended with a row of small beads following a row of beads the same size as those used in row 12.

Refer now to the diagram for the threading pattern required to complete that part of the necklace that goes around the neck. The necklace may be finished by simply tying the two ends of the threads together or by fastening one end of the necklace to a small bar and the other to a small ring. The necklace is closed by placing the small bar through the ring.

THIS NECKLACE WITH PENDANT AND FRINGE looks quite complex, but it is made using the methods you already know. The diagram on the next page shows the construction. (Illus. 8.)

Beadcraft need not be limited only to jewelry, although that is surely its most obvious use. It can also be used to create a room divider or a covering for a window. For the latter, buy a bead rack—or a simple, adjustable curtain rod—at a specialty hardware shop. String beads on wire filament of whatever length is needed to fall from the top of the window to the bottom. Use wooden beads, which can be left natural or painted, in a pattern which pleases you (one suggestion—thread one oval-shaped bead, then three round beads, then another oval, and so on, until the wire is filled). Fasten the wire to the bead rack and then mount the rack at the top of the window or at ceiling level, if you wish. The effect—light and airy. The cost in money and time—minimal.

Beads can also be embroidered on to fabric or inserted with pins into plastic foam balls for gay and festive Christmas ornaments.

1
2
3
4
5
6
7
8
9
10
11
12
13

DIAGRAM OF A NECKLACE WITH PENDANT AND FRINGE: Start with the eight shaded beads. Secure a double thread on either side of them with the macramé knot and proceed as instructed in the text. (Illus. 9.)

CANDLE-MAKING

A candle is simply a cylinder of tallow, wax or other solid fat which contains a wick to give off light when burning. But besides light, a candle can give color and fragrance, and even esthetic pleasure by means of a pleasing design.

Little is known of the history of candles, though we do know that they were used by the Romans. The modern candle probably evolved from the medieval custom of dipping cores of wood, rush or cords in household fat and burning these tallows as a source of light. About 1825, the use of tallow, beeswax and vegetable wax—bayberry in America, candleberry in the East, and waxberry in South America—was supplemented by stearin. At the same time, twisted cord was replaced by a plaited wick as the candle's core. Fifty years later, paraffin was added to the list of waxes used.

Methods and Materials

There are three main methods of making candles by hand: rolling sheets of beeswax around a wick, dipping the wick into hot wax, and pouring hot wax into a mould.

Artificial honeycombs of beeswax are used to roll candles. They can be obtained from beekeepers, candle dealers, honey wholesalers and hobby shops.

Paraffin is a translucent, glasslike, waxy substance which is distilled from petroleum. Paraffin drips considerably because of its low melting point, and candles made purely of paraffin are not practical. Paraffin is usually added to beeswax to improve the consistency when the beeswax is heated.

Stearin (ester of glycerol and stearic acid) is a soft, white, odorless solid made of natural animal and plant fats (palmitin). Stearin becomes malleable at about 120 degrees F. Adding paraffin to stearin will help in the casting. These candles burn well and do not bend as a result of heat.

Moulding wax is a combination of paraffin, stearin, sometimes a small addition of beeswax, and coloring and dyeing material. Moulding wax is used in a hot, fluid stage for dipping candles.

Modelling wax is a mixture of equal amounts of bleached beeswax and paraffin, with dyes added.

Drop wax consists of collected remnants of wax or leftovers of candles and candle drippings.

Wicks are made from cotton yarn in various thicknesses. The candle thickness and amount of wax required determine the thickness of the wick. For paraffin candles, use the thinnest kind

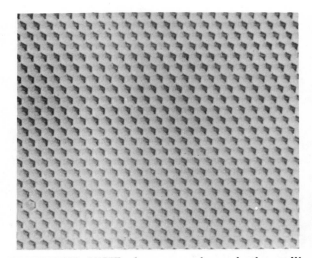

A HONEYCOMB SHEET of pure wax is used when rolling candles.

Condensed from the book, "Candle-Making" by Susanne Strose | © 1968 by Sterling Publishing Co., Inc., New York

of wick; for stearin, medium-thick ones; and for beeswax candles, use very thick wicks. It is advisable to obtain wicks from a candle shop rather than make your own. Wicks which you buy have a bottom and top. The bottom is indicated by a knot.

Rolling Candles

Probably the easiest method of candle-making involves wrapping or rolling a honeycombed sheet of beeswax round a wick. Cut the wax sheet to the desired size. The width of the sheet determines the diameter of the candle. If you cut the top portion on an angle, the candle will be tapered.

Leave approximately 1 inch of wick free at the top. The rolling method is excellent for small children to use because no heat is involved.

Dipping Candles

Producing a dipped candle requires more equipment than a rolled candle. Beeswax and moulding wax are best to use here. A wax-paraffin mixture will do in the absence of the others. You also need a tall narrow tin or aluminum can to serve as a wax container, a saucepan for boiling water, and an electric hot plate or stove.

Place some wax in the can, and place the can in the saucepan half-filled with water. Heat the water until the wax in the can begins to melt. Continue to add wax, melting it as it is added, until the contents are within an inch of the top.

Now take a wick about 40 inches long and dip it quickly into the liquid wax. Pull it out immediately, stretch it straight, and allow it to dry. Then cut the long wick into several shorter ones the height of the can, plus 2 inches to hang over the top.

Quickly dip one of these pieces into the liquid wax, making sure it does not bend, and let it harden again. Repeat this procedure several times until the wick has accumulated the desired thickness. Continue to add wax to the can so the volume is always an inch from the top. Always keep the temperature constant to prevent the wax from catching fire. If the wax does ignite, smother the fire with a tight metal cover—never use water to extinguish burning wax.

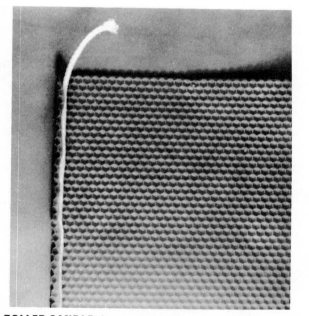

A ROLLED CANDLE: Leave an extra amount of wick at the top. Press the wick into the edge of the beeswax sheet.

TAPERED CANDLE: Cut the top of the wax sheet at an angle.

DIPPING CANDLES: In (a), the wick has been dipped once; in (b) the wick has been dipped several times; in (c) the candle has been straightened; in (d) the bottom has been cut into shape with a warm knife.

Shaping Your Candles. First, cut the bottom of the candle with a heated knife to make it flat. Now roll the candle back and forth on a glass or marble surface to make it smooth and round. Once this is done, your candle is finished.

In order to free yourself from the seemingly endless job of dipping and holding wicks until they dry, construct a small rack to take your place. Attach several hooks to a ledge, about 3¼ inches apart. Tie your wicks to these hooks. To make sure the wicks hang straight, attach a bead or other weight to the bottom of the wicks. Melt your wax in a container with a handle that is easy to grip.

Instead of dipping the wick into the wax, reverse the procedure by raising the container to the wick. In this way you can coat each wick one after the other, pausing only to reheat the wax when it becomes too cool.

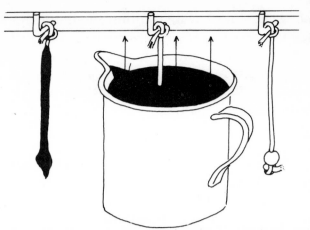

HANG WICKS from a ledge to dry so that you don't have to hold them by hand. Once they are tied to the ledge, it is easier to bring the container of wax to the wick rather than dip the wick into the container.

Moulding Candle Shafts

Use the same equipment as you did for dipping candles, plus an additional assortment of different-size cans and a tray for cold water. You will also need knitting needles and thick wicks. Moulding wax or a combination of stearin and paraffin are best suited for this technique.

With a sharp object, punch a hole in the middle of the bottom of an empty can. Pull a wick through the hole, making a knot on the underside of the can to prevent the can from sliding off the wick. At the top, tie the wick to the middle of the needle. Keep the wick as taut as possible without bending the knitting needle.

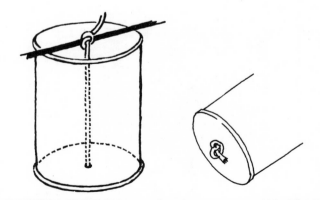

MOULDED CANDLES are made using cans as moulds. Tie the wick on the underside of the can and to a knitting needle above the can to keep it taut.

Melting the Wax. Just as you did with the liquid wax for dipping candles, place wax into a can and then place the can into the saucepan to heat. When the wax melts, pour it into the can with the stretched wick. Now place this can, which is the mould, into the tray with cold water. This will speed the hardening process.

Once the wax is solid (8 to 10 hours later), you can remove the moulded candle from the container. First remove the knot at the bottom and untie the knitting needle. To remove the candle from the can, pull firmly on the wick. Because of the waxy surface, the candle should slide out fairly easily.

If the candle sticks in the can, put the can under hot water, constantly turning it around to prevent any one spot from being heated too long. This will melt the wax around the outside slightly, and will loosen the wax. If there are any bumps or curves in the wax, roll the candle on a glass or marble surface to smooth it.

Multi-Layered Candles

Multi-layered candles are very decorative yet easy to make. Using different colored waxes and the same procedure for melting the wax as you did in moulding, pour a small amount of the liquid wax into a container which is resting in a tray of cold water. Be sure to pour carefully directly into the middle to avoid splashes on the sides of the container. When the wax hardens, add another color (again, only a small amount). Repeat this until the container is filled. When the contents have hardened, place the container in a tray of warm water to help loosen the wax. If the sides are damaged, roll the candle on a flat surface to smooth it out.

Transparent, heat-resistant plastic cups make good moulds for multi-layered candles because you can see exactly how much wax to pour for each layer.

Designing Ornamentation

Use your imagination to create a unique "fancy" candle. Since the chances of making something beautiful are quite good, even children can make candles with professional results.

Roll some partially hardened wax on a flat surface until it is a long and narrow tube. Wrap this around your candle to form spiral ridging, attaching the ridging with a small amount of melted wax if necessary. This method may be used to apply vertical stripes, serpentine lines, or any number of other designs.

Either the same color as the candle or a contrasting shade can be used; this choice depends upon your esthetic sense and the materials for coloring which you have on hand.

THIS RIDGED CANDLE was made by wrapping partially hardened wax around a candle.

LAYERED CANDLES: Let each layer cool before adding the next. Add extra wax to even the top around the wick.

MORE DECORATIVE CANDLES: Ridges can be either horizontal or vertical. When using tools to make designs on candles, warm the points of the tools first so that the wax can be softened.

Dots or points (small wax balls) can also be attached to add interest and color to the original candle.

Designing with Tools. Once you have developed the technique of moulding by hand and have produced some candles that you like, try decorating with tools. This requires a little more concentration. There are several tools you can use: metal knitting needles, long nails, a palette knife, an awl, an old ballpoint pen—all are good for carving in wax.

Use one of these pointed tools to carve a design on a small flat piece of wax. Heat the tip of the tool in a candle if the wax is not sufficiently soft. When the design is complete, stick the small pieces to the candle.

Create and decorate cube, round or oddly shaped candles to use for any occasion. Your creativity can lead to many fun-filled hours making something both useful and attractive.

COLORED WAX SHEETS were first cut and then joined to the candle shaft by gentle heating to create this unusual candle.

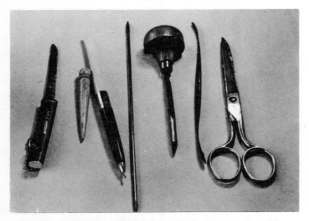

METAL INSTRUMENTS to make designs on candles.

LEATHERCRAFT

Animal skins are quite easy to work with, and with the multitude of inexpensive choices available in hobby and leather shops this has become a popular craft in recent years. Some craftsmen prefer the decorative aspect of leathercrafting, which includes tooling, modelling, incising, leather mosaic, embossing and embroidery, as well as the more complicated processes of inlaying and enamelling on leather. Even the simple fashioning of useful articles, from boxes to clothing, is a rewarding pastime.

Types of Leather

Although it is helpful to know the standard uses for different types of skins, there is no reason to be limited by them except when something obviously demands a special kind of skin. A large bag, for example, which will be used to carry relatively heavy things, should be made of a sturdy leather. In general, *cowhide* is used for anything which must wear well, including shoe soles and suitcases, while *cowhide split*, the least expensive grade of cowhide, is used for leather mosaics and inlaying, since it splits and tears easily. *Calfskin* is one of the most beautiful leathers, and is ideal for almost anything, from handbags to bookcovers. This durable leather is perfect for tooling and modelling, and is comparatively inexpensive as well. Versatile *sheepskin* is most often used for clothing, bags and modelling, and is very inexpensive. *Pigskin* and *goatskin* are common choices for gloves. Because of their texture, the more expensive *lizard*, *snakeskin* and *alligator* skins are not suitable for tooling or modelling, but their durability and beauty make them ideal for wallets, cases of all kinds, and coverings. There are three different kinds of *suede*, which is the flesh side of leather: calfskin, which is used for footwear; and goatskin and sheepskin, generally used for clothing. For bookmarks, inlays, leather mosaics, and other small items, *leather remnants* can be purchased by the pound (skins are sold by the foot). All leather should be stored with the grain side out, whether it is flat or rolled.

Lacing and Threads

While *leather lacing* is fairly expensive, *plastic lacing* is both inexpensive and entirely suitable for many projects. Lacing is used to join two pieces of heavy leather when it is undesirable to glue them. Lacing is also often used for decorative purposes.

Sewing is done with various kinds of thread: *saddler's thread* for heavy-duty articles; *bookbinder's thread*, which comes in different thicknesses; *linen* and *nylon thread*, which are quite strong; and *buttonhole silk*, often used for gloves. No matter what kind of thread you use, it must be waxed before sewing.

Tools

Three kinds of needles are necessary: a *two-prong lacing needle* for lacing; blunt *harness needles;* and *saddler's needles*, which include triangular *glover's needles*.

Other important tools are a *leather knife*, a *hole punch*, a *diamond awl*, a *leather shears*, and a *stitch-marking wheel*. You can make a stitch-marking wheel from the gear wheel of a discarded alarm clock. For leathers which are not

Condensed from the book, "Creative Leathercraft" by Grete Petersen | © 1960 by Sterling Publishing Co., Inc., New York

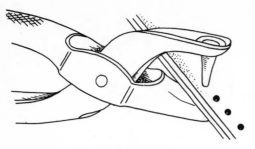

A HOLE PUNCH (Illus. 1).

too heavy, use a sewing machine without thread to pierce the holes.

Heavy leathers require careful advance preparation for sewing. The edges of a hem to be turned must be *skived*, or pared down, with a razor blade in a holder to reduce bulk. Always pare towards the outer edge, slanting down so that the stitch line is thick and only the outermost edge quite thin.

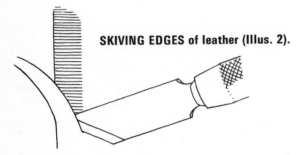

SKIVING EDGES of leather (Illus. 2).

Next, it is usually wise to *groove* the stitching line with a *bone folder*, so that the stitches will have a trough to lie in and will not be exposed to wear. Place a ruler along the line and make a depression with the point of a bone folder along it.

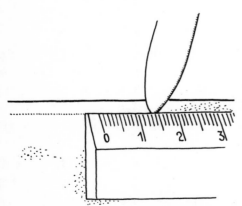

GROOVING THE STITCHING LINE (Illus. 3).

To mark holes for the stitches, roll a stitch-marking wheel along the line, guiding it with a ruler. If the leather is going to be laced, or is very thick, punch out the holes cleanly with a hole punch or a diamond awl along the stitch marks. Always do the corners first so they will be identical.

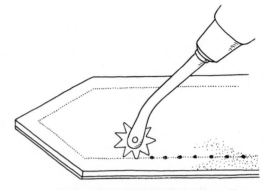

A STITCH-MARKING WHEEL (Illus. 4).

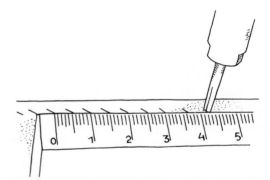

PUNCHING HOLES with a diamond awl (Illus. 5).

Stitches

One practical and easy way of joining two pieces of leather together is to lace them. You can buy both leather and plastic laces in many different colors and widths or you can make your own thongs. Cut strips from a lightweight skin—goat split, for example—and glue them together to make long laces. (For instructions on glueing, see page 337.)

To estimate how long the laces should be for your work, make a test lacing through ten holes. Count the total number of holes that require lacing, divide the amount by ten, and multiply the result by the length of the thong you used for the ten holes. Plastic laces go through the holes easily if you cut the ends diagonally to a point. Leather thongs and laces must be pushed through with a needle or wire, or you can buy a special lacing needle.

There are many different ways to lace edges to add interest to the object you are making. The simplest overcasting can produce a differ-

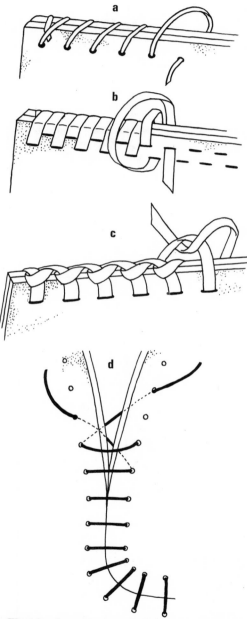

LACING: The simple overcast stitch in *a* is used in *b* also, only in *b* the lace is thicker and the holes are alternately spaced. The lacing will be very decorative if you use the method shown in *c*. Lacing the two pieces of leather together is shown in *d* (Illus. 6).

ent look by varying the thickness of the laces and the distance between the holes. A fancy crocheted effect is obtained by running the thong through the previous loop, as in Illus. 6c. You can also give your lacing bright results by using two or more colors.

Begin by tucking the end of the lace under the first lacing stitch. Take a couple of extra stitches in the last hole and glue the end down where it will not show.

You can also attach two pieces of leather together shoelace fashion, using two laces. If you overcast with only one lace the pieces can easily be pulled apart.

In lacing two curved pieces together, be sure to adjust the distance between holes around the curve, and mark the same number of holes on each side.

Reinforcing seams is a good idea, particularly if the seams will be subject to a great deal of stress. Fold a strip of leather in half and insert it between two adjoining pieces. Sew through all four layers.

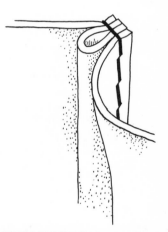

HAND-SEWN REINFORCED SEAM (Illus. 7).

With thin leathers you can sew a reinforced seam on the sewing machine in two operations. Spread one of the pieces with the right side up. Fold the reinforcing strip together and lay it at the edge of the leather, and sew. Lay the other piece of leather on top, wrong side up, and sew again, this time a little deeper, so the first stitches do not show.

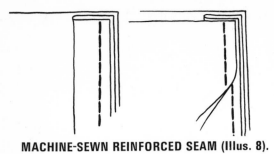

MACHINE-SEWN REINFORCED SEAM (Illus. 8).

You can reinforce and trim at the same time by sewing on an edging strip along with the seam. Sew the right side of the edging to the right side of the leather by hand or machine. Fold over and sew again from the other side.

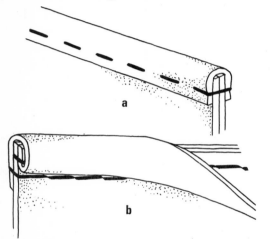

EDGE THE SEAM by sewing another strip of leather over the edge of the two pieces (Illus. 9).

To make a mitered corner seam, cut the edges of the leather obliquely, the amount of slant depending on whether the angle is to be obtuse or acute. Pierce oblique holes with your awl and saddle stitch with two needles. This will keep the corner from "yawning."

You can also stitch seams so that they are "hidden," with the stitching barely showing. With a sharp knife, cut a groove in each piece of leather at an angle, along the line of the seam, and punch the holes. The threads will be hidden and will not wear out. Use a curved saddler's needle to sew with, poking it down in one groove and up through the other. This is a good technique to use when sewing soles, as the stitches will not wear when they are hidden.

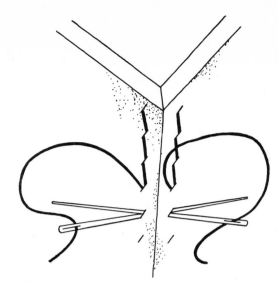

A MITERED CORNER SEAM should be used when two pieces are being joined that are not going to lie flat, such as the corner of a box (Illus. 10).

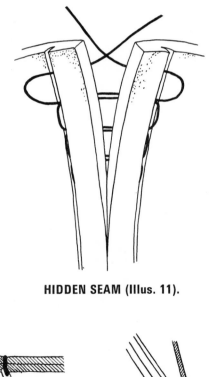

HIDDEN SEAM (Illus. 11).

WHEN SEWING SOLES, make hidden seams so the stitches do not wear out (Illus. 12).

Glueing

You can find several kinds of leather glue in craft shops, both in tubes and in jars. Remember that glue that can be thinned with water is the easiest to work with.

Spread the glue out evenly with a flat brush on the surface of each piece. Press the surfaces together from the middle out towards the edges. If the edges do not line up, tear the pieces apart immediately and begin again.

To make a lined corner, include enough leather when cutting the corner to fold over for a margin. Skive the margin, if necessary, and glue it down. Push the pleats at the corner down firmly with a lacing needle or paper knife. Cut the paper or leather lining a little smaller than the underlayer and glue it down.

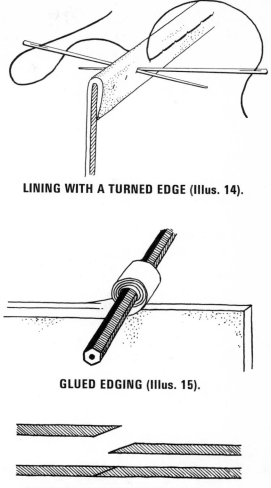

LINING WITH A TURNED EDGE (Illus. 14).

GLUED EDGING (Illus. 15).

GLUEING STRIPS TOGETHER (Illus. 16).

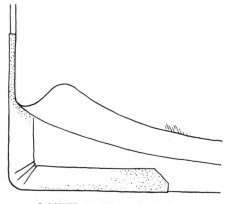

A LINED CORNER (Illus. 13).

If you would like the lined side of an article to look as attractive as the outside, make a lining with a turned edge. Fold the edge of the leather over, having skived it if necessary. Glue the folded-over portion tightly, and sew this hem by hand or machine. To aid you, most sewing machines have margin followers to keep the edges and seams parallel.

Edges can be glued instead of sewn. Smear the edging and the edge itself with glue. Roll the edging up on a pencil and then unroll it on to the edge of the leather.

To glue leather strips together, to make longer strips for laces, cut the surfaces that are to be joined at the same angle. Smear them with glue and push them evenly together.

Coloring Leather

There are various ways to color the leather you are working with. Water and oil dyes can be brushed on and partially wiped away, giving an antique effect. Waterproof ink dyes, which come in many colors, can be used to draw designs or color the edges of a design. Bronze or gold powders moistened with clear varnish are very attractive on leather, and gold leaf can be pressed or tooled into prepared outlines for a striking accent. All leather dyes come with detailed instructions for application, and these should be followed exactly.

Generally, the leather dyes fall into three categories: brushing dyes, spray dyes and dipping dyes. Brushing dyes are the trickiest; you must apply the color quickly and evenly or it will streak. Dipping is not difficult, but use a container large enough to lay the leather flat in the dye bath. Remove the leather quickly and place it on a flat surface to dry. Since leather dyes are strong, always use gloves when working with them.

A Tooled Bookmark

Make a pattern for a bookmark out of cardboard, and place it over the middle of the piece of calfskin you have selected (the middle is usually thicker than the edges of any skin and should always be used for the main body of the article to be made). Trace the design on to the skin with a pencil, and place the leather on a flat, sturdy cutting board. Cut it out carefully with a very sharp leather knife or a razor blade in a holder. Lightweight skins can be cut with leather shears.

In order to tool or model the leather, the skin must be damp. Do this with a wrung-out cloth, and keep the leather damp throughout the tooling process. After planning a design (use primarily straight lines until you are skilled)

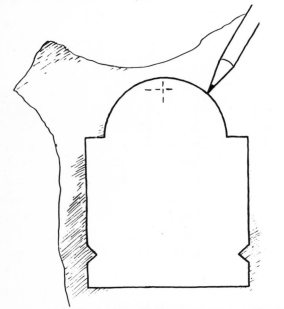

PLACE THE CARDBOARD PATTERN on the wrong side of the leather skin and trace the pattern with a pencil. Cut the leather with a razor blade, shears or knife (Illus. 17).

TOOL THE LEATHER with a ballpoint tracing stylus to make your own designs. Or buy a stamp in a hobby store and make a repeating motif, as shown here (Illus. 18).

on a separate piece of paper, place the pattern over the leather, which should be right side up. Using a ballpoint tracing stylus, trace the outlines of the design, making indentations in the leather.

You can add to the design by *stippling*, which is pressing little dots into the leather using the pointed end of the tool. Another possibility is *stamping*: various stamps can be found in any hobby store. If you press them down on the right side of the damp leather you will be *embossing* a concave pattern; if you turn the leather over to press in the design you will form a *relief* design. Reliefs can also be done with any sharp tool in a freehand design without stamps: turn the leather right side down, dampen the right side, and trace the design on the skin side. Go over the outlines with your stylus while holding the leather against the palm of your hand. If you want to *incise* part of the design, thus making it more distinct, carve away about half the thickness of the leather (right side up) along the outlines of the design. Then use a modelling tool to depress the areas near the cuts, making the design stand out in higher relief.

A Leather Mosaic Box

Another interesting project for a beginner is to cover a cigar box with leather in a mosaic pattern. After making a cardboard pattern for each part of the box *except the top*, cut out various pieces and glue them carefully to the box with any good leather glue, preferably one that can be thinned with water. While the

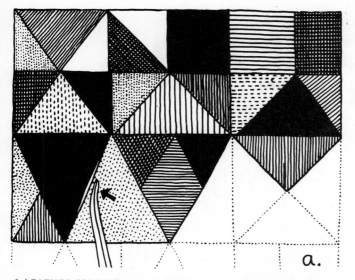

A LEATHER MOSAIC is made from scraps of leather you have collected. The arrow points to the bone folder smoothing the leather out to the line (Illus. 19).

glue is drying, plan the mosaic design for the top.

Draw an outline exactly the size of the box top on transparent paper, and plan a design composed of many small shapes. Cut out scraps of leather in various colors to fit the small spaces. Place them over the design as you go to make sure they fit tightly. The only requirement is that the scraps should all be of the same thickness, so that the surface will appear level. Trace the design on to the box top and glue down the scraps, pushing out the edges of each one to fit the outline with your bone folder or modelling tool. The finished box can either be lacquered or waxed and polished.

For bookcovers or boxtops where the mosaic is not to reach to the outer edge, glue a whole piece of leather on the surface of the object and cut out the area where the design will be. Make a design by cutting up the piece you removed (trace a design on it and cut out the pieces along the lines) and then glue it back into position. Or, use only part of the cut-away piece, and add various colored scraps from other leather skins.

Folding Clutch Purse

A folding clutch purse is made from two leather rectangles placed right sides together and stitched along three sides. The purse could be lined in an attractive fabric such as silk moire, although you may prefer a more practical lining of thin plastic vinyl or cotton hopsacking. Fancy stitching, completed before the bag is stitched, would decorate this purse even more, but even without the additional work it is attractive due to the soft leather.

Cut two $10\frac{3}{4}$ by 10 inch pieces of suede or any other thin leather, and two $9\frac{2}{3}$ by 10 inch pieces of lining material. Or, you could use one piece of leather $10\frac{3}{4}$ by 20 inches with a lining $9\frac{2}{3}$ by 20 inches. Since the leather is not thick, you can use the sewing machine. With the wrong side of the leather out, stitch three sides to make a bag $10\frac{3}{4}$ inches high. Make another bag from the lining material, $9\frac{3}{4}$ inches high. Leave a section of the seam in the fabric bag open so that you can later turn the bags through it. Sew the bags together right side to right side along the top opening, and turn out the pouch through the hole you left. Overcast the hole by hand.

A CLUTCH PURSE made of soft leather is as attractive to carry as it is practical to hold (Illus. 20).

PLASTIC FOAM CRAFTING

You can make your own lightweight boats, baby seats, bathtub toys, bird houses, flower pots and many other durable projects with plastic foam. Known in the United States by the trade name Styrofoam, plastic foam is manufactured in such a way that it is moisture-proof, non-absorbent, and resistant to vermin and corrosion.

Requiring only a minimum of tools, plastic foam can be cut and shaped with any tool as sharp as a kitchen knife, and stuck together with toothpicks in the absence of glue. Though some varieties of foam can be twisted and bent, plastic foam is not very flexible. It will snap under pressure or any attempt to change its shape.

Tools

Working well with foam will depend on your selection of tools. Of prime importance is a sharp knife. The blade should be fairly rigid to permit cutting through ½ inch thick foam.

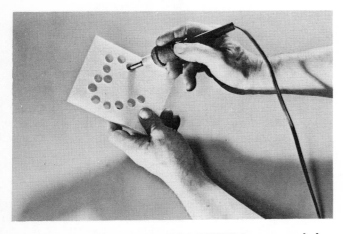

AN ELECTRICAL WOOD-BURNING PENCIL bores even holes in plastic foam. It is also a good cutting tool.

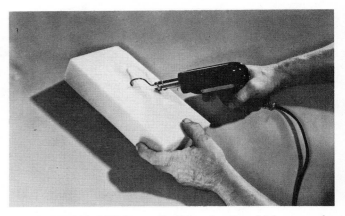

A SOLDERING GUN has a flexible wire tip which can make deep cuts in plastic foam.

Applying soap to the edge helps greatly with all cutting tools. To measure and also guide cutting operations, use a steel ruler or carpenter's square.

With thin sheets of plastic foam, a sharp-edged cookie cutter will do. Of course, wood saws, band saws and planes will work, too, but they tend to leave rough edges.

An electrical wood-burning pencil is a tremendous convenience for certain cutting jobs, especially for boring holes and for making sculptured designs.

In some projects, you will find that you need special tools to make 3-dimensional cuts. A small electrical soldering gun will fill this need. Operating on the same principle as the wood-burning pencil, a soldering gun is capable of finer cutting strokes and will make slices in the foam.

As with many crafts, it is wise to first work with a small scrap piece of the material and get the feel of how foam will cut and how each of the tools vary in function.

Condensed from the book, "Plastic Foam for Arts and Crafts" by Brock Yates | © 1965 by Sterling Publishing Co., Inc., New York

Joining

Attaching portions of a project requires only a small amount of glue. Any glue will do an excellent job of bonding foam. This includes airplane glue, rubber cement, all types of epoxy cements, and old-fashioned organic-based glues. Simply apply adhesive to both surfaces, let them partially dry and then push them together. Let them dry completely overnight.

For larger projects involving heavier pieces of plastic foam, choose an adhesive known for its strength. Apply pressure to the joint area using a U-clamp.

Painting

For indoor use, almost any paint can be used. There are, as well, special paints produced for use with plastic foam. Water-base or poster paints are well suited.

For outdoor use, latex-base paints do a very good job as both a protective cover and for decorative purposes. It is best to put an underlying coat of primer over the foam before painting it. This prevents weathering and stains from setting.

Simple Boats

After you have gotten the feel of the tools and plastic foam, try constructing an easy

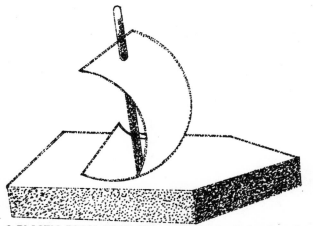

A PLASTIC FOAM BOAT: This is the basic design for a boat. Use paper or cloth for a sail, and float the boat in any container of water, from a bathtub to a lake.

boat as your first project. Because of its buoyancy, your boat will ride higher in the water and tend to be more stable than its wooden counterpart. Consequently, should you decide to construct a more complex ship, building will be a lot easier.

Using a sharp knife or single-edged razor blade in a holder, cut a simple design from the foam. Next, with a pencil and a small piece of cloth or paper, add the sail. Be careful not to push the pencil through the bottom of the boat. If the pencil is too tall or heavy, it will cause the boat to tilt to one side and even fall over. Ice cream sticks can be utilized for both mast and side decorations.

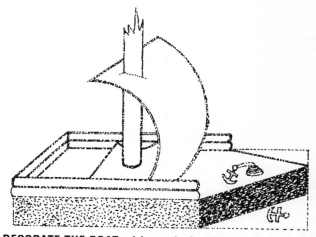

DECORATE THE BOAT with nautical emblems and ice cream stick rails. Layer the surface to represent decks.

Baby Seat

With 1-inch thick plastic foam, a portable baby seat can be constructed for a new baby ranging from age "very new" to 1-year-old. The seat will be light and strong enough to carry on trips. Most important, it will resist any accidents which might occur. A strong adhesive is recommended for adequate strength and long-lasting bond.

The side panels can be shaped conventionally or artistically carved into animal forms to be played with when the child gets too big and heavy to use the seat. Bright paints can be employed to enhance the appearance, but be sure to use non-toxic lead-free paint.

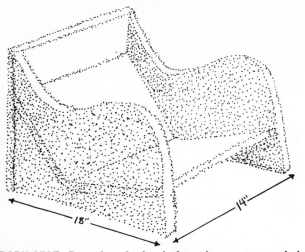

A BABY SEAT: Even though plastic foam is easy to cut, it is sturdy enough to support a small infant. Use a strong glue such as epoxy to hold the pieces together.

Bathtub Toys

Children have always loved to play with toys while they are in the bathtub. Many toys which float can now be made with plastic foam.

Using a 1-inch or 2-inch thick piece of plastic, you can slice out as many as seven different toys from a small square. Rings, fish, boats and almost any type animal can be designed in one solid piece. Design a small turtle and watch your child float his new toy around the tub.

Outdoors with Plastic Foam

Because of plastic foam's ability to weather the elements, you can make an outdoor shelter that your cat or dog can enjoy in any kind of weather. (See illustration on next page.)

Constructed out of 1-inch or 2-inch foam and secured to the ground, the house presents very little difficulty in preparation. To build, cut 2-inch foam into two pieces 18 inches $\times$ $33\frac{1}{2}$ inches for the ends, shaping an archway door in one of them. Then, cut two lengths 18 inches $\times$ 36 inches for the sides.

The roof is made of one piece, 40 inches $\times$ 18 inches, and a piece, 40 inches $\times$ 19 inches —overlapping at the top. Put the entire structure together with nails and strong outdoor glue. In order to make the shelter secure, you can attach it to a piece of marine plywood, 20 inches $\times$ 38 inches. Be sure to paint the wood on both sides to protect it from the damp ground. Fill any empty gaps left by uneven cutting with adhesive cement.

Once you have completed the doghouse project, you are ready to put some of your own ideas down on paper and finally into construction. An excellent move from this point would be to construct a bird feeder or bird house to be placed in your back yard or neighborhood tree. (See next page.)

TOYS FOR THE BATHTUB are easy to construct from plastic foam. The toys will float in the water and last through many bathtime games.

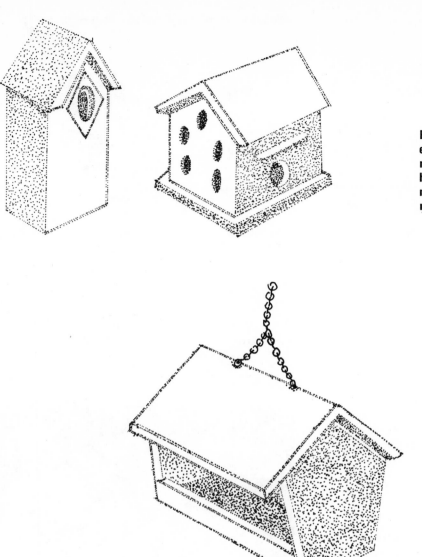

BIRDHOUSES: Plastic foam is sturdy enough to remain outdoors, through almost any kind of weather. Instead of hanging the birdhouse from a branch, you might want to mount it on a pole. Use a metal pole, however, to prevent hungry cats from climbing up.

Flower Pot/Window Box

Make a decorative flower pot or window box to go on your window sill (inside or out). The box can be utilized in one of two ways or in daring instances—both ways. You can choose to use plastic foam designed flowers or plant your own flowers. A combination of both can turn out to be fascinating.

Cut five pieces of plastic foam to the prescribed proportions (see illustration). You can easily fit the planter together. Leave the bottom portion for last, allowing an area for easier handling. While the bottom portion is

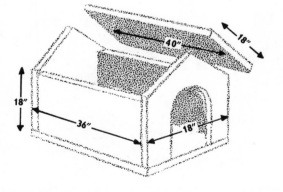

A DOGHOUSE: If you own a small, quiet dog, he will enjoy a plastic foam house. Lively animals, however, might be too rough on the material.

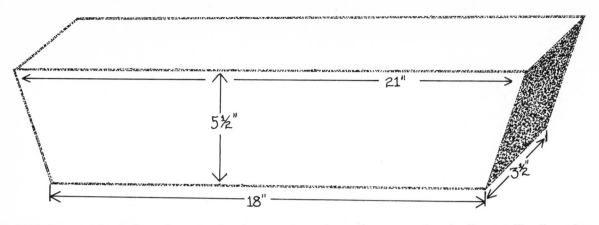

WINDOW BOX: Because plastic foam does not absorb water, it can be used as a container for flowers. The dimensions above will make a box which is balanced and structurally sound.

off, you can paint and carve designs into the front and sides. If you choose to paint the bottom section, do this while you are free to move it around. As a last phase, place the bottom section into place, using ample amounts of adhesive.

The finished project is both sturdy and impervious to water. It can be filled with soil and your selection of flowers. If you really feel creative, style your own flowers from plastic foam and colored paper.

Holiday Decorations

Using an ordinary pair of scissors, you can make an infinite variety of simple shapes and forms from plastic foam. Dress them up with buttons, hat pins, ribbons, and even glue and glitter. The glue and glitter process is extremely simple. Just apply a small amount of glue over the area you choose to cover and sprinkle the glitter over the glue. The excess will fall away and the rest will remain decorative and shiny.

The Hot-Wire Cutter

If you really like working with plastic foam, you will want this device, which rounds the edges as you cut. Designed exclusively for use with foam, the hot-wire cutter looks like a simple coping or fret saw—with a wire substituted for the conventional thin saw blade. A low voltage current passing through the nickel-chrome resistance wire creates heat in

proportion to the current applied and the rated wire resistance. The heat of the wire melts a small layer of the plastic, which spreads in a thin film over the cut face of the foam. This plastic film adds considerable strength to the finished shape and smooths the cut face.

ORNAMENTS OF PLASTIC FOAM are lightweight and can be colored with an assortment of paints, sequins, glitter and other articles. A variety store can supply these, as well as beads and ribbons for decorating.

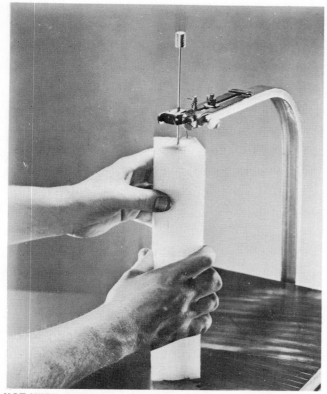

HOT-WIRE CUTTER: Insert the hot thin wire into the plastic foam slowly. Pushing the foam faster than the wire can melt it creates uneven edges.

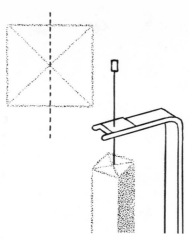

TO FIND THE MIDDLE OF A BLOCK, draw pencil lines diagonally through opposite corners.

The hot-wire cutter can be purchased in hobby shops and from art material suppliers. Special attachments are available for the shaping of cones, cylinders, etc.

Cutting foam with a hot-wire cutter requires slow, even feeding of the foam. Forcing the foam will result in distortion of the wire and uneven edges on the cut surfaces.

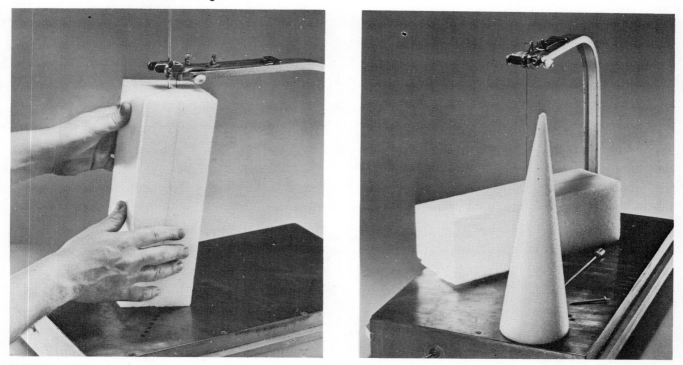

CUTTING CONES: Begin with a rectangular block of plastic foam. A short spindle, which is available where you buy the cutter, fits into a hole in the plate at the base. Clamp the long spindle to the arm of the cutter. It will serve as an axis for the cone as you revolve the rectangular block.

 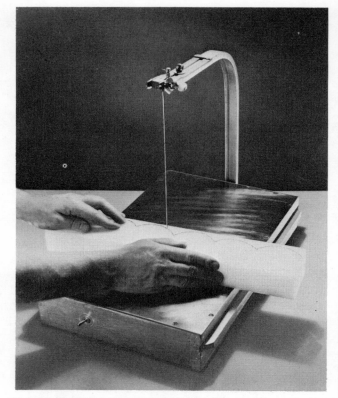

MAKING CUTTING EASIER: If you are making straight cuts with the hot-wire cutter, use a block of wood or a ruler as a guide.

TO MAKE MORE COMPLICATED DESIGNS, draw them on the plastic foam with a pencil before cutting them.

SCULPTURE AND COLLAGE IN PLASTICS

The use of plastics as materials in the shaping of works of art is a modern phenomenon. Some artists began to use plastics as early as the 1940's, but the medium has been more generally used only since the 1960's. Today, plastic sculpture and collage is one of the more important aspects of contemporary "new material" sculpture and an exciting field for the beginner to explore.

The use of plastics in art today extends across a wide territory and covers acrylic painting (acrylic is a plastic-based paint), sculptures in clear lucite, plexiglas, plexiglas and distilled water, plexiglas and light, acrylic-painted sculpture cast in polyester resin, uvex butyrate plastic constructions and constructions in flex polyurethane, extrusion sculpture of vinyl and galvanized steel, fiberglas and steel sculpture, vacuum-formed plastic, fiberglas used alone or in combination with other materials, constructions from mylar sheet plastic, cast acrylics, and even lithographs on lucite and paper, to mention only a few.

There are several categories in which plastic sculpture and collage can be placed. Sculpture can stem directly from geometric-based shapes, constructed of rigid material, in logical form. One group of plexiglas geometric sculpture is the "container" concept in which a plastic material like plexiglas is used to build a container which then holds another material visible through the transparent synthetic. In the container school, another concept is to use acrylic with a tube of light connecting two parts of the sculpture with light.

Another large category is that of combined plastic materials. This includes cast polyester resin pieces painted with bright acrylic, polyester casting, extrusion of liquid vinyl with

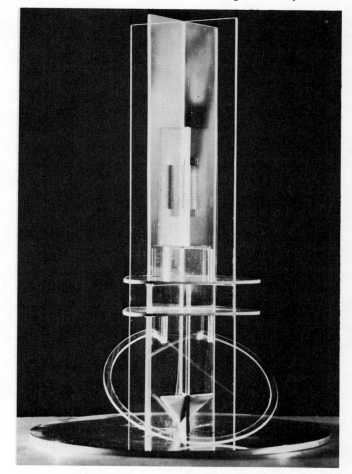

A PLASTIC MODEL OF A FOUNTAIN: Plastic is a modern invention currently in vogue as a modelling material. It is superior to glass because of its chemical construction, which makes it almost non-breakable, yet it retains the same clear beauty which glass has. (Naum Gabo, *Model for glass fountain,* Yale University Art Gallery, gift of Collection Société Anonyme.)

Written especially for this volume by Ruth Ullmann

other materials, and the simulation of natural objects in flex polyurethane.

A third group into which plastic sculpture and collage may be divided are those works which combine several materials, some of which may be plastics. This would include, for example, relief sculptures of acrylic lacquer over stretched fiberglas, curved abstractions made of fiberglas stretched over shaped wooden forms, crumpled mylar sheets (a plastic paper-like substance) over concealed motors to provide movement, etc.

There is still a great deal to be explored in this new field, and the beginner is limited only by his own imagination and technical skills. Many of the modern methods of working in plastics require a great deal of specialized equipment and blower arrangements to take out toxic fumes formed by the materials. However, some of the materials are safe to use in a studio and do not require a heavy investment in equipment. All you need for these are working surfaces, light and the materials themselves.

Plexiglas

Plexiglas is a trade name for a specific kind of acrylic sheet, weighing half as much as glass and available in many colors, transparent or opaque, textured or smooth.

The tools needed to cut plexiglas are either a small handsaw or jig. Since it is a relatively expensive material, the beginner is advised to obtain factory remnants. Here is what is needed to make some sculptures:

> plexiglas remnants
> large pieces of plexiglas, plywood or other
>   material for bases
> plastic cement (ethylene dichloride)
> handsaw or jig
> sandpaper (wet or dry, 32)
> eyedropper with which to apply cement to
>   join narrow surfaces.

The Block Construction. Take several pieces of plexiglas cut into rectangles or squares and

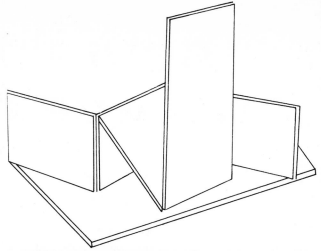

A PLEXIGLAS SCULPTURE made from sheets of plexiglas is easy to construct. The sheets are held together with plastic cement.

visualize a small sculpture. Then start a working drawing of the various parts to scale.

Now assemble the pieces. Paint the plywood base white. Place the pieces into position. If they appear "right," sand the edges to be cemented and apply the plastic cement with the eyedropper. Hold the bonded pieces together until they are firm; allow to dry. If the surface becomes scratched, sandpaper off the marks or polish at the end with jeweler's polish or with a copper cleaner.

The Container. This requires more careful work. It is wise to start with a 12″ × 12″ × 12″ container of transparent plexiglas, and to plan the interior design carefully. Make an assemblage of plastic objects which can be cemented to the floor or sides of the container. When dry, sand the seams and cement the walls of the container together. In a professionally formed piece the seams of the box might be outlined with stainless steel ribbon and a fluid, used inside to hold the objects or just to create interesting effects, might be liquid mercury, distilled water or mineral oil.

Plastic Collage

To make a collage of plexiglas, take a number of cut squares, rectangles or other shaped pieces. Make a geometric plan both for

A PLASTIC COLLAGE: Sheets of plexiglas placed over a collage break up the collage into separate geometric areas. Attach the sheets to the collage with plastic cement. Use an eyedropper to avoid applying too much cement.

placement and for color and design. Consolidate these sketches into a single drawing the size of the finished collage to form a "working" drawing. Take a piece of clear plexiglas shaped to size as the base. Place the objects on the sheet as a trial. Then sand the sheet and the edges of the pieces to be cemented and apply the cement with the eyedropper on the edges of each piece. Cement placed in the middle of a piece will flaw the collage.

The transparent plexiglas collage permits use of pieces on the back as well as the front, and the beginner can experiment with free-form shapes cut with a jigsaw.

Polyester Resin

Polyester resin is a liquid which can be used with other materials such as fiberglas to make either a "bubble-type" sculpture or one which can be cast.

To make a free-form bubble sculpture, the following ingredients are needed:

polyester resin—sold in quarts or gallons
catalyst MEK peroxide
fiberglas cloth—at least 1 yard
plastic bowls
plastic or rubber gloves
glass stirrer
measuring spoons
chicken wire (1″ mesh)

To make the polyester resin harden it must be catalyzed. The general formula is 4 tablespoons polyester resin to $\frac{1}{4}$ teaspoon MEK. The formula should be mixed only in the amount that can be used within 20 minutes.

First construct an armature out of the chicken wire, then drape the fiberglas cloth over this. Now undrape it and cut the fiberglas into several pieces. Mix the solution and dip the cloth pieces one at a time into the solution. Apply carefully to the armature, and smooth into shape. While the drying is going on, press the fiberglas into the final desired shape.

For simple polyester resin casting, the beginner needs first to obtain an assortment

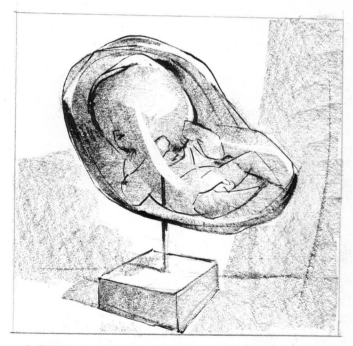

A SHEET OF POLYESTER RESIN encases another sculpture. The transparent plastic gives the entire piece the look of floating in mid-air.

of polyethylene or polypropylene containers. Mix a heavier catalyzed solution of polyester resin and then pour this solution into the plastic containers. Allow it to dry or "cure." Then squeeze it out of the molds. These will be the building blocks of the sculpture. Mix another batch of the catalyzed solution (still heavier) and use this to cement the blocks together. The piece may be finished with a spray of polyester resin gel or the pieces might have been colored initially by adding 2 or more drops of acrylic paint to small solutions of the polyester resin before pouring into the molds.

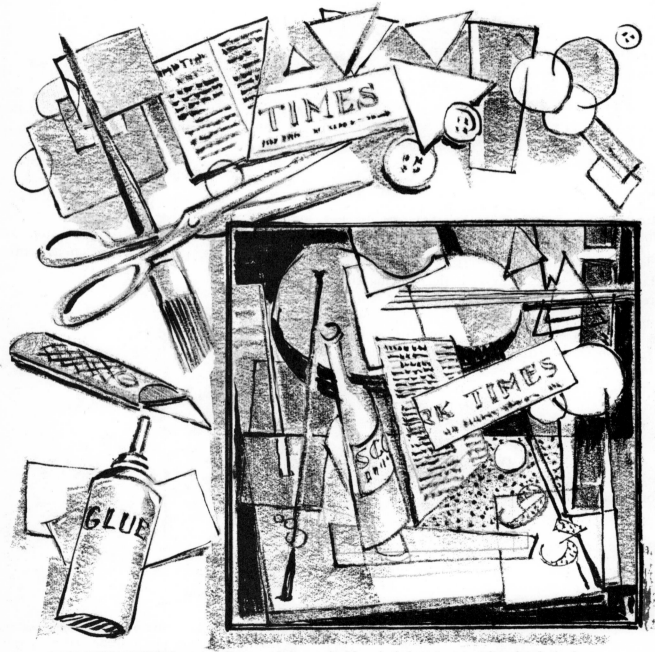

USING VINYL SHEETS: A paper collage can be covered with a vinyl sheet to protect it and make it glossy.

Vinyl

Spray vinyl is highly toxic and not suitable for use in a workshop without adequate safeguards. Therefore, sheet vinyl in transparent, opaque, colored or clear form is recommended. For a wrapped vinyl sculpture obtain some sheet vinyl, medium thickness; heavy cardboard for relief backing; white liquid (Elmer's) glue; plywood or cardboard for the base; and clear liquid cement.

To experiment first with a relief collage, collect a supply of 3-dimensional objects. Arrange these for effect on the base and think about color. Then glue down the pieces on the board, and paint with acrylic paint where needed. Wrap the entire collage under the vinyl sheet. Experiment and, when satisfied, wrap the vinyl around the back and fasten it down with the clear cement.

Plastic Foam

Plastic foam, known as Styrofoam, is a polystyrene, a rigid, porous plastic, foam-like substance which can be carved with a knife or an ordinary carving tool. For good abstract design, it is best to treat this material simply. All you require are some plastic foam blocks, a kitchen knife, buffer, china marking pencil, and superfine plaster.

PLASTIC FOAM is soft and easily cut. To make the sculpture more permanent, it should be coated with epoxy resin or plaster.

First, carefully plan your design. Transfer the drawing to the block with the china pencil. Now begin to carve in a slow, exploratory way, using a shaving, not a digging, motion. When completed, the sculpture will be porous. Preserving it requires a coating of epoxy resin or fine plaster. The plaster-coated work can then be brightly painted with acrylic paints.

print

ETCHINGS AND OTHER INTAGLIO PRINTS

The word "etching" is derived from the German "atzen" which literally means "to make to eat." Etching, therefore, is a method of making a printing plate on metal by using an acid solution to eat away certain areas of the metal. Only a print made from an etched plate is an "etching."

Etchings differ from prints made from engravings in the way in which the lines are incised, making the printed effect much softer. Engravings are made from plates which have been directly incised with a metal tool or burin. Prints produced by engraving, dry point, mezzotint, or aquatint are not etchings. But all these prints, including etchings, are known as "intaglio" prints, because the lines that print are below the surface of the plate. When the plate is printed, the result is an image that seemingly is built up of ink in low relief on the paper; this is the main distinguishing characteristic of intaglio printing.

The Etching Process

The actual process of etching a metal plate consists of about seven steps. First, you coat the thin metal sheet on its face (the surface to be used) with acid-resistant ground, and the back and sides with an acid resist. The ground is then smoked black and you draw a design on the coating with a needle or other tool. This tool puts lines in the ground and exposes the metal in those places. You put the plate into an acid bath for a length of time and, when it is removed, you wipe the ground from the plate. Then you ink the plate, being sure to fill the etched areas. The surface has to be wiped off so that the only ink remaining is in the crevices. Dampened paper is then placed on the plate and, by forcing the plate and paper through a special press at high pressure, you get a print from the ink that has been picked out of the etched cavities.

Tools and Supplies

The requirements for producing etchings are best listed in the categories or steps in which they are used.

Basic Equipment: Copper or zinc plate(s) and a metal file. A heater and a stand as high as the heater top (called a jigger). Ink slab; rollers; and printing press. For the student, a press at an art studio or school can be used initially.

Needling Tools: Needles (sewing needles, phonograph needles, etc.); mimeo styli; ball-point pens; roulettes; brushes, including a badger-hair brush; liquid ground or other ground; and stop-out varnish.

Etching the Plate: This requires various acids and diluted baths stored in labelled glass bottles with glass or plastic tops; rubber or plastic acid trays; cloths; a feather, etc. The acids generally used are: nitric acid; hydrochloric acid and potassium chlorate for Dutch bath; or iron perchloride. Whiting (chalk) also is needed for the hand-wipe operation.

Paper and Press: Hand-made papers are most

Condensed from the book, "Etching and Other Intaglio Techniques" by Manly Banister | © 1969 by Sterling Publishing Co., Inc., New York

ETCHING WORKTABLE: On the table are an ink slab with spatula and muller, behind which is an ink storage crock. Next on the right is an electric griddle, with a foil-covered jigger. Chalk is handy, and ink rollers hang from the shelf above. On the shelf itself are oil cans with kerosene and turpentine; containers of wiping compound and copper polishes; putty and palette knives; ink pigments and oils; and dabbers.

suitable for etching because of their higher quality and durability. Rag papers and machine-made papers can also be used, but in all cases the sizing must be softened by soaking. It is wise to have a large supply of newsprint available also for trial runs, etc.

The etching press consists of a flat metal bed upon which the plate and paper are laid, then passed between two large steel rollers. Because of the pressure needed, the rollers are attached to a gear system and three blankets are laid over the paper when printing to force the paper into the cavities of the plate.

Ink: Specially prepared inks can be purchased in either black or in colors. Purchasing inks is recommended for the beginner or occasional etcher. Otherwise inks can be made from dry ingredients mixed on the ink slab and ground with a muller. Ink is applied to a dabber with a palette knife and then spread on the plate. Dabbers, rollers, and tarlatan pads (for cleaning) and other clean cloths are required.

These are the essential tools and supplies; other, more specialized tools and supplies will be discussed with the various intaglio techniques.

Preparing and Grounding the Plate

The Plate: Any fairly hard or hard metal can be used for etching, but copper and zinc are generally used. Do not experiment with steel or iron. Though more expensive, copper is hard, takes a fine line and is the traditional etching metal. Copper and zinc photo-engraving plates, with backs already pre-coated with acid resist, can be obtained from a photo-engraving supplier. Zinc is softer, produces wider lines and takes a deeper etch. The gauge most frequently used is 16 to 18. Buy plates in the size you will use. Economical purchase of large sheets (18 by 36 inches) is possible, but then you should have access to a metal guillotine cutter.

Be sure the edges of the plate are bevelled to a 45° angle, or else the edge of the plate may damage the press blankets and paper in printing. You can bevel the edges yourself with a metal file.

Preparing the Plate: Remove scratches by running a burnisher lengthwise over the scratch with a little oil and polishing with 4/0 emery paper. Wipe the plate with a clean rag dipped into turpentine to remove grease. Then scrub the plate with a rag dipped into dilute ammonia, followed by a scrubbing with whiting. After washing the plate under running water in a sink (and repeating if necessary), wipe the plate dry with a clean chamois cloth.

Next heat the plate to a temperature of 150° to 200° F. over a hotplate, or a Bunsen burner covered by a steel plate, or other suitable heating device. Remove the plate on to an aluminum foil-covered jigger (a box or raised surface placed level to the heater to facilitate sliding back and forth). Now lay on the ground.

Grounding: One prepared ball ground—either hard or soft—should be purchased, as one ball will ground many plates. Liquid ground also is available, as is transparent ground (used only for regrounding) or ground can be prepared from dry materials.

Melt the ground on to the heated plate by moving the ball around on it. Next, level and smooth the ground with a leather-covered roller, rolling evenly. An alternate method is to apply ground with the use of a dabber (a wooden instrument resembling a pestle that

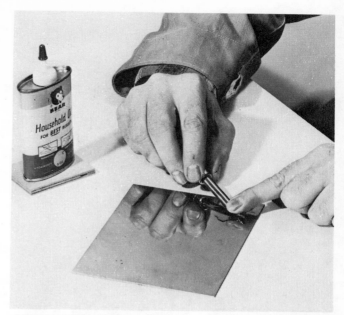

BURNISHING: Polish out light scratches with the burnisher before grounding the plate. Lubricate with ordinary machine oil and rub the length of the scratch.

has been covered with padding and chamois or silk).

Rock this back and forth on the hot plate. Or both methods may be used in combination. The color of a grounded plate should be an *even* dark brown.

Smoking the Ground: Smoking adds a layer of soot to the melted hard ground. (Soft ground does not have to be smoked.) It hardens the ground and will make the drawing show up in greater contrast; it also shows up any flaws so they can be patched. To smoke a hot, grounded plate, pick it up from the heater with

HARD GROUND BALL rests next to a leather roller in its protective box.

SMOKING THE PLATE: Hold a kerosene flame or a wax taper an inch or more away from the surface of the plate. Note that smoke is being drawn up through a filter in a hood.

a hand vise or pliers (the jaws of which are protected with blotting paper). Hold the plate with the ground facing downward and pass a wax taper (six-stranded) with all wicks lit across the ground at a distance of one inch until the surface is an opaque black. A kerosene lamp or other device also could be used. Care must be taken not to scorch the ground.

Needling the Plate (Hard Ground)

Before drawing through the ground to create the design, it is wise to make a preliminary drawing or sketch in pen and ink or pencil. Then you can trace it on to parchment-type tracing paper and transfer it to the grounded plate. This can be done by burnishing with a spoon or a hard-rubber roller. Or, you can place the plate face down on the tracing, folding back the margins of the drawing and taping them to the back of the plate, and then run the plate face up through the press. The image will be in reverse. If you are copying a photograph or painting or a picture post card, look at it in a mirror as you copy.

Complete the drawing on the plate by needling. Work spontaneously, and only use the tracing as a guide. All types of points can be used as etching needles, but you will need at least three sizes: small, medium and large points. Blunt needles won't skid on the plate. Hold the etching needle vertically, regardless of the point, and apply a firm, even pressure. Make wide lines by laying several fine lines side by side. To simulate an engraved line you need to use an échoppe, an instrument which has an angled point. Always draw on a cool ground.

After needling, coat the back and edges of the plate with an acid-resist (liquid asphaltum or stop-out varnish).

Needling the Plate (Soft Ground)

After the soft ground has been laid on the plate in exactly the same manner as the hard ground, but with a different roller or dabber, lines can be drawn directly on the ground with a pencil. The traditional technique is to lay a piece of paper over the soft ground and draw on the paper with a pencil; the pressure causes the paper to adhere to the ground, and when it is lifted it takes the ground with it.

Corrections

Mistakes in needling the plate can be corrected with the use of stop-out, obtained commercially or made with one part shellac to two parts alcohol. Use a clean brush and keep alcohol handy to clean the brush. Paint the stop-out over the unwanted lines. If the whole drawing has gone awry, remove the ground, and start all over again.

Etching the Plate

Wear rubber gloves for this work.

The strength of the acid solution will vary

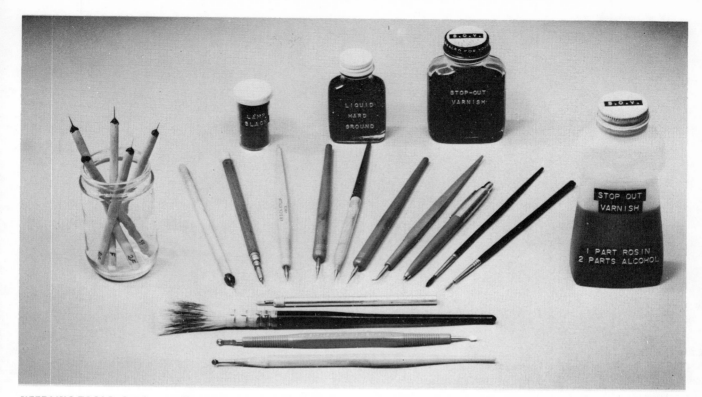

NEEDLING TOOLS: Sewing needles are in the jar at the left, then in the semi-circle are two phonograph needles, mimeo styluses, a ballpoint pen, and two brushes. Surrounding these are jars containing lampblack, liquid ground, and stop-out varnish. In the foreground are roulettes, a badger-hair brush, and an X-Acto knife.

according to the metal plate used and the kind of bite desired. Always pour *acid into* water and not vice versa.

Acids should be stored in clearly labelled glass jars. Do not use the same solution for copper and zinc. Do your etching in Pyrex dishes or plastic photo trays. Place the plate in the tray and add the acid bath.

Acids are caustic and rubber gloves should be worn during the etching process. Keep bicarbonate of soda handy for placing on skin if it is touched by acid and ammonia for washing acid from clothing.

Nitric Acid: For copper, a ratio of 3 parts acid to 5 parts water will be just right. For zinc plates, the proportion would be 1 part acid to 9 parts water. Fumes will be kept to a minimum with these formulae.

Dutch Mordant: This acid bath is used for etching very fine lines. It is made by first dissolving a small amount of chlorate of potassium crystals in a little water by boiling.

When this is cool, add it to the water and then add hydrochloric acid to the water mixture. Use a ventilator or keep a window open as this solution gives off fumes.

The ratios for preparing Dutch mordant would be as follows:

COPPER—25 ounces water, 5 ounces hydrochloric acid, 1 ounce potassium chlorate; ZINC—22 ounces water, $2\frac{1}{2}$ ounces hydrochloric acid, and $\frac{1}{2}$ ounce potassium chlorate.

Iron Perchloride: This is a good consistent mordant, but it produces a sediment. So (unlike the other mordants) when using this acid bath, lay the plate face downward in the acid, resting the plate carefully where there is no etching on wedges of wood or glass. Iron perchloride is used only on copper. Mix 1 pound of iron perchloride crystals with $1\frac{1}{2}$ pints of water. Dilute with $\frac{3}{4}$ pint of water. Adding 10% of hydrochloric acid dissolves the sediment and permits face-up etching of the plate.

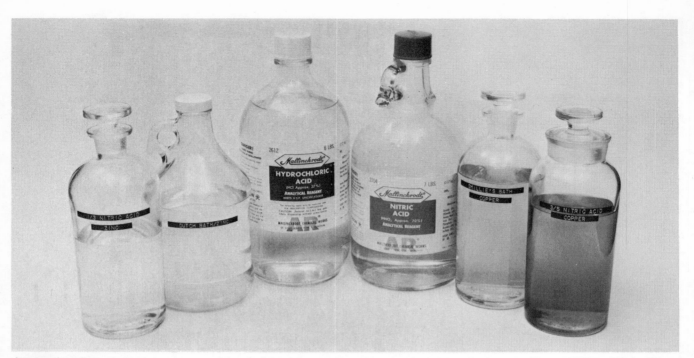

ETCHING ACIDS and diluted baths are stored best in glass bottles with ground-glass or plastic tops. Note that the used zinc baths on the left are clear, and the used copper baths on the right have a tone.

Biting the Plate: For best results first soak the needled plate for 5 minutes in 28% acetic acid. This removes the grease and oxidation from the lines and permits prompt starting of the etch in the acid bath.

Even though no exact timing is possible for an etched plate (this will also depend on the temperature of the bath), here is a guideline. In a fresh bath of 1 part nitric acid to 2 parts water a simple, one-bite copper plate will etch in 20 to 30 minutes. In a bath of 3 parts nitric to 5 parts water, the plate will etch to a reasonable depth in 10 or 15 minutes. A zinc plate bathed in a fresh solution of 1 part nitric to 9 parts water will etch in 10 or 15 minutes.

In a nitric bath, bubbles form along the line and should be lightly removed by brushing with a feather.

Before placing the etched plate in the bath be sure to place stop-out on the edges of the plate and the back. When this is dry, place the plate face-up in the acid bath (only face-down in an iron perchloride bath). Brush bubbles away. As soon as the lightest lines have been etched, take out the plate, wash it under water, dry and apply stop-out to the lines that do not need more etching. Repeat until all varying depths of etched areas have been achieved.

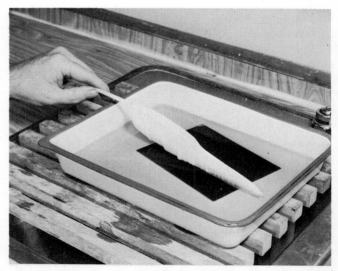

FEATHERING: Remove the bubbles that form in a nitric bath by brushing the plate lightly with a feather like this.

Be sure to wash the plate in water and dry it every time it is removed from the acid bath. The leftover acid may be poured back into the jar and used again.

Reworking the Plate

A scraper and a burnisher are the common tools used to rework an etched plate. The burnisher rubbed lengthwise will eliminate fine lines. Use the scraper to remove deeper unwanted lines, then rub a Scotch stone, followed by snake slip or charcoal under running water over the area and finally polish the area with dry emery polishing paper. Where a severe dent has been made in the plate, *repoussage* (see page 177) must be performed to bring the area up to its former level. The plate can then be reground and new lines applied to the reworked area.

Preparing the Paper

Any paper can be used if it can be *evenly* dampened without excessive cockling. Water-leaf papers do not contain sizing and are not expensive. The best sized papers are made from rag pulp, but in this case the sizing must be softened by soaking in water or dampening with a sponge before the paper can be used

in the etching press. Place the sheets of paper, handling one at a time, between large sheets of damp blotting paper stacked under a heavy glass, or formica (plywood) and weight down.

The Etching Press

An etching press is a highly specialized piece of printing equipment. On a flat bed (supported on a frame) the plate and paper and etching blankets are placed, and then the bed and all are passed between a pair of heavy steel rollers by turning a hand wheel called a star wheel. Most such presses can adjust the pressure and can print from high wood blocks, etc., as well as from etched plates. Generally speaking, the press bed should be twice as large as the etched plate.

Usually three etching blankets are used. On their quality depends the quality of the print. The thinnest blanket (a $\frac{1}{16}$-inch felt layer) is called the sizing catcher. It is placed on the bottom, next to the press bed, just over the plate and a sheet of protective newsprint. Next comes the heaviest blanket ($\frac{3}{16}$-inch)

THE ETCHING PRESS: (Left, below) A 14-inch press built by Manly Banister. (Below) The bed has been removed to show the construction. Note the gearing on the drive roller to reduce the effort of turning. The top roller runs free.

INKS: Ink pigments must be kept in closed glass jars (left). Raw linseed and other oils are best kept in syrup dispensers (right). Prepared inks come in tubes. You also need palette knives and putty knives, an ink slab (litho stone) and mullers, if you are going to make your own ink.

called the "cushion," and then the topmost blanket ($\frac{1}{8}$-inch), known as the pusher. The blankets must be kept clean and may be hand washed in a mild detergent. When not in use, they should be placed flat on a shelf near the press. When worn, they should be replaced.

Inking the Plate

INK. It is possible to prepare etching ink from powdered ingredients and oils, but the beginning or occasional etcher is best off buying prepared inks. You can add a little raw linseed oil to loosen the ink, and some burnt umber to speed the drying process.

If a great deal of etching is to be done, then a good black ink mixture to prepare is comprised of: two parts Frankfort black to one part Vine black mixed with burnt umber and heavy burnt plate oil. Do your mixing on an ink slab with a palette knife.

INKING THE PLATE. Place the etched plate on the heater and heat it until just too hot to touch. Then slide it on to the jigger and force ink into all the etched lines with a dabber. After use, scrape the dabber clean and wrap it in plastic.

Clean the plate with scrim, that is, wipe it with pads made from a stiff, coarsely woven cloth called tarlatan. Mosquito netting or starched cheesecloth can also be used. Wipe lightly lengthwise; turn the plate; wipe across; repeat. Then dip your hand into whiting and wipe the plate with the side of your hand. Perform the hand-wipe quickly and without pressure. Wipe your hand after each chalking. Some etchers prefer *retroussage*, in which a soft, rolled cloth is whisked over the plate. Finally clean the edges of the plate.

Printing the Plate

Place newsprint over the bed of the press. Place the plate face up on the paper with the longest side parallel, if possible, to the rollers.

Next, position the dampened paper over the plate using clips to prevent smudging the paper. Place a blotter or piece of newsprint over the paper to protect the first blanket. Then position the blankets in proper sequence (see illustration) and prepare to print. During the printing process, keep the rollers moving, as otherwise a line will develop on the print where the rollers have stopped.

Carefully remove the newsprint and the print. Dry prints in two stages. First, place the prints between dry blotters as they come from the press. Change blotters until the prints are dry.

Then, if the prints buckle, resoak or dampen them and leave them between blotters under a weight. Once dry, the prints may be stored in a drawer by stacking them and interleaving them with tissue paper.

Etchers usually number each print in an edition in the order in which the prints were pulled. For example, if an edition is to number 50, the first print would be numbered 1/50 in the lower left-hand corner under the etched area.

Finally, it is important to clean up after each printing run. Wipe ink smudges from the press with a kerosene-dampened rag. Clean the plate by flooding it with kerosene and scrubbing. Dry with a clean, soft cloth. Clean the ink slab (storing leftover ink in a crock or jar of water), and clean all tools. Put rollers and dabbers away and be sure to protect all equipment from dust.

History of Etching

The origins of etching are not precisely known; however, it is believed the process,

REMBRANDT was the world's greatest etcher, as this plate, called "The Rat Killer," shows.

like engraving, was invented by armourers or silver and goldsmiths north of the Alps to accelerate the process of making designs on

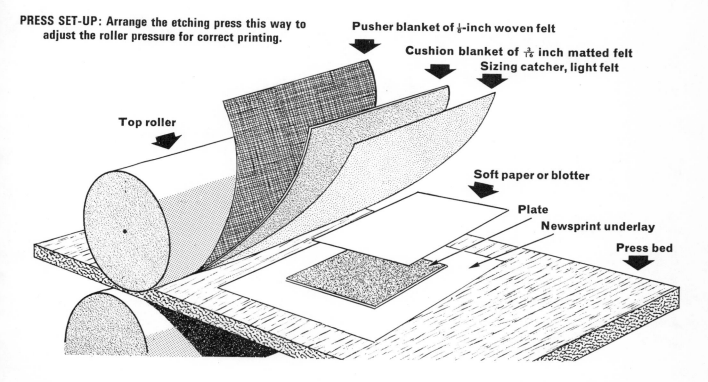

PRESS SET-UP: Arrange the etching press this way to adjust the roller pressure for correct printing.

Pusher blanket of $\frac{1}{8}$-inch woven felt

Cushion blanket of $\frac{3}{16}$ inch matted felt

Sizing catcher, light felt

Top roller

Soft paper or blotter

Plate

Newsprint underlay

Press bed

MASTERPIECES OF ETCHING: (Above) Rembrandt's "Landscape with Cottage and Haybarn" shows the fine line that the Dutch master was able to achieve. This plate is $5\frac{1}{8}$ x $12\frac{5}{8}$ inches, and is the gift of R. Horace Gallatin to the National Gallery of Art, Washington, D.C. (Below) An American, John Marin (1875-1953), made this interesting etching, "Cloitre St. Maclou, Rouen," which hangs in the Art Institute of Chicago.

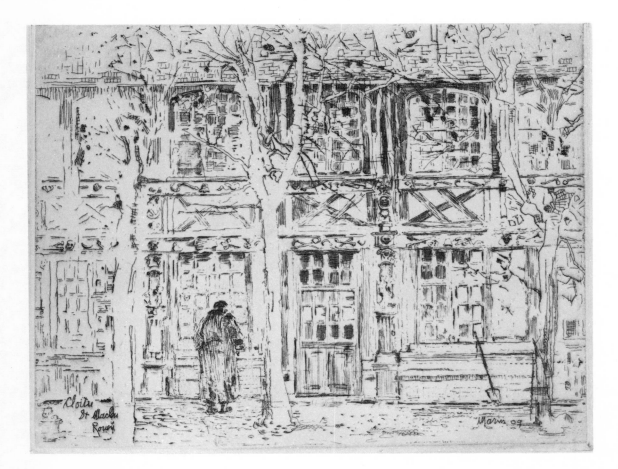

metal. Although etching was practiced as early as the 15th century, the first etching to which a date can be assigned is a portrait by Daniel Hopfer, a German artist living *c.* 1493–1536. The earliest dated etching was produced in 1513 by a Swiss goldsmith. The Italians recognized etching as an independent graphic medium in the 16th century, but it was not until the 17th century and the great Dutch artists—Rembrandt and Van Dyck—that etching really became a developed art form. Other great artists, including Goya and Whistler, subsequently created fine etchings, but the great revival of interest in etching and combined intaglio printmaking has come about in the 20th century.

Other Intaglio Plates

There are other methods of preparing plates for intaglio printing which can be used alone, or in combination with etching. These are the sugar-lift aquatint, direct drawing with stop-out, aquatint, mezzotint, dry point, and engraving.

Sugar-Lift Aquatint: This technique permits you to draw directly on to a plate in tone in such a way that the black marks will print as black marks on the paper. Drawing is done with a solution known as a sugar-lift solution. To make this, dissolve sugar in a little water until the water is saturated and no more sugar will dissolve. Then mix India ink with the solution in equal parts. Draw with the solution directly on an ungrounded but polished and grease-free plate. Leave it to dry until the black reaches a sticky thick texture.

When ready, cover the entire surface of the plate with a layer of asphaltum and turpentine mixed in equal parts. Apply quickly and gently so as not to disturb the drawing. Dry the plate over a gentle heat and then submerge it in water. This will cause the sugar-lift to expand

and crack off the plate, leaving the asphaltum stop-out intact except where the drawing was made. Once all the sugar-lift solution has lifted, the plate is ready for biting. Proceed, using stop-out on the back and side. Then clean, ink and print as if the plate were a regular etching.

Drawing with Stop-Out: Direct drawing on an ungrounded, polished and clean plate with stop-out will produce a print similar to the sugar-lift method except that all the marks made on the plate will print as white areas, while the unpainted areas will print as open, bitten, mottled-grey tones.

To achieve these effects, simply paint directly on the polished, grease-free plate with a stop-out solution made up of equal parts of asphaltum and turpentine. Once this is dry, the back and sides of the plate can be stopped out and the plate can be bitten in acid. As large parts of the plate are likely to be exposed, there will be much activity and bubbling and

AQUATINT: (Left) The texture is attractively grainy in this type of plate, as used by Degas for his "Au Louvre: Musée des Antiques," which is in the Metropolitan Museum of Art, New York City.

AQUATINT: Box with the plate resting on a paper underlay. Better than the bellows shown would be a vacuum-cleaner exhaust.

care should be taken not to inhale the fumes. Keep a window open, or use an exhaust fan.

Other stop-out solutions can be substituted, such as shellac mixed with alcohol.

Aquatint: Aquatint is a process that enables you to produce a plate that will print areas of controllable tone ranging from light grey to black or the equivalent in color. It is frequently used in connection with etching. In aquatint you use the acid the same way as in etching, but the ground is different. The ground is rosin dusted on to a plate with a rosin bag or through an aquatint box. The plate must then be heated carefully until the rosin melts enough to stick to the plate; it should not melt together. The plate is then bitten in acid. Aquatint is used as a means of making hard-edged areas of tone, but there are ways of graduating the tone—by scraping and burnishing, by pouring acid and water directly on to the plate or by pouring diluted acid into a tilted tray.

Mezzotint: This method of making a plate is similar in its final effect to a plate made by the aquatint method, but mezzotint, if carefully used, can achieve even subtler effects. It is a technique which demands much practice. In mezzotint, the copper plate must first be scoured with a "mezzotint rocker."

This tool is shaped like a large chisel. The bevelled edge of the blade is curved; on the unbevelled flat side of the blade, parallel lines are engraved terminating at the curved edge in tiny teeth. The rocker blade in general use is $2\frac{1}{2}$ inches wide, but other widths also are available.

The rocker blade is set into a rocker arm or rocking-pole device. When this is moved over the plate it leaves a line of pits which print as closely spaced dots. Each pit has a burr thrown up around it and ink is retained in both the pit and under the surrounding burr. The soft velvety black which is characteristic of mezzotint cannot be produced by any other method.

SOFT-GROUND ETCHING WITH AQUATINT: "The Farm" by Manly Banister is a combination plate, 5 x 9 inches on zinc. The soft ground was bitten in a 1:3 nitric bath, and the aquatint in a Dutch bath. The cloud edges were faded with the touch of a litho crayon.

Mezzotint relies upon ink being held in a burr raised *above* the surface of the plate rather than in a cavity bitten or cut into it.

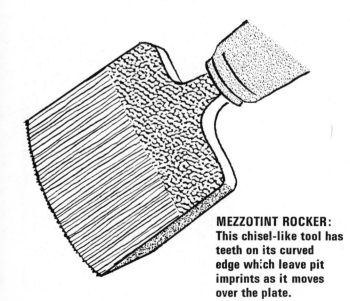

MEZZOTINT ROCKER: This chisel-like tool has teeth on its curved edge which leave pit imprints as it moves over the plate.

To make a mezzotint, the first step is to etch the design into the plate. Etched lines are visible through the burr and this method makes it possible to avoid extra work by rocking only those areas where greys and blacks are wanted. To rock the plate takes a good deal of time and patience. The plate must be rocked in eight different directions. Following the rocking procedure, you use a variety of burnishers and scrapers to flatten the burr to achieve the right strength of grey tone desired. Roulettes also are used in retouching areas.

Care must be taken in inking and printing the mezzotint plate so as not to wear out the burr. Make the ink thinner with raw linseed oil and apply it with a dabber or wad of soft cloth. Wipe with tarlatan cloth and print on a thick, soft paper.

Burin Engraving: The earliest method of creating an intaglio printing plate was to

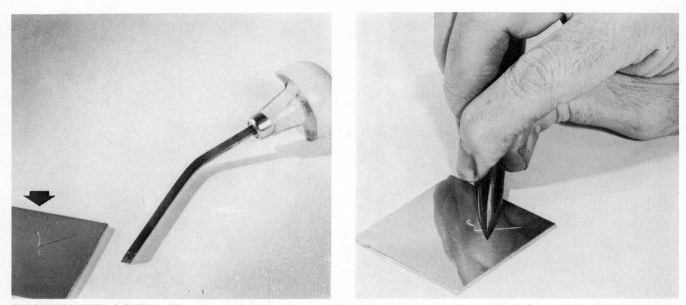

ENGRAVING WITH A BURIN: When you push the tool across the plate you turn up a burr or curl of metal ahead of it (left). The burr is well anchored and sharp. Cut it off with a scraper (right) at intervals before it gets too long.

engrave it by hand with an engraving tool or burin. The burin comes in many shapes and sizes and is used for various purposes. The most commonly used engraving tools are: the square-shank burin, lozenge-shaped burin, tint tool, multiliner, and scorper. Since the burin blunts quickly, sharpening stones are needed— a carborundum for grinding and an Arkansas stone for finishing. Sharpening is a difficult process to master and the beginning engraver should seek out an experienced master engraver to provide a practical demonstration.

In a burin engraving, all lines are incised into the plate with the burin, and all tones are achieved by either cross-hatching or stippling. When cutting, the important thing to remember is that the plate must move, not the hand or the burin. To facilitate this movement of the plate it is traditional for the engraver to work on a stuffed leather bag, but a smooth-surfaced table will do as well. As with etching, the depth and width of the incised line will govern the depth of tone and the width of the printed line. Copper is probably the best metal for burin engraving, but since it is hard to see lines on polished copper surfaces, engravers

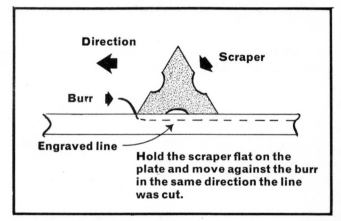

HOW TO CUT OFF THE BURR (above). How the engraved line looks (below).

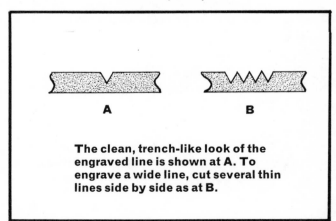

The clean, trench-like look of the engraved line is shown at A. To engrave a wide line, cut several thin lines side by side as at B.

DRY POINT: Hold the needle (diamond in use here) loosely but apply it firmly to the plate. As you work, rub lampblack into the lines to make them more visible on the plate. View your subject in a mirror.

will often dull the plate by immersing it in a bath of dilute acid for a few seconds. Once the cutting is finished, the plate is polished, the edges bevelled and it is inked and printed exactly the same way as the etched plate.

Dry Point: The difference between burin engraving and dry point is that in engraving the burin cuts a furrow through the metal, but in dry point the lines are only scratched enough to raise a burr above the surface of the plate that will hold ink. In engraving, the metal removed is scraped away. Many artists specialize in dry point, since it eliminates the chemical aspects of etching as well as the array of tools needed for engraving. Three types of points are used in the "dry point needle": steel, cemented tungsten carbide, and diamond. The needle is set into a steel shaft.

Dry point needles can be held much like a pen or pencil. The finest lines are made by holding the point vertically at an angle of 90° to the plate. The greater the slant of the needle, the wider the burr.

Copper or zinc plates can be used. To print, use regular etching ink, but render it more fluid with the addition of raw linseed oil. Do not use a dabber, but apply the ink with a wad of soft cloth. Use soft cloth for wiping also. Finish with the chalked hand-wipe, working around the lines rather than over them. Then print on a thick, soft paper and ease the pressure on the press a little.

Metal Graphic and Shaped Plates

Two other techniques are popular with contemporary printmakers. The first is to cut an etched plate into an expressive shape or to produce a complex print by printing a number of cut plates together. Plates can be cut with metal cutters and the edges filed to a smooth

COLOR PRINT made with dry point and aquatint by Mary Cassatt (1844-1926). This is the third and final state of "Afternoon Tea" which hangs in the National Gallery of Art, Washington, D.C., Rosenwald Collection.

45° bevel, so as not to tear the paper during printing.

In the metal graphic, any kind of metal can be used. The metal graphic process starts with a thin plate as a base and builds up heights by cementing other metal to it. It may be printed by intaglio method, relief method or a combination of the two. The effects are infinite and limited only by the imagination of the artist and the capacity of the press.

Color

Etching at times has been considered an unsuitable medium for color. But color can be used. The beginner may produce colored etchings by first printing the plate in a regular black ink on cold-pressed watercolor paper, and when dry coloring the print with watercolors.

More elaborate methods of color printing of intaglio plates involve the separate plate method, the single plate method and the offset method.

POTATO PRINTING

If you want the rewards of block printing without investing time and money in the special skills and tools required for linoleum or wood, the common potato makes a remarkably versatile and satisfying substitute.

Because this inexpensive vegetable can be so easily carved into a variety of shapes which have a sharp and firm printing edge and face, potato printing has become an increasingly popular method of repeating designs on practically any material—paper, fabric, wood, even plastic.

A sharp kitchen knife is all that is needed for carving most stencil designs. While it is possible to create quite complex relief designs in a single potato, more varied and fanciful results will come from "building" a composite design. The flamboyant fighting cocks on page J were created entirely of simple geometric shapes plus the imaginative use of color.

PRINTING EASTER EGGS in brilliant colors is easy with potato stamps.

Materials

Potatoes: Peel and clean several potatoes. Be sure you have enough on hand to complete your project. If you plan to print the same design in different colors, you will need a separate stencil for each color. The potato, for all its marvelous printing qualities, is nevertheless permeable and will absorb some ink or paint when it is used as a stamp.

To make sure each color prints sharp and clear, fresh stencils are essential. Make fresh stencils each day you print, because the organic potato will soon decompose and become too soft to use for printing.

Colors: If you are printing on paper, all watercolors, tempera and poster paints are suitable. For fabric printing, you will want something more permanent: use dyes specially intended for use on fabrics. By printing one color over another, a third will be created; by diluting the dye, a color a few shades lighter than the original will result. To ensure a uniform color, however, the potato stencil must be recolored before *each* new impression.

Paper: Try a variety of papers to see the different effects which each produces. Use absorbent typewriter paper and unprinted newspaper, or surfaces that are more glossy,

Condensed from the book, "Potato Printing" by Susanne Strose / © 1968 by Sterling Publishing Co., Inc., New York

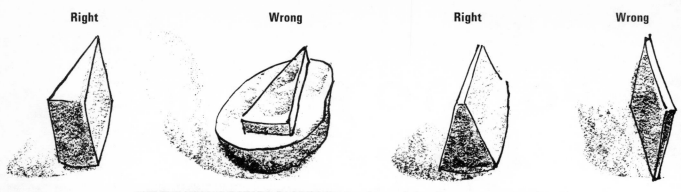

| Right | Wrong | Right | Wrong |

CUT THE WHOLE POTATO BLOCK into the shape of the area you want to print.

such as transparent paper or lightweight cardboard.

Fabrics: Coarsely textured fabrics do not give very good results. More finely woven materials such as cotton, linen, and silk absorb the dye more fully and evenly. Of course, for some articles the coarser look may be desired.

For printing fabrics you need permanent colors which do not run or wash out in the laundry. Pour some color over a folded rag of felt or cloth and spread the color carefully with a brush or knife. Now press your potato stamps on this "stamp pad" and color them evenly.

Next, cover a work table with newspaper

and fasten your fabric over it with thumb-tacks. Stencil the fabric with your colored potato stamp. You must proceed with caution because spots and stains cannot be removed.

After the color-stamping is complete, take the material off the table and iron it on the unprinted side. Now your fabric is colorfast and you can wash it without fear that your design will fade or run.

Other equipment: To cut the potato stencil, use a sharp kitchen knife or a razor blade in a holder. A camel's-hair brush about $\frac{1}{2}$-inch wide will help you apply the paint evenly to the stencil. A jar of water should be nearby to rinse the brushes.

Cutting the Stencil

When cutting the potato in the design you have chosen, do not merely take a potato half and cut the design in relief. Instead, cut the whole piece into the shape of your design. This will not only help you distinguish one stencil from another, but also allow you to see the rest of the design when you are printing. Remember to make a fresh stencil for every color and every day that you print.

For your first project, cut a stencil in an elementary geometric shape and print it several times, to get the feel of the medium. Notice how much paint you need to apply with the brush to achieve an even and attractive impression, and how much pressure is necessary. When you feel that your technique has

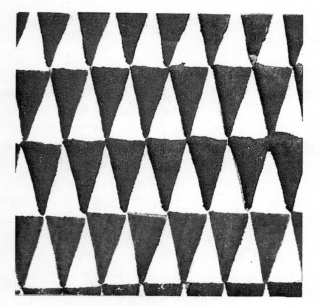

A SIMPLE WEDGE made this design.

become regular and predictable, try using two stencils of different patterns—perhaps a triangle and a rectangle, or two different rectangles—and two different colors. Overlapping the stencils can produce a third color, while letting the paper show through in spots can create another shade. Thus, even with only two basic designs and two primary colors, you can achieve a variety of different patterns and tones.

Stars and Blossoms

So far you have made prints by using only the most basic stamp patterns. But you can use scraps of potato which you have set aside to create pictures, by adding triangles, bars, petals, dots and rays to a main shape. For example, cut and print a large circle; this can serve as the center for a flower. Then cut smaller circles, and print them around the original large one. Using a narrow triangle stencil, print a stem and some leaves. Place these flowers in a row along the border of a place mat (using permanent dyes instead of paint), or decorate paper in a haphazard fashion to make a garden out of your gift wrappings. Stars can be made by cutting narrow strips or squares, and arranging them around a central dot.

For more elaborate flower arrangements, proceed in the same way as you did to make individual flowers. You might print bouquets on the corners of napkins or postcards, or make a series of designs for a calendar. Each month could show a flower which blossoms during that time of year.

SQUARES used twice in different colors.

THIS PINE BOUGH was made from printing with a small stamp used eleven times.

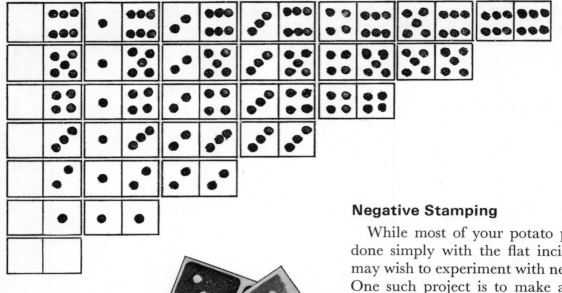

DOMINO CARD SET made from potato stamps, positive and negative.

Negative Stamping

While most of your potato printing will be done simply with the flat incised design, you may wish to experiment with negative printing. One such project is to make a set of domino cards with potato stamps. Cut out seven stamps with the number of dots varying from 0 to six. The 28 cards in the illustration above show how the dots will normally print. The lower illustration shows how the stamped cards will look with the dots as negative space surrounded by color. Gouge the dots out of the potato with a small punch. Color the stamp and print your cards.

RUBBINGS

If you ever placed a sheet of blank paper over a coin and then rubbed a pencil lightly over the paper to produce an "impression" of the coin, you were practicing the ancient Chinese craft of *T'a-pen*, known more familiarly today as frottage (fro-*tazh*) or rubbing. Quite simply, the technique of frottage is the "lifting" of a design from a pre-formed or carved surface—bas-reliefs, manhole covers, old gravestones, brick walls, leaves, bark, coins, etc. In China, where the technique may have had its birth as early as 300 B.C., rubbing was responsible for the spread of art and literature to all corners of the far-flung empire; pictures of the gods, the edicts of the emperors, and Buddhist and Confucian texts were first carved in stone for the purpose of producing copies by means of the rubbing technique.

Although rubbing spread throughout the Far East—particularly in Japan, where it is known as Ishizuri—it was very slow to gain any measure of popularity in the West, mainly because it was regarded primarily as a means of reproduction and not as a fine art. Today, however, perhaps because of the influence of the Pop artists who have shown that any product or by-product is suitable material for a work of art, the frottage techniques are being used by thousands of people around the world. The inexpensiveness of the necessary materials and the simplicity of the techniques (even very young children can become rapidly adept) also account for the new-found popularity of frottage.

There are two basic techniques—dry and wet. The dry technique is held in more esteem by most people because it is easier to master;

the wet technique to produce ink rubbings requires a great deal more practice and patience.

Manhole Cover Rubbing Using the Dry Technique

For this project you will need a stiff brush for cleaning the surface; toothbrush for cleaning small details; putty knife for scraping away foreign matter; scissors; roll of masking tape; paper for final rubbing (rice papers, charcoal paper, speed-ball printing paper, detail paper, or 3M rubbing fabric); rubbing media (primary crayons, charcoal, tailor's chalk, lumber crayons, or graphite sticks); pre-moistened paper towels for keeping hands clean and avoiding smudges; and spray fixative.

Selecting the proper manhole cover is very important. Don't choose one in the middle of the road. Also, some are much too worn to guarantee an effective final product. Once the cover has been decided upon, clean away all foreign matter with your stiff brush, toothbrush, and putty knife. After the surface is thoroughly clean, cut the paper to size, allowing at least a 1-inch border on all sides. Place the first piece of masking tape in the middle of the top edge, the second opposite at the bottom, the third at the middle of the right edge, and the fourth opposite on the left. Before applying each piece of tape, the paper should be smoothed out from the middle with your free hand. It is most important that the paper be held securely in place because the slightest shifting during the rubbing operation will cause a blurring of the image.

Written especially for this volume by Jon Teta

SOME MANHOLE COVERS have elaborate designs as emblems. If you only want to make a rubbing of this portion of the cover, cut a round piece of paper to the proper size and place it over the middle.

Grasp the crayon or other rubbing media firmly, and carefully apply it to the paper's surface, working delicately from the middle out. After you have established the entire design lightly, repeat the procedure, this time using a moderate pressure and working carefully from the edges in.

Before removing the paper, study the finished design from a distance for evenness of color.

Small imperfections that register as white spots can be doctored up later at home. Free the print by peeling the masking tape *off* the paper gently, never toward the paper. Spray the entire design with a spray fixative, following the directions on the label.

Naturally, if you live in an area where there is heavy street traffic, a manhole cover may not be the object to practice the dry technique upon. Look for a wall or plaque with an interesting surface.

Gravestone Rubbing
Using the Wet Technique

For this project you will need a stiff brush; toothbrush; putty knife; scissors; rice papers (haruki, moriki, kinwashi, or natsume); ink (India ink or printer's ink); beeswax; methycellulose (tablets or powder, available from most drugstores under the brand name of "Cellothyl"—prepare a liquid solution by mixing a level teaspoon of powder in a pint of warm water and shake vigorously until completely dissolved); elephant ear sponge for applying methycellulose mixture; clothing brush; atomizer or squeeze bottle of water; paper towels or tissues; and dabbers of various sizes (make dabbers by covering balls of sponge with several layers of cotton cloth and

DECORATIVE GRAVESTONES are not common, but there are some to be found if you look hard enough. Many universities, libraries and other large institutions have carved stone or metal decorations from which rubbings can be made.

surround them with pieces of chamois, tying off the ends with thin wire or string).

Choose a stone bearing a finely cut design. Clean with the brushes and putty knife (lichen on old stones may be a minor problem and scraping is the only method to remove them). When the stone is clean, measure and cut the rice paper. Holding the paper in place on top of the design, wet the paper liberally with the methycellulose mixture, using the fingers or a small elephant ear sponge; tape is not necessary since the methycellulose is a mild glue. Place the rice paper on the stone. While the rice paper is still wet, remove all air bubbles with your hands, working gently from the middle out. Allow the paper to dry thoroughly.

The next step is optional and should be done only when the inks and colors you intend to use contain little or no water.

Using a soft bristle clothing brush, apply beeswax to the dry paper, brushing in all directions, delicately at first and then with more vigor until the paper surface is polished; this will prevent the ink from penetrating the paper and will assure a sharp image.

You are now ready to apply the ink. Saturate a large dabber with ink, then use it as you would a stamp pad, transferring ink from this large pad on to a smaller dabber which will be used to make the rubbing. Remove excess ink from the small dabber by touching it to a piece of scrap paper, repeating this step after every inking. Brush the small dabber very delicately across the paper, always moving horizontally and never letting the dabber come to rest on the paper; this requires a great deal of practice and the novice should not be too discouraged with failure.

Allow the finished rubbing to dry thoroughly, then remove the paper by gripping firmly at the bottom and peeling up with a constant, even pull. The methycelullose will cause the paper to curl. This can be eliminated by pressing under a flat board or by mounting with photographic dry mount tissue.

As you become proficient in the wet and dry rubbing techniques, the design possibilities of many hitherto neglected objects will occur to you. Automobile tire treads, for example, can be used to create interesting repeat designs, and startling results can often be achieved by taking a rubbing of a collage made of quite ordinary objects such as buttons, haphazard loops of string, twigs, and pebbles.

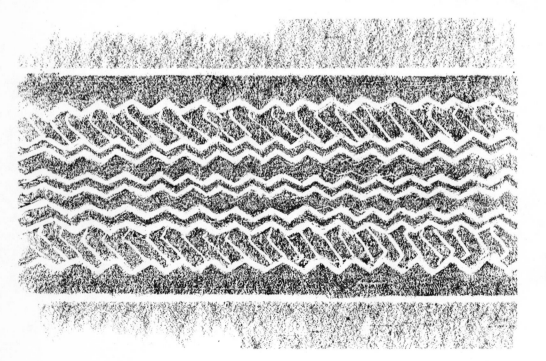

TIRE TRACKS form unusual repeating patterns.

SCREEN PROCESS PRINTING

The screen process is a technique for making black, single-color or multi-color prints inexpensively with stencils of silk and simple equipment. The process which is used both in industry and by artists today is a perfection of an early type of stencil printing that has been in use for hundreds of years. It is actually a technique that can simulate the subtle transparent washes of watercolor, the heavy impasto of oil painting, the qualities of gouache, pastel or wood block, or reproduce drawings in some lines and large solids.

Commercial display studios and sign shops have long recognized the value of the process for creating signs and posters. Craftsmen, too, began to experiment. Today, with the use of lithographic tusche and films, stencil-making has expanded and so has the scope of silk screening. In fact, screening is an important part of the graphic arts industry as it can produce both line and halftone by a photographic process. It can be done by the artist-craftsman by hand or in industry with a screen process press. In fact, it can be used to print on anything—paper or cardboard of any thickness, wood, textiles, plastic and glass bottles.

The Basic Principles

Artists and craftsmen use hand-cut stencils which are affixed to a piece of silk (or cotton, which is adequate for a beginner printing on textiles) that is stretched tight on a wooden frame. The non-image areas (the areas not to be printed) are blocked out and ink is forced through the open areas of the fabric screen with a rubber blade called a squeegee on to the object (such as paper) being printed. The prints are made one at a time by hand. One great advantage of the process is that the screen can be large—almost any size—and that the printing comes out clearly on any kind of material.

There are two types of printing: reverse printing and direct printing. In the case of reverse printing, the design is blocked out and the background is printed, leaving the design "in reverse." In direct printing, the design is

THE PROCESS: The outer lines show a table top. Secured to it by hinges is a liftable rectangular frame with reinforced corners. Stretched over the base of the frame is silk. The inside of the frame is covered by a cut-out stencil. When ink is pushed through the cut-out parts of the stencil with a squeegee, an image of the artwork is printed on the material (paper or textile) below the frame.

Written especially for this volume by Ruth Ullmann

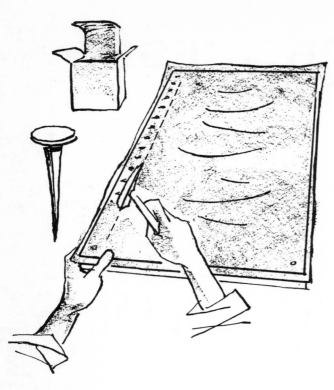

left open for the penetration of paint, and the surrounding area or background is blocked out by the stencil.

Equipment

The wooden frame acts both as a support for the fabric screen and as a basin for the paint or ink used in printing. The frame should be rectangular and is best constructed from seasoned wood free from knots. Any seasoned wood may be used and white pine is inexpensive. The frame must be rigid and well constructed, especially in the corners and joints. If it warps easily it will not serve as a good stretcher for the silk and it will be impossible to register color prints accurately.

The size of the frame will, of course, vary with the size of the print, but it must be larger than the area to be printed. For a 6″ × 9″ print, the relative dimensions of the screen should be 9″ × 17″ (inside dimensions). Paint has to be placed at one end, and at the other end room has to be left for the squeegee to follow through on its run.

The time spent in constructing the screen frame accurately is well worth while, for this is the basic tool. The simplest form of construction is to cut some straight white pine furring strips, nail them together and reinforce the joints with angle irons on top. Another method is to make an interlocking type of frame with a half-lap joint; or the joints can be put together with a mitered or picture frame corner, but this requires use of a miter box. Always use angle irons for reinforcement.

The most professional means of joining the strips is with a tongue-in-groove type of frame corner which is a stronger method of joining.

The finished frame, properly joined and right-angled, should be sandpapered smooth to remove any splinters or rough edges. Coat the frame with shellac or lacquer to prevent warping and to act as a sizing to keep paint from penetrating the wood.

A number of different kinds of fabric can be used for the screen, but the best is #12 mesh silk, which is medium fine and is good for all work. For finer work a #14, #16, or #20 mesh silk may be used. The higher the number, the finer the mesh and the sharper

STRETCHING: Next, tack the short side (Step 3, above), starting again in the middle. The wrinkles at the end will come out when you tack the last side (Step 4, right).

the print, but also the harder to keep from clogging. Nylon and wire mesh are also usable. In the beginning, you might use a fine mesh cotton, which does not hold its stretch so well on large screens, but this will not matter.

The next step is to stretch the silk or cotton on to the frame. First, place the frame on your worktable and center the cloth over the frame. Drive a carpet tack into each corner to hold the cloth temporarily in place. Then stretch one long side at a time. Grip the cloth firmly and pull it taut towards you. Starting in the middle, insert tacks about 1 inch apart all along the side, radiating out from the middle. Then start at the center of the opposite side, and do the same. Finally stretch the short sides the same way and insert tacks. If properly stretched, the last side should take up any wrinkles, leaving the screen firm and taut. Just one word of advice: be sure that the heads of the tacks sink flush with the wood.

Now trim off any excess cloth, and cover the four rows of tacks with brown gummed paper.

Fold strips of gummed paper lengthwise,

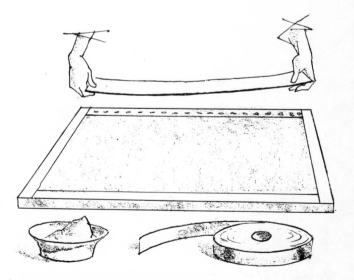

COVERING THE TACKS: Use gummed tape. Seal the edges of the basin side the same way.

gum side out. Turn the frame so the basin side is up, and seal the four inside edges of the frame by pasting the paper strips on so that one half glues to the cloth and one half to the wood. Use as much gummed paper as necessary. The overlap on the cloth will not matter as you don't use every inch of the frame. Shellac or lacquer the frame to prevent the paint from oozing into the wood, and spreading on to your work that way.

Besides the frame for the screen, you need a flat board that is absolutely level and larger than the frame, for a printing bed. Any flat board that will not warp easily can be used—an old drawing board or artist's table top, or a piece of ¾-inch plywood—but get it clean and smooth. Sandpaper the board carefully because any bump can ruin a print, particularly if the printing is to be done on thin paper. Preferably, cover the board with ⅛-inch hardboard, or a piece of formica. You will also need some 2-inch high blocks of wood.

Use three guides or gauge pins to control registration. These can be made of paper, cardboard, fiberboard, celluloid or metal. Register guides should be equal in thickness

to or slightly thinner than the paper to be printed, as otherwise they will cause ridges on the screen and interfere with the printing.

Place the guides only after much thought and experimentation. They will determine where you place your "copy" (artwork) in making the stencil, they will guide your frame placement, and later your printing paper. Place two guides on the long side of the board and one at the short end. The guides may be nailed to the base, but this will ruin the board, so it is recommended that unless metal guides are used, the guides be fixed to the base with water-soluble glue or rubber cement. Using colored guides is also helpful.

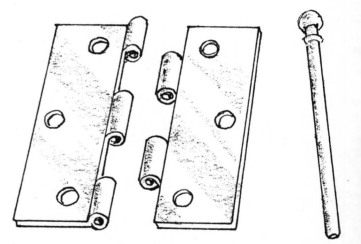

PUSHPIN HINGES: Since you will be lifting your frame off continually, it is best to have hinges like this, which come apart when the pin is removed, but are tight-fitting when hinged together.

Two sets of hinges are needed for the frame. Use pushpin hinges which are held together by a sturdy shaft or pin that can be pulled out to release the frame. For a start, 2½-inch or 3-inch pushpin hinges should be all right. Attach the hinges by first centering the frame, silk side down, on the base. Use ¾-inch flat-head screws to fasten the hinges, placing one male and one female hinge at each end of the long side of the frame and the mates of these hinges at the same point on the base. This type of construction permits the frame to be raised

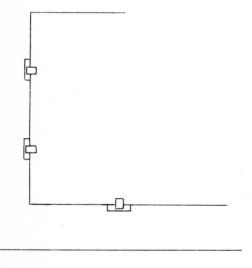

GUIDES: To be sure your artwork prints in the same position each time, you need these gauge pins set up this way, to hold the paper as you slide it into place.

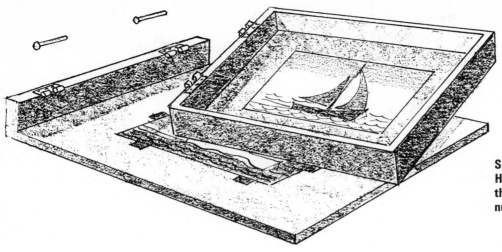

SET-UP WITH UNIVERSAL HINGE: If you make a base like this, you can use it for any number of screens.

and lowered like a horizontal door always falling back into exactly the same position.

Place the pushpin hinges on the base at a point which will permit you to use the same hinges with any size screen. When putting a hinge half on a screen, line it up with the hinge half on the base. By placing the hinges the same distance apart and in the exact same position on all frames, any frame can be used on the same printing bed without shifting hinges. The base thus becomes the master printing bed for any number of frames. It is wise also to check the screws occasionally to see that they have not been loosened or else you will not get accurate registration with your multi-colored prints.

One last attachment is needed on the frame —a device to hold up the screen. The simplest method is to attach an arm or drop stick to one side of the frame. The stick, about 1 foot long, should drop by its own weight to a perpendicular position when the frame is raised. A door spring or old metal support used to prop up the lid of a phonograph can be used instead. Such folding metal supports are available at hardware stores.

The other required tool is a squeegee. This rubber blade tool is used to push the paint through the mesh screen and deposit it on the paper, textile or other stock to be printed. One run of the squeegee will scrape paint from one side of the screen to another, each run resulting in an impression.

There are two types of squeegees: the grip handle type or one-handed squeegee, and the two-handed squeegee. Either type works well. The important consideration for the squeegee is size. For a 6″ × 9″ print, with a screen of 9″ × 17″, an 8-inch squeegee should be used. This permits a play of $\frac{1}{2}$ inch on either side. (See next page.)

DROP STICK: The arm will hold up your screen frame (even with the squeegee in it) while you are working on the press bed or table top below it. Here the hinges were mounted flat on the bed.

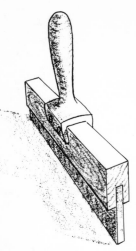

SQUEEGEES: The one-hand kind (left) is easier for small screens, and is best for experienced printers. The two-handed (right) is necessary with large screens and a great deal of paint. (Below, right) The proper method of running the squeegee. Pull towards you at a very slight angle.

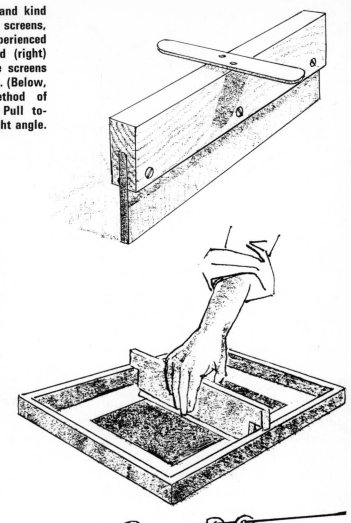

Buy a good hard rubber squeegee to start with. Later, after practicing with the screen process, you may wish to make your own squeegees. If the rubber dulls after much use, sharpen it by stroking the blade over a long sandpaper board or abrasive garnet cloth. Be sure to keep your squeegee sharp and square at the point where it comes into contact with the screen. The squeegee should be carefully cleaned after each printing, for paint left on a squeegee will rot the rubber.

Drying time for prints will vary with the type of paint used, the paper, and the climate. Small editions can be dried easily by clipping each individual print to a strong wire line with paper clips or clothespins.

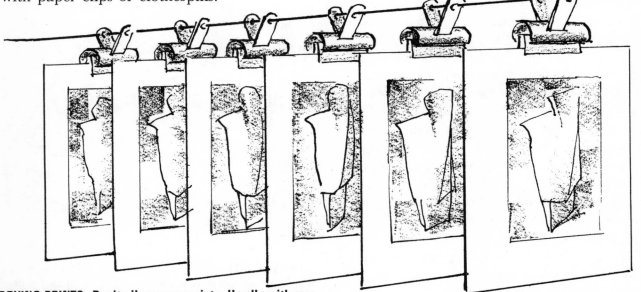

DRYING PRINTS: Don't pile up your prints. Handle with care until they dry.

Making the Stencil

There are five methods of making a stencil: with paper, block-out, tusche, film, and by photographic methods. A beginner might find the paper stencil least troublesome to make right.

The Paper Stencil: For printing a simple bold design this type of stencil is all right. You will need stencil paper, a stencil knife, a sharpening stone, and cellophane tape.

Step 1. Raise the screen frame up on its arm and place the drawing or whatever you are going to copy on the wooden base, pushing it up against your register guides. If the guides do not allow your drawing to be properly centered, move the guides. Let the frame down to be sure you have the drawing where you want it in relation to the frame.

Step 2. Cut a sheet of stencil paper to cover the area of the drawing with some overlap. To make sure it is not too large, test by lowering the screen. Now lift the screen up and off its hinges. With the stencil paper directly over the drawing, tape the corners down securely.

Step 3. Trace cut the design with your stencil knife, but don't remove the areas to be stripped out yet. Use an X-acto knife or single-edge razor blade in a holder. Hold the blade perpendicularly and do not press down too heavily, just enough to cut through the paper without digging into the original.

Step 4. Remove the tape from the corners of the stencil but do not move the stencil. Replace the screen on its hinges and lower it over the stencil. Put paint in the screen at one end and spread it evenly with the squeegee. This will make the stencil paper stick to the underside of the screen. Now lift the screen and the stencil paper will come up with it. Tape the overlapping edges of the paper stencil to the sides of the frame.

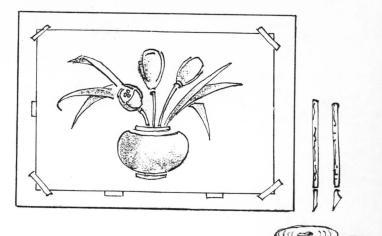

DRAWING READY for stencil cutting is taped down on the base, up against the register guides.

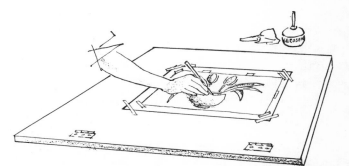

CUTTING A PAPER STENCIL: Don't start until you have the stencil paper taped down directly over the drawing in a good position for screening later.

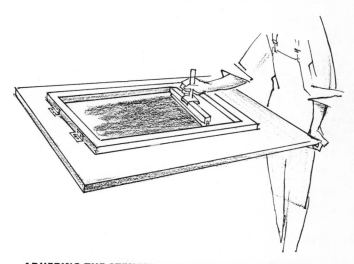

ADHERING THE STENCIL to the underneath side of the screen is achieved by use of paint and squeegee in this fashion. When the stencil is lifted up with the screen, tape it firmly to the edges of the frame.

SCREEN PROCESS PRINTING ■ 385

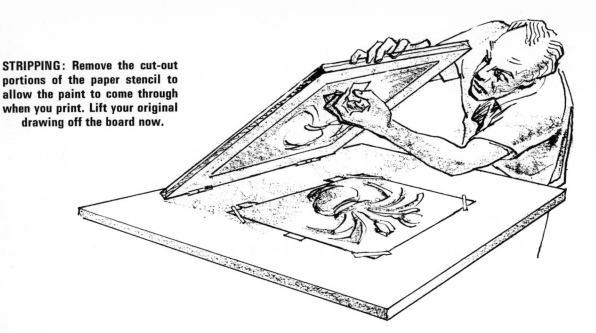

STRIPPING: Remove the cut-out portions of the paper stencil to allow the paint to come through when you print. Lift your original drawing off the board now.

Step 5. Strip away the parts of the stencil that have been cut free. This will open up areas where the paint will now come through. These will be the areas that you want to print.

Step 6. Remove your original drawing from the board and put down a sheet of waste newsprint on the base in its place. Lower the screen and, with the squeegee, move the paint from one end of the frame to the other end, spreading it evenly. The paint coming through the cut-away areas of the stencil and the silk should give you a rough impression or "proof" of what you will print. You have now "made ready" and are ready for printing.

The paper stencil allows a heavy layer of paint to come through, which should last for several hundred impressions. With a paper stencil, you can use printer's ink or any paint except tempera or watercolor, as water-based paints will wrinkle the paper and make sharp printing impossible.

Printing

First you must decide what you want to print on. The easiest is a fairly smooth, stiff paper. However, at the start, you might want to use cardboard or even cloth. The problem with a textile is getting it into the guides for good register. In any event you will use paper for your first prints. Once you have your stencil ready, your paint mixed, and the paper in place in the guides, you are ready to print.

Check to see that the screen hinges are tight, the guides fastened firmly and accurately, the squeegee well sharpened. The squeegee to be used should be at least 1 inch larger than the width of the design to be printed. If it is smaller, two scrapes will be needed to cover the area and a streak will show where these overlap. On your first attempt at silk screen printing, just put a few spoonfuls of paint at one end of the screen and see how many impressions you get from that amount. If you can control more paint, pour in a greater quantity the next time you refill the screen.

On the actual run, place the paint at one (end) side of the screen. Place the squeegee in the paint on the screen. Hold the squeegee firmly and pass it once from end to end. Hold the squeegee at a slight angle, tipping it slightly in the direction of the stroke. Lift the screen up on its arm, peel off the paper, and examine your first impression. It will probably be uneven. Next time you run the squeegee down the length of the screen, make it smoother.

After each print, raise the screen, propping it on its arm, remove the print and insert another sheet. You will soon get the knack of screening.

On your first few prints, keep them simple and single-colored. As you soon become more proficient in the technique, you can experiment with multi-colored prints.

After printing, to remove the stencil, simply raise the screen and peel the stencil off. Then wash the screen with a solvent compatible to the type of paint used.

You might prefer another type of stencil for finer or more detailed work. These are your alternatives:

The Block-Out Stencil: This method simply calls for blocking or masking out portions of the screen with a liquid, such as glue, shellac or lacquer, leaving the cloth untouched where the paint is to go through. When printing with tempera or watercolors, use lacquer or shellac as the stop-out medium. Use glue with oil-based paints.

There are two methods for making a block-out stencil. The first is to brush in the glue, lacquer, or shellac directly on the screen. The second method calls for first sizing the silk or cotton.

PINHOLES left in the blocked-out areas will allow paint to come through. Check in front of a strong light and fill in the holes with glue.

Working on unsized silk:

Step 1. Raise the screen and center the original art on the base, using your register guides.

Step 2. Lower the screen and check to be sure the original is entirely visible through the silk. Now trace the drawing with pencil or pen and ink on to the silk.

Step 3. Prop up the screen, remove the original, and lower the screen again on to a few sheets of newsprint. Brush the stop-out medium on the parts which are to stop out

BLOCK-OUT (Method 1): On unsized silk, using a brush and glue as a stop-out, trace or paint right on the silk the areas you want not to print. The open areas (those you leave) will print.

the paint, painting around the design, or in certain areas inside it. Allow the stop-out medium to dry. Glue will dry within an hour, lacquer will dry within 15 minutes, and shellac generally dries within a half hour. When dry, hold up the screen against the light. If there are any pinholes, stop out these leaks. You are now ready for makeready and printing.

After printing, if you have used glue, all you need to dissolve the coating is water. Use warm or cold water on both the top and bottom sides of the silk. Be sure to dry the screen thoroughly before storing. For lacquer, use lacquer thinner. For shellac, use shellac thinner (denatured alcohol).

A sized screen is used only for lacquer or shellac stencils. For the sizing, use glue diluted in water, 1 part glue to 3 parts water.

Step 1. Disengage the screen and place it on top of some waste newsprint on a flat table, with the screen basin up. Then pour a little of the diluted glue along one bank of the screen. Using a piece of stiff cardboard, scrape the glue mixture over the screen. Smooth the glue across the screen several times to cover the entire silk surface with an even coating. Let dry.

Step 2. Follow the same procedures as before in setting up the drawing to be copied on the board. Push it up against the guides.

Step 3. After the sizing is dry, hinge the screen and lower it over the design. The sizing will not affect the transparency of the silk and the drawing will be clearly seen through the sized screen. With lacquer or shellac, trace paint the design with a brush directly on the sized silk. Again, paint only the areas you want *not* to print.

Check the silk to detect any pinholes and touch up any leaks. Let the lacquer or shellac dry.

Step 4. Disengage the screen and prop it up on your two blocks of wood so that the silk surface does not touch anything. After making sure that the lacquer is dry, dissolve the glue sizing by washing it off with water. Use a wet sponge on *top* of the silk. The water will not affect the lacquer or shellac but it will quickly dissolve the exposed glue. Take great care not to tip the screen or flood water into other areas.

Step 5. Dry the screen, using a cloth pad to wipe out all traces of melted sizing, but do not touch the underside of the screen. Rehinge the screen and you are ready for printing.

A sized screen will last for large editions of prints and may be preserved for later use. To dissolve a sized stencil, rub both sides of the screen with a water-laden sponge. This will dissolve the glue sizing and lift off the lacquer or shellac.

SIZING THE SILK for Block-Out Method 2: Using 3 parts water to 1 part glue, put the mixture on the basin a little at a time and use the squeegee to spread it.

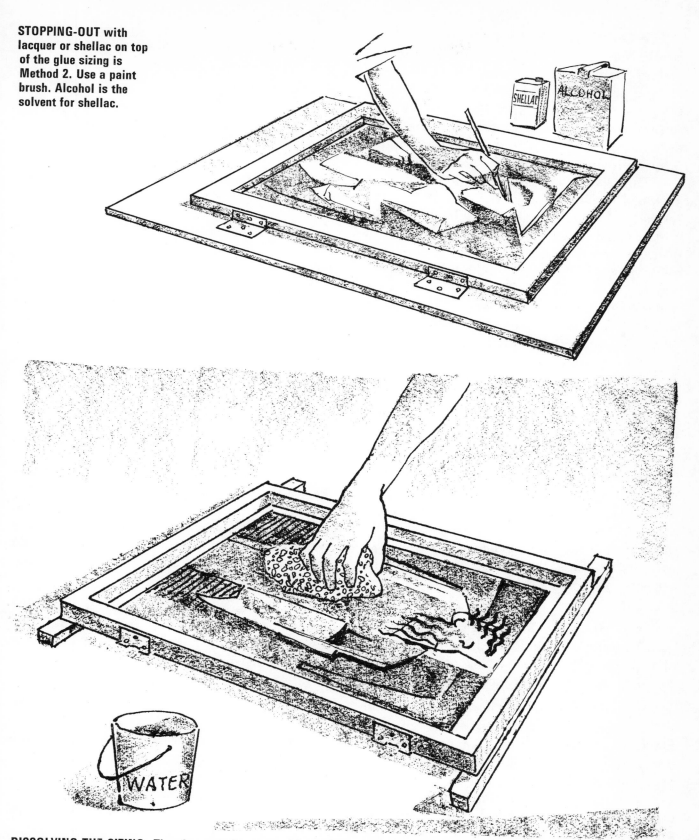

STOPPING-OUT with lacquer or shellac on top of the glue sizing is Method 2. Use a paint brush. Alcohol is the solvent for shellac.

DISSOLVING THE SIZING: The glue must be removed from the silk after the design has been painted with lacquer or shellac. Water and sponge will do the job.

The Tusche and Litho Stencil: This is by far the most practical and adaptable method for producing fine art prints. Tusche is an opaque paint that contains wax and works on the principle of chemical resistance of a greasy substance to water and glue. When you paint an area of the silk screen with tusche and draw on it with a litho grease pencil, then coat the whole screen with glue, the painted-in area acts as a stop-out against the glue. When the tusche and grease are later dissolved, the glue that covered the art breaks away, leaving an open area on the silk through which the paint easily passes. With the tusche-litho method, you have the same freedom as if you were making an original drawing. Each tusche stroke on the silk is a latent paint stroke in the print. You can make solids with the tusche and shaded areas with the pencil.

The tusche stencil may be prepared either on a raw silk or on a sized silk screen. You need the lithographic tusche, a lithographic pencil or crayon, a brush, glue, and kerosene to dissolve the tusche.

Step 1. Raise the screen, center the original art in the guides. Lower the screen and make an exact tusche facsimile of the drawing as seen through the screen. Any mistakes can be touched up with litho pencil, or washed out with water while the tusche is wet, or with kerosene once it has dried.

Step 2. Disengage the screen and prop it up on your two blocks. Now glue in the screen by pouring some glue along one bank of the screen and scraping the glue across with a sharp-edged cardboard. Allow the glue to dry.

Step 3. Dissolve the tusche by rubbing both sides of the silk thoroughly with a kerosene-soaked rag, concentrating mainly on the underside of the silk in the tusched areas. When no black appears on the rag, all the tusche in the area has been dissolved. Wipe up the kerosene, and dry the stencil. Check it to see that all the tusched areas are washed out, that glue has blocked out the rest of the screen

MATERIALS for tusche and litho method: jar of opaque and a simple grease pencil and litho crayon.

and that there are no pinholes left. Touch up with a brush and glue any areas that need it, replace the screen in the hinges, and you are now ready to print.

Prints made this way are noted for a softness that comes from mesh marks of the silk along the edges. The stencil, once cleaned, can be stored for future use, or it can be cleared for a new stencil. Use cold or warm water on both sides of the silk to dissolve the stencil and plenty of clean rags or sponges.

A sharper image can be obtained by making a tusche stencil on a sized silk screen. A sized screen provides a smoother surface and therefore is better for making prints which require a fine line, crosshatching or other intricate detail. In this case, use a sizing of ordinary household cornstarch diluted in warm or cold water, a heaping tablespoon to a glass of water.

Step 1. This is the same as for all the other methods. Raise the screen and set down the original in the guides as before. Lower the screen and make a key tracing in pencil or pen and ink directly on the silk.

Step 2. Remove the screen and prop it up on blocks so that it is not in contact with the table, and size the screen. Use a sponge dipped into the starch solution, passing it across the silk several times to deposit as smooth a coat as possible. If the drawing has been pencilled in, place the sizing only on the underside of the silk screen. Allow the starch sizing to dry thoroughly and then replace the screen on the hinges.

Step 3. Tusche in the design, applying it as before. Then unhinge the screen, apply glue to the screen, allow the glue to dry, and then dissolve the tusche as before.

Step 4. Dry and check the stencil, replace the screen on its hinges and you are ready to print. For sharp prints, use a #14, #16 or #20 mesh silk screen.

To dissolve the tusche-glue stencil use water. To dissolve a tusche-lacquer stencil use lacquer thinner.

Film Stencil: This method of preparing the stencil is recommended whenever precision and sharp line are required. The film stencil is made from a double-layered stopping-out film; the design is cut and stripped out of the top layer and the rest of the film is adhered to the silk. Finally the undercoating is peeled off and this leaves the silk exposed in the shape of the design. All you require are sheets of lacquer stencil film, adhering thinner appropriate to the particular film, removing thinner, a film stencil knife, some soft absorbent lint-free rags, clear fill-in lacquer and an adjustable lamp needed for close work.

Step 1. Raise the screen, place the original on the base in your guides as before.

Step 2. Unhinge the screen, cut a sheet of film with its backing sheet larger than the area to be printed and center the film over the original art, lacquer side up. Fasten the film down with masking tape. Trace the design, cutting the film surface without penetrating the glassine backing. When cutting film, remember that it takes four cuts to make a line regardless of its width. Next strip the film by sliding the knife under a corner of a cut section and pulling it off. Check your film and brush off any stray particles of film or dust. Remove the tape and replace the screen.

Step 3. Adhere the film stencil to the screen by taking a soft cloth pad, saturating it with adhering thinner and rubbing it along a small portion of the silk once or twice. Repeat with a dry rag right away. It takes only a little thinner to make the film adhere.

Step 4. Raise the screen. The film will have to come up with it. Allow this to dry and set, and then strip off the backing sheet. Stop out the surrounding area (if any) by filling in lacquer over the silk around the film. (See next page.)

Step 5. The film stencil is practically imperishable and can be used over and over again. It can be used with any type of paint, except lacquer.

To dissolve the film stencil, spread several layers of newspaper on the printing base. Saturate the newspaper with removing thinner

FILM STENCIL: This is a double-layer stencil. After the design has been cut, the stencil has to be adhered to the silk. It is done (left) with adhering thinner. One hand holds the saturated cloth, the other a dry rag. A little thinner is enough.

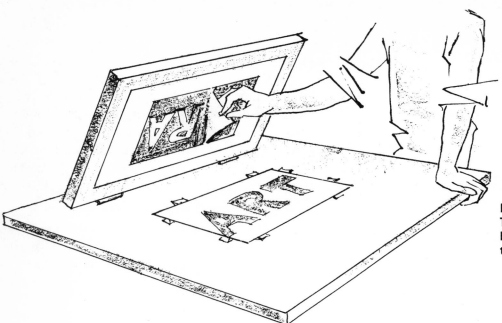

and lower the screen. Spread some saturated newspaper on top of the silk. The film should come off, but if not, use a rag soaked in thinner to remove stubborn parts. Dry immediately, wiping away any traces of lacquer thinner.

Commercial screens are made by photographic methods but these are too complicated for the studio craftsman.

Color Printing

You will need a screen for each color. If your original art is in full color, you will need to trace only the red parts for your red screen, blue parts for blue, etc. For green, you would trace the area in both yellow and blue. Where multi-color prints are planned, it is vital that each screen be in perfect register. Print the first color (usually the lightest color—yellow—first) right through the entire edition. When this is dry, print the second color (usually red or blue), and so forth. Where transparent process colors are involved (such as green made from yellow and blue), you will get a paint build-up, so be sure that the paint below is dry before you overprint.

On rare occasions, a single stencil may be used to print two or more distinct colors, but this occurs only when the colors in the art are well separated from one another and the screen can be partitioned off to print the separate colors simultaneously.

The trick to multi-color registration lies in the register guide system used to synchronize any number of colors to form a perfectly registered print with as many colors as the original. The first step is to place the register guides accurately on the printing bed, as previously described. Next draw fine cross-lines on each of the four sides in the margin of the original, as in this illustration.

Duplicate these cross-marks in the exact same place as you lay down each stencil for each color. The marks will seem to be part of the design. In a perfectly registered print, the marks for the last color in the series will fall directly over all the previous cross-marks. This is the professional way of checking the registration.

It is also a good idea to proof a color printing before making the actual run. List the order in which the colors are to be run, and pull a proof of each color so that it becomes a record

WITH THE FILM STENCIL you must stop out any clear area around the film with lacquer on a pad.

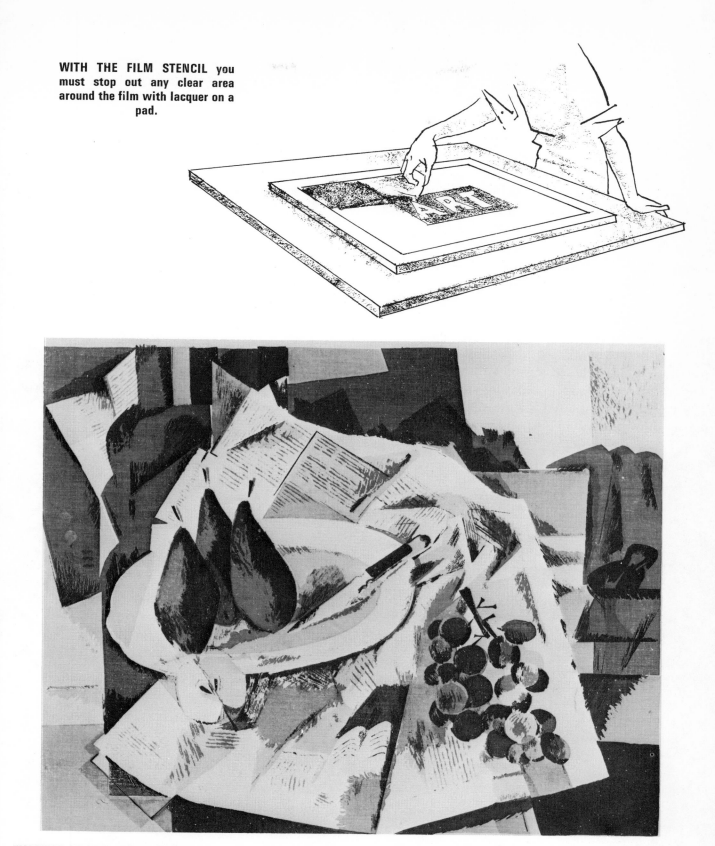

EXAMPLE OF SILK SCREEN PRINTING: "Still Life of Fruit in Shades of Grey," made with a paper stencil. From the book "Screen Printing" by Heinrich Birkner.

of the color separations. When you are satisfied with the colors and overlapping, then make your run.

Another method of helping to get good registration is to allow a small leeway for overlapping colors. Extend the area of the first color into the second just a hair's-breadth to compensate for any possible discrepancies in registration during the printing. With opaque colors there will be little if any indication of the overprinting. With transparent colors the over-print area will form a third color or gradation of color. Where an additional tone is not wanted, no overlap should be made.

While the silk screen process is suited to reproduce flat colors, some blending and shading is possible by cross-hatching.

Silk screen can use almost any type of paint and today the craftsman has opaque and transparent inks available that have been specially formulated for the silk screen process, besides process oil and watercolor paints.

Process oil colors must be thinned before being used as they are too heavy as they come from the can. Varnish makes the best thinner. To make an opaque color transparent, mix it with a clear transparent base.

Process tempera or gouache paints may be thinned with plain water, eliminating the need for expensive varnishes and solvents. Process tempera paints are naturally transparent; only white and black tempera paints are opaque. The use of such paints is limited to stencils where glue is not a stopping-out medium, and are mainly used for simulating watercolor paintings.

Enamels, dyes, lacquers, and other paints are available also, but these are not recommended for the novice. There are even fluorescent paints specially formulated for screen process work which provide luminosity far exceeding ordinary paints. Whatever type of paints you use, cover them well when not in use.

WOOD BLOCKS
CUTTING, ENGRAVING AND PRINTING
(including Linoleum Blocks)

Although the woodcut, the wood engraving, and the linoleum block differ from each other in important ways, they are all printed in the same manner, called "relief printing." This makes it possible to consider them all in the same general category.

Every block consists of two types of area—the "deeps," or areas that are cut away, and the "reliefs," or areas left standing on the original face of the block, which collectively form the printing surface.

The earliest printing from wood blocks was done in China in the 9th century A.D. By the 15th century, the art of the woodcut was being vigorously practiced in the Western world.

The first printed books were called "block books," because each page, both illustration and type, was carved completely from a single plank of wood. To make a book, a number of such blocks were cut and printed, and the prints were gathered and bound. In the same way, woodcuts were printed, often in color, on thin cardboard in the manufacture of playing cards.

Later, the woodcut was used only for illustration, the type being set separately much as it is today. Albrecht Dürer, the German artist, was one of the most prolific practitioners of the woodcut, though it is doubtful that he ever cut a block himself. It was customary in his time for the artist only to draw the subject on the block, which was then cut by a block-cutter, who was not an artist but a member of the local carpenters' guild.

The woodcut was finally replaced by the engraving and the etching, and fell into disuse.

EARLY WOODCUT: Working in the 16th century, Albrecht Dürer made many large blocks like the one from which this is a detail.

(From "The Complete Woodcuts of Albrecht Dürer" by Dr. Willi Kurth, courtesy Dover Publications, Inc.)

Written especially for this volume by Manly Banister

WOOD ENGRAVING: Cut into the end-grain of a wood board, this well-known engraving by Rockwell Kent, entitled "Big Baby," is just slightly larger (6 x 4½) in the original.

(From "Woodcuts" by John Biggs, courtesy Blandford Press)

In the 18th century, the use of wood for printing illustrations received a new start with the development of the wood engraving to a high state of perfection by Thomas Bewick, the English printmaker. Until relatively few years ago, the wood engraving was still used for illustrating catalogues.

The wood engraving is not to be confused with the woodcut, for these are two entirely different things. Whereas the woodcut is gouged from the flat side of a board, the wood engraving is engraved in the end-grain, using burins and other engraving tools, similar to the manner in which a copper engraving is made. There, however, all similarity to copper ceases, for the wood engraving can only be printed by the relief method, while the copper or other metal engraving (as well as the etching) is printed by a process known as "intaglio printing," on a press made especially for that purpose.

The wood engraving was developed in order to produce prints more cheaply—prints could compete in fineness of line and profusion of detail with the engraving from metal. This meant that engraving tools, not gouges and knives, had to be used. Such tools will not work in plankwood, as they only tear up the grain instead of cutting it.

Since only wood of the highest quality can be used, the engraving block is consequently small, and wood engravings themselves are generally made quite small compared to the woodcut. Larger blocks can be made by glueing smaller ones edge to edge. The rarity of suitable wood and the difficulty of preparing it for the market make the engraving block somewhat expensive.

The linoleum block, from which many exhibition prints are made today, is a wholly modern development. It came into being long after the original invention of linoleum, a composition of hardened linseed oil, ground cork and other things, named and first patented by the Englishman, Frederick Walton, in 1836.

Many myths still cling to the use of linoleum for printing such as: it crumbles easily; not many prints can be made from a block; it is useless for cutting fine detail; and so on. If such allegations were ever true, they no longer are. Modern linoleum is the result of over a century and a quarter of research and development in the field of floor coverings. You can count on making from your linoleum block many times over the number of prints you are likely to want from it.

Tools and Materials for the Woodcut

Almost any kind of wood can be used to make a woodcut, though some kinds are more suited to the purpose than others. Even boards having knots or a surface that is splintered and weatherbeaten can be used for special effects.

Generally, though, a smooth-surfaced board with grain that is not too prominent should be chosen. Fruitwoods such as pear, apple, cherry, and so on, are often preferred, not only for the smooth, textureless surface they provide, but also for their durability in printing, as all are hardwoods. Oak, mahogany and maple are also used, though these are often too hard and, in the case of oak and mahogany, complicate the design with an open grain that shows up in the printing.

For the beginner as well as the old hand, white pine makes an excellent woodcut. It cuts easily without splintering. Also, it is available in a thickness called 5/4 (five-quarter), which means that it is $1\frac{1}{4}$ inches thick before being planed, after which it is $1\frac{1}{8}$ inch. It is available in widths up to 18 inches. The extra thickness of the plank helps to deter warping, a problem that can be serious when using a screw-type printing press. (Blocks of such thickness cannot be printed on standard printing presses, which accept blocks only type high; i.e., 0.9186-inch thick).

A choice of plywoods can also be bent to the block-cutter's use. Fir plywood makes a good background block (to be described later on), particularly if it has an interesting grain which has been heightened by scrubbing it with a wire brush. In cutting, it tends to splinter, however. Plywood surfaced with either birch or maple veneer cuts very nicely—a slight open grain of the birch is noticeable in the print. All plywood should be used in the $\frac{3}{4}$-inch thickness.

LINOCUT: A wholly different look is obtained from a lino-block print. This is "Sunflower" by Manly Banister.
(From the book, "Prints from Linoblocks and Woodcuts" by Manly Banister.)

PREPARING WOODBLOCK to receive design by sanding.

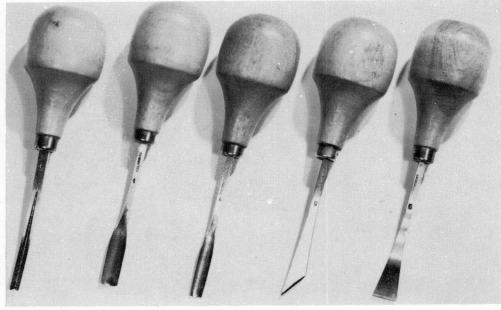

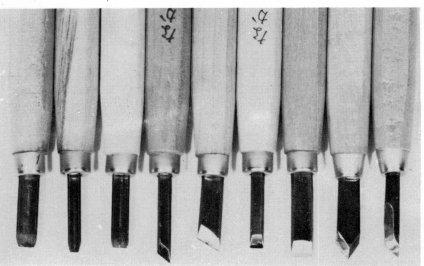

WOODCUTTING TOOLS: The American V-cutters, knives and gouges (above) are ruggedly built.

SPECIAL WOODCUT KNIFE, shown full size, is for top cutting efficiency.

JAPANESE WOODCUT TOOLS (left): Blades differ from Western design, allowing wide range of effects. Inexpensive, they are of good quality steel.

Two manufacturers make sets of tools for the woodcut, and these can be bought at art supply or hardware stores. Knives, gouges and V-cutters can also be purchased separately, in various sizes, from some mail order houses specializing in woodworking tools. Also on the market are sets of Japanese woodcutting tools which are very good.

A set of woodcut tools may consist of an angled blade for use as a knife, two or more sizes of round-bottomed gouge, a V-cutter or two, and a curved chisel for smoothing the bottoms of the gouged areas. For heavy cutting, the Japanese-style knife is excellent. More readily available and also good is the Stanley utility knife, at hardware stores, which is used with the replaceable, heavy-duty blade.

Both V-cutters and gouges are used by pushing the tool away from you. Therefore, you need a benchhook, or a board clamped to your worktable with a C-clamp, against which the block can be held to absorb the thrust of the tool.

The V-cutter cuts with one stroke a thin line that prints white in an area that elsewhere prints black. The gouge is used to clean out excess wood from the broad, white-printing (negative) areas.

A dull tool may slip and cut your free hand if you are not careful how you hold the block, so keep your tools sharp. Sharp tools also produce a better job. Buy an India stone for general sharpening, a hard Arkansas stone for honing to a keen edge, and a slip stone with round edges for removing burr from the hollow lips of gouges.

If the blade is very dull, start with the coarse side of the India stone. Use plenty of oil—any household oil. Hold the tool with the bevel flat upon the stone, press down firmly and rub it back and forth. Turn the blade over and grind for a while on the opposite edge, if the blade has two bevels. If it has only one, grind only the beveled edge. When the bevels are bright looking and you can feel a coarse "wire edge" by carefully touching it with the tip of your finger, turn the stone over and repeat the process on the fine side.

Having achieved the finest possible edge, turn next to the Arkansas stone, which is a hard, dense, translucent white stone that rapidly hones the edge to polished smoothness, removing the wire-edge burr in the process. Oil is also used with the Arkansas stone.

When sharpening the V-cutter, hold the

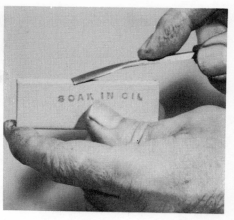

SLIP STONE: Use this for removing burr from inside curve of gouge by rubbing on rounded edge.

bevel on the side of the V flat against the stone and sharpen as described above. Count the strokes to make sure both sides of the V receive equal wear, as a lop-sided V-cutter is worthless until it has been completely reground.

The bevel of the gouge is on the bottom, or outside, of the curve. This provides a little difficulty in sharpening, as the tool must also be rolled from side to side as it is rubbed on the stone, to ensure sharpening of the entire curve. The round-edged slip stone is given a few strokes against the inside of the curve to remove the resulting burr.

Making the Woodcut

As in all printing procedures, you must put your drawing down on the block backwards to the way it will look in the print. In other words, the design, picture or image is reversed as if being seen in a mirror.

You may, if you wish, make a complete drawing, with shading and all the rest of it, then make a soft-pencil tracing of this on parchment tracing paper. Or, you may make a somewhat more sketchy drawing directly on the tracing paper with a soft, graphite pencil. Your third, and not highly recommended, alternative is to make your original drawing directly upon the block itself.

To transfer a drawing, tape the tracing paper face-down to the block and go over every line, visible through the back, with a used-up ballpoint pen. Don't bear down hard enough to indent the wood, as this will show up in the

TRANSFER your drawing to the block by taping it face down and tracing with a stylus.

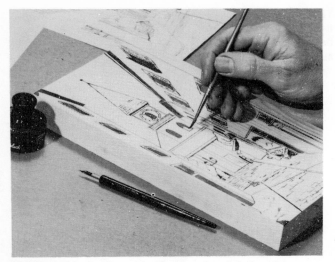

DRAW on block after transferring, then ink in with pen or brush.

print. Check the transfer from time to time as you go along by lifting a corner of the paper, holding the remainder firmly so that it does not shift on the block. When you have transferred the entire drawing, without missing any lines, strip off the tracing paper and spray the block with prepared fixative, or brush it with shellac diluted with twice its quantity of shellac thinner. The shellac prevents the India ink from bleeding into the wood as you next go over every line with a pen and fill in with ink and a brush all the areas that are intended to print black.

All you have to do now is cut away all the white spaces in your (mirror) image on the block, leaving all the lines and ink-covered areas to be printed.

The first step is to isolate every printing line and area with V-cuts. Never use a V-cutter or gouge to cut along a line or to outline a printing area. Always use a knife for this work.

Start anywhere in the design. Hold the knife as if it were a dagger, with your thumb on top of the handle, and stab it into the wood beside the line and angling away from it at about 45 degrees. This leaves support under the line in much the same way that a highway fill slopes away from the road surface. With the cutting edge of the blade facing towards you, draw the knife slowly and carefully towards yourself, holding the block with your free hand to prevent it from moving. You will discover that the knife cuts more easily and accurately when moving with the grain than across it. For making very light cuts, you may hold the knife as if it were a pencil and thus achieve closer control.

Cut the full length of whatever individual line you have chosen, then turn the block completely around and repeat the cut in the opposite direction, in the negative space beside the first cut and a brief distance removed from it. Angle the blade again so that the second cut contacts the first below the surface. This stroke completes the V-cut and the waste wood is immediately removed.

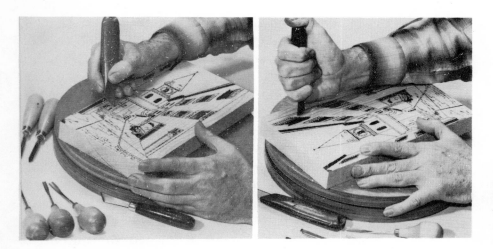

KNIFE HOLDS: When cutting fine detail, hold knife as you would a pen, and allow your fingers to work the point. When cutting long, straight or curving lines, use a dagger grip and pull the blade towards you.

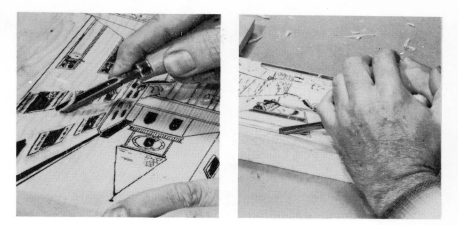

GOUGE with a thrusting movement away from you. Use two hands on the V-cutter for best control.

Treat both sides of every line and the perimeter of every printing area in this same way. Make sure always that the knife angles *away* from the line it is following, as an undercut line will quickly break down in printing.

When you have all lines and areas thus isolated, start removing the excess wood from the negative spaces with one or another of the gouges. The wider the negative space, the deeper it must be gouged to avoid getting ink into the bottoms and subsequently having a trace of them appear upon the print.

If you want to put some white lines into a black-printing area, or to make ragged edges (such as simulating clumps of grass), use the V-cutter. Criss-crossed V-cutter lines also serve to create tones and texture in the print.

Your finished woodcut shows the mirror-image of your drawing in relief and is very much a work of art in itself, without consideration of the prints to be made from it.

Suppose, however, that you have made a mistake and have cut away a line that should have been left standing? How do you replace it? It isn't easy, so first determine whether the drawing can do without that line. If it can, fine. Forget it. If not, and the error is small, you may fill the space with plastic wood. Since this material shrinks on drying, fill to well above the surface. When it is dry, sand it even with the block face. Undercut lines and small voids may also be filled with plastic wood. Unless you are a skilled woodworker who possesses a router and knows how to use

it, big mistakes are practically impossible to repair. The whole area must be routed out to an equal depth then re-filled by glueing in a piece of wood.

Textures

You may wish to produce a texture in some area of your print . . . or to use the grain of the wood in some interesting fashion, as for clouds in a sky or waves on a sea. Such textures and effects are generally achieved by wearing or abrading the wood in some manner to give it a roughened surface.

A file card (a kind of brush having short,

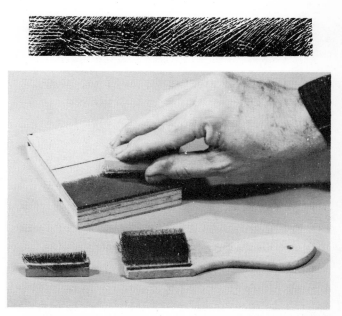

FILE CARD: This brush, when scrubbed on the surface, gives you the effect shown above.

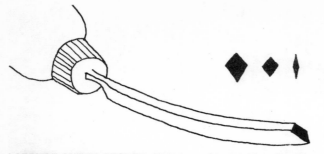

LOZENGE-SHAPE GRAVER: This cuts deep, makes fine lines. Point is bevelled to 30° angle. The heavier the graver, the wider the line it cuts.

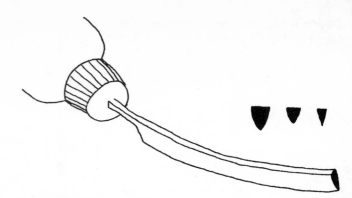

SPITSTICK (elliptic engraver or tint tool): For outlining, and easy turning in the wood. Twelve sizes are available.

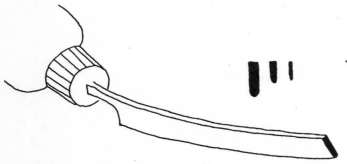

ROUND SCORPER OR GOUGE: This comes in numerous sizes. For gouging out wide lines or scooping broad negative spaces.

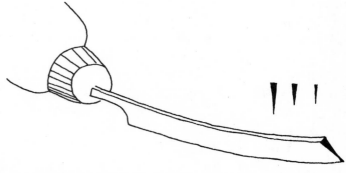

ANGLE TINT TOOL: This comes numbered in sizes from 1 to 12 for cutting areas of fine lines one beside the other to make tones, or tints, in the print.

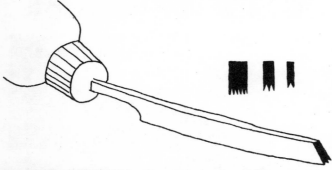

MULTIPLE LINING TOOL: Many sizes are available, designed to cut two to twelve lines at once, for quickly cross-hatching tones or laying adjacent lines for tints.

SQUARE SCORPER, or flat graver: Also comes in numerous sizes. For planing bottoms, making wide lines and textures.

ENGRAVING TOOLS: Though these come in an array of a dozen or more sizes each, a beginner will get off to a good start with a fine and a medium each of the spitstick (elliptic tint tool), the round scorper and the flat scorper.

steel bristles, which is used to clean metal particles from the teeth of a file) may be scrubbed over the surface. The card may be cut into pieces with a hacksaw for working small areas more readily. Or the surface may be scratched with coarse steel wool or sandpaper, or abraded by a revolving wire brush chucked in a small, electric hand drill. The result will be not only to scratch the surface but also to heighten the grain by wearing away the soft spaces between the hard ridges.

Prepare the finished block for printing by rubbing it all over with boiled linseed oil. Wipe off the excess and let stand until the oil absorbs into the block, usually overnight.

The Wood Engraving

The wood engraving requires not only a different kind of wood from the woodcut, but also different tools. You will not be able to find the wood you need at your local lumberyard. Wood engraving blocks are purchased readymade from a dealer in such materials. The block may be of pear wood, maple, boxwood, or whatever the dealer has in stock.

The wood-engraving block is manufactured type-high (0.9186-inch thick), as it must be printed in a printing press in order to derive from it all the advantages of which it is capable. The surface is sanded smooth and ready to work on. Although the blocks are relatively expensive, the cost can be pro-rated over several uses, if you don't mind the extra work involved. A used block may be ground down and smoothed on a belt sander for re-use. To return it to type-height, thin cardboard and paper can be pasted to the bottom as needed.

The tools used in wood engraving are similar to those used for copper engraving, though generally cheaper, as they are made of carbon steel instead of the more expensive tool steel required to work metal.

The burin (or graver) used by the wood engraver differs from the copper-engraving tool by having its tip angled back more sharply — at 30 degrees. The spitstick, an-

other type of engraving tool, is made especially for wood engraving. It has an elliptical cross-section, which makes it easier to control in engraving both thick and thin lines. The tint tool comes in various sizes to cut lines of varying widths. The lining tool, or multiple graver, is also available in several sizes, one cutting two lines simultaneously, another three, and so on, up to six. It is used to create areas of tone, composed of mingled black and white, as in cross-hatching.

The difference between copper engraving and wood engraving is that the engraved line in copper prints black while in wood it prints white. It is the portions between the lines in the wood engraving that print. The wood engraving, therefore, is a white-line print upon a black background. However, when many white lines are engraved side by side, the printed result obviously has the appearance of many black lines with white spaces between.

The wood engraving gouge has a rounded bottom like a woodcutting gouge, but it is a great deal smaller and solid instead of hollow. It is used for the same purpose as the woodcut gouge.

The scorper has a rectangular cross-section and is used to make the bottoms flat and smooth. Occasionally, woodcut tools may be used.

The gravers must be kept sharp to avoid tearing the wood. For this purpose, the same India and Arkansas stones used to sharpen woodcutting tools are employed. Each tool is sharpened by standing it on end and rubbing the cut-off section on the stone. It is difficult to do this by hand without spoiling the flatness of the angle, and special tool holders are on the market to hold the tool in the correct position while it is rubbed back and forth on the oilstone.

Before transferring the drawing to be engraved, paint the face of the block with India ink and let it dry. The traced-on drawing will show up in shiny, graphite lines against the black. Strengthen where necessary by going over lines with a pencil, then fix with spray fixative or brush with thinned shellac.

Hold the graver with the knobbed end in the palm of your hand, so that the tang lies almost flat against the face of the block. Visualize the image on the block as printing in white lines and negative spaces and cut out the design to correspond. Professional wood engravers hold the block on a leather sandbag while cutting to facilitate control, but a smooth table top will work very well for the beginner. When cutting curved lines, the tool is neither turned nor twisted. It must be held firmly and steadily while the block is turned against it.

As lines and areas are removed from the blackened surface, they show up startlingly white and the surfaces remaining upon the block show clearly the progress of the design in reverse.

Before printing, treat the engraved block with boiled linseed oil as recommended for the woodcut.

The Linoleum Block

If there are no broad, open areas to be cut out, linoleum may be used unmounted. For general use, however, it is glued to a backing of $\frac{3}{4}$-inch plywood.

For the beginner, readymade blocks may be bought at art supply shops. These are made type high with a white surface, ready for drawing.

If you plan to do a great deal of work in this medium, however, buy your linoleum at a considerable saving from a linoleum store in remnants measuring 2 feet or 3 feet in each direction. Ask for "battleship linoleum." This is a heavy-duty floor covering, $\frac{1}{8}$-inch thick with a backing of heavy burlap. The thin, paper-backed "linoleum rug" is of no use to the block-cutter.

To cut linoleum, score the face side with a knife point, then bend the lino backward. The composition will break along the scored line and then you can use the knife to cut through the burlap backing.

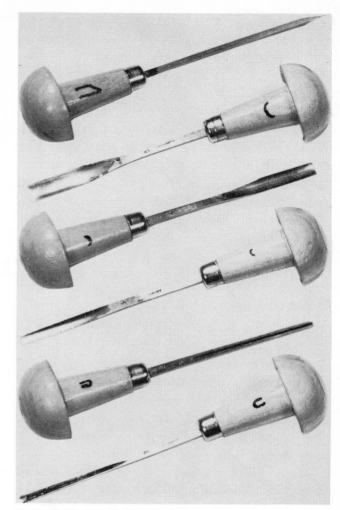

LINO-CUTTING TOOLS: These have push-handles and flat gouges for fast clean-out.

LINO BLOCKS mounted on plywood can be made into hand stamps by insertion of a dowel.

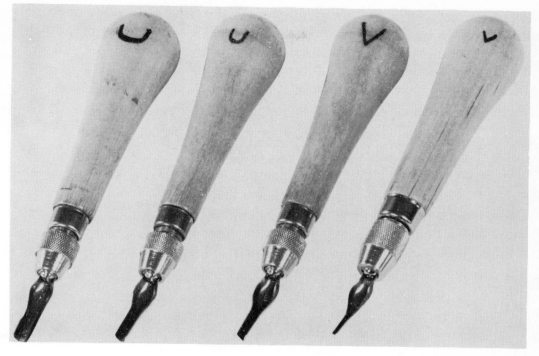

REPLACEABLE BITS in various sizes that fit into a chuck-handle are the feature of Speedball tools. Use a separate handle for each type bit. For convenience, draw a picture of the shape of the cutter on the handle with a soft-tip pen.

Where accurately sized blocks are required, a power-driven circular saw is needed. First square the remnant off, then glue it down to a sheet of ¾-inch plywood. To assure a good bond, turn the linoleum-side down upon the floor and pile weights on the plywood. When the glue has set, the plywood-linoleum combination may then be accurately cut into blocks of varying sizes.

Sand the surface of the linoleum with 6/0 sandpaper to remove the shine and any eggshell appearance that may be present (which would otherwise be visible in the print). Unless the lino is white or light-colored to begin with, it must now be given a coat, sprayed or brushed on, of flat white enamel undercoater to which thinner has been added. This allows the drawing to show up.

You may now transfer the drawing to the block and ink it in (the isolating coat of fixative or shellac is not needed on lino) as described in making a woodcut.

Linoleum is not only easier to cut than wood, it also has no grain to worry about in planning the design. Linoleum cuts as easily and accurately in one direction as in any other.

Since linoleum becomes hard, brittle and impossible to cut in cold weather, warm the block by a heater before starting work. Heat softens it, so do not place the block too close to the source.

The tools used for cutting linoleum are the same in style as those used for woodcuts, but generally lighter in construction. Complete sets of permanent-type lino-cutting tools are sold in art supply shops. Use and maintain lino-cutting tools in the manner described for woodcutting tools.

Excellent lino tools also are Speedball sets featuring chuck-handles with inexpensive, replaceable cutting tips. A separate handle for each cutting tip is advisable.

Lino is worked in the same manner as wood in both cutting and texturing. When gouging out large voids, remove the burlap backing down to the wood. Even broad mistakes are easily corrected in linoleum. Simply remove the offending area down to the wood and glue in a new piece of lino. Where only a small piece has been gouged out of a line, gouge a similar piece from a waste area and glue it into the mistake with Elmer's glue.

Printing the Relief Print

Any professional printer is equipped to print your woodcut, wood engraving, or linoleum block, by itself or in company with type, so long as the block is type high. If thicker than 0.9186 of an inch, it cannot be printed in a platen press. If thinner, the thickness can be built up by pasting paper or thin cardboard to the bottom of the block.

Blocks may also be printed on some etching presses, particularly the modern ones which support the top roller on heavy springs, permitting it to ride type high above the press bed.

Unless a platen press or etching press is available to you, either at home or in a shop, or some other kind of a block-printing press, you will have to consider printing your woodcut or linoblock by hand.

Practically any paper will do for printing your first proofs. Newsprint is readily available and cheap. Do not use it for permanent prints, as it quickly turns yellow and ugly-looking. You can also print on colored construction paper and pastel paper, as well as on special, inexpensive block-printing papers made for the purpose. If you get to the point where you are selling your work, buy the more expensive —and more durable—hand-made rag papers and the various Japanese unsized papers such as Hosho, Torinoko, Kochi and so on.

Although both water-base and oil-base block-printing inks are on the market, the oil-base inks are best (unless children are to use them, then water-soluble inks wash easily from hands and clothing). Regular printers' ink may also be used, and best for single-block printing is a black called "job black." Such ink may be bought from a supplier to the printing trade.

With block, ink and paper on hand, you

need only a slab of stone or plate glass to roll the ink out on, an ink roller, and a baren. Ink rollers made of soft rubber may be bought in several sizes at art supply shops. Get one about 6 inches wide. Place several small dabs of ink on the stone and roll it out with the ink roller, rolling it in every direction until the ink lies in an even, glistening film. Do not roll the film out too thick or too thin. After pulling a few proofs, you will understand just how thick to make it so that a proper film of ink will be transferred to the block. Too little ink makes a light, anemic-looking print; too much makes the print look sloppy.

Pass the ink-charged roller once across the block, then roll it again upon the stone to pick up more ink, and again pass it over the block. Do this several times, until the block is well inked. Now roll the ink out on the block both lengthwise and crosswise a number of times to distribute it evenly.

Some printers like to dampen the paper before printing to make it take the ink more readily. First take a number of blotters, wet one in a tray of water and lay it on a sheet of plastic. Lay on a dry blotter, then wet another and lay it on. Continue this until all the blotters are piled, alternating wet and dry. Lay on top a sheet of glass (or plastic-covered plywood) and leave under a weight for an hour or so, until the moisture equalizes throughout the pile.

Soak rag papers in a tray of water until limp, then take out one sheet at a time, drain it, and place it between the damp blotters, one sheet to each pair of blotters. Unsized papers such as the Japanese papers must never be wetted in water. Such are placed *dry* between the damp blotters. Lay on the covering and weight, bring the bottom plastic up and over the covering to keep in the moisture, and let sit for one or two hours until the moisture again equalizes.

Every sheet of paper has two sides—a face side and a screen side. The screen side is the side that lay against the screen in the process of manufacture, and it is rougher in texture than the face side. Where a paper shows a rough side and a smooth, it is better to print upon the smooth side. Where a paper has a

INKING THE BLOCK: Roll ink out on the block lengthwise and crosswise until it is well inked.

BAREN: This hand device can be used to make a print from a block without a printing press.

readable watermark, the face side is the side from which the watermark can be read.

Print on paper enough larger than the block to permit trimming the margins when the ink has dried. Lay the piece of paper, damp or dry, face down upon the inked block. Place it carefully, without twisting; for, if the paper moves at all after it is down, the imprint will be smeared. Secure the paper in place by lightly rubbing with the fingertips over the solid printing areas. Over all lay a sheet of heavy paper or thin manila. This will protect the print paper from tearing.

The baren is a round device which, in the case of the Japanese style, looks like a large button covered with dry corn husk. Speedball manufactures a baren made of plastic with a teflon cover. Yet, many artists use nothing more complicated than a common tablespoon or, preferably, a large, wooden spoon.

The baren is now rubbed carefully and with moderate pressure upon one corner of the block to offset the ink upon the print paper.

After a bit, carefully peel back the corner and see how the print is coming along. Perhaps more pressure or longer rubbing will be needed. If neither produces good results, the block probably needs more ink. It takes a few proofs to catch on to just how much you need of everything—of ink, rubbing and pressure—to produce a good-looking print.

An advantage of hand printing is that you can deliberately relieve the pressure in certain areas to produce a lighter tone, or mealy effect, that will suit your artistic purposes. Where more ink is required, peel the paper carefully back from one end, past the middle. Then re-roll the exposed part of the block with more ink. Carefully replace the paper, lift it at the opposite end, and then re-ink that part of the block. As long as a large part of the print remains firmly stuck to the block, this lifting and re-inking procedure may be followed without fear of smearing, if the whole process is done with care.

Keep examining the print as you rub. When

satisfactory, strip it from the block (use extreme care, particularly if the paper is damp), and lay it aside to dry. Also, the print may be hung on a line with clothespins at the corners or, in the case of very large prints, hung over a line like a bedsheet, with the printed side facing outward.

Relief Printing with a Press

Use of a printing press brings to light certain printing problems not at all inherent in the hand method. Whether or not the printing press requires the block to be type-high, every block must be of an equal thickness over its entire area in order to print well. This seldom happens. Where the block is even minutely thinner, it will print lighter than where it is thicker, owing to the fact that the pressure upon such areas is consequently reduced.

If you are using a "clam-shell" or job press, you must first bring your block to type-high, then clamp it in the chase with furniture and quoins. Lay padding on the platen and stretch a tympan (or covering) sheet over it. Pull a proof on a piece of newsprint (frisket sheet) taped to the tympan. (See illustration on next page.)

It will be a living wonder if the block prints properly the first time off, though a very small one just might. From the proof, you will see that some parts of the block print in a lighter tone than desired. These areas will have to be built up, or thickened by pasting *torn* bits of paper under them. Paste these to the bottom of the block. Such corrections are called "makeready." Often several thicknesses of paper are required, and each must be a little smaller than the previous one in order to graduate the reduction of pressure at the edge of the treated area.

In very small areas, the makeready may be pasted to the underside of the tympan sheet. Stick a pin through the area on the proof to be doctored, and where it comes out on the backside of the tympan sheet, paste on the makeready. Makeready can also be placed under the packing on the platen, and this is

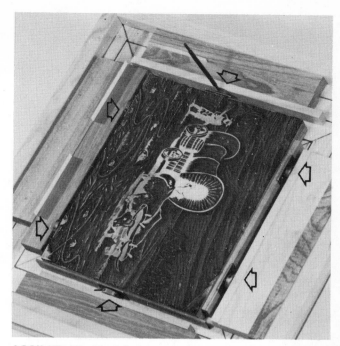

LOCK-UP: The block is in a rectangle called a chase. Arrows point to the quoins (pronounced "coins") which are clamps that expand as you adjust them. The wood strips on the side of the block are called furniture. Note the quoin key standing in the quoin at the head of the chase.

MAKEREADY: To bring up a low spot on your block, tear a bit of paper (do not cut it as that will form a ridge) and paste it on the underside of your block. Paste on as many bits as necessary.

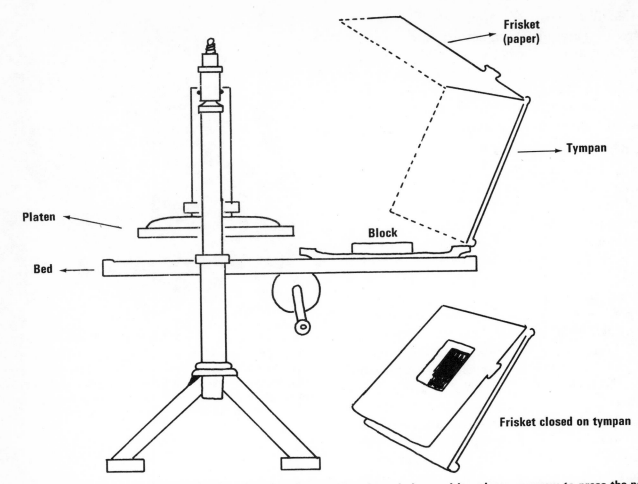

Friset (paper)

Tympan

Platen

Bed

Block

Friset closed on tympan

PRESS: This hand press shows the principles and various parts. The platen is lowered by a lever or screw to press the paper against the inked block on the bed when the bed is rolled beneath it. Over the block is placed a tympan pack consisting of a piece of paper with a window cut out of it (called a frisket) to allow the wanted areas of the block to print and the unwanted areas to be shielded, along with a covering sheet called a tympan. The paper for printing is placed in the pack between the frisket and tympan. Makeready bits of paper can be pasted to the tympan as well as to the block.

usually advisable to prevent the demarcation from showing up on the print.

The advantage of pasting makeready to the block, however, lies in the fact that it remains with the block when that is stored away, and therefore is always present and ready when the block is to be reprinted.

When you have finally got your woodcut, wood engraving, or linoblock to print evenly all over, you can set your gauge pins (as guides) and go ahead and make as many prints from it as you wish, just as you would print from a forme of type.

If you use a so-called "block-printing press"

or something similar made from a bench-screw, or an etching press, the principle of making ready is still the same. However, since work cannot be done on the platen as it is with the platen press, you must substitute for the tympan sheet a piece of pressboard covered with tympan paper or thin manila. This is laid paper-side down on the printpaper covering the block when it is run through the press.

Whatever kind of press you use, a small block requires a harder platen than a large one. So does a block that is mostly cut away as compared to one that prints with large, black areas.

The hardness or softness of the platen is controlled by the paper padding placed behind the tympan sheet, or between the paper and the pressboard. When proofing, start with a hard platen consisting of a sheet of tympan paper or manila over a sheet of pressboard. Add sheets of newsprint between them as may be required to even the tone, or color, of the print. Do this before adding any other make-ready, as a soft platen may be all that will be needed.

When using an etching press, the block should be locked up in a chase, as in platen press work, for consistently good prints. A chase can be made by welding a rectangle from $\frac{3}{4}'' \times \frac{3}{4}''$ angle iron. A block run through the etching press by itself will invariably tilt up as it passes out from under the top roller, and this will have to be avoided by holding it down by hand with every proof . . . a real nuisance.

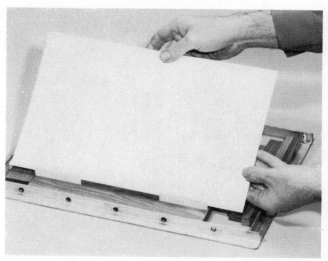

GUIDES (gauge pins) set up at the edge of the chase help you to get your paper into position without smearing.

Printing Multiple Blocks

To achieve a printed effect of several colors, a separate block will have to be cut for each color. A wood engraving does not readily lend itself to color printing, so we will consider here only the woodcut and the linoblock.

The simplest color print is composed of two colors, a color for the background print and the "key block" to be printed in black or some dark color. In any color series, of however many colors, all the blocks must be cut to

COLOR GUIDE: On a proof of your key block, color in your scheme to use as a guide.

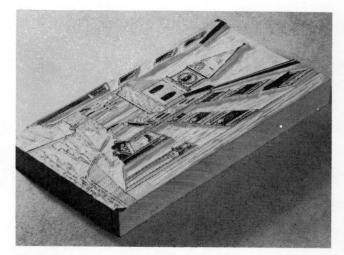

KEY BLOCK: This is the black plate. Note the corner triangles left on for assuring register in transferring the design to the other color blocks.

COLOR SET: This series of five wood blocks shows the key block and those portions of the linear design that have been transferred to the yellow, red, blue and brown blocks.

exactly the same size. The key block carrying the design is cut first, leaving the corners uncut, whether they belong in the final print or not. A proof is then made on wax paper. While the ink is still wet, lay the proof face-down on the secondary block, using the printed corners to line it up correctly (the imprint can be seen through the wax paper, as well as the block, so lining up is easy to do). Either run the block through a press or rub down the proof to set off the design upon the secondary block. A separate proof has to be pulled for each block in the series.

When the key design has thus been transferred to all the blocks, sprinkle the wet ink with talcum powder and brush it off. This dries the ink so that the blocks can be worked on immediately.

Often, a two-block print is composed of simply a tone block that is printed first in

TRANSFERRING: Make a print of your key block on wax paper. The ink design will show through. Place the paper with the ink still wet on another block, using the corner triangle for line-up (register) and print down. This will give you an outline for cutting the secondary color.

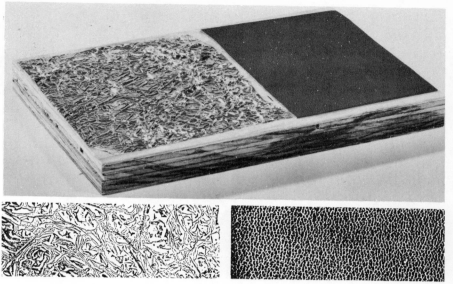

TONE BLOCKS can be made easily and used with good effect in two-color printing. This block was set up with crumpled aluminum foil on the left and Morocco leather on the right. Texture is particularly interesting when printed in colored ink as an underprint.

some light color. When the ink has dried, the key block is printed over it. In this case, the tone block does not need cutting, except to the same rectangular size as the key block. The surface may be textured with a wire brush or by other means so that the grain will be heightened to print prominently, or the surface may contain knots or be unplaned or weather-beaten, so as to result in an interesting pattern when printed.

Also, tone blocks may be created by glueing on crumpled aluminum foil, cloth, leather, coils of string, fiberglass mat, embossed paper or cardboard, and so on. Where such texturing materials would absorb ink, isolate with a coat of shellac before printing. Such materials may be glued to the block with Elmer's glue.

To lighten a colored ink, mix a small quantity of it with "extender," a colorless base.

When printing a series of color blocks, the lightest color, usually yellow, is printed first. After the ink of the first printing has dried (by the next day), the next darker color can be laid on. A transparent blue printed over yellow will result in green, and this will give you two colors with one printing, and save your cutting an extra block.

The easiest way to achieve register—i.e., the matching of one imprint upon another so that all the colors fall into their proper places—is to lock up the block in a chase with furniture and quoins. A block-high guide of thin cardboard is inserted between the furniture blocks at the head and to the left of the block. A similar guide is placed off the tail, or bottom, of the block. This gives three points for lining up the paper with the block. When the paper is placed carefully with each printing, each imprint is bound to fall into its proper place on the print. (See photo on page 409.)

Mounting the Print

The easiest way to mount a print is to trim the margins even all around, then attach it with a dab of paste at each corner to a backing of white or colored mounting board.

Matting a print is somewhat more difficult. A mat is composed of two pieces, a backing board of illustration board, which comes with a white paper facing, and the mat-frame itself, which is made of mat board. Many kinds and colors are available.

Make the mat considerably bigger than the print and cut an opening in it that will extend $\frac{1}{4}$ inch beyond the printed area on both sides and the top, and $\frac{3}{8}$ inch at the bottom. This extra size will allow a strip of the print paper to remain visible all around the print. The

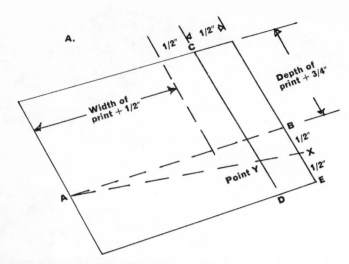

A.

1/2" 1/2"

Width of
print + 1/2"

Depth of
print + 3/4"

C

B

1/2"

X

1/2"

Point Y

E

A

D

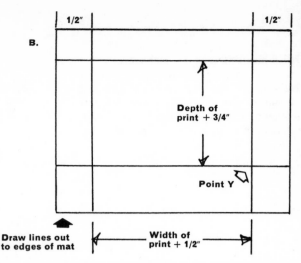

B.

1/2" 1/2"

Depth of
print + 3/4"

Point Y

Draw lines out
to edges of mat

Width of
print + 1/2"

MATTING THE PRINT: The first step is to measure the width and depth of the print (right). To the width add ½ inch and to the depth add ¾ inch for the visible paper margins. Transfer the measurements to the top left corner of the back of the mat, as shown in (A). Divide the remaining distance on the right in two and draw the line C-D. Indicate A-B with pencil marks, divide B-E at point X. Lay ruler from point A to point X and mark point Y where it crosses line C-D, as shown in (A). With point Y as the bottom right corner of the opening, lay out the entire opening as shown in (B).

wider space at the bottom allows room for title and your signature.

Rather than center the print in the mount, establish it with equal side margins and the bottom margin a little wider than the top for a more balanced and eye-pleasing effect. Cut the opening in the mat, using a steel straight-edge and a mat-cutting knife.

Paste the print to the backing board at its two top corners and paste the mat board over it, with the print showing through the opening. Weight the assembly down to assure a good bond with the paste.

Before the print is matted, however, it must be titled and signed. Write the title in hard pencil (2H) under the print, at the middle. Under the right-hand corner, write your signature. Under the left corner place the print number and the edition number. If you plan to make twenty prints (or any other number of prints), that is your edition number. All the prints are numbered from 1 to 20. The first print is marked 1/20, the second 2/20, and so on. The number in front of the slant merely keeps track of the prints numerically and has no special significance, except to indicate the order in which they were printed. You can have any number of prints you want in an edition. The principle of numbering remains the same.

scrap
materials

COLLAGE

Collage consists of making designs from materials not normally associated with one another, cut into different shapes and forms and pasted to sheets of paper or canvas to form a composition.

Closer to the panel or mural idea than the sculpture or diorama techniques, collage should be a unified, flat or multi-level composition with interesting planes, colors and textures.

Collage is great fun for those who feel they lack artistic talent. Creating a composition from pieces of junk, paper, photographs, and so on, without resorting to actual painting or sculpture techniques, is both challenging and less demanding than many art forms. Objects can be nailed, glued or stapled to the background.

THIS BARNYARD SCENE is assembled from different thicknesses of paper, ranging from heavy construction paper to newspaper to tissue paper. Even though the original collage used only black and grey paper, a great variety of textures and shades was still achieved.

Written especially for this volume by Maurice Siegel

Barnyard Scene

A bright and colorful barnyard scene can be easily pieced together using red construction paper for the barn, and real twigs for trees in the distance. Sticks or toothpicks can form a fence.

Use straw for the haystack, feathers for the chickens, and even a toy car, cut in half, driving into a garage. Your ability to relate the various materials will determine the success of your composition.

Collage does not necessarily have to be a scene. It can be a collection of a multitude of bright colors. A collage can be an assemblage of pictures which bring together fond memories of the past.

Paper Collage

For paper collage, colored construction paper or tissue paper, some paste and scissors are all you need. Cut or tear large and small pieces of the colored paper and paste them in random positions. You can place them side by side or overlap them alternately, but remember, if tissue papers overlap, the colors get darker.

You can cover a book or album with an attractive collage. Use lightweight background paper, such as paper bags, newspapers and typing paper, and cover it with tissue paper. Collage on harder background surfaces, such as cardboard or wood, can be framed.

A MONTAGE consists of photographs pasted together to tell a story. The background here is newspaper; you might prefer to paint a picture behind the photographs.

Scrapbook Collage

Tracing family histories and one's heritage has long been an exciting hobby. A special form of collage called montage uses photographs as the component materials, and an interesting family scrapbook could be made from photographs you have collected through the years.

Piece the pictures together to tell a story or depict a memorable event. These items will be a constant reminder of exciting details which would otherwise be forgotten with time. Black page albums provide an excellent background for arranging and pasting. Arrange in free-form fashion, with overlapping and layering, but avoid covering up important sections of type or picture. Use rubber cement for easy mounting, so you can lift if you don't like your arrangement.

Letters, handbills, posters or other large objects could occupy the central area of the page. Smaller items such as wallet photographs, post cards, trading cards, wrappers, etc., might be placed around the central object.

Collect the different items which tell your story and lay them out in order of events. Doing one event at a time, simply place the various objects down on a background. Move them around and look at them from various angles. Your aim is to design a story with many items without covering or losing their intended value. Once you have chosen the final positions, paste all down with rubber cement. If the page tells a time sequence, draw in little arrows so the viewer can follow the story line.

To avoid the square sharp corners which might sometimes show in your arrangement, you can make a negative from the complete montage, and with an air brush blend in the edges of the individual photographs. The print which results from this negative will be a much softer, more pleasing montage, and an extremely personal and creative scrapbook.

CORRUGATED CARTON CRAFTING

If you are looking for new handicraft materials, you will discover that corrugated carton cardboard offers many possibilities. It is a material which can be used to construct both decorative and practical objects. After developing a "feel" for this material, you will find new uses yourself, as corrugated carton cardboard offers great inspiration and challenge to those working with it. An important attraction of corrugated cardboard is that it is easily obtainable, often free. Most of the time, boxes are discarded as worthless.

Condensed from the book, "Corrugated Carton Crafting" by Dick Van Voorst / © 1970 by Sterling Publishing Co., Inc., New York

Types of Board

Single-wall board (also called double-faced board) consists of two plain cardboard facings, enclosing fluted corrugated cardboard. Double-wall board has two sets of flutes with a cardboard facing in the middle, and a facing on each outside. In Illus. 1 is a cross-section of double-wall board. The layers 1-2-3 and/or 3-4-5, if they were separate, would be called single-wall board.

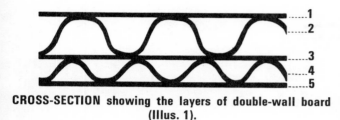

CROSS-SECTION showing the layers of double-wall board (Illus. 1).

Cartons thrown away or delivered by grocery stores or supermarkets are usually single-wall board, as are drugstore cartons of small size. Cartons from hardware stores that sell large appliances, such as refrigerators and television sets, are likely to be double-wall board. Both types come from department stores. Since most stores are happy if you take away their used cartons, and the supply is endless, be selective—do not take soiled or damaged boxes, only clean and relatively undamaged ones.

Tools

A knife or single-edged razor blade in a safe holder, a pair of scissors, and a ruler are most important for working with corrugated cartons. The knife blade should be sharp, thin and pointed. The best type for your purpose is one that can be pushed in or out. Some knives of this type have a scored blade and the front part of the blade may be broken off when it becomes dull, so that you can always work with a sharp edge and point.

Warn children who are too young to handle a knife themselves that they will need help from adults in their cutting.

Scissors are easier for children to use. They are used primarily for cutting "folded" and "bent" strips (Illus. 12 and 13) but can be used in place of a knife blade at times.

You will not need other tools. The only additional things you will need are an adhesive—either a tube of glue, a pot of paste, or a can of rubber cement—and some sticks or cane of matchstick size and some cane or dowels, longer, but no thicker, than matchsticks.

Start by Experimenting

Don't try to make an object right away. If you do, you will quickly find that you need experience in every phase of the craft in order to make an airplane, for example, and you will be disappointed with the plane you create. If you start by simply experimenting, you will build up enthusiasm and your mind will become filled with ideas of ways you can cut, strip, peel, and glue. In just handling the material and working with it you will become familiar with its possibilities.

Cut one side from a carton of double-wall

KNIFE BLADES are the only tools you will need for cutting. Heavy-duty scissors can substitute for knives if necessary (Illus. 2).

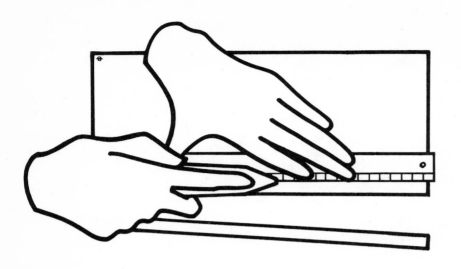

CUTTING a strip of double-wall board (top view) with a ruler and blade. Keep your blades sharpened so your cuts will be clean (Illus. 3).

board and have a good look at the board. Notice that the two layers of fluted or corrugated board are not exactly alike. In one, the "waves" are short and in the other the "waves" are long—you are going to make use of this fact.

Now look again at Illus. 1—the cross-cut of double-wall board. The layers have been numbered for easy reference. Cut away part of layer 1 (this is easier with some types than with others) and you will expose layer 2, the long wave. If it is difficult to remove layer 1, moisten the board with a sponge and after a short time it will be easy to pull off the top layer.

If you cut a rough circle just in layers 1 and 2, you will make a kind of hole with a flat bottom. If you continue to cut deeper, the hole will go through five layers. Or you can start cutting another hole through layers 5 and 4 only.

How to Cut Strips

Always cut across the waves. You will be surprised how sturdy even $\frac{1}{2}$-inch-wide strips of double-wall board turn out to be.

Illus. 3 and 4 show how to cut strips with a ruler and a blade. Hold a knife at the same angle to the board all the time as you draw the blade along the edge of the ruler. Press with one hand on the ruler to hold it steady as you cut.

If you do not succeed in cutting through all the layers the first time, repeat the process, holding the knife at the same angle. The sharper your knife, the cleaner the cut.

Strips are basic for making almost every conceivable project with corrugated board, so practice until you can cut strips cleanly with one or two strokes.

Your $\frac{1}{2}$-inch-wide strips can be used straight, bent or folded. Straight strips used for con-

CUTTING a strip of double-wall board (side view). Before beginning a project, practice cutting strips until you are able to do it with one clean stroke (Illus. 4).

struction are almost always placed in a flat or lying-down position so that the wavelike shape of the corrugation can be seen from the side. If you glue such double-wall strips together in regular fashion you can obtain an open-work type of design (Illus. 5 and 6).

If, instead, you first peel off layer 1 and attach layer 2 to layer 2, and layer 5 to layer 5, you will make bigger waves between the layers (Illus. 7).

Now you can vary this still more by removing with your blade some of the short

STACK of double-wall strips glued with layer 1 to layer 5 at each level (Illus. 5).

STACK glued with layer 1 to layer 1 and layer 5 to layer 5 (Illus. 6).

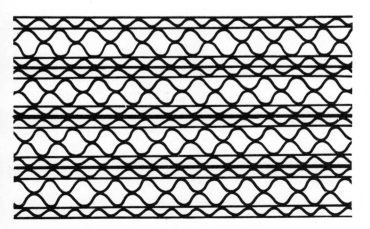

STACK glued with layer 2 to layer 2 and layer 5 to layer 5. Layer 1 has been peeled off (Illus. 7).

STACK glued as in Illus. 7, but with some areas cut away (Illus. 8).

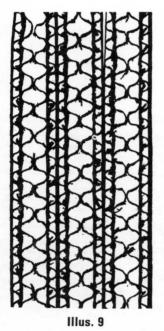

Illus. 9

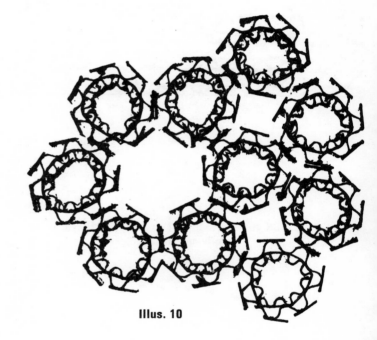

Illus. 10

OPEN-WORK PATTERNS

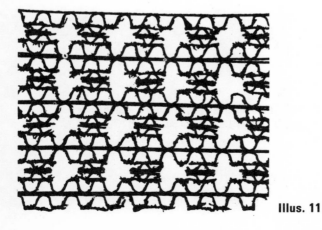

Illus. 11

waves and layers 3 and 5 at intervals, such as at every second or third large wave (Illus. 8).

You will discover for yourself how to make many other nice open-work patterns. Just a few further suggestions are shown in Illus. 9, 10 and 11.

Bending

Start with straight strips, either $\frac{1}{2}$ inch wide or wider. You will "bend" these, not by rolling the board but by making incisions with your scissors at certain points. You can make these cuts in layer 1 in between each of the large waves, and also in layer 5 but only in alternate waves (Illus. 12). Then you can bend the strip easily. You can vary this by making incisions at every wave in both layers which will allow an even sharper bend (Illus. 13).

You can even bend without scissor cuts. Just remove layers 1 and 5, and you will have a very pliable strip that will coil like a snake (Illus. 14).

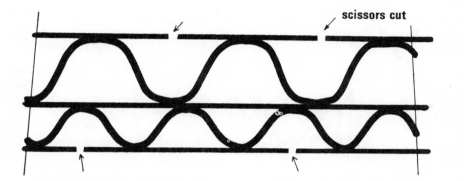

EACH LONG WAVE has been cut, but only alternating short waves (Illus. 12).

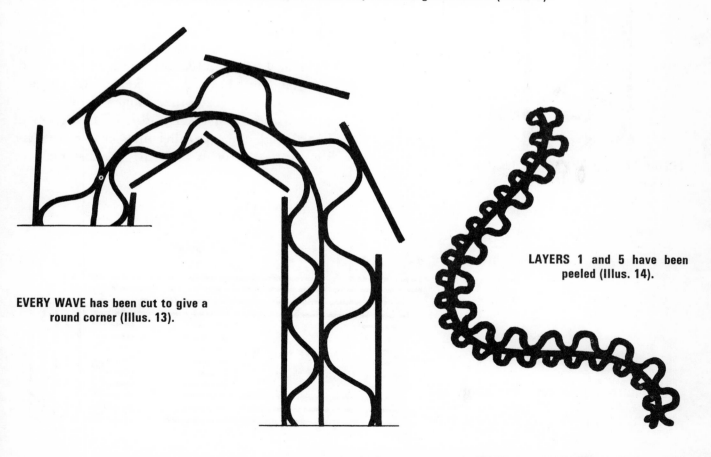

EVERY WAVE has been cut to give a round corner (Illus. 13).

LAYERS 1 and 5 have been peeled (Illus. 14).

Folding

If you cut through layers 1, 2 and 3 you can put a definite fold in a straight strip. The same type of incision through layers 5, 4 and 3 will allow you to fold the strip in the opposite direction (Illus. 15).

Building a Straight-Strip House

Now that you have made various types of strips, you are ready to start using them. Choose a house first, any type. The description and illustrations of the house here are meant only to acquaint you with the technique. The design is up to you.

For a start, try a house like the one in Illus. 16. The walls (*a*) are $\frac{1}{2}$-inch wide strips glued in a regular pattern with waves dovetailed at the corners. For windows and doors you merely leave out strips (*b*), or cut out parts of strips.

The roof and awning (*c*) are a little more complicated. They are made from a piece of corrugated board cut in a rectangle. There are two possible variations:

1. Make horizontal and vertical incisions in layer 1 of your rectangular piece of board, so that you have a checkerboard pattern. Then pull off every other square (Illus. 17).

2. Use only layers 1 and 2 of a single-wall board and make parallel lines cross-wise over the waves (crushing them) at distances of

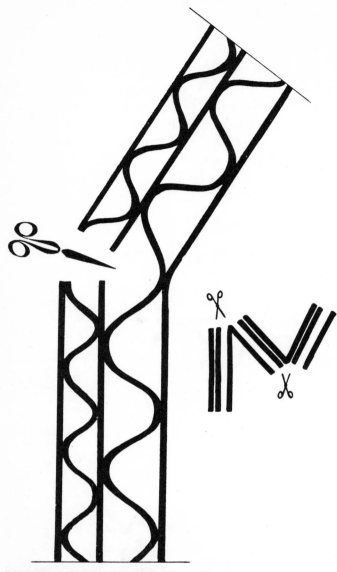

FOLDING A STRAIGHT STRIP (Illus. 15).

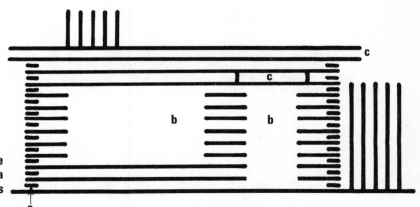

A STRAIGHT-STRIP HOUSE. Try a simple type of house first. Do not make too small a house—it is easier to work with large strips (Illus. 16).

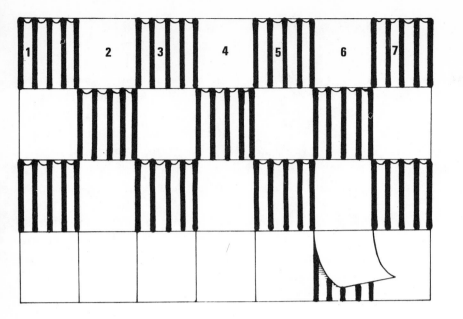

1 inch or 1½ inches apart. You can make the lines with either the flat side of a knife blade or with the closed points of a scissors. The crushed waves will produce a zigzag pattern.

The assembling of the parts is left to you. Just be sure you have a stable base. Illus. 18 shows you how one house was constructed of straight strips.

Making Mobiles

A mobile is an object or combination of objects attached by string or wire to the ceiling or any high place, floating freely in space as the currents of air move it. Because a mobile needs to be light, corrugated board is an ideal material.

The possibilities are almost endless. You can

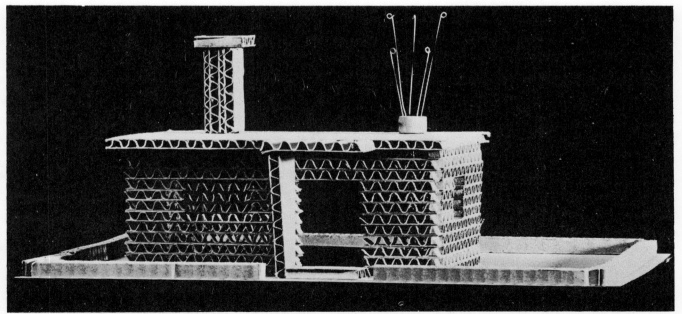

THIS HOUSE was made of single-wall board and the chimney of double-wall board. The inside of an old light bulb was used for the television aerial (Illus. 18).

use strips of wallboard and ½-inch-wide wheels, for example, as in Illus. 19.

The wheels are made as before by bending (see Illus. 12 and 13) the ½-inch-wide strips. You can roll your wheels tightly, but for this purpose it is better to roll them loosely instead, allowing the many small holes to show. You may want to glue colored transparent paper to some of the wheels. Another alternative is to attach a second wheel to the first with adhesive tape.

You will discover very quickly how to balance your wheel mobile when you hang the wheels with string to corrugated board strips (see Illus. 19).

The rewards of working seriously to master the basic techniques of corrugated cardboard crafting can be quite satisfying. The material lends itself to a variety of objects that will come within your scope as you proceed in the craft. Corrugated cardboard is strong enough to support a mirror—hence, a mirror frame. It can be pasted to an armature and made to support candles; it can be constructed into a base to hold a piece of sculpture or a plant. It can be used to make a serving tray or a place mat.

As you become more proficient with the techniques of the craft, you will soon see that almost anything that can be constructed out of wood can also be made out of cardboard—and for a fraction of the cost.

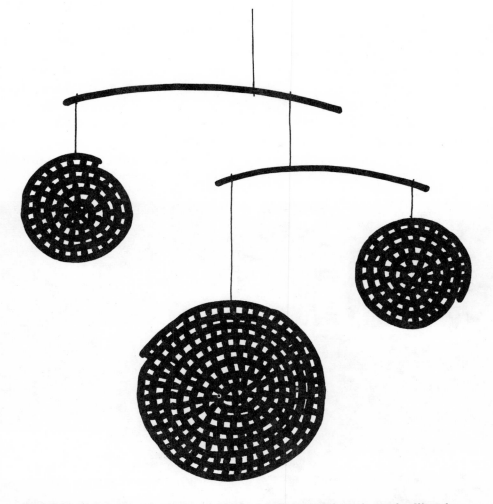

A MOBILE. A wheel mobile is constructed by bending straight strips and rolling them —either loosely as shown here, or tightly (Illus. 19).

DÉCOUPAGE

Découpage is the art of decorating with paper cut-outs. It originated in Venice during the 17th century, and rapidly spread to France, England and Germany, where it flourished for two centuries. It was revived in the United States in the 20th century.

This craft requires few tools, no heavy equipment, and is enormously variable. The paper cut-outs can be applied to almost any surface, from wood and glass to metal and fieldstones. Even porous surfaces are acceptable if they are first sealed. Lamps, paperweights, tables, boxes, trays and lamp shades are only a few possibilities for which *découpage* is an ideal decorative art. The cut-outs themselves can come from magazines, gift wrappings, Christmas cards or even wallpaper, or you may design and paint them yourself.

The object is to select an appropriate motif (birds, cupids, coats of arms, boats, landscapes) for the object you want to decorate,

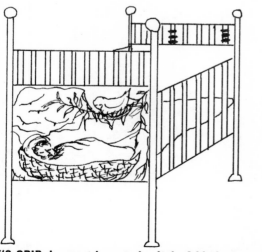

A BABY'S CRIB does not have to be drab. Add photographs, magazine clippings and birth announcements. If the crib was used for an older brother or sister, the new decorations will personalize it for its current occupant.

Written especially for this volume by Barbara Klinger

WALL HANGING: Attach a colorful magazine page to a piece of wood with a layer of varnish. If you wish, make the edges of the picture ragged, to look older, by carefully scorching the corners with a low flame.

apply the cut-outs, and then cover them with several coats of varnish until they are "submerged," and cannot be felt through the surface. The surface is then sanded, and may be treated further with paint, enamel, or gold leaf. The paper cut-outs seem almost but not quite to be a part of the original surface, and often have a misty, antique quality.

For *découpage* on wood, the surface to which the paper cut-outs are to be applied must be absolutely clean and smooth. Sand the wood carefully and wipe the surface with a soft, lint-free cloth. Next paint the surface in an appropriate background color, and allow this to dry thoroughly. Meanwhile, cut out the selected paper designs as carefully as possible. Use sharp scissors. Glue the cut-outs down smoothly. A little roller or any tool for applying pressure will help you to press down the edges. Be careful not to mar the paper cut-outs, and remove any excess glue with cotton moistened with vinegar.

When the glue is completely dry, seal the *découpage* surface with a mixture of half alcohol and half clear shellac. Again, let dry completely before going on to the next step, which is applying the varnish. This may take several hours or even overnight. Apply the varnish in very thin coats, brushing in *one direction only*. Allow lengthy drying periods between each coat. You must apply as many coats of varnish as are necessary to cover the cut-outs until they can no longer be "felt." Sand the surface with fine sandpaper or steel wool until there are no rough edges and the surface feels glassily smooth. The final step is a coat of wax, applied a little bit at a time over a small area with a circular motion.

When applying *découpage* to metal, sand off any finish on the metal and remove any rust spots with a good rust remover or steel wool. Apply a rust-proofing liquid with a soft brush, and allow this to dry completely. When the surface is absolutely clean and dry, proceed just as you did with the wooden surface.

METAL TRAY: Metal is also a good surface for decoupage. Gold leaf can be applied around the border.

LUNCH BOX: Metal lunch boxes are sometimes very drab, but one decorated with fancy pictures will please anyone. These can also be used as handbags.

Glass surfaces for *découpage* must be absolutely grease-free, so clean the surface meticulously before you begin, using gloves to prevent finger marks. Outline the design on the opposite side of the glass, and glue the cut-outs in the outline that shows through on the front. Work from the middle of each cut-out towards the edges, smoothing down the

edges carefully. Seal with alcohol and shellac and then varnish as you did with the wooden surface. On glass, you may use a plastic-spray finish instead of wax, but the latter is easier to work with. Gold leaf or colored papers, glued to the back or front of the glass, make especially attractive backgrounds for *découpage* on glass.

A LAMP with pictures on its base is a welcome addition to any room. Use either an old lamp or a bottle which has been wired for electricity.

The procedure for *découpage* on stones or other porous surfaces is the same as for wood, except that the surface must first be sealed completely. Try to select rocks which have a relatively smooth surface; egg shapes are particularly desirable for paperweights. After sanding away loose particles, apply a coat of acrylic spray or other sealer, and then follow

EVEN STONE OBJECTS are suitable for decoupage by being coated with a sealer before the cut-outs are applied. Make a paperweight or a door stop.

the rules for *découpage* on wood. Remember that you do not have to cover the entire surface of the rock with paper cut-outs, but it is best to apply the varnish over a relatively larger area than that to be covered by the design.

Gold leaf may be used to enhance your design. This material is very brittle, so it must be handled with extreme care. Paint the area to be covered with adhesive and gently apply the gold leaf one sheet at a time. Use a soft brush to pick up the gold leaf, and smooth it down. Allow it to dry for several hours, and seal it with clear varnish just as you seal the paper cut-outs.

Antique glazes make very attractive finishes for *découpage*, and many colors are available in ready-to-use form. Paint on the glaze as it comes from the jar and allow it to dry for a few moments. Wipe the surface with a soft cloth, removing parts of the glaze. Experiment first as it takes practice to achieve the nicest effects.

MASK-MAKING

Masks have been used by man to emphasize, distort, or hide emotion during rituals, hunts, festivals, and theatrical performances in virtually every culture. Probably, the most familiar masks recognized by young children are the Indian witch doctors seen regularly on television.

A large selection of materials is available for the manufacture of masks, each requiring a special method of handling. Masks have been formed from such materials as wood, ivory, paper, wax and gold. Paint and mosaic tile are added in many instances to enhance the appearance.

AN ECUADOR INDIAN is wearing a mask for a ceremonial dance.

Monofold Masks

Monofold masks are simple to make and add liveliness to any celebration—from birthdays to Halloween. First trace the mask outline on a colored background paper or corrugated paper. Then cut out the tracing. Using tempera paints or crayon, or colored bits of paper, emphasize shapes and color. Shapes can even be built through the use of papier mâché. Other materials can be employed to add texture and interest, such as pipe cleaners for earrings, buttons for eyes, tin foil for ears, hair and beard, etc.

Attach a piece of elastic behind each of the ears to hold the mask on your head. Now you are ready for a rain dance!

Paper Bag Masks

A paper bag can easily be transformed from a drab, lifeless receptacle into the source of an exciting afternoon for a young child.

Using a pair of scissors, glue, packing straw, construction paper and some pipe cleaners, you can make masks of clowns, witch doctors, devils, monsters and many more.

Choose a paper bag large enough to fit over your head. Locate the position of your eyes and carefully cut out two circles large enough for you to see through. Cut up some construction paper in the form of ears and a tongue. Glue these into their respective places. If desired, cut an opening for your mouth.

Decorate the paper bag in any fun style you desire. The more colors used and the larger the ears, the funnier the mask gets. If available, a plastic funnel will make a very funny nose. Crayons, paint, or just colored pencils will provide additional features.

Written especially for this volume by Gordon Lander and Maurice Siegel

Create a ferocious monster face by topping the mask with packing straw for hair and cone-shaped paper for horns. Fangs can be drawn in or built from contrasting colored paper. Outline the eyes and mouth with dark colors to emphasize your dangerous monster's features.

Papier Mâché Masks

Children love to work with papier mâché because it is easy to mold.

For younger children, it is best to begin with an oval-shaped piece of cardboard. This will serve as the shape of the head and base for you to place the strips of papier mâché. The bigger the pieces of cardboard, the easier it is for the children to handle.

To begin, take several strips of paper (newspaper is best) and soak them in a paste-water solution. Then lay each strip, side by side, over the oval-shaped piece of cardboard. After you have put down several layers in one direction, crisscross the strips and continue putting down layers until approximately $\frac{1}{4}$ of an inch of paper has been placed on the oval. At this point, punch two holes in the wet paper to serve as eyes. Let the face dry.

To raise specific areas (nose, lips and eyebrows) wad up some dry paper in the desired shape and place it in its respective position. Next, place strips of paste-wet paper (one at a time) over the features until they reach the desired height.

Mold the strips into shape as they begin to dry. This will give the features of the face a more realistic quality. Do not be afraid to mold the paper. If you push too hard and cause a space, all you have to do is add a few more strips to fill it in.

When your mask has dried, it is then ready to be painted. Select several colors to finish off your mask. Make it friendly or evil. Put a few pipe cleaners into the top of the head and through the ears. Cut a hat from colored construction paper and glue it (on a slant) to the head. Hold the mask to your face and look through the two eyeholes.

IN A MEXICAN PARADE, masks add color and excitement to the festivities.

Chicken Wire Masks

Large masks like those used in Mardi Gras and carnival parades must be strong to support long use, and yet, be light enough for a person to carry around without too much strain. These masks are made with chicken wire and paste-wet paper and are easier to construct than you might imagine.

First twist the chicken wire into the desired head shape and then smooth out or clip all ends. The head is usually $2\frac{1}{2}$ to 3 feet high and round enough to allow a person's head to rest within. The shoulder portion of the mask must also allow room for your head to pass and rest comfortably. Place some foam rubber pads between the wire and your shoulders.

Shape the nose, mouth and ears separately and then attach them to the frame by entwining the excess wire into the proper areas of the head with pliers.

Prepare a paste-and-water solution and then place soaked pages of paper over the frame. Put on several layers, allowing each layer to dry before applying the next. When the head is formed and dry, apply the paint.

Place the finished mask on your shoulders. When comfortably fitted, locate the eyes and mark the spots. With a sharp blade, cut through the paper so that you can see. The eyes may not necessarily be where you might think. In other words, should the wearer's eye level be below the approximate location of the painted eyes, then you will cut holes large enough to see, and still paint eye circles. Do not cut additional holes unless they are needed.

Do not cut the wire. For ventilation, cut small holes above the ears and in the nostrils of the nose. Additional holes can be made in the rear of the head if ears and nose are not enough.

The rest of the costume can be prepared before or after the mask is complete. Work on it while the different layers are drying. The costume is made from inexpensive material and is usually oversized to add to the humor.

MATCHBOX CRAFTING

With a small assortment of ordinary household matchboxes, you can construct miniature furniture for a doll house, such as a dresser, couch, bed, or even a piano. Making your own furniture will save you a tremendous expense and give you the satisfaction of completing a special project by yourself. All you need are matchboxes in assorted sizes, index cards or plain stiff paper, poster paints and a small brush, and a single-edged razor blade in a holder for cutting.

A Matchbox Couch

Select six small rectangular matchboxes and empty the matches into another match container. If there is any advertising on the box, peel off as much of it as you can. Now piece these boxes together, one at a time, in the arrangement you have chosen. After glueing two boxes together, allow the glue to dry before attaching another box. To construct the sides and seat of the couch, apply glue only three times, as shown in the illustration. The back of the couch can be formed by attaching two matchboxes slightly higher than the sides, or an index card or two old playing cards. When all the pieces are glued together and have dried, paint your new couch.

A Miniature Piano

Probably the hardest part of making your piano will be painting it, as the construction is certainly not difficult. Using a large box of household matches, you can make a piano with a few simple cuts of the single-edged razor blade. First, remove the drawer section of the box and cut the two sections as indicated in the illustration. Now, put the drawer back into its cover.

To form the piano keys, use an index card

CONSTRUCTING A COUCH: The first stage in making a matchbox couch is glueing together the separate boxes. Apply glue only at the places indicated by the numbers; this will make the couch sturdy enough without using too much glue.

THE COMPLETED COUCH has seats, arm rests and a back.

Written especially for this volume by Maurice Siegel

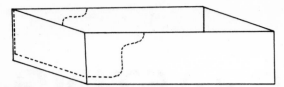

THE INSIDE OF THE MATCHBOX should be cut away along these lines.

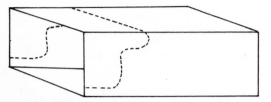

CUT THE OUTSIDE of the matchbox to fit over the cut portion of the inside.

or the piece of box which you cut from the drawer cover. With the razor blade trim the paper to the appropriate width of the keyboard. Sketch and paint the contrasting keys before glueing them into place. Unless you have a very steady hand and are sure you will not smear the paint, it would be best to paint the rest of the piano before inserting the keyboard.

Using a piece of paper which curves easily, cover the S-shaped curve of the piano and glue it. Attach wooden matchsticks (after the heads have been burned), toothpicks or sturdy pipe cleaners as legs. Apply your choice of tempera

paints to the instrument. After your piano has dried, start your own doll music class. Make a piano bench by attaching legs to a narrower box in the same fashion as you did to the piano.

A Doll's Dresser

No doll collection would be complete without a storage place for doll clothes. Make a dresser by simply placing a few boxes on top

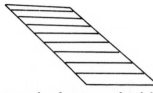

KEYBOARD: Cut a strip of paper to the right size and paint piano keys on it.

PIANO BENCH: Attach legs to a matchbox so your dolls can sit while they play.

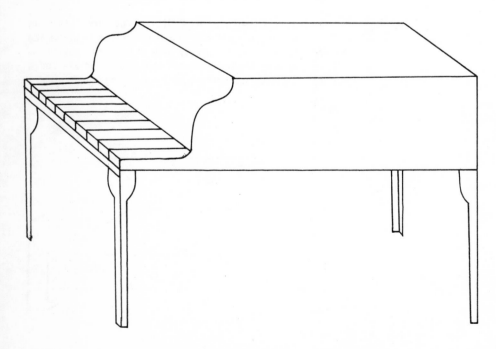

A MATCHBOX PIANO: By carefully cutting and glueing the pieces, you can make a piano that any doll could play.

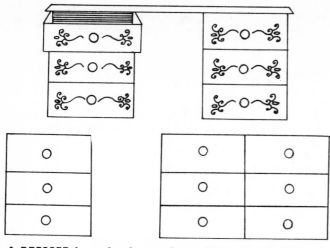

A DRESSER is made of several matchboxes stacked on top of one another. Make a dresser with a space between the two sets of drawers, one with the drawers next to each other, or a simple chest with only one row of drawers.

RESTAURANTS often give away matchboxes with their name on them. Either peel the name off or paint over it.

of each other. Construct a matchbox with a built-in drawer, so dressers are easy to put together.

Remove the drawers from the boxes and glue the boxes together, painting them as desired. Next, decorate the drawers themselves, and replace them in the boxes. Use buttons or bits of aluminum foil as handles for the drawers. The double dresser with a space between the sets of drawers uses a piece of cardboard or an index card for the top.

Matchbox Funnycar Racers

Every year, and in some parts of the country every weekend, thousands of people gather to watch car races such as the Indianapolis 500 or the Grand Prix. Children are no exception to this hobby. The thrill of auto racing can now be brought right to a child's fingertips.

Your child can make his own Funnycar Racers with an assortment of matchboxes, a few buttons for wheels, some cardboard, paint and a little glue.

Many restaurants have matchboxes made for advertising purposes and are glad to give them away, so you should have no trouble finding supplies for this craft. For the Funnycar projects, you will need narrow and long boxes, as well as other smaller shapes.

Peel off as much of the advertising as possible. Use black tempera paint to cover the entire box. Take a piece of paper and glue it around the opening for the drawer section. At the other end of the box, glue a piece of cardboard which extends about 1 inch above the box and is slightly bent at the top. This is a racing stabilizer, shown on the next page.

Make a windshield the same way you made the stabilizer in the rear. This time, use a piece of cardboard which stands only $\frac{1}{4}$ inch higher than the hood of the car.

Glue small buttons to their respective places to represent wheels. You now have the makings of an Indianapolis 500 racer. Check the nearest hobby shop for wheels and axles which can be attached and actually move.

A SIMPLE MATCHBOX like this one can be turned into a racing car. Long thin boxes are the best shape to use.

There are many different styles to design as well as wacky creations which have never been seen before. Put two matchboxes together (each a different size) and see if you can invent a new model.

Painting Your Funnycar

Begin by painting the entire car black. This will cover all the advertising and make the surface appear as neat as possible. Racing stripes and numbers in red and yellow stand

THE RACING STABILIZER on this car gives it protection against tipping when it travels at high speeds.

out very well. Give the wheels a once-over with gold paint. Collect or trade Funnycars with your friends.

MOBILES

Balanced, moving, sculptural forms have an ancient history. As a distinct art form, however, "mobile sculpture" dates from the early 1930's when Alexander Calder, the "father of mobiles," began experimenting with the artistic effects mobiles produce. Since then, mobiles have gained enormous popularity, not only in the professional world of art, but as a craft that can be executed and enjoyed by everyone.

An innumerable range of materials and objects can be used to make mobiles, from wood to glass, and eggs to ping-pong balls. There are no strict rules in mobile construction regarding shape, composition, or color. There are, however, certain fundamentals that are very helpful for balance and arrangement.

Balance and Composition

Trial and error is the best method to use to determine the balance point. Balancing a mobile is the same, in principle, as balancing on a seesaw: if two objects of equal weight are at either end of your mobile, the balance point will be exactly in the middle of the objects. If one end supports a heavier weight than the other, however, the balance point will be nearer the heavier object.

By using a ruler as a seesaw and a variety of coins strung from threads, you can see for yourself how the balance point changes depending on which weights are used.

When creating equilibrium in a mobile, it is not necessary for the objects to be lined up horizontally. As long as the objects and the supporting wires and threads maintain vertical equilibrium (that is, do not tilt the supporting

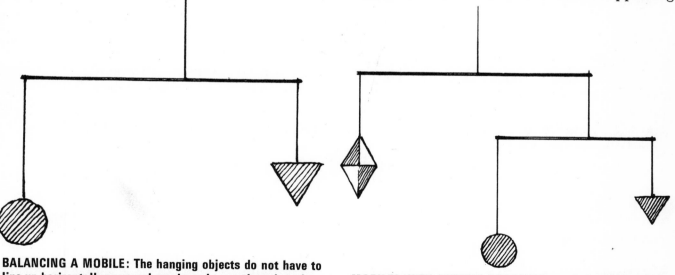

BALANCING A MOBILE: The hanging objects do not have to line up horizontally; one end can hang longer than the other. The mobile should be balanced so that the main supporting rod is parallel to the ground.

MOBILES WITH SEVERAL BRANCHES can balance also. Just remember that the side with more weight or more figures should be the side with the shorter length of supporting rod.

Condensed from the book, "Make Your Own Mobiles" by T. M. Schegger | © 1965 by Sterling Publishing Co., Inc., New York

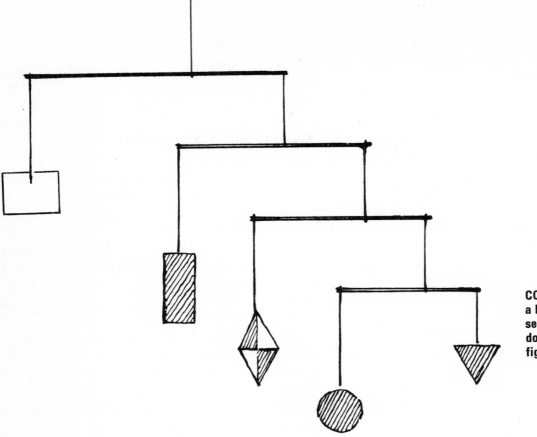

COLOR: Dark colors give a heavy appearance and seem to pull the form downward, while light figures seem to float in air.

rod), the hanging structures can be strung from threads of any length. In fact, asymmetrical hangings often make a mobile more interesting.

Color

Color can play an important rôle in the balance and composition of a mobile. The example above is a simple experiment in the effect of color on balance. You can try this yourself by cutting out shapes from grey cardboard and suspending them from lengths of wire with heavy thread. Then one by one, paint the shapes on both sides with crayon or poster colors. As you will see, the effect is completely different when the shapes are all colored and can move around.

Materials

Cardboard: Two different thicknesses are necessary. For large mobiles, use medium-weight or heavy-weight artist's illustration board or poster board. When bending or folding is necessary, oak-tag, which is a flexible and easily cut glazed cardboard, is ideal. While ordinary scissors are adequate, an X-Acto or a mat knife make neater cuts.

Paper: Fairly stiff paper is more flexible and lighter than cardboard. It also moves freely in air currents.

Plastic: Colored or clear plastic comes in large sheets and is a very good material to work with. It can be easily cut and does not require painting.

Metal: Sheet tin is very useful in making mobiles and can be easily obtained from a roofer's supply house. Two thicknesses, 0.006 inch and 0.012 inch, are satisfactory for most purposes. Compound leverage shears or tin snips (with serrated edges) are used for cutting tin. (See Tin-Can Crafting for tips on working with tin.)

Glass: Glass is more difficult to work with

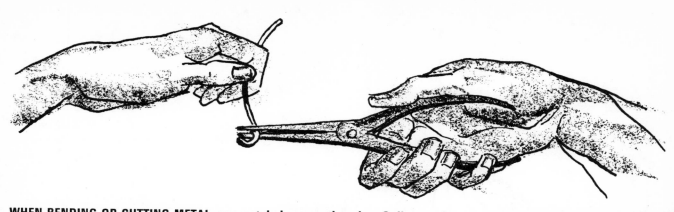

WHEN BENDING OR CUTTING METAL, use metal shears or tin snips. Ordinary scissors are not suitable and will be ruined if used on metal.

than most materials. It comes in a wide variety of colors, however, and has many desirable properties, such as transparency or translucency and iridescence. The results when working with glass are usually very pleasing. There are certain important rules in glass cutting that must be observed. A simple glass cutter's wheel is easy to use. Glass must always be cut on a flat surface. Remember that the glass is only *scored* with the cutter, not cut through. After scoring, a slight tap on the glass while holding the scored line on the edge of a table will break it.

Paints: Poster colors (tempera) are suitable for indoor mobiles; for use out-of-doors, oils should be used to withstand the effects of moisture.

Thread and Wire: Although heavy sewing thread is satisfactory, nylon thread and nylon fishing line are best for mobiles since they are sturdier, stiffer and practically colorless. For heavier or more permanent mobiles, galvanized iron wire is available in various thicknesses. Long-nosed pliers with side cutters are necessary for cutting and bending wire.

Glue: Acetone-base household cement is adequate for most mobiles and dries very quickly. When a stronger bond is required, polyvinyl resin or epoxy cements should be used.

Hangings and Supports: If even a very light mobile is to be hung from a ceiling, it needs some kind of device that will hold it firmly. Tape and ordinary nails are not adequate. The three types of fasteners shown below are the most suitable.

HANGING MOBILES: Plugs and screws are the best devices to secure mobiles for hanging. These three are some common types that should be used.

A Paper Mobile

A gay little carousel is simple to make and
will serve as an inspiration to proceed to more
complicated mobiles. Cut a circle 10 inches
wide from heavy glazed paper to form the roof.
Make a cut from the outer edge to the exact
middle with a knife or scissors, and overlap
the two cut edges and glue them together to
form the cone shape. Make the scalloped
border from a strip of colored paper $\frac{1}{2}$ inch

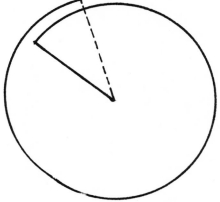

WHEN CUTTING OUT THE CAROUSEL, make two parts: the border, which you can cut in any decorative pattern you like, and
a circle, with a section removed, for the top.

wide and 31 inches long, and glue it around the bottom edge of the cone. Then a variety of simple animal shapes can be cut out and suspended from the underside of the roof with thread. The carousel must be balanced exactly, so experimenting and juggling is necessary. The animals can be colored with paints or crayon, or cut from colored paper.

METAL MOBILES have few restrictions as to size, color and shape. Since these will be heavier than most mobiles, they will not move around as much as paper. Their artistic value will have to come from the unusual shapes and colors you provide them with.

A Metal Mobile

Abstract forms can be hung singly or in groups in a large mobile. Cut a top and bottom for each form; these do not have to be the same shape or size. Punch the plates at the corners. These can be painted with bright colors on both sides. Then suspend the bottom plate from the top plate with colored nylon thread, and knot both the top and bottom of each to hold them securely. Here, where a feeling of random shape and movement is desired, the exact balance point is unimportant and actually undesirable. A mobile from these abstract shapes should be hung in a lopsided way to achieve the most interesting effects.

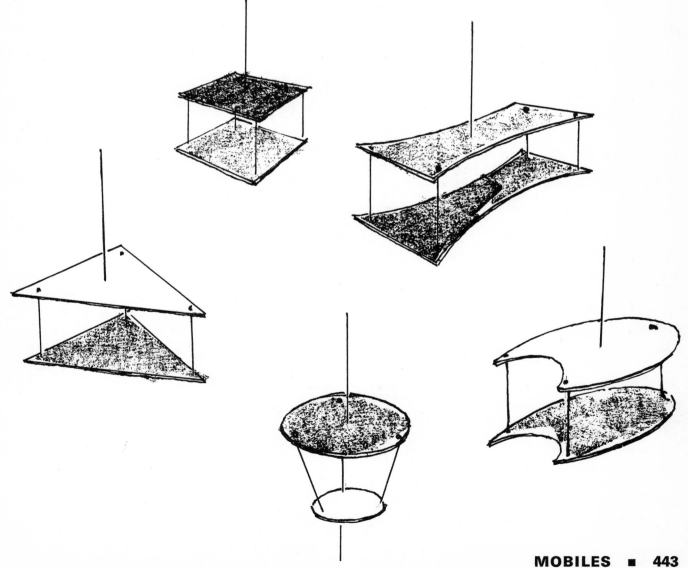

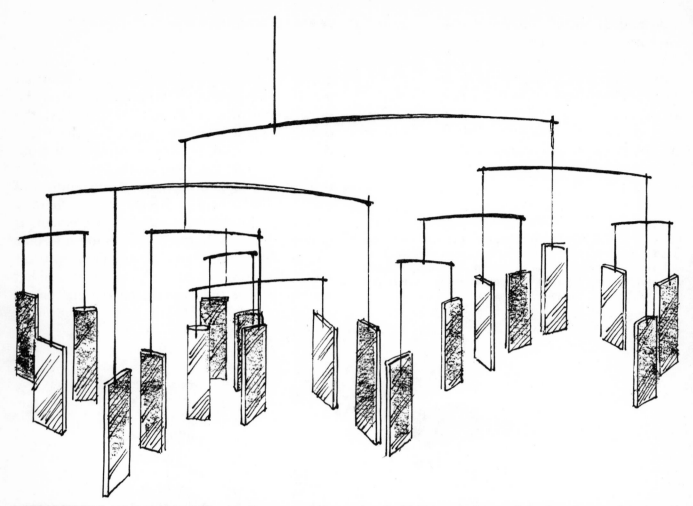

A GLASS MOBILE makes gentle sounds when it moves and hits against itself. The transparency of the glass is part of the beauty here: to add spots of color, however, use acrylic paint, which is particularly suited to glass.

A Glass Mobile

From a sheet of thin glass, cut 1-inch wide strips of varying lengths and dye them with special glass colors which are available at most art supply shops.

Thread for hanging the glass pieces can be glued to the glass with acetone-base cement. If a glazier is available, however, he can drill tiny holes in the end of each strip for the suspending nylon thread. In most mobiles, the hangings should be placed so they do not touch each other. One of the important effects of the glass mobile, however, is the tinkling sound created when the strips hit each other while they move. Experiment to discover the best position for the glass strips to create the most melodious sounds.

MUSICAL INSTRUMENTS

With a little time and ingenuity, you can create a wide variety of musical instruments. You can unearth the raw materials for musical treasures from the kitchen, the basement, the garage, and nearby stores. The basic materials needed for the instruments described here are cardboard tubes, tin cans, soda bottle caps, miscellaneous pieces of wood and a rubber inner tube.

Tin-Can Drum

Drums were probably the first musical instruments, since they are among the easiest

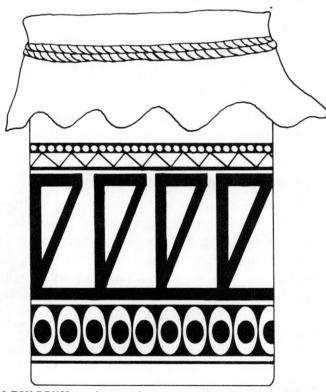

A TOY DRUM can be any size you want it to be, depending on the size of the can that you use to make it. Paint a bright design on the can before you stretch the inner tube over the top.

to construct. All the materials you need for making one are a large juice can or a 2-pound coffee can, some string, and a piece of inner tube about 7 inches in diameter.

Using a can opener, remove any remaining rough edges from the top of the tin can. A pair of pliers will smooth out any remaining rough edges. Next, with the assistance of another person, stretch the piece of rubber over the open end of the can. While your assistant holds the rubber piece in place, secure the drumhead to the drumshell by winding heavy string below the ridge of the frame.

The drum can be decorated in any style you want. Be sure to let the drum design dry properly before you attach the skin.

If you have different sized cans and more than one piece of rubber, you can make more than one drum and produce more than one sound. The different tones will allow you more flexibility when you accompany another musician.

A variety of drum beaters are available in your home. Try a chicken or turkey drumstick, a whisk broom, or a flexible shoetree. Regular drumsticks can also be purchased.

Tin-Can Maracas or Shaker

For your Latin American tunes you'll need this one. It's a variation of an old Indian rattle, and you can make a maracas very much like those offered in the stores.

For this exotic shaker, find two tin cans of the same size. Remove the contents, but don't entirely remove the lids so you can push them back into place later. Scrape off the labels under hot water.

Into one can, throw a half dozen kernels of

Condensed from the book, "Make Your Own Musical Instruments" by Muriel Mandell and Robert E. Wood | © 1957 by Sterling Publishing Co., Inc., New York

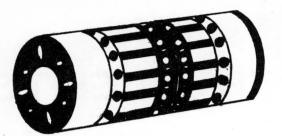

A LATIN AMERICAN MARACAS, made of small tin cans with a few bits of gravel or hard seeds inside, adds a foreign flavor to any music you play.

rice or dry cereal or a cupful of sand. Into the other, put several paper clips, nails, pebbles, or bottle caps. Reseal the cans with cellophane tape. Bind the two cans together with adhesive tape.

Paint an interesting design with enamel on the cans, being sure to cover the adhesive tape. Or paste stretched crepe paper streamers over the entire rattle.

Play it by shaking energetically or by tapping quickly and lightly with your fingers.

Jingle Ring

Jingle rings are used frequently today by many rock and folk groups to accompany other instruments as well as singers. Following a few simple directions, you can make your own jingle ring.

A JINGLE RING makes lively accompaniment for any type of music. The bottle caps knock against each other and sound like bells.

A wooden or metal embroidery hoop will give you a ready-made frame. If this is unavailable, you can fashion a hoop by working off the ring around the top of an opened coffee can. Be careful not to cut yourself.

You will need 10 to 14 soda bottle caps. Soak the caps and pry out the inside corks. Then hammer around the edges of the tops and flatten them. Use a small nail to make a hole in the middle of each cap.

Attach them in pairs to the hoop with colorful yarn, safety pins, or loops made from wire coat hangers. You can disguise the ring by winding crepe paper or material scraps around it, or by painting it bright red. If you use safety pins or wire, paint them a contrasting color.

Play the jingle ring by holding it in one hand and striking it with your other hand. Shake it, or if you prefer, put a short stick through the hoop and swing it round and round in a small circle.

A CARDBOARD TUBE becomes an excellent kazoo. Hold the tube up to your lips and hum a tune. The sound travels in the tube and changes the tone of your humming.

Humboard Kazoo

Cover the end of a cardboard tube with a piece of waxed or wrapping paper larger than the opening. Hold the paper tight with a rubber band or a string around the tube, or by pasting it down. Use a nail to punch eight small round holes an even distance from one another in a straight line along the middle of the cardboard tube.

Put your lips to the open end and hum away. Holding your fingers over the holes (as with a flute), you can vary the sounds. Paste on aluminum foil and your humboard will look like a flute.

You can use cardboard tubes to make rattles or rubber-band strummers.

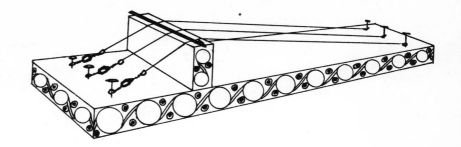

A STRINGED INSTRUMENT depends upon the length and thickness of its strings for the different notes. A my-olin can be plucked or bowed like a violin.

My-olin

The hardware store will supply most of the simple materials you need to make this rugged stringed instrument. It will stand a good deal of rough treatment and reward efforts to play it with a genuine understanding of the string family of instruments. You can pluck or thump or bow it, and each different way of playing the my-olin makes a different kind of music.

For the body of your instrument, use wood 2 inches thick, 4 inches wide and about 36 inches long, but the piece of wood need not be regular in outline. An odd-shaped strip makes a more attractive instrument.

In addition, you will need a piece of wood 1" × 1" × 4" to act as a stationary bridge, and another ½" × 1" × 1" for a movable bridge to vary the tones.

At the hardware store, pick up six heavy large-headed nails (roofing nails), a few light nails, and three small turnbuckles.

For strings, get steel piano wire of different gauges if possible (#13, 15, 19). You don't need more than 3 feet for your lowest string. If you can get very thin wire, you will need less than 2 feet for that string. For high sounds, use thinner wire. Make the thin strings shorter than the thicker ones and the sound will be higher still.

If you can get only one size of wire, order about 12 feet for your strings. This will give you a little extra in case a string breaks.

Drill three holes an inch in from one end of your board. These are for fastening the turnbuckles you will use as pegs to tighten the strings. The heavy nails should slip in and out of the holes but should fit fairly tightly.

Cut off a small triangle from the bottom end if your wood is symmetrical and you want to vary the shape. Sand your wood smooth. Shellac, varnish or paint if you like—it will not influence the tone.

Bend with pliers or cut with wire cutters a piece of your heaviest wire (perhaps No. 19 or 20) about 3 inches shorter than the length of your board. Fasten one end to one screw eye of the turnbuckle.

Unscrew the two hooks of the turnbuckle until they are almost completely out so that the turnbuckle is about as long as you can make it.

Slip one heavy nail through the screw eye not attached to the wire and push it into the first hole in your board.

About ½ inch below the turnbuckle at its longest length, nail the stationary bridge strip across the board.

Lay your wire over the bridge and along the length of the board. At a point about 1 inch from the end, bend the wire as a marker for the loop for the other nail.

If you have a small vise, fasten your nail upright in the vise and using both pliers to grip the wire, wrap it around the nail so as to make a neat loop.

With the loop around its neck, take the nail and stretch the wire along the board. Scratch a mark at the point it reaches. At that point, drill a hole so that the nail will go in up to the head. If the nail comes through on the other side of the wood, cut or saw off the extra length of nail.

You will have plenty of room on the turnbuckle to tighten the wire and get a variety of pitches. If a buzz or rattle persists, cut a piece of coat hanger wire slightly shorter than the width of the board. Loosen the string, slip the hanger wire under the string and across the bridge, and tighten the string on top of it. Try tuning it to low G on the piano or on the violin pitchpipe.

Make each of the strings you put on shorter (and thinner if possible) than the one next to it so that you can stretch each to a higher pitch. With the help of the piano or pitchpipe, you may be able to tune the second string to D and the third to A.

If you get thin enough wire, the last string you put on can be anchored 12 inches from the turnbuckle. Take a look at the strings behind a piano keyboard and see how the shorter wires at the high end are thinner.

Playing the My-olin

If you have spent some time tuning your my-olin, it should play very well. Pluck it with a feather quill or hit it with a dowel stick (approximately 1 foot long) and listen to the strings vibrate. Using a section of rubber hose (1 foot long), rub it back and forth as you would a violin bow. Prop your second strip of wood underneath the strings and play different notes by sliding the bridge back and forth.

Washtub Bass Viol

You don't need magical powers to transform an old washtub into a bass fiddle. The tub itself, if not already available, can be purchased in a hardware store for a minimum cost. Aluminum tubs cost the least and produce the best vibrations. The necessary materials are: a broomstick, a length of clothesline and an eye bolt, two washers and a nut.

Take your washtub and turn it upside down, so that the open portion of the tub is facing the ground. Next, puncture a small hole in the middle—just large enough to allow the screw to pass through. Cushion the screw with a washer and thread it through the hole. On the inside of the tub, place the other washer and

tighten with a nut. Be sure to tighten the nut as much as possible.

An old broomstick or mop handle is the next item to put into place. Saw a $\frac{1}{2}$-inch notch at the end of the stick so it can fit over the lip of the tub. To prevent the stick from splitting, place a wire brace just above the notch. Strong adhesive tape will provide the same protection if wire is not available.

Take the piece of clothesline and tie it to the eye bolt securely. Then, place the stick notch into the lip and stand the stick upright. Stretch the line to the top of the stick. Do *not* bend the stick forward to meet the line. Now tie the clothesline around the uppermost part of the stick, so it does not slide down.

Playing Your Bass

Playing the bass is easy. Place the basin against your legs. Hold the stick with your left hand and pluck the string with your right.

Tilt the stick as far away from the middle as possible, making the line very tight. This will produce your highest note when you pluck the line. To vary the sounds, tilt the stick towards the middle and move your hand down the clothesline. The lower you move your hand, the lower the note. Avoid excess slack in the line.

With a little practice, you can accompany another musician and even play your own melodies. The washtub bass makes a fine companion to banjo, drum or recorder.

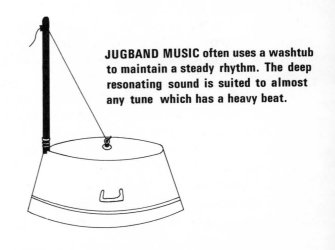

JUGBAND MUSIC often uses a washtub to maintain a steady rhythm. The deep resonating sound is suited to almost any tune which has a heavy beat.

PAPIER MÂCHÉ

Papier mâché has been a popular art form for over 2,000 years, having originated in China. Traditionally, it consists of building up layers of paper strips soaked in flour and water to form sculptures, dishes, masks, or toys—in fact, almost every object has at one time or another been reproduced in papier mâché. The finished pieces are light in weight and, until recently, somewhat fragile. Modern epoxy finishes strengthen papier mâché to the point where it is possible to make chairs strong enough to sit on. In addition, epoxy finishes render the paper surface impervious to practically anything from alcohol to water.

The use of mash, or liquefied paper pulp, and flour, is a variation of the paper strip method. It is handled much like modelling clay, and enables the craftsman to make objects of almost any size and shape, as well as affording new possibilities to exploit textural effects.

The Paper Strip Method

While newsprint is the traditional basic material of papier mâché, rag or tissue papers make interesting substitutes.

Whatever paper you choose, the addition of resin glue to the flour and water paste mixture will give your constructions much more strength and durability. The following mixture is recommended as a dipping solution for the paper strips in all cases: Mix together half a cup of ordinary flour, a quarter of a cup of powdered resin glue, and one pint of water. Stir well until there are no lumps or bubbles. Do not try to save this mixture, but make up a fresh batch of glue mixture before beginning each new project.

Since so many layers are required with the strip-building technique, the following is a great time-saver: tear, with the grain, a thick section of newsprint at the middle fold into two sections of single pages. Tear these in quarters, and tear off the cut outside edges as well, so that all edges will be "feathered." Shuffle a few sheets one at a time into a bucket of tap water, making sure that none stick together. Remove the wet sheets and place them next to the glue mixture. Using your hand, cover the top sheet with glue mixture. Tear this sheet in half, place the two halves together, and tear in half again to make one laminated strip composed of four individual strips of newspaper joined by thin layers of paste with none of the four edges exactly together. Making these laminated strips will enable the building-up

HAT BOX made of papier mâché strips.

Condensed from the book, "Papier Mâché and How to Use It" by Mildred Anderson | © *1965 by Sterling Publishing Co., Inc., New York*

process to go along about four times as fast as it would if you used only single strips.

A Papier Mâché Bowl

To make a bowl, select a mould (a glass dish) approximately the size you want your finished bowl to be. Place the first strip on the bowl through the middle. Repeat this process, adding strips through the middle to make a star-like pattern on the bowl. Put the first layer of strips on, paste side up, so that you will be able to free the mould later on. Press each strip from the middle towards the ends as you layer it over the mould to remove air bubbles and excess water and paste; this will make your construction firm. Apply layered strips parallel

THIS IS THE BOWL you will make in your first strip project.

NEXT, paste strips parallel to the base. Then paste strips diagonally, in every direction until you reach the desired thickness. Then bake it in the oven.

FIRST, using a glass bowl as a mould, paste on your prepared glued strips radiating from the middle outwards.

to your body until you have covered the mould; then apply a second layer at right angles to the first. Apply the next layer of strips diagonally in one direction, and the fourth layer diagonally in the opposite direction. The edges of your bowl will be thinner, of course, because not all the strips will reach to the edge, but this will give the bowl strength at the bottom, where it is needed, without making the entire dish seem heavy. When you have built up the desired thickness, remove the mould.

Press the bottom and sides of your bowl to squeeze out any excess water, and bake the bowl in a 250 degrees F. oven for five to ten minutes on a baking sheet covered with aluminum foil.

Trim the ragged edges of the bowl with a pair of sharp scissors, and cover the edge with short paste-soaked strips, forming a sturdy, even edge. Bake again until the bowl is completely dry but not overly brown. If you want it to be waterproof, coat the bowl with linseed oil and bake once again until it is dry.

To finish, sand the bowl with fine emery paper and decorate it with three or four coats of opaque brushing lacquer, sanding between coats.

AFTER FIRST BAKING, cut off the ragged edges of your paper strips.

REINFORCE the edge with more and shorter strips before baking again.

The strip technique can be employed to make any number of objects: boxes, baskets, lamp shades, dolls, etc. Figures should be constructed by layering around an armature made of wire, netting or rolled paper tubes, and most objects with a definite form (boxes, bowls, plates, flower pots) will benefit from the support of a mould. Your armatures need not be elaborate; just use whatever you have on hand (coat hangers are ideal) and bend it approximately into the shape you want the finished construction to have.

Other variations of the paper strip method are weaving with the laminated strips, or rolling them tightly round a knitting needle to form beads.

ANGEL made over wire armature.

LAMP SHADES made by the pasted strip method, later hardened with epoxy.

Working with Mash

Mash opens up new horizons in papier mâché, for in this "mushy" state the paper can be modelled, moulded, shaped and incised just like clay. Using a paper or wire armature makes it possible to construct almost any shape with mash and achieve a subtlety impossible with the strip method. Even more important is the fact that there is almost no limit to the textural variations you can achieve with mash. It can be combined with the paper strip method as well: a quarter-inch layer over any strip construction will enable you to incise designs or have an icy smooth surface.

Traditionally, mash was made by boiling paper until the fibers broke down, and beating the pulp until it formed a smooth mass. An improved version is this: Tear two sheets of newsprint into strips about $\frac{3}{4}$ by 2 inches long, and place them in an electric blender filled with 3 cups of water. Blend until smooth, and drain in a colander. You should have approximately $1\frac{3}{4}$ cups of pulp. Repeat the procedure until you have enough pulp to fill the top of a large double boiler—one that will hold several quarts if possible. To each quart

UNBEAUTIFUL ALARM CLOCK: The tall papier mâché mash case hides the ugliness.

pan with water, and cook, uncovered, until the mixture is stiff and dark in color (four and a half quarts will probably cook in about three hours). To preserve the mixture, add half a teaspoon of oil of wintergreen to the mash. The mash may be used as soon as it is cool enough to handle, or it may be stored in the refrigerator in a plastic bag.

If you are in a hurry, or want extremely fine pulp, unroll enough toilet paper to fit into the top of the double boiler. Add water to cover, and cook until disintegrated. Add a cup of flour to each quart of pulp, and cook until thick enough to work with.

The mash should be quite thick when you begin work, but flexible enough to mould. Always apply it in thin layers, allowing each to dry before applying the next.

A Mash Clock Case

This case can be made to cover an unbeautiful alarm clock, case and all.

CLOCK CASE made with mash. Notice how a punched border can enhance the appearance.

of pulp in the top of the double boiler add one cup of ordinary flour, fill the bottom of the

Select a cardboard box for an armature, and cut a hole for the clock face. Cover the outside of the box with mash, and bake.

Lay the case face down on the table and fit the face of the clock into the hole in the case. If your clock needs a support to hold it exactly in position, build one with a stiff piece of cardboard and tape. Now cover the inside of the box (except for the top of your clock support) with mash and bake again until the case has dried thoroughly.

Decorating Papier Mâché

Most papier mâché constructions benefit from a minimum of decoration, since their texture is what makes them attractive, but for certain objects there are decorative techniques particularly suited to this medium. Among them is incising (punching) designs into the surface of semi-solid mash. Sticks, buttons, coins, and almost any household utensils (forks, spoon backs) make interesting depressions in the mash which will become wonderfully distorted as the mash dries.

Fabric, leather, furniture, food or batik dyes are all excellent coloring agents for mash, as well as the more traditional water or poster colors. The advantage of these over opaque pigments is that they are transparent enough to allow the rough textures to be seen. A subsequent covering of epoxy or lacquer will protect them.

A paper "collage" pasted on as the final layer is another effective decorating technique. Collage may be used to carry out a theme (boats, hats, landscapes, still lifes), or it may be simply a collection of colored papers torn from magazines and greeting cards. The final coating of epoxy or lacquer will again ensure the protection of the finished surface.

Whether you use paints, dyes, paper decorations, or a textured finish on your creations, always remember that papier mâché is not a precise art form, and that you should allow your imagination full rein.

COLLAGE was the technique used to decorate this papier mâché wastebasket after it had been hardened with epoxy. Lacquer was brushed over the collage.

UNUSUAL CANDLEHOLDER decorated in the semi-solid mash stage by incising with a pencil, using both pointed and blunt ends.

Finishes

Among the opaque finishes, colored brushing lacquer, the traditional finish for papier mâché, is the best choice. It must be applied in thin coats, however. If you want a glossy finish, sand each dry coat before applying the next. While 25 coats are necessary for a truly traditional lacquer finish, you will rarely need to apply more than five or six. Ordinary oil and water paints can be used as the final finish, but are not recommended for most projects. Substitute lacquer whenever you can as the final coat.

In the transparent finishes, clear lacquer is again appropriate, and definitely to be preferred to shellac, which is unsuitable for those objects which will be exposed to water or alcohol. However, both these finishes do blend into the paper surface, giving a lovely soft quality, unlike varnish and paints which seem to lie on top of the surface without becoming an integral part of the piece.

As has been stressed, by far the best finish for almost any papier mâché piece is epoxy. Many brands are available, and all come with detailed instructions. It is absolutely essential to follow these to the letter, and to observe all recommended precautions such as protecting the eyes and skin. Where strength is a requisite epoxy will give results well worth the effort.

CANDLESTICKS made of mash over armatures of rolled paper. The nail point holds the candle in place. The same structure could be used to make chessmen.

NAPKIN RINGS can be made with mash over a rolled paper armature, the same armature you use for candlesticks.

SCRAPCRAFT

In this age of instant obsolescence, every home abounds in wastebasket scrap items—egg cartons, bottle caps, cigar boxes, old records, corks, etc.—that are the perfect fodder for scrapcraft. With a little imagination and working with the simplest of tools (scissors, razor blades, pen knives) and the simplest materials (glue, cellophane tape, poster paint, library paste), these humble throwaway items can be fashioned into useful household aids, colorful toys, interesting additions to the wardrobe, or decorations for every room in the house. Scrapcraft has always been popular with arts and crafts groups, and no one is too young or too old to participate in and enjoy "making something out of nothing."

The projects here require scrap items that either may be found around the house or are "found" objects, such as sea shells, leaves, seeds, etc., that are discarded by nature.

Cigar Box

PROJECT: Beach Scene Shadow Box
Materials:

 cigar box, at least 1 inch deep
 beach sand
 colored construction paper
 drawing paper
 tissue paper
 sandpaper
 cotton
 poster paints
 small sea shells
 razor blade in holder
 scissors
 glue
 picture hook

If there are no cigar smokers in your house, you can ask your druggist or tobacco store clerk to save a flat, 1-inch-deep cigar box for you. Remove the cover from the box, as well as all papers on the four sides. Sand lightly if necessary. Paint the outside of the box in a color that will harmonize with the room in which you plan to hang the finished shadow box. When dry, paint the inside with blue (for sky) poster paint.

While waiting for this to dry, plan your scene on a piece of drawing paper to prevent errors. Placing the cigar box lengthwise on its side, spread an even layer of glue along the bottom inside edge. Sprinkle real beach sand over the glue and let dry.

To give a 3-dimensional effect, extend the beachline $\frac{1}{2}$ inch up the inside vertical sides and along the back of the box, following the

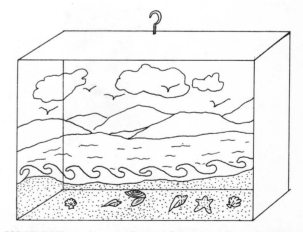

A CIGAR BOX can be transformed into a small stage. Paint a scene inside the box, and add other objects—paper, pipe cleaners, sea shells—to decorate the setting. See Papercraft (page 271) for other ideas.

Adapted in part from the book, "Creating from Scrap" by Lillian and Godfrey Frankel | © 1962 by Sterling Publishing Co., Inc., New York and edited and added to by Jon Teta

same procedure—spreading glue, sprinkling with sand, and allowing to dry.

Cut "waves" from light blue construction paper, making certain you follow the beachline all around. Cut "hills" from light brown and dark brown construction paper. Position the hills about $\frac{1}{4}$ inch above the waves; the portion left exposed (the sea) will thus be the same blue as the sky. The clouds can either be cut from white tissue paper or made of tufts of cotton and glued in place.

With black poster paint, paint birds in flight in the sky and ripples in the sea. In the final step, position and glue down firmly a number of small sea shells along the inside bottom edge. Attach a picture hook to the back of the box and your scene is ready for hanging.

Corks

PROJECT: Toy Cork Soldier
Materials:
   2 large corks
   2 medium corks

CORK SOLDIER is fashioned from different sizes of corks and pipe cleaners. Paint military stripes on his body to identify his regiment or country.

   12 small corks
   pipe cleaners
   ice pick
   poster paints

A cork soldier is a popular toy for little boys to play with, or an unusual ornament for a Christmas tree. Start by piercing each cork through the middle with an ice pick. Use the pipe cleaners to connect the corks, using medium-size corks for the soldier's head and hat, large corks for his waist and body, and small corks for his arms and legs. Turn the ends of the pipe cleaners so that the corks won't slip off. After the figure has shaped up, paint on the soldier's eyes, nose and mouth with black poster paint and a pen. With a brush, color his hat red and his uniform blue with yellow buttons. If the cork soldier is to be hung on the Christmas tree, insert a hook into the top of his hat.

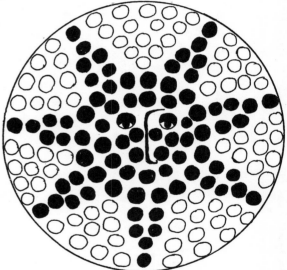

A HOT PLATE made from bottle caps attached to a piece of plywood is decorative enough to put right on the dinner table. Rest a hot dish on top of it—the metal and wood will absorb the heat so it does not damage the table.

Bottle Caps

PROJECT: Hot plate
Materials:
   64 pop bottle caps
   8-inch square of plywood
   enamel paints

glue
hammer
sandpaper
small paint brush
small artist's brush

Trim and sandpaper your piece of wood until it is smooth, especially around the edges. Paint one side of the wood and the sides with blue enamel paint. Arrange some of the bottle caps in the shape of a sun. Put glue on the rough edges of each cap in turn and tap it down into the sheet of wood with your hammer. Arrange the rest of the caps around the sun design and hammer and glue them to the wood.

When the glue is dry, paint the caps of the sun design with bright red enamel; paint the surrounding caps with the same blue enamel paint that you used to paint the wood. When dry, your hot plate is ready for service on the dining table.

Egg Carton

PROJECT: Pot of Tulips
Materials:

    plastic molded egg carton
    coffee can
    green food dye
    pipe cleaners
    sand or gravel
    green construction paper
    scissors
    poster paints
    knitting needle
    glue
    aluminum foil

Start out by separating the 12 holders or cups of the egg carton and examining each to make sure it is intact. If it is not perfect, throw it away and choose another.

Cut out small triangles from the tops of the holders, then poster paint them, inside and outside, in gay tulip colors of red, yellow, and blue.

Use green pipe cleaners for stems (if colored pipe cleaners are not available, dip white ones into a solution of water and green food dye).

EGG CARTON CUPS are just the same size and shape as tulips. Paint them floral colors and add leaves and stems for a permanent flower arrangement.

Poke a small hole through the bottom of each egg holder with a knitting needle. Bend the pipe cleaners down about $\frac{1}{4}$ inch, then thread the straight ends through the holes in the cups.

Fill an empty coffee can with sand or gravel. Making sure that the pipe cleaner "stems" differ in length, push them into the sand in a pleasing floral arrangement. Cut leaves out of green construction paper; stiffen the leaves with pipe cleaners glued to the backs. Add the leaves to the floral arrangement, cover the coffee can with aluminum foil, and your Easter plant is finished.

Glass Etching

Etching or engraving on glass is one of the oldest of arts, so old in fact that an authentic date as to its origin does not seem to be available. While most methods are very difficult, requiring the services of experts, etching cream, available at most handicraft shops, makes the art of etching on glass so simple and safe that even a child can do excellent work.

Plain ordinary tumblers and jelly glasses can thus be decorated and turned into unusual pieces, at a very low cost.

PROJECT: Decorated jelly glass

Materials:

    aluminum stencil foil
    etching cream
    medium-hard pencil
    heavy cardboard
    razor blade in holder or stencil knife
    jelly glass
    tracing paper
    teaspoon

To start, select a simple design, perhaps that of a swan in profile. Trace the design on tracing paper. Place this tracing over a sheet of aluminum stencil foil, then trace the design all over with a medium-hard pencil, using a firm, even pressure to be sure that the design is pressed into the foil.

Place the stencil foil on a sheet of light cardboard, and cut out the design with a razor blade. Placing the stencil on the glassware is probably the most important step. If all the edges around the design are not firmly pressed down, the etching cream will creep under and cause a ragged appearance. After making sure that the glass surface to be etched is thoroughly clean, position the stencil on the glassware.

Using the smooth end of a teaspoon, firmly press down all the edges around the stencil

ETCHING CREAM is a modern discovery which makes designing on glass almost as easy as designing on paper. The cream corrodes the glass, leaving a rough etched appearance after it is washed off.

design. Then apply the etching cream directly from the tube to the open spaces of the stencil. Allow the cream to remain for 2 minutes, then wash off under warm water. Carefully remove the stencil, dry the glass carefully, and your etching is completed.

Macaroni

PROJECT: Necklaces

Materials:

    food colors
    macaroni
    needle
    yarn or elasticized stretch thread
    absorbent paper towels
    water

MACARONI SHELLS come in many different shapes. The tubular ones can be strung with macaroni wheels and worn as jewelry.

Macaroni comes in a number of fascinating shapes and sizes. To lend variety to your necklace, choose several different kinds. Macaroni can be dyed different colors by dipping it into a solution of water and food colors. Drain on absorbent paper towels and allow to dry thoroughly overnight.

If you are making a necklace with large macaroni, such as ziti or rigatoni, thread heavy yarn through the openings, and knot the thread at the back. If you are using the smaller variety, such as pastene, use a needle and elasticized stretch thread.

MILK BOTTLE TOPS can be painted and glued to a piece of ribbon. Depending on its length, the resulting article can be worn as a belt or collar which closely fits the neck.

Milk Bottle Tops

PROJECT: Floral Belt
Materials:

  cardboard milk bottle tops
  glue
  poster paints
  ribbon
  heavy books

Measure bright, ½-inch ribbon to fit around the waist, including enough to tie a bow, and leave dangling ends from 6 to 8 inches. Next, space the cardboard milk bottle tops along the ribbon evenly. The tab side with the printing should be against the ribbon. Glue them down with a strong adhesive. (Elmer's Glue is especially recommended.)

When you have pasted down enough tops, cover each of them with a heavy book and allow to dry for at least an hour. When you are assured that the tops are secure, turn the entire belt over. Spread glue over each of the tops, and "face" each with another top, so that you have discs on both inside and outside. When you have finished, cover the tops with the heavy books once again, and allow to dry overnight. Using bright poster paints, paint a floral design on each of the tops, so that the belt is reversible.

Milk Carton

PROJECT: Telephone Booth

A toy telephone booth can easily be made from an empty cardboard milk carton. First draw the outline of the windows on all four sides of the carton with a ballpoint pen. Now cut the cardboard along the pen lines. To make the door, cut one of the window sides down to the base and also along the base as shown. Fold the door out on the dotted line. You can then crayon the carton or cover it with paper.

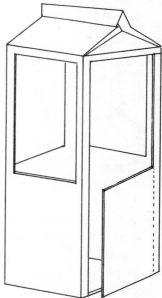

TELEPHONE BOOTH can be cut from a waxed cardboard milk carton. Make a door that can open and close easily, by folding the cardboard along the "hinges."

Nut Shells

PROJECT: Walnut Fish Mobile
Materials:

  walnut shells
  colored construction paper
  quick-drying spray paints
  glue
  nylon thread
  wire clothes hangers or galvanized iron wire
    in No. 14 or 16 gauge thickness (available
    at the hardware store)
  pliers
  scissors

The next time you are eating walnuts, try to save both halves of the same shell; this will ensure a better fit and a better final appearance to your walnut fish. Spray or paint the empty walnut halves with quick-drying colors. From colored construction paper, cut out the dorsal fins and tails in a variety of shapes—half-moon, jagged-edge, scalloped edge, or feathery. Glue a fin and tail to half of each walnut shell.

Now glue the two halves of each shell together. Allow to dry thoroughly before proceeding with the mobile.

THE **CONSTRUCTION OF A FISH MOBILE** of walnut shells is shown in the upper right corner here. Paper fins are glued on, and then the shell halves are attached to each other. To hang the mobile so that it balances evenly, try placing the central support thread on different places along the wire.

The iron wire will be the support arms of the mobile from which the walnut fish will be suspended. Using a pair of long-nosed pliers, make round loops of any size at either end of each length of wire; to do this, grasp the end of the wire in the jaws of the pliers near the tip and form a loop with a quick twisting motion of your wrist.

Tie a length of nylon thread through each loop. Attach a walnut fish to the end of each length of thread by knotting the thread through a small hole punched in the dorsal fin.

Build your mobile from the bottom up, suspending each support arm from the lower one with a length of nylon thread. You will have to decide whether you want your mobile to hang in symmetrical balance or to be balanced in asymmetrical equilibrium. Once the mobile is hung from the ceiling, you can experiment by moving the nylon thread between the support arms. (See Mobiles, page 441, for hanging instructions.)

Paper Clips

PROJECT: Chain Mail Vest
Materials:
    paper clips
    needle
    thread
    old vest (or woman's bolero)

You will need lots of paper clips for this project, so plan on using up all those you have saved or purchase at least a dozen boxes (100 clips to a box) from your local stationery store. Link the clips together to form "chains" of varying lengths—30 to 50 clips for each "chain." Using an old vest as a base, drape your paper clip chains over the shoulders, overlapping them and sewing them in place with needle and thread.

For the most interesting effect, have some of the chains short in front and longer in the back, and vice versa. Next, sew more chains along the neck of the vest and around both armholes.

Phonograph Records

PROJECT: Fruit Bowl
Materials:
    old scratched breakable phonograph record
    pliers or tongs

Heat the kitchen oven to 350 degrees. Place the record in the oven for 10 minutes. Using a pair of pliers or tongs, remove the record and

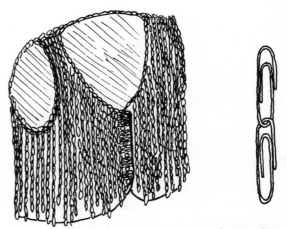

PAPER CLIPS strung together make a dazzling surface. Sew the paper clips on an old vest to prevent them from becoming caught on other things as you move.

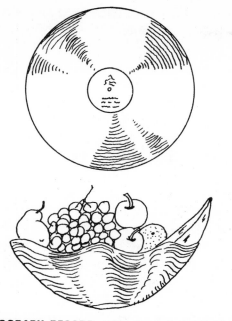

A PHONOGRAPH RECORD, when heated, is pliable enough to shape into a bowl. Do not bend the part where the label appears; leave it as a flat base.

try to bend it. If it is not pliable, put it back in the oven a little while longer. Don't touch the heated record with your bare hands. Test the record again until it bends easily.

Working with the pliers, shape it into a bowl. You will be able to handle it with your hands a few minutes after you take it out of the oven. Once you have molded it into a suitable shape let it cool and harden. Next, paint your bowl with enamel or poster paints, using bold, broad strokes to cover all the surfaces.

Spools

PROJECT: Spool Tie Rack
Materials:

    board, $18'' \times 3'' \times \frac{3}{4}$
    wire coat hanger
    8 empty thread spools
    hammer and small nails
    hand saw
    screw eyes
    hooks
    sandpaper
    drill
    varnish
    paint brush
    hooks

Saw the board into three pieces—one piece 12 inches long and the two end pieces each 3 inches long. Sandpaper each piece. Measure 1 inch from the end of each 3-inch piece and drill a hole to hold the coat hanger. Nail or screw the 3-inch pieces to the ends of the long piece. Untwist a wire coat hanger and cut off a 14-inch section.

Slide the spools over the wire, put the wire ends through the drilled holes, and turn down the ends to keep it in place. Varnish the entire rack. Place a screw eye at each end of the back of the tie rack and hang it on hooks in your closet.

A SPOOL TIE RACK is a practical gift. The size of the spools you use, as well as the length you want your rack, will determine how many spools you need to save.

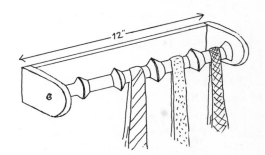

Tin Cans

PROJECT: Pencil holder

Materials:

 frozen juice can
 glue
 yarn

Cover the top 1 inch of the outside of the frozen juice can with glue. Wind the yarn row by row, making certain that each is as close as possible to the previous row. Add more glue and yarn until the entire can is covered.

PENCIL HOLDERS are good favors to give away at parties. They can be filled with candy or other surprises, and later put to a more practical use.

Soap

PROJECT: Soap Carving

Materials:

 carbon paper
 paring knife, or a penknife with a thin,
  pointed blade
 pencil
 paper napkins
 soap cake (white)
 lollypop stick
 toothpicks

Soap has a great many advantages over other kinds of sculpture material. It is cheap and, if a project turns out to be something less than a masterpiece, little but time is lost. It is

firm yet responds to gentle pressure and only the simplest of tools are needed to carve definite marks in it. With the paring knife, smooth the cake of soap, removing any lettering and raised edges.

Create a simple design on a piece of paper, such as a dog in profile seated on a pedestal. Transfer the design to the cake of soap, using carbon paper and tracing lightly with a soft pencil.

Begin the carving by laying the soap flat on a hard surface and removing all the excess soap from around the design. From this point on, you can hold the soap in your hands and carve as in peeling potatoes, working all around the design rather than doing one section first.

When finished, smooth by rubbing lightly all over with the flat side of the knife. Use a sharpened lollypop stick and toothpicks to incise details such as eyes, mouth, and dog collar. Set the carving aside to dry for a day or so, then polish gently with paper napkins.

Toothpicks

PROJECT: A Flag

Even the youngest child can make his own toothpick flag before he learns how to sew one out of cloth. The staff is 3 toothpicks high, the area for stars 1 toothpick deep. The stripes can

SOAP is a popular sculpturing material because of its low cost and the ease with which it can be carved. First outline the area to be cut with a pencil on top of carbon paper, and then carefully cut away the excess soap.

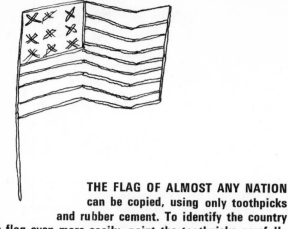

THE FLAG OF ALMOST ANY NATION can be copied, using only toothpicks and rubber cement. To identify the country of the flag even more easily, paint the toothpicks carefully with a small brush.

be $2\frac{1}{2}$ or 3 toothpicks long. Make the stars out of equal sized broken bits.

To give permanence to the flag, coat a piece of paper with rubber cement. Let it dry. Give it another coat and while it is still sticky, embed the toothpicks in position. When the cement has fully dried, with a finger rub away very carefully the excess from the clear outside areas only.

Ice Cream Sticks

PROJECT: Trivet
Materials:

  16 ice cream sticks
  16 small wooden beads
  48 large wooden beads
  spool of nylon thread
  gimlet

With a gimlet, bore tiny holes in each ice cream stick $\frac{1}{2}$ inch from one end and $1\frac{1}{2}$ inches from the other. Take the nylon thread and tie a double knot in it about 2 inches from the end. String a small bead on it up to the knot. Next place an ice cream stick on the thread and then a small bead. Continue until all the sticks and small beads have been laced, then tie the two ends together fairly tightly. Do not cut off the excess yet.

Now lace another thread in the same way through the other holes in the sticks, putting 3 beads of the larger size between the sticks. Tie this loosely, too. Go back and make the

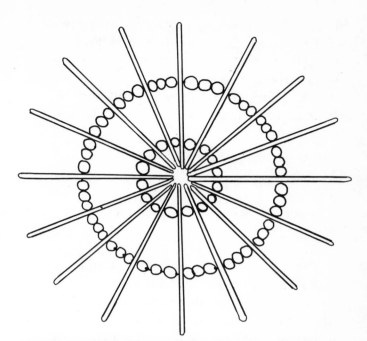

A TRIVET MADE OF WOODEN MATERIALS is most practical; it will not scratch the table surface on which it rests. Because of the nylon thread, however, this trivet is not suited for holding hot dishes.

inner circle as tight as possible and cut off the excess thread. Do the same with the outer circle. You will have a tight little trivet when you finish. It can be used as a place mat for a cereal or other dish, but not a hot dish on a polished table.

String

PROJECT: String sculpture
Materials:

  20 yards of string or yarn
  toy balloon
  flour and water or wallpaper paste

Inflate the balloon to its full size and tie the end. Soak the string in a bowl of paste until it is thoroughly saturated. Wipe any excess paste off the string with a rag.

Now wind the string around the balloon in any way which pleases you. The more different directions in which you wind, the more interesting shapes you will create, as the string crosses and recrosses itself. When the design is as intricate as you want, stop winding the string.

Hang the balloon and string up to dry.

Leave them overnight, and the string will be stiff by morning. Puncture the balloon with a pin, and carefully remove the pieces by pulling them through one of the openings in the string. Hang the sculpture from the ceiling. If you don't handle it roughly, it should last for years.

PROJECT: String figures
Materials:

string
paper
water
salt

You can make string into flat shapes also. If flour and water or wallpaper paste is not available, use heavily salted water. Soak the string in the salt water until it is saturated. Remove it and let most of the excess drip off.

Working on a flat piece of paper, manipulate the string into human or animal shapes. Create a whole family, including a dog or a cat. Leave the string to dry for several hours or overnight. When all the water has evaporated, the salt will have made the string stiff, and the shapes you designed will be fairly permanent.

STRING FIGURES which you design from string saturated with salt water can be decorated even more: add buttons or fabric to make faces, a thin layer of cotton for wispy clouds, and tissue paper for fragile-looking flowers.

Wire and Tissue

PROJECT: Wire Figures

Using only pliers, lightweight wire or pipe cleaners (or both together), glue (clear drying), and tissue paper in assorted colors, you can create a miniature circus, a boxing match or a football game. Because the paper is already colored, you do not need messy paints.

Precut several pieces of wire into 6-inch and 12-inch lengths. Many pliers have joints that are sharpened for use as wire cutters. In many instances, simply bending light wire back and forth will cause it to break at a desired point.

After you decide on a design, twist the wire lengths into a model or armature. Trim off sharp edges or excess wire. Save all the excess wire in a paper cup or envelope in case you need extra pieces later for something (feet, hands, hat, etc.).

The next step is adding the tissue paper body to the miniature model. Getting the first layer to stick will probably present the biggest problem. To do this, slightly dilute your clear-drying glue with water in a paper cup and dip the wire figure in or use a paint brush to coat the wire with glue. Make sure the section to be tissued is covered with glue. Now take a strip of colored tissue paper and wrap it loosely or tightly around the desired area. Allow this to dry and then repeat until the proper thickness is reached.

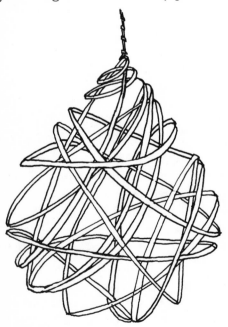

AN ABSTRACT STRING SCULPTURE is fascinating to study. By just looking at it, no one will be able to figure out how it was made!

WIRE FIGURES covered with tissue paper can be bent into any position. To balance a tightrope walker on a piece of cord, wrap a small piece of wire around his feet and the cord.

Set your models into an empty shoebox or carton which has had the long side cut out. For a circus scene with a tightrope walker or a man on a flying trapeze, suspend a wire from one wall of the box to the opposite side. Construct a trapeze from wire and a match-stick. Draw the audience and clowns on the sides of the box.

For a boxing scene, elevate the boxing ring from the floor of the box by simply placing a small, square, upside-down box into the middle of the larger box. This will be the ring. Glue down four matchsticks into the corners and twist wires around them to form the ropes of the ring. Place your fighters in the middle of the square. On the walls of the larger box, draw in enthusiastic faces.

Set up a tennis match using your miniature models. Draw in the lines of the court on the base of a shoebox, or use wires. Set the wire and tissue figures upright by anchoring their feet in the base as illustrated. The racket can be made of wire mesh (screening). For additional realism, attach a small ball to a suspended wire for an "in play" effect.

A TENNIS MATCH can be played by two wire figures. Their rackets and the net are made of a small part of a wire screen.

Found Objects

Found objects are those objects that are discarded by nature—sea shells, leaves, seeds, driftwood, etc. In more recent times, the term has also come to include interesting items discarded by man to be found in dumps, fields, attics, and garbage pails.

Who was the first person to fashion a neck-lace out of sea shells, or preserve the beauty of a golden autumn leaf by pressing it between the pages of a book? No one knows, of course, but what is known is that man has always had a fascination for nature's discards. At no point in history, however, was the passion for found objects more feverish than in the 19th century. It was a man's world and refined young ladies of the day were judged not on their ability to hold up their end of an intellectual conversation but rather on their skill and cleverness at transforming nature's products into ornamental "works of art." Such periodicals as *Godey's Ladies Book, Harper's Bazaar,* and *Mrs. Leslie's Magazine* warned that a lady could not be considered "useful" unless she was capable of making a rustic frame of twigs and acorns and pine cones, or a wreath of the reddened October blackberry. Sea shells, porcupine quills, bird feathers, straw and dried leaves were among the natural materials that were fashioned into the "fancy pretties" that crowded every inch of the Victorian home and ultimately came to be known as "dust- catchers."

Today, found objects are especially dear to the heart of the collagist, who refers to them as

objets trouvés. These objects are usually incorporated into an *assemblage.*

Pine Cones

PROJECT: Christmas Wreath
Materials:

    pine cones
    walnuts
    pecans
    large sheet of heavy cardboard
    glue (Elmer's Glue is recommended)
    gold paint or gold glitter
    mahogany stain
    red ribbon, 2 inches wide
    clear shellac
    scissors or knife
    ruler
    small artist's brush
    paint brush for staining
    sturdy hook

From the large sheet of heavy cardboard, cut out a circle the size you would like to make your wreath. Measure in at least 4 to 6 inches from the outer circumference, and cut another circle out of the center.

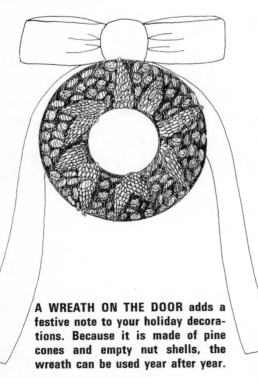

A WREATH ON THE DOOR adds a festive note to your holiday decorations. Because it is made of pine cones and empty nut shells, the wreath can be used year after year.

Glue the pine cones to the wreath shape, varying the placement to lend interest. Be as lavish as possible with the glue, squirting it between the cones where they meet as well as on the cardboard base; the white glue will not show when the wreath is completed.

Glue walnuts and pecans all over the wreath —on top of the pine cones, around the base, and between any large gaps. Again, be lavish in your use of glue.

Place the wreath aside to dry at least for a day or so. When dry, check for any pine cones or nuts that may be loose. Next, stain the entire wreath with mahogany or dark brown stain; don't strive for an even, over-all color since a more interesting effect is to have the wreath darker in some spots than in others. Allow the stain to dry for at least three days.

Next, using a small artist's brush and the smallest amount of gold paint (you might touch the brush to a newspaper after you have dipped it into the paint to get off the excess), lightly brush some of the pine cone leaves at random all around the wreath. This will give an antique effect. You may prefer to use gold glitter, instead; if so, you should add the glitter shortly after you stain the wreath, when all of the excess stain has been absorbed and it is still tacky.

Next, spray the entire wreath with clear shellac. Allow to dry, then spray a second coat. When ready to hang, put a sturdy hook on the back and add a large red bow with long dangling ends.

Leaves

PROJECT: Spatterwork Tray
Materials:

    oak and maple leaves
    old tray
    spray paint
    newspapers
    rubber cement
    toothbrush
    India ink
    small piece of window screening

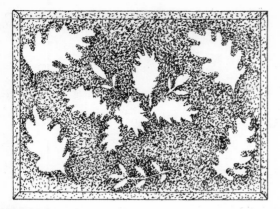

SPATTERWORK TRAY: Spatterwork adds a delicate layer of color wherever it is applied. Glue leaves on the tray before you paint, to keep some areas the original background color.

Spatterwork dates back to about 1860, and the ladies of the time used the technique to decorate fabrics, old trays, papier mâché table-tops, as well as to create interesting patterns that were framed and hung on the wall.

Place newspapers over your work area. Begin by spray painting an old tray in a warm, neutral tone of beige or off-white. This may require several coats of paint if the tray has a design that has to be covered. Let the paint dry thoroughly.

Arrange the leaves in a pleasing pattern on the tray. Tack them down with rubber cement, lightly but being certain the leaves lie flat. Dip the toothbrush into the India ink. Blot off the excess by brushing the toothbrush across a sheet of newspaper. Holding the small piece of window screening a foot or so above the tray, rub the toothbrush across the screening *towards* you. Spatter in this fashion all over the tray.

When finished, do not remove the leaves. Allow the tray to dry for several days, then pull off the leaves. The rubber cement can be removed by rubbing lightly with your fingers.

Sea Shells

PROJECT: Apple Blossom Shell Earrings
Materials:

a pair of earring blanks (available at most hobby stores)

10 small cup shells, about $\frac{1}{4}$ inch in diameter
two small yellow baby cup shells
tube of shell cement
lacquer pink pearlizer (a special shell-tinting agent)
two round plastic discs
toothpicks
tweezers
package of green garfish scales (if available)

Shells of all kinds are obtainable from shops that specialize in this field, but if you live close to the ocean, it is really more fun to gather up your own. The best time to collect shells is in the early morning or when the tide is far out. When you have gathered up enough evenly matched small cup shells, you will be ready to make these simple earrings in the classic apple blossom pattern.

First, squeeze a drop of shell cement in the middle of a round plastic disc. Using tweezers, set the smooth side of the shell into the cement, cut side up. Set the second shell into the cement slightly overlapping the first; continue until five shells are set in an even circle. These are the "petals" of your apple blossom.

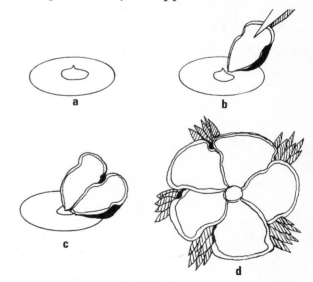

SHELL EARRINGS: These are the four steps to follow to construct an earring. In (a), a drop of glue is in the middle of a plastic disc. Tweezers place the first sea shell into position in (b). Two "petals," one overlapping the other, are glued down in (c). The finished earring in (d) has been decorated with green garfish scales around the edges and a small shell in the middle.

Place a very small drop of cement in the middle of the "flower" and, using the tweezers, drop a small yellow baby cup shell in. Tint the outer edges of the shells with lacquer pink pearlizer.

If green garfish scales are available, you may want to decorate the apple blossom with "leaves." To do this, dip the end of each scale into shell cement and slide under the "petals" at desired intervals (toothpicks will come in handy in positioning the scales).

In the final step, place a drop of cement on top of the earring blank and attach the shell "flower." Repeat the same procedure for the second earring.

Seeds

PROJECT: Seed Mosaic
Materials:
   variety of seeds, such as poppy, sunflower, watermelon, etc.
   heavy cardboard
   glue
   rice

On a piece of heavy cardboard, sketch a simple design such as the one in the illustration. Working with one type of seed at a time, coat with a layer of glue all parts of the

A MOSAIC OF SEEDS can either be all one color or several contrasting ones, depending upon the seeds you use. Watermelon seeds are dark, for example, while pumpkin seeds are light. See page 44 for another picture of a seed mosaic.

design that will include that seed. Large seeds should be handled individually, while the small varieties can be sprinkled on.

Repeat with another part of the design, and continue until the entire design is covered. You can add some color, if desired, by dying some rice in a solution of water and food color; when the rice is thoroughly dry, add it to your seed mosaic.

wood

WOODWORKING

Woodworking is a satisfying craft that utilizes ordinary and easily available materials. It is an activity that will enable you to express both the practical as well as the aesthetic sides of your personality. You can make wooden objects that are unique, hand-crafted, sturdy, appealing, and less expensive than comparable works bought commercially. A relatively small area of your home, such as a corner of your basement, is all the room that is needed.

Here, enough basic information will be given to help you learn some of the rudiments of woodworking. These basic instructions are applicable to the crafting of a wide range of objects, whose creation will serve to help make your home more appealing and functional, both inside and out.

What You Will Need

The only tools needed to succeed at woodworking are those found in the toolbox of the average home handyman. A good hammer is the first tool required, and the best all-purpose type is the *claw hammer*. A *crosscut saw* is also a necessary tool. As the name implies, it is used for cutting across the grain of the wood, such as when you cut off the end of a board. A *rip saw*, whose teeth are coarser and set at a different angle from those of a crosscut saw, is used for sawing with the grain. Other necessary tools for basic woodworking include: *coping saw; ruler; try square; brace* and *bits* of various sizes; *pencil; paint brushes; hand drill* and assorted *twist drills; tin snips; screwdrivers; nail set; smoothing* or *jackplane; metalworking file* with handle; and a *woodworking file,* or *rasp,* with handle.

Written especially for this volume by Gordon Lander

For a working surface, any solid table will be adequate, but since the table top will take some hard usage, a workbench is preferable, especially if it is equipped with a vise.

Basic Woodworking Joints

Three simple ways to join pieces of wood together are the *butt, lap,* and *miter* joints.

In the butt joint, the side of one board is nailed into the end of the other. Since the nails going into the end piece travel with the grain, the butt joint is not a particularly strong one. Corner irons, brackets, or glueing blocks may be used on the inside of the butt joint to strengthen it.

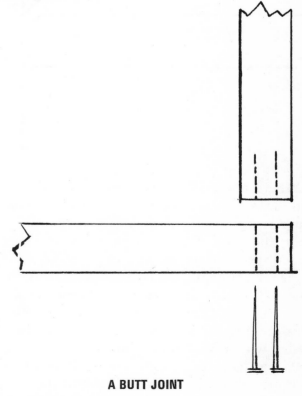

A BUTT JOINT

The lap joint is a variation of the butt joint, and makes up in strength for what it lacks in beauty. Most crates are joined almost entirely by lap joints, as are ladders and other objects which must be able to withstand stress and strain. In the lap joint, the two pieces to be joined are overlapped, face to face, so that the nails go through the grain on both pieces. This joint generally does not require additional bracing.

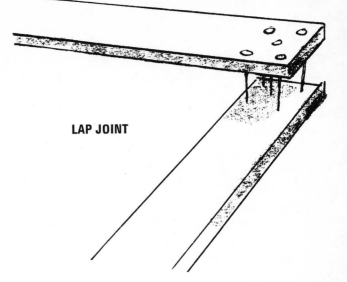

LAP JOINT

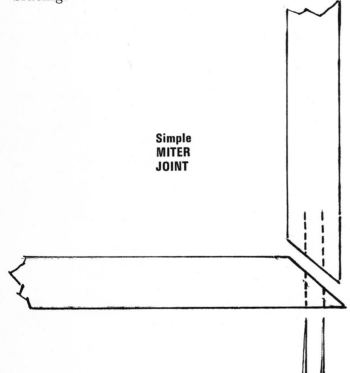

Simple MITER JOINT

tenon joint. The three basic joints described here are sufficient, however, for most projects, as you will see when you begin to use them.

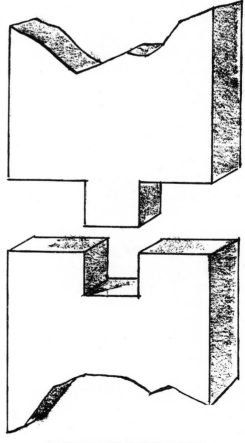

Where a smooth joint is required, with no end grain showing, such as in a picture frame, the miter joint is used. In a simple miter joint, the ends of the two pieces to be joined are cut at a 45° angle. The ends are joined to make a right angle and fastened with nails and glue. The nails are driven in perpendicular to the outer surface of each joining member after the angled faces of the joint have been coated with a good wood glue.

As you gain experience and skill in woodworking, you will want to experiment with more elaborate joints, such as the *mortise and*

MORTISE AND TENON JOINT

Making a Bird Feeding Station

One of the pleasures of woodworking is found in making an object that is not only useful, but that will also provide endless hours of entertainment. A bird feeding station is one such project. By building this relatively simple object, you can enhance the appearance of your yard and establish a sanctuary for birds in your area.

Two pieces of pine and 16 1¼-inch (3d) common nails are all the materials you will need to build the bird station. The bottom piece should be at least ½ inch thick, 10 inches wide, and at least 10 inches long. The frame, or feeding box, is made from a piece of pine ½ inch thick, 2 inches wide, and 23 inches long.

Start your feeding station by cutting the 10 × 10 inch bottom. Choose the straightest end of your 10-inch-wide board, and, by placing the handle of the try square along the edge, make sure the end of the board is square. Then, using your ruler, make a mark 10 inches from the end of the board. Hold the try square against the edge of the board and draw a straight line across the board at the 10-inch mark.

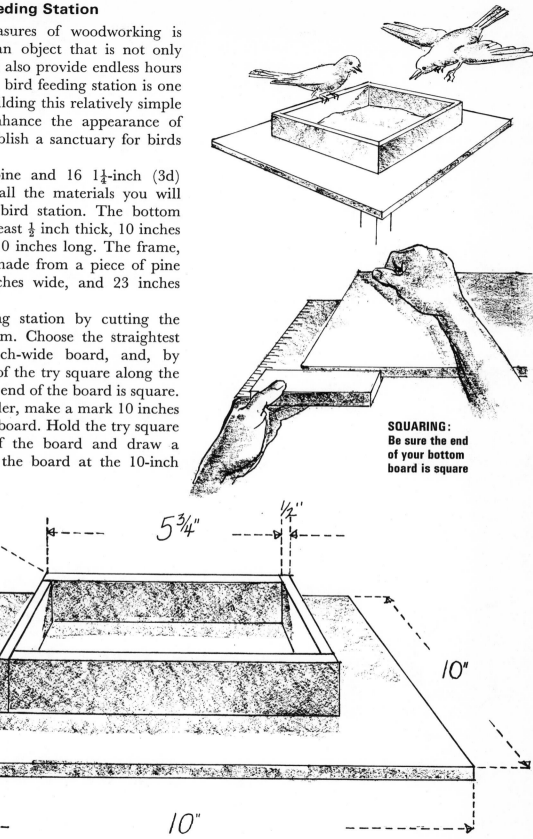

SQUARING:
Be sure the end of your bottom board is square

Use your crosscut saw to cut the bottom board. To use the saw most efficiently, hold it at a 45° angle to the edge of the board and guide the saw carefully with your right hand as you hold the wood firmly on the workbench with your left hand (if you are right-handed). Draw the saw upward lightly to make a starting groove on the line you have marked. Push down firmly to begin your cut. Remember that the saw cuts only on the downward stroke, so when you draw it back, relax and make sure you are cutting straight along the line.

To make a perfectly square cut, it is also necessary to make sure the side of the saw is perpendicular to the face of the board. Test this angle from time to time—especially as you begin your cut—by putting the handle of your try square flat on the board with the blade extending up along the side of the saw.

When you have cut almost through the wood, saw slowly and carefully so you do not split the small piece of wood that remains to be cut.

The frame for your bird feeder comes next. To begin, use your try square to divide and mark the 23-inch piece of pine into four sections $5\frac{3}{4}$ inches long. If you have a vise on your table, use it to hold the wood and cut the piece with your crosscut saw.

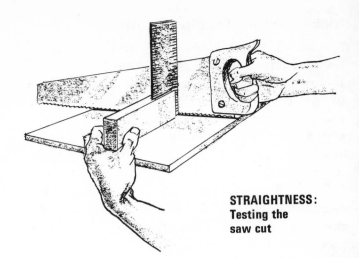

STRAIGHTNESS: Testing the saw cut

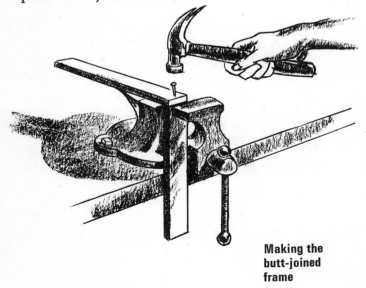

Making the butt-joined frame

Assemble the frame by means of butt joints. Start by placing one of the $5\frac{3}{4}$-inch pieces in the vise. Placing another piece squarely on the end of the piece in the vise, nail them together with two $1\frac{1}{4}$-inch common nails. Be sure you nail the pieces as shown—one *side* to one *end*. Repeat the procedure until all four sides are nailed together. This method will give you a perfect square with each side measuring $6\frac{1}{4}$ inches.

To assemble the bird feeding station, use your try square and ruler to mark a square $2\frac{1}{8}$ inches in from the edges of the bottom section. These pencil lines are simply guides to show where the nails should go when the bottom is fastened to the frame.

Putting two $1\frac{1}{4}$-inch nails to a side, drive eight nails through the bottom so that they barely stick out on the other side—not more than $\frac{1}{16}$ of an inch.

Take the completed frame, and position it squarely over the protruding points. When the frame is satisfactorily positioned, give it a light tap with your hammer so the tips of the nails will sink into the frame and keep it in position when you turn the feeder over to finish driving the nails in.

To protect your feeding station from harsh winter weather, you may wish to oil or stain it. A small can of boiled linseed oil will be enough to give adequate protection. Paint on a liberal amount with your brush. Wait about 15

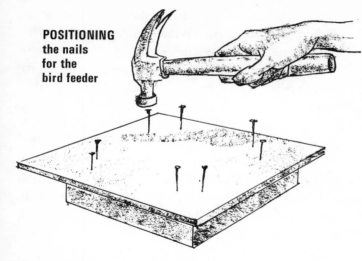

**POSITIONING
the nails
for the
bird feeder**

minutes; then wipe off the excess with an old cloth or paper towel. Apply several coats—lengthening the time between application and wiping so that the oil may penetrate and preserve the wood.

If you prefer to stain your feeding station, one of the many outdoor preservative-type stains is best for your purposes. Instructions vary according to the composition of the stain, so read the directions on the can and follow them carefully.

Your bird feeding station can now be nailed to a post or fence. Even better—particularly if there are squirrels in your area—suspend it from the branch of a tree with wire. By putting seeds, bread crumbs, or suet in the feeder every day during the winter, you may enjoy hours of entertainment and education watching the birds gather at your backyard feeding station.

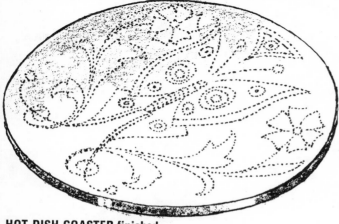

HOT-DISH COASTER finished

A Hot-Dish Coaster

Now you may wish to try something more ambitious. Making a hot-dish coaster will enable you to use more tools and practice more difficult woodworking skills. Decorative and useful, this attractive addition to your home will be a conversation piece whenever guests sit down for dinner.

To make the coaster, you will need a piece of $\frac{3}{8}$-inch plywood at least 6 inches square, a large tin can at least 6 inches high, a small box of $\frac{1}{4}$-inch *bright steel wire nails*, one 2-inch (6d) common nail, and an ordinary sheet of paper. To finish the coaster, you will require a small jar of alcohol, a small container of orange shellac, and some polishing wax.

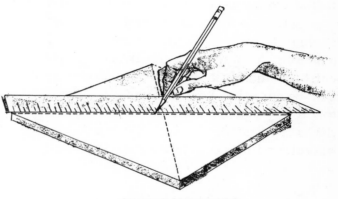

FINDING THE CENTER

To make the hot-dish coaster, first use a pencil compass to draw a 6-inch circle on the piece of plywood. (Plywood is made in a shop from thin sheets of soft wood that have been glued together at right angles to prevent splitting and warping.) An easy way to find the center of the piece of plywood is to draw diagonal lines across the wood, from corner to corner. The center will be the point where the lines meet. If you adjust the compass so the metal tip is 3 inches from the pencil's point, you will be able to make a 6-inch circle. Place the metal tip at the center point on the plywood and rotate the pencil to draw a 6-inch circle.

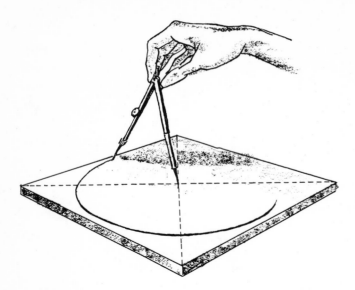

Use your coping saw to cut out the plywood circle. Keep the plywood steady by placing it in the vise or by holding it firmly against the workbench as you saw. Be certain to keep the coping saw outside the line of the circle as you cut along the plywood. After the circle has been cut out, smooth its edge with a woodworking file. Be sure that your file has a handle on it, to protect yourself from accidental cuts from the sharp end of the file. Make the edge as smooth and round as possible.

The metal top for your coaster will be made from a large tin can. To do this, first remove the top of the can; then use your tin snips to cut along the seam and remove the bottom. Flatten the body of the can so you have a large, flat piece of tin. Next use your compass to draw a $5\frac{3}{4}$-inch circle on the tin. (The distance between the metal tip and the pencil's point should be set at $2\frac{7}{8}$ inches.) Cut out the circle with the tin snips. Use a metal file to make the edges of the tin circle smooth. (A metal file has teeth that are smaller and harder than the teeth on a woodworking file.)

From a piece of paper, cut a circle whose size is equal to the size of the tin circle. Now draw or copy on the paper any design you wish to use for the surface of your hot-dish coaster.

Next, put the tin circle, shiny side up, on the wooden circle. Allow a $\frac{1}{8}$-inch border to show. Place the paper circle on top of the tin circle. Then use the small steel wire nails, $\frac{1}{2}$ inch apart, to affix both the tin circle and the paper circle to the plywood. Press the circles tight as you hammer in the nails, to prevent slippage.

You can make a handy tool for stamping

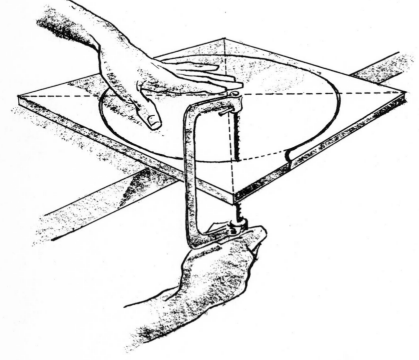

COPING SAW: Holding your plywood firmly on the edge of your workbench, use the saw to cut the circle.

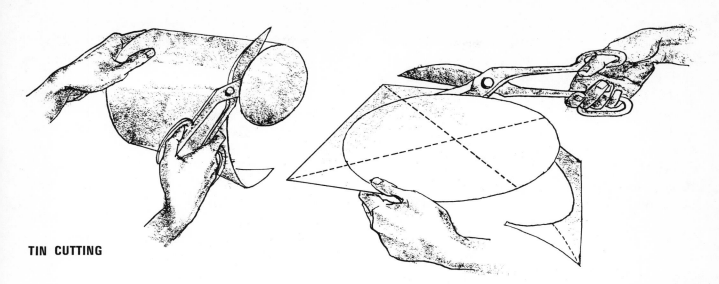

TIN CUTTING

your design on the tin by filing off the point of a 2-inch (6d) nail until the end is smooth and round. Use this stamping tool to tap evenly spaced dents along the lines of the design you have drawn. Be careful not to puncture the tin. After you have tapped in your design, tear off the paper.

Apply a coat of shellac to the wooden parts of the coaster. Clean your brush with alcohol. Wait two hours and then apply a second coat of shellac, remembering to clean your brush when you have finished. In four hours the shellac should be thoroughly dry. You may wish to cover both the tin and the wood with a

coat of wax, polishing both sides of the coaster to make it shine. Before polishing, clean the tin with the tip of a rag dipped in alcohol to remove any shellac that may accidentally have dried there.

Enamel Designs on Wood

An enamel design is a colorful alternative to stamped tin. Creating a scene or design on a wood surface causes fewer problems than one might imagine. Simply trace or draw a design on thin paper. After sanding the top of the plywood circle smooth, lay the design in the position you wish the final decoration to fill.

TACKING the paper circle to the tin circle and the plywood.

STAMPING: Use a blunted nail for incising the design in the tin.

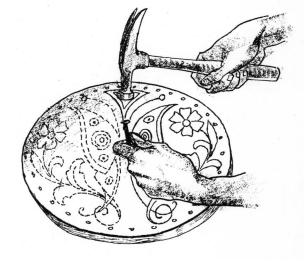

Now go over the drawing with a pencil, pressing slightly harder than you would ordinarily. This will imprint your design on the surface of the wood. Check periodically to see that the design is transferring legibly.

Now you are ready to paint in the design with enamels of various colors. After the first coat has dried, apply a second.

When both applications of enamel have dried, finish the surface with several clear coats of shellac, allowing two hours between coats.

The enamel design will show through clearly.

Hot-dish coasters can be made in any shape, size, or design. So by all means, experiment.

Your imagination and energy may lead you to some truly exciting results. Before long, your newly acquired skills in woodworking will enable you to make more and more beautiful and useful objects for your home, including toys, sleds, candle-stick holders, and even chairs and cabinets.

DOLL-MAKING

One of the delights of this age-old craft is that a doll made from just an old glove or stocking can give as much pleasure and exhibit as much imagination as a fully developed doll carved from wood, with a carefully moulded head and with arms and legs that move. Anyone who wants to can make a simple doll, and anyone who is interested in acquiring skills to make a more complicated doll can also do so. The techniques can be learned and refined by experience; the materials are easily obtained; the tools required are few. And the craft is one for men as well as women, for children as well as adults.

The tools you will need are a small knife, a file for wood, a rasp (a coarse file with a surface of raised points), a small drill, and perhaps a small vise for holding wood pieces as you work with them. For modelled dolls, you will also need a modelling knife. If, however, you intend to stay with dolls made of fabric, all you will need are a needle and thread or yarn.

When fashioning dolls, it is helpful to remember the proportions of the various parts of the body, keeping in mind that the proportions vary according to the age of the figure you plan to construct. The head of a doll meant to be a young child will be larger in proportion to its body than the head of a doll meant to be an adult. For example, the total size of a doll meant to represent a two-year-old is four times the length of its head, while the total height of a doll meant to represent an adult is the length of six heads. The average width of the body equals one head. Remember too that just as the legs get longer in relation to the length of the body as a child grows, so too should the legs of a doll. Arms (including the hands) are approximately as long as the legs when the leg is measured from the hip joint to the sole of the foot. The knee should be located midway between the hip joint and the sole of the foot, and the elbow should be located midway between the shoulder and wrist.

These general guidelines for proportioning dolls are for creating lifelike dolls; for stylized figures, let your imagination help you "feel" what the right size for the doll should be.

A Handkerchief Doll

A doll almost guaranteed to captivate any child is the handkerchief doll. To make it, you will need a white handkerchief, a discarded pair of nylon stockings, and a ball of white woollen yarn.

Put the handkerchief in front of you and, having rolled one stocking into a very tight ball, place the ball on the top middle of the handkerchief. Turn the top of the handkerchief over the nylon ball. The ball will become the head of the doll; the two flaps of the handkerchief that form on either side of the head will become the arms. See the illustrations on the next page.

Holding the folded handkerchief in your left hand, use your other hand to start winding the woollen yarn around and around exactly where the neck belongs. Pull all folds of the head on the side facing you, leaving the other side smooth for the face. Take the other stocking and roll it tightly, pressing it into the shape of an egg. Place it under the throat, and wrap the handkerchief vertically over this second ball.

Condensed from the book, "Making Dolls" by H. Witzig and G. E. Kuhn | © 1969 by Sterling Publishing Co., Inc., New York

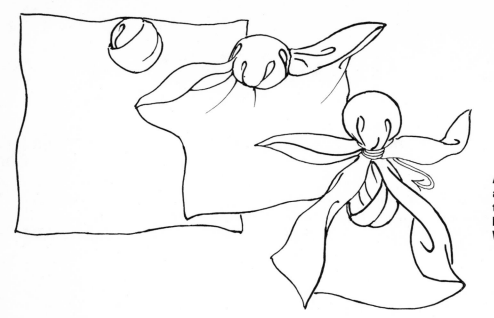

A HANDKERCHIEF DOLL begins with a stocking which is rolled up into a tight ball and wrapped inside the handkerchief to form the head. Wind yarn tightly around the neck (Illus. 1 to 3).

Begin winding yarn around this second ball just at the point where you made the throat. Continue winding the yarn back up around the body and then across each shoulder, forming the arms from the flaps left free on top. Keep the ends of the flaps free for the hands. Repeat the winding process a third time down the body.

There is a wide flap below the torso that will be used for legs. Divide the flap into two equal parts by cutting up from the bottom towards the torso. Wind yarn around these flaps, tightening it where you think the ankles should be, and then continue winding to form the feet. Finally, wrap the yarn up and down, under the legs and over the shoulder. Continue with another layer of yarn until the doll is solid. Now take moistened colored pencils and paint the eyes, nose and mouth. Make a wig by sewing strands of wool yarn to the head, tie on a little apron, and you have the kind of waif-like little creature that appeals to every child. Your child will soon be making such dolls for him or herself.

THE BODY of the doll is made by wrapping the handkerchief around a second stocking. Wind the yarn around the torso and down the arms, leaving a small portion loose for hands (Illus. 4 and 5).

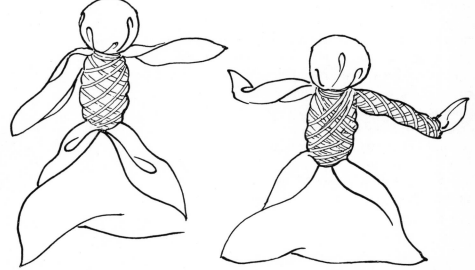

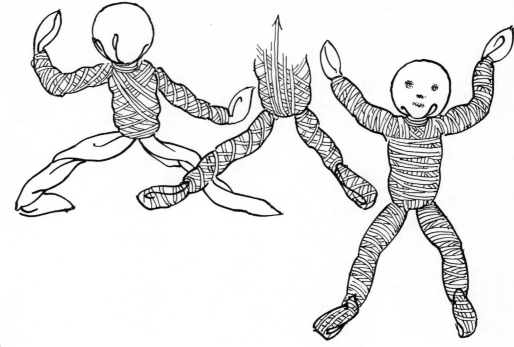

WRAPPING THE LEGS:
Separate the legs and continue winding yarn. Wrap each leg and foot tightly, paint a face, and the doll is complete (Illus. 6 to 8).

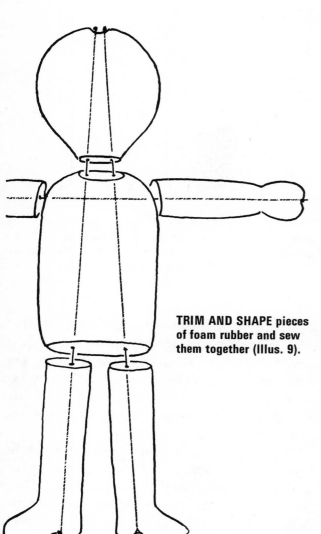

TRIM AND SHAPE pieces of foam rubber and sew them together (Illus. 9).

A Foam Rubber Doll

With proper supervision, a child can make one of these dolls as a present for a friend or a younger brother or sister. Cut three pieces of foam rubber into blocks $1\frac{1}{2}$ inches thick, $2\frac{1}{2}$ inches long and 2 inches wide. Divide two of these blocks in half lengthwise, to provide the four pieces that will be used for the arms and the legs. The third whole block forms the body of the doll. A 2-inch cube forms the head. The six pieces of foam rubber are now trimmed and shaped with scissors into rounded, lifelike forms. Follow the standard guidelines for realistic proportions.

Align the pieces in front of you—head resting on torso, arms extended like the cross of a "T" from the torso, legs underneath. To join the pieces, use a thick needle and string. Insert one string into the top of the head, pushing it through the torso and down through the left leg. Insert another to the right of center, down through the torso and through the right leg. Insert a third string into the end of one arm, through the torso near the top, and out through the other arm.

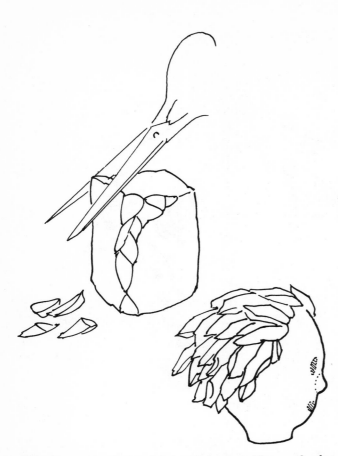

FORMING HAIR: Cut strips of foam rubber and glue them on the head. Begin at the bottom of the head and layer the strips to make the hair look realistic (Illus. 10 and 11).

COMPLETED, the foam rubber doll will look like this. The head should be securely sewn to the torso with threads running through the body (Illus. 12).

Knot all threads at each end and cover any depressions by glueing on small pieces of foam rubber. If you wish, use beads or yarn for the features of the face, and fashion hair from strips of dark-colored foam rubber. A gaily colored tie around the neck gives a finished, jaunty air to one of the little dolls on the next page.

A Twig Doll

An enchanting doll can be made from a twig. Ideally the twig should be approximately as thick as a thumb and about 8 inches long. Although the completed doll will be shorter, the extra length can be used as a handle while working.

Using a saw, make a first cut around and into the twig about an inch from the top and another about an inch down from the first. With a knife, surround each sawed cut with a circle of diagonal notches. Notch the edge at the top end of the wood, too. The area from the notched top to the first sawed and notched cut is the doll's head. Cut two notches for the eyes and another for the mouth.

If you have chosen your twig with foresight, there will be a knob in the appropriate place for a nose; if not, another notch will do. Dress this doll in a paper cloak and you have a king. Or give him a bushy mane and he becomes a fierce lion.

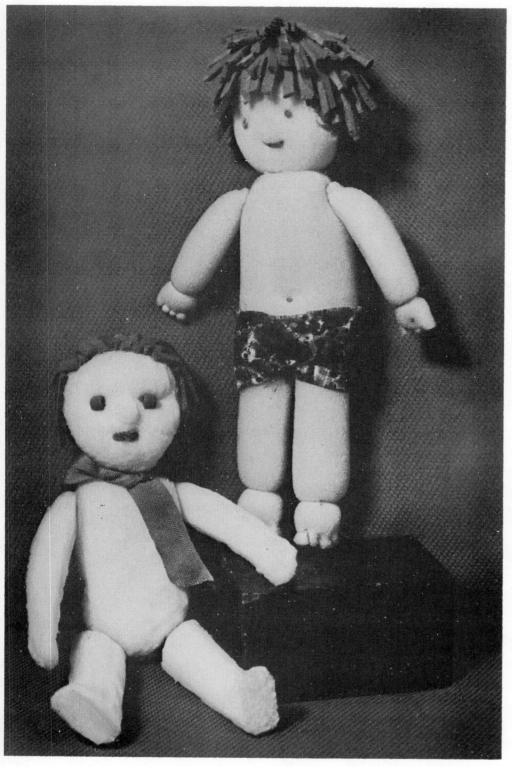

Use your imagination when selecting twigs and you can rapidly improve upon the basic totem pole design described above. A simple forked twig, for example, will make a realistic standing figure with two clearly defined legs. And, by following the instructions given below, you can even give your twig dolls limbs that move.

TWIG DOLLS are not difficult to make if you choose your twig carefully. While it is best to start with a smooth piece of wood, undesirable bumps can be filed off. If you want your doll to have legs, use a forked twig and carve the head on the end opposite the fork. The twig dolls in the photograph have disc jointed arms and legs that move. See the next page to learn how to make disc joints (Illus. 14 to 18).

Disc Joints

It is relatively easy to fashion arms and legs that move, for they will turn on an axle that is placed through the doll's body. Small diameter wood dowels ($\frac{1}{16}$- or $\frac{1}{8}$-inch) can be used for easy, if rigid, joints. After a hole *the same size* as the dowel has been drilled through the limbs and torso, push the axle through the torso, leaving ample length on each end to attach the limbs. Swab the exposed ends of the dowel with glue and attach the limbs. Be sure there is adequate space between the surfaces of the joint for free movement of the limbs. After the glue has dried, sand the ends of the dowel to fit the contours of the limb.

For realistic leg movements, the turning points for the legs have to be made in the torso by using diagonal saw cuts. Imagine the hip joint of the doll as a turning spool. The spool is divided into three parts by saw cuts that face each other at equal, acute angles.

For twig dolls, the hip joint is made by first drilling a hole through the branch, and then making the two diagonal saw cuts.

The dowel axle described above has two disadvantages: it is not particularly flexible and one limb cannot move without the other moving also. By using four dowel "pegs" instead of two axles, the limbs can be made to move independently; but real flexibility can best be attained by using solid rubber tubing for the axle.

Solid rubber tubing can be bought in various sizes at most craft and hobby shops or from

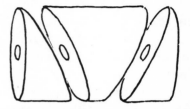

TO MAKE THE LEGS of the doll movable drill a hole through the hip (Illus. 20).

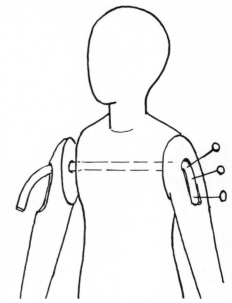

DIVIDE the hip area into three parts. The middle section is connected to the torso, and the two side areas extend into the legs (Illus. 21).

rubber products dealers. Insert the tubing axle by turning it slowly through the holes. Each end of the rubber tubing is sunk into a groove, made with a knife, in the limb, and then glued. Hold the ends of the tubing in place with pins until the glue sets. Fill over the groove and tubing with appropriate modelling material—plastic wood, for example, if your doll is made of wood.

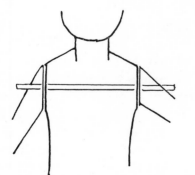

DISC JOINT: To make this, a wood dowel is inserted through the doll's torso and arms (Illus. 19).

TO MAKE JOINTS that allow independent movement of one side, use rubber tubing instead of wood dowels. Pin and glue the ends of the tubing in a groove on the doll; then coat the area with modelling material to hide the rubber (Illus. 22).

Dowel Dolls

Standing dolls can be made from large wood dowels or an old broomstick. The dowel you use should be about five times longer than its width. (The line labelled *m* in Illus. 23 is at the ·middle of the dowel.) First draw a pencil line (*t*) to indicate the throat, about one-fifth of the way down from the top of the dowel. From there, measure down about one-quarter the length of the dowel and draw a line (*w*) to indicate the waistline. Make saw cuts around these lines.

The cuts should not be made too deep; you can always cut deeper at a later time. Use a damp cloth or some cardboard while holding the dowel between the teeth of the vise. This is necessary to avoid slippage of the dowel and to keep it free from any damage.

Now, with your rasp, shape the form of the waist and the throat (Illus. 24). Round the rough edges of the waist and chest smoothly with the file (Illus. 25). After you have shaped the throat as shown, the head will appear in a ball-like form.

As viewed from the side, the bottom piece (*a*) remains unchanged. But the chest and back (*b*) should be shaped as shown in Illus. 26.

THIS LITTLE DOLL was carved from a piece of wood and then dressed and decorated in a peasant costume (Illus. 27).

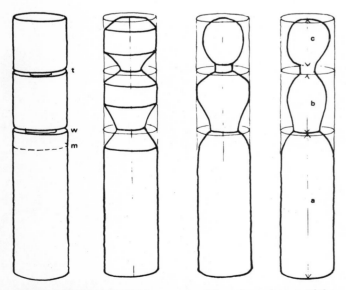

DOLLS CAN BE CARVED from a wood dowel or a broomstick. It is important to make the carved areas as round as possible (Illus. 23 to 26).

You also round off the head (*c*), on which you will paint facial features and hair.

At a point a little above *b* in Illus. 26, drill a hole through the torso. After smoothing the entire body with sandpaper, pull a thick cord (which should be approximately five times the length of the head) through the hole you have drilled. This cord will form the arms; position the cord so the arms are of equal length. To indicate the wrist and hand, tie and fray the end of the cord. These flexible and revolving arms will make it possible for you to pull a dress over the head of the doll. You can make the cord more stable by glueing it into position within the body of the doll.

Such wooden dolls with arms lend themselves well to dressing in traditional costumes. Older children will enjoy the research needed to discover the type of clothing to use.

To create faces for these dolls, you can paint features with moistened colored pencils. You can either paint on hair or paste on woollen yarn to give the hair a natural style.

Modelled Dolls

A new dimension can be added to your crafting if you decide to learn how to model dolls. The material you use for modelling should be easy to knead, but after being shaped it should become hard and stable enough to be sawed, filed, smoothed, etc.

One of the problems with modelling dolls is finding the right modelling material—one that is easy to handle yet durable. Plastic and prepared clays can, of course, be used.

PIPE CLEANERS were used as arms and legs on the modelled dolls in the foreground, while those in the background have modelled arms and legs as well as modelled bodies (Illus. 28).

Those who wish to stay with materials that are not costly can mix their own modelling compounds. One mixture that is easily prepared is made of sawdust, cellulose glue, and water.

To prepare the sawdust mixture, place the amount of sawdust you are going to use in a bowl and sift out the coarse particles. Sprinkle binding glue in another bowl. Add water and mix the powder until it is thick and jelly-like. Add the sawdust to this paste and mix it well. Take the mixture from the bowl and knead it with your hands. If the mixture sticks to your fingers, add more sawdust. Once this material has been mixed, it has to be used immediately.

Papier mâché is another inexpensive modelling compound. Tear some newspaper into strips about ⅜-inch wide. Tear the strips into pieces about 1 inch long until you have enough

to fill a quart jar. Sprinkle these bits of paper into a quart of boiling water, and boil the mixture gently until the paper has completely disintegrated. Take the mixture from the stove and beat it with a rotary beater until it is smooth. Drain the mixture in a strainer or colander. Add a cup of flour to the mixture and stir well. Heat the mixture using a very low flame for about an hour. When the mash has reached the right consistency, it should stand in small piles.

This papier mâché mash can be used as soon as it is cool enough to work, and it can be kept in the refrigerator for indefinite periods.

Remember that whatever modelling material you use will have to be oven-dried and made waterproof with lacquer, paint, or wax.

To make modelled dolls, a frame—either of wire, wood, or cardboard—must first be con-

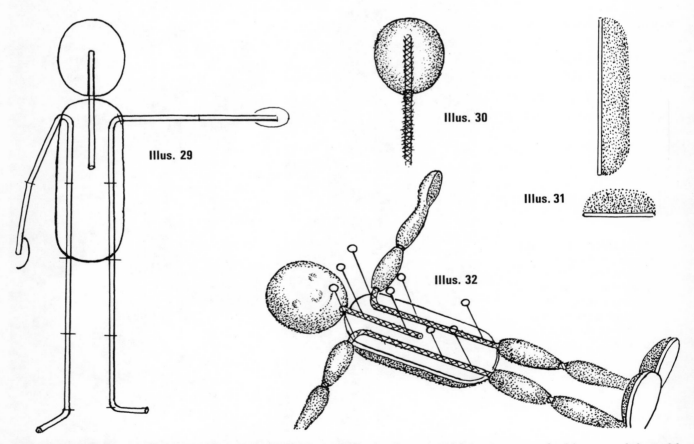

THE WIRE SKELETON of a modelled doll is shown in Illus. 29. The head, arms and legs are wrapped with yarn and then with modelling material (Illus. 30 and 31). The cardboard torso is covered with modelling material also, first the back and then the front. The pins secure the wire frame to the cardboard back and are removed when the front of the doll is modelled (Illus. 32).

structed and the modelling material built on to the frame. A wire frame can support modelling material and result in a sturdy little doll. Make the head for this doll 1 inch long and use this as the basis for all measurements. Take two wires 6 inches long with an additional half-inch on each for each foot. Bend each wire into an "L" shape. The shorter sides—2 inches—will be used as the frame for the arms; the longer—$4\frac{1}{2}$ inches—will support the torso and make frames for the legs. A third wire—2 inches long—will support the head. A cardboard pattern is shaped and cut to be used as a basic form for the torso. This, as well as the arms, legs and head, will be covered with modelling material. For the material to adhere firmly, the frame must be coated with glue and then wrapped with yarn.

Each arm and leg has to be modelled like a spindle. Apply the modelling material to the yarn-covered wire and shape the hands and feet. Using the modelling material, roll the head like a ball and stick it on to the edge of the wire you have chosen to support it.

Then cover one side of the cardboard form of your torso with the modelling material to form the back of the doll. When it is dry, glue and pin the wire frame with head, arms, and legs attached to the front of the cardboard, and apply material to form the front of the doll's body, removing the pins when the

material is dry. Fill in the pinholes with modelling material. For a good standing position, a cardboard form should be pasted under each foot. Leave all joints exposed, so that you can bend the wire into the positions you desire.

Hard Modelled Heads

There are several ways of making heads from modelling material. First make a paper silhouette of the head (Illus. 33). The size of the head depends upon the size of the body. You will need the silhouette as a pattern when forming the head. The inner line shown at the skull should be taken into consideration when the doll is to have a thick wig.

Construct a paper core around a stick. You should be able to use the projecting end of the stick as a handle while working. Wind smooth paper around the top of the stick, and glue it into place to make sure it will not unwind again. Now wrap another layer of paper—soft, thin paper, such as tissue or napkins—over the first layer. Repeat this process several times by

HARD MODELLED HEADS need a paper pattern as a guide for size. They are made on top of paper wrapped around a stick (Illus. 33 and 34).

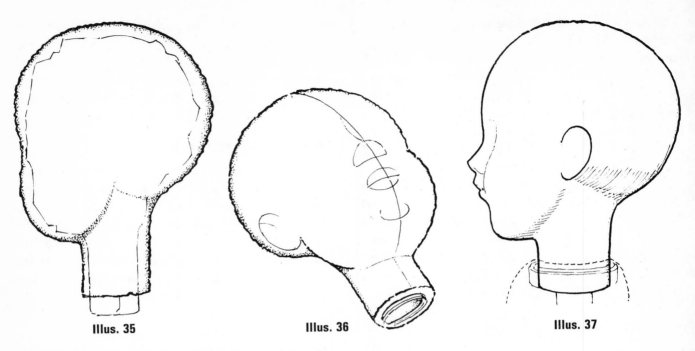

Illus. 35   Illus. 36   Illus. 37

wrapping paper piece by piece to build up the core. Then wind sewing yarn very tightly over the paper (Illus. 34). When doing this work, keep comparing the head with the size of your paper pattern, and make sure it is about $\frac{1}{4}$ inch smaller than the pattern. Then moisten the dry core with glue.

Apply your modelling material in an average layer of $\frac{1}{4}$-inch thickness and try to produce the fundamental form of the head. When this is done (Illus. 35), the head must dry.

Check the hard form. When it is hard enough, measure the symmetry of both halves of the face. A line in the middle of the face may be helpful (Illus. 36).

After all uneven parts have been corrected, the head must dry again; then form the facial details (Illus. 37). They may still not look satisfactory to you. It is possible that you will have to form the head a fourth or a fifth time. When it comes to forming the nose or the mouth you can use a small knife, but otherwise you should always use your fingers. Only your fingers can give the soft and smooth form required of a head. The final smoothing and polishing is done last.

A throat ring made from thick paper strips which are wrapped around the neck and glued

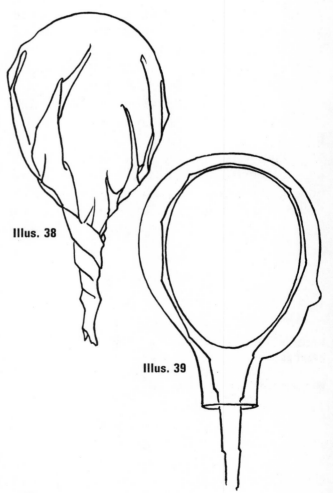

Illus. 38

Illus. 39

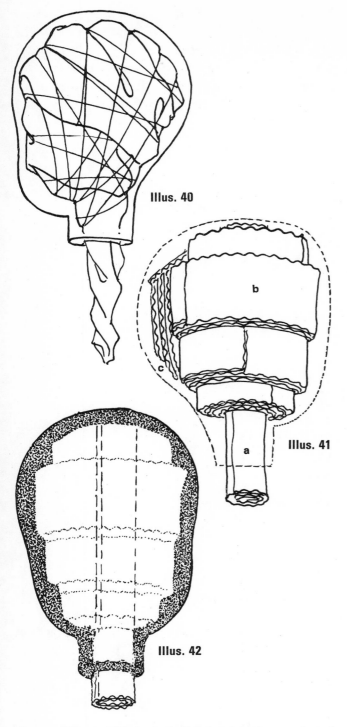

Illus. 40

Illus. 41

Illus. 42

of the paper into a taper and let everything dry (Illus. 38).

Cover the wrapped eggshell with a layer of your modelling material $\frac{1}{8}$ to $\frac{3}{8}$ of an inch thick (Illus. 39). The paper taper, which will have become hard in the meantime, will be convenient for holding the head. The upper part of the taper is used as a base for the throat. The final shaping of the head will involve another effort. We do not recommend forming details on small heads such as these. Shaping of the nose and ears are enough to indicate the face.

You can use the eggshell form to make an enlarged head. Begin as you did with the small eggshell head. Then put a few layers of napkins or tissue paper over the first cover. Using yarn, wind a net over the head. After this is done, you may give the head a final shape with the help of your modelling material (Illus. 40).

A head with a corrugated paper core is particularly convenient for a doll of 20 inches or more in length. In this case, corrugated paper will supply the complete core of the head as well as of the throat (Illus. 41). The bottom extends into a handgrip (a). You roll and glue strips of corrugated paper counterclockwise in a vertical series as shown (b).

In this way, you shape the form of a head. For the back of the head add a few extra pieces of corrugated paper (c).

Next, cover the core of the head with your modelling material and you will get the final form (Illus. 42). Proceed with the details, including the throat ring, as previously described.

To dry the formed heads, stick the handgrip of the head into a bottle. Be sure to have everything shaped and dry before removing the handgrip with a saw cut.

Because of the nature of the modelling material and the firmness of the inner layers, only suggestions of a nose, mouth and eyes are possible. You will probably want to add more of a face than this to your doll, and the type of features you add will do much to make the doll attractive.

there (Illus. 37) is helpful in putting a head into the body of a stuffed doll.

Another method of forming the core is to use the shell of an egg. The core will be no less solid than the other heads. First obtain the shell of a raw egg that you have emptied. Paste some newspaper over it. Wind the bottom part

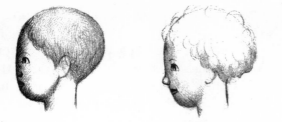

THE FACE on the left seems flat and artificial because the nose is painted on. The right face is more lifelike because of the modelled nose (Illus. 43 and 44).

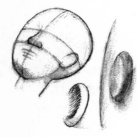

THE EAR: Notice the proportions of the ear in relation to the rest of the head (Illus. 45).

The nose is the feature which gets the most attention on a face, particularly in profile. You should notice that children's noses are smaller and narrower than adults', so remember this when forming the nose from modelling material. While some features can be realistically painted, the nose demands a three-dimensional representation.

Eyes, mouth, eyebrows and chin can be detailed with moistened colored pencils or oil paints, however. Ears, which are difficult to draw, can be hidden by a wig. If you do decide to draw them, notice that the bottom of the ear is on a line with the tip of the nose, and that the top extends to fill the second lowest quarter of the head. The shape of the ear is more or less a rolled oval.

Wigs can be made from yarn, fur, or artificial hair. First draw the appropriate hairline on the head, so that you have limits to fill in with whatever type of hair you choose. You may glue the hair on the head piece by piece, to create a realistic layered look. Or, you may prefer to form the wig off the head, and then glue it on. One successful technique consists of

fitting a piece of lightweight fabric such as tulle or organdy to the head where you will want the wig to sit. Stitch this fabric in enough places so that it retains its shape when removed from the head. Then sew the wig material to this fabric, and glue the whole piece on the head.

PLACE FABRIC on the modelled head and stitch it to itself so that it stays the proper shape when it is off the head. Sew hair to the fabric wig and glue it to the head (Illus. 46 and 47).

Stuffed Dolls

For those who enjoy sewing, a stuffed doll is most rewarding. An easy first project is to make the head and body from one piece of cloth material. (In cutting a pattern do not forget to leave a margin of cloth around the paper outline to serve as a seam.) The paper pattern for the tubelike head-body is shown in Illus. 49. Cut two layers of cloth, placing the dotted line *a* on the fold of your material, and sew the seam at *b*; *c* remains open to serve as a hole for stuffing; *d* has to be sewn. The wig will cover this part later. The head has to be stuffed to a firmly rounded ball which is then wrapped at the area (*e*) where the throat joins

HAIR FOR MODELLED HEADS can be painted on, or wigs made of real hair, yarn or synthetic fibers can be glued to the head (Illus. 48).

PATTERN for the head and body of a stuffed doll (Illus. 49).

the body. The body should be less firmly stuffed. Sew the small hole at the bottom of the doll between the place where the legs will be (see stitches in Illus. 49 *c*).

Following the paper pattern in Illus. 50, cut out the legs, two layers of cloth for each one. Make your seams, leaving the tops open. After stuffing the legs, sew the top hole together. The legs have to be pushed into the body and sewn to it with running stitches. The feet (*e*) have to be indicated with backstitches.

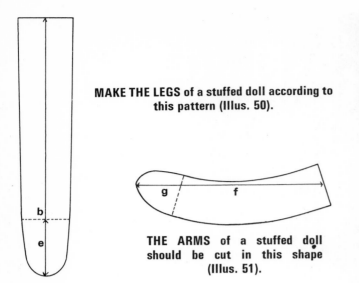

MAKE THE LEGS of a stuffed doll according to this pattern (Illus. 50).

THE ARMS of a stuffed doll should be cut in this shape (Illus. 51).

The arms of your doll are made in the same manner as the legs, following the pattern in Illus. 51. They have to be placed loosely at the body and sewn. They can be bent slightly if desired. Hands are indicated by winding yarn around the wrist. The face is painted with moistened colored pencils. A wig can be made from fur or curled wool.

Stuffing the material will be new for you. Re-used wool, cotton, gauze, or used nylon stockings are most convenient for stuffing these dolls. The stuffing of dolls is a work which requires patience, care, and a feeling for form. Any lumps or any empty spots cannot be made to disappear once the doll is fully stuffed. Carelessness and uneven stuffing can ruin the best paper pattern and your design. Therefore, you always have to start at the joints first and then push the material in small portions into the holes, distributing it immediately with your fingers and if necessary with a pointed object.

Always begin to stuff by coming from the middle and pushing against the walls. When you stuff the hands, the stuffing material has to be pushed with a thick knitting needle into the thumb. If you fill arms and legs loosely, the doll can be seated better. Once the limb is stuffed, close it with pins, roll it on the table so that uneven spots are corrected, and then sew it to the body with even stitches.

THE BODY OF THIS DOLL is stuffed, but her head is modelled and painted. The hair is a wig of synthetic fibers (Illus. 52).

A stuffed doll can be made much more interesting by substituting a hard modelled head for the stuffed one described above. Simply shorten the pattern in Illus. 49 so that it is for a torso only. After you have finished stuffing and sewing the doll, snip open a short length in the top of the torso where the neck should be. Push the throat ring of the modelled head into the opening, gather and sew the material securely above the ring, and your stuffed doll is complete.

KITE-MAKING

Since their origin in China some 2500 years ago, kites have had an impressive and varied history. The practical and religious uses of kites spread quickly throughout Asia as far west as India, south to Burma, Malaysia, and Indonesia, and into the Pacific as far east as Easter Island.

The Samoans used kites to tow their canoes from island to island, and fishing kites made of sewn leaves are still used in Malaya. In New Zealand, bird kites were an essential part of the Maori religion. In elaborate and secret ceremonies, Maori priests foretold the outcome of battles by interpreting the complex flight of their kites.

Kites were the source of one of the earliest examples of psychological warfare. In the second century B.C. a Chinese general, surrounded by a superior force and facing certain defeat, hit upon the ingenious idea of flying kites with small harps attached over the enemy camp on the night before the battle. In the darkness, the enemy took the weird notes of the harps to be the voices of their ancestors warning them of defeat and they hastily abandoned their camp.

Kites are still immensely popular in Asia where prizes are given in design competitions and large sums are wagered on kite fights. Kite flying is the national sport of Thailand, and huge crowds gather to watch kite fights between the large star-shaped male *chula* kites and the smaller female *pakpao* kites. The larger kites are handled by teams of six to ten men,

THIS MAORI BIRD KITE is an example of the tremendous constructions which are used in the Maori religion. (Illus. 1.)

Written especially for this volume by Gordon Lander

MOON KITES FROM MALAYSIA, called "wau bulan," are elaborately decorated. The kites sometimes resemble birds, fish, cats and human beings. (Illus. 2.)

and the object of the competition is to invade the territory of the smaller kites, entangle one and draw it back and down into male territory. Although the odds are two to one against the smaller kites, they are skillfully managed and often succeed in bringing a large *chula* down in their own territory.

Although kites were known in Arabia by 400 A.D., and crude kites of the windsock variety were flown in Europe during the Middle Ages, it was not until the Renaissance explorers brought back sure-flying Eastern designs that kite flying became popular in Europe. The sport quickly gathered enthu-

KITES ARE NOT ONLY FOR EXHIBITION in Malaysia, but are flown competitively. The kite which flies the highest is the winner. (Illus. 3.)

IN THAILAND ALSO, kite-makers strive for size as well as beauty. The most pleasing designs are given awards in the Annual Kite Decoration Contest. (Illus. 4.)

siasts, and in 1732 France had to outlaw kite flying for a time because of the rioting at flying competitions.

The technological applications of kites were soon recognized in Europe and the development of kites was towards stability and strength. In the early 19th century George Pocock patented his *char volant*, a carriage drawn by kites that worked amazingly well.

Benjamin Franklin is probably the most famous person to have used a kite for scientific purposes. He demonstrated in June, 1752, that lightning and electricity were identical forces by flying a kite into a storm and collecting electricity by means of a key attached to the end of the rain-dampened string.

Almost simultaneously in the late 19th century, two types of kites were invented that had great technological potential for strength and stability. They were the bow kite of William A. Eddy (1891) and the box, or cellular, kite of Lawrence Hargrave (1893). Both kites were of great value to meteorologists, and, until displaced by aircraft and efficient balloons, the U.S. Weather Bureau depended almost entirely upon them. In 1910, at the Bureau's weather station at Mt. Weather, Virginia, the American altitude record was set when a train (more than one kite flown in

BENJAMIN FRANKLIN'S FAMOUS EXPERIMENT with a kite and a key led to the invention of lightning rods to protect buildings. (Illus. 5.)

tandem) of ten Eddy kites reached a height of 23,385 feet. The great strength and lifting power of the Hargrave box kite is illustrated by their use in lifting observers above German submarines to increase their range of vision during World War I.

The ordinary box kite still found practical application during World War II when they were used to raise wireless antennae from liferafts so that downed airmen could radio their position.

The non-rigid, flex-wing kites developed by Francis Rogallo of the National Aeronautics and Space Administration show how complicated modern kites have become. It is nevertheless not at all difficult to build a kite that will fly successfully, and only the simplest equipment is required in kite construction. A block plane, sandpaper, a knife and a pair of scissors are really all the tools you need. Some sticks of wood, string, glue, and paper or cloth to cover the frame are all the materials that are necessary, and this material costs little or nothing.

NASA, the National Aeronautics and Space Administration, built this kite, attached here to a mock-up Mercury space craft. The Rogallo wing, as the kite is called, will replace the parachute now used in landings. The kite can be controlled by the astronaut for landing spacecraft. (Illus. 6.)

Kite Construction

The wood used in the construction of kite *frames* should be well seasoned, straight-grained, and light. Spruce and white pine are excellent. Balsa wood, available in a variety of sizes at hobby stores, is easy to work, extremely light, and good for making small kites. Balsa wood is not as strong as other woods, however, and a brisk wind or a severe landing can demolish a balsa kite. Ordinary wood dowels are also available in a variety of sizes at lumber and hobby stores. While not quite so easy to work as balsa, dowels have the great advantage of flexibility and strength. If the kite design calls for sticks that must be bent, small diameter dowels can be used, but bamboo, reed, or rattan is better. Before trying to bend any stick, soak it in hot water for at least half an hour.

Each stick used in a kite should be balanced as shown in Illus. 7. If one end is heavier than the other, sand it or shave it off with a block plane until it balances perfectly on your finger.

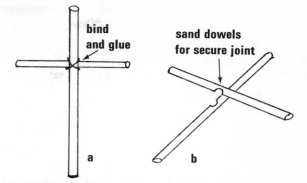

FASTENING JOINTS: Never use nails in a kite; the extra weight will cause an imbalance. (Illus. 8.)

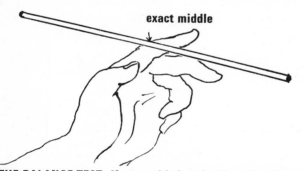

THE BALANCE TEST: If one end is heavier than the other, the stick will not balance on your finger. The heavy end will have to be sanded or shaved. (Illus. 7.)

Never nail wood joints; bind and glue them instead (see Illus. 8). After they are bound and tied with thread, coat the binding with airplane cement or epoxy glue for added strength. When joining crossed dowels, a more secure joint can be made by sanding a flat or concave area on each piece where it is to be joined. Wrap some sandpaper around a short length of dowel to make the concave joining areas shown in Illus. 8b.

While the frame gives basic form and strength to the kite, weight is kept to a minimum by using an *outline* of thread or string to give shape to the outer edges. In the two-stick kite in Illus. 9, the ends of each stick are notched to hold the thread. The outline thread is then tied with a slipknot to one end, looped and drawn taut around the next end, and so on, until the starting point is reached where the thread is securely tied. Measure the sides of the kite to see that the frame is equal and

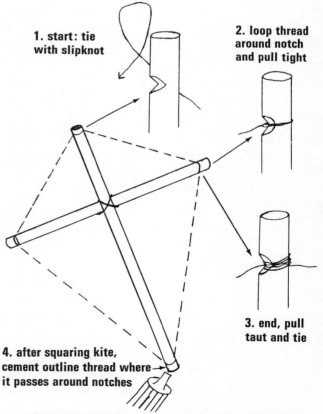

1. start: tie with slipknot

2. loop thread around notch and pull tight

3. end, pull taut and tie

4. after squaring kite, cement outline thread where it passes around notches

TYING THE STRING to make the outline. (Illus. 9.)

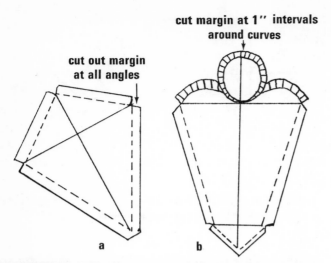

cut out margin at all angles

cut margin at 1″ intervals around curves

a   b

COVERING A KITE: Use paper and cloth, and fasten with flour and water paste or white glue. (Illus. 10.)

symmetrical, then glue the thread where it passes over and around the notches.

Small kites should be covered with tissue paper, preferably the strengthened model airplane tissue sold in hobby stores. For larger kites you can use newspaper, rice paper, brown wrapping paper, waxed freezer paper, or cloth. If cloth other than silk is used, it should be treated with a coat of model airplane "dope," varnish or shellac after it has been glued to the frame. Lay the kite on the cover paper and cut the paper, leaving a 1½-inch margin around the outside edges of the frame and outline. Cut out notches in the cover at all the angles, as in Illus. 10a, so the paper will not bunch at the corners or angles when the margin is folded over the frame. If the edges of the kite are rounded, the margin should be clipped every inch, making the cut from the outside edge of the margin as far as the frame. See Illus. 10b. This makes it possible to fold the margin smoothly over the rounded sides of the frame.

Use flour paste or white glue to fasten the paper covering to the frame. Paste one edge at a time, folding each edge over the frame until all sides of the cover paper are firmly and smoothly attached to the frame.

All flat kites require *tails*. The tail's wind resistance—and to some extent its weight—helps keep the kite at the proper angle to the wind. By dragging from the bottom of the kite, the tail helps to dampen the play of wind forces under the kite's flat surface and keeps the kite from tipping backward and forward and weaving from side to side. The length of the tail is generally four times the length of the longest frame stick, but this length can be shortened or lengthened to achieve the best flying results. The simplest tail is made by tying pieces of cloth or paper about 3 inches wide and 6 inches long at 8-inch intervals along a string, so the tail looks like Illus. 11a. Lay the string over itself into a ring (Illus. 11b) and make a loop (c). Pull the loop (c) through the ring (b), and then stick the cloth strip through the loop (c). Pull the string tight around the center of the strip to form a knot. Using these slipknots will speed up the work.

Most kites cannot be properly controlled by a flying string tied to a single point. Kites therefore have *bridles*—systems of strings tied at strategic points on the kite which meet at a point where the main flying string is attached. Since bridles vary considerably from kite to kite, they can best be explained in the discussion of individual kites which follows.

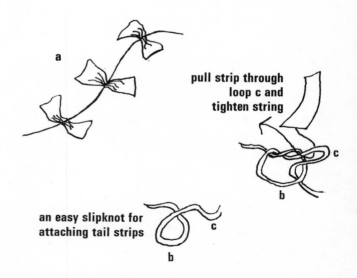

a

pull strip through loop c and tighten string

c

b

an easy slipknot for attaching tail strips

c

b

TYING THE TAIL by using a slipknot. (Illus. 11.)

The Arch-Top or Pear Kite

This kite had its ancient origins in Malaya and Java, and was popular among English children in the 18th century. It is one of the simplest kites to make. You need only two sticks and two outline strings. The center stick A-B (Illus. 12a) is of white pine or spruce, $\frac{1}{2}$-inch square and 36 inches long. The bow stick C-A-D is a piece of bamboo $\frac{1}{8}$ inch by $\frac{1}{4}$ inch by $37\frac{1}{2}$ inches. Cut and balance these sticks. Soak the bamboo in hot water for half an hour.

Notch the ends of the bamboo. Now find the exact center of the bamboo stick C-A-D and mark it with a pencil. Bend the bamboo into an arc, as shown on the plan, and tie it with a string at C and D so this form will hold. Bind and glue one end of the stick A-B to the bow at the exact center you have marked with the pencil. Bind the stick A-D to the center of the string C-D. Tie an outline string at C, pass it around B, and tie it at D.

Now place the frame on the cover paper (Illus. 12b) and cut out and fasten the cover to the frame. The diagram shows how the margin should be cut to ensure a smooth fit around the curved edge of the frame.

The bridle (Illus. 12c) consists of two strings, one attached at A and B, the other at C and D. The bridle strings should be long enough so that, when they are tied to the flying string as shown, the joining point is 12 to 15 inches from the kite and slightly higher than the brace string C-D.

The pear kite must have a tail which is attached at B.

Star Kite

Star kites can be made any size so no definite dimensions will be given. Decide how large a kite you wish to make and then draw a circle on the cover paper (see Illus. 13). Divide the circle into five equal parts. The distance between the points AD, AC, and EB determines the length of the sticks. Three $\frac{1}{4}$-inch square sticks or dowels of equal length are used.

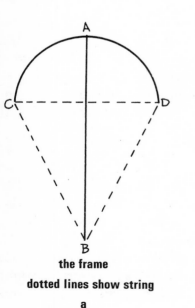

the frame

dotted lines show string

a

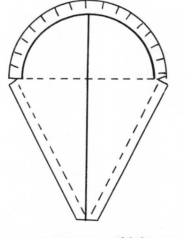

cut cover paper with 1"
margin around frame

b

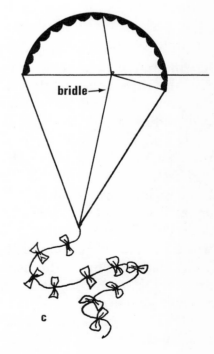

c

AN ARCH-TOP KITE. (Illus. 12.)

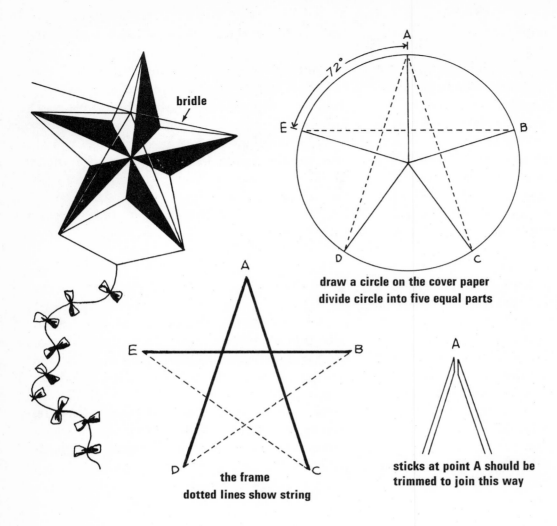

bridle

72°

draw a circle on the cover paper
divide circle into five equal parts

A STAR KITE. (Illus. 13.)

the frame
dotted lines show string

sticks at point A should be
trimmed to join this way

Cut and trim the three sticks to the proper length and give each one the balance test. Lay the three sticks in their proper places on the circle. Bind and glue them together. Attach two outline strings between the points E and C, D and B, and the frame is complete. Lay the frame on the paper circle, cut the paper, and fasten it to the frame. To form a bridle, three strings are required, two long ones of equal length which are attached at points A and D, E and B, and a third shorter string which is attached at C and tied at the gathering point at the center of the horizontal stick E-B and slightly above it. At this point the flying string is attached.

This kite needs a tail. Tie it to the center of a tail bridle attached at points D and C.

After the kite is covered, it can be decorated with poster paints or different colored papers in the manner suggested by the illustration.

The star kite is only one of the many geometric figures that can be easily made and flown.

Eddy Bow Kite

Sometimes called a Malay kite, the Eddy kite is named after William Eddy, who brought the design to perfection in the 1890's.

The Eddy kite is a superb flyer because the bowed crosspiece pulls the two sides of the kite away from the keel-like centerpiece and lets the changing air forces slide around and under the kite much as water moves along the curved sides of a boat's hull.

A simple Eddy kite can be made with two dowels 36 inches long. The vertical piece A-C is $\frac{3}{8}$ inches and the crosspiece D-E is $\frac{1}{4}$ inch in diameter. It is very important that this kite balance, so after notching each end of the crosspiece D-E, make sure it balances at point B. Soak the crosspiece in hot water for half an hour before assembling the kite. Cross A-C and D-E so they resemble a small letter "t". Point B should be approximately 8 inches from point A. Bind and glue the joint. Now tie the outline string at point A and pass it around points D, C, E, and back to A. After checking to see that the length of outline A-D is the same as A-E, and that D-C is equal to C-E, cement the outline where it passes around the end of each stick. Cover the kite.

Now tie another string securely to the previously prepared notch at D. Pass it around the other notch at E. Pull the string slowly and firmly, bowing the crosspiece until the distance between the crosspiece D-E and the bow string is about 4 inches at point B. See Illus. 14b. Tie off the string at E.

Because the bow string and the crosspiece D-E are under stress, be sure to remember to add glue to the notches where the string passes around D and E. Since you have altered the shape of the kite by bowing the crosspiece after covering it, the cover may sag slightly. This distortion will not affect performance.

The Eddy kite requires a two-leg bridle, attached at point B and at a point about 6 inches above point C. (See Illus. 14c.) Owing to the angled flying surface, the Eddy kite, if carefully built, will not require a tail.

Hargrave Box Kite

Up to a certain point, the larger a kite is, the better it will fly. So aerodynamically stable is Hargrave's kite, however, that very small kites, properly made, will climb the full length of a reel of cotton in a light breeze. Box kites are powerful lifters, as you will discover if you build the 24-inch model described here.

The standard box kite is an open-end rectangle made of four sticks with two bands of covering at either end. These bands are each $\frac{1}{3}$ the total length of the kite, so an open space $\frac{1}{3}$ the total length remains in the middle of the

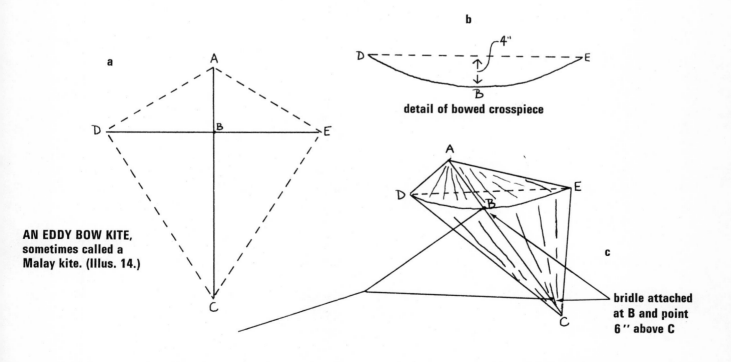

AN EDDY BOW KITE, sometimes called a Malay kite. (Illus. 14.)

detail of bowed crosspiece

bridle attached at B and point 6″ above C

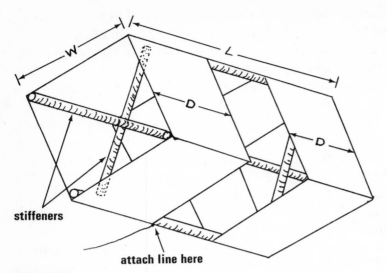

stiffeners

attach line here

Illus. 15a

Illus. 15b

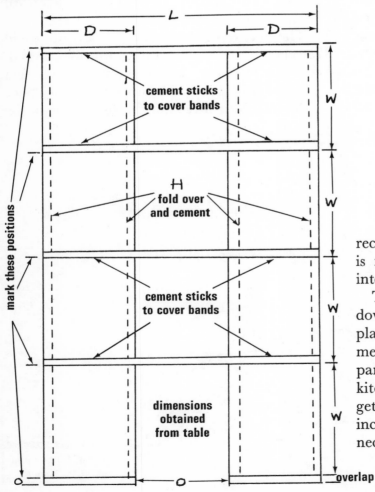

L

D ‹———› D

cement sticks
to cover bands

H
**fold over
and cement**

cement sticks
to cover bands

mark these positions

dimensions
obtained
from table

W

W

W

W

overlap

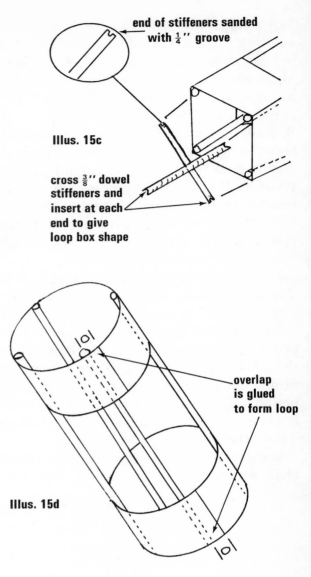

**end of stiffeners sanded
with $\frac{1}{4}$″ groove**

Illus. 15c

cross $\frac{3}{8}$″ dowel
stiffeners and
insert at each
end to give
loop box shape

**overlap
is glued
to form loop**

Illus. 15d

rectangle. The square shape of the kite's ends is made by two crossed pairs of *stiffeners* set into each end of the kite.

To build a 24-inch box kite, cut four $\frac{1}{4}$-inch dowels 24 inches long. The dimension W in the plan and in the Table of Stick Sizes and Dimensions represents only the width of a single panel. This figure—$9\frac{1}{2}$ inches for a 24-inch kite—must therefore be multiplied by four to get the total length for each band. ($4 \times 9\frac{1}{2}$ inches = 38 inches.) An extra margin is necessary so that the ends of the bands can be fastened securely together. A 2-inch margin is sufficient for a 24-inch kite, so the total length of each band is 40 inches. The dimension D represents the depth of the band. Following the $\frac{1}{3}$ rule mentioned above, the depth of the bands for a 24-inch kite is thus 8 inches.

Since the edges of the bands are exposed to the wind, it is a good idea to strengthen them with a "hem"—an extra margin added along the edges of the band which is folded over and glued down. A 1-inch margin is best for the 24-inch kite so add 2 inches to the depth of each band. The total dimensions of each band will be 10 × 40 inches.

Lay out the covering bands parallel on the floor. Fold back the 1-inch margin on each edge and glue it down. Now, with pencil and ruler, mark off four sections $9\frac{1}{2}$ inches apart. See Illus. 15b. At the bottom of each band mark off the 2-inch overlap. Lay the four $\frac{1}{4}$-inch dowels on the cover where you have marked it and cement them to the bands with airplane glue. When the glue has thoroughly dried, loop the margin ends of the bands up to the first dowel and cement the 2-inch margin carefully over the first dowel as shown in the plan.

Cut four $\frac{3}{8}$-inch dowels $13\frac{1}{8}$ inches long. Wrapping sandpaper around a short length of $\frac{1}{4}$-inch dowel, sand the ends of these four dowels so that they are slightly concave. (See Illus. 15c.) Slide two stiffeners diagonally into each end of the kite to a depth of 3 inches as shown. After making sure the kite is square, glue the end of each stiffener where it is braced against the corner. The stiffeners will bow slightly, stretching the loop into a tight, strong box shape.

The box kite needs no tail or bridle, and flies edgewise into the wind. The flying string should be attached to one of the long sticks right below the top band.

Flying Kites

You must have at least a slight breeze (the leaves of trees should be rustling) of 4 miles per hour for successful kite flying. Gentle and moderate breezes of from 8 to 15 miles per hour (leaves and twigs in motion, small branches moving) are ideal for most kite flying. Except for large box kites, winds above 20 miles per hour will either rip the kite or break the string.

Most hobby stores have reels of cotton or nylon kite-flying line, but smaller kites can be flown with ordinary cotton string, fishing line, or button thread. Never use wire for a kite string.

Do not fly your kite near power lines, and never fly a kite in the rain.

To launch a small kite, stand with your back to the wind, holding the kite by a corner at the right flying angle. Wait until the wind seems steady, toss it upward, and step backward, keeping the string taut. Remember that it is the force and drag of the string just as much as the wind which keeps a kite in the air. If the angle of launch is right, and if the tension on the string is correct, the kite will begin to rise upward and backward. Let out line steadily, keeping good tension. If you let out too much line, all control will be lost.

To launch a larger kite, lay it flat on the ground with its top pointing into the wind and its tail stretching out straight behind it. Unroll about 50 feet of line and wait for a strong, steady breeze. When one comes, a gentle tug on the line will lift the top of the kite; allow the wind to pass under the kite, and lift it up at the correct flying angle.

TABLE OF STICK SIZES AND DIMENSIONS

LENGTH L	STICK SIZE	W	O	D	H	STIFFENER
3"	1/16" SQ.	1 1/4"	1/4"	1"	1/4"	1 1/16"
6"	1/16" "	2 3/8"	1/4"	2"	3/8"	3 9/32"
9"	3/32" "	3 1/2"	1/2"	3"	1/2"	4 13/16"
12"	1/8" "	4 3/4"	1/2"	4"	1/2"	6 1/2"
18"	3/16" "	7"	1"	6"	1"	9 5/8"
24"	1/4" "	9 1/2"	2"	8"	1"	13 1/8"

Box kites are launched in much the same way. Place the kite on the ground with the corner with the flying string attached facing the wind. Unroll about 30 feet of line and wait for a steady breeze. When one comes, a gentle tug on the line will tilt the kite to its proper angle and the wind will lift it up as you play out the line.

To bring your kite in it is a good idea, particularly in a strong breeze, to use a technique called *underrunning*. When you have wound the string in to the last 100 feet or so, anchor the line and walk out to the kite, pulling the string in firmly hand over hand. This technique will force the kite downward gently and prevent damage to a kite you may have spent hours building and decorating.

PUPPETS AND MARIONETTES

Articulated clay figures controlled with fine wires have been found in Egyptian tombs. The Greeks have left stage directions for puppet productions of Homer, which, according to the ancient historians, were highly popular.

Puppets have been associated with religion throughout the world, and still play an active part in ceremonies and festivals. Puppets reached their most exalted status in the Christian religion during the Middle Ages when they were used within the church to present miracle and mystery plays. It is thought that the name "marionette" originated at the time of these church presentations to describe the small, articulated figures of the Virgin Mary. The term is now used generally to apply to that branch of the puppet family operated by strings.

Puppets—and particularly marionettes—thus have a venerable and highly developed tradition which is outside the child's domain. The construction of marionettes is an intricate craft in itself. When the techniques of stagecraft, play production, and realistic manipulation of the marionettes are added, the knowledge and skill required for even the simplest Punch and Judy rendition can be appreciated.

So diverse, however, is the puppet family that there is at least one member suitable for every age and degree of interest. And from finger puppets to many-stringed marionettes,

TWO FAMOUS PUPPETS, Spejbl and Hurinek, take their bows in the puppet theatre named for them in Prague, Czechoslovakia.

Written especially for this volume by Anne Kallem and Gordon Lander

FINGER PUPPETS, easy to make, are very talented. They can dance, sit, and express all kinds of emotion. Make one for each hand and you can stage a performance.

puppets have one thing in common: an almost uncanny ability to please and enchant children and adults alike.

Walking Finger Puppets

Draw the head, arms, and torso of a character on a firm piece of cardboard. Leave plenty of space at the bottom of the torso. Color your character appropriately and cut it out. A third dimension can be given to your character by adding button or bead eyes and a wig made from cotton or yarn.

Next cut two holes in the torso just large enough for your index and middle fingers. Color your fingers with felt-tip pens or poster paints to match your character.

With a little practice, you will soon pass beyond merely making your finger puppet walk, run, and sit. You should be able, with appropriate leg motion alone, to make your puppet express joy, agitation, impatience, boredom, and anger.

Now you are ready to make a second finger puppet and put on a show. You will be amazed at how quickly your audience becomes absorbed in the puppet action and dialogue, oblivious of your hands providing the action in full view.

Moving Models

Simple, reciprocating action—such as two boxers—can be easily achieved. Draw and color your figures on stiff paper. Cut them out and place them on two flat (ice-cream) sticks, the feet of both figures on one stick, the heads of both on the other. Fasten the figures to the sticks with four tacks. Hold the top stick with your right hand and the bottom stick with your left. By alternately pushing and

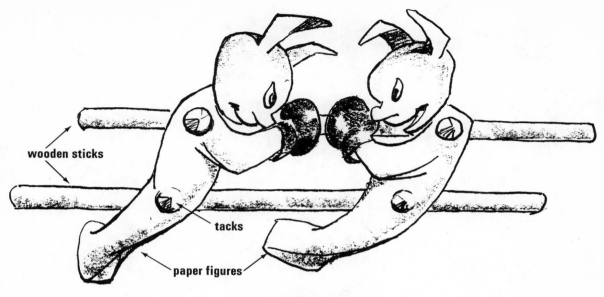

BOXING BUGS

wooden sticks

tacks

paper figures

pulling the sticks, the figures will eagerly begin their show.

Puppets on upright sticks are easy to make and easiest to handle in a puppet show.

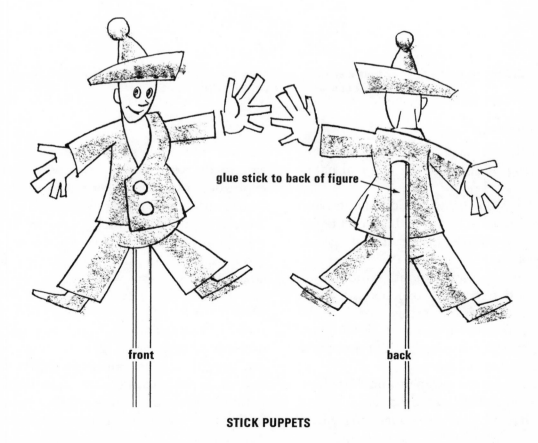

glue stick to back of figure

front

back

STICK PUPPETS

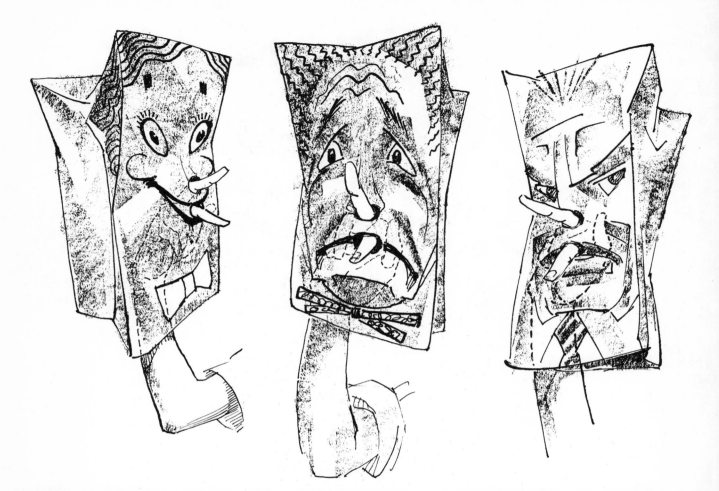

PAPER BAG PUPPETS are so simple to make from material that is always on hand that you can create an entire cast of players for a show in a short time and with little effort.

Paper Bag Puppets

By using different-sized paper bags you can construct a gang of grotesque or comical hand puppets.

Draw the faces on the wide side of the bag, the ears on the narrow side. Use plenty of bold color to emphasize the facial expressions you wish to portray.

Cut out the puppet's mouth and nose. With your hand inside the bag, extend your thumb or a finger through the mouth, your index finger through the nose, and let your moving fingers give motion to the puppet's antic speech.

Make several of these puppets and, with the help of a friend, plan and produce a show. Remember that if you are operating your puppets beneath a sheet-covered doorway, you can greatly increase your range of dramatic expression by making more than one of each character with varying expressions to fit the moods required by your play. In an instant transition—by ducking your hand below stage level and changing puppets—a laughing character becomes a weeping one.

Potato Puppets

With nothing more than a pocket knife, some potatoes, cloth, raisins, and pins, you can produce a very amusing puppet show.

Peel a potato and carve a simplified face with eye sockets, a nose and a mouth. Put raisins in the eye sockets and fasten them with straight pins. Do not strive for meticulous realism in your carved potato—stylized and exaggerated features are much better for representing various personalities and emotions.

At the bottom of the potato cut a deep hole for your finger. After you have placed the puppet on your finger, cover the rest of your hand with a piece of cloth. If you wish to have more body detail, push a pointed stick or wood dowel into the potato head and "dress" the stick to fit the potato head. While you may add arms and even legs to the vertical rod, a loosely draped cloth is often enough.

Making potato puppets will give you an opportunity to get the feel of wood carving. Carving potato features will also help you when you move on to papier mâché puppets.

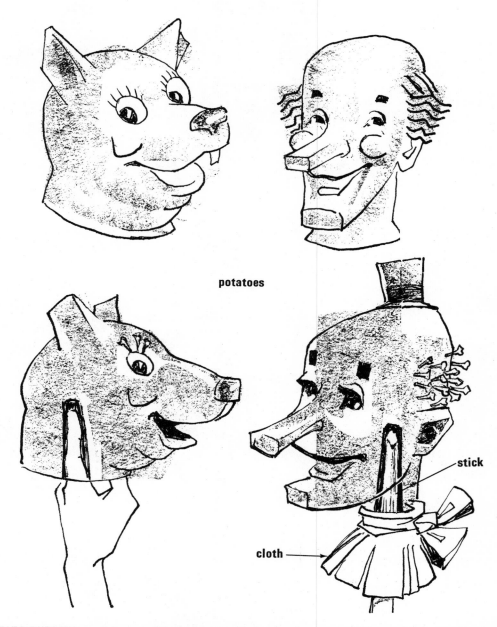

potatoes

stick

cloth

POTATO PUPPETS provide you with an opportunity to exercise your skill in carving, as well as your ingenuity in creating.

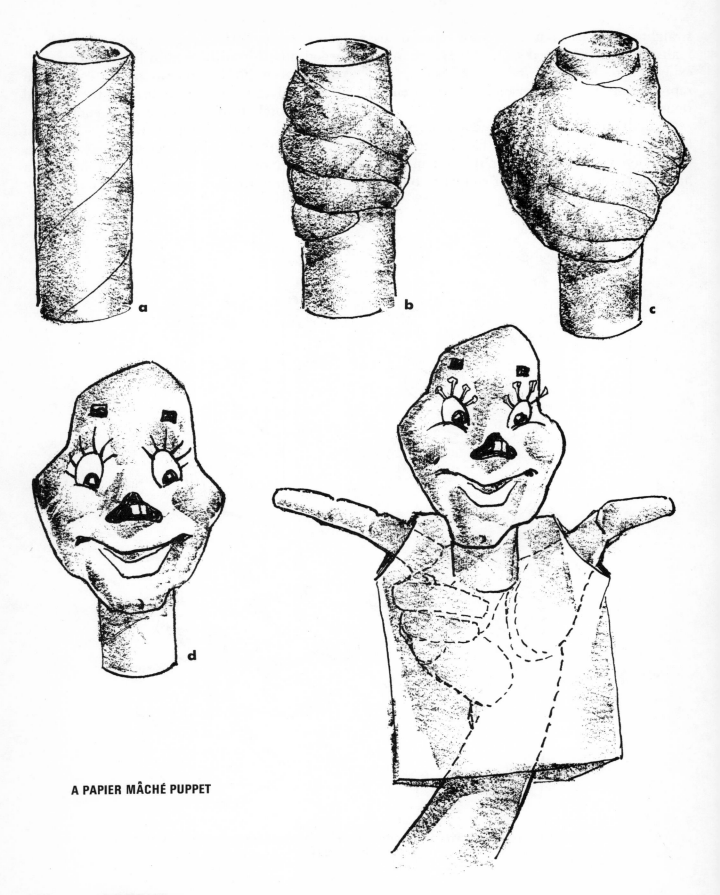

A PAPIER MÂCHÉ PUPPET

Papier Mâché Puppets

Once you have made a few different type puppets and have gotten an idea of how parts are joined and which parts will move, your next project should be puppets made of papier mâché. The advantage here is the firmness of the material and its ability to be molded. It is capable of withstanding fine detail. (See Papier Mâché, page 449 for full details on the process, if you want to go beyond the simplest level.)

Start with a pot of wallpaper or library paste, some old newspaper, and a tissue paper roll. Make narrow strips of the newspaper and wet them thoroughly with the paste. Circle some strips around an old tissue paper roll. Continue to add paper until you have built up a thickness of about $\frac{1}{4}$ inch. This is the puppet's head. Next, roll some paper into tiny tube-like strips, dip them in the paste solution and then place them where the puppet's eyebrows, nose and mouth will be. After placing these features, put strips (paste-wet) over them to hold them in place.

Adding the features to the main section of the head should be done while it is still damp. At the same time, using your thumbs, mold the areas around these features by pushing them in to form realistic or comical creases. The ears should be made separately and added after as the last feature. When the head has dried completely, paint it with poster or tempera paints. Follow a simple pattern for the cloth body.

A Simple Marionette and Control

The complexities of making and operating marionettes have been discussed. If you would like to experiment with these intriguing puppets, however, the accompanying illustration shows you how to make a simple wooden marionette with an "airplane" control.

The puppet's limbs are made from wood dowels of the appropriate size, the torso and feet from scrap wood, and the head modelled in papier mâché or carved, whichever you

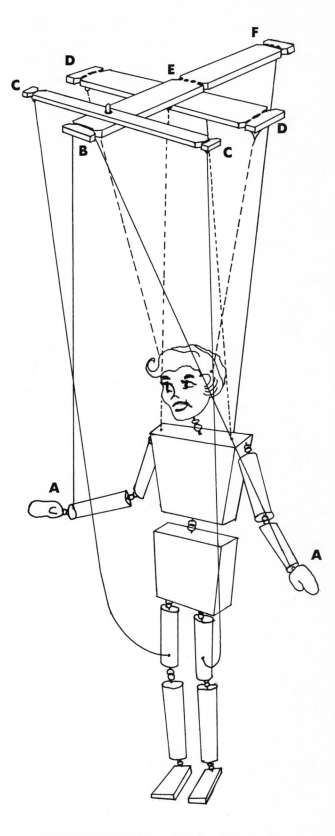

MARIONETTE with an "airplane" control.

prefer. Small marionettes are extremely difficult to manipulate, so think in terms of a total body length of at least 16 inches and proportion the body accordingly. (See Doll-making for body proportions.) All joints in the puppet are made with eye screws. You will have to bend open the eye of one screw with a pair of needlenose pliers to join the two screws together. Be sure to bend the eye closed after the joint is complete.

The marionette control is made from lath— or an ordinary wooden yardstick. The long piece (B-F) should be about 10 inches long, the two cross pieces about 8 inches. Note that the cross piece, C-C, has a hole in the middle and rests upon the control by means of a $\frac{1}{4}$-inch dowel which is glued to piece B-F. The cross piece C-C must be constructed in this manner so that it can be lifted from the rest of the control to manipulate the marionette's legs.

Although the marionette may have as many as 20 strings, the standard number is 9, which is sufficient for a wide variety of movements. Nylon fishing line is recommended for the strings, although buttonhole thread will serve.

The two control strings at C-C, as described, are attached to the thighs slightly above the knees and are used to walk the marionette.

The two strings at A-A (actually one long string) that pass over the control at B are used to move the arms. By lifting this string off the control, both arms are moved simultaneously. By leaving the string looped over the control, either arm may be manipulated separately while the other hangs naturally.

The two strings at D-D are tied to either side of the marionette's head to control it. These strings hold the puppet's head erect, and they also are used to make the marionette shake his head.

The two strings (again one long one) which are attached to either shoulder and pass over the control at E are—like the head strings— used mainly for support, although you may use them to exaggerate your marionette's walk. By pressing back on the strings, the puppet will nod his head.

The last string, attached to the control at F and to the middle of the puppet's back, is used to make the marionette bow, lean forward, or jump back.

The control is generally held in the left hand between points E and F, while the strings are manipulated with the right hand.

As you practice making your marionette walk, sit, jump, and gesticulate, bear in mind that controlled movements, however slow, are preferable to fast, jerky action. Keep the marionette's feet lightly touching the stage. It is easy, when concentrating on a complex gesture, to forget this detail, and suddenly learn from your laughing audience that your puppet's pathetic speech is being made high in the air.

By experimentation, you will soon learn to operate your puppet realistically enough to put on a play. Two fundamental motions do, however, require explanation.

To sit your marionette, it is not enough simply to back him up to the chair and plunk him down. The knee strings must be operated also, lifting and bending the puppet's legs as you simultaneously lower the main control to seat him. To make your marionette lie down, he must first kneel or sit. From this position you can then make him recline gracefully.

Dress your marionette to please yourself and the character he is to play, but bear in mind that loose, stylistic clothes give a more natural impression when the marionette is in motion than do the most carefully designed realistic costumes.

Making a Puppet Theatre

Once you have made your puppets and are ready for a show, you must find a place to perform. The important thing to remember is that the stage must be able to accommodate your needs. If you have several friends performing with the puppets at the same time, you will need a larger area than if you had only a one-man show.

You can put together a theatre simply by

placing a blanket in different positions. Tie it from a doorknob and extend it to a table, allowing it to hang nearly to the floor. Squat down behind the blanket and maneuver the puppets from this position. Using safety pins, you can draw (on paper) some scenery for additional enhancement. This stage will accommodate several puppeteers.

If you have a doorway leading into an open room, you can place the blanket (or sheet) across the doorway and perform from behind the blanket. This stage area is good for one or two puppeteers.

If you are performing by yourself and have a small table, place the blanket around the table with scenery pinned to the blanket. The

A PUPPET STAGE can be made easily by hanging a sheet or a blanket across a doorway.

PUPPET THEATRES have had a long-standing tradition in Europe, and there are many professional puppet troupes who perform only for children, such as this group presenting a folk tale in Czechoslovakia.

PUPPET FILMS : These puppets are acting in a film created by Jiri Trnka, world-famous puppetmaster and children's book illustrator.

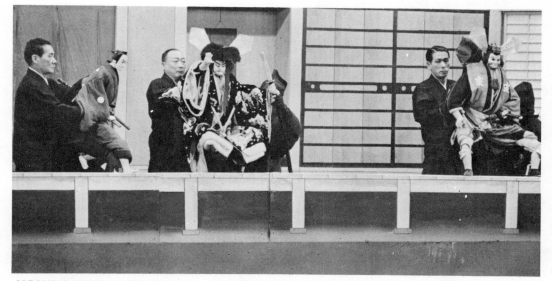

JAPANESE PUPPET THEATRES are called "bunraku" and are considered one of the high dramatic arts. Unlike western puppet theatres, the actors who manipulate the puppets are in full view of the audience.

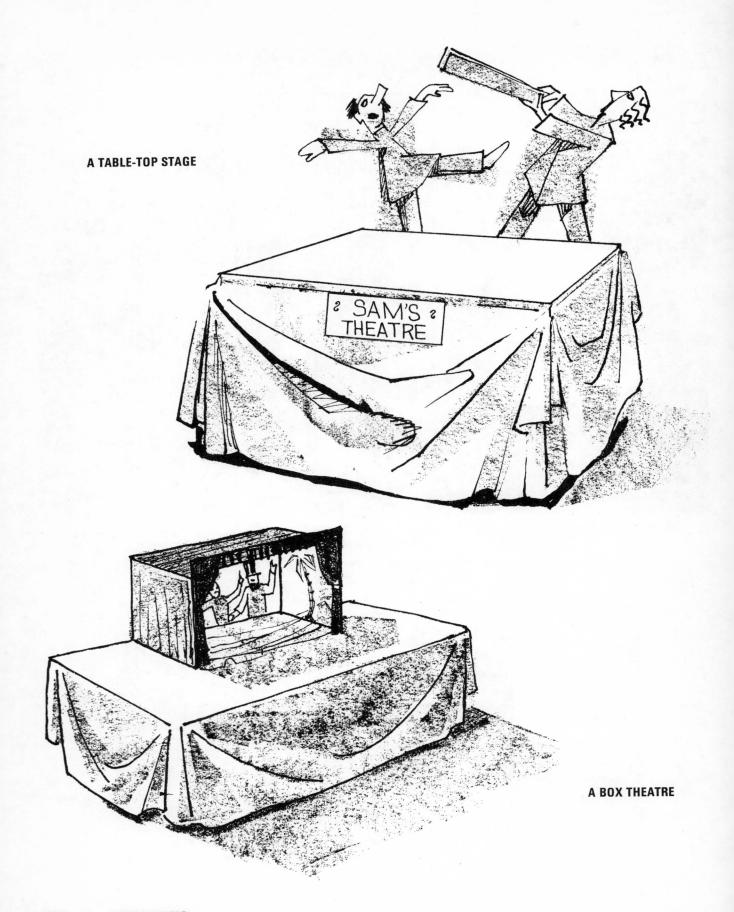

A TABLE-TOP STAGE

SAM'S
THEATRE

A BOX THEATRE

AN OPEN WINDOW STAGE

larger the table, the more performers can be accommodated.

Many theatres are closed in. To make a theatre like this, cut the bottom from a large box and place it on the table that you are performing from. Additional scenery can be drawn on the sides of this box. Maneuver your puppets so that all motions stay within the confines of the boxed walls.

If the weather is warm and your friends want to sit in the backyard, open a low window and use this as your stage. For the audience, place several chairs in the grass. Now you are ready to put on your own puppet show. Use your own patter, or get it from a book. Also, there are many records available today which tell interesting stories which you can perform along with. These are inexpensive, colorful and educational.

MONUMENTAL WOOD SCULPTURES: During a symposium in Quebec with wood as its theme, seven sculptors created what they considered monuments to nature. This is the one that Otani, a Japanese artist, prepared by whittling with an axe.

WOOD CARVING AND WHITTLING

Wood carving by the whittling process is more than just a pleasant pastime. It provides an opportunity to create useful objects with decorative qualities. Whittling allows you to turn a plain object into a beautiful ornamented work of art.

If creating a beautiful design on paper is not difficult for you, then the actual whittling or carving of the design will not be hard. Many delicate and diversified tools are available and should be used if you want the little extras which will make your product better than the next.

A Walking Staff

Carving a walking staff is probably the oldest form of whittling known. Sticks are still being whittled today in many parts of the world. All you need are a sturdy branch or square bar about 4 feet long and a sharp pocket knife. Always cut away from your body.

Begin by deciding which end will be the top, as this will bear the design. With a ruler, draw some horizontal guidelines on the four sides of the bar or circle the branch evenly. Cut above and below each line at a slant so that you gouge out an indentation that is attractive. Bevel the corners carefully or otherwise they will crack if rubbed or dropped.

If you decide to make a very detailed design, draw it out on paper first and even pencil it on the staff before carving. If you use a square bar, a vise or clamp can hold it in place while you work. Most important, if you live in the city and have no use for a walking staff,

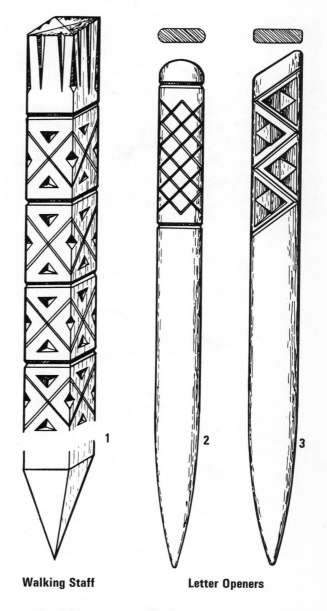

Walking Staff   **Letter Openers**

THE PRINCIPLES of wood carving are shown in these staffs: gouging (1), incising (2), relief (3) and beveling (all).

Adapted in part from the book, "Whittling and Wood Carving" by H. Hoppe | © 1969 by Sterling Publishing Co., Inc., New York and added to by Maria and Louis DiValentin

you can use exactly the same technique to make a letter opener or a fancy pole to support plants in a windowbox.

Tools

For more complicated carving work, a wide variety of chisels and gouges are helpful, each to make a special cut or groove. Two or more different-sized mallets will be used as hammers. The lighter mallet is for removing small quantities of wood, the heavier for removing larger masses.

If your project gets into finer detail, you will use flat chisels and small gouges with a light mallet. For sawing you need a rip-saw and a crosscut saw for large cuts and a fret saw, coping saw or jigsaw for scroll-like cuts. You might also need a wood file and a rasp; a compass; calipers and a try square for measuring and ruling; a vise or C clamp; and a long screw (bench screw) for holding your work steady.

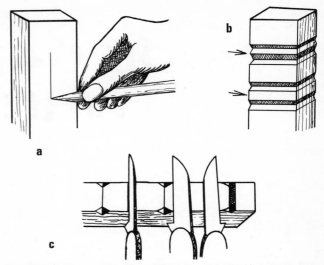

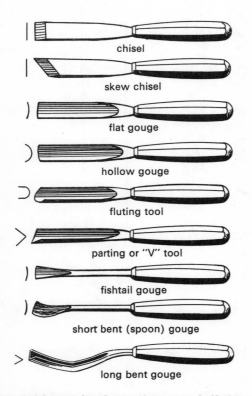

chisel

skew chisel

flat gouge

hollow gouge

fluting tool

parting or "V" tool

fishtail gouge

short bent (spoon) gouge

long bent gouge

TOOLS needed for cutting deeper than a pen knife into wood and for carving out forms include these chisels and gouges.

WHITTLING is wood carving with a pen knife. (a) shows how to use a pencil as a scratch gauge; (b) shows that you must leave bars—either pointed or flat—between cuts to prevent corners breaking away; (c) shows how to cut notches if the wood is hard by making oblique cuts inward before hollowing out.

Your work area must have adequate lighting, especially when you work in fine detail. It must be a large enough area to hold your biggest project. The worktable itself should be high enough for you to work comfortably standing up.

For neatness and safety purposes, never keep more tools on the working surface than are needed for the immediate task. After each use, return the tools to their proper storage area. This will protect the cutting edges as well as prevent accidents.

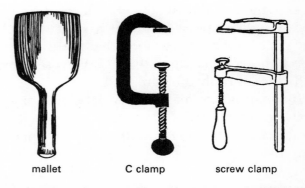

mallet   C clamp   screw clamp

OTHER TOOLS are a mallet for hammering the chisel, and clamps for holding your work.

For practice, take a small piece of scrap wood and tap each chisel into it to see what effect it has.

Incised Carving

The easiest carving is decorative incising (literally, cutting in) of wood. Draw your design in pencil on a flat piece of wood. If your drawing or pattern is on tracing paper, trace it on to the wood. Trace it top, bottom and sides. Now you want to incise the drawn lines, leaving the background plain. To incise, use a veining tool or V tool, $\frac{1}{8}$ inch or $\frac{1}{16}$ inch. Clamp the wood in place on your worktable so it will not move while you work. Hold and guide the tool in your left hand and push it along with your right. Make a light marking cut first—do not cut full depth. Use chisels and gouges from any direction but stay in one position. Follow the drawn design, making a continuous line instead of a number of short cuts. Make each line the same width. If the tool tears the wood it can be smoothed and cleaned out by going over the cut in the opposite direction.

The background may be threaded-in or stippled. Threading-in consists of a number of parallel lines cut with a V tool. Stippling is done with a metal punch.

Practice at the start on a few odd pieces of wood—preferably pine. Do simple, single line designs. Silhouette designs are not difficult. Copy pictures from magazines and books, or try profiles of members of your family.

Incised decorations on trays, picture frames, panels, and book-ends are also easily done. Unfinished wooden articles or furniture may be bought inexpensively and finished with unique and attractive carvings, all these with a hook-billed knife or V tool.

Relief Carving

In relief carving the basic steps are the same: drawing, lining, wasting away and grounding out. The only difference is that in relief, you bring the design up by cutting down and cutting away the unwanted wood, then the background, slicing, rounding and modelling.

As a relief project, design a simple rose. Start with a square piece of wood. Draw on it. Cut the corners and make it round. Designate the center, make four concentric circles and show the lines between where the petals will be. Cut around the center. Then carve down

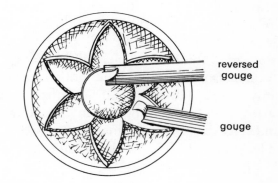

ROSE DESIGN: Carve hollows with the gouge, and reverse the tool to make the rounded shapes.

RELIEF CARVING: Going over a pressed-in design with vertical cuts (a); carving away negative (unwanted) areas (b); finishing off details (c).

towards the center. Carve the large petals, then carve away the inner portion of the petal. Cut grooves between and round the central pearl. Deepen with a gouge, where the edges of the inner petals meet the central pearl.

Ornamental Carving

To ornament a carved box with a relief design, start by transferring the design which has been first drawn on paper. With a sheet of carbon paper, trace the outlines of the design on the wood. Now go over each line and press it into the wood with the point of your pen knife. Next, depending on the size of the wood, use one or more clamps to secure the board to your worktable.

Now you are ready for the actual carving.

Outline the design further with vertical gouge cuts. Then remove the unwanted (negative) background. Don't cut deeply. Work slowly, getting deeper in stages. Next, finish by shaping final details into your design. Be careful not to crack the outstanding (positive) portions of the design. If this should happen, simply glue the broken piece back on.

When carving, hold the gouge or chisel firmly in your left hand and tap it from behind sharply with a mallet held firmly in your right hand. (Reverse the position of the tools if you are left-handed.) The mallet should hit the tool

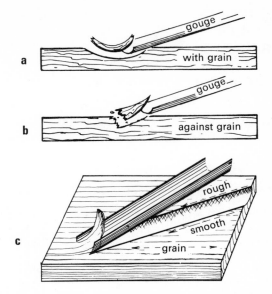

GRAIN is important. Carve with the grain (a), not against (b). You can cut diagonally across the grain (c).

at a right angle. Begin your swing from the elbow, not from the shoulder.

Carve hollow forms with a gouge that is slightly smaller than the intended cut-out. Carve rounded forms—like grapes and pearls—with a reversed (tool turned over) chisel or gouge.

Practically any design can be relief carved with the chisels, mallet and pen knife. The same procedure is followed by the finest wood craftsman.

CARVING: Mallet should strike the chisel at right angles. Push the gouge with both hands.

Lettering

Lettering can take on many different forms to fit any purpose. Usually, wood with a striking grain pattern will distract from the over-all effect, but it can sometimes enhance the design.

As with all of your whittling projects, sketch your letters on paper first and then transfer it to the wood surface. Work the letters into each other, as the LOW has been done in the illustration. Recognize that some letters are wider than others, and some do not fill an entire block. The W is wide, but the O can nestle into it. Lettering requires study.

You can incise letters fairly easily on soft-wood with your chip-carving knives and a parting tool, or on hardwood with your mallet, chisels and gouges. Make a vertical cut in the middle of the letter and chip or chisel the wood away obliquely on either side leaving two slopes that meet in the middle. The carving of letters in relief is more difficult. Basically, you use the same technique as you do for ornamental relief carving, cutting away the negative areas.

Before you go into sculpture with wood you need to know more about the wood itself.

The Grain of Wood

Grain has a bearing on carving because in some woods the grain is hardly visible, and in others it is quite strong and close. You have to design your carving with an idea to the

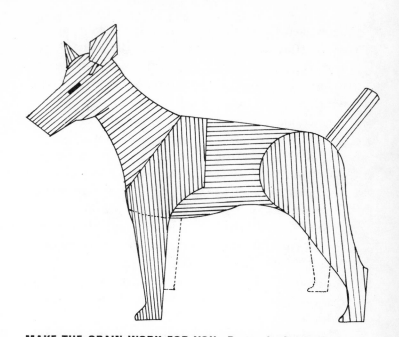

MAKE THE GRAIN WORK FOR YOU: Down the legs, along the body, up the tail, across the face—this is the way to piece a sculpture together.

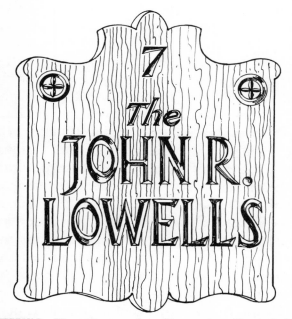

LETTERING: The strong grain adds to the effect of this signpost. Nestle the letters into each other.

direction of the grain. If you are making an animal, you would want the grains to run down the legs, not across. There would be a tendency for them to break off when carved from a main block if there was a cross-grain.

If you can get a diagonal run of grain that is fairly strong, this can be helpful to you in planning your design. Most pieces of wood have grain running diagonally and twisting.

Characteristics of Woods

While there are styles in woods, the wood sculptor does not need to be too concerned because he can use almost any wood that is available and reasonable enough in price to suit his purse. A good carver is ready to try any variety of wood that comes his way provided it is seasoned.

In only a few minutes you will discover the carving quality of any wood. Experiment on small pieces.

Sometimes, the texture of a wood and its true color are hidden by the fact that it has been stored in the open air for seasoning. A wood that looks dull grey may be truly warm and reddish inside. You will also find some woods that you like to carve, some that carve well. A beginner would do well to try some soft woods first.

Pine: This wood is generally whitish or yellowish, straight-grained and durable. A soft wood, it presents no difficulty for the beginner and can easily be carved by hand. The grain is generally even and stable.

Sycamore: This is a white wood that turns light brown in the open air and is very easy to carve. The grain is straight and indistinct. Since it rots very easily, it should not be placed out-of-doors. It is hard enough to be used for a tabletop.

Willow: This is a straight-grained soft but tough wood. In appearance it is whitish to pale brown in the center. Since it seasons without difficulty, it is suitable for carving, especially things like toys.

Douglas Fir: As you get experienced in wood sculpture, you can use this very strong wood which is quite hard. It has a great tendency to crack, split, shrink and swell so you must be sure it is seasoned.

Teak: A rich golden brown, teak carves readily but has a rather coarse and uneven texture. Its aromatic oils act as a preservative. Be careful that you use sharp tools because the tough nature of teak tends to blunt edges. The grain is undulating but generally straight.

American Walnut: For a beautiful carving, walnut is probably the best hardwood. You know its use in furniture and veneers but for distinctive sculptures, this cannot be beaten.

Elm: For large wood carvings, elm is tough and strong. It is easy to obtain and relatively inexpensive.

Ash: This is a rather tough wood to carve but not too difficult. Reasonable in price, it varies in color from white to light brown. Its grain is broad and strongly marked.

Beech: This is plentiful and a reliable all-purpose hardwood with an even texture that can be worked in all directions. It carves and polishes well and can readily take stain.

Wild Cherry: Like other fruitwoods, this is a very good carving wood but it needs slow seasoning and tends to split if dried quickly.

Seasoning

Do not use green freshly cut timber for carving. This kind of wood contains water in its cells and cell walls. Only in the process of drying out does the wood reach its final form which is known as "seasoned." Your work will be distorted or will crack and split if you use green wood.

There are two methods of seasoning—by air and by kiln. Rather than season wood yourself, buy seasoned wood either in plank or block form. Look at the end of whatever wood you buy and make sure that there are no splits in it. Also examine any wood you use to avoid knots.

Carving in the Round

To begin, do not use the hardwoods such as oak or walnut and until you are quite expert, avoid mahogany, maple or birch. Don't use too soft wood either because your work will be wasted. Such woods as balsa are all right for children, but pine or willow are better to begin with.

Using the same worktable that you use for other crafts, be sure that you work at the height that is comfortable for you. Use a vise or not, but you will probably not need large clamps unless you make large statuary that needs glueing together. If you prefer to work standing upright, then try a sculptor's revolving stand. Make it stationary by screwing a piece of board on the bottom side, as large in diameter as the top of the revolving table, and clamp the board to the table top. You can keep the top steady while carving by hooking the stand and top with an eye-and-hook arrangement (as for a screen door).

Besides the cutting tools, you will need grinding tools to keep your tools in good

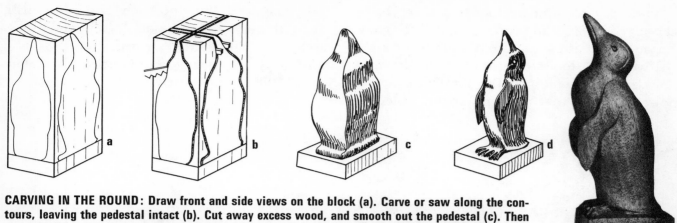

CARVING IN THE ROUND: Draw front and side views on the block (a). Carve or saw along the contours, leaving the pedestal intact (b). Cut away excess wood, and smooth out the pedestal (c). Then carve the figure (d). The finished penguin should be sanded, holes or cracks filled with plastic wood, then waxed or lacquered to prevent warping.

condition. Wipe them with an oily rag to keep them from rusting. You will need oilstones such as carborundum for sharpening and an Arkansas stone for giving your tools the final edge.

For wood sculpture you would do well before you begin to make a small model of your figure in clay or plaster. Start with simple geometric shapes. Do an egg, a cylinder, a cone and a sphere. Try a simple-shaped toy, a clown, a Humpty-Dumpty, a fish, and a bird. Draw side views, upper and lower, front and back. Then secure the block of wood and using one gouge, cut with the grain. Cut deep where necessary, and round off the edges. Cut V shapes as you did with the walking stick wherever you have a large area to gouge out. To prevent the grain from splitting, make a stop-cut vertically with your knife wherever you want the gouge to stop. Cut step by step slowly.

Let's say you are carving a small dog. Start with the body first, then the legs and ears. Observe the form and the planes, and carve carefully. Where your animal design has slim legs, do most of the carving and shaping before cutting out the waste wood which separates the legs. Leave this until last so there is less danger of breaking the legs.

After you have your object carved out of the block or plank, finish it with sandpaper. Then shellac it or wax it or stain it. If you mount your carving with a contrastingly colored background, you will get a good visual effect. If you paint your object, give the carving a coat of one-half shellac and one-half denatured alcohol first to fill the pores of the wood.

Advice for the Wood Carver

In carving across the grain, always make deep cuts, then chip away the wood around and towards the cut.

Never place your hands in such a position that a slip of a tool can inflict injury. Keep your tool edge always visible.

If you are putting a long arm on a figure, such as on the Statue of Liberty, you cannot carve this from a single block. This has to be carved separately and glued or pinned on with dowels or peg joints. When glueing, make sure that both the wood and the glue are heated as this will ensure proper adhesion.

Whenever cracks develop, fill in with beeswax or a sliver of wood of the same kind, if you want to preserve your carving.

One trick to avoid too many cracks, or checks, in a wood is to drill a hole through the bottom center of the block up into the midsection. This will enable the wood to dry out evenly by allowing air in.

Some of the same methods used in stone carving (see page 261) can be applied to wood carving, such as carving from a plaster model.

If you want to attach a limb to a body with dowels, drill a hole first the same size as the dowel. Be sure that you line up the holes in the body and limb precisely. You can drill right through from the outside. If you do it well, you will hardly see the dowels at all, after they are hammered in, especially if you match the color properly.

ORNAMENTAL CARVING is traditional in Morocco for architectural use. Geometric designs are first carved and then either inlaid or painted, as can be seen on this mosque door. The Muslim religion prohibits carving of humans or animals.

appendix

SUPPLIERS

The following list of suggested suppliers has been compiled from catalogues received, and is not necessarily complete. The editors of this volume have reason to believe, but will not guarantee, that these suppliers will give you satisfaction.

Acme Glass Company
2215 West Roosevelt Road
Chicago, Illinois 60608
Stained glass crafting: glass, lead, zinc, acid, tools and Tiffany lamp shades.

Allcraft Tool and Supply Company
215 Park Avenue
Hicksville, New York 11801
Ceramics: kilns and kiln accessories.
Enamelling: binders, hand tools, decorating materials, metals (copper and silver) in sheets, circles and various shapes, enamel colors, jewelry findings (also in yellow gold), gold and silver wire, and a wide variety of jewelry mountings in 14K and 10K gold (white or yellow) and sterling silver. Kilns and kiln accessories.
Etching: chemicals (acid) and engraving tools.
Lapidary: tumblers, facetors, grinders, saws, laps, accessories, chemicals, hand tools, and stones.
Metalcrafting: anvil heads, mandrels, surface plates, stake holders, T-stakes, flat and round topped stakes, hammers, mallets, wooden mallets, vises, cutting tools, shafts and shaft accessories, metals and wire (silver, gold, pewter, copper, brass, nickel silver).
Repoussage: metal (in sheets) and carving tools.
Sculpture: complete line of casting equipment and waxes for model making.
Stained glass crafting: stained glass (fired and unfired), lead, polishers, cutting tools, soldering tools and accessories.
Wirecrafting: wire (silver, gold, pewter, copper, brass, nickel silver), cutting tools, soldering irons and solder, all metalcrafting tools.
Woodworking and engraving: saws, hard woods, hand tools, chisels, mallets and drills.

Amaco Art and Craft Products
American Art Clay Co., Inc.
4717 West Sixteenth Street
Indianapolis, Indiana 46222
Ceramics: kilns and kiln accessories, wheels, clays, glazes, and a variety of shaping and modeling tools.
Claywork: modeling clays, doughs and modeling tools.
Enamelling: kilns, metal enamels, copper shapes and general enamelling supplies.
Paints: (polymer-based, water colors, finger paints and temperas), chalks and chalk pastels.

American Handicrafts
P.O. Box 791
Fort Worth, Texas 76101
General arts and crafts supplies for: acrylics, basketry, burlap crafting, candle-making, découpage, enamelling, felt crafting, mosaics, repoussage, and stained glass crafting. Beginner's kits.

Bon Bazar
149 Waverly Place
New York, N.Y. 10014
Burlap crafting: a wide variety of colors sold by the yard or as remnants.

The Brown Leather Company (Skil-Crafts)
305 Virginia Avenue, P.O. Box 105
Joplin, Missouri 64801
Leathercraft: a complete line of leather including carving cowhide, calf finish cowhide, maverick kip, tooling bellies, tooling calf, tooling pig, harness leather, latigo and saddle skirting; lining leathers including skivers, bag stiffener, suedette, sheepwool, saddle sheep, moccasin and chap cowhide and ostrich grain on pig; and special leathers including embossed calf, pigtex leather skins, skivers, hair-calf skins, suede splits, lining suede skins, lammies and suede splits. See Skil-Crafts listing for *Leathercraft* tools and miscellaneous materials.

R. M. Catterson-Smith Limited
Exhibition Grounds
Wembley
ENGLAND

Ceramics: electric pottery kilns, potters' wheels, banding wheels.

CCM Arts and Crafts Inc.
9520 Baltimore Avenue
College Park, Maryland 20740

General arts and crafts supplies for: acrylics, basketry, batik, beadcrafting, bookbinding, candle-making, ceramics, claywork, corrugated carton crafting, crayoncraft, enamelling, etching, felt crafting, lapidary, leathercraft, macramé, metalcrafting, mosaics, origami, paper flower making, papier mâché, plastics, plastic foam crafting, screen process printing, sculpture, stained glass crafting, stone carving, weaving, wirecrafting, wood blocks, wood carving, woodworking.

Commonwealth Felt Company
211 Congress Street
Boston, Massachusetts

Felt crafting: colored felt and felt transfer patterns.

Charles Cooper
Hatton Garden Ltd.
London, E.C.1
ENGLAND

Scrimshaw: scorpers.

Covington Engineering Corporation
112 First Street
Redlands, California 92373

Lapidary: a complete line of power tools and accessories.

The Craftool Company
1 Industrial Road
Wood-Ridge, New Jersey 07075

Bookbinding and paper making: presses, beaters, beginners' kits.
Ceramics: potter's wheels (manual and electric), spray booths, cabinets, ball mills.
Etching: etching and block presses, printers' cutters, and beginners' kits.
Lapidary: combination units, tumblers, saws, laps, buffers, hand tools, beginners' kits.

Weaving: looms (various types and sizes), rug frames and spinning wheels.
Beginners' kits for batik, wood carving and clay and stone sculpture.

Craftsmen Potters Association of Great Britain
William Blake House, Marshall Street
London, W.1
ENGLAND

Ceramics and claywork supplies.

Craftsmen's Distributors Ltd.
1597 London Road
London, S.W.16
ENGLAND

General craft supplies.

Crafts Unlimited
49 Shelton Street
London, W.C.2
ENGLAND

General craft supplies, especially for basketry, batik, ceramics, claywork, lapidary, mosaics, screen process printing and tie-and-dye.

Creative Crafts Magazine
Model Craftsman Publishing Corp.
31 Arch Street
Ramsey, New Jersey 07446

While not a source of material supplies, this magazine, available by subscription, offers additional suggestions for a variety of crafts projects.

Dick Blick
P.O. Box 1267
Galesburg, Illinois 61401

General arts and crafts supplies for: acrylics, basketry, batik, beadcrafting, bookbinding, burlap crafting, cardboard crafting, ceramics, claywork, crayoncraft, découpage, etching, felt crafting, lapidary, mosaics, origami, paper craft, paper flower making, screen process printing, sculpture, stone carving, tie-and-dye, weaving, wirecrafting and wood carving.

Dollspart Supply Company, Inc.
5-06 51 Avenue
Long Island City, New York 11101

Doll-making: wigs, body parts, shoes and accessories, doll stands, wire and small tools.

Economy Crafts
47–11 Francis Lewis Blvd.
Flushing, N.Y. 11361
  General crafts supplies for: basketry, beadcrafting, burlap crafting, candle-making, ceramics, découpage, enamelling, etching, felt crafting, leathercraft, mosaics, needlework, papier mâché, sculpture, stained glass crafting, weaving, wirecrafting, wood blocks.

Frances Paul Crafts
3033 La Madera Avenue
El Monte, California 91732
  Lapidary: gem drills (and parts), mandrels, grippers (for stones and beads), carvers, bead mills, and small carving tools and accessories.

Friedlein Natural Products
Kudu House
The Minories, E.C.3, London
ENGLAND
  Scrimshaw: cleaned whale's teeth.

Great Western Equipment Company
3444 Main Street
Chula Vista, California 92011
  Lapidary: saws, grinders, sanders, polishers, combination units, laps, tumblers and accessories, grits and polish compounds.

Hvalur Ltd.
Hafnarfjordur
ICELAND
  Scrimshaw: fresh whale's teeth.

J. Johnson and Company
33 Matinecock Avenue
Port Washington, New York 11050
  Wood carving and engraving: gravers, knives and complete carving sets, brayers, Norton stones and wood, oil base inks and print paper.

Lily Mills Company
Shelby, North Carolina 28150
  Weaving: various types of hand looms (table and floor models), bobbin and warp winders, and yarns (cotton, wool, linen, novelty yarns, chenilles and carpet yarns).

The Needlewoman Shop
146–148 Regent Street
London W1R 6BA
ENGLAND
  Needlecraft: yarn, patterns, canvases, background materials, packaged kits, needles, hooks and other implements for all kinds of needlework including crewel, embroidery, needlepoint, rug hooking, crochet work and knitting. Services are also available for mounting finished needlework (pillows, hand bags, etc.).

Nervo Art Stained Glass Works
4911 Telegraph Avenue
Oakland, California 94609
  Stained glass crafting: stained glass sold by the foot and as scraps, lead came, copper foil and glass tools, flux, etc.

New York Doll Hospital
787 Lexington Avenue
New York, New York 10021
  Doll-making: wigs, clothes, body parts, doll stands, doll heads and facial parts.

Rytime-Robilt Pty. Ltd.
218 Bay Road
Sandringham, Vic., 3191
AUSTRALIA
  Lapidary: power tools and accessories.

Sy Schweitzer and Company, Inc.
P.O. Box 71, Gedney Station
White Plains, New York 10605
  Beadcrafting: Beads (wooden, glass and pearls), adhesive cements, jewelry parts and findings.
  Lapidary: glass cabochons, jewelry parts and findings.

Sculpture House
38 East 30th Street
New York, New York 10016
  Ceramics: kilns and kiln accessories, potter's wheels, trimming tools, banding wheels, glazes and clay.
  Sculpture: carving and modeling waxes, carving stones, bronze modeling kits, modeling paste, clay, plasticine, plaster and plaster casting accessories, modeling tools and knives for all sculpture mediums, plaster casts, armatures and modeling stands.

Skil-Crafts (a division of the Brown Leather Co.)
305 Virginia Avenue
Joplin, Missouri 64801

General arts and crafts supplies for: basketry, bead-crafting, candle-making, claywork, crayoncraft, dé-coupage, doll-making, enamelling, felt crafting, leathercraft (see below for complete listing), mosaics, paper flower making, plastic foam crafting, re-poussage, sculpture and collage in plastic, tin-can crafting, wirecrafting, wood blocks, wood carving and woodworking.

Large selection of supplies for *Leathercraft* (see also the Brown Leather Company): complete kits, tools and cutters, saddle stamps, craftaid patterns, sewing supplies, leather "hardware," leather cleaners and dressers.

Soriano Ceramics
2021 Steinway Street
Long Island City, N.Y.

Mosaics: trivets, swivel rings, backings and frames.

Stained Glass of Hanover
D/B/A/ Whittemore Durgin Glass Company
Box 2065
Hanover, Massachusetts 02339

Stained glass crafting: stained glass, lead cames, stained glass tools, "Tiffany" type lampmaker's supplies, dalle glass, glass cutters, glass pliers, glass adhesives, glass lens cutters, copper foil, soldering irons, solder, sheet lead, lead wire, glass nuggets, glass jewels, stained glass books and instructions.

X-Acto Inc.
48–41 Van Dam Street
Long Island City, N.Y. 11101

Beadcrafting: beads, complete kits and supplies.
Etching: routers, gouges and miscellaneous cutting tools.
Leathercraft: cutting and punching tools.
Metalcrafting: carving, cutting tools and soldering irons.
Nail sculpture: vises and soldering irons.
Repoussage: cutting and carving tools.
Tin-can crafting: cutting and carving tools.
Wire sculpture: soldering irons and cutting tools.
Wood blocks: wood and linoleum cutters.
Wood carving: carving tools and cutting tools.
Cutting tools for use on paper and cardboard are also available.

Yarn Depot, Inc.
545 Sutter Street
San Francisco, California 94102

Macramé: jute, straw and a variety of yarns.
Needlecraft: wide variety of yarn (wool, linen, rayon, jute, metallics, chenille, bouclé and mohair) suitable for crewel, needlepoint, knitting, embroidery and crocheting.
Weaving: yarn (see *Needlecraft*).

BIBLIOGRAPHY

The following list of books was compiled to help the beginning craftsman further his knowledge. In most cases, the authors of the articles suggested these books, to supplement the basic instructions given here with more advanced information. The editors have not had the opportunity to examine each of these books in detail (other than those published by Sterling), and the methods used in them may differ from those in the Encyclopedia.

Acrylic

Acrylic and Other Water-Base Paints
Torche, Judith
Sterling Publishing Co., Inc., 1966
Oak Tree Press Co., Ltd.
Guide to Polymer Painting
Fabri, R.
Van Nostrand Reinhold Co., 1966
Introducing Acrylic Painting
Pluckrose, N.
Watson-Guptill Publications, 1968
Painting with Acrylics
Gutierrez, Jose and
Roukes, Nicholas
Watson-Guptill Publications, 1966

Basketry

Basketry
Christopher, F. J.
Dover Publications, Inc., 1952
Baskets and Basketry
Wright, Dorothy
Charles T. Branford Co., 1959
Weaving with Cane and Reed
Kroncke
Van Nostrand Reinhold Co., 1968

Batik

Batik: Art and Craft
Krevitsky, N.
Van Nostrand Reinhold Co., 1967
Batik as a Hobby
Stein, Vivian
Sterling Publishing Co. Inc., 1969
Oak Tree Press Co., Ltd.
Book of Batik
Mueling, Ernst
Taplinger Publishing Co., Inc., 1967
Introducing Batik
Samuel, Evelyn
Watson-Guptill Publications, 1968

Beadcrafting

Bead Design
Harris, Edith and
Wasley, Ruth
Crown Publishers Inc., 1969

Bead Embroidery

Edwards, Joan
Taplinger Publishing Co., Inc., 1967
Creating with Beads
La Croix, Grethe
Sterling Publishing Co., Inc., 1969
Oak Tree Press Co., Ltd.

Bookbinding

Basic Bookbinding
Lewis, A. W.
Dover Publications, Inc., 1952
The Binding of Books
Horne, H. P.
Haskell House Publishers, Ltd., 1968
Bookbinding for Beginners
Corderoy, John
Watson-Guptill Publications, 1967
Creative Bookbinding
Johnson, Pauline
University of Washington Press, 1965
Introducing Bookbinding
Robinson, Ivor
Watson-Guptill Publications, 1968

Burlap Crafting

Creating with Burlap
Fressard, M. J.
Sterling Publishing Co., Inc., 1970
Oak Tree Press Co., Ltd.

Candle-Making

Candle-Making
Strose, Susanne
Sterling Publishing Co., Inc., 1968
Oak Tree Press Co., Ltd.
Kitchen Candlecrafting
Monroe, Ruth
A. S. Barnes and Company, Inc., 1969
Modern Art of Candle Crafting
Olsen, Don and Ray
A. S. Barnes and Company, Inc., 1965

Cardboard Crafting

Building with Cardboard
Lidstone, John
Van Nostrand Reinhold Co., 1968

Cardboard Carpentry

D'Amato, Janet and Alex
The Lion Press, Inc., 1966
Cardboard Crafting
Granit, Inga
Sterling Publishing Co., Inc., 1964
Oak Tree Press Co., Ltd.

Ceramics

Ceramic Design
Kenny, John B.
Chilton Book Co., 1968
Ceramics, A Potter's Handbook
Nelson, Glenn C.
Holt, Rinehart and Winston, Inc., 1966
Ceramics for the Artist Potter
Norton, F. H.
Addison-Wesley Publishing Co.,
Inc., 1956
Modern Ceramics
Beard, Geoffrey
E. P. Dutton & Company, Inc., 1963
Practical Pottery and Ceramics
Clark, Kenneth
The Viking Press, Inc., 1964

Claywork

Clay in the Classroom
Barford, George
Davis Publications, Inc., 1963
Creating with Clay
Seidleman, James
Crowell Collier and Macmillan,
Inc., 1967
Creative Clay Design
Rottger, E.
Van Nostrand Reinhold Co., 1963
Creative Claywork
Isenstein, Harald
Sterling Publishing Co., Inc., 1969
Oak Tree Press Co., Ltd.

Collage

Collage: Personalities, Concepts, Techniques
Blesh, R. and
Janis, H.
Chilton Book Company, 1967

How to Make Collages
Lynch, J.
The Viking Press, Inc., 1961

Coloring Papers

Coloring Papers
Strose, Susanne
Sterling Publishing Co., Inc., 1968
Oak Tree Press Co., Ltd.
Creative Paper Design
Rottger, Ernst
Van Nostrand Reinhold Co., 1961
One Hundred Watercolor Techniques
Kent, Norman
Watson-Guptill Publications, 1968

Corrugated Carton Crafting

Corrugated Carton Crafting
Van Voorst, Dick
Sterling Publishing Co., Inc., 1969
Oak Tree Press Co., Ltd.
Creating with Corrugated Paper
Hartung, Rolf
Van Nostrand Reinhold Co., 1966

Crayoncraft

The Complete Crayon Book
Alkema, Chester Jay
Sterling Publishing Co., Inc., 1969
Oak Tree Press Co., Ltd.
Crayon Techniques
Girdler, R.
Pitman Publishing Corp., 1969
Creating with Crayons
Kampmann, Lothar
Van Nostrand Reinhold Co.
Creative Expression with Crayons
Boylston, E. R.
Davis Publications Inc.
Introducing Crayon Techniques
Pluckrose, H.
Watson-Guptill Publications, 1968

Découpage

Découpage
Nimocks, Patricia
Charles Scribner's Sons, 1968

Doll-Making

Complete Book of Doll Making and Collecting
Christopher, C.
Dover Publications, Inc., 1970
The Doll Book
Worrell, E. A.
Van Nostrand Reinhold Co., 1966
Dolls and How to Make Them
Hutchings, Margaret
Charles T. Branford Company, 1963
How to Make Dolls
Edwards, N.
Associated Booksellers, Inc.

Making Dolls
Witzig, H. and Kuhn, G. E.
Sterling Publishing Co., Inc., 1969
Oak Tree Press Co., Ltd.

Enamelling

Beautiful Art of Enameling
Dutton, Nanette
Arco Publishing Co., Inc., 1968
Creative Enamelling and Jewelry-Making
Zechlin, Katharina
Sterling Publishing Co., Inc., 1965
Oak Tree Press Co., Ltd.
Enameling: Principles and Practice
Bates, Kenneth
World Publishing Co., 1951
Enamelist
Bates, Kenneth
World Publishing Co., 1967
Metal Enameling
Rothenberg, Polly
Crown Publishers, Inc., 1969
Technique of Enamelling
Clarke, G.
Van Nostrand Reinhold Co., 1967

Etching

Craft of Etching and Lithography
Woods, G.
Charles T. Branford Co., 1966
Creative Printmaking
Andrews, Michael F.
Prentice-Hall, Inc., 1964
Etching and Engraving: Techniques and the Modern Trend
Buckland-Wright, John
Dover Publications, Inc.
Etching (and Other Intaglio Techniques)
Banister, Manly
Sterling Publishing Co., Inc., 1969
Oak Tree Press Co., Ltd.
Simple Printmaking
Cooper, Mary and
Kent, Cyril
Watson-Guptill Publications, 1967
Techniques of Etching and Engraving
Brunsdon, J.
Van Nostrand Reinhold Co., 1966

Felt Crafting

Felt Crafting
Janvier, Jacqueline
Sterling Publishing Co., Inc., 1970
Oak Tree Press Co., Ltd.
Felt Dolls to Make and Dress
Tearle, P.
Hobby House Press, 1949
Felt Toys
Mochrie, E.
Hobby House Press, 1964

Fresco

Art of Fresco Painting
Merrifield, Mary
Transatlantic Arts, Inc.

Ikebana

Flower Arranging by Tat
Shinno, Tat
Lane Magazine and Book Co., 1965
Ikebana (Japanese Flower Arranging) Simplified
Bowes, Olive Scofield
Sterling Publishing Co., Inc., 1969
Oak Tree Press Co., Ltd.
Stepping Stones to Japanese Floral Art
Carr, R. E.
David McKay Co., Inc., 1959

Kite-Making

Chinese Kites, How to Make and Fly
Jue, David F.
Charles E. Tuttle Co., Inc., 1967
Kites: How to Make and Fly Them
Downer, Marion
Lothrop, Lee and Shephard Co., Inc., 1959
Twenty-five Kites that Fly
Hunt, Leslie
Bruce Books, 1964

Lapidary

Art of Gem Cutting
Drake, Henry
Simpson Printing and Publishing Co., 1963
Art of Lapidary
Sperisen, F. J.
Bruce Books, 1961
Facet Cutters Handbook
Soukup, E. J.
Simpson Printing and Publishing Co., 1962
Gemcraft: How to Cut and Polish Stones
Quick, L.
Chilton Book Co., 1959
Gem Cutting
Sinkankas, John
Van Nostrand Reinhold Co., 1962
Handbook of Gemstone Carving
Wertz, E. & L.
Gembooks

Leathercraft

Creative Leathercraft
Petersen, Grete
Sterling Publishing Co., Inc., 1960
Blandford Press Ltd.
Fun with Leather
Leeming, Joseph
J. B. Lippincott Co., 1941
General Leathercraft
Cherry, R.
McKnight and McKnight Publishing Co., 1958

Leathercraft
    Groneman, Chris H.
    Charles A. Bennett Co., Inc., 1963
Leatherwork-Procedure and Designs
    Klingensmith, W. P.
    Bruce Books, 1968
Working with Leather
    Williams, Guy R.
    Emerson Books, Inc., 1967

Macramé

The Ashley Book of Knots
    Ashley, Clifford W.
    Doubleday and Co., Inc., 1944
Macramé
    Pesch, Imelda Manalo
    Sterling Publishing Co., Inc., 1970
    Oak Tree Press Co., Ltd.
Macramé: The Art of Creative Knotting
    Harvey, Virginia I.
    Van Nostrand Reinhold Co., 1967

Mask-Making

Mask Making
    Baranski, Matthew
    Davis Publications, Inc., 1966
Masks and How to Make Them
    Slade, Richard
    Transatlantic Arts, Inc., 1966
Paper Faces
    Grater, Michael
    Taplinger Publishing Co., Inc., 1968

Metalcrafting

Creating with Metal
    Granstrom, K. E.
    Van Nostrand Reinhold Co., 1968
Metal and Wire Sculpture
    Gruber, Elmar
    Sterling Publishing Co., Inc., 1969
    Oak Tree Press Co., Ltd.
Metalsmithing for the Artist-Craftsman
    Thomas, R.
    Chilton Book Co., 1960
Metalwork Essentials
    Blide, D. C.
    Kranzusch, R. F. and
    Tustison, F. E.,
    Bruce Books, 1962

Mosaics

The Art of Making Mosaics
    Jenkins, L., Mills, B.
    Van Nostrand Reinhold Co., 1957
Making Mosaics
    Arvois, Edmond
    Sterling Publishing Co., Inc., 1969
    Oak Tree Press Co., Ltd.
Modern Mosaic Techniques
    Lovoos, J. and
    Paramore, F.
    Watson-Guptill Publications, 1967

Mosaic Making
    Hutton, Helen
    Van Nostrand Reinhold Co., 1966
Mosaics
    Aller, Diane and Doris
    Lane Magazine and Book Co., 1959
Mosaics
    Garnett, Angelica
    Oxford University Press, Inc., 1967
Mosaics: Hobby and Art
    Hendrickson, E.
    Hill and Wang, Inc., 1957
Mosaics, Painting in Stone: History and Technique
    Rossi, Frederico
    Praeger Publishers, Inc., 1969
Mosaic Techniques: New Aspects of Fragmented Design
    Stribling, Mary L.
    Crown Publishers, Inc., 1966

Mobiles

How to Make Mobiles
    Lynch, John
    The Viking Press, Inc., 1953
Make Your Own Mobiles
    Schegger, T. M.
    Sterling Publishing Co., Inc., 1970
    Oak Tree Press Co., Ltd.
Making Mobiles
    Moorey, Anne and Christopher
    Watson-Guptill Publications, 1957

Musical Instruments

Make Your Own Musical Instruments
    Mandell, Muriel and
    Wood, Robert E.
    Sterling Publishing Co., Inc., 1959
    Bailey Bros. & Swinfen, Ltd.

Nail Sculpture

Nail Sculpture
    Gruber, Elmar
    Sterling Publishing Co., Inc., 1969
    Oak Tree Press Co., Ltd.

Needlecraft

Appliqué Stitchery
    Laury, Jean Ray
    Van Nostrand Reinhold Co., 1966
Canvas Embroidery
    Springall, Diane
    Charles T. Branford Co., 1969
The Complete Book of Needlework
    Hirst, Irene
    Taplinger Publishing Co., Inc., 1963
    Ward Lock Ltd.
Creative Embroidery
    Nicholson, Joan
    Crown Publishers, Inc., 1960
Crewel Embroidery
    Wilson, Erica
    Charles Scribner's Sons, 1962

Embroidery Design
    Mason, Enid
    Charles T. Branford Co., 1969
Embroidery Stitches
    Butler, Anne
    Praeger Publishers, Inc., 1968
Fun with Crewel Embroidery
    Wilson, Erica
    Charles Scribner's Sons, 1962
Making Pictures in Paper and Fabric
    Honeywood, Mary
    Watson-Guptill Publications, 1969
Metal Thread Embroidery
    Dawson, Barbara
    Taplinger Publishing Co., Inc., 1969
Needlepoint
    Hanley, Hope
    Charles Scribner's Sons, 1964
Patchwork Quilts
    Colby, Averil
    Charles Scribner's Sons, 1966
Practical Embroidery
    Haupt-Bottoglea, Heidi
    Charles T. Branford Co., 1969
Quilting as a Hobby
    Brightbill, Dorothy
    Crown Publishers, Inc., 1963
Quilting Manual
    Hinson, Delores A.
    Hearthside Press, 1966
The Stitchery Book
    Lubell, W. and
    Miller, I. P.
    Doubleday and Co., Inc., 1965
Technique of Creative Embroidery
    Risley, Christine
    Watson-Guptill Publications, 1969

Origami

Art of Origami: Paper Folding Traditional and Modern
    Randlett, Samuel
    E. P. Dutton and Co., Inc., 1961
Living Origami
    Honda, Isao
    Charles E. Tuttle Co., Inc., 1962
Modern Origami
    Sakoda, James M.
    Simon and Schuster, 1969
Paper Folding to Begin With
    Simon, Elaine and
    Temko, Florence
    The Bobbs-Merrill Co., Inc., 1968

Papercraft

Creating with Paper
    Johnson, P.
    University of Washington Press
Creating with Colored Paper
    Kampmann, Lothar
    Van Nostrand Reinhold Co.
Creative Paper Crafts in Color
    Alkema, Chester Jay
    Sterling Publishing Co., Inc., 1967
    Oak Tree Press Co., Ltd.

Creative Paper Design
 Rottger, E.
 Van Nostrand Reinhold Co., 1961
How to Make Things Out of Paper
 Sperling, Walter
 Sterling Publishing Co., Inc., 1960
 Oak Tree Press Co., Ltd.
Make It in Paper
 Grater, Michael
 Taplinger Publishing Co., Inc., 1962
Papercraft for Fun
 Seidman, Sy
 Associated Booksellers, Inc.
Paper Sculpture
 Johnston, M. G.
 Davis Publications, Inc., 1965

Paper Flower Making

Flower Making
 Lobley, Priscilla
 Taplinger Publishing Co., Inc., 1969
Making Paper and Fabric Flowers
 Wilder, Carolyn
 Hearthside Press, 1969
Making Paper Flowers
 Strose, Susanne
 Sterling Publishing Co., Inc., 1969
 Oak Tree Press Co., Ltd.

Papier Mâché

Art and Design in Papier Mâché
 Kuykendall, Karen
 Hearthside Press, 1968
Exploring Papier Mâché
 Betts, V. B.
 Davis Publications, Inc., 1966
Original Creations with Papier Mâché
 Anderson, Mildred
 Sterling Publishing Co., Inc., 1967
 Oak Tree Press Co., Ltd.
Papier Mâché
 Johnson, Lillian
 David McKay Co., Inc., 1958
Papier Mâché and How to Use it
 Anderson, Mildred
 Sterling Publishing Co., Inc., 1970
 Oak Tree Press Co., Ltd.

Plastic Foam Crafting

Plastic Foam
 Benning, C. J.
 J. Wiley and Sons, Inc., 1969
Plastic Foam for Arts and Crafts
 Yates, Brock
 Sterling Publishing Co., Inc., 1965
Rigid Plastic Foams
 Ferrigno, T. H.
 Van Nostrand Reinhold Co., 1967

Potato Printing

Potato Printing
 Strose, Susanne
 Sterling Publishing Co., Inc., 1969
 Oak Tree Press Co., Ltd.

Puppets and Marionettes

Creating and Presenting Hand Puppets
 Bodor, J. J.
 Van Nostrand Reinhold Co., 1967
Practical Puppetry
 Mulholland, J.
 Arco Publishing Co., Inc., 1962
Presenting Marionettes
 French, S.
 Van Nostrand Reinhold Co., 1967
Puppet and Pantomime Plays
 Howard, Vernon
 Sterling Publishing Co., Inc., 1962
Puppets
 Snook, Barbara
 Charles T. Branford Co., 1966
Simple Puppetry
 Jackson, Sheila
 Watson-Guptill Publications, 1969

Repoussage

Repoussage
 Meriel-Bussy, Yves
 Sterling Publishing Co., Inc., 1970
 Oak Tree Press Co., Ltd.

Rubbings

Brasses and Brass Rubbing
 Gittings, Clare
 Blandford Press Ltd.
Creative Rubbings
 Andrew, Laye
 Watson-Guptill Publications, 1968
Rubbings and Textures
 Bodor, John J.
 Van Nostrand Reinhold Co., 1968

Scissorscraft

Chinese Paper-Cut Pictures
 Kuo, Nancy
 Taplinger Publishing Co., Inc., 1965
Scissorscraft
 Grol, Lini
 Sterling Publishing Co., Inc., 1970
 Oak Tree Press Co., Ltd.
Silhouettes, Shadows and Cutouts
 Laliberte, N. and
 Mogelon, A.
 Van Nostrand Reinhold Co., 1968

Scrapcraft

Art from Scrap
 Orye, J. and
 Reed, C.
 Davis Publications, Inc., 1960
Creating Art from Anything
 Meilach, Dona Z.
 Reilly and Lee Books, 1968
Creating from Scrap
 Frankel, Godfrey and Lillian
 Sterling Publishing Co., Inc., 1962
Designing with String
 Seyd, Mary
 Watson-Guptill Publications, 1968

Screen Process Printing

Block and Silk Screen Printing
 Ahlberg, G. and
 Jarneryd, O.
 Sterling Publishing Co., Inc., 1961
Practical Screen Printing
 Russ, Stephen
 Watson-Guptill Publications, 1969
Screen Printing on Fabric
 Clayson, R. and
 Searle, V.
 Watson-Guptill Publications, 1968
Screen Process Printing
 Kosloff
 Signs of Times, 1968
Serigraph: Silk Screen Techniques for the Artist
 Auvil, Kenneth W.
 Prentice-Hall Inc., 1965
Silk Screen as a Fine Art
 Chieffo, Clifford T.
 Van Nostrand Reinhold Co.
Silk Screen Printing
 Eisenberg, James
 McKnight and McKnight
  Publishing Co.
Silk Screen Printing for the Artist
 Marsh, Roger
 Transatlantic Arts, Inc., 1969

Sculpture

Art of Sculpture
 Read, Herbert
 Princeton University Press, 1961
Modelled Sculpture and Plaster Casting
 Auerbach, Arnold
 A. S. Barnes and Co., Inc.
Sculpture for Beginners
 DiValentin, Maria and Louis
 Sterling Publishing Co., Inc., 1969
 Oak Tree Press Co., Ltd.
Sculpture: Techniques in Clay, Wax, Slate
 Eliscu, F.
 Chilton Book Co., 1959
Starting with Sculpture
 Dawson, Robert
 Watson-Guptill Publications, 1968

Sculpture and Collage in Plastics

Plastic Sculpture and Collage
 Schwartz, Therese
 Hearthside Press, 1969
Sculpture in Plastics
 Roukes, N.
 Watson-Guptill Publications, 1968

Scrimshaw

All Hands Aboard Scrimshawing
 Barbeau, Marius
 Peabody Foundation for Archeology,
  1966
Scrimshaw, Art of the Whaleman
 Flayderman, E. M.
 N. Flayderman and Co.

Stained Glass Crafting

Glass Craft: Designing, Forming and Decorating
    Kinney, K.
    Chilton Book Co., 1962
Stained Glass
    Armitage, E. L.
    Charles T. Branford Co.
Stained Glass Crafting
    Wood, Paul W.
    Sterling Publishing Co., Inc., 1967
    Oak Tree Press Co., Ltd.
Technique of Stained Glass
    Reyntiens, P.
    Watson-Guptill Publications, 1967

Stone Carving

Creation of Sculpture
    Struppeck, J.
    Holt, Rinehart and Winston, Inc., 1952
Direct Carving in Stone
    Batten, Mark
    Transatlantic Arts, Inc.
Materials and Methods of Sculpture
    Rich, J. C.
    Oxford University Press Inc., 1947

Tie-and-Dye

Tie-and-Dye as a Present Day Craft
    Maile, Anne
    Taplinger Publishing Co., Inc., 1963

Tin-Can Crafting

Tin-Can Crafting
    Howard, Sylvia W.
    Sterling Publishing Co., Inc., 1959
    Mills & Boon Ltd.

Weaving

A Handweaver's Workbook
    Thorpe, Heather G.
    The Macmillan Co., 1966
Handweaving
    Plath, Iona
    Charles Scribner's Sons, 1964
The Weaver's Book (Fundamentals of Handweaving)
    Tidball, Harriet
    The Macmillan Co., 1961
Weaving as a Hobby
    Ickis, Marguerite
    Sterling Publishing Co., Inc., 1968
    Oak Tree Press Co. Ltd.
Weaving Is for Anyone
    Wilson, Jean
    Van Nostrand Reinhold Co., 1966

Wirecrafting

Welded Sculpture
    Hale, Nathan
    Watson-Guptill Publications, 1968
Wire Sculpture and Other Three-Dimensional Construction
    Brommer, G. F.
    Davis Publications, 1968

Wood Blocks: Cutting, Engraving and Printing

The Craft of Woodcuts
    Biggs, John
    Sterling Publishing Co., Inc., 1963
    Blandford Press Ltd.
Introducing Woodcuts
    Woods, G.
    Watson-Guptill Publications, 1969
Linocuts and Woodcuts
    Rothenstein, Michael
    Watson-Guptill Publications, 1964

Linoleum Block Printing
    Kafka
    McKnight and McKnight Publishing Co., 1958
Prints from Linoblocks and Woodcuts
    Banister, Manly
    Sterling Publishing Co., Inc., 1967
    Oak Tree Press Co., Ltd.
Sunset Woodcarving Book
    Aller, D.
    Lane Magazine and Book Co., 1951

Wood Carving and Whittling

Contemporary Carving and Whittling
    Hunt, W. B.
    Bruce Books, 1967
Creative Wood Design
    Rottger, E.
    Van Nostrand Reinhold Co., 1961
Sculpture in Wood
    Rood, John
    University of Minnesota Press, 1950
Sculpture in Wood
    Norman, P. E.
    Transatlantic Arts Inc., 1966
Whittling and Woodcarving
    Hoppe, H.
    Sterling Publishing Co., Inc., 1969
    Oak Tree Press Co., Ltd.
Wood Carving and Whittling Made Easy
    Gottshall, F. H.
    Bruce Books, 1963
Wood Design
    Willcox, P.
    Watson-Guptill Publications

Woodworking

Basic Woodworking Processes
    Fowler, E. W.
    Bruce Books, 1961

If you are unable to find any of the books listed here at your bookstore, write to one of the following specialty book suppliers. They carry many crafts books and should be able to help you.

Craft and Hobby Book Service
P.O. Box 626
Pacific Grove, California 93950
    Specializing in books for weaving and needlework.

Crafts Unlimited
49 Shelton Street
London, W.C.2
ENGLAND
    Offering general craft supplies and books.

The Needlewoman Shop
146–148 Regent Street
London, W1R 6BA
ENGLAND
    Books pertaining to all kinds of needlework.

The Library Corner
Box 1137
Boynton Beach, Florida 33435
    Dealing in designs and books pertaining to crafts and ceramics.

INDEX